STUDIES AND TEXTS 218

Dislocations

Maps, Classical Tradition, and Spatial Play in the European Middle Ages

ALFRED HIATT

PONTIFICAL INSTITUTE OF MEDIAEVAL STUDIES

Acknowledgements

Publication of this volume was generously supported by Ann M. Hutchison, James P. Carley, and the Janet E. Hutchison Foundation, Toronto.

Library and Archives Canada Cataloguing in Publication

Title: Dislocations : maps, classical tradition, and spatial play in the European Middle Ages / Alfred Hiatt.
Names: Hiatt, Alfred, author. | Pontifical Institute of Mediaeval Studies, publisher.
Series: Studies and texts (Pontifical Institute of Mediaeval Studies) ; 218.
Description: Series statement: Studies and texts ; 218 | Includes bibliographical references and index.
Identifiers: Canadiana (print) 2020015009X | Canadiana (ebook) 20200150235 | ISBN 9780888442185 (hardcover) | ISBN 9781771104043 (PDF)
Subjects: LCSH: Literature, Medieval – History and criticism. | LCSH: Geography in literature. | LCSH: Geography, Medieval – Europe. | LCSH: Place (Philosophy) in literature. | LCSH: Space in literature. | LCSH: Maps in literature.
Classification: LCC PN682.G45 H53 2020 | DDC 809/.9332–dc23

Pontifical Institute of Mediaeval Studies
59 Queen's Park Crescent East
Toronto, Ontario M5S 2C4
Canada
www.pims.ca

Dislocations

Maps, Classical Tradition, and Spatial Play in the European Middle Ages

In Europe, during the Middle Ages, classical Greek and Roman geography continued to provide the fundamental structure for knowing the world's places and peoples. From encyclopedic compendia such as the *Natural History* of Pliny the Elder and its redaction in Julius Solinus's *Polyhistor* to the works of canonical Roman poets such as Virgil, Ovid, and Lucan, the geographical content of antique texts invited study and explication.

Yet medieval authors well knew that classical spatial order, itself full of lacunae, only infrequently corresponded to their own reality. *Dislocations: Maps, Classical Tradition, and Spatial Play in the European Middle Ages* considers the ways in which medieval and, later, humanist geography absorbed and reinvented classical spatial models in order to address key questions of historical change, migration, and emerging national, regional, and linguistic identities.

Drawing on a wide range of literary texts, maps, and geographical descriptions – and utilising the ancient but now largely discarded scholarly genre of the dialogue – *Dislocations* argues that medieval spatial representation was complex and richly textured, whether in the form of a careful gloss in a manuscript of Lucan's *Civil War*, or as the exuberant sexualized allegories of the fourteenth-century papal notary Opicinus de Canistris.

The book also explores a further kind of dislocation: the surprising connections between medieval geographical thought and twentieth- and twenty-first-century visual arts, including Dadaism and the remarkable *Mappamundi Suite* of the Gujarati artist Gulammohammed Sheikh. While past spatial orders may be relegated to obscurity, they just as often linger – in archives, memories, and ruins – to be retrieved and reanimated in revealing ways.

Contents

Acknowledgements

I received support and encouragement from a number of people and institutions in the course of writing this book. I would particularly like to thank the Leverhulme Trust for awarding me a Research Fellowship in 2009–10, and the School of English and Drama at Queen Mary, University of London, which granted me two periods of sabbatical leave, in 2013 and 2017, and provided a subvention to help defray the costs of publication. Beyond material assistance, the School has offered a remarkably pleasant and harmonious working environment, and for that I am very grateful to all my colleagues, especially fellow medievalists Tamara Atkin, Julia Boffey, and Jaclyn Rajsic. Much of this book was researched and written in the incomparable environment of the Warburg Institute Library, while the resources of the British Library and the Institute of Classical Studies, London, also proved invaluable. Particular thanks are due to Margaret Clunies Ross and Andy Merrills, both of whom read and commented most helpfully on draft chapters. Gulammohammed Sheikh responded with great generosity to my questions about his *Mappamundi Suite*; it was Ananya Kabir who alerted me to his work in the first place.

Some of the ideas and arguments that appear in this book were first presented as conference and seminar papers, and I am grateful for the comments and discussion engendered in all instances. In 2010 Marica Milanesi's invitation to participate in the international colloquium on "Fonte cartografiche tra medioevo ed età moderna" at the Fondazione Centro Studi sulla Civiltà del Tardo Medioevo, San Miniato, provided the stimulus for the first version of Chapter 7. Parts of Chapter 4 were delivered in 2014 at the École Pratique des Hautes Études, Paris in the seminar of Patrick Gautier Dalché, a particular honour, since it is no exaggeration to say that, without Gautier Dalché's scholarship, this book would not have been possible. Audiences at Birkbeck, University of London, and the Centre for Medieval and Renaissance Culture, Southampton, heard sections of Chapters 6 and 8, respectively. The Austrian Historical Institute in Rome generously hosted a conference on the subject of *translatio imperii et studii*, in 2011, at which I presented an early version of Chapter 5. I hope the Institute will not mind me making it the scene of the fictional dialogue in Chapter 6, which began life as a monologue as long ago as 2005, when Anke Bernau and David Matthews invited me to a colloquium on "medieval nation" at the University of Manchester.

Part of Chapter 4 has previously appeared as "A Map of Ovid's *Tristia* I.10 in Dublin, Trinity College MS 632," *Journal of the Warburg and Courtauld Institutes* 75 (2012), 31–51, while elements of Chapters 5 and 9 appeared in "Maps of Empires Past," in *Post-Empire Imaginaries? Anglophone Literature, History, and the Demise of Empires*, ed. Barbara Buchenau and Virginia Richter (Leiden, 2015), 3–23. I am grateful to the Journal and to the editors of *Post-Empire Imaginaries?* for permission to reproduce this material.

It is, finally, a pleasure to acknowledge the assistance of the editorial team at the Pontifical Institute of Mediaeval Studies. I would like to make particular mention of James Carley for initially welcoming the project; Kirsten Schut for her exemplary copy-editing; and Megan Jones for advice on images. Above all, I thank Fred Unwalla for all his help in seeing *Dislocations* into print, and especially for his consistent and thoughtful engagement with the book. Three anonymous readers for the press wrote warm, extensive, and properly critical reports on the entire manuscript, which have greatly improved the final version.

Preface

Readers of this book will notice some elements that may appear unusual. In the course of the introductory chapter "Dislocations," an authorial monologue is interrupted by the disgruntled voice of an imagined reader (or listener). This voice, still rather unhappy, returns in the conclusion to pose a number of questions. Chapter 6 contains within it an imagined dialogue between three academics on the subject of nations and the representation of space in the Middle Ages. Finally, a "dialogue in hell between two readers" (different ones, I imagine, to the interlocutor of the introduction and conclusion) appears between Chapters 4 and 5, and again prior to Chapter 8. The initials of these readers ("WS" and "RF") derive from Wallace Stevens's poem "The Idea of Order at Key West," but their comments are not intended to approximate the thoughts of Stevens or of the apostrophised Ramon Fernandez. These dialogic elements seemed for the most part to accrete organically to the project as I wrote, rather than being the result of a conscious decision taken at any one moment. I am sure that they emerged from a sense of frustration with the limitations of academic prose as it tends to be practiced today. But the dialogues were also a practical response to particular problems, such as the difficulty of treating a subject like "nation," with its sizeable intellectual baggage, marked by a huge bibliography, in a relatively compact and engaging manner. Readers – actual ones rather than the phantoms in these pages – can judge whether this approach has been successful or not.

List of Figures

Illustrations appear following page 156.

Sources of all illustrations are indicated below. Every effort has been made to ensure that owners and photographic sources are accurately credited; if there are any errors or omissions, please bring them to the attention of the Pontifical Institute of Mediaeval Studies, so that appropriate corrections may be made in any future edition.

CHAPTER ONE

Dislocations

I turned to the man and spoke.

"Are you Uruguayan or Argentine?"

"Argentine, but I've been living in Geneva since '14," came the reply. There was a long silence. Then I asked a second question.

"At number seventeen Malagnou, across the street from the Russian Orthodox Church?"

He nodded.

"In that case," I resolutely said to him, "your name is Jorge Luis Borges. I too am Jorge Luis Borges. We are in 1969, in the city of Cambridge."

"No," he answered in my own, slightly distant, voice, "I am here in Geneva, on a bench, a few steps from the Rhone."[1]

In "The Other" (*El otro*), the opening story of Jorge Luis Borges's *The Book of Sand* (1975), two times converge, then contradict and disambiguate. At the outset of the narrative Borges explicitly invokes the ancient *dictum* of Heraclitus that "one cannot step twice into the same river."[2] Borges sits on a bench by the

---

1. Jorge Luis Borges, "The Other," in *The Book of Sand and Shakespeare's Memory*, trans. Andrew Hurley (London, 2001), 3–11, at 4; "El otro," in *El libro de arena* (Buenos Aires, 1975), 9–21, at 10–11: "Me le acerqué y le dije: —Señor, ¿usted es oriental o argentino? —Argentino, pero desde el catorce vivo en Ginebra — fue la contestación. Hubo un silencio largo. Le pregunté: —¿En el número diecisiete de Malagnou, frente a la iglesia rusa? Me contestó que sí. —En tal caso —le dije resueltamente— usted se llama Jorge Luis Borges. Yo también soy Jorge Luis Borges. Estamos en 1969, en la ciudad de Cambridge. —No —me respondió con mi propia voz un poco lejana. Al cabo de un tiempo insistió: —Yo estoy aquí en Ginebra, en un banco, a unos pasos del Ródano."

2. Charles H. Kahn, *The Art and Thought of Heraclitus: An Edition of the Fragments with Translation and Commentary* (Cambridge, 1979), 168 (fr. 51); see also *Heraclitus: The Cosmic Fragments*, ed. G.S. Kirk (Cambridge, 1962), 366–84. The saying, which was known to Plato, and subsequently cited (with different interpretations) by Aristotle and Seneca, was recorded by Plutarch, who related it to the phantasmic nature of every being; it is similar to another fragment ("Upon those who step into the same rivers different and again different waters flow"), also of debated meaning.

Charles, looks at the river, which "made me think of time ... Heraclitus' ancient image." He suddenly senses that he "had lived this moment before," notices someone else sitting on the bench, hears the other man whistling, then singing, and "with horror" recognizes the other's voice.[3] The ensuing conversation flickers, briefly sparks, but finally stalls in mutual awkwardness. Borges the younger reads Dostoyevsky and writes poems on the brotherhood of mankind; Borges the elder has moved on ("Only individuals exist").[4] What gives the story its strangeness and poignancy is the symmetry of the benches by the rivers, the shock of the cohesion of the Charles in Cambridge, Massachusetts, with the Rhone in Geneva.

It is, for the moment of the story, as if the flow of those waters could overcome distance, becoming "the flow of time," of a non-linear history ("As for history ... There was another war ... the cyclical Battle of Waterloo"). History that moves in circles allows memory to work against the effects of time and space: "The tune carried me back to a patio that no longer exists and to the memory of Alvaro Melián Lafinur, who died so many years ago."[5] The dialogue between the two versions of Borges leads to a third place: their point of origin. "Mother is well, living happily in her house in Buenos Aires, on the corner of Charcas and Maipú, but Father died some thirty years ago ... Our grandmother had died in the same house."[6] If there is a triangle in "The Other" between a home and two abroads – Europe, North America – the overriding experience of the story is one of the suspension of geometry. Two benches in two places at two times become a single bench by the river of time: a river with many names.

Geography is most obviously understood as the establishment of spatial order. Literally a writing of the earth, its lines, names, and measurements all work to make space comprehensible, navigable, and susceptible to representation. To represent the earth is to make it legible, repeatable. It is to identify places, distinguished from other places: "We are in the city of Cambridge"; "I am here in Geneva, a few steps from the Rhone." Geography is currently constituted as an academic discipline, but this was not always the case. In the past, as it still does,

3. "The Other," 3–4; "El otro," 9–10: "... el río hizo que yo pensara en el tiempo. La milenaria imagen de Heráclito ... Sentí de golpe la impresión ... de haber vivido ya aquel momento."

4. "The Other," 7.

5. "The Other," 6, 4; "El otro," 14, 10: "Hubo otra guerra ... la cíclica batalla de Waterloo"; "El estilo me retrajo a un patio, que ha desaparecido, y a la memoria de Álvaro Melián Lafinur, que hace tantos años ha muerto." Melián Lafinur, a poet, was Borges's cousin.

6. "The Other," 5; "El otro," 13: "Madre está sana y buena en su casa de Charcas y Maipú, en Buenos Aires, pero padre murió hace unos treinta años. ... Nuestra abuela había muerto en la misma casa."

spatial representation found expression across diverse disciplines and practices. In Europe, in classical antiquity and the Middle Ages, these disciplines included the study of grammar, rhetoric, geometry, astronomy, and the arts of history and poetry. Then as now, forms of representation varied according to social needs and generic conventions. The world, its regions, and cities could be expressed as a sumptuous map, a workaday diagram, or by means of a written description. Geography could be found in a poem, a painting, or a legal document.

Naturally, the representation of the earth, and the establishment of spatial order, will always bring with it questions of ownership and control. Such questions go beyond the matter of who makes a map – government, individual, corporation, religious order, or combinations of these and other categories – and extend to the nature of representation. On what basis is geographic order recognised? What constitutes order: what are its requirements? The answers to these questions were, and are, far from universal.

The following chapters argue that the representation of geographical space can only fully be understood by reference to elements of disorder and dislocation within representation. Such elements need not be seen as anarchic. Geometry, the measurement of the earth, remains central to the geography of dislocation. The novelty and alternative of dislocative geographies lie instead in the premise that place is read through place, that the understanding of a location is never entirely pure, never completely separate from other locations. In the modern era this experience is most obviously realised as one of the effects of colonialism – the Old World place name replicated in the New – and as the (often related) experience of migration, voluntary or enforced. It is also the mark of certain artistic movements of the twentieth and twenty-first centuries – Dadaist collage, Borgesian fiction and their successors – in which apparently distinct experiences of time and space co-exist. Spatial overlay, the repetition and reiteration of places, may consequently seem a mark of modernity, but neither colonialism, nor migration, nor artistic layerings of place were invented in the "modern" era. Dislocation has a long history.

In this book, the discussion of that history takes as its focal point the European Middle Ages, understood as a period extending from the transformation of the western Roman Empire in the fifth century until the religious Reformations of the sixteenth century. No attempt will be made to claim this period, or the European region, as one of special significance for the concept of dislocation. Nevertheless, medieval Europe witnessed four manifestations of a "geography of dislocation" that seem particularly significant, both in their own right and for their profound connections with modern spatial dislocations. These were the medieval reworking of classical Greek and Roman spatial representation, itself abounding in acts of disruption of various kinds; the reconfiguration of space around emergent regnal and national identities and in terms of vernacular languages, but also from c. 1350–1600 in terms of a powerful humanist spatial ethic; the figuration of migration, wanderings, and mission in which particular individuals (saints, tribes, heroes, and heroines) are read as vectors of place; and the emergence of the map as a form of text existing in diverse genres, and susceptible to various forms of textual play. The organisation of chapters in this study corresponds roughly to these themes within geographical thought. An opening section on classical geography and the medieval reception of *geographica* in classical poetry leads on to an exploration of the challenge to geographical order posed by temporal and spatial change (*mutatio*), by translation both linguistic and metaphoric, and by narratives of migration and nation. A final section considers the role of medieval spatial practices in the work of certain twentieth- and twenty-first-century artists. The forces of migration, the mutation of place names across time and across languages, and the literary dismantling of order all left their traces on medieval maps, verbal and graphic, and in turn these heterogenous texts have generated playful yet highly intellectual responses in which tenets of modernity can be dismantled by reference to the medieval.

At some times deliberate, at others accidental, always creative, geographic disorder is itself part of order, an essential element that constitutes meaning. To return to Borges's "The Other," one fundamental question is what allows this fiction to take place: what are its grounds? How is it possible to imagine the temporal and spatial fusion of Geneva c. 1918 with Cambridge c. 1969? The starting points for these breaches of order are the orders themselves: chronology and geography. (And they too come marked by the threat of confusion: which "city of Cambridge"? "Since '14" of which century?). The story itself advances a number of explanations to account for its temporary dismantling of norms, its doubling of selfhood. The possibility that the encounter between the two Borgeses takes place in a dream is raised early in the narrative, and it returns in the conclusion: "The other man dreamed me, but did not dream me *rigorously.*"[7] Memory, but also the loss of memory, similarly take on the guise of explanatory frameworks which allow confusion and mingling: "the other man spoke to me in a dream, which is why he could forget me; I spoke to him while I was awake, and so I am still tormented by the memory."[8] Yet the reader is left with a parody of reasoning: neither of these Escher-esque representations of logic ultimately explains anything. Order resumes, more or less, leaving the dialogue between

7. "The Other," 11; "El otro," 21: "El otro me soñó, pero no me soñó rigurosamente." The lack of rigour explains the anomaly that, during the encounter, the elder Borges hands the younger a banknote dated 1964, only to learn later that banknotes are not dated.

8. "The Other," 11; "El otro," 21: "... el otro conversó conmigo en un sueño y fue así que pudo olvidarme; yo conversé con él en la vigilia y todavía me atormenta el recuerdo."

selves across space and time temporary. However, the implication lingers that the conjunction of places is best seen not a rupture, but as a condition of spatial order.

Modes of Dislocation

Thank you for this introduction. But it leaves me with some questions. Are you going to stick to historical sources or literary ones? And if – as looks likely – you plan, no doubt fashionably, to mix the two, are you saying that "geographies of dislocation" are historical phenomena, in the sense of being experienced by real people in real time and space? Or literary phenomena, which is to say products of the imagination, without an impact on how people actually understand geography? Borges, presumably, was under no delusion that the Rhone flowed into the Charles ...

I hope you do not stop reading now, but these kinds of distinctions between historical and literary sources, real and imaginary, are not particularly helpful when one looks at certain problems of spatial representation. My argument is that geographies of dislocation are both experienced historically and given imaginative expression. So one starts with Borges as a way of encapsulating dislocation; but the next step might be to think about the remarkable tendency of medieval churchmen, architects and builders, to construct replicas of the Holy Sepulchre in Jerusalem in parts of Europe, so that by the end of the fifteenth century one could find a Jerusalem in Bologna, in Brindisi, in Wiltshire, in Augsburg, in Pisa, in Fulda, in Torres del Rio, in Cambridge, in Mtskheta, Georgia ... These were and in some cases still are real buildings, and it is reasonably conjectured that they were intended to draw visitors towards an experience of Jerusalem – an experience of its space and of all the spiritual significance that space entailed – in somewhere other than Jerusalem itself.[9] But it is not clear to me that there can be

9. Richard Krautheimer, "Introduction to an 'Iconography of Medieval Architecture,'" *Journal of the Warburg and Courtauld Institutes* 5 (1942): 1–33; Geneviève Bresc-Bautier, "Les imitations du S. Sepulcre de Jérusalem (IXe–XVe siècles)," *Revue d'histoire de la spiritualité* 50 (1974): 319–42; Robert Ousterhout, "The Church of S. Stefano: A 'Jerusalem' in Bologna," *Gesta* 20 (1981): 311–21; Robert Ousterhout, "Flexible Geography and Transportable Topography," in *The Real and Ideal Jerusalem in Jewish, Christian and Islamic Art*, ed. Bianca Kühnel (Jerusalem, 1998), 393–404; Colin Morris, "Bringing the Holy Sepulchre to the West: S. Stefano, Bologna, from the Fifth to the Twentieth Century," in *The Church Retrospective*, ed. R.N. Swanson (Woodbridge, 1997), 31–59; Bianca Kühnel, "Virtual Pilgrimages to Real Places: The Holy Landscapes," in *Imagining Jerusalem in the Medieval West*, ed. Lucy Donkin and Hanna Vorholt (Oxford, 2012), 243–64; Bianca Kühnel, Galit Noga-Banai, and Hanna Vorholt, eds., *Visual Constructs of Jerusalem* (Turnhout, 2014); Pnina Arad, "Is Calvary Worth

a meaningful categorical separation between that experience of space as something historical and real, and – for example – the well-known epithet hurled by Francis Petrarch at papal Avignon: "Babylon on the Rhone." The dislocations involved in constructing both Jerusalem in Bologna, and Avignon as Babylon, are actions that require symbolic but also literal interpretation; they rely on the same processes, whereby a known geographical order is realigned. As for Borges, he may or may not have experienced all sorts of delusions, but his conjunction of those two rivers makes possible their conjunction in the mind of a reader, including a reader who has experienced neither.

Alright. But I wonder what your next step is going to be. You say that there is nothing "special" about spatial dislocation in the Middle Ages, though you go on to assert that there is something "significant" about it. But how are you planning to situate this "significant-but-not-special" dislocation? Will you, for instance, attempt to reconstruct the mentalities by which people in the Middle Ages perceived space, and (consequently?) spatial disorders of the kind you are interested in? In other words, how thorough are you going to be?

It is certainly possible to imagine a painstaking reconstruction of the mentality of a medieval society with particular reference to the society's sense of space: how its members perceived and represented their surroundings, but also how they conceived of larger spaces – their region, nation or empire (if applicable), the Catholic church in its local and supra-local manifestations, the world and ultimately the cosmos. All the while acknowledging the differences within that "they": the different perceptions of literate and non-literate, highly and moderately educated, aristocratic and common, male and female, adult and child, native and non-native, and so on. A sort of spatial *Montaillou*. In fact something similar has been attempted for medieval Marseille, with interesting results.[10] However, this is not the way I intend to proceed. Even if the study of a single village or town can be assumed to be representative of some larger mentality (and that is a big

Restoring? The Way of the Cross in Romans-sur-Isère, France," in *Between Jerusalem and Europe: Essays in Honour of Bianca Kühnel*, ed. Renana Bartal and Hanna Vorholt (Leiden, 2015), 154–72; Laura Venesky, "Jerusalem Refracted: Geographies of the True Cross in Late Antiquity," and Lucy Donkin, "Earth from Elsewhere: Burial in *terra sancta* beyond the Holy Land," both in *Natural Materials of the Holy Land and the Visual Translation of Place 500–1500*, ed. Renana Bartal, Neta Bodner, and Bianca Kühnel (London, 2017), 64–75; 109–26.

10. Daniel Lord Smail, *Imaginary Cartographies: Possession and Identity in Late Medieval Marseille* (Ithaca, 1999); *Montaillou* itself contains a short chapter on concepts of time and space among the villagers: Emmanuel Le Roy Ladurie, *Montaillou: Village occitan de 1294 à 1324* (Paris, 1975), 419–45.

"even if"), it seems preferable to outline some of the fault lines within spatial order that extend across a range of times and societies. A microhistory of spatial perceptions might not, that is, tell us very much without a lot of contextualisation and it would not be able to escape the role of texts in mediating and shaping the experience of space.

For that reason I make no apology for concentrating on representation: this is at base a study of dislocation as a textual phenomenon, and such a study cannot be confined to any particular genre. Geography did not exist as a discipline in the Middle Ages. As I have already indicated, that had the effect of diffusing intellectual engagement with geographical matters across a wide range of genres. Geographic learning was embedded in classical poetry; it was attached to chronicles and absorbed within encyclopedic compendia. It can be found in letters, in romance and epic narrative, in saints' lives, biblical exegesis, legal documentation. It can most obviously be found in maps – which, in the Middle Ages as in classical antiquity, took the form of purely verbal descriptions of the earth, its topography, and peoples, as well as graphic representation in which word and image, *scriptura et pictura*, were considered vital.[11] As these remarks suggest, maps in this period especially cannot be understood in isolation from other texts. The following pages follow the topic of dislocation across narratives that produced, celebrated, and tried to resolve spatial disorder, without drawing firm boundaries between historical periods. The focus of this book is almost entirely on spatial representation in the Latin west; inclusion of materials from the Byzantine east and the Islamic world would have required a comparative dimension beyond its scope. Nevertheless my hope is that the study of spatial dislocation as the product of the intersection of history and textuality, with its attendant problems, can reveal points of convergence or difference with these and other related fields.

So what is "dislocation"?

Let me offer some basic starting points for this discussion by outlining some of the different modes of "dislocation." In no way an exhaustive list or rigidly defined system, the following pages identify four significant processes by which the texts discussed in this volume recast geographic order: superimposition; exile; translation and mutation; and error.

---

11. See particularly Margriet Hoogvliet, *Pictura et Scriptura: Textes, images et herméneutique des Mappae Mundi (XIIIe–XVIe siècles)* (Turnhout, 2007); Patrick Gautier Dalché, "De la glose à la contemplation: Place et fonction de la carte dans les manuscrits du haut Moyen Âge," *Settimane di studio del Centro italiano di studi sull'alto medioevo* 41 (1994): 693–771.

1. Superimposition

Perhaps the most straightforward mode of spatial dislocation is that in which a spatial form – a river, mountain, building, street, or entire city, for example – is replicated or relocated in another place. The act of superimposition requires a kind of transparency: the superimposed place is read both in terms of its standard associations, and in terms of its newly-acquired significance in the site of its relocation. The Holy Sepulchre must continue to signify as the Holy Sepulchre of Jerusalem, even as it is recast across the cities of Europe; but its meaning is also that of an agent of dislocation, since it is "in" and "at" so many places. In its turn, the site of relocation acquires new spatial significations, as the host of an alien spatial form. This mode of superimposition changes significance when it multiplies – the many Jerusalems refer not just to the original, but to all the other replicas, never liberated from a powerful investment in the space of the first.

Yet it is not necessarily the case that superimposition of places demands a relationship of priority, in which one place is removed from its original position and relocated elsewhere, in a secondary site. In some instances, rather than x in y, the relation between the two (or more) superimposed parties is one of equivalence. One of the clearest examples of superimposition as a mode of spatial play in the Middle Ages is the work of Opicinus de Canistris. Opicinus (1296–c. 1354) was a papal notary who expressed as the fruit of certain mystical visions a series of figures, in which he literally superimposed city and regional maps upon a sea chart showing the Mediterranean basin, including parts of northern Europe, north Africa, and the near east; in some of Opicinus' images, Europe and Africa are anthropomorphized and placed on top of one another (Figure 1).[12] As already indicated, the nature of superimposition is not to erase one text with another. The result is not a palimpsest, in the technical meaning of that term as a manuscript in which one text has been scraped away or otherwise removed to make way for another text or texts (and in which some elements of the initial text may nevertheless survive, or be recoverable). Rather, Opicinus intended both maps (of the city and the region, of Europe and Africa) to be read together, without one taking priority over the other.

All the same, superimposition tends towards assertions of control, whether political or artistic. The replication of the design of a church and its surrounding topography, the relocation of an expropriated monument, the overlay of one map upon another, all require an authorial presence to manipulate materials in such a way as to allow their realignment and recognition.

12. See Chapter 8.

2. Exile and the Out of Place

In a twelfth-century primer on the study of the liberal arts (*Didascalicon de studio legendi*), the theologian Hugh of St Victor asserted an apparently simple proposition: for those who philosophize, the entire world is a place of exile; hence "he is perfect to whom the entire world is as a foreign land." Hugh described a progression, from the love of homeland, to the perception of homeland everywhere, to the renunciation of home and the embrace of exile.[13] Alien land (*aliena terra*) drives a person to intellectual effort. Such thinking was deeply rooted in classical philosophy, and manifest in literary texts: Hugh managed to cite tags from Virgil, Ovid, and Horace in support of his proposition. The notion was also entirely cohesive with a Christian morality that rejected the transitory things of the world and looked instead to the world to come, which was eternal and unchanging. The letters of Paul, and subsequent exegesis, had established the figure of the believer as a *peregrinus*, a foreigner or pilgrim on earth, one who awaited his homeland in the celestial city of God.[14] To attain a sense of the world as exile was to experience temporality, and the body, as alien forms.

Hugh of St Victor may have deployed the idea of homeland as exile in the *Didascalicon* at the level of a pious abstraction, but another twelfth-century example shows it directed towards more immediate political ends. In the *Gesta Regum Anglorum* of the English monk William of Malmesbury, the idea appears in the extraordinary sermon of Pope Urban II that launches the first Crusade in 1095. Other versions of Urban's sermon at the Council of Clermont survive, most written closer to the event than William's chronicle of c. 1125; whatever its veracity, the speech shows strikingly the level and nature of geographical consciousness available to educated churchmen of the period. In William's account, Urban provocatively lists Christian lands of Asia and Africa now in the hands of the Saracens or Turks. Yet the geography is typically layered: first a roll call of provinces derived from Isidore of Seville's early seventh-century *Etymologiae* (14.3.38),

13. Hugh of St-Victor, *Didascalicon de studio legendi: A Critical Text* 3.19, ed. Charles Henry Buttimer (Washington, DC, 1939), 69: "perfectus vero, cui mundus totus exsilium est." Translations throuogut this book are my own unless otherwise indicated. On classical and medieval representations of exile see, inter alia, Jan Felix Gaertner, "The Discourse of Displacement in Greco–Roman Antiquity," in *Writing Exile: The Discourse of Displacement in Greco-Roman Antiquity and Beyond*, ed. Jan Felix Gaertner (Leiden, 2007), 1–20; Thomas Ehlen, "Bilder des Exils–das Exil als Bild: Ästhetik und Bewältigung in lyrischen Texten," in *Exil, Fremdheit und Ausgrenzung in Mittelalter und früher Neuzeit*, ed. Andreas Bihrer et al. (Würzburg, 2000), 151–232.

14. 2 Cor 5:6; Hebr. 11:13–16; Ambrose's commentary on Psalm 118: *Opera V: Expositio Psalmi CXVIII* 7.28, ed. M. Petschenig (Vienna, 1913), 144: "qui enim domesticus est dei, exul est mundo, qui conuersatur in caelestibus, peregrinus est terris."

buttressed by references to Lucan's first-century AD epic, the *Bellum civile*. Then a call on his audience – people from "the world's more temperate provinces" – to reclaim the lost territory. Finally, in answer to the possibility that these sturdy Christians might baulk at leaving their homelands, Urban deploys the neo-Stoic leitmotif: "to the Christian the whole world is at once a state of exile and a fatherland: exile is fatherland; fatherland is exile."[15] It was not the case that Urban (or William) had no access to contemporary geographical information. The twelfth century saw the burgeoning of description of contemporary space, often as a direct result of crusading activities,[16] as well as an increase in the production of *mappae mundi*. Indeed, William's gloss on the sermon identifies contemporary peoples of the European north in a way that verges on the popular medieval genre of national stereotype: zeal for crusade seized not only Mediterranean peoples, but also induced the Welshman to leave his hunting, the Scot his fleas, the Dane his continual drinking, and the Norwegian his raw fish.[17] Instead, the relentless classicism of the sermon – apart from references to Lucan and Prudentius, its final appeal to virtue is based on the Latin translation of Flavius Josephus' account of the speech of Eleazar to Jewish survivors at Masada[18] – must be seen as a cultural preference. The geographical descriptions contained in classical texts, accessed through late antique compilations, not only bore authority; they also brought historical and literary resonance which could be mobilised to contemporary religious and political ends. The result was a deliberately eclectic swirl of reference, in which contemporary and antique were not opposed categories.

The dramatic success of the first Crusade only added to themes of spatial dislocation. Not only did the crusaders achieve the view of the Holy Sepulchre *in situ* that Urban had promised them; occupation of the Holy Land also brought,

---

15. William of Malmesbury, *Gesta Regum Anglorum: The History of the English Kings* 4.347.1–16, at 15, ed. and trans. R.A.B. Mynors, R.M. Thomson and M. Winterbottom, 2 vols (Oxford, 1998), 1: 598–606, at 604–6: "quia diuersis respectibus Christiano totus est mundus exilium et totus mundus patria; ita exilium patria, et patria exilium."

16. *Du Yorkshire à l'Inde: Une "géographie" urbaine et maritime de la fin du XIIe siècle (Roger de Howden?)*, ed. Patrick Gautier Dalché (Geneva, 2005); Patrick Gautier Dalché, "Le renouvellement de la perception et de la représentation de l'espace au XIIe siècle," in *Renovación intelectual del occidente europeo (siglo XII)* (Pamplona, 1998), 169–218.

17. *Gesta Regum Anglorum* 4.348.2, 1: 606: "Tunc Walensis uenationem saltuum, tunc Scottus familiaritatem pulicum, tunc Danus continuationem potuum, tunc Noricus cruditatem reliquit piscium."

18. *Gesta Regum Anglorum*, 2: 305–6; Neil Wright, "'Industriae Testimonium': William of Malmesbury and Latin Poetry Revisited," *Revue Bénédictine* 103 (1993): 482–531, at 511–19; Neil Wright, "Twelfth-Century Receptions of a Text: Anglo-Norman Historians and Hegesippus," *Anglo-Norman Studies* 31 (2009): 177–95; Eleazar's speech is at *Hegesippi qui dicitur Historiae Libri V* 5.53.1, ed. V. Ussani (Vienna, 1932–60), 408–16.

at least for some, a relocation of identity. "For we who were Westerners have now become Easterners," Fulcher of Chartres proclaimed in his chronicle of the first Crusade. "He who was a Roman or a Frank is a Galilean or Palestinian in this land. He who was of Rheims or Chartres, now is styled 'of Tyre' or 'of Antioch.' ... He who was a foreigner is now as though a native, and he who is a visitor is everywhere made a resident."[19] Here though the boast of "at home in exile" is turned around, as the exile claims possession of alien soil. In the later Middle Ages, the ultimate failure of the crusading project added a further layer of spatial memory: the vestiges of Crusader rule, ruined strongholds, churches converted to mosques.

The emergence of humanism in the fourteenth century added a new twist to the meaning of exile. In the thought of Francis Petrarch, the Christian's exile from the city of God becomes also exile from classical civilization. This version of exile is not a state that can be remedied by a return to homeland: one may imitate and even correspond with antiquity, but one may not inhabit it. Yet it was also an immensely productive sensibility. The exilic intellect travels widely, traverses the extremes of the world, while the unlettered remains static, domestic, rural.[20] This contrast emerges strikingly in a famous letter written by Petrarch to the poet and courtier Philippe de Vitri. Philippe had apparently complained that, while in Italy, his master, the Cardinal Gui de Boulogne, had endured "exile" from Paris. Petrarch's rebuke contains not only patriotic praise of Italy, but also a lament for the loss of Philippe's youthful curiosity about the world – the curiosity of a noble mind that knew no boundaries, unlike that of the peasant who remains tethered to his own land, "in proprio rure."[21] This is the same *rus* that is the subject of cel-

19. Fulcher of Chartres, *Historia Hierosolymitana (1095–1127)* 3.37.3–5, ed. Heinrich Hagenmeyer (Heidelberg, 1913), 748–49: "nam qui fuimus Occidentales, nunc facti sumus Orientales. qui fuit Romanus aut Francus, hac in terra factus est Galilaeus aut Palaestinus. qui fuit Remensis aut Carnotensis, nunc efficitur Tyrius vel Antiochenus. ... qui erat alienigena, nunc est quasi indigena, et qui inquilinus est, utique incola factus."

20. A similar sentiment is maintained by Palla Strozzi in Francesco Filelfo's dialogue *De exilio* (On Exile) 1.184, ed. Jeroen de Keyser, trans. W. Scott Blanchard (Cambridge, 2013), 134–35: "Educatio igitur atque institutio vitae plus interdum valet quam ortus" (So education and training for life sometimes has greater influence than birth).

21. Francis Petrarch, *Le Familiari* 9.13, ed. Vittorio Rossi, 4 vols (Florence, 1933–42), 2: 246–56, at 252. Exile was a recurrent theme in Petrarch's writing: see particularly the letters of consolation on exile (*Fam.* 2.3 and 2.4) and *De Remidiis utriusque fortunae* 2.67; 2.125; for commentary see, among an abundant literature, Giuseppe Mazzotta, *The Worlds of Petrarch* (Durham, 1993), 66–72, 187–92; and recently Célia Filippini and Anne-Marie Telesinski, "Métaphores et métamorphoses de l'exil dans le *Canzoniere* de Pétrarque," and Enrico Fenzi, "Petrarca e l'esilio: Uno stile di vita," in *Écritures de l'exil dans l'Italie médiévale*, ed. Anna Fontes Baratto and Marina Gagliano (Paris, 2013), 141–55; 365–402.

ebration, even idealisation, in Virgil's *Eclogues* and *Georgics*, where it is contrasted in similarly stark terms with the outside world of Rome's imperial expanse. In Virgil too that knowledge of places beyond the native soil, intimately connected with empire, but also with mythology, furnishes a spatial order subject to figurative acts of dislocation. In the first *Eclogue*, Tityrus prompts Meliboeus' vision of invasion with an apparently casual simile, designed to express the strength of impression a certain "youth" (presumably Octavian) had made on him:

> ante pererratis amborum finibus exsul
> aut Ararim Parthus bibet aut Germania Tigrim,
> quam nostro illius labatur pectore uultus.[22]

> the Parthian exile will drink from the Arar, and Germania from the Tigris, having wandered the boundaries of each other's lands, before that one's face will pass from our heart.

The figure of the exile out of place, drinking from the "wrong" river, epitomises length of time (sooner that than this), but at the same time reveals the casual inversions of order that order itself – the order of places, of names – makes possible. These classical tropes of spatial play contributed to a way of thinking about the world, its rivers and peoples, that was available not only to a Petrarch, but also to those of a classicist bent who came before him.

3. *Translatio* and *mutatio*

The very idea of the "Middle Ages" is marked by certain spatial dislocations. Framed at one end by the disintegration of empire and at the other by the emergence of new imperial and national powers, the period saw the redefinition of the city of Rome as an ecclesiastical, rather than political, centre within Europe. Powerful and pervasive narratives of translation developed to explain not only the movement of political power (*translatio imperii*) across historical space and time, but also the transfer of what would now be called cultural capital (*translatio studii*), both conceived as a translation from east to west. To these narratives of spatial dissemination, according to which the Christian religion, imperial and in some cases royal power, and much of intellectual culture all acknowledged non-European points of origin, recursive practices such as pilgrimage, and genres such as epic, demanded the revisitation of places of memory, frequently located in a temporal and spatial elsewhere.

---

22. *Ecloga* 1.61–63, in P. *Vergili Maronis Opera*, ed. R.A.B. Mynors (Oxford, 1969), 3.

Ideologies of translation generally emphasise continuity; they acknowledge relocation, rather than dislocation. The crucial element is control, neatly expressed in the lapidary statement of the first-century AD rhetorician Quintilian concerning metaphor (*translatio*): "thus the noun or verb is translated from the place which is proper to it (*ex eo loco in quo proprium est*) into a place which is either not its own or which is better than its own."[23] *Translatio* is legitimate, indeed the mark of a more advanced level of eloquence, so long as the new "site" for the translated word is appropriate. "Do not always allow a word to reside in its usual place (*in proprio loco*)," urged Geoffrey of Vinsauf's early thirteenth-century manual of composition, the *Poetria nova*, in an apparent echo of Quintilian's dictum: "let it avoid its proper place and wander elsewhere (*perigrinetur alibi*), to find a pleasing seat in another's ground: let it be a new sojourner (*novus hospes*) there and please by its novelty."[24] The use of spatial language here is not coincidental. As I will outline in subsequent chapters, the sovereign disruption of order was a function of rhetoric which shaped conceptions of historical and political legitimacy. Empires, kingdoms, peoples, monasteries, universities, holy relics, the Bible itself: all derived authority, at one point or another during the Middle Ages, from acts of translation. Nevertheless, if we understand translation as something that encompasses imperfections as well as successes, it is possible to find dislocation within it. If by translation we also understand mistranslation, mishearing and mis-speaking, and even untranslatability, all of which contribute to its processes, then it is possible to say that dislocation informs translation, and perhaps that it is necessary to it.

In the course of this book I will argue that another concept – *mutatio* – complicates *translatio*, sometimes overlapping, sometimes working in concert with it, but at other times opposing and disrupting it. *Mutatio* is in its simplest meaning a change, and as such could be encompassed within *translatio*. As Quintilian put it in his remarks on metaphor, "a trope is the change (*mutatio*) of the word or phrase from its own meaning into another with improvement."[25] But in a spatial context *mutationes* functioned in less predictable and ordered ways. Certain kinds of *mutatio* were unplanned, the product of historical forces. Such *mutationes*

23. Quintilian, *Institutionis oratoriae libri duodecim* 8.6.5, ed. M. Winterbottom, 2 vols (Oxford, 1970), 2: 463: "Transfertur ergo nomen aut uerbum ex eo loco in quo proprium est in eum in quo aut proprium deest aut tralatum proprio melius est." Compare Cicero, *De oratore* 3.37, ed. K. Kumaniecki (Leipzig, 1969) 320: "iis [verbis], quae transferuntur et quasi alieno in loco conlocantur."

24. Translation from Ernest Gallo, *The* Poetria Nova *and its Sources in Early Rhetorical Doctrine* (The Hague, 1971), 54–55 (ll. 763–68).

25. *Institutionis oratoriae libri* 8.6.1, ed. Winterbottom, 2: 462: "Tropos est uerbi uel sermonis a propria significatione in aliam cum uirtute mutatio."

include, at their most banal, the loss of a place name over the course of time, or conversely the preservation of a place name without knowledge of what and where exactly it signified. Crucially, spatial mutation does not depend on movement from one place to another (*translatio*'s transfer from the original/proper to new/non-proper/better), but can be the product of stasis, where what changes is not the location but times, languages, or peoples. Lacking the self-licensing confidence of *translatio*, mutation may signify the arbitrary, the imposed, the illegitimate. Finally, *mutatio* does not only apply at a local level to the individual toponym. It can instead describe the passage of entire systems of spatial representation through different historical periods, with all the lacunae and errors that result from the reception of the record of past places.

4. Error

The notion of the Middle Ages as an era tolerant of error, devoid of critical sense, sacrificing reality at the altar of symbolism, is untenable. It is not based on a serious, open-minded engagement with medieval sources, but on an intellectual and – at a certain level – ideological commitment to the notion of the European Renaissance against which the Middle Ages must be seen literally as a death (of art, learning, civic sensibility) or at best as a childhood.[26] Error exists in all eras: it is a natural condition of order. In spatial terms, to construct order – to draw, to calculate, to name – is to create the possibility for mistakes. The interesting question to ask concerns the way in which societies define, identify, and regulate error. Which kinds of error are permitted, which punished, and who is authorised to judge error? What does the possibility of particular errors reveal? With regard to the representation of space, the Middle Ages inherited no shortage of error, and argument about error, from classical antiquity. Literally a wandering, error has both figurative and practical functions. Canonical texts, such as Virgil's *Aeneid*, embedded error in their structure, returning to the idea as a condition of foundation; late antique or medieval commentators (a Servius, for example, or an anonymous medieval glossator) tried to unpick the geographic convolutions of a Virgil or a Lucan, and sometimes added their own; medieval chroniclers

---

26. This ideology, which has a fundamental expression in Jacob Burckhardt's *Die Kultur der Renaissance in Italien* (Basel, 1860), is reasonably complex: it is secularist, though sympathetic to the Protestant critique of the "Catholic Middle Ages"; it is positivist, committed to notions of progress, particularly evident in its treatment of spatial representation; in certain manifestations it is aggressively Europhile; it is, often, the basis of a professional investment in "Renaissance Studies", but also – in ways that go back to the fourteenth-century invention of humanism – of "Classical Studies." For critique on spatial matters see Patrick Gautier Dalché, *L'espace géographique au Moyen Âge* (Florence, 2013), esp. 31–42 ("Considérations intempestives sur l'objet 'espace médiévale' et sur sa construction").

attempted to reconcile information from conflicting sources; humanists developed philological techniques so as to identify the correct modern location of ancient cities; sixteenth-century intellectuals argued about the language spoken in the earthly paradise and its possible preservation in place names. All these examples are made possible by a conception of error, and by the desire to disambiguate, to choose between different ways of representing space. They also show an ongoing commitment to making past spaces, their places and their peoples, legible for a contemporary audience.

In Macrobius's early fifth-century *Saturnalia* an unflattering comparison with Homer sees Virgil accused of mangling spatial order. While Homer is praised for listing places "as he would were he making the journey," obeying the "discipline of description" (*disciplina describentis*), Virgil "observes no sequence in the places he mentions but jumps around and cuts the sequence up."[27] In book 10 of the *Aeneid*, the list of troops allied with Aeneas against his rival Turnus veers from Pisa in furthest Etruria to places near Rome, then leaps to Liguria and across to Mantua. However seriously this criticism is meant, it indicates an expectation that poetic order should correspond to spatial order, that both operate within a fundamentally rhetorical function, and that to disrupt spatial order, and particularly to move in leaps (*saltibus*), obeying no particular order (rather than, for example, inverting), was highly unsatisfactory from the point of view of poetry. The *Saturnalia* strongly implies that an educated person will be able to judge such descriptions of space against a mental roll-call of places: "no more will you find that he followed an unbroken territorial sequence in the catalogue of Turnus' allies [in book seven], if you mentally review the places' locations."[28] The rhetorically-trained reader had internalised the position and sequence of places – *situs et series locorum* – and so recognised deviation where it occurred. Yet classical poetry – notably in the exuberant anti-geographies of Lucan's *Bellum civile* – could revel in manipulations of spatial order. Lucan's epic bequeathed a rich dislocative inheritance to its many medieval readers: mountains piled on mountains, rivers swapping characteristics, places that were neither land nor sea, seas or rivers so filled with corpses that they became land, land flooded to the point that it became a sea. Whether this was error, or poetic license, the medieval commentators on the *Bellum civile* and other classical texts that distorted geography

---

27. Macrobius, *Saturnalia* 5.15.3–4, ed. and trans. Robert A. Kaster, 3 vols (Cambridge, 2011), 2: 384: "disciplina describentis velut iter agentis accedit, nec ullo saltu cohaerentiam regionum in libro suo hiare permittit ... contra Vergilius nullum in commemorandis regionibus ordinem servat sed locorum seriem saltibus lacerat."

28. *Saturnalia* 5.15.5, trans. Kaster, 2: 386: "sed nec in catalogo auxiliorum Turni, si velis situm locorum mente percurrere, invenies illum continentiam regionum secutum."

tried to explain, and in explaining they sometimes drew diagrams, or even small maps. Lucan's spatial disordering was productive, not just of interpretation, but of new texts and images in their own right. Error, then, is not simply and not always a matter of mistakes. It can encompass deliberate and informed distortion, as well as misrepresentation. The identification of error may consequently involve not its correction but its commemoration.

You seem to be covering a lot of territory, rather rapidly. Is there an argument here?

Fundamentally this book is about trying to understand something, rather than trying to construct a neatly structured and convincing argument. There is an argument – or arguments – but within a wider exploration of the nature of what I am calling "dislocation." The initial starting point for this exploration is the dislocative nature of classical geographical thought and representation. I propose that classical geography was filled with lacunae, contradictions and uncertainties, but also marked by the capacity for dextrous play – as seen particularly in works of canonical poets such as Virgil, Ovid, and Lucan, though this point could also be made of Horace, Statius, and many other classical authors. The second starting point is the idea that the medieval reception of this unstable geography was thoughtful and creative, rather than inert. (Incidentally, neither of these points is original, but both represent a departure from a still influential paradigm, according to which classical texts exhibited intellectual and practical mastery over space, which medieval readers either ignored or ineptly copied). To those starting points I add the fundamental question: what happens when a society inherits a spatial order that comes with significant cultural authority but that manifestly no longer corresponds to the reality of space, because it dates from several centuries past, and because it is itself not the product of a synoptic vision but rather a patchwork of information from diverse sources? One answer might be to jettison it, or to take certain essential concepts and frameworks but rewrite the detail (medieval Islamic geography, influenced as it is by Persian and Indian traditions, essentially does this to its inheritance of ancient Greek texts). Another is to preserve the antiquated order, tactfully supplementing omissions and only updating where most necessary. It is this last response that in my view best characterises the western medieval reception of classical geography. But how does such an approach – classical foundations, medieval supplementation – understand and represent change? Broadly, this is the question addressed in the central section of this book. There I argue for the importance of *mutatio* as a major concern of medieval geographical thought, rather than the more normative *translatio*; there I debate the spatial understandings of *natio* in the Middle Ages; there

I argue for the constant interplay of Latin and vernacular spatial representation up to 1600, rather than a simple rise of the vernacular.

There are certain lines of argument that run across these discussions. First, that the emergence (or perhaps better the invention) of humanism in the fourteenth century is a crucial fault line for spatial representation, more significant than the discovery of the New World at the end of the fifteenth. Yet while humanism represents a change in the terms of engagement with classical texts, and while it has a marked impact on spatial representation (visual and verbal), it does not erase continuities with the preceding centuries. The same concerns, the same concepts, remain: *mutatio* and *translatio*; the location of historically attested places, whether in sacred or secular narrative; the relationship between Latin and vulgar tongues as vehicles for spatial representation. The second line of argument is that narrative, and the representation of narrative, contribute to the fracturing of space that is characteristic of dislocation. Narrative might seem at first sight to lend itself to coherence and order. But the multiplication of narratives – stories of different peoples, different places – pluralises spatial meaning. Where is Thebes? Which Babylon? What are the Syrtes? It depends which narrative you are glossing. The textual power of a single toponym lies in the wealth of stories that it can contain.

The final section of this book turns to examples of the textual effects of dislocations, rather than to thematic problems. Here too there is an argument about continuity, namely that – as certain modern artists have perceived – the move away from linear perspective as the foundation of western art prompted the identification of affinities with medieval art, including medieval maps. That identification operates at a generic level in a comparison between the *oeuvre* of the fourteenth-century visionary Opicinus de Canistris with Dadaist and surrealist art; it is specific and unambiguous in the spectacular adaptations of the Ebstorf *mappa mundi* produced by the contemporary Indian artist, Gulammohammed Sheikh. The "medieval" image is alive in modern representational practices; and the latter animate the former in unpredictable ways. Dislocation goes on, in other words, because spatial representation cannot help but be dislocative, but also because it is a powerful mode of imaginative and affective expression.

Limits of Dislocation

May I say that I remain unsatisfied? There seem to me to be at least two problems with the notion of dislocation as you have advanced it so far. These are in some ways practical problems, but there is an ethical dimension to them too. First, one could very easily reduce "dislocation" to a banality. I mean, pretty much everywhere you look you will find a dislocation of some sort, whether it is somebody in Yorkshire with a Persian rug in her living room, a Pole with a Thai baht in his wallet, a Floridian couple with an Eiffel Tower mug in their dishwasher, and so forth. Should a person in Europe or Africa who wears a t-shirt with the label "Made in China" be thought to "perform an act of dislocation"? Isn't this going to become a bit silly? And then, if we confine ourselves only to literary sources, open any book and you will find numerous characters, things, words and ideas that are in some way or another "out of place." So you could spend a lot of time sniffing out these dislocations and be none the wiser because in complex societies which are interconnected in numerous ways with other societies and cultures – above all, through trade, diplomacy, migration, and intellectual exchanges now including the internet – dislocations are entirely normal and unremarkable. And this brings about the second objection.

There is an implicit tendency in your analysis so far to view dislocation favourably: to be interested in it as a marker of pluralism, to value it for enabling alternative views, "textual play," "swirls of reference," and the like. No doubt there are numerous cases where the confusion of spatial order – or, if you like, the inherent disorder within spatial order – serves useful, and democratic, purposes. At the same time there are far more questionable deployments of alternative spatial orders: the country whose citizens proudly and provocatively sport maps showing their fatherland with borders vastly expanded, at the expense of neighbouring peoples and ethnic groups within and without the current boundaries. And further: certain dislocations (actual ones, not fantasies) are imperialist, expropriative, violent. So one may well smile wryly at the thought of Ovid relegated to first-century Tomis, or become fascinated by the deployment of chinoiserie in eighteenth-century English drawing rooms; but that smile might fade rather quickly when contemplating the dislocations wrought by slavery, war, and social exclusion. Dislocations, as the name rather suggests, can be painful. A final, related, objection is to ask about those relatively self-contained societies whose spatial orders (because they are not constructed out of conquest, conflict, or migration) contain few if any elements of dislocation.

There are certainly histories of relationships to land that are not ones of dislocation in the sense of migration, or of exile; and there are certainly histories of displacement from land that are not "creative" or playfully disruptive. The object of this study, however, is not to embrace dislocation as inherently redemptive or liberatory, but to understand some of its practices and effects, and thereby to complicate the notion of order. For order is usually negotiated, and always requires reinforcement and dissemination. Would you bear with me while I conclude with an example that may seem very distant, but which I believe will help to answer the question of what spatial dislocation, and the representation thereof, is and can be?

Do I have a choice?

The Canning Stock Route was established in the early part of the twentieth century by the eponymous Alfred Canning as a means of transporting cattle from the north-west to the south-west of Australia. Since almost the entirety of the 1850-kilometre-long route passes through desert, Canning needed to determine the precise points at which wells could be constructed. To find water in the arid landscape Canning and other members of his expedition resorted to inhumane methods. During the survey that mapped the route in 1906, they relied on local Aborigines to identify wells and soaks. While some apparently volunteered, Canning later admitted that his men captured and chained others; Aboriginal oral histories record that Canning deprived the captives of fresh water, then released and followed them as they sought out the nearest supply.[29] When eventually constructed, the Route consisted of 48 wells, many of which had the effect of impeding access to native water supplies. Although some were destroyed by indigenous populations soon after their completion, the wells were re-established between 1929 and 1931 and have become indelible markers of the region.[30] The Stock Route cut across the lands traditionally owned by indigenous groups, serving to undermine spatial orders underpinned by belief structures traditionally expressed in song, visual arts, and oral narrative. The Route also led to the widespread displacement of Aboriginal people, through movement "off the land" to population centres (missions, towns, settlements), through employment as labourers on the Stock Route itself, or through a variety of consequences resulting from contact with white settlers, not excluding abduction. The Stock Route, and the processes of colonisation of which it was a product and agent, had the effect of taking people from their lands, both literally and also metaphysically, as they lost the conceptual and parental relationship with land that is such a strong feature of traditional indigenous – and particularly Australian Indigenous – societies.

29. Allegations of cruelty made against Canning and his deputy, Herbert Trotman, by Edward Blake, a white member of the exploratory party, led to a Royal Commission: see *Royal Commission to Inquire into the Treatment of Natives by the Canning Exploration Party 15 January – 5 February 1908*, ed. Phil Bianchi et al (Carlisle, 2010). On the Aboriginal oral histories see "Of Mining and Meat: The Story of the Canning Stock Route," in *Yiwarra Kuju: The Canning Stock Route* (Canberra, 2010), 33–37, at 33–35.

30. "Of Mining and Meat," 33–37.

This familiar narrative of the imposition of power and culture in their various forms, with motivations by turn malevolent, indifferent, and well-meaning, has had somewhat unexpected effects on spatial representation. A sponsored programme of workshops involving over 100 native artists and curators, on multiple sites across the Western Desert,[31] has in recent years given the dislocations of the Canning Stock Route an unexpectedly rich expression in a revived practice of indigenous art. In numerous paintings, indigenous artists incorporate traditional narratives of the Dreamtime origins of natural features such as wells and soaks with their own experiences of the land, including removal forced and voluntary, and in several cases, violence. The discourse of the artists is nostalgic, recuperative: but at no point does it seek to evade the post-colonial landscape. In numerous artworks the wells of the Stock Route form crucial reference points. Others reproduce the line of the route itself, sometimes slender, vestigial, seemingly in danger of being reclaimed by the sandhills it once defined – yet never forgotten.

At stake in some recent artworks created by Western Desert peoples is both the idea of the map and the right to map. As one artist put it: "When you look at this painting, don't read it like a whitefella map. It's a Martu map: this is how we see the Country."[32] The "hybrid maps" of a group of Paruku (Lake Gregory) artists dramatise this concern in striking ways. A conventional map of part of the Stock Route, marked with wells, soaks, lakes, and camps, is redrawn on a landscape coloured by the dotting characteristic of indigenous art (Figure 2).[33] The intentions of the artists are to assert native title: the works are said to have been triggered by the legal recognition of indigenous land rights in a 2001 judgement of the Federal Court of Australia.[34] And yet if, following the crucial Mabo case of

31. Carly Davenport, "The Story behind the Canning Stock Route Project," in *Yiwarra Kuju*, 3–11; *Ngurra Kuju Walyja: One Country, One People. The Canning Stock Route Project, 2006–2011*, ed. Monique La Fontaine and Elisha Buttler (Perth, 2011).

32. Ngalangka Nola Taylor, commenting on "Martumili Ngurra" (2009), quoted in *Yiwarra Kuju*, 179; John Carty, "Drawing a Line in the Sand: The Canning Stock Route and Contemporary Art," in *Yiwarra Kuju*, 23–31, at 31: "These paintings are not, individually, maps in a Western sense. But *collectively* they emerge as a kind of map: not a map for orienting oneself in the landscape, but for re-orienting oneself in history." [Emphasis in original.]

33. See further the "Map of Dreaming tracks ... imposed over Canning's map": Monique La Fontaine, "Listening to Country: The Inseparable Links between Family and Dreaming on the 'Canning Stock Road,'" in *Yiwarra Kuju*, 13–21, at 18; and the "True Map of Canning Stock Route Country," an image drawn in sand by a senior Martu man in 2008, in which the route cuts through a grid of song lines and native itineraries: Carty, "Drawing a Line in the Sand," 27.

34. See "Paruku" (2007), in *Yiwarra Kuju*, 144.

1992, the legal requirement for native title is the continuous and unalienated use of, and presence on, land by traditional owners,[35] the rendering of the map of the Canning Stock Route tells a somewhat different story. The very construction of the map is testament to the colonial disruptions that were predicated upon non-recognition of the rights of indigenous peoples: its lines, names, and numbers ("Well 31," "New Delivery Camp") carry that history. Yet the redrawn map also carries the languages of Western Desert peoples, memorialised in place names, and it carries the land itself – in an aesthetic sense, as in a moral one, never wholly alienable, and susceptible to striking acts of reclamation.

This book will consider, for the most part, classical and medieval European dislocations of spatial orders. As the real and fictive dislocations already discussed indicate, however, there is little sense in a restrictive periodisation of dislocation. Instead, the task is to recognise the presence of dislocation within certain spatial orders, but also to see it as the effect of a collision or combination of diverse ways of describing the world. If there is a positive conclusion to be drawn from such a study, it concerns the survival of those spatial orders deemed superseded, unscientific, pre-modern. For it would seem that, while past spatial orders may be relegated to obscurity, they just as often linger – in archives, in memories, in ruins – to be retrieved and reanimated in surprising and revealing ways.

35. *Mabo and Others v State of Queensland* (1992), 107 Australian Law Reports 1.

CHAPTER TWO

The Dislocations of Classical Geography

In the penultimate book of his *Naturalis historia* (*Natural History*), Pliny the Elder conjured a startling vision of Rome. Writing around 75 AD, Pliny imagined all the noteworthy structures of the city, across a span of eight hundred years, piled on top of each other. Such a heap would certainly have been eye-catching, if unwieldy. Pliny mentions iconic imperial structures such as the Circus Maximus; the Basilica Aemilia, with its Phrygian columns; the Forum of Augustus; Vespasian's Temple of Peace; palaces, theatres, aqueducts and sewers. The point of the image was the extraordinary magnitude that such a pile would attain: "with everything piled up and thrown together in a single mass, it would rise to a size as if some other world were described, all in one place."[1] The pile, a statement of rhetorical control as well as political command, takes the catalogue of the buildings of Rome and raises it into a vertical structure, in a virtuosic display of both learning and imagination, a fitting triumph for Pliny's own accumulation of knowledge in the *Naturalis historia*. Architecture is an articulation of empire; writing its tributary. But is this an image of order or disorder? The pile is still a pile, a mass "thrown together." The fantasy seems to show the malleability of these imperial structures more than their durability, to invite awe rather than advance knowledge, to lump together rather than distinguish. There is something primal – chaotic, violent, even unhinged – about the pile.

Pliny's pile may serve more generally as a suitable emblem of the attempts of Greek and Roman authors to bring order to spatial representation. Like the pile of Rome's buildings, classical spatial order was the product of remarkable practical and intellectual achievements. The geographical writings of Pliny and many

---

1. Pliny the Elder, *Naturalis Historiae Libri XXXVII* 36.101, ed. C. Mayhoff, 6 vols (Leipzig, 1892–1909), 5: 343–44: "universitate vero acervata et in quendam unum cumulum coiecta non alia magnitudo exurget quam si mundus alius quidam in uno loco narretur." For discussion of this well-known but ambiguous passage see Valérie Naas, *Le projet encyclopédique de Pline l'Ancien* (Rome, 2002), 1, 207–8, 374–76; Sorcha Carey, *Pliny's Catalogue of Culture: Art and Empire in the Natural History* (Oxford, 2003), 73–74, 94–101; Mary Beagon, *The Elder Pliny on the Human Animal: Natural History Book 7* (Oxford, 2005), 29–30.

other ancient authors attest to an astonishing wealth of knowledge of peoples and places, as well as a highly developed understanding of the shape and size of the earth. This achievement is all the more impressive given the large number of ancient texts that do not survive: those parts of the pile now fragmentary or entirely missing. At the same time, in spite of its magnitude, the spatial order of Greek and Roman antiquity was neither fixed nor complete. It carried lacunae, errors, and points of uncertainty, to which were added the vagaries of textual transmission and the difficulties of interpreting often obscure lists of places, peoples, and natural features. In turn, the extent and detail of classical spatial representation formed the basis for spatial description in medieval Europe. Like much else in medieval culture, geographical thought was deeply rooted in classical antiquity. Those roots determined the ways in which the world could be conceived and represented, but they also transmitted the disorders of classical geography. Such disorders, and the attempt to define spatial order from which they arose, provide the necessary starting points for an understanding of the dislocations of medieval geographical thought. For in many ways the Middle Ages inherited a pile – a rich array of information that had never been completely stable.

Geography in classical Greece was not a subject in its own right, but a body of knowledge spread across a range of genres.[2] Among the wide variety of ancient Greek texts that display geographical thought of one kind or another, it is possible to discern two different – but by no means mutually exclusive – approaches to ordering the world: those of cosmology and topography. Cosmology understood the earth in relation to the stars and the passage of the sun. This perspective sought to determine the size of the earth, the relationship between seas and lands, and the effects of the sun's movement on human life. Cosmological models specified the number and direction of winds (usually eight or twelve),[3] and sought schematic ways of representing a spherical earth, of which only a part was actually known. One theory, which appears to date from at least the fifth century BC, divided a spherical earth into five zones from pole to pole. By analogy with a corresponding division of celestial zones, there were two habitable terrestrial

---

2. On Greek geography see *Géographes grecs* 1, ed. and trans. Dider Marcotte (Paris, 2000); Francesco Prontera, *Geografia e storia nella Grecia antica* (Florence, 2011); Duane W. Roller, *Ancient Geography: The Discovery of the World in Classical Greece and Rome* (London, 2015); Serena Bianchetti, Michele R. Cataudella, and Hans-Joachim Gehrke, eds., *Brill's Companion to Ancient Geography: The Inhabited World in Greek and Roman Tradition* (Leiden, 2016); also Christian Jacob, *La Description de la terre habitée de Denys d'Alexandrie ou la leçon de géographie* (Paris, 1990).

3. Aristotle describes twelve winds in *Meteorologica* 2.6; Pliny, who prefers an eight-wind system, synthesizes different Greek traditions: *Naturalis historia*, 2.119–21.

zones, one in either hemisphere; one central zone of extreme heat; and two polar zones of extreme cold.[4] An alternative mode of division, perhaps slightly later in date, identified seven *klimata*, or latitudinal bands, which ran from the equatorial region to the northernmost extent of human habitation.[5] Knowledge of the distances between places and their relative direction stimulated mathematical calculations that could be applied to the entire world. Eratosthenes of Cyrene (c. 285–194 BC) used the distance between Alexandria and Syene (modern Aswan, below the first cataract of the Nile) to calculate the degrees of latitude between the two cities, and from that figure he posited the circumference of the earth to be 252,000 stades, an impressively accurate measurement cited repeatedly in later classical and medieval texts.[6] From Pythagoras onwards the conviction that the expanse of the sphere encompassed space beyond the known world encouraged speculation about unknown yet habitable portions of the earth. The Stoic commentator on Homer, Crates of Mallos, is credited with devising a model by which the world was divided into four large land-masses, two in each hemisphere, divided by an equatorial ocean and a longitudinal ring of ocean running from pole to pole.[7] Well before Crates, Plato's *Timaeus*, which hypothesized circumnavigation of the earth, and his *Republic*, whose concluding "myth of Er" sees the world viewed from the heavens, had shown the way in which theories of the

4. The theory of the zones was attributed to Parmenides (fifth century BC), though modified by his successors: Strabo, *Geography* 2.2.2–2.3.3, ed. and trans. H.L. Jones, 8 vols (London, 1917–33), 1: 360–76; Plutarch, *De placitis philosophorum*, 895E, in *Œuvres morales*, vol. 12.2: *Opinions des philosophes*, ed. and trans. Guy Lachenaud (Paris, 1993); Cleomedes, *Caelestia* 1.4.58–62, ed. Robert Todd (Leipzig, 1990), 21–23.

5. Strabo credited Eudoxos of Knidos (fourth century BC) with being an expert on *klimata*: *Geography* 9.1.2, ed. Jones, 4: 240; there is scholarly argument about whether Eratosthenes (who is thought to have applied Eudoxos's idea) or Hipparchus (who used trigonometry) deserves credit for inventing the schema: see Didier Marcotte, "La climatologie d'Ératosthène à Poséidonios: Genèse d'une science humaine," in *Sciences exactes et sciences appliquées à Alexandrie*, ed. Gilbert Argoud and Jean-Yves Guillaumin (Saint-Étienne, 1998), 263–77.

6. *Eratosthenes' Geography*, trans. Duane W. Roller (Princeton, 2010), 58–65; for reception, see e.g. Pliny, *Naturalis historia* 2.247, ed. Mayhoff 1: 228; Macrobius, *Commentarii in Somnium Scipionis* 1.20.20, ed. and trans. M. Armisen-Marchetti (Paris, 2001–3), 1: 117; Martianus Capella, *De nuptiis Philologiae et Mercurii* 6.596–98, ed. James Willis (Leipzig, 1983), 209. A stade is a measurement of distance containing 600 feet, but the length of foot varied among classical authors, so the precise length of Eratosthenes's stade is not certain: see Germaine Aujac, *Ératosthène de Cyrène, le pionnier de la géographie: Sa mesure de la circonférence terrestre* (Paris, 2001), 50–63; Claude Nicolet, *Space, Geography, and Politics in the Early Roman Empire* (Ann Arbor, 1991), 60–61.

7. Strabo, *Geography* 1.2.24, 2.5.10, ed. Jones, 1: 112, 448.

nature of the earth, and its position within the cosmos, could function as an essential component of philosophical works.[8]

If the world could be understood from the elevated perspective of the cosmos, it was equally subject to description at ground level. The principal modes of description of the known world (*oikoumene*) comprised local and regional topographies as well as itineraries over land or sea. The genre of the "periodos" was a circuit of the inhabited world, and could be presented in visual form; that of the "periegesis" consisted primarily of regional descriptions; the "periplus," meanwhile, offered a detailed topographic and ethnographic account of coastal regions from the view-point of the sea.[9] Geographical texts of these kinds did not exist in isolation and could be combined to form more over-arching accounts of lands and seas. Spatial description infused texts across many genres, with the boundaries between creative and scientific works either porous or non existent. The works of Homer were treated as veritable textbooks by some later scholars, while theoretical scientific works such as Aristotle's *Meteorologica* were filled with details of rivers and seas.[10] Spatial representation played a significant, often essential role in historical writing: the *Histories* of Herodotus became fundamental sources of geographical and ethnographical information for generations of later classical authors, and ultimately for their medieval successors. The Aegean and Mediterranean basin, along with the Black Sea, remained the core regions of geographical description throughout the classical period, but horizons expanded significantly – in all directions – over the course of the centuries. Alexander the Great's conquests in the east (334–323 BC) produced an array of contradictory reports which later commentators struggled to digest, with the result that India, central Asia, and parts of northern Asia became integrated into standard descriptions of the known world.[11] The legacy of Alexander in Egypt, in the form of the foundation of Alexandria and the establishment of the Ptolemaic dynasty, also

8. *Timaeus* 63A; *Republic*; *Phaido* 110b.

9. On genres see Marcotte, *Géographes grecs*, lv–lxxii. For examples of the periplus see the fourth-century BC *Pseudo-Skylax's Periplous: The Circumnavigation of the Inhabited World*, ed. and trans. Graham Shipley (Exeter, 2011); Arrian's Periplus of the Pontus-Euxine, second quarter of the second century AD, and the late second-century "Navigation on the Bosforus" by Dionysius of Byzantium, both edited in Stefano Belfiore, *Il Periplo del Ponto Eusino di Arriano e altri testi sul Mar Nero e il Bosforo: Spazio geografico, mito e dominio ai confini dell'Impero romano* (Venice, 2009); *The Periplus Maris Erythraei*, trans. Lionel Casson (Princeton, 1989), mid first-century AD, is a-typical in its emphasis on trade.

10. *Meteorologica* 2. On the influence of Homer see Francesco Prontera, "Sull'esegesi ellenistica della geografia omerica," in *Geografia e storia nella Grecia antica*, 3–14.

11. See Strabo, *Geography*, book 15; Pliny, *Naturalis historia*, book 6; Roller, *Ancient Geography*, 90–104; Marcotte, "La climatologie d'Ératosthène à Poséidonios," 268–69.

contributed to increased knowledge of the Nile and Red Sea, in part thanks to sponsored expeditions.[12] For the north-west, the fourth-century BC voyage of Pytheas of Massalia beyond Britain as far as the enigmatic island of Thule was a controversial but well-known source, used by Eratosthenes but rejected in the early first-century AD by his critic, Strabo.[13]

Classical Rome inherited both the cosmological and the topographical perspective of the Greeks. The reception of Greek cosmological texts in Rome is particularly evident from the first century BC. Some works, such as Aratus's third-century BC poem, the *Phaenomena*, were translated into Latin at this time,[14] while others underwent adaptation. Cicero's *Somnium Scipionis* (Dream of Scipio), the final section of *De re publica*, notably responded to Plato's "myth of Er" at the end of his *Republic*: Scipio's dream sees the Roman general look down on the earth from the perspective of the heavens, as his grandfather encourages him to observe the meagre portion of the earth that Rome controls.[15] As this instance suggests, Roman appropriation of Greek geographical learning involved the addition of imperial perspective and reach. By the time Pliny the Elder wrote his thirty-seven-book encyclopedia, the *Naturalis historia*, in the 60s and 70s of the first century AD, Roman military expeditions had advanced at least as far south as Meroe, had conquered Britain, and had penetrated as far as the mouth of the Elbe in Germania. In the east, detailed surveys of Dacia, Armenia, and the Pontic region had been submitted to the emperor;[16] Pliny's work also attests to strengthened commercial and diplomatic links with India and Taprobana (modern Sri Lanka). Such surveys and reports comprised only one of the sources of information available to Pliny, however. The *Naturalis historia*, in some ways the culmination of Roman geography, drew on all available models, and included earlier Greek authors such as Herodotus, Eratosthenes, Polybius of Megalopolis (c. 200–118 BC), Artemidorus (fl. c. 100 BC), and Posidonius (c. 135–c. 50 BC).

The work of its codifiers reveals that classical geography was far from a settled and complete body of knowledge. Instead, its governing modes were contestation, change, and doubt. Herodotus's *Histories* provides perhaps the earliest example. Book four of the *Histories* sees Herodotus vigorously oppose an image of the world, which he implied was standard or at least commonly accepted, in

12. Roller, *Ancient Geography*, 109–14.

13. See Monique Mund-Dopchie, *Ultima Thulé: Histoire d'un lieu et genèse d'un mythe* (Geneva, 2009), 28–29.

14. There are fragments of translations by Cicero, P. Terentius Varro Atacinus, and Ovid; a late first-century translation is traditionally attributed to Germanicus Caesar.

15. Cicero, *De re publica* 6.13–6.33, ed. J.G.F. Powell (Oxford, 2006), 135–47.

16. Nicolet, *Space, Geography, and Politics*, 85–88.

which an encircling Ocean surrounds Asia, Libya, and Europe.[17] Europe, he thought, was wrongly reduced in size by such a scheme, and the idea of an encircling Ocean was a fiction he attributed to poets, possibly Homer himself.[18] More fundamentally, Herodotus drew attention to the arbitrary nature of division. The Nile divided Libya from Asia, and the Tanais (the modern river Don) was held to split Europe from Asia, but on what basis? As he pointed out, these three known parts of the earth – Asia, Libya and Europe – had contested histories, as arguments about the origins of their names revealed.[19] Indeed, much of them remained unknown: the south of Libya, the north of Europe, and the east of Asia all lacked credible descriptions.

The same tone of energetic debate, even polemic, informs later descriptions of the earth. It characterises the two monumental geographical works to survive from the first century AD: the *Geography* of Strabo of Amaseia, and books three to six of Pliny's *Naturalis historia*. Both works summarise and critique scores of previous authors, in numerous cases providing the only extant witnesses to authorities whose texts are otherwise lost. Strabo's seventeen-book *Geography* seems to have been composed primarily during the reign of the emperor Augustus, although references to events in the reign of Tiberius suggest that it was still in progress up to 24 AD.[20] Despite writing at the height of Roman power, however, Strabo consistently represented the perspective of the Hellenic world. Scion of a distinguished family from the Black Sea region, Strabo's education in Anatolia and Rome, and his travels in the eastern Mediterranean and Egypt, brought him into contact with leading Greek-speaking intellectuals.[21] He gravitated to Alexandria, a city he describes in some detail, in which a Hellenic elite had recently come under direct Roman governance following the overthrow of the Ptolemaic dynasty.[22] Towering over the *Geography* is the figure of Homer, with whose works Strabo seems to have enjoyed an encyclopedic familiarity. The *Geography*'s first two books mounted a strident defence of Homer's spatial concepts, particularly those that underlie the *Odyssey*, against the contrary views of

17. Herodotus, *Historiae* 4.36.2, ed. N.G. Wilson, 2 vols (Oxford, 2015), 1: 353.

18. *Historiae* 4.42 and 2.23, ed. Wilson, 1: 355 and 1: 140, respectively.

19. *Historiae* 4.45, ed. Wilson, 1: 357–58.

20. *The* Geography *of Strabo*, trans. Duane W. Roller (Cambridge, 2014), 1–16 reviews the evidence; cf. Daniela Dueck, *Strabo of Amasia: A Greek Man of Letters in Augustan Rome* (London, 2000), 146–51; Aubrey Diller, *The Textual Tradition of Strabo's Geography* (Amsterdam, 1975), 6.

21. Evidence for Strabo's life comes solely from his own work: e.g. *Geography* 2.5.11, ed. Jones, 1: 450 (travels); 12.3.15, 12.3.39, ed. Jones, 5: 396, 444–48 (patria); 14.1.48, ed. Jones, 6: 262 (studies).

22. *Geography* 17.1.8–13, ed. Jones, 8: 32–54.

scientists such as Eratosthenes and his successors.[23] The polemical tone abates in subsequent books, but throughout the *Geography* Strabo felt compelled to compare discordant authorities, whose contradictions he was not always able to resolve. Aristotle and Posidonius disagreed about the cause of a stony plain between Massalia and the Rhone (earthquakes or a solidified lake); Polybius criticised Timaios's claim that the same river possessed five mouths; Artemidorus disputed Eratosthenes's account of the climate and cities of Africa, but in turn Artemidorus's account of African rivers (many and large) was contradicted by that of Posidonius (few and small).[24] More problematic were the many discrepancies found in the descriptions of Asia recorded by members of Alexander the Great's military expedition, not helped by the inaccurate accounts of more recent travellers. The size of India was almost impossible to determine due to the wildly differing estimates: "Ktesias says that Indike is no smaller than the rest of Asia, Onesikritos that it is one-third of the inhabited world, and Nearchos that it is a four-month journey simply through the plain. But Megasthenes and Deimachos are somewhat more moderate, for they make it over 20,000 stadia from the southern Ocean to the Kaukasos ... ."[25] Perhaps most striking in a work packed with detailed topographic and ethnographic information is Strabo's frank ignorance about the northernmost parts of Europe. He rejected the testimony of Pytheas of Massalia, with the result that he was reliant on the reports of Roman authors such as Julius Caesar. What lay beyond the Elbe was, he admitted, "totally unknown" (*agnosta*):

> But what is beyond Germania and that which is next to it ... is not easy to say, nor whether they extend to the Ocean, stretching alongside it for its entire length, whether some of it is uninhabitable because of the cold or another reason, or whether there are other races of people situated successively between the sea and the eastern Germans. This same ignorance exists concerning others successively toward the north, for I do not know about the Bastarnians, Sauromatians, or, simply, those living above the Pontos, and how far they are from the Atlantic Sea, or whether they adjoin it.[26]

23. *Geography*, 1.2.3–5, ed. Jones, 1: 54–62; 1.2.10–40, ed. Jones, 1: 74–172.

24. Respectively, *Geography* 4.1.7; 4.1.8, ed. Jones, 2: 182–91; 17.3.8–10, ed. Jones, 8: 168–76.

25. *Geography* 15.1.12, ed. Jones, 7: 16–18; trans. Roller, 648. Ctesias of Cnidos wrote a history of Persia (c. 400 BC); Onesikritos of Astypalaia and Nearchos of Crete were members of Alexander's fleet who wrote reports of their voyages; Megasthenes and Deimachos were Greek ambassadors who both wrote accounts of India.

26. *Geography* 7.2.4, ed. Jones, 3: 172; trans. Roller, 291.

A somewhat similar admission of ignorance concluded Strabo's description of the southernmost portion of Africa: the boundaries of Ethiopia and Libya were unknown, and it was not clear what lay beyond Egypt nor what could be found on the west coast.[27] The limits of knowledge were clearly drawn, but even in the known areas, including those familiar to the author, the discordance of authorities frequently rendered spatial representation unstable.

A little over a century after Strabo, the *Geography* of Ptolemy of Alexandria propounded a significantly different mode of spatial representation. Instead of the rich mix of historical, ethnographic, and topographic detail that seems to have characterised Greek geography, Ptolemy presented a mathematically-based cartography dependent on the location of places according to degrees of latitude and longitude. Ptolemy, who seems not to have known Strabo's work, outlined three different ways of accurately constructing maps so as to represent part of a sphere on a flat surface, supported by lengthy lists of toponyms and their co-ordinates. His world image notably dispensed with an encircling outer ocean, positing instead a land bridge between Africa and Asia. A series of twenty-six regional maps allowed geography to be broken down into component parts, to be examined at the level of the region as well as that of the entire known world.[28] The *Geography* (c. 150 AD) began by emphasising the empirical basis of description in the measurement of distance and the observation of the stars. Yet Ptolemy readily conceded that the size of the known world, as well as the carelessness of observers, and changes in the features of the land over time, all inevitably contributed to error in even the most up-to-date representation of the earth.[29] Travellers' records of distance and direction between places were unreliable and inconsistent, particularly in the case of little-known parts of the world for which few reports existed.[30] Ptolemy favoured the use of astronomical data to determine the location of places, but in its absence he endorsed the evidence of the forms and colours of local animals and peoples. If it was at the Nubian capital of Meroe that (heading south) one first encountered very black people ("pure Ethiopians"), elephants, and other "more wonderful" animals, then the same phe-

27. *Geography* 17.3.23, ed. Jones, 8: 208.

28. Ptolemy subdivided Europe into ten maps; Asia received twelve, and Africa four. This subdivision did not reflect administrative geography so much as geographic and ethnographic boundaries: see Didier Marcotte, "Ptolémée et la constitution d'une cartographie régionale," in *La invención de una geografía de la Península Ibérica*, ed. Gonzalo Cruz Andreotti et al. (Madrid, 2007), 161–72.

29. Klaudios Ptolemaios, *Handbuch der Geographie* 1.2; 1.5, ed. and trans. Alfred Stückelberger and Gerd Graßhoff, 3 vols (Basel, 2006–9), 1: 56–60, 66.

30. *Handbuch der Geographie* 1.8; 1.9, ed. Stückelberger and Graßhoff, 1: 74–80.

nomena should exist at the corresponding parallel to the south of the equator: since Meroe lay 16°25′ north, Agisymba, land of the Ethiopians, must lie on the parallel 16°25′ south.[31] Ptolemy was acutely aware of the capacity of visual representation not simply to reflect error, but actively to induce it. He criticized the data and maps of his predecessor Marinos of Tyre, alleging numerous errors and inconsistencies, and complaining that Marinos had presented a significantly distorted world image. Not only did repeated copying (*metapherein*) eventually create significant distortions (the sum total of minor changes from copy to copy),[32] the restrictions of the material basis of maps had, Ptolemy thought, encouraged "errors of drawing" which in turn had fuelled "confused" narratives, such as the doctrine of the encircling world ocean.[33] All the same, Ptolemy freely admitted that his own calculations, particularly for more remote places, relied on a significant level of approximation and estimation. For this reason he presented his data in columns, so as to facilitate correction resulting from subsequent research.[34]

Like Strabo's work, the impact of Ptolemy's *Geography* on medieval European spatial representation was indirect until the fifteenth century, when both texts were translated for the first time from Greek into Latin.[35] The classical source that had the greatest influence on medieval geographical thought in the Latin west was Pliny's *Naturalis historia*. Unlike the geographies of Strabo and Ptolemy, Pliny's work was copied and studied directly throughout the Middle Ages.[36] More importantly, it was also known by means of its widely disseminated third- or fourth-century reworking at the hands of Iulius Solinus. The scope of Pliny's geography, which constituted just over a tenth of his great encyclopedia,

31. *Handbuch der Geographie* 1.9.9–1.10.1, ed. Stückelberger and Graßhoff, 1: 80.

32. *Handbuch der Geographie* 1.18.2, ed. Stückelberger and Graßhoff, 1: 104.

33. *Handbuch der Geographie* 8.1.4, ed. Stückelberger and Graßhoff, 2: 768–70.

34. *Handbuch der Geographie* 2.1.2–3, ed. Stückelberger and Graßhoff, 1: 138.

35. For the history of Ptolemy's reception see Patrick Gautier Dalché, *La Géographie de Ptolémée en Occident (IVe–XVIe siècle)* (Turnhout, 2009); for Strabo see Diller, *The Textual Tradition of Strabo's Geography*.

36. L.D. Reynolds, "The Elder Pliny," in *Texts and Transmission: A Survey of the Latin Classics*, ed. L.D. Reynolds (Oxford, 1983), 307–16; Birger Munk Olsen, *L'étude des auteurs classiques latins aux XIe et XIIe siècles*, 4 vols (Paris, 1982–2014), 2: 244–73; Charles G. Nauert, Jr, "Caius Plinius Secundus," in *Catalogus translationum et commentariorum: Mediaeval and Renaissance Latin Translations and Commentaries: Annotated Lists and Guides*, vol. 4, ed. F. Edward Cranz (Washington, DC, 1980), 297–422; Marjorie Chibnall, "Pliny's *Natural History* and the Middle Ages," in *Empire and Aftermath: Silver Latin II*, ed. T.A. Dorey (London, 1975), 57–78; Vanna Maraglino, ed., *La Naturalis Historia di Plinio nella tradizione medievale e umanistica* (Bari, 2012). On the complex manuscript history of the *Naturalis historia* see particularly Michael D. Reeve, "The Editing of Pliny's *Natural History*," *Revue d'histoire des textes*, n.s. 2 (2007): 107–79.

was vast. The opening of the *Naturalis historia* offered a description of the world magisterial in its detail, an unrivalled summation of physical and human geographical knowledge as it stood in late first-century Rome. This description, which fills the four "geographical" books of the *Naturalis historia* (books 3–6), conforms to no single genre. It is in part indebted to the coastal itineraries of the periplus tradition. Yet the multitude of his sources – including reports of military expeditions and envoys, the monumental map of Marcus Vipsanius Agrippa, which Pliny states was displayed in Rome during the reign of the emperor Augustus,[37] and a host of earlier (predominantly Greek) geographical authorities – meant that Pliny included many details of interior topographies and populations, and that his survey did not stop at the frontiers of the Roman Empire. Pliny's description of Europe (books 3–4) works its way around the Mediterranean, Adriatic, and Aegean coasts, but it incorporates a lengthy description of Italy, uniquely divided into eleven regions, apparently following administrative divisions made by Augustus;[38] it concludes by moving westward across Germania to Britain, Gaul and finally Spain. Similarly, the account of Africa (book 5) moves from west to east along its north coast as far as Egypt, but then details peoples of the interior as far as Ethiopia. Pliny's account of the sources of the Nile shows just how varied was the material at his disposal.[39] He draws on the report of Juba II, king of Mauretania (c. 48 BC–23 AD), but also refers to Homer, the mathematician Timaeus (whose theory that the river rises from a spring and then disappears underground Pliny distrusts), Herodotus, Artemidorus, and Aristocreon along with other unnamed authorities; in addition to these ancient sources, he adduces readings of the level of the Nile from as recently as the principate of Claudius. A comparable mix of information sustains the description of Asia (books 5–6). Beyond the Roman provinces from Syria and Judaea to the Hellespont and the Black Sea coast, Pliny moves through Armenia and the Caspian Sea as far as the Seres (usually understood as the Chinese); he concludes an important description of India with a detailed account of the island of Taprobana, apparently based in part on the testimony of envoys to imperial Rome.[40] Finally, having completed the circuit of Asia by returning to the Red Sea and Persian Gulf, Pliny concluded the geographical books of the *Naturalis historia* with an entirely different mode of description. This was a list of the seven climatic zones

---

37. Pliny, *Naturalis historia* 3.17, ed. Mayhoff, 1: 238.

38. Pliny, *Naturalis historia* 3.38–138, ed. Mayhoff, 1: 247–88.

39. Pliny, *Naturalis historia* 5.51–58, ed. Mayhoff, 1: 381–85). See particularly Andy Merrills, *Roman Geographies of the Nile: From the Late Republic to the Early Empire* (Cambridge, 2017), 279–97.

40. Pliny, *Naturalis historia* 6.81–92, ed. Mayhoff 1: 464–68.

(*klimata*) that run from India in the south through to the northern parts of the Caspian Sea.[41] Pliny explicitly identifies the *klima* as an idea of Greek invention, which merited translation into Latin geography: by dividing the earth into "segments" ("which we call 'circles,' the Greeks 'parallels'") that run latitudinally from east to west, one can perceive association and natural connection between peoples and cities based on their shared experience of the stars, of the length of days and nights, and of the "curve of the earth" (*convexitas mundi*).[42] Significantly, Pliny supplemented this division "worked out by the ancients" (*antiquorum exacta*) with further segments devised by "the most scrupulous of their followers": three in the north, and two additional circles in the south.[43] As a result, this final overview of the known world ultimately extends from Syene in the south as far as Thule in the north, and includes Dacia, the northern Gallic provinces, Britain, and the far-northern "Hyperboreans." This was no inert transfer of dated knowledge, and neither was it systematic or smooth. Here again, Pliny wrestled with more than one source, with the result that the neat schema of the seven *klimata* sprawled across twelve circles, encompassing places and peoples ancient and contemporary, current and defunct, real and mythical.

Frank acknowledgements of mutability recur throughout Pliny's description of the world in the *Naturalis historia*. Pliny notes in a matter-of-fact tone that fifty-three peoples recorded as inhabiting ancient Latium had died out without trace (*sine vestigiis*).[44] The city of Dioscurias, which according to Timosthenes of Rhodes once attracted three hundred tribes (*nationes*) speaking different languages, was now deserted.[45] The region of Etruria was noted for its changeability of name (*mutatis saepe nominibus*), the result of successive occupations by warring tribes, while the province of Hispania Citerior (i.e. near, or eastern, Spain) had significantly changed shape since the days of Pompey the Great.[46] Like his Greek predecessors, though without their polemical tone, Pliny criti-

---

41. Pliny, *Naturalis historia* 6.211–18, ed. Mayhoff 1: 517–21.

42. Pliny, *Naturalis historia* 6.211, ed. Mayhoff 1: 517–18. On Pliny's Greek sources (perhaps through the Latin intermediary P. Nigidius Figulus, a friend of Cicero) see Jehan Desanges's notes to the Budé edition 6.4 (2008), 266–68.

43. Pliny, *Naturalis historia* 6.219–20, ed. Mayhoff, 1: 521–22: "sequentium diligentissimi."

44. Pliny, *Naturalis historia* 3.70, ed. Mayhoff, 1: 259.

45. Pliny, *Naturalis historia* 6.15, ed. Mayhoff, 1: 434.

46. Pliny, *Naturalis historia* 3.50, ed. Mayhoff, 1: 251, and 3.18, ed. Mayhoff, 1: 238: "aliquantum vetus forma mutata est." Pliny seems to be referring to administrative boundaries; "forma" can be understood as "map" (the Budé edition's "carte"), but here "the old map of Hispania Citerior has changed" seems unlikely. "Aliquantum" can mean "a little" or "quite a lot"; the context of Pliny's remarks suggests to me the latter.

cized the errors of other authorities, and attempted to disentangle elements of myth from empirical knowledge, such as the towns of north Africa recorded by Hanno the Carthaginian which, suspiciously, had left "not the slightest recollection nor physical trace."[47] Elsewhere, the problem was one of inconsistent nomenclature: Pliny was particularly exercised by the error of many who called the mountain pass in Hiberia the "Caspian gates" (*Caspiae portae*) when it was in fact properly known as the "Caucasian gates" (*Caucasiae portae*). Unfortunately, he found, even maps (*situs depicti*) sent back to Rome marked the pass "Caspian gates", rather than gates of the Caucasus.[48] Ultimately, in the *Naturalis historia* the insecurity of spatial order stems not just from faulty reporting, the intrusion of fictive narratives, or the changes to places and peoples over time, but also from the inability to resolve contradictions in source material. In the passage in which he commented on Hanno's towns, Pliny described the region in the vicinity of Mount Atlas as "immense and uncertain," a comment not simply on its size but on the difficulty of reconciling the account found in Hanno with that of other authors, such as Polybius, whose periplus Pliny used for the north-west of Africa.[49] The same could be said of northern Europe and Asia, where the vast number of nomadic peoples that inhabited Scythia had resulted in "an inconsistency of authorities greater than for any other region."[50]

As a number of scholars have pointed out, Pliny's survey is imperial in its articulation and in much of its foundation.[51] Yet it does not follow that the order of space presented was consistent or agreed. Pliny's geography is provisional and contingent, rather than permanent. As the examples noted above suggest, the act of compiling the description of the world that occupies books three to six of the *Naturalis historia* involved Pliny in some profoundly dislocative manoeuvres. Far from a seamless or "timeless" survey, Pliny noted change, variance of sources, incomprehensibility. The picture of the world under the empire was, as a result, far from chronologically consistent. Just as Strabo subordinated more recent descriptions to the overarching authority of Homer ("there is no successful accomplishment of any proposition at present unless nothing is in conflict with him"),[52]

47. Pliny, *Naturalis historia* 5.8, ed. Mayhoff, 1: 363: "nec memoria ulla nec vestigium exstat."

48. Pliny, *Naturalis historia* 6.40, ed. Mayhoff, 1: 445–46.

49. Pliny, *Naturalis historia* 5.7, ed. Mayhoff, 1: 363: "spatium ad eum inmensum incertumque."

50. Pliny, *Naturalis historia* 6.51, ed. Mayhoff, 1: 451: "nec in alia parte maior auctorum inconstantia."

51. Carey, *Pliny's Catalogue of Culture*; Trevor Murphy, *Pliny the Elder's* Natural History: *The Empire in the Encyclopedia* (Oxford, 2004).

52. *Geography* 8.3.3, ed. Jones, 4: 24; trans. Roller, 339–40.

so in describing regions such as Asia Minor and the Black Sea area, Pliny combined the ancient accounts of Herodotus and even more antique sources with relatively recent information.[53] More remarkable still is Pliny's (possibly deliberate) exaggeration of the number of places and peoples in Italy itself, resulting in a large number of ghost towns and ghost tribes. Around 100 place-names in Italy cannot be identified with any modern toponym, or with a known ancient site, and there are instances of towns in Pliny's list appearing in more than one region, or twice in the same region.[54] Pliny may have been dealing with Augustan-era material that inflated the population of Italy for propagandistic purposes, but it is striking that in the regions at the heart of the Roman world his geography can be characterised by ambiguity and imprecision, as well as by its depth of detail. Such aspects of the works of Pliny and other classical authors – above all, the use of multiple sources, from different periods, resulting in a-chronic presentations of space, and the consciousness of mutation – laid a foundation for medieval spatial representation that was already filled with dislocations.

From Solinus to Isidore:
The Early Reception of Classical Geography

The story of the medieval reception of classical geography begins in late antiquity with acts of translation, commentary, and preservation, but also with acts of construction and reconstruction. Greek geography did not survive the classical era intact, but important fragments remained in circulation and major works gradually resurfaced. Ptolemy's *Almagest* reached the Latin west in the twelfth century by means of translation from Arabic, but his *Geography* was only partially known until its Latin translation by Jacopo Angeli in the first decade of the fifteenth century.[55] Strabo's *Geography*, meanwhile, had to wait until 1458 for its translation into Latin at the hands of Guarino Veronese.[56] Within the Latin tradition, manuscript evidence suggests that the text of Pliny's *Naturalis historia* was rarely copied or read whole before the ninth century at the earliest. However, the first six books, including the geographical section, were among parts of the encyclopedia that circulated separately. This part of

53. Fausto Bosi, "Sulla descrizione dell'area pontica nella Naturalis Historia di Plinio," in *Plinio il vecchio sotto il profilo storico letterario* (Como, 1982), 231–38.

54. See Edward Bispham, "Pliny the Elder's Italy," in *Vita Vigilia Est: Essays in Honour of Barbara Levick*, ed. Edward Bispham and Greg Rowe (London, 2007), 41–67.

55. Gautier Dalché, *La Géographie de Ptolémée en Occident*, 23–142, esp. 61–71 (Cassiodorus).

56. Diller, *Textual Tradition of Strabo's Geography*, 126–29.

Pliny's work was certainly known to Bede (d. 735), and to the early ninth-century Irish author Dicuil.[57] Other works experienced a more spotty transmission. Knowledge of Pomponius Mela's first-century AD survey of the known world, *De chorographia*, was limited until its dissemination among humanist circles in the fourteenth century, when it became an important authority.[58] The *Periegesis tes oikoumenes* (Geographical description of the known world) of Dionysius of Alexandria, a text of some 1185 hexameters, seems by contrast to have been well known in Carolingian Europe in its early sixth-century Latin translation by the grammarian Priscian; the work enjoyed an oblique yet significant connection with early examples of medieval world maps,[59] but it suffered a steady drop in popularity from the twelfth century until a resurgence of interest in the fifteenth.[60] Another influential source of geographical information came from the narratives of Alexander the Great's eastern expedition, such as Quintus Curtius Rufus's first- or early second-century prose *Historiae Alexandri Magni*, although the reports of Alexander's conquests could equally be apprehended through general descriptions such as that found in Pliny's *Naturalis historia*.

Only one, relatively small, part of the medieval inheritance resided in practical texts designed to facilitate Roman travel and administration, such as the treatises on surveying compiled by the Agrimensores, or the register of imperial officials and army units known as the *Notitia Dignitatum*, which probably dates

57. Reynolds, "The Elder Pliny," 309; Elisa Tinelli, "La *Naturalis Historia* di Plinio nel *De natura rerum* di Beda il Venerabile," in *La Naturalis Historia di Plinio nella tradizione medievale e umanistica*, 77–104; *Dicuili Liber de mensura orbis terrae*, ed. J.J. Tierney (Dublin, 1967).

58. Catherine M. Gormley, Mary A. Rouse, and Richard H. Rouse, "The Medieval Circulation of the *De chorographia* of Pomponius Mela," *Mediaeval Studies* 46 (1984): 266–320; Nathalie Bouloux, *Culture et savoirs géographiques en Italie au XIVe siècle* (Turnhout, 2002), 159–67.

59. Patrick Gautier Dalché, "Mappemonde, milieu du VIIIe siècle," in *Le Scriptorium d'Albi: Les manuscrits de la Cathédrale Sainte-Cécile (VIIe–XIIe siècle)*, ed. Matthieu Desachy (Rodez, 2007), 24–27; a copy of the Latin *Periegesis* appears in the same manuscript as the eleventh-century Cotton *mappa mundi* (British Library, MS Cotton Tiberius B.V (1), fol. 56v) and a "Priscianus gramaticus de situ et nominibus terrarum cum mappa mundi" is recorded at Glastonbury Abbey in a thirteenth-century library catalogue: *English Benedictine Libraries: The Shorter Catalogues*, ed. R. Sharpe et al. (London, 1996), 188.

60. *La Périégèse de Priscien*, ed. Paul van de Woestijne (Bruges, 1953). Marina Passalacqua, *I codici di Prisciano* (Rome, 1978), 382–85, lists forty-two manuscripts of the *Periegesis* from the ninth (an impressive six) to the eighteenth centuries; fifteen of these date from the fifteenth century, but only one from the thirteenth and none from the fourteenth centuries.

from the early fifth century.[61] Among surviving itineraries, the most comprehensive is the third-century Antonine itinerary (*Itinerarium provinciarum
Antonini Augusti*), which records distances between places in Roman provinces
stretching across north Africa, the Mediterranean islands, and Europe. The existence of later medieval manuscripts of this itinerary, and the presence of some
details from it on later medieval world images, including the Hereford map (c.
1300), testifies to its limited but significant impact in the Middle Ages.[62] The
adaptability of the written itinerary as a genre was evident as early as the fourth
century, when the Bordeaux itinerary recorded a pilgrimage route from Bordeaux
to Jerusalem;[63] meanwhile, antique itineraries seem to have underpinned more
elaborate descriptions of the world, such as the anonymous eighth-century
Ravenna Cosmography.[64] A more significant category of classical geographical
literature comprised works of a scholarly nature, designed to inform and in some
cases also to entertain. These ranged from unadorned lists of provinces, peoples,
rivers and other natural features,[65] to more developed commentaries, such as the
fourth-century *Expositio totius mundi et gentium*.[66] Works such as the *Cosmographia* of Iulius Honorius – attributed in certain manuscripts to Julius Caesar
himself – gained particular prestige from their explicit association with the
Roman Empire.[67]

Yet it was not simply works dedicated solely or in part to geographical
description that conveyed classical spatial representation to the Latin west.
Numerous classical authors were read during the Middle Ages who, in one way
or another, represented terrestrial space in the course of historical, philosophical
and poetic works. In addition to Cicero's *Dream of Scipio* (for most medieval

61. M.D. Reeve, "Agrimensores"; "Notitia dignitatum," in *Texts and Transmission*, 1–6;
253–57.

62. *Itineraria Romana*, vol. 1, ed. Otto Cuntz (1929, repr. Stuttgart, 1990), 1–85; see
G.R. Crone, "New Light on the Hereford Map," *Geographical Journal* 131 (1965): 447–62;
The Hereford Map, ed. Scott D. Westrem (Turnhout, 2001), xxix–xxx.

63. *Itineraria Romana*, 1: 86–102.

64. *Itineraria Romana*, vol. 2, ed. Joseph Schnetz (1940, repr. Stuttgart, 1990), 1–110.

65. See for example the *Laterculus Polemii Silvii*, the *Cosmographia* of Iulius Honorius –
a systematic list of names which was in circulation by the mid-sixth century when cited by
Cassiodorus in his *Institutiones* – and the *Cosmographia* of pseudo-Aethicus: all in *Geographi
Latini minores*, ed. Alexander Riese (Heilbronn, 1878; repr. Hildesheim, 1964), 21–55; 71–
103; 130–32; Vibius Sequester, *De fluminibus fontibus lacubus* etc., ed. R. Gelsomino (Leipzig,
1967) supplied lists of topographical names derived from classical literary texts.

66. Ed. Jean Rougé (Paris, 1966).

67. Claude Nicolet and Patrick Gautier Dalché, "Les 'Quatre Sages' de Jules César et la
'Mesure du Monde' selon Julius Honorius: Réalité antique et tradition médiévale," *Journal des
savants* (1986): 157–218.

readers the only surviving part of his *De re publica*), Sallust's *Bellum Iugurthinum*, the oeuvre of Virgil and Ovid, and Lucan's *Bellum civile* all contained descriptions or scattered references to geographical space to which medieval readers, commentators and authors responded – not least through the construction of maps and diagrams.[68] As this last point suggests, the medieval reception of classical geography involved both visual and verbal representation. In turn, the use of graphic representation raises the question of whether medieval mapmakers, as well as those compiling written descriptions, relied on Roman maps. The unique surviving example of a Roman world map is the Peutinger map, a fourth-century depiction of itineraries from Britain to India which is extant in an early thirteenth-century copy. Its preservation in southern German and northern Italian regions suggests that the Peutinger map was regarded as an important artefact, although evidence for its influence on medieval maps is limited.[69] Other (no longer extant) maps and plans from the early Roman Empire may have informed medieval spatial representation, but the origins of medieval *mappae mundi*, zonal maps, and other purely verbal descriptions of the earth seem to lie more in the labours of late antique grammarians and rhetoricians to compile and distil classical learning into a form that could be digested – and, importantly, committed to memory – by their pupils.[70]

The role of grammarians and rhetoricians was significant because geography did not constitute a discrete subject of knowledge during the Middle Ages. The term was scarcely known in the Latin west, and it certainly did not possess a separate pedagogical identity. Instead, the representation of geographical space existed within and alongside mainstream subjects and genres. Within the liberal arts, the description of the earth was a facet of geometry, the "measurements and dimensions of the earth":[71] the description of the world given by the figure of

---

68. Sallust, *Iugurtha*, ed. L.D. Reynolds (Oxford, 1991), 17–19. The reception of Virgil, Ovid, and Lucan is discussed in the following chapters.

69. Patrick Gautier Dalché, "La trasmissione medievale e rinascimentale della Tabula Peutingeriana," in *Tabula Peutingeriana: Le antiche vie del mondo*, ed. Francesco Prontera (Florence, 2003), 43–52; Richard J.A. Talbert, *Rome's World: The Peutinger Map Reconsidered* (Cambridge, 2010), 163–72.

70. See particularly Patrick Gautier Dalché, "L'héritage antique de la cartographie médiévale: Les problèmes et les acquis," in *Cartography in Antiquity and the Middle Ages: Fresh Perspectives, New Methods*, ed. Richard J.A. Talbert and Richard W. Unger (Leiden, 2008), 29–66, and on pedagogical contexts Gautier Dalché, "L'enseignement de la géographie dans l'antiquité tardive," *Klio* 96 (2014): 144–82.

71. Isidore of Seville, *Etymologiarum sive originum libri xx* 1.2.3, ed. W.M. Lindsay, 2 vols (Oxford, 1911), 1: 25–26: "Sexta [disciplina] geometrica, quae mensuras terrae dimensionesque conplectitur."

Geometria in Martianus Capella's fifth-century allegory *De nuptiis Philologiae et Mercurii* (On the Marriage of Philology and Mercury) enjoyed considerable popularity in the Middle Ages.[72] However, there is good evidence to suggest that knowledge of the location of places and peoples (the *commemoratio locorum*) was a standard part of rhetorical training: the good rhetor was able to summon from memory the names of provinces, cities, and peoples from throughout the known world.[73] Descriptions of the world perhaps initially composed for pedagogical purposes could circulate independently, but perhaps more frequently they accompanied or existed within other texts. The nature of these other texts was very diverse, including biblical commentary, philosophical treatises, chronicles and other forms of historical writing, encyclopedic works, calendrical and computistic material, and travel and pilgrimage narratives.[74] As an index of this variety, maps are attested not only in books, but also in a variety of settings, secular and religious – palaces, libraries, dining halls, bedrooms, floors and walls of churches – with functions ranging from public display to private contemplation.[75]

The sources of medieval spatial representation were numerous, and cannot always be securely identified. However, certain texts exerted particular influence, due to their wide dissemination, and their utility in providing authoritative distillations of classical geography. Contrary to what is sometimes imagined, the Christian Bible was not among the more frequently used sources for geographical description. Biblical sites and narratives certainly appeared within medieval spatial representation, and Christian exegesis naturally sought to explicate references to places and peoples, but the Bible lacked the kind of compendious survey of the known world that was the preferred basis for most medieval descriptions and maps. Instead, those in search of a geographical resource turned more often to Solinus (occasionally, directly to Pliny), or to one of the other two pillars of medieval geography: the second chapter of Paulus Orosius's *Historiarum adversum paganos libri vii* (Seven books of histories against the pagans), and books nine, thirteen, fourteen and fifteen of Isidore of Seville's *Etymologiae*. While these texts differed from each other in significant ways, each came to serve as a

72. Natalia Lozovsky, *"The Earth Is Our Book": Geographical Knowledge in the Latin West ca. 400–1000* (Ann Arbor, 2000), 113–38.

73. Gautier Dalché, "L'enseignement de la géographie," 149–52, 155–63; see too Félix Racine, "Teaching with Solinus: Martianus and Priscian," in *Solinus: New Studies*, ed. Kai Brodersen (Heidelberg, 2014), 157–70, and J.L. Lightfoot's introduction to Dionysius Periegetes, *Description of the Known World*, trans. J.L. Lightfoot (Oxford, 2014), 183–93.

74. On contexts see particularly Hoogvliet, *Pictura et Scriptura*; Evelyn Edson, *Mapping Time and Space: How Medieval Mapmakers Viewed Their World* (London, 1997).

75. See Gautier Dalché, "De la glose à la contemplation"; Marcia Kupfer, "Medieval World Maps: Embedded Images, Interpretive Frames," *Word and Image* 10 (1994): 262–88.

pivot between imperial geography and the altered reality of post-imperial space. Copied and excerpted up to and beyond the fifteenth century, the works of Solinus, Orosius, and Isidore gave access to an image of the Roman world.[76] That image, far from coherent, flecked with admissions of uncertainty, was adapted and updated in a variety of ways.

At some point in the third or fourth century AD, Iulius Solinus compiled a "collection of memorable things," a work he subsequently retitled the "Polyhistor."[77] Solinus, about whom next to nothing is certainly known, substantially based his *Polyhistor* on Pliny's *Naturalis historia*, salted with extracts from Mela's *De chorographia*. He mentions neither source, but he does make it clear in the first dedication to his work that he had preferred "the diligence of antiquity" to innovation.[78] Despite that preference, Solinus did something radical with Pliny. The *Polyhistor* is neither a redaction nor a simple compilation: it re-orders Plinian material in a way that breaks down and remixes the carefully constructed categories of the *Naturalis historia*.[79] This reordering is evident from the text's opening. Pliny had followed the geographical books of the *Naturalis historia* with book

76. The number of extant manuscripts of these authors testifies to their popularity: just under 300 manuscripts for Solinus, the earliest dating from the ninth century; around 200 "full or substantial" manuscripts of Orosius's *Historiae*, rising to around 300 if fragments and excerpts are included, from the sixth century onwards; somewhere in the vicinity of 1000 manuscripts of the *Etymologiae* if fragments are included: M.E. Milham, "Solinus," in *Catalogus translationum et commentariorum*, vol. 6, ed. F. Edward Cranz (Washington, DC, 1986), 73–85, at 73, and Kai Brodersen, "A Revised Handlist of Manuscripts transmitting Solinus' Work," in *Solinus: New Studies*, 201–8; for Orosius see Lars Boje Mortensen, "The Diffusion of Roman Histories in the Middle Ages: A List of Orosius, Eutropius, Paulus Diaconus, and Landolfus Sagax Manuscripts," *Filologia Mediolatina* 6–7 (1999–2000): 101–200, at 112–14, 119–65, and Orosius, *Histoires*, ed. Marie-Pierre Arnaud-Lindet, 3 vols (Paris, 1990–91), 1: lxvii–lxix, who reports "at least 275" manuscripts and fragments; for Isidore, the list compiled by Eduard Anspach in José Maria Fernández Catón, *Las Etimologías en la tradición manuscrita medieval* (León, 1966), gives some indication of the scope of the manuscript tradition.

77. Solinus, *Collectanea rerum memorabilium*, ed. Theodor Mommsen, 2nd ed. (Berlin, 1895), 217. For criticism of Mommsen's editorial practice, and the argument that the *Polyhistor* is a fourth-century compilation, see Peter Lebrecht Schmidt, "Solins Polyhistor in Wissenschaftsgeschichte und Geschichte," *Philologus* 139 (1995): 23–35. The work was often known in the Middle Ages as "De mirabilibus mundi" (On the marvels of the world).

78. *Collectanea* prol. 5, ed. Mommsen, 2: "antiquitatis diligentia." See Barbara Pavlock, "Paradox and the Journey in the Dedicatory Preface of Solinus' *Collectanea*," in *Solinus: New Studies*, 24–31.

79. Gautier Dalché, "L'enseignement de la géographie," 161: "bien plus qu'une compilation, c'est une véritable réécriture." See also Arwen Apps, "Source Citation and Authority in Solinus," and Tom Hillard, "Prosopographia Shared by Pliny and Solinus: The Question of Solinus' Source(s)," in *Solinus: New Studies*, 32–42; 43–74.

seven, a searching and at times mordantly humorous commentary on the human condition. The first book of the *Polyhistor* reverses this order. Solinus moves from a description of Rome and its history, of largely unknown source so possibly his own composition, to a disquisition on the different modes of calculating years and the Julian reform of the calendar, then to a section on human nature heavily dependent on Pliny's book seven, and only thereafter to the description of the world. Pliny's self-contained geography in books three to six itself underwent significant revision at the hands of Solinus. Whereas the *Naturalis historia* separated *geographica* from *animalia*, *naturalia*, *mirabilia*, and *lapidaria*, Solinus reintegrated material from other books – especially books eight (animals), ten (birds), twelve (trees), and thirty-seven (stones) – into the geography of books three to six. If the over-arching order remained spatial, it now encompassed within its frame animals and natural resources, as well as lands and peoples. Solinus's account of Africa, for example, takes as its spine book five of the *Naturalis historia*, moving from the Atlas mountains, through Mauretania, Numidia, Carthage, and the Syrtes, to Egypt, but it also includes long sections on elephants, bears, lions, and serpents, all derived from book eight, and shorter remarks on precious stones from book thirty-seven.[80]

If one effect of reworking the *Naturalis historia* was to break up the flow of specifically topographic and ethnographic detail, another was – on the contrary – to construct coherent commentaries. Solinus's treatment of the Mediterranean owes much to his sources but is ultimately significantly different. The *Polyhistor* brings together scattered comments on the strait of Cadiz, the columns of Hercules, the Mediterranean coasts, and the Black Sea from books three and six of the *Naturalis historia*, and adds discussion of the causes of tides found in Mela's *De chorographia*.[81] Solinus himself supplies overarching remarks to glue these extracts together. The result is a commentary on the multiplicity of toponomy: a single sea possesses an almost countless number of names. This point is implicit in Pliny's description,[82] but Solinus amplifies it. Ocean bursts from the west between the columns of Hercules, dividing Europe to the left and Africa to the right as it progresses to the east. From Spain to the west coast of Italy alone it is called the Hiberic, Balearic, Gallic, Ligurian, Tuscan, Ionian, Tyrrhenian, or "lower" Sea. Its names derive variously from the provinces it passes along (Asiatic, Phoenecian), from the islands within it, from towns, from peoples who live on it, from people drowned in it (Myrtoum or Hellespont), from the commemoration of a king (Ionian), from the transit of cattle (Bosphoros), from the cus-

80. *Collectanea* 24.1–31.3, ed. Mommsen, 107–37.
81. *Collectanea* 23.14–18, ed. Mommsen, 105–7.
82. E.g. Pliny, *Naturalis historia* 4.51, ed. Mayhoff, 1: 320.

toms of the inhabitants (Euxine, or "Axine," inhospitable), and from the direction of its flow (Propontis).[83] This reflection on naming generates something that resembles an image of the Mediterranean, defined by topography, ethnography, and history. That in turn leads Solinus to a similarly expansive outline of the exterior ocean, one that systematically moves in a circuit around the known world. The outer Ocean itself is, we are told, known by various names according to the shores it embraces: Arabian, Persian, Indian, the "eastern" (Eous), Seric, Hyrcanian, Caspian, Scythian, German, Gallic, Atlantic, Libyan, and Egyptian.[84] This sequence of names, running from near east through the far north, then to the west and south, could be remembered and depicted. Even when relying upon him, Solinus did not simply copy Pliny and, paradoxically, for all his recapitulation of old materials, Solinus constructed an image of the world more readily graspable than that of his master.[85]

In neither case, however, was geographic order established with any degree of rigidity. Both Pliny and Solinus presented geography in motion – or rather, in history. To the endless updatings and comparisons between now and then, sometimes with moral emphasis, evident in the *Naturalis historia*, Solinus added some of his own. In a passage found neither in Pliny nor Pomponius Mela, Solinus commented on the boundaries of Cilicia. These, the *Polyhistor* asserts, were once very different from what they are today, and if you followed the old boundaries you would have something discordant (*absonus*) from the present. Therefore the best way was to follow both times at once.[86] Cilicia's founder Cilix, a Phoenecian, had lived in an age now almost hidden beyond the reach of memory. The region once extended as far as Pelusium in Egypt, and included within its domain the people of Lydia, the Medes, the Armenians, Pamphilia, and Cappadocia. But the Assyrians reduced it, and it is now bounded by the gulf of Issus, and the Taurus and Amanus mountains.[87] Here and elsewhere in the *Polyhistor* the attempt to bring order is not in doubt, but the order requires consciousness of change, and a sometimes critical reading of sources which takes the form of their rearrangement. The explicit objective of Solinus's work was the "commemoratio locorum," a phrase which implies both commemoration of places and rather more actively

83. *Collectanea* 23.14–16, ed. Mommsen, 105–6.

84. *Collectanea* 23.17, ed. Mommsen, 106–7.

85. Kai Brodersen makes a similar point, albeit with over-emphasis on the linear nature of Pliny's spatial representation: "Mapping Pliny's World: The Achievement of Solinus," *Bulletin of the Institute of Classical Studies* 54 (2011): 63–88.

86. *Collectanea* 38.1, ed. Mommsen, 161: "si terminos sequimur quos habuit olim, absonum est a contemplatione rerum praesentium. ergo inter utramque culpam factu optimum est amborum temporum statum persequi."

87. *Collectanea* 38.2–3, ed. Mommsen, 161.

their commitment to memory through the construction of spatial order.[88] Yet the acts of recalling and ordering places detailed by Solinus had to contend with the multitude of names, and the mutations of history that beset classical geography. Derivative of the old imperial geography, the "commemoratio locorum" was constitutive of a new one: the mixed, mobile geography that was born of empire, and that outlived it.

The survival of empire and its structures in a world increasingly under the moral and spiritual governance of the Christian church is the underlying theme of Orosius's *Historiae*. Orosius's description of the world, coming as it did at the opening of his seven books of history, positioned geography as an adjunct to historical and moral commentary. The stated objective of his books "against the pagans" was to confound the notion that the world was unusually infested with evils because the worship of Christ had replaced the worship of idols.[89] Instead, the vast scope of human history from the creation of the world to the early fifth century, when Orosius was writing, revealed a narrative of prolonged misery, alleviated by the birth of Christ. At the same time, Orosius's history tells a different story, a narrative of the genesis, expansion, and transformation of the idea of Rome; or to put it another way, a meditation on the meaning of the terms "Roman" and "barbarian," designed to accompany the work of Orosius's teacher, Augustine of Hippo.[90]

Orosius, "a Roman and a Christian," had witnessed at first hand the disruptions of the late empire, having fled barbarian invasions of his native land (usually thought to be Spain) for north Africa in the years before 414.[91] Yet the picture he presents of "barbarian" identity is a complex one, mediated by the figure of Christ. Book seven of the *Historiae* closes with an account of the Gothic king Athaulf, which Orosius apparently heard narrated to Jerome in Bethlehem by a native of Narbo (in southern Gaul) who knew the Goth intimately. According to

---

88. *Collectanea* prol. 3, ed. Mommsen, 1–2: "locorum commemoratio plurimum tenet, in quam partem ferme inclinatior est universa materies. quorum meminisse ita visum est, ut inclitos terrarum situs et insignes tractus maris, servata orbis distinctione, suo quaeque ordine redderemus."

89. Paulus Orosius, *Historiarum adversum paganos libri vii* prol. 9, ed. C. Zangemeister (Vienna, 1882), 3.

90. On the complex relationship between Augustine's *De civitate dei* and Orosius's *Historiae*, see Theodor E. Mommsen, "Orosius and Augustine," in *Medieval and Renaissance Studies*, ed. Eugene F. Rice (Ithaca, 1959), 325–48, and the persuasive reassessment of Peter Van Nuffelen, *Orosius and the Rhetoric of History* (Oxford, 2012), 197–205.

91. *Historiarum ... libri vii* 5.2, ed. Zangemeister, 280: "ad Christianos et Romanos Romanus et Christianus accedo"; Orosius earlier gives what appears to be an autobiographical account of initial accommodation to, and subsequent flight from, barbarian invasion (3.20, ed. Zangemeister, 183).

the informant's story, Athaulf initially wished to obliterate the Roman name, to become a Gothic version of Caesar Augustus, and to replace one empire (*Romania*) with his own (*Gothia*). But Athaulf realised that the unbridled barbarity of the Goths, and specifically their inability to follow laws, meant that they could never successfully govern a state. Under the benign influence of his wife Placidia, he resolved instead to use the military force of the Goths to preserve and augment the Roman name, so that – if he could not be known as its transformer (*immutator*) – Athaulf would be remembered as the author of Rome's restitution (*restitutionis auctor*).[92] Orosius writes at a moment in which Rome stands on a precipice, but at which it may emerge regenerated by barbarian energies, since it is only in Roman terms (*Caesar, Romania, leges reipublicae*) that imperial power can be expressed. This too is a world in which the barbarians, whether or not they become Roman, may become Christian, in which the unifying (and expansionist) properties of Christianity make it the true *immutator imperii*. If, writes Orosius, "through the East and the West the churches of Christ are filled with Huns, Suevi, Vandals, and Burgundians, and with diverse and innumerable peoples of faith," surely the mercy of God would seem to be praised and exalted, since "even if at the price of our [i.e. Roman] tottering (*etsi cum labefactione nostri*)" so many people had accepted divine truth.[93]

The geographical description provided by Orosius divides the world into three parts (Asia, Europe, Africa), then breaks them down into regions, in a way that offers a conceptual frame for his readers.[94] The overriding principle is one of contiguity. The characteristic mode of description locates each region or province in relation to what surrounds it to the east, west, north, and south, whether another region, a natural feature such as a sea, river or mountain range, or a people. The absence of chronological precision is perhaps the point of such a description. The core of the geography is the Roman provincial system of the high empire, but it incorporates later additions and transmutations, contemporary information (including information about places beyond the empire) and – particularly in Asia – information dating from the reign of Alexander, and therefore several centuries old at the time Orosius wrote.[95] The mode is accretive, and it does not ostensibly distinguish old from new information. Consequently the Massagetae, a people not attested after the third century BC, appear in the same

92. *Historiarum ... libri vii* 7.43.4–8, ed. Zangemeister, 559–61. See Van Nuffelen, *Orosius and the Rhetoric of History*, 176–85.

93. *Historiarum ... libri vii* 7.41.8, ed. Zangemeister, 554: "quod uulgo per Orientem et Occidentem ecclesiae Christi Hunis Suebis Vandalis et Burgundionibus diuersisque innumeris credentium populis replentur."

94. *Historiarum ... libri vii* 1.2, ed. Zangemeister, 9–40.

95. See Yves Janvier, *La Géographie d'Orose* (Paris, 1982), 221–70.

text as the Scotti, who were first recorded by Ammianus Marcellinus in the fourth century AD, "out of date" information (but evidently within date, for Orosius and his readers for centuries to come) alongside contemporary knowledge.[96]

Geography, in the complex and dynamic context of world history viewed from the early fifth century, has a double function. Located prior to the narration of history, as a prelude to action, it cannot hope to keep pace with the events Orosius narrates, and in particular with the border-shifting irruptions of barbarian peoples. As a result, it cannot correspond in comprehensive detail to the history that it announces: places and peoples described in the sweep of events from creation onwards are absent from Orosius's description of the world, a synthesis that does not capture any single historical moment, and which notably omits any mention of Jerusalem. Rather than an inert appendage, however, Orosian geography might be seen in theatrical terms as a backdrop that precedes the play of history, and that itself informs and is transformed by the actors that perform on its stage.[97] It is not simply that it is impossible to conceive of Alexander the Great without recourse to spatial description, just as the Roman Empire itself cannot exist outside of geography. It is that, beyond the function of reference, Orosius's history shows the construction and reconstruction, consolidation and dissolution, of geographies. Empires form and retract, change, are restored or obliterated, and the same fates befall their provinces, places, and peoples.

The position of geography within the *Etymologiae* of Isidore, bishop of Seville (d. 636), is wholly different to its location in Orosius's *Historiae*. The principal treatment of the known world comes in book fourteen of the *Etymologiae*, immediately after cosmography and hydrography (book thirteen), before book fifteen's catalogue of cities and other human constructions, and some distance from book nine's account of peoples and government. It is not attached to history, and – at least ostensibly – it does not serve a moral purpose. In some ways, then, Isidore restored the categorisation established by Pliny, in which the description of the earth could be separated from other features of the known world. Yet Isidore's objectives were distinctive.[98] True to the function of his work as an account of the origins of words, he emphasised the etymologies of place names. India derived its name from the river Indus, Syria from "a native of the

---

96. *Historiarum ... libri vii* 1.2.41, ed. Zangemeister, 18 (Massagetae); 1.2.81, ed. Zangemeister, 30 (Scotti); e.g. Ammianus Marcellinus, *Res gestae* 26.4.5, 27.8.5, ed. Wolfgang Seyfarth, 2 vols (Leipzig, 1978), 2: 9, 47; see Janvier, *La Géographie d'Orose*, 227, 230.

97. Cf. A.H. Merrills, *History and Geography in Late Antiquity* (Cambridge, 2005), 50–99; Lozovsky, *"The Earth Is Our Book"*, 73–78; Van Nuffelen, *Orosius and the Rhetoric of History*, 170–76 argues for the rhetorical and gestural nature of the geographical opening.

98. See Jacques Fontaine, *Isidore de Seville et la culture classique dans l'Espagne wisigothique*, 3 vols (Paris, 1959–83), 2: 770–84, 828–30.

land" named Syrus, Numidia from the nomadic life of its inhabitants, Gallia from the whiteness of its people, since the Greek "gála" means milk, Etruria from "héteron" (other) and "hóros" (end) because it extended as far as the river Tiber – or from a prince named Etruscus.[99] Knowledge of the earth and its peoples was part of the knowledge of the history of the Latin language and related tongues, in turn the key to knowledge *de rerum natura*. Isidore compiled the *Etymologiae* in the first half of the seventh century, with the result that he was able to draw heavily on Solinus (the principal source of book fourteen), Orosius, and Servius's commentary on the works of Virgil, along with a variety of other sources.[100] In its format, Isidore's description follows Orosius, moving from general remarks about land and the world to descriptions of Asia, Europe, Africa, and islands in the Mediterranean and further afield. Unlike Orosius, and consistent with his topic of the earth and its different manifestations, Isidore concludes book fourteen with discrete sections on promontories, mountains, and other natural formations (tumulus, valley, field, soil, etc.), and on lower regions (caves, vents, depths). Despite the relative absence of overt moralising, Isidore's description was more explicitly Christian than Orosius's, beginning with Paradise and including Jerusalem, "as if the navel of the entire region."[101] Isidore's representation of the known world is far from synchronic: if nothing else, his heavy use of Solinus (more than 100 borrowings) and Orosius (just over fifty borrowings) meant that his description could no more present an image of the earth at a particular point in time than his sources had done.[102] The reliance on Solinus had the additional result that, especially in Asia, Isidore includes animals and stones within the description of places and topographical features.[103] Nor does Isidore display a consistent attitude to the *mutatio locorum*, the changes in geography over time. In some cases Isidore omits his source's record of a change of name: in his description of the African province of Mauretania Tingitania he follows Orosius

99. Isidore of Seville, *Etymologiae XIV: De Terra* 14.3.5, 14.3.16, 14.5.9, 14.4.25, 14.4.22, ed. Olga Spevak (Paris, 2011), 11, 23, 89, 77, 75. For a typology of the various etymologies presented in book fourteen see Olga Spevak, "Isidore de Séville: Le livre XIV des *Etymologiae* et la tradition étymologique," *Revue des Études Latines* 87 (2009): 231–48.

100. *Etymologiae XIV*, ed. Spevak, xxxv–xxxix; cf. Hans Philipp, *Die historisch-geographischen Quellen in den Etymologiae des Isidorus von Sevilla*, 2 vols (Berlin, 1912–13).

101. *Etymologiae* 14.3.21, ed. Spevak, 27: "quasi umbilicus regionis totius." The source is "Hegesippus" (translating Josephus, *The Jewish War*, 3.52): *Historiae libri V* 3.6.5, ed. V. Ussani (Vienna, 1932–60), 1: 198: "in medio autem Iudaeae ciuitas Hierosolyma quasi umbilicus regionis totius ... nuncupatur."

102. See *Etymologiae XIV*, ed. Spevak, xxxvii. For discussion of Isidore's reliance on "obsolete" information, see Hervé Inglebert, "Isidore de Séville en son monde: Lieux, peuples, époques," *Antiquité Tardive* 23 (2015): 109–22.

103. See for example the description of India: *Etymologiae* 14.3.7, ed. Spevak, 15.

in noting a nomadic people called the Gaulaules, but leaves out Orosius's observation that this tribe was once known as the Autololes.[104] Elsewhere, however, Isidore retains the *mutatio* as noted by a source, or actively supplies information. He observes, perhaps thanks to Jerome's *Epitaphium Sanctae Paulae*, that the city of Samaria in the Palestinian region of the same name was once a royal city in Israel, "which now is named Sebastia after the name of Augustus."[105] On the basis of "Hegesippus" (the Latin translation of Flavius Josephus), or possibly Orosius, Isidore states that Pentapolis, named after the five cities of the impious that were consumed by celestial fire, was once more fertile than Jerusalem, "but now is abandoned and scorched."[106] This awareness of *mutatio* is not confined to the Holy Land. Scythia, Isidore tells us, was once huge, extending from India as far as the ends of Germania. Now, though, it is much reduced, bounded to the west by the Caspian Sea, and to the south by the Caucasus.[107] So while Isidore's description of the earth put spatial representation in the frame of etymology, it retained many of the aspects that characterise the works of the late antique authors he drew on. Isidore, like Solinus and Orosius before him, consolidated classical geographical description while recasting it as part of historical or universal knowledge. Whatever the incongruities, whatever the slippages between periods – and whatever the errors – a geographical corpus had been reshaped.

The medieval preservation of this refashioned geographical corpus can be considered a particular form of classicism. Since so much of medieval culture derived from the ancient world, it made sense to preserve an image of that world, not for sentimental or "conservative" motives, but for the utilitarian purpose of understanding better the classical texts and political structures that had survived into the Middle Ages: of understanding history as a spatial as well as a temporal concept. Imperial spatial formations, such as the Roman provincial structure, articulated powerfully the imprint of the Roman Empire across a swathe of ter-

104. *Etymologiae* 14.5.12, ed. Spevak, 93: "a meridie Gaulalum gentes ... pererrantes." Orosius, *Historiae* 1.2.94: "a meridie gentes Autololum quas nunc Galaules uocant." See Spevak's comments, xl.

105. *Etymologiae* 14.3.22, ed. Spevak 27: "ciuitas quondam regalis in Israel quae nunc ab Augusti nomine Sebastia nuncupatur"; *Sancti Eusebii Hieronymi Epistulae* 108.13, ed. I. Hilberg, 3 vols (Vienna, 1996), 2: 322–23: "uidit ... Sebasten, id est Samariam, quae in honorem Augusti ab Herode Graeco sermone Augusta est nominata." Isidore gives a slightly more detailed account in book fifteen: *Etymologiae* 15.1.25.

106. *Etymologiae* 14.3.24, ed. Spevak, 29: "Terra amplius ab Hierosolimis olim uberrima, nunc autem deserta atque exusta." *Hegesippi ... Historiae Libri V* 4.18.1, ed. Ussani, 271: "nunc autem ea locorum deserta atque exusta incendio sunt"; Orosius, *Historiarum ... libri vii* 1.5.9–10, ed. Zangemeister, 46.

107. *Etymologiae* 14.3.31, ed. Spevak, 35. The basis here is Orosius, *Historiarum ... libri vii* 1.2.47, ed. Zangemeister, 20.

ritory in the three *partes* of the known world, and *ipso facto* showed the limits of that empire. In turn, such formations offered points of connection with contemporary political structures – the kingdoms, duchies, counties, cities, and more recent empires – that had succeeded imperial space. The goal of this classicism was evidently not to construct chronologically precise depictions of a past spatial order. Rather, the picture that emerged in the works of Solinus, Orosius, and Isidore was temporally mixed, and wholly adaptable to the purposes of Christian narrative. It was within Roman imperial space that Christ was born and killed; into the provinces, along with Rome itself, the apostles had spread the gospels; there they had been martyred. Given the pressing relevance of this spatial history, medieval scribes, authors, and readers – like Orosius's barbarian king Athaulf – saw value in maintaining and interpreting the map of empire, rather than erasing it and starting afresh.

CHAPTER THREE

Aeneas and Ovid between Troy and Rome

Good Lord, what in fact do you expect me to invent? Practically everything's been invented by other people already. It gets more and more difficult every day.[1]

Classical geographical description came entwined with literary expression. Among the major conduits of classical geography to the Middle Ages were the epics of Virgil and Lucan, and the oeuvre of Ovid. For each of these authors, geography and geographic order offered a crucial fabric from which to weave narrative. In each, too, geography's confusions – epitomised in the wanderings, exiles, flights, colonisations, foundations, and violent encounters experienced by a range of characters – generated intellectual energy. In different ways Virgil, Ovid, and Lucan manipulated a detailed knowledge of the world, infused with historical and mythographical significance, to invest their poetry with density of meaning. Such density was then explored by centuries of commentators, readers, and authors. For the Middle Ages, Virgil, Ovid, and Lucan were foundational: they provided works that acted not simply as texts to be read, copied, and appreciated, but as resources of learning, whose riches could be re-worked in manifold ways. Starting in late antiquity, commentators such as Virgil's Servius sought to explain, unravel – and, inevitably, add to – the underlying geography of these texts, always with the possibility of further confusion. But as well as explication, there were realignments: allegorical readings, modernisations, and translations, as well as maps, both visual and verbal. Following the thread of classical geography in and out of texts and across histories and languages, an account emerges not of disintegration from order to disorder, nor of ludic experimentation unpicked and flattened, but of passage from one dislocation to another.

Some insight into the literary fashioning of geography, and into the puzzles and pregnant meanings left behind by such fashioning, can be gained by a comparison of two narratives of exile. One, of tremendous importance for the cultural memory of the centuries that followed, is the story of the Trojan exodus as

1. The complaint of the charlatan Hjalmar in Ibsen's *The Wild Duck*, Act 5, ed. and trans. James Walter McFarlane (London, 1960), 235.

recounted by Aeneas in book three of Virgil's *Aeneid*. The other narrative, less momentous but never forgotten in the Middle Ages, is the account of Ovid's own relegation from Rome to the Black Sea, as told by the poet himself in his two volumes of exile poetry, *Tristia* and *Ex Ponto*. The story of an exile is inherently one of spatial dislocation. These stories, though, contain multiple dislocations, temporal as well as spatial; moreover, they are conjoined by Ovid's conscious reversal of Virgilian narrative. From them arise certain recurrent aspects of dislocation, which extend beyond the representation of migration and the consequent transfer and layering of spatial identity. In Virgil and Ovid dislocation emerges as a practice intimately connected with acts of foundation. It is a precondition for foundation, yet one that carries the threat of the disintegration of a secure polity. The *Aeneid* traces the foundation of Rome back to the exile of Aeneas and his fellow Trojans from the sacked city of Troy. For Ovid, meanwhile, banishment opens a trajectory in which the linguistic and political fabric of foundation starts to fray, in which the nature and meaning of Rome is both intensified and unsettled. These stories also reveal an aspect of dislocation which has particular significance for the representation of geographical space. Evident in the *Aeneid* as in the *Tristia* and *Ex Ponto* is the dislocation that lies within toponyms, the problem of understanding and assigning place through a name or names, which may change, lead elsewhere, or unexpectedly vanish. This is the problem of mutation, which lies at the heart of the medieval reception of classical geography.

AENEID 3

New Mistakes, Old Lands

Book three of Virgil's *Aeneid* sees the hero in flight, and in imitation of Ulysses. If his wanderings are less exotic than Homer's hero, their nature is more complex: whereas the *Odyssey* narrates a return home from Troy, the third book of the *Aeneid* tells of departure from the Trojan homeland in search of a new one. To complicate matters further, the narrator is Aeneas himself; the narrative is unresolved, because at the time of its telling the new fatherland remains unreached; and the story's immediate audience, Dido, Queen of Carthage, is about to become another obstacle, and victim, in the quest for Italy. The story of wandering told by Aeneas veers toward the comic. He, his father and son, and a band of Trojan comrades know that they must leave Troy (whose conquest and destruction by the Greeks was the subject of book two) and refound it elsewhere, but only in the course of the book do they discover exactly where this new *patria* is, and how to reach it. Consequently, Aeneas leaves scattered behind him a series of mistakes. He confidently founds or intends to found new cities in Thrace (the modestly named Aeneadae), and in Crete, before learning the identity of the correct place, which itself has at least three names, and which he will not reach before making a tour of Sicily, being blown all the way to north Africa, narrating his story to Dido, and losing (one per book, and possibly in increasing order of importance) his father, lover, and helmsman.

The reasons for the false starts vary. First, in Thrace, the ground seeps the blood of a murdered Trojan ambassador, Polydorus, and the ill omen deters the Trojans (*Aen* 3.19–68).[2] Next an act of misinterpretation compounds their misfortunes: Aeneas's father Anchises makes a "new mistake about old lands." On the island of Delos, where Aeneas asks the god Phoebus for guidance towards another Troy, a divine voice instructs the Trojans to search for the land that first brought them forth from their ancestral stock, indeed a land described as their ancient mother, which awaits "with bountiful breast" (*ubere laeto*), ready to become the "house of Aeneas" (*domus Aeneae*) and that of his children's children (*Aen* 3.85–98).[3] Anchises decides that the god must be speaking of Crete, the island from which Teucer, the first Trojan, set out to found a kingdom on Rhoetean shores. "Pergamum" is duly founded in Crete, and just as quickly abandoned after a disastrous plague. More divine advice follows, this time explicit: the land the Trojans should look for is called Hesperia by the Greeks, but known by its inhabitants as Italia. As Anchises now remembers, the ignored prophetess Cassandra had mentioned Hesperia and the Italian lands as the destiny of the Trojans; his mistake in interpreting the oracle was that he did not consider the "twin parents" of Troy. It is the homeland of another ur-Trojan, Dardanus, not Teucer, that they should seek: "he acknowledged the two-fold descent from dual founders, and that he had been deceived by a new mistake about old lands" (agnouit prolem ambiguam geminosque parentis, / seque nouo ueterum deceptum errore locorum: *Aen* 3.180–81).[4] Further reflection on refoundations follows during a curious interlude in the city of Buthrotum (*Aen* 3.294–520).[5] There

2. All references to the *Aeneid* are to the text contained in *P. Vergili Maronis Opera*, ed. R.A.B. Mynors (Oxford, 1969).

3. On the motif of the ancient mother see Nicholas Horsfall, *Virgil, Aeneid 3: A Commentary* (Leiden, 2006), 107.

4. The "enigmatic colonial oracle" was a standard feature of ancient Greek colonial discourse: Carol Dougherty, *The Poetics of Colonization: From City to Text in Archaic Greece* (Oxford, 1993), 45–60; Nicholas Horsfall, "Aeneas The Colonist," *Vergilius* 35 (1989): 8–27.

5. See Horsfall, *Aeneid 3: A Commentary*, 233–37 for the Homeric, Apollonian and Euripidean sources of this episode and general discussion; also Maurizio Bettini, "Ghosts of Exile: Doubles and Nostalgia in Vergil's *parva Troia* (*Aeneid* 3.294ff)," *Classical Antiquity* 16 (1997): 8–33.

Aeneas encounters yet another new Troy, this time the Pergama founded by fellow exile, and son of Priam, Helenus. Conveniently, Helenus has the gift of prophecy, which enables him to give precise directions along the "pathless path" (*uia inuia*) to Italy (*Aen* 3.383). Aeneas is told to round the island of Circe, avoid the west coast of Italy (which is populated by "evil Greeks"), look for Sicily, but beware of Scylla and Charybdis.

The proliferation of new Troys, false new Troys, effigies, and colonies amounts to a prelude to foundation in which ancestors and exiles are entwined in a search for identity and its relationship to territory. If Troy is the book's spatial ghost, it is only one of several shades encountered by Aeneas and his men. There is Polydorus, the unburied corpse whose blood flows from the earth when Aeneas attempts to found Aeneadae. There is Hector, whose wife Andromache, encountered in Buthrotum, figures the fate of the Trojans – her homeland incinerated (*patria incensa*), she was claimed by Pyrrhus, son of Achilles, as a trophy, child-bearing in servitude, then passed on to Helenus (a servant given to a servant: "*famulo famulamque*"), before settling in her new husband's "Ilian citadel", repatriated in the effigy (*Aen* 3.320–55; 497). There is Achaemenides, a Greek warrior discovered on Sicily, one of Ulysses's men who unluckily failed to flee the Cyclops, and who now dwells in lonely terror on the island. Achaemenides retells the story of the Cyclops, bringing the presence of Ulysses powerfully into focus as a model for Aeneas (*Aen* 3.613–54).[6] In so doing Virgil acknowledges the literary ghost of Homer,[7] as well as invoking the "Sicilian muses" credited in his own early volume, the *Eclogues*. These literary shades contribute to the insistent clash of temporalities evident in the *Aeneid*'s third book. Troy past meets Troy present and future; Italy and Sicily present confront Italy and Sicily past; Homeric epic is invoked by Virgilian epic in the making. The Trojans visit places built in effigy of those destroyed, and through prophecy glimpse places not yet built. Foundation itself emerges as an act of imitation, and all claims of originality are dispelled. The mode is one of return (to Dardanus), reunion, repetition, and assimilation.

At the turn of the fourth century, a grammarian resident in Rome compiled an extensive commentary on the works of Virgil which was to enjoy vast influence in late antiquity and the Middle Ages.[8] It appeared in the margins and between

6. Horsfall, *Aeneid 3: A Commentary*, 406–9.

7. See *Il libro terzo dell'Eneide*, ed. Pier Vincenzo Cova, 2nd ed (Milan, 1998), lxviii–lxxxii, and for contrast Georg Knauer, *Die Aeneis und Homer: Studien zur poetischen Technik Vergils mit Listen der Homerzitate in der Aeneis* (Göttingen, 1964), 184–98.

8. On Servius see Robert A. Kaster, *Guardians of the Language: The Grammarian and Society in Late Antiquity* (Berkeley, 1988), 169–97, 356–59, who emphasises Servius's role as an active teacher.

the lines of hundreds of medieval manuscripts of the work, as well as independently of its source.[9] One effect of Servius's work was to explicate and thereby open out the spatial reference contained within the *Aeneid*. The commentary begins with a statement that goes to the heart of the spatial complexity inherent in Virgil's epic. It responds to the opening of the *Aeneid*, in which Aeneas is described as "the one, exiled by destiny, who first came from the shores of Troy to Italy and Lavine coasts" (Troiae qui primus ab oris / Italiam fato profugus Lauinaque uenit / litora: *Aen* 1.1–3):

> WHO FIRST. Many ask why Virgil said that Aeneas was the first to come to Italy, when shortly after he states that Antenor had founded a city before the arrival of Aeneas. He did indeed say that, but Virgil spoke most wisely in reckoning times. For at the time when Aeneas came to Italy, Italy extended as far as the river Rubicon – something that Lucan recalled ("and [the Rubicon], a fixed boundary, cuts Gallic fields off from Italian farmers"). From this it is apparent that Antenor did not come to Italy, but to Cisalpine Gaul, which is where Venice is located. The limits of Italy were subsequently extended as far as the Alps, and this changed situation created Virgil's "error." Many however want this question to be resolved as follows: that Virgil seems to have added "to Lavinian shores" to avoid signifying Antenor. However, the first explanation is the better one.[10]

---

9. P.K. Marshall, "Servius," in *Texts and Transmission: A Survey of the Latin Classics*, ed. L.D. Reynolds (Oxford, 1983), 385–88, provides a brief overview of the textual complexity of Servius's *Commentary*. See John J.H. Savage, "The Manuscripts of the Commentary of Servius Danielis on Virgil," *Harvard Studies in Classical Philology* 43 (1932): 77–121; John J.H. Savage, "The Manuscripts of Servius' Commentary on Virgil," *Harvard Studies in Classical Philology* 45 (1934): 157–204, and Birger Munk Olsen, *L'étude des auteurs classiques latins aux XIe et XIIe siècles*, 4 vols (Paris, 1982–2014), 2: 673–826, for listing of Virgil manuscripts of the eleventh and twelfth centuries. Early in its transmission the commentary of Servius became entwined in some manuscripts with the earlier commentary of Aelius Donatus. Efforts of nineteenth- and twentieth-century scholars to disentangle the two commentaries have been largely unsuccessful.

10. *Servii Grammatici qui feruntur in Vergilii carmina Commentarii*, ed. G. Thilo and H. Hagen, 3 vols (Leipzig, 1881–87), 1: 6–7 (at *Aen* 1.1): "QVI PRIMVS quaerunt multi, cur Aeneam primum ad Italiam venisse dixerit, cum paulo post dicat Antenorem ante adventum Aeneae fundasse civitatem. constat quidem, sed habita temporum ratione peritissime Vergilius dixit. namque illo tempore, quo Aeneas ad Italiam venit, finis erat Italiae usque ad Rubiconem fluvium: cuius rei meminit Lucanus 'et Gallica certus limes ab Ausoniis disterminat arva colonis' [*Bellum civile*, 1.215–16]. unde apparet Antenorem non ad Italiam venisse, sed ad Galliam cisalpinam, in qua Venetia est. postea vero promotis usque ad Alpes Italiae finibus, novitas creavit errorem. plerique tamen quaestionem hanc volunt ex sequentibus solvi, ut videatur

In classical antiquity foundation is not as straightforward as it seems: other people have discovered almost everything already. Antenor's dangerous usurpation of Aeneas's role as founder of Italy can be explained away by shifting the northern border. Yet, as Servius points out, the insistence that Virgil was thinking of Italy as far as the Rubicon, supported by a famous line from Lucan, is merely the better of at least two possible explanations, both of which acknowledge that Aeneas's primacy can only be asserted with significant limitations. The doubleness of place, encountered at the very beginning of the epic, will recur again and again, compelling Servius to situate Virgil's poem within a web of prior action, whether in the distant or more recent past. Anchises's mistaken identification of Crete as the destined site for a new Troy, for example, demands explication of the complex history of the Trojan ancestors, Dardanus and Teucer:

> CRETE. Dardanus, son of Jupiter and Electra, having departed from Corythus, a city of Tuscany, first came to Troy and there erected some small buildings. After Dardanus' death, Teucer came from Crete and found the comrades of Dardanus living in valleys. Teucer built walls and fortifications. So at this point Anchises makes a mistake; not being mindful of the arrival of Dardanus, he argues that the oracle signifies Crete ... .[11]

Dardanus himself is "primus," like Aeneas in book one, yet his narrative coalesced with Teucer's: both Tuscany and Crete turn out to be identifiable as ancestral sites for the Trojans, and as if to disrupt primacy further, Servius narrates a brief history of colonisation. Teucer is the one who builds the walls and citadels, moving the populace out of valleys, and ultimately giving them his name. Anchises's error is to think etymologically; Dardanus must be substituted as the true "auctor," yet the contestation embedded in Virgil's narrative draws Servius into cross-narration, into inclusion of the incorrect guess of Aeneas's father. Subtly Aeneas's "foundation" becomes ever more tenuous: a repetition of Troy's foundation, a reversion to the Tuscan origins of Dardanus, a second or a third guess.

---

ob hoc addidisse Vergilius 'ad Lavinia litora', ne significaret Antenorem. melior tamen est superior expositio." See further Mathilde Mahé-Simon, "Servius et le nom de l'Italie," in *Servius et sa réception de l'Antiquité à la Renaissance*, ed. Monique Bouquet and Bruno Méniel (Rennes, 2011), 89–100.

11. Servius, *Commentarii*, 1: 359 (at *Aen* 3.104): "CRETA Dardanus Iovis filius et Electrae, profectus de Corytho, civitate Tusciae, primus venit ad Troiam et illic parva aedificia collocavit. post cuius obitum Teucer venit ex Creta et invenit Dardani socios habitantes in vallibus. qui constituit arces et moenia. modo ergo errat Anchises, nec respiciens adventum Dardani oraculum Cretam significare argumentatur ... ."

The Rise of Allegory

So familiar was the *Aeneid* to learned early Christian authors that it could be invoked in passing, as assumed knowledge. The effect was to entwine Virgil's poem in unexpected ways with Christian narrative, with the result that Aeneas's wanderings were displaced yet further afield.[12] For Augustine of Hippo the very phrase "City of God" and its analogue "house of God" came with a Virgilian subtext. He maintained that Virgil's description of Romans as the "house of Assaracus" (*Aen* 1.284) and elsewhere as the "house of Aeneas" (*Aen* 3.97) "imitated holy scripture in which the 'house of Jacob' is used to describe the entire Hebrew people."[13] The narrative of the Trojans, in which Italy is at once a destiny and a point of origin, thereby was made to align with that of the Israelites, the two peoples drawn together by the metonymic quality of "house."

A further step in the Christian appropriation of the pagan literary corpus was to wrench spatial reference outside of its literal frame, and to construct from geography a series of moral metaphors: in other words, to read allegorically. Allegorical readings of the *Aeneid* are certainly present in Augustine, and they are even visible in Servius's commentary. Servius identified the third book of the *Aeneid* as the book of "errores," wanderings, after the omens and pathos of the first two books, and before the "ethos," "festivity," and "knowledge" of the next three.[14] The sixth-century mythographer Fulgentius understood books two and three in terms of youthful folly, a prelude to adult wisdom attained in the later books.[15] But the most striking reading of the poem as an allegory of human life was achieved in the twelfth-century *Commentum super sex libros Eneidos Virgilii*

---

12. A useful overview of the reception of book three of the *Aeneid* can be found in Pierre Courcelle, *Lecteurs païens et lecteurs chrétiens de l'Énéide: I. Les témoignages littéraires* (Paris, 1984), 225–79; for medieval reception of the *Aeneid* in general see Domenico Comparetti, *Virgilio nel medio evo*, rev. ed., 2 vols (Florence, 1896); *The Virgilian Tradition: The First Fifteen Hundred Years*, ed. Jan Ziolkowski and Michael C.J. Putnam (New Haven, 2008). More focussed studies are offered by Christopher Baswell, *Virgil in Medieval England: Figuring the Aeneid from the Twelfth Century to Chaucer* (Cambridge, 1995); Craig Kallendorf, *In Praise of Aeneas: Virgil and Epideictic Rhetoric in the Early Italian Renaissance* (Hanover, 1989).

13. *De civitate dei* 15.19, ed. B. Dombart and A. Kalb, 2 vols (Turnhout, 1955), 482: "imitatus namque est poeta ille litteras sacras, in quibus dicitur domus Iacob iam ingens populus Hebraeorum."

14. Servius, *Commentarii*, 1: 458 (at *Aen* 3.718).

15. "Expositio Virgilianae continentiae secundum philosophos moralis," in *Opera*, ed. Rudolf Helm (Leipzig, 1898), 93–94. John of Salisbury articulated a similar scheme: the first six books of the *Aeneid* equate to different ages, the third being the errors of youth: *Policraticus* 8.24, ed. Clement Webb, 2 vols (Oxford, 1909), 2: 415–16.

(Commentary on six books of Virgil's *Aeneid*) attributed to the schoolmaster and Chartrian philosopher Bernardus Silvestris.[16] This commentary, which in its current state extends from book one to 6.636 of the *Aeneid*, interprets the opening book as a mirror of infancy; book two (fall of Troy) as childhood; book three (wanderings) as adolescence; book four (affair with Dido) as early manhood; and book five (funeral games for Anchises) as "virilis aetas" (the age of full manhood). Book six – in which Aeneas is granted access to the underworld – is interpreted as a profound declaration of philosophical truth requiring word by word interpretation.[17] As a consequence, fundamental geographic and topographic terms are transposed: the city becomes the human body, the "arcs" (citadel) the head; the dwellings of suburban farmers correspond to the hands and feet, and the fire that destroys Troy is "the natural fervour of first youth."[18] Aeneas's travels become a moral journey to manhood. Antandros, near to which the Trojans construct a fleet, signifies that which is contrary to manhood, and which must be left behind. Thrace represents avarice and its ruler Polimestor "aggregatio pecunie"; Delos is understood as "clarity" and honour, the result of departing from avarice.[19] Crete and Italy are connected by the injunction to "seek the ancient mother." Crete represents bodily nature, while Italy is the nature of the soul: it comprises rationality, immortality, virtue, and knowledge (*rationalitas, immortalitas, virtus, scientia*).[20] The Trojans' error of initially choosing Crete over Italy thus becomes the mistake of favouring body over soul. Dangers of the voyage are interpreted as moral obstacles. The Strophades are the "recurrence of vices" (*revolutiones vitiorum*), storms the commotions of the flesh that draw the subject back to vice, the Cyclops the "great amount of roaming around that adolescents suffer" (*girovagationum multitudinem quam patiuntur adolescentes*), mount Etna elation; Poliphemus himself, whose one eye signifies the consideration of temporal matters only, is arrogance. Drepanum, site of the burial of Anchises, is "boyish anguish, to be understood as the hasty temper which disturbs boys with the greatest vehemence."[21]

Allegory in one way undoes geography, translating physical features into the language of emotion and intellect. The homeless, rootless state of the Trojans becomes the predicament of the human alienated by bodily desires from the

16. Bernardus Silvestris, *Commentum super sex libros Eneidos Virgilii*, ed. Julian Ward Jones and Elizabeth Frances Jones (Lincoln and London, 1977).

17. *Commentum*, xiii.

18. *Commentum*, 15–16.

19. *Commentum*, 17–20.

20. *Commentum*, 20–21.

21. *Commentum*, 21–23: "acerbitas puerilis, interpretatur que est iracundia que pueros maximo fervore solet infestare."

immortality and rationality of the soul, yet led on by its guiding presence. At the same time, allegory relies on geographical structure. It derives meaning not simply from the concept of the journey but from the notion of distance between locations. The meaning of Italy as Italy is not entirely erased, since it continues to underlie its signification as the soul. The sign the commentator operates under is that of the "integumentum" (veil, cover), and the object of the commentary is to expound, but also expose the *integument*.[22] Reading geography allegorically could be seen as constraining, as an imposition of an insistent, alien medieval structure on a classical narrative. But viewed from another perspective, it takes to radical lengths the moral understanding of Virgil's poem that was present in the text from its creation, without closing down other, more literal readings.

Mapping Error

Among the opportunities offered by the *Aeneid* to medieval readers was the possibility to direct the poem's narrative of exile and foundation towards their own patriotic or dynastic ends. By the end of the twelfth century, numerous European peoples were able to assert a Trojan genealogy, based on the claim that exiles from Troy had founded colonies to the city's west. Trojan ancestry, often conflated with biblical history, became an important foundation stone of English, Norman, French, Spanish, and of course Italian historical consciousness; the same logic could be applied to the ancestors of Germans, Bohemians, and the counts of Flanders.[23] Numerous cities asserted a Trojan lineage,[24] or an active role in the events described in the *Aeneid*;[25] even the University of Oxford, goaded by its rivalry with Cambridge, claimed to have been founded by Trojan

---

22. See Winthrop Wetherbee, *Platonism and Poetry in the Twelfth Century: The Literary Influence of the School of Chartres* (Princeton, 1972), 104–25.

23. Susan Reynolds, "Medieval *origines gentium* and the Community of the Realm," *History* 68 (1983): 375–90; Richard Waswo, "Our Ancestors, the Trojans: Inventing Cultural Identity in the Middle Ages," *Exemplaria* 7 (1995): 269–90; Colette Beaune, "L'utilisation politique du mythe des origines troyennes en France à la fin du Moyen Âge," in *Lectures médiévales de Virgile* (Rome, 1985), 331–55; for bibliography see Kordula Wolf, *Troja – Metamorphosen eines Mythos: Französische, englische und italienische Überlieferungen des 12. Jahrhunderts im Vergleich* (Berlin, 2009), 16–17 n4.

24. Beaune, "L'utilisation politique," 352; Wolf, *Troja*, 110–23.

25. The twelfth-century *Liber Guidonis* gave one thousand expert soldiers from Pisa ("*civitas nobilissima*") a role in Aeneas's victory over Turnus: *Liber Guidonis compositus de variis historiis*, ed. Michele Campopiano (Florence, 2008), 133; cf. *Aen* 10.179–80.

intellectuals.[26] The central theme of book three of the *Aeneid* – exile and refoundation – proved infinitely adaptable, and desirable. The indigenous was shunned in favour of the foreign arrival, bearing all the authority of classical epic. The history of the Trojans thereby became part of the history of the Christian peoples of Europe.

In the early fourteenth century the allegorical possibilities of the third book of the *Aeneid* were conjoined with a form of geographic literalism to advance a powerful political sentiment. Dante's *Monarchia*, written as a defence of the independence of imperial power from the papacy, contained a passage that confidently and controversially proclaimed the nobility of the Roman people, and their *de jure* possession of empire, on the basis of the nobility of Aeneas.[27] This nobility rested precisely on the mixed nature of the hero's origins, derived from each of the three parts into which the world was divided. Asia contributed Aeneas's forebears Assaracus and the rulers of Phrygia (*Aen* 3.1–2); Europe his most ancient male ancestor, Dardanus (*Aen* 3.163–67); Africa his most ancient female ancestor, Electra (*Aen* 8.134–37), a daughter of Atlas, whose African origins are attested by the presence of the Atlas mountain in Africa.[28] Aeneas's marriages only confirmed his claims to a global nobility: his first wife, Creusa, was the daughter of Priam, king of Troy, and thus an Asian noblewoman; his second spouse Dido was "queen and mother of the Carthaginians in Africa";[29] and his final mate, Lavinia, daughter of King Latinus, came from Italy, the most noble region of Europe.[30] Those ancestors and wives, a "double concourse of blood" (*duplex concursus sanguinis*), ensured the greatest nobility of the Roman people.[31]

Such a formulation serves to obfuscate the doubleness of space so evident in Servian commentary, in which histories of place move away from unity. Dante read a world geography into the person of Aeneas, and superimposed the world-man onto Rome: the presence of the foreign on Italian soil was paradoxically formed into a sign of integrity. Elsewhere the poet showed himself alert to the

26. Alfred Hiatt, *The Making of Medieval Forgeries: False Documents in Fifteenth-Century England* (London, 2004), 70–101.

27. Dante Alighieri, *Monarchia* 2.3.6–17, ed. Pier Giorgio Ricci (Milan, 1965), 177–81. An indignant refutation came swiftly from the friar Guido Vernani of Rimini: Anthony K. Cassell, *The* Monarchia *Controversy* (Washington, DC, 2004).

28. *Monarchia* 2.3.10–13, ed. Ricci, 178–79; Orosius, *Historiarum ... libri vii* 1.2.11, ed. Zangemeister, 11.

29. *Monarchia* 2.3.14–15, ed. Ricci, 179–80: "regina et mater Cartaginensium in Affrica"; Dido calls her love "marriage" (coniugium) at *Aen* 4.171–2.

30. *Monarchia* 2.3.16–17, ed. Ricci, 180–81.

31. *Monarchia* 2.3.17, ed. Ricci, 180–81.

ambiguities involved in spatial history, in ways that suggest hidden echoes of book three of the *Aeneid*. This sensitivity is nowhere more evident in Dante's oeuvre than in a remarkable passage in canto 20 of *Inferno*, in which the pilgrim is treated by his guide to a brief narrative of the foundation of Virgil's home town, Mantua. The context is a valley of hell in which the inhabitants are turned around (*travolto*), their heads twisted to face backwards. Among these sorry shades is a female figure, identified by Virgil as "Manto," a native of the "city of Bacchus" (that is, Thebes), who wandered through many lands, before settling on an uninhabited piece of marsh land in Italy "to flee all human society" (*per fuggire ogne consorzio umano*).[32] In a few lines Dante, in the voice of Virgil, sketches a map of the region:

> Suso in Italia bella giace un laco,
> a piè de l'Alpe che serra Lamagna
> sovra Tiralli, c'ha nome Benaco.
> Per mille fonti, credo, e più si bagna
> tra Garda e Val Camonica e Pennino
> de l'acqua che nel detto laco stagna.
> Loco è nel mezzo là dove 'l trentino
> pastore e quel di Brescia e 'l veronese
> segnar poria, s'e' fesse quel cammino.[33]

Up in fair Italy, at the foot of the mountains that bound Germany above Tirol, lies a lake which is called Benaco. By a thousand springs, I think, and more, the region between Garda and Val Camonica and Pennino is bathed by the water which settles in that lake, and in the middle of it is a spot where the pastors of Trent and Brescia and Verona, if they went that way, might give their blessing.

The passage is elegant, regular: it moves from the large geographical unit (*Italia*) to the natural feature (*giace un laco*), deftly associated with the Alps, and the natural border with Germany (*Alamagna*). In its course it manages to capture both national (*Italia bella*) and local pride, as well as acknowledging ecclesiastical oversight of the area in the form of the three *pastore*. Thereafter, attention

32. Dante Alighieri, *Inferno* 20.85, in *La Commedia secondo l'antica vulgata*, ed. Giorgio Petrocchi, 4 vols (Milan, 1966–67), 2: 339.

33. *Inferno* 20.61–69, ed. Petrocchi, 2: 336–37. *The Divine Comedy*, vol. 1: *Inferno*, trans. Charles S. Singleton (Princeton, 1970), 207. "Tiralli" was a castle, and by extension the name of the county of Tiralli or Tirolo.

shifts to the river Mincio, which emerges from the Benaco and becomes a tributary of the Po. Aspects of this map – the fertility of the landscape in particular – suggest a *locus amoenus*, but they are soon undermined. A history of local conflict is implied (the fortified city of Peschiera "confronts" – *da fronteggiar* – the Brescians and the Bergamaschi across the lake), while the river goes on to form a marsh, "grama" (l. 81: unwholesome? unbearable?) in summer, which attracted the a-social Manto. This "cruel virgin" (*vergine cruda*) took advantage of the spot's isolation to perform her magic arts, and left her body there; upon those "dead bones" (*ossa morte*) men built a city and called it Mantua.[34] It has recently, Virgil pointedly concludes, seen a decline in population following political machinations. We hear no more of Mantua, nor Manto, but the narrative implies an inherent volatility which may be understood to be diffused more widely throughout "Italia bella." The idea of foundation upon the dead bones of an exile – one, learned commentators on *Inferno* quickly pointed out, who came from the fratricidal city of Thebes[35] – seems reminiscent of Aeneas's failed attempt to found a new Troy on the body of Polydorus, an event recalled by Dante later in the *Inferno*.[36] As foundation myths go, this is outstandingly bleak, mysterious, and in obvious contrast to Virgil's account of Rome's origins.[37] It is no suprise to find within the works of an author such as Dante a number of different ways of apprehending spatial history. But the presence of the Manto story within *Inferno* indicates once again the entwined nature of foundation narratives. As the story of Manto also suggests, toponyms had the capacity to hold much beneath their surface. Like the soil itself, they could reveal unsettling histories when probed.

Some decades after the *Monarchia*, another highly influential reader of Virgil and Servius recognized the secondary nature of Aeneas and the exilic nature of the Trojans as a central aspect – and potential problem – of the Roman foundation myth. The difficulties of stabilising space, and movement through spaces, are evident in Francis Petrarch's annotations of his manuscript of the *Aeneid*, apparently added at various intervals between 1338 and the years leading up to

---

34. *Inferno* 20.82–93, ed. Petrocchi, 2: 339–40; cf *Inferno*, trans. Singleton, 209. See Angelo Mazzocco, "Dante, Bruni and the Issue of the Origin of Mantua," *Modern Language Notes* 127 (2012): 257–63.

35. See for example *Guido da Pisa's Expositiones et Glose super Comediam Dantis*, ed. Vincenzo Cioffari (Albany, 1974), 390; Pietro Alighieri, *Il "Commentarium" di Pietro Alighieri*, ed. Roberto della Vedova and Maria Teresa Silvotti (Florence, 1978), 315–17; Cristoforo Landino, *Comento sopra la Comedia*, ed. Paolo Procaccioli, 4 vols (Rome, 2001), 2: 774–75.

36. *Inferno* 30.18.

37. It also contrasts with Virgil's own brief allusion to Mantua's foundation in *Aen* 10.198–200, where Ocnus, son of Manto and the river Tuscus, gives the town its name.

his death in 1374.[38] The clearest indication of what was at stake in the humanist reading of Virgilian (but, also, Servian) geography emerges in Petrarch's lengthy gloss on *Aeneid* 3.531, in which Virgil referred to a "templum ... in arce Minervae": a temple on the hill of Minerva, or perhaps in her citadel, at any rate the first landmark of Italy seen by Aeneas and his men. Thereafter, the Trojans, mindful of Helenus's advice, press onwards past Tarentum (modern Tarento), Caulon, and Scylaceum before glimpsing Mount Etna and the Sicilian coast (*Aen* 3.548–60). But where is, or was, the "temple of Minerva"? Petrarch attempted to resolve the doubts, but not without acknowledgement of the vicissitudes of textual transmission. He wrote in his manuscript a very long comment, in fact a mini-essay on spatial dislocation and textual commentary, which is worth quoting in full for its contemplation of the fundamental difficulty of recovering ancient places:

> There are indeed many things that give rise to error in the knowledge of places, and they are these, among others: the remoteness of regions inaccessible to people of our era; change of place names; the small number and obscurity of writers on the subject and their not infrequent disagreements; and, above all, carelessness of intellect and sluggishness of attention for anything at all not directly in front of the eyes. For this reason, not only readers but often even commentators themselves skip over these matters. We however, more scrupulously investigating this question to the best of our ability both among writers, especially cosmographers, and in written descriptions of the earth, as well as in certain very old maps which came into our possession, conclude that the place [referred to by Virgil] which is called Castrum or Castra Minerve is in that corner of Italy above or beyond Otranto. This place is the first on the Italian shore to present itself to those coming from Epirus. This is what Virgil describes. ... as [the description] bends around from the Adriatic to the Tyrrhenian sea, the correct order of progress along the coast is followed: Tarentum, Crotonis, Caulon, Scylaceum, from here the view of Etna etc. Therefore for this place we either simply accept "temple of Minerva" just as the text states, which perhaps was the first sight that they encountered there, or that, wanting to name the place, [Virgil] used "templum" instead of "Castra," using one term for another as was his wont. Indeed there is another place of this name, that is the "temple of Minerva" – although Pomponius Mela calls it a "promontory" – in the same region of

38. Milan, Biblioteca Ambrosiana A 79 inf. On the manuscript see *Le Postille del Virgilio Ambrosiano*, ed. Marco Baglio, Antonietta Nebuloni Testa, and Marco Petoletti, 2 vols (Rome, 2006), 1: 6–29.

Campania, on a different coast, so far as can be understood, between the rivers Sileris and Sarnus, between the towns of Salerno and Sorrento.[39]

This investigation – notably conducted with recourse to cosmographers such as Pomponius Mela, as well as "very old maps" – succeeds in identifying the place to the satisfaction of Petrarch, but only after eliminating certain obstacles and confusions: Virgil's use of "templum" for "castra/um"; the presence of another place of the same name, on a different shore, which in turn encourages Petrarch into a brief appendicization of confusable places.[40] Why does the location of the *templum Minervae* matter? This question is not addressed by Petrarch, and the obvious answer is that, in a rhetoric of primacy, the identification of the first always matters. Beyond that, though, the importance of clarifying location seems to lie in an investment in a rigorously literal reading of the *Aeneid* as a means of re-vivifying the concept of Italy. Topography becomes crucial to such a reading, in part because the ancient map affirms and re-animates the modern one, revealing the depths of historical meaning held by the land.[41] Could it be in part too because the very prolixity of the land – its homonyms or near homonyms – and the poet's elisions between architectural (but also spatial) forms, generate intel-

39. *Le Postille del Virgilio Ambrosiano*, ed. Baglio et al., 1: 329–31: "Errorem sane circa locorum notitiam multa pariunt, atque hec inter cetera: regionum inaccessarum nostris hominibus longinquitas, nominum mutatio, scriptorum raritas obscuritasque eorundemque nonnunquam dissensio, sed super omnia incuriositas ingeniorum ac segnities nichil omnino curantium nisi quod ante oculos est. Hinc non comunes modo lectores, sed sepe ipsi etiam glosatores suspenso gressu ista pretereunt. Nos autem hoc quantum potuimus scrupulosius inquirentes tam apud scriptores, presertim cosmographos, quam in descriptionibus terrarum et quibusdam cartis vetustissimis que ad manus nostras venerunt, deprehendimus locum esse in ipso Ytalie angulo supra sive ultra Ydruntem, qui dictus est Castrum vel Castra Minerve. Is locus venientibus ex Epyro in litore ytalico primus occurrit. Hunc Maro describit. ... dum a supero ad inferum mare circumflectitur, optimo occurrentium ordine usus est, Tarenti, Crotonis, Caulonis, Scyllacei, hinc Ethne prospectus et cetera. Hoc igitur loco vel simpliciter accipimus templum Minerve scilicet dicatum, quod forte ibi erat primum sui prospectum exhibens, vel nominare locum volens pro Castris templum posuit, aliunde transferens more suo. Est enim locus alter huius nominis, scilicet templum Minerve, quanquam Pomponius [Mela 2.69–70] 'promontorium' vocet, in ipso Campanie tractu diverso litore, quantum intelligi datur, inter Silerim et Sarnum flumina, inter Salernum et Surrentum oppida."

40. See *Le Postille del Virgilio Ambrosiano*, 1: 330–31 for echoes elsewhere in Petrarch's writing. Scholars currently identify the temple as capo Santa Maria di Leuca, near modern Castro at the base of the "heel" of Italy.

41. On the significance of Petrarch's gloss for the humanist understanding of ancient space as well as the "stigmatisation of the errors of the copyist": Nathalie Bouloux, *Culture et savoirs géographiques en Italie au XIVe siècle* (Turnhout, 2002), 108–10, 196–201.

lectual energy? Confusion, that is, is a productive force, posing questions, demanding the articulation of order. Confusion attests to the passage of time, to the long history of place, to a multiplicity of rivers and towns.

In the fifteenth and sixteenth centuries allegory remained an attractive mode of interpreting Aeneas's wanderings. Coluccio Salutati, the humanist chancellor of Florence, followed Macrobius and Fulgentius in interpreting the flight from Troy as the soul's exile from heaven; but he understood allegory flexibly, as open to *inventio*, a way of generating multiple, not necessarily conflicting, meanings.[42] At the same time, Salutati carefully observed the geographic content of Servius's glosses, inscribing in his copy of Virgil notes such as "'Butroti urbem,' that is Buthrotum, the source of the Timavus. This city is in Epirus, part of which is Chaonia, which was previously called 'Molosia'."[43] As this example suggests, literal and allegorical readings were complementary rather than opposed: the same culture – indeed the same person – could easily sustain both. The fifteenth century saw a new allegorisation of book three within the *Disputationes camaldulenses* of Cristoforo Landino, in which Troy represented vice, Helenus became the light of truth, Italy true knowledge, Polyphemus political tyranny, and the straits of Messina the course between the Scylla of lust and the Charybdis of avarice.[44] But the same century also saw a sustained literal reading of book three in the form of the rather melancholic *Liber insularum* produced by the Florentine Cristoforo Buondelmonti for Cardinal Giordano Orsini. Buondelmonti's *isolario* – which survives in at least four versions dating from c. 1420 to 1430, as well as subsequent translations and adaptations[45] – takes the form of an itinerary around the Aegean, in which, in good humanist fashion, the classical past is exhumed and juxtaposed with the present. Maps and texts identify key sites of ancient history and invoke the classical literary record; the reader also learns of the contemporary state of the islands and their peoples, living in the shadow of Ottoman advance. The first part of the *Liber* sees Buondelmonti trace the steps of Aeneas in reverse, from Italy back to Troy, repeatedly quoting book three of the *Aeneid* as he travels from Corfu past Mt Leucata, to the islands of Dulichium, Zacyn-

---

42. *De laboribus Herculis* 3.31.13–16, ed. B.L. Ullman (Turici, 1951), 347–49.

43. Kallendorf, *In Praise of Aeneas*, 82–84: "Butroti urbem, id est Butrotium, ut fontem Timavi. Haec civitas est in Epiro, cuius pars est Caonia, que ante 'Molosia' dicta est." The text derives from Servius, *Commentarii*, 1: 393 (at *Aen* 3.292).

44. Cristoforo Landino, *Disputationes Camaldulenses*, ed. Peter Lohe (Florence, 1980), 133–59. For discussion, including comparison with Landino's 1488 commentary on Virgil, see Kallendorf, *In Praise of Aeneas*, 129–65.

45. See the lucid summary in Emmanuelle Vagnon, *Cartographie et Représentations de l'Orient méditerranéen en Occident (du milieu du XIIIe à la fin du XVe siècle)* (Turnhout, 2013), 275–81.

thus (modern Zante), the Strophades, Crete, and Delos. On Gallipoli, Buondelmonti notes the peninsula's proximity to ancient Troy, as well as the location of King Xerxes's bridge between Asia and Europe. But he also complains of the largesse of the Byzantine emperor, who has ceded this land to the Turks, with the result that the province has been filled with foreign peoples and foreign tongues (Figure 3).[46] Asia stands ready to invade Europe once more, and later copyists of the *Liber insularum* were able to update Buondelmonti's detailed map of Constantinople to reflect the Ottoman capture of the city in 1453.[47] Spatial representation, never static, could always respond to the changing contemporary significance of places, while maintaining a framework of ancient reference.

Buondelmonti was far from the first to attempt to locate Virgilian antiquity by reference to a map. Petrarch, after all, claimed to have used maps to help locate the troublesome "templum Minervae." Yet the text of the *Aeneid* itself only rarely generated maps. It is true that one of the earliest surviving manuscripts of the works of Virgil, from the fourth century AD and therefore perhaps contemporaneous with Servius, contains two map-like illustrations, both of which pertain to book three. There is a representation of Sicily, triangular in shape, with seven cities and the island of Ortygia. The image corresponds to *Aen* 3.692–715, in which Aeneas describes Sicily, and mentions the port of Drepanum, where his father, Anchises, will die: here the city appears as a semi-circular colonnade to which a Trojan ship, sail billowing, approaches. Some pages earlier an image of Crete alongside five small islands, representing the Cyclades, illustrates Virgil's account of the search for a new Troy, and the foundation of Pergamum (*Aen* 3.124ff).[48] Such illustrations did not generate a sustained tradition within Virgil manuscripts,[49] however, and it was only at the end of the sixteenth century that a cartographic work was dedicated solely and explicitly to the wanderings of Aeneas. Abraham Ortelius's "Aeneae Troiani Navigatio (Ad Virgilii sex priores

---

46. Cristoforo Buondelmonti, *Librum insularum archipelagi*, ed. Gabr. Rud. Ludovicus de Sinner (Leipzig, 1824), 118 (no. 61); cf. Cristoforo Buondelmonti, *Liber insularum archipelagi: Transkription des Exemplars Universitäts und Landesbibliothek Düsseldorf Ms. G13*, ed. and trans. Karl Bayer (Wiesbaden, 2007), 48 (no. 63).

47. Vagnon, *Cartographie et Représentations de l'Orient méditerranéen*, 298–301.

48. BAV, Vat. lat. 3225, fols. xxxi and xxvii respectively. The account of Pierre de Nolhac, *Le Virgile du Vatican et ses peintures* (Paris, 1897) remains useful.

49. See though the para-Virgilian landscape of Fiesole added to a late fourteenth-century manuscript of Ovid's *Metamorphoses*: Eleonora Mattia, "L'illustrazione delle 'Metamorfosi' di Ovidio nel codice Panciatichi 63 della Biblioteca Nazionale di Firenze," *Rivista di storia della miniatura* 1–2 (1996–7): 45–54, at 50–51. Zonal diagrams were sometimes used to illustrate *Georgics* 1 and very occasionally *Aeneid* 7: Alfred Hiatt, *Terra Incognita: Mapping the Antipodes before 1600* (London, 2008), 76–78.

Aeneidos)," from the 1595 edition of his great atlas, the *Theatrum Orbis Terrarum*, enables the reader to trace the trajectory of the first six books of the *Aeneid*, including its most significant place names (Figure 4). The major landmarks of book three are certainly present: a reader could follow Aeneas's wanderings from "Antandros, unde Aeneae classis solvit" (Antandros, from where the fleet of Aeneas set out), to Thrace, then through Delos to Crete, where the failed colony of Pergamea appears on the north coast alongside another Trojan foundation, Rhoeteum. On the Ionian coast there is "[Mount] Leucata, where the shrine of Venus of the Trojans, is located" (*Leucata, in qua Veneris Aeneadis fanum*), and the city of Buthrotum, while at the very heel of Italy appears "Atheneum, or the temple of Minerva" (*Atheneum, sive Minervae templ.*) just where Petrarch thought it should be. Off the coast of Africa, Ortelius depicts the dire storm that drives the Trojans away from Italy by means of a fleet of ships in various stages of submersion. No fewer than three Troys appear: one in Phrygia, another next to Buthrotum, and a third in the Adriatic, the ancestor of Venice, just a short journey from "Patavium [Padua], city of Antenor" (*Patavium Antenoris vrbs*). Italy begins far south of the Alps at the river Po (*Eridanus flu.*), forcefully marked, but true to his Virgilian source and Servian commentary Ortelius records no less than three names for the land: "Hesperia Saturnia et Italia." Carthage too is a subtle and persistent presence on the map. Its complex histories are indicated by its designation "Carthage which was the city of Agenor, and Byrsa" (*Carthago, quae Agenoris urbs, et Byrsa*), a reference to the legendary Phoenecian king and the name given by Dido to the city's citadel. Moreover, Ortelius presents as a subtext to the "Aeneae Troiani Navigatio" the story of Dido's forced migration from Phoenecia to the African coast: he shows the departure of seven ships from Tyre,[50] and marks "Tyrians and Phoenecians" (*Tyrij et Poeni*) alongside Carthage.

There is, however, a counter-narrative to Virgil, fittingly expressed on the reverse side of the map. Here Ortelius supplied a commentary on his image, including a cool debunking of the myths of both Dido and Aeneas, courtesy of Pausanias's second-century AD description of the region of Phocis, Dionysius Halicarnassus, Livy, Macrobius, Appian, Pompeius Trogus, and the late antique poet Ausonius. In the posthumous 1601 edition of the *Theatrum*, readers were informed that there were even some who thought Aeneas had never left Troy: "they regard the entire journey as a fiction" (*fictam totam hanc nauigationem*

---

50. Abraham Ortelius, "Aeneae Troiani Navigatio," in *Theatrum Orbis Terrarum* (Antwerp, 1595), sig. f ir: "Naves quae forte paratae / Corripiunt, onerantque auro, portantur avari / Pygmalionis opes pelago, dux femina facti" (*Aen* 1.362–64).

putant).[51] Such doubts about the historicity of the *Aeneid* had a long history. Even in late antiquity Servius noted the historical impossibility of Aeneas's affair with Dido, and others, including Macrobius, Augustine, and Jerome, drew attention to the fictive nature of the story.[52] Petrarch pointedly observed these reservations; some years later, Coluccio Salutati reassured one of his correspondents that this looseness with history need not diminish the importance of Virgil's story.[53] By the end of the sixteenth century, Ortelius was able to add Greek sources, such as Strabo, Appian, Dionysius, and Pausanias, that were not available to Petrarch or Coluccio, but which had gradually become known in humanist circles in the course of the fifteenth century. In his commentary on Aeneas's navigation, Ortelius accordingly supplements Virgil's narrative with the testimony of other ancient authors, noting numerous points of disagreement, alternative names, uncertainties of reference, likely falsehoods. Aeneas had probably not sailed up the Tiber, his band may not have numbered more than 600, the voyage lasted perhaps two and certainly not seven years. Did it matter? Consciousness of the fictive nature of Aeneas's journey seems to have done nothing to diminish its cultural potency, as Ortelius's map triumphantly shows. The "Aeneae Troiani Navigatio" achieved the humanist aim of making geographical reference in classical verse legible in cartographic form. The diffusion of Servius seems resolved within a Petrarchan finality of judgement, the multiple narratives of foundation somehow distilled and contained. West of Egypt, an inscription from book one of the *Aeneid*, "I am pious Aeneas ... " (*Sum pius Aeneas*), echoes the ideas in Dante's *Monarchia* in which Aeneas acts as a unifier, but also as a node between three *partes* that frame the map around its literary, historical and intellectual centre: the Mediterranean.

---

51. *Theatrum Orbis Terrarum* (Antwerp, 1601), sig. xxxiii. Book thirteen of Strabo's *Geography* (presumably 13.1.53) was the main source for this claim.

52. Servius, *Commentarii*, 1: 98–99 (at *Aen* 1.267); Macrobius, *Saturnalia*, 5.17.4–6, Augustine, *Confessiones*, 1.13.22, Jerome, *Adversus Iovinanum* 1.43 (where Dido dies a chaste widow, and Aeneas is not mentioned).

53. Petrarch makes the point at various places in his writings: see particularly his letter to Federico d'Arezzo in the *Rerum Senilium Epistolae: Lettres de la Vieillesse* 4.5.38, ed. Elvira Nota, trans. F. Castelli et al., notes by Ugo Dotti, 5 vols (Paris, 2002–13), 2: 93. Coluccio's letter to Astorgio Manfredi is in *Epistolario di Coluccio Salutati*, ed. Francesco Novati, 4 vols (Rome, 1896), 3: 232–38, esp. 237–38. The problem of the historical impossibility of Aeneas's affair with Dido was equally noted by non-humanist authors: see Ranulph Higden, *Polychronicon Ranulphi Higden monachi Cestrensis*, ed. Churchill Babington, 9 vols (London, 1865–86), 1: 21.

ipse ignotus, egens, Libyae deserta peragro,
Europa atque Asia pulsus. (*Aen* 1.384–85)

I, unknown, needy, wander the deserts of Africa, driven from Europe and
Asia.

Out of this state of ignominy – and precisely because of it – a story of profound
significance for national and international identities will be crafted. The reject, the
exile, carries the seed of a people, a city, but also an empire.

Look at it another way, however, especially with the conflicts and uncertainties of Ortelius's commentary on the image in mind, and the map can start to
tell different stories. On it the teeming nature of classical geography and its modern inheritance offers points of distraction to the undisciplined eye. There is
Mount Ida, "renowned for the judgement of Paris" (*Paridis iudicio memoratus*),
which along with Paphos on Cyprus, and several references to Venus (two
shrines, two temples and the town of Aphrodisum, added to the 1601 edition)
suggest readings of this space that verge on the allegorical: more the triumph of
Aphrodite than virtue in flight from eroticism. Then there is the consciousness
available to Ortelius's readers that, in yoking together Aeneas and Dido, Virgil
had anachronistically conjoined (at least) two times: that the coherence of space
was thus working to cover the temporal fracture at the heart of his fable of exilic
love. Finally, Ortelius's *Theatrum* allows this image to be read in conjunction
with many others contained within his atlas – with other maps of the classical
world, but also with the maps of modernity, in which Byzantium will transform
into Constantinopolis and Carthago be joined by Tunis: in which some places
will vanish and others, including "Troia," stubbornly persist.

SAINT OVID'S EXILE

By a curious twist of fate, the wanderings of Aeneas found an echo in the biography of the poet Ovid, exiled by the emperor Augustus from Rome to the Black
Sea town of Tomis in AD 8. The reasons for Ovid's banishment remain obscure,
but the nature of his punishment was to have lasting literary significance. Ovid's
status was, technically, that of a "relegatus non exul." Not simply forbidden to
return to Rome, he was required to remain in a designated place, with hope but
no certainty of pardon.[54] Characteristically, Ovid wrought this experience of

54. R.J. Dickinson, "The *Tristia*: Poetry in Exile," in *Ovid*, ed. J.W. Binns (London,
1973), 154–90, at 154–55.

dislocation into poetic form. Two collections of verse, known as the *Tristia* (Sorrows) and *Epistulae ex Ponto* (Letters from the Black Sea), survive from Ovid's period of relegation. They frequently operate, perhaps somewhat deceptively, in the mode of autobiography. The *Tristia* begins with the figurative return of the book, in place of the poet, from the Black Sea to Rome, and continues with an exploration of the imperial centre from the periphery. Ovid imagines his wife and his friends in Rome, and their distress (or, in the case of disloyal friends, indifference) as a result of his exile, represented unambiguously as a form of death, with the torments of Tomis reminiscent of the underworld.[55] Above all, the figure of Caesar dominates, and with it the theme of the poet's relation to sovereign power. Ovid's longing to return to Rome puts him in a position of supplication and entreaty towards Augustus, encapsulated in the 579-line appeal to the emperor contained in book two of the *Tristia*. Already by the end of book one, though, the spatial dynamic is beginning to alter. As the poet narrates his journey into exile, he introduces the notion of the Black Sea as mythopoetic space: a space on the boundary of empire, comprehensible only by reference to mythical narratives.

The geographic site of Tomis was important for Ovid's poetics of exile. Apparently unknown, or little known, to most Romans, it was located on the western shore of the Black Sea. Its position to the east and north of Rome allowed Ovid to associate it with extremes of cold, and with local peoples of known ferocity, such as the Scythians. At the same time, its location meant that Tomis occupied a place decidedly within the Greek cultural orbit. For Ovid, as for his Roman readership, strata of Greek history and mythology were an unavoidable presence in the Black Sea region, and they could be made to work polemically against Roman political and literary authority.[56] In *Tristia* 1.10, for example, Ovid provides what is ostensibly a factual account of his journey towards Tomis, in the form of a prayer for the safety of the ship that carried him part of the way. The poet departs from Corinth, sails to the island of Samothrace, and from there he continues his journey to Tomis by land through Thrace. The ship, meanwhile, makes its way from Samothrace through the Hellespont, passing Dardania, Lampsacus, Cyzicos, Byzantium, and Mesembria along the way, and encountering the "citadel of Bacchus" (*arces Bacche*) and the "exiles from Alcathoi" (*profugi Alcathoi*), before finally reaching Tomis (the "Milesian city").[57] The stops Ovid

---

55. Gareth D. Williams, *Banished Voices: Readings in Ovid's exile poetry* (Cambridge, 1994), 12–13.

56. Cf. Williams, *Banished Voices*, 7.

57. Ovid, *Tristia*, ed. John Barrie Hall (Stuttgart and Leipzig, 1995). Subsequent references are to this edition.

mentions, while all identifiable with real places, inevitably evoke a variety of myths and deities, several of which lend an erotic cast to the itinerary. Aside from the explicit reference to Bacchus (his otherwise unnamed citadel is usually thought to be Dionysopolis), the reference to the Hellespont and the cities of Sestos and Abydos conjures the doomed love of Hero and Leander, while Lampsacus was notorious for licentiousness befitting its tutelary deity, Priapus. One axis of alignment is with Jason and the Argonauts, perhaps a result of Ovid's use of Apollonius of Rhodes's *Argonautica*: Samothrace and Cyzicos both have associations with Jason or other Argonauts. Another set of associations, here and elsewhere in *Tristia* and *ex Ponto*, is with Ulysses: on more than one occasion in the series Ovid will compare his wife to Penelope.[58] Two further shadows lurk: Medea, a native of the Black Sea region, Jason's lover, figure of murderous magic in book seven of Ovid's *Metamorphoses* and subject of his lost play;[59] and Aeneas. In the first part of his journey, Ovid and his ship "turned course away" from "Hector's city," probably a reference to the site of Hector's tomb, Ophrynium, rather than Troy,[60] but in any case an oblique invocation of the Trojan war. Mention of Dardania evokes the twinning of Italian and Trojan ancestry familiar from the *Aeneid*, and in particular echoes *Aen* 8.134: "Dardanus, first father and founder of the Trojan city" (*Dardanus, Iliacae primus pater urbis et auctor*). Yet any sense of reassurance generated by this Trojan reference is immediately unsettled by the addition of Priapic Lampsacus and the "arces Bacchae." The subtle elaboration of a coastline imbued with Bacchic association arguably recalls book seven of the *Aeneid*, where Amata, maddened instrument of Juno, provokes war between the Trojans and the Rutuli while in the grip of Bacchic frenzy. Do the "profugi Alcathoi" mentioned towards the end of the poet's journey similarly recall Aeneas himself, "fato profugus" at the beginning of the *Aeneid*?[61] It is at least possible that in the short space of *Tristia* 1.10 Ovid intended not merely to describe a journey but to establish an erotic, fugitive landscape that by implication and association opposes the foundational narrative of the *Aeneid*, and instead recalls and reverses the exilic, amatory path taken by Aeneas but ultimately rejected in the

---

58. Anne Videau-Delibes, *Les Tristes d'Ovide et l'élégie Romaine: Une poétique de la rupture* (Paris, 1991), 51; for other sources and comparison with Ovid's previous verse see Jan Felix Gaertner, "Ovid and the 'Poetics of Exile': How Exilic is Ovid's Exile Poetry?," in *Writing Exile: The Discourse of Displacement in Greco-Roman Antiquity and Beyond* (Leiden, 2007), 155–72.

59. Éléonora Tola, *La métamorphose poétique chez Ovide: Tristes et Pontiques: le poème inépuisable* (Louvain, 2004), 341.

60. See Luck's commentary: Ovid, *Tristia*, ed. and trans. Georg Luck, 2 vols (Heidelberg, 1967), 2: 83.

61. As suggested by Tola, *La métamorphose poétique*, 260.

name of Rome and *imperium*. Ovid, the love poet, turns his back on Hector and finds himself in a landscape associated with flight and desire, where he will not found a civilization, but instead experience its unravelling in barbarous surrounds.

Subsequent books of the *Tristia* introduce more information about Ovid's new environment, its people (the Getae), and their language. Subtly the position of the relegated poet changes. The harsh, uncultured, and unforgiving nature of the place and the violence of its inhabitants remain constant, but *Tristia* and *ex Ponto* witness the slide of Ovid's own identity away from cultured Roman towards barbarity, a duality already complicated by traces of prior Greek colonisation in the region. In *Tristia* 3.9 Ovid suddenly takes an interest in the origin of Tomis:

> hic quoque sunt igitur Graiae – quis crederet? – urbes
> inter inhumanae nomina barbariae;
> huc quoque Mileto missi uenere coloni,
> inque Getis Graias constituere domos. (3.9.1–4)

> here there are also Greek cities – who would believe it? – among names of savage barbarism; colonists came here from Miletus, and they built Greek homes among the Getae.

Later, in the course of an ethnographic description, Ovid will note some retention of the Greek language, but "made barbarous with a Getic twang" (*Tristia* 5.7.52). The corruption of Greek remnants offers a model for Ovid's own cultural decomposition. His position in relation to the inhabitants of Tomis is sometimes expressed through a reversal of perspective, in which difference is intensified: "I am the barbarian here; nobody understands me and stupid Getae laugh at Latin words" (barbarus hic ego sum, qui non intellegor ulli / et rident stolidi uerba Latina Getae: *Tristia* 5.10.37–38). Yet gradually the surrounding peoples and their languages infiltrate identity. The Roman bard is forced to utter things Sarmatian style. He talks to himself to keep words alive, fears he has "unlearned" Latin, because has learned to speak Getic and Sarmatian (*Tristia* 5.12.57–58), concludes that he has become almost a "Getic poet" (*poeta Getes*) (*ex Ponto* 4.13.18). From this vantage point of corroded Latinity, Roman origins can be examined all the more clearly. Early on, a tour of Rome includes the place where the city was founded (*Tristia* 3.1.32), and it continues to be explored through imagined triumphs (*ex Ponto* 2.1), or through the portal of a medallion in Ovid's possession containing images of Augustus, Livia and Tiberius (*ex Ponto* 2.8). If Ovid is Rome relegated, his disintegration figures and presages the city's disintegration amid hostile terrain and a plurality of tongues.

Ovid's exile to the Black Sea, in short, offered him new opportunities for poetic discourse, as well as countless miseries.[62] It recast his relation to imperial Rome, from an urbane voice at its centre to a stranded plaintiff at its outermost periphery, creating a new dynamic centred around loss, distance, and exclusion: "the furthest of lands has me, the furthest of worlds" (ultima me tellus, ultimus orbis habet: *ex Ponto* 2.7.66).[63] Pontic exile forced Ovid to make a subject of himself, to elaborate an autobiographical discourse, in which the ego takes centre-stage, writes after its own death from beyond the grave of exile, and engages in a self-reflexive perusal of fame. Crucially, exile brought Ovid into contact with barbarian societies, causing a progressive rethink of Roman identity which took the form, variously, of a repetitious discourse of cultural superiority, a return to origins, a sense of his own barbarity resulting from not being understood, and most importantly a process of unlearning – of losing the ability to speak and write properly – culminating in his reincarnation as a Getic poet. The *Tristia* and *Ex ponto* helped to define the meaning of exile as the dislocation of self within the space of the periphery, a space initially marked by distance and hostility in which the exilic subject finds himself gradually, reluctantly, implicated.

The first concerted response to Ovid's exile poetry occurred in Carolingian Europe, where the *Tristia* and *ex Ponto* seem to have enjoyed some popularity within monastic circles. Florilegia and booklists attest to copies of *ex Ponto* in St Gall from the ninth century and by the eleventh and twelfth centuries in monasteries of northern and central Europe, including Blaubeuern, Tegernsee, Bamberg, Egmond, and Cracow.[64] Few early manuscripts of the *Tristia* survive, but it was known to certain ninth-century poets such as Theodulf of Orléans, Walahfrid Strabo, and Mico of Saint-Riquier.[65] From the eleventh and twelfth centuries, as interest in, and imitation of, his verse reached new heights, the works of Ovid were increasingly accompanied by sets of glosses and commentaries. Geography was not necessarily at the forefront of commentators' concerns, but the nature of

---

62. On "generic dislocation" in Ovid's exile poetry see Gareth Williams, "Ovid's Exilic Poetry: Worlds Apart," in *Brill's Companion to Ovid*, ed. Barbara Weiden Boyd (Leiden, 2002), 337–81, at 340–53.

63. Ovid, *Ex Ponto libri qvattvor*, ed. J.A. Richmond (Leipzig, 1990).

64. R.J. Tarrant, "Ovid," in *Texts and Transmission*, 257–84, at 263; John Richmond, "Manuscript Traditions and the Transmission of Ovid's Works," in *Brill's Companion to Ovid*, 443–83; on the relative modesty of the manuscript tradition up to and including the twelfth century see Birger Munk Olsen, "Ovide au Moyen Âge (du IXe au XIIe siècle)," in *Le strade del testo*, ed. Guglielmo Cavallo (Bari, 1987), 67–96, with the counter-analysis of Jean-Yves Tilliette, "Savants et poètes du moyen âge face à Ovide: Les débuts de l'*aetas Ovidiana* (v. 1050–v. 1200)," in *Ovidius redivivus: Von Ovid zu Dante*, ed. Michelangelo Picone and Bernhard Zimmermann (Stuttgart, 1994), 63–104.

65. Tarrant, "Ovid," 282–83.

the exile poetry demanded at least incidental consideration of place. The site of Ovid's exile was frequently thought to have been the island of "Pontus," sometimes understood to be in Thrace, or more vaguely of or "towards" Scythia.[66] The toponym Tomis, however, could generate more complex discussion. One eleventh- or twelfth-century commentary on *ex Ponto* commences with the following gloss on the first line of Ovid's opening letter in the series, "Ovid (Naso), by now no new inhabitant of land of the Tomitanae ..." (*Naso Tomitanae iam non novus incola terrae*):

> Thomitanae are a people so called from the name of the land, which is called Thomos, as if to say "divided from other lands," or because it was there that Medea killed her brother Absyrtus and dismembered him. "Thomos" in Greek means "divisio" [division] or "sectio" [cutting up] in Latin.[67]

The gloss's opening etymological move leads on to mythography, with the concept of division emerging as pivotal. Ovid is the inhabitant of a land named after dismemberment itself, the act of fratricide committed by Medea to ensure escape from her homeland with Jason.

The trope of longing from distance informed medieval and post-medieval understandings of the exile poetry. Carolingians substituted Angers, Strasbourg, or Speyer for Scythia as places of exile,[68] but retained the central dynamic of alienation from political and cultural power, and the author's paradoxical – even perverse – recuperation in a harsh soil. Some (Ermoldus Nigellus, Modoin of

---

66. See the appendices to Fausto Ghisalberti, "Mediaeval Biographies of Ovid," *Journal of the Warburg and Courtauld Institutes* 9 (1946): 10–59.

67. Copenhagen, Kongelige Bibliotek, Gl. Kgl. S. 2015 4° fol. 1r: "*Thomi(tanae)* dicti sunt populi a nomine terre, quae Thomos dicitur, quasi ab aliis terris diuisa, uel quia Medea ibi fratrem suum Absirtum occidit et membratim diuisit. Thomos grece diuisio latine, uel sectio." Cited in Ralph J. Hexter, *Ovid and Medieval Schooling: Studies in Medieval School Commentaries on Ovid's* Ars Amatoria, Epistulae ex Ponto, *and* Epistulae Heroidum (Munich, 1986), 116. A very similar explanation is given in an accessus to *ex Ponto* contained in several twelfth- and thirteenth-century manuscripts: *Accessus Ovidiani*, ed. Gustavus Przychocki (Kraków, 1911), 26–27. In his commentary on Dante's *Comedia*, Boccaccio identified "Tomitania" as an island in the Euxine (*mar Maggiore*), near to the river Phasis in Colchis: *Esposizioni sopra la Comedia di Dante* IV.122, ed. Giorgio Padoan (Milan, 1965), 201.

68. For Angers see the exchange between Theodulf and Modoin of Autun ("*Naso*"), in *Poetae Latini Aevi Carolini*, ed. E. Dümmler, 4 vols. (Berlin, 1881–1923), 1: 563–73 (nos. 72 and 73); for Speyer: "Walahfridi Strabi carmina" 76, in *Poetae Latini Aevi Carolini*, 2: 413–15; for Strasbourg: the elegies to Pipin by Ermoldus Nigellus, in *Poetae Latini Aevi Carolini*, 2: 79–91. See too Arrigo da Settimello's heavy use of the *Tristia* in his elegy of 1193: *Elegia*, ed. Clara Fossati (Florence, 2011); Hexter, *Ovid and Medieval Schooling*, 90–91.

Autun, Walahfrid Strabo) coupled Virgil with Ovid as part of a canon of poetic exiles, possibly based on an interpretation of Virgil's *Eclogues*, while for others the epistolary nature of the poetry seems to have liberated creative energies. In the poetry of the learned and witty cleric Baudri of Bourgueil (1045/6–1130), Ovid becomes a recipient as well as a writer of letters, and Rome itself a site of exile and frustrated desire. Baudri imagines a certain "Florus" writing to the relegated Ovid in frankly amatory terms, in which Rome and Pontus become no longer centre and periphery but reciprocal and interchangeable. "In body I am at Rome," Florus tells Ovid, "but in my desires I am with you in exile" (*Corpore sum Romae, sed uotis exulo tecum*):

> Nam nulli potius quam michi carus eras [cf. *Tristia* 3.6.3].
> Roma michi locus est, tibi Pontus: uel michi Roma
> Sit Pontus, Pontus uel tibi Roma foret![69]

For you mattered to no-one more than to me. Rome is my place; yours Pontus. Let Rome become Pontus for me, or let Pontus become Rome for you.

The trope of letter writing as a breach of geography, at once an acknowledgment and victory over distance, enjoyed a continuity of use from classical antiquity onwards.[70] The letter holds place, marks distance in its formal features – an address, a farewell – and at the same time not only bridges the distance, but also circulates in the place it is read. In the context of exile, it effects a return by proxy, as Ovid imagined powerfully in both the *Tristia* and *ex Ponto* (*Tristia* 1.1, 3.1; *ex Ponto* 2.8). Baudri's verse reduces the experience of exile to an exchange between two sites so intense it brings them to the point of mutual superimposition. Yet lost in the swirl of exile and *patria* is the irruptive, corrosive presence of alien peoples and their chattering tongues.

---

69. Baudri de Bourgueil, "Florus Ouidio," in *Poèmes*, ed. and trans. Jean-Yves Tilliette, 2 vols (Paris, 2002), 1: ll. 75–78; Sabine Schülper, "Ovid aus der Sicht des Balderich von Bourgueil, dargestellt anhand des Briefwechsels Florus-Ovid," *Mittellateinisches Jahrbuch* 14 (1979): 93–117; Tilliette, "Savants et poètes," esp. 102–4; Ralph J. Hexter, "Ovid and the Medieval Exilic Imaginary," in *Writing Exile*, 209–36, at 225–30.

70. A fine example is Petrarch's letter to Barbato da Sulmona: Francis Petrarch, *Dispersa* 33 (Var. 22), in *Lettere disperse*, ed. Alessandro Pancheri (Parma, 1994), 262–78.

Sanctus Naso ... conversus ab errore

On another reading, however, distance from Rome allowed for proximity to faith: Ovid's exile became his conversion. Several short biographies of Ovid had accompanied his oeuvre in the Middle Ages, offering an account of the poet's life and works, with different theories as to the cause of his relegation. The three most frequent explanations for exile were the outrage to morality caused by his *Ars Amatoria*; an affair with the emperor's wife, Livia; or his observation of Augustus *in flagrante* with his boyfriend (*amasio suo*).[71] One version of events even posited the treacherous intervention of Virgil, who having observed Ovid ascending a ladder to Livia's bedroom, removed some rungs, and caused his rival to break his leg.[72] Most accounts assumed Ovid's death in exile, although one tradition held that he had in fact achieved his desire and returned to Rome – only to be crushed to death by the crowd that greeted him.[73] At some point during the Middle Ages a counter-history of the poet's later years emerged, the earliest surviving expression of which was recorded in the thirteenth century, in the form of a note in a manuscript of south German or Swiss origin.[74] The startling proposition of the annotator of this manuscript was that Ovid had died a Christian. Here geography played its part. Tomis was not far from Patmos. Surely Ovid had encountered that island's most famous inhabitant, and fellow exile, the evangelist John. Why then would the poet not have heard the truth and received baptism? And, once admitted to the Christian faith, would he not have performed missionary work among the Getae in the manner of the early apostles? After all, he himself stated in the *Tristia* that he had learned their language: "Now that I have learned to speak Getic and Sarmatian, I seem to have unlearned Latin" (ipse mihi uideor iam dedidicisse Latine, / iam didici Getice Sarmaticeque loqui: *Tristia* 5.12.57–58).[75] Such an erudite and prudent man would have made an obvi-

71. *Accessus ad Auctores*, ed. R.B.C. Huygens (Leiden, 1970), 35. See Hexter, "Ovid and the Medieval Exilic Imaginary," 213–14.

72. Accessus to the *Tristia* in Paris, Bibliothèque nationale de France, lat. 8255: see Ghisalberti, "Mediaeval Biographies of Ovid," 50.

73. Repeated in the fourteenth century by Boccaccio and Giovanni del Virgilio: J.B. Trapp, "Ovid's Tomb: The Growth of a Legend from Eusebius to Laurence Sterne, Chateaubriand and George Richmond," *Journal of the Warburg and Courtauld Institutes* 36 (1973): 35–76, at 44–45.

74. Freiburg, Universitätsbibliothek, MS 380, a manuscript originally of the tenth or eleventh century, contains the *Collationes* of Johannes Cassianus, and an excerpt from Bede's *Ecclesiastical History*; in the late thirteenth century it was in the possession of the Chorherrenstift Beromünster.

75. Bernhard Bischoff, "Eine mittelalterliche Ovidlegende," *Historisches Jahrbuch* 71 (1952): 268–73, at 272.

ous candidate to become the first bishop of Tomis; that he subsequently suffered for his faith was more than credible. Sanctus Naso? Why not, after all?

This legend, which in various versions entered Italian humanist circles in the fourteenth century and continued to circulate as late as the sixteenth,[76] was an exemplary act of assimilation: a personage of antiquity, and an established fragment of his biography, re-interpreted in terms of the omnivorous genre of the saint's life. It seems to have required some rethinking of spatial order. Tomis/Pontus had been understood in the accessus tradition to be an island,[77] representative of exilic isolation perhaps, but in the fugitive tradition of the note its insularity evokes a spatial sympathy with Patmos. At the same time, the story's radicalism, and its comedy, lie in the consciousness that its source was Ovid's verses themselves, their complaints, their expression of a *vox clamantis*, an educated voice talking back to the metropolis from a distant shore: a position of striking similarity to that of the evangelist sent to convert a pagan people, surrounded by them, nursing a light, always in danger of submersion.[78] Ovid's Pontic tomb was, then, a site of some literary productivity. From it originated not only the conversion narrative, but also the most popular work of pseudo-Ovidiana of the later Middle Ages, the *De vetula*, a poem allegedly contained in an ivory capsule and buried with the poet, only to be disinterred and sent to Constantinople by a people now unable to read Latin.[79] Well past the Renaissance learned visitors looked for Ovid's grave, and many claimed to find it,[80] until the age of nation states intensified its meaning, and Ovid became the first Romanian poet, inspiring a series of authors, some exiles themselves, for whom the settlement once Tomis, now Constanța, became a point of departure.[81]

On *mappae mundi* Ovid makes occasional appearances in ways that confirm his partial assimilation within Christian legend. The thirteenth-century Vercelli *mappa mundi* locates him in the region of Caesarea: "this region is called Pontus

76. Trapp, "Ovid's Tomb," 43–44.

77. Ghisalberti, "Mediaeval Biographies of Ovid," 35.

78. The outstanding example in late medieval English letters is John Gower's *Vox clamantis*, a lament for the state of England shortly before and during the time of the English Rising of 1381, which draws heavily on the *Tristia* and *ex Ponto*: *The Complete Works of John Gower*, vol. 4: *The Latin Works*, ed. G.C. Macaulay (Oxford, 1902).

79. *Pseudo-Ovidius de vetula: Untersuchungen und Text*, ed. Paul Klopsch (Leiden, 1967), 193. *De vetula* also contains an account of Ovid's conversion to Christianity.

80. Trapp, "Ovid's Tomb."

81. See Theodore Ziolkowski, *Ovid and the Moderns* (Ithaca, 2005), 112–24; Nicolae Lascu, *Ovide: Le poète exilé à Tomi* (Constantza, 1974), 103–22. Landmarks include Vasile Alecsandri's play *Ovidiu* (1885); Nicolae Iorga's poem *Ovidiu* (1931); Sigismund Toduta's symphony *Ovidiu* (1957); most famously Vintila Horia's novel *Dieu est né en exil* (Paris: Fayard, 1960); and Martin Mincu's *Il diario di Ovidio* (1997).

Cesarea; in it Ovid was relegated."[82] Following Honorius Augustodunensis's twelfth-century survey, the *Imago Mundi*, the Ebstorf *mappa mundi* of c. 1300 identifies Pontus as the region "in which Ovid and Clement were relegated into exile" (Figure 5).[83] The location of this inscription directly opposite Mt Ararat, Noah's ark, and the sepulchre of the first-century apostle Bartholomew (*Sepulchrum Bartholomei apostoli*), and directly above the sepulchre of the apostle Phillip (*Sepulchrum Philippi apostoli*), indicates the way in which Christian history had marked the territory, demanding a reading in terms of martyrdom and the apostolic spread of the faith. Clement, the first-century AD pope and saint, seems at first an unlikely companion. But there were symmetries. He too was – according to his fourth-century *Acta* – exiled by the emperor Trajan from Rome to an island in the Black Sea region, where he made numerous converts, founded churches, and was eventually martyred.[84] The presence of mythographic elements balances the Christian territorialization. Ovid's position on both Vercelli and Ebstorf maps is near to the Golden Fleece and Colchis, and hence to the roots of the Trojan war: "Kingdom of the Colchi. Here philosophers imagine the Golden Fleece, about which they say Jason attained it and from that the conflict between the Greeks and Trojans developed." "The Argonauts under Jason made off with this Golden Fleece, or hide, during the reign of King Oeta [i.e. Aeetes]."[85] The place of the relegated Ovid within medieval cartography is far from promi-

82. Carlo F. Capello, *Il mappamondo medioevale di Vercelli (1191–1218?)* (Torino, 1976), section F.III: "Haec regio vocatur Pontus Cesarea. In hac fuit ovidius religatus." My thanks to Helen Davies and the Lazarus Project (University of Rochester) for allowing me access to high resolution images of the Vercelli map, against which I have checked, and in some cases emended, Capello's transcriptions.

83. *Die Ebstorfer Weltkarte*, ed. Hartmut Kugler, 2 vols (Berlin, 2007), 1: 74 (no. 23.12): "Pontus regio ... in quo Ovidius et Clemens exilio relegantur." Honorius Augustodunensis, *Imago mundi* 1.20, ed. Valerie I.J. Flint, *Archives d'histoire doctrinale et littéraire du Moyen Âge* 49 (1982): 7–153, at 59: "Exin Pontus, regio multarum gentium a qua et Ponticum mare appellatur, in quo Ovidius et postea Clemens exilio relegantur"; Gervase of Tilbury repeats Honorius but throws in the possibility that Clement's exile may have pre-dated that of Ovid: *Otia Imperialia: Recreation for an Emperor* 2.6, ed. and trans. S.E. Banks and J.W. Binns (Oxford, 2002), 236. Matthew Paris's partial *mappa mundi* (Cambridge, Corpus Christi College, MS 26, fol. vii verso) includes the inscription in the Black Sea "Pontos insula ubi Ovidius exul."

84. "Martyrium S. Clementis," in Patrologia Graeca, 2: 617–32.

85. *Ebstorfer Weltkarte*, ed. Kugler, 1: 74 (no. 23.3): "Regnum Colchorum. Hic phylosophi fingunt aureum pellem, de qua J[as]onem penetrasse dicunt, unde etiam G[recorum] et Tro[i]anorum effecta est conflictio"; (no. 23.8): "Hanc pellem vel vellus aureum [Argo]naute sub Jasone abstulerunt Oeta rege regnante." *Il mappamondo di Vercelli*, Section F.1: "hic est regnum colchos; hic fuit aries qui habuit aurum vellus, quem Jason cum aliis argonautis rapuit. Rex istius terre dicebatur Oeta."

nent, and would not be apparent to any but the most scrupulous readers of these detailed *mappae mundi*. But it does attest to the enduring association of his name with the Black Sea region, however conceived, as well as to his insertion between myth and history: on the "margins of empire" (*Tristia* 2.200: haeret in imperii margine terra tui), and for his medieval audience, also on the margins of faith.

The presence of Troy in general tends to be rather muted on medieval *mappae mundi*, and both Ovid and Virgil were on occasion curiously enlisted in a reading of the erasure of the pre-Roman past. In its depiction of Troy (*Ilium*) the Ebstorf map does provide a rather impressive representation of a city, with heavy walls, towers, and fortifications, and with a quotation designed to show the vicissitudes of fortune. Something odd has happened to this quotation, however. It was apparently intended to be a remark made by Penelope to Ulysses in the first book of Ovid's *Heroides*, that "now there is a cornfield where once there was Troy" (*iam seges est, ubi Troia fuit*),[86] itself an echo from the third book of the *Aeneid*: "and [I leave] fields where Troy used to be" (*et campos ubi Troia fuit*).[87] However, the inscription on the Ebstorf map actually reads "now there is a cornfield where once was trodden (*trita*)" (*Nunc seges est ubi trita fuit*).[88] The intention of the mapmaker appears to have been to display an image of Troy at the height of its power, accompanied by an inscription that observes its disappearance. That simultaneous exhibition of two extremities of power is entirely consistent with the popular doctrine of fortune's wheel most obviously associated with Boethius's *Consolation of Philosophy*. The textual complexity of Ebstorf's Ilium is greater than a straightforward gesture towards *fortuna*, however. The voice of the inscription is double. It is at once that of the wife left behind, observing the passage of history, reproving an errant husband, and at the same time that of the Roman poet reflecting on the foundation narrative of his own city: in the continuation of the quotation, Penelope adds that the fields are made fertile by Trojan blood. So the viewer of the Ebstorf map sees Troy and its disappearance, and may just grasp the irony of its proximity to the end point of Ovid's own exilic fortune alongside Clement in the Pontus. Yet to this interweaving of histories, lives, and literature, the misreading of Troy as "trita" (trodden) adds another utterly unpredictable layer: rather than elevating past glories and Roman origins, the inscription anonymises the city, treading it into the earth.

86. Ovid, *Heroides* 1.53, ed. G.P. Goold, trans. Grant Showerman, 2nd ed. (Cambridge, 1977), 14.
87. *Aeneid* 3.11, ed. Mynors, 153.
88. *Ebstorfer Weltkarte*, ed. Kugler, 1: 102 (no. 37.10).

Virgil and Ovid – contemporaries and rivals, classical and medieval poets – offer contrasting modes for understanding relations between Rome, its pre-history, and its imperial expanse: the mode of mythography and allegory, and that of biography sliding on occasion into hagiography. In both authors, however, the motif of exile remains fundamental, whether imperial centre figures the end of relegation or its starting point. To exile inheres the transfer of place, the reiteration of a former identity in new surrounds, and at times too the violent imposition of one place upon another. Lucan, the first-century AD successor to the literary legacy of Virgil, Ovid and other authors, and caustic observer of the political legacy of the Caesars, intensified these strands of Roman dislocation. In his poetry, civil war sees the expansive energies of empire turned inwards, with the result that the dismemberment of spatial order becomes the sign of political violence. Reworking Virgilian epic, amplifying Ovidian complaint, Lucan produced the most thorough upending of geography in the Latin literary corpus, an exuberant catalogue of confusion that his many medieval readers sought to comprehend, explicate, and emulate.

CHAPTER FOUR

Lucan's Geography of Dislocation

Corduba me genuit. rapuit Nero. proelia dixi
quae gessere pares hinc socer inde gener.
Continuo numquam direxi carmina ductu,
quae tractim serpant: plus mihi comma placet.
Fluminis in morem quae sunt miranda citentur:
haec uere sapiet dictio quae feriet.[1]

Cordoba gave birth to me. Nero snatched me away. I told of battles fought
by comrades, a father-in-law and a son-in-law. With unbroken line I never
ordered my verses, which creep along at length: the caesura pleases me more.
Let wondrous things be put in motion in the manner of a river: let this utter-
ance savour truly of the things it bears.

"Epitaphion Lucani"

Born in Spanish Cordoba in 39 AD, the poet Lucan was snatched by Nero in at
least two senses. Well known in Rome for his literary talents and his family connections (his uncle was the moralist Seneca), Lucan seems, for a time at least, to
have been a favourite of the emperor. It was to Nero that Lucan dedicated a for-
mulaically praising, or perhaps deeply ironic, encomium at the beginning of his
epic, the *Bellum civile*.[2] But the two eventually fell out dramatically and publicly.
Accused, along with Seneca, of participation in the conspiracy of Gaius

1. *Commenta Bernensia*, ed. Hermann Usener (Leipzig, 1869), 6–7; on the similar
epigram that Virgil attracted see Irene Frings, "Mantua me genuit – Vergils Grabepigramm auf
Stein und Pergament," *Zeitschrift für Papyrologie und Epigraphik* 123 (1998): 89–100.
2. *Bellum Civile* in *Lucani Opera*, ed. Renato Badalì (Rome, 1992), 1.33–66 (subsequent
references are to this edition, by book and line number). For representative contributions to
the debate about the praise of Nero see Frederick Ahl, *Lucan: An Introduction* (Ithaca, 1976),
47–54, Michael Dewar, "Laying it on with a Trowel: The Proem to Lucan and Related Texts,"
Classical Quarterly 44 (1994): 199–211, and Emanuele Narducci, *Lucano: Un'epica contro
l'impero* (Rome, 2002), 22–28; more recently *De Bello Ciuili Book I*, ed. Paul Roche (Oxford,
2009), 7–10.

Calpurnius Piso against the emperor, Lucan was forced to commit suicide in 65.[3] At that time the *Bellum civile* was unfinished. Its first three books had been published in 62 or 63 AD; a further six had been completed, with a tenth in progress when Lucan died. It was enough, as it turned out, for the work to become his monument: the *Bellum civile* rapidly garnered admiration and imitation, and remained a staple of European literature for the next nineteen centuries.[4]

Lucan's *Bellum civile* tells the story of Julius Caesar's war with his erstwhile ally and former son-in-law, Gnaeus Pompey, in 49–48 BC. In so doing, the poem engages literary combat at close quarters with two influential precursors: Caesar's own commentary on the Civil War, and Virgil's *Aeneid*. Lucan offered a pungent alternative to Caesar's *Civil War* – not simply another view, but at times a knowing distortion of the earlier account.[5] He also sought to present a counterweight to Virgil's narrative of the foundation of imperial rule on Italian land.[6] In both cases, geographic revisions have the effect of destabilising Roman history.

Caesar's commentary on the Civil War rests on a sure grasp of the geography of the Mediterranean region, as he describes the movement of his campaign against Pompey from Europe into Asia Minor and ultimately North Africa. Routes, distances between places, and a clear sense of provincial demarcation inform Caesar's narrative and acquire strategic significance. The commentary depends on detailed topographic descriptions of key sites in the conflict, and

3. Lucan's role in the plot is described in Tacitus, *Annales*, ed. H. Heubner, 2 vols (Stuttgart, 1983), 1: 15.49, 56, 70. Further biographical details come from Statius, *Silvae* 2.7, and three late antique *vitae Lucani* conveniently printed by Badalì: *Lucani Opera*, 399–407.

4. On the reception of the *Bellum civile* see generally Walter Fischli, *Studien zum Fortleben der* Pharsalia (Lucerne, 1945); *Lucans Bellum Civile: Studien zum Spektrum seiner Rezeption von der Antike bis ins 19. Jahrhundert*, ed. Christine Walde (Trier, 2009); *Brill's Companion to Lucan*, ed. Paolo Asso (Leiden, 2011), 435–545; Peter von Moos, "Lucain au Moyen Âge," in his *Entre histoire et littérature: Communication et culture au Moyen Âge* (Florence, 2005), 89–202; Paolo Esposito, "Sulla prima fase della fortuna lucanea," *Giornale italiano di filologia* 66 (2014): 163–81.

5. John Henderson, *Fighting for Rome: Poets and Caesars, History and Civil War* (Cambridge, 1998), 165–211; Jamie Masters, *Poetry and Civil War in Lucan's Bellum Civile* (Cambridge, 1992), e.g. 18–25; Jan Radicke, *Lucans poetische Technik: Studien zum historischen Epos* (Leiden, 2004), 29–43, sees Livy rather than Caesar as Lucan's source, but given that Livy's account is for the most part lost, and would have itself drawn on Caesar's commentary, the argument is circular.

6. On the *Bellum civile* as anti-*Aeneid* see especially Emanuele Narducci, *La provvidenza crudele: Lucano e la distruzione dei miti augustei* (Pisa, 1979), Narducci, *Un'epica contro l'impero*, 75–87, and *inter alia* Sergio Casali, "The *Bellum Civile* as an Anti-*Aeneid*," and Alison Keith, "Ovid in Lucan: The Poetics of Instability," both in *Brill's Companion to Lucan*, 81–109, 110–32.

human interventions therein: on the construction of barricades, ramparts, and causeways, on floods, and on Caesar's willingness, where necessary, to divert the courses of rivers.[7] Such descriptions, amplified and often altered, form the kernel of Lucan's *Bellum civile*. Like Caesar's account of the conflict, Lucan's poem is about a civil war on a world stage. Its focal point may be the "Emathian" (that is, Thessalian) fields of the poem's opening line, where Caesar and Pompey fight a decisive battle in book seven, but the text's action sweeps from Gaul, through Italy, to Massilia (modern Marseille), Ilerda in Spain, north Africa, Greece, then Thessaly, Egypt, and (unlike Caesar's commentary) deep into the African desert. The *Bellum civile* is imbued with geographic and ethnographic learning: the names of rivers, mountains, cities, and their peoples are frequently and strategically deployed. Yet Lucan loves to unsettle geographic order. The poem's subject matter seems to demand corresponding disruptions in nature, often imagined, rather than actual: rivers burst, mountains clash, cities are transplanted.[8] This will to upturn order contributes to the fantastical nature of the political conflict that occupies much of the *Bellum civile*. So much so that priority can be hard to determine: are monstrous geographic distortions imagined in order to serve the theme of civil war, or are they themselves the theme? There are times when Caesar's conflict with Pompey seems to offer merely a convenient pretext for envisaging different worlds, different orders of things.

No complete manuscript of the *Bellum civile* survives from before the ninth century, but there is evidence of a nearly continuous history of reading and commentary on Lucan's poem from the time of his death onwards. The works of late antique authors, pagan and Christian alike, cite the *Bellum civile*: Augustine, Servius, and Macrobius all drew upon it, as did the poets of Vandalic Africa, Dracontius and Corippus.[9] Lucan informed Isidore of Seville's *Etymologiae* and influenced Bede, while study of the *Bellum civile* flourished during the Carolingian

---

7. *C. Iuli Caearis Commentarii*, ed. Alfred Klotz, 2 vols (Leipzig, 1952–57), vol. 2, esp. 1.25 (the siege of Brundisium); 1.61 (Caesar attempts to divert the course of the Sicoris); 3.49 (Caesar dams rivers to deprive Pompey's men of water); 3.97 (Caesar cuts off a river to entrap Pompey's men).

8. For studies of Lucan's "cosmic disorder" see in particular Masters, *Poetry and Civil War*; A. Loupiac, *La poétique des éléments dans* La Pharsale *de Lucain* (Brussels, 1998); Michael Lapidge, "Lucan's Imagery of Cosmic Dissolution," *Hermes* 107 (1979): 344–70, revised slightly in *Lucan*, ed. Charles Tesoriero (Oxford, 2010), 289–323; Micah Y. Myers, "Lucan's Poetic Geographies: Center and Periphery in Civil War Epic," in *Brill's Companion to Lucan*, 399–415.

9. Augustine, *De civitate dei*, 3.27; Macrobius, *Commentarii in Somnium Scipionis*, 2.7; influence is evident in Dracontius' *De laudibus Dei* and Corippus' *De bellis libycis* and *In laudem Iustini minoris*. On Servius see Paolo Esposito, "Virgilio e Servio nella scoliastica lucanea," in *Gli scolii a Lucano ed altra scoliastica latina*, ed. Paolo Esposito (Pisa, 2004), 25–77.

Renaissance.[10] From the tenth century onwards the *Bellum civile* was copied with increasing frequency: hundreds of manuscripts are extant, testament to the poem's status as an essential schoolroom text, but also to sustained interest in it in centres of learning throughout Europe.[11] That interest can be attributed to many qualities: to the style of the *Bellum civile*, its epic diction, its examples of oratory, its perceived value as a historical source, its handy provision of *sententiae* and exemplary narratives. Perhaps above all else, the poem offered its readers a connection – visceral in its intensity – with the ancient world: Lucan's narrative was potent, but also dense. As "Lucan's epitaph," a short verse that accompanies biographical material on the poet in some early manuscripts, put it, the poem was like a river.[12] The simile suggests the potential for rapid movement but also for serpentine meanderings: for digression and drifting as well as torrent.

The density of the *Bellum civile*, its erudition and richness of allusion, meant that it demanded commentary in order to be understood and appreciated. During the Middle Ages the poem was relatively rarely read without the accompaniment of glosses and marginal notes. In some cases the *Bellum civile* generated free-standing commentaries, such as the "Commenta Bernensia," a collection of notes on the poem copied in the ninth century, which is preserved in the same manuscript as another commentary, the "Adnotationes super Lucanum."[13] Major commentaries followed in the succeeding centuries, often in response to the needs of school and university teaching. The twelfth-century master Arnulf of Orléans produced one of the most extensive medieval commentaries on the poem, and the later medieval period saw commentaries from *magistri* such as the

10. Isidore of Seville, *Etymologiae*, e.g. 12.4. For Bede and Anglo-Saxon England more generally see Michael Lapidge, *The Anglo-Saxon Library* (Oxford, 2006), and for Carolingian Europe Harold C. Gotoff, *The Transmission of the Text of Lucan in the Ninth Century* (Cambridge, MA, 1971).

11. R.J. Tarrant, "Lucan," in *Texts and Transmission*, 215–18. Birger Munk Olsen counts over 200 surviving Lucan manuscripts from the ninth to twelfth centuries alone, including extracts and fragments: *L'étude des auteurs classiques latins*, 2: 17–83; 3.2: 91–96. See also Eva Matthews Sanford, "The Manuscripts of Lucan: *Accessus* and *Marginalia*," *Speculum* 9 (1934): 278–95.

12. The textual history of the "epitaph" is somewhat complex: see *Commenta Bernensia*, ed. Usener, 6; *Le vite antiche di M. Anneo Lucano*, ed. Cecilia Braidotti (Bologna, 1972).

13. Bern, Burgerbibliothek, Cod. 370. The "Commenta Bernensia" were edited as *M. Annaei Lucani Commenta Bernensia*, ed. Hermann Usener (Leipzig, 1869; repr. Hildesheim, 1967). The "Adnotationes" – *Adnotationes super Lucanum*, ed. Ioannes Endt (Leipzig, 1909) – were frequently intermingled with other glosses: hence the *Supplementum Adnotationum super Lucanum*, ed. G.A. Cavajoni, vol. 1 (Books 1–5) (Milan, 1979); vol. 2 (Books 6–7) (Milan, 1984); vol. 3 (Books 8–10) (Amsterdam, 1990). Late antique commentaries on Lucan did not survive intact into the Middle Ages, as they did for Virgil: Shirley Werner, "On the History of the *Commenta Bernensia* and the *Adnotationes super Lucanum*," *Harvard Studies in Classical Philology* 96 (1994): 343–68.

grammarian Zono of Magnali, the Dante commentator Benvenuto da Imola, and the humanist Pomponio Leto.[14] Yet Lucan was read for pleasure and instruction outside of academic contexts. One extant commentary was written in 1355 by an Italian in the entourage of the Holy Roman emperor Charles IV: this anonymous commentator included glosses in which he used his own experience of the Po in flood to affirm the validity of Lucan's description of the river in book two of the *Bellum civile*.[15] Malleable texts themselves, commentaries on the *Bellum civile* were far from static. Sets of glosses could be combined, refined, supplemented, or juxtaposed. Commentary accreted to the original text, but rarely displaced it. Glosses directed the reader towards a meaning, towards another text, or to an image – enriching, enlarging, and at times misleading.

The abundant glosses and scholia in manuscripts of Lucan's *Bellum civile* make the text the location for what can be termed an interlinear and marginal geography. Medieval commentators on Lucan sought to understand the poem's geographic content, not by forming some kind of an overview of the spatial meaning of the *Bellum civile*, but by explicating, and also often expanding upon, its references to particular places and peoples. At a basic level, glosses identified the nature of the topographic features referred to in the poem, labelling a toponym "island," "city," "river," "region," or "mountain." Yet commentators and glossators frequently added information to the basic gloss, including mythographical and etymological explanations. In certain cases they glossed the poem with diagrams. Explanatory images, several of which contain topographic elements, accompanied the poem from at least the ninth century – the *Commenta Bernensia* contains no fewer than nineteen small illustrations of passages from the *Bellum civile*[16] – and such images were still being copied and adapted in the fifteenth.[17]

---

14. See Paolo Esposito, "Early and Medieval *Scholia* and *Commentaria* on Lucan," in *Brill's Companion to Lucan*, 452–63.

15. Johannes Endt, "Ein Kommentar zu Lucan aus dem Mittelalter," *Wiener Studien* 32 (1910): 123–55 and 272–95, at 126, 128.

16. O. Homburger, *Die illustrierten Handschriften der Burgerbibliothek Bern. Die vorkarolingischen und karolingischen Handschriften* (Bern, 1962), 119–24. The *Commenta*'s illustrations include the Apennines (2.399–438); the site of Brindisi (2.610–27); "how Caesar surrounded/besieged Massilia" (3.375–87); the site of the battle of Ilerda (4.11–23); north Africa (4.666–75); Olympus and Parnassus (5.4, 72–78); Euripus (5.230–36); mount Garganus (5.379–80); the isthmus of Corinth (6.57–58); the mountains of Thessaly (6.333–42); Syrtes (9.300ff); a world map (9.411); and a sketch of the straits of Bosforos, Propontis, and Hellespont (9.954–60).

17. Patrick Gautier Dalché, "Les diagrammes topographiques dans les manuscrits des classiques latins (Lucain, Solin, Salluste)," in *La Tradition Vive: Mélanges d'histoire des textes en l'honneur de Louis Holtz*, ed. P. Lardet (Paris and Turnhout, 2003), 291–306.

Glosses performed several different functions beyond that of identification. Most obviously, they could draw analogies between one place and another. When, in book eight of the *Bellum civile*, the defeated but still scheming Pompey entrusts his ally Deiotarus with a mission to seek aid from the Parthians, he makes reference to "Caspian enclosures" (*Caspia claustra*) (*BC* 8.222). "He means the Caspian mountains which enclose the kingdom of the Parthians, just as the Alps Italy, and the Pyrenees Spain," noted Arnulf of Orléans.[18] But the effect of the gloss might equally be to identify problems, and to offer alternative readings without deciding on a correct interpretation. Far from simply policing spatial order by distinguishing islands from mountains, or rivers from regions, glosses and scholia instead had the effect of diffusing and even overwhelming spatial order. In the same speech, Pompey imagines the entry of a Parthian army into Europe, and obscurely refers to a town they will overrun as "Pellean Zeugma" (*BC* 8.237). Arnulf's twelfth-century commentary responds: "Zev(g)ma is a city between Egypt and Parthia which Alexander [the Great] from the city of Pella built to enclose the Parthians so that they might not harm him."[19] The gloss perfectly reasonably seeks to explain what "Zevma" was, and why it is termed "Pellean." Yet it necessarily intrudes weighty historical narratives: here Zeugma not only divides two regions, but by virtue of its role in the Alexander narrative finds another place, Pella, conjoined with it. For the *Commenta Bernensia*, in its geographical context "Zeugma" was originally a bridge constructed by Alexander, which subsequently became the name of the city.[20] A further significance, so obvious it did not need to be glossed, was that the word zeugma, literally a "yoking" or "junction," was known to all medieval commentators on the poem as a rhetorical term for the use of one word to govern more than one clause: in fact, the name had been given to the city because it was formed from the union of two cities, Seleuceia and Apamea. City, bridge, rhetorical term, Pellean Zeugma bore a heavy freight, and the glosses drew out, rather than closed down, its meanings.

Where did these openings, sometimes inspired, sometimes misguided, leave Lucan's distinctive and insistent resort to topography? Medieval readers and authors grappled with the world image they found in Lucan's poem, an image

18. Arnulf of Orléans, *Glosule super Lucanum*, ed. Berthe M. Marti (Rome, 1958), 403: "uocat Caspios montes qui claudunt regnum Parthorum sicut Alpes Italiam, Pirenei montes Hispaniam."

19. Arnulf of Orléans, *Glosule*, ed. Marti, 403: "ZEVMA Ciuitas est inter Egyptum et Parthiam quam edificauit Alexander de Pellea ciuitate ut Parthos concluderet ne illi possent nocere." Arnulf's gloss resembles that of the *Adnotationes*, where Zeugma was placed by Alexander "Pellaeus" as a barrier against the defeated Parthians: *Adnotationes*, 308.

20. *Commenta Bernensia*, ed. Usener, 264: "... ab Alexandro Macedone quondam pons factus est qui hodieque Zeugma appellatur."

already manipulated, subject to poetic distortions, and at times inhabiting the borders of incomprehensibility. But it was a world image that offered valuable information – such as the names of ancient peoples and places – and demanded responses pedantic and creative in equal measure. This chapter considers Lucan's geography of dislocation through the lens of his medieval readers. Within the manuscripts of the *Bellum civile*, and in the many texts that responded to the poem, it is possible to discern a number of passages whose content caused readers to consider spatial order, and the deconstruction of that order performed by Lucan. Some of these passages were clearly marked for their significance, by illustration or by commentary; others may have occasioned no more than a routine level of explication. All however reveal the mutability of Lucanian geography, its complex intertextuality, and its potential to generate new ways of seeing the world.

Geography in the Subjunctive Mood

One medieval commentator argued with some justification that Lucan was a poet precisely because "in topography – that is, in the descriptions of places – he invents."[21] The topographical fictions of the *Bellum civile*, as evident to a medieval readership as they are to a modern one, often find expression in grandiose visions. The nature of these visions is usually violent, involving floods, droughts, human assaults on natural formations, and the conjunction of distant places. They characteristically require the dissolution of boundaries, particularly the division between land and water. Rather than pure invention, however, the crucial element of this mode of spatial representation was its proximity to reality, and its simultaneous distortion of it. The governing spirit of Lucan's imagined geography was the subjunctive, a grammatical mood of possibility and uncertainty, where "would," "might," and "could" triumph over "is."

Caesar's relationship to Italy – conqueror and despoiler – acts as a particular catalyst for visions of alternative geographies. In a remarkable passage in book two of the *Bellum civile*, Lucan describes the Apennines and the rivers that flow from the mountains. The opening for this display is the simple statement that Pompey intended to meet Caesar's forces in the middle of Italy, where the Apennines rise in wooded hills; 41 lines of geographical description follow (*BC* 2.394–

21. "[I]n topographis id est in descriptionibus locorum fingit unde vocatus est poeta": Berlin, Staatsbibliothek Preussischer Kulturbesitz, MS Lat. 2 34-I, fol. 1r; Munich, Bayerische Staatsbibliothek, Clm 4593, fol. 146r; both are twelfth-century manuscripts. The interest of the Munich manuscript in topography is noted in Sanford, "The Manuscripts of Lucan," 294.

439). There are two ifs, two moments in which geography is expressed in the subjunctive mood. The first is that the size of the river Po would have equalled or bettered the Nile or the Danube were it not for the plains of Egypt (which allow the Nile to expand), and were it not that the course of the Danube through the world allows it to collect waters that would otherwise empty into various seas (*BC* 2.416–20).[22] The second alternative topography concerns the Apennines, which apparently once connected the Italian mainland to Sicily:

> longior Italia, donec confinia pontus
> solueret incumbens terrasque repelleret aequor;
> at, postquam gemino tellus elisa profundo est,
> extremi colles Siculo cessere Peloro. (*BC* 2.435–38)

(the range was) longer than Italy, until the pressing sea dissolved its boundaries, and the ocean thrust back the land; after the earth was cut off beneath the two seas, the range's furthest mountains fell to Sicilian Pelorus.

As is the case elsewhere in the poem, land recedes.[23] The notion that the mainland and Sicily had originally been part of the same land mass was something of a geographical commonplace,[24] but despite being a passing thought in Lucan's poem, the idea somehow lingers. Italy was longer, its river could have been the equal of the Nile and Danube. With part of the land submerged, Sicily's mountain, Pelorus,[25] becomes the reminder of a lost unity. The immediate juxtaposition of this image with a "Caesar in arma furens" (*BC* 2.439), lusting for battle, rejoicing to fight Pompey on Italian soil, aligns Caesar with the sea – an overwhelming, sundering force.

More extreme topographic distortions follow. When Caesar lays siege to the town of Ilerda (modern Lleida) in book four, snows melt on the Pyrenees, causing the river Sicoris to flood. The arms of Caesar are shipwrecked (*naufraga ... arma*), and geography erased.

---

22. On Lucan's treatment of the Nile (and other rivers), see Andy Merrills, *Roman Geographies of the Nile: From the Late Republic to the Early Empire* (Cambridge, 2017), 251–78.

23. For example *BC* 1.100–106: Crassus, as the mediator between Caesar and Pompey, is compared to the Isthmus of Corinth: if land receded ("si terra recedat"), the Ionian would dash against the Aegean.

24. For example, Sallust, *C. Sallusti Crispi Historiarum Reliquiae*, ed. B. Maurenbrecher (Leipzig, 1891–93), 494, as well as a number of other classical sources including Virgil, *Aeneid*, 3.414–19; Ovid, *Metamorphoses*, 15.290–91; Strabo, *Geography* 6.1.6; Pliny, *Naturalis historia*, 3.86. See also Isidore, *Etymologiae*, 14.6.34.

25. The Sicilian range referred to is the modern-day Monti Peloritani.

Iam tumuli collesque latent, iam flumina cuncta
condidit una palus uastaque uoragine mersit,
absorpsit penitus rupes ac tecta ferarum
detulit atque ipsas hausit subitisque frementis
uerticibus contorsit aquas et reppulit aestus
fortior Oceani. (*BC* 4.98–103)

Now mounds and hills lie hidden; now a single swamp joined all the rivers
together and submerged them within its vast depths: it completely absorbed
the cliffs, it carried off the shelters of wild beasts and consumed the creatures
themselves. Howling with rapid eddies it contorted the waters and, stronger,
thrust back the tides of Ocean.

Rivers unite into a single body of water, night no longer recognises the rising sun,
the known world of the northern temperate zone approximates its antithesis, the
Antarctic, in which stars are never seen, and nothing grows in the sterile cold.[26]
At this point the poet offers up a prayer to Jupiter and Neptune:

Non habeant amnes decliuem ad litora cursum,
sed pelagi referantur aquis concussaque tellus
laxet iter fluuiis: hos campos Rhenus inundet,
hos Rhodanus, uastos obliquent flumina fontes;[27]
Riphaeas huc solue niues, huc stagna lacusque
et pigras, ubicumque iacent, effunde paludes
et miseras bellis ciuilibus eripe terras. (*BC* 4.114–20)

Let the rivers not run down to the shores, but let them be carried backwards
by the waters of the sea, and may the ruptured earth unbind their course:
may the Rhine flood these fields and the Rhone too, let the rivers divert their
vast well-springs. Melt Riphaean snows here, here release swamps and lakes,
pour forth sluggish marshes, wherever they lie: and snatch wretched lands
from civil wars.

Rivers and mountains define spatial order; Lucan invokes them so as to imagine
its dissolution, and the consequent obliteration of human conflict. The Rhine

26. Lapidge, "Lucan's Imagery of Cosmic Dissolution," 316, links the passage to
Seneca's description of Stoic "ekpurosis" (cosmic conflagration) and the consequent dissolution of all things into one mass.
27. Badalì prints "fontis," but "fontes" is equally supported by manuscript evidence;
intriguingly some manuscripts have "montes": "let the rivers divert vast mountains."

and Rhone represent Germania and Gaul respectively; the Riphaean mountains stand for Scythia and the far north. All converge in Spain. The capacity of water to erase geography, to spread across and ultimately dissolve borders and wars, turns out to be at once a potent fantasy and hopeless digression: immediately after the prayer, the sun comes out, floods recede, and Caesar deals punishment to the river Sicoris by dividing it into canals.[28] Yet along with other moments of topographic exuberance, the flood at Ilerda constitutes a sequence of imaginative reformulations of spatial order in which alternative, or occluded, geographies come briefly to light. The following pages trace some of the more spectacular instances of Lucan's disruption of order, as the poem and its protagonists make their way from the Italian mainland, through western Europe, Asia Minor, and finally into Africa.

Brundisium

Towards the end of the second book of the *Bellum civile*, Pompey, on the run from Caesar, is about to leave Italy to raise an army. "Rouse the Euphrates and Nile," he commands: Egyptians, Armenians, Scythians, Greeks, Macedonians – indeed the entire East – is imagined rallying to his cause (*BC* 2.632–48). But as Caesar closes in, the port city of Brundisium threatens to become Pompey's prison, and he is forced to flee in something approaching ignominy. Sign of doomed heroism, Brundisium at the same time becomes emblematic of Caesar's challenge to nature as well as to history, as he seeks to change the balance between sea and land in order to ensnare his adversary. Lucan did not miss the opportunity to provide a description of place at once learned and creative:

> Vrbs est Dictaeis olim possessa colonis,
> quos Creta profugos uexere per aequora puppes
> Cecropiae uictum mentitis Thesea uelis.
> Hinc latus angustum iam se cogentis in artum
> Hesperiae tenuem producit in aequora linguam,
> Hadriacas flexis claudit quae cornibus undas.

28. Here as elsewhere, Lucan's narrative has some basis in the account of the Civil War given by Caesar and other historians, and bears strong similarities to a passage on universal flood in his uncle's *Naturales Quaestiones*, written around 62 AD: Seneca, *Naturales quaestiones* 3.27.8–10, ed. Harry M. Hine (Stuttgart, 1996), 152–53. For commentary see Masters, *Poetry and Civil War*, 30–34; Matthew Leigh, *Lucan: Spectacle and Engagement* (Oxford, 1997), 44, 74, *Bellum civile (Pharsalia) Libro IV*, ed. Paolo Esposito (Naples, 2009), 104–6; Merrills, *Roman Geographies of the Nile*, 275–76, and cf. Ahl, *Introduction*, 76–81.

Nec tamen hoc artis inmissum faucibus aequor
portus erat, si non uiolentos insula coros
exciperet saxis lassasque refunderet undas.
Hinc illinc montes scopulosae rupis aperto
opposuit natura mari flatusque remouit,
ut tremulo starent contentae fune carinae.
Hinc late patet omne fretum, seu uela ferantur
in portus, Corcyra, tuos, seu laeua petatur
Illyris Ionias uergens Epidamnos in undas.
Hoc fuga nautarum, cum totas Hadria uires
mouit et in nubes abiere Ceraunia cumque
spumoso Calaber perfunditur aequore Sason. (BC 2.610–27)

The city was once occupied by Dictaean settlers, exiles from Crete carried across the sea on Cecropian ships with sails that falsely reported the defeat of Theseus. From here the side of Hesperia, now forcing itself into a narrow strait, extends into the ocean a slender tongue, which encloses the Adriatic waves with curved horns. However, the sea, admitted in narrow channels, would not form a harbour here if an island did not block with its rocks the violent Corus, and fling back the languid waves. Here and there nature opposed masses of rocky cliffs to the open sea and drove away the gusts, so that keels might rest content on a quivering line. Far beyond, all the sea opens up, and sails are either borne to your harbours, Corcyra, or they turn left, heading towards Illyrian Epidamnos in Ionian waters. This is the refuge of sailors, when the Adriatic moves at full force, when the Ceraunian mountains are covered in clouds, and when Calabrian Sason is drenched by the foamy sea.

Medieval commentators supplemented Lucan's deliberately obscure display of *topographia* with their own learning. They glossed the city's etymology, explaining that "Brunda" meant "deer's head," and quoting Isidore of Seville's claim in his *Etymologiae* that "in its situation the city resembles not only horns, but a head, and a tongue."[29] Some commentaries gave more detail about Brundisium's Cretan origins, offering multiple explanations for the presence of Cretans in southern Italy, including shipwreck, a punitive expedition against Daedalus following his escape from the labyrinth, and the relocation of comrades of Theseus fol-

29. Isidore, *Etymologiae* 15.1.49: "ut et cornua videantur et caput et lingua in positione ipsius civitatis." Strabo, *Geography*, 6.3.6 describes Brundisium, and derives its name from "Brunda," stag's head. The poetic model for Lucan was *Aen* 1.159–64, while he derived detail from Caesar's *Commentarii*, 1.25–30.

lowing his defeat of the Minotaur and the subsequent debacle of his father's suicide, when the colour of the sails on Theseus' ships mistakenly led the old man to believe that his son had been killed.[30] As for geography, the commentators did their best to distinguish islands and cities from mountains: Epidamnos was a city, Corcyra an island (called Corfu in the vernacular and located in the Ionian sea, a fifteenth-century humanist commentator noted) or perhaps a city;[31] Sason was, depending on the commentator, a port, a town, or perhaps a mountain (it is in fact an island); Hesperia meant Italia,[32] and Coros meant the winds.[33] At least one set of glosses was alert to Virgilian echoes. Lucan's use of "Dicteis" echoed a line from book three of the *Aeneid*: "Dictea negat tibi Iuppiter arva" (Jupiter denies you Dictaean fields) (*Aen* 3.171). Similarly, "Cecropiae" two lines later meant "Athenian" but it also brought to mind Virgil's use of the same word in relation to the fable of the Minotaur, in the sixth book of the *Aeneid*: "Tum pendere poenas Cecropidae iussi ..." (then the Cecropian children, ordered to pay a tribute) (*Aen* 6.20–21).[34] Such comments on the *Bellum civile* unwound the mythology that lay coiled within the poem, but they also at times revealed a shared poetic topography, inviting their readers to remember the Crete denied to Aeneas during his search for a new Troy, and perhaps too to see some irony in Pompey's flight from a city of exiles at the end of Italy.

The diagrams that glossed the Brundisium passage in medieval manuscripts took up Lucan's construction of the city as a projection of Italy (Hesperia), and a synecdoche.[35] Like Italy, the city was a tongue jutting into sea, narrow enough to invoke alternative geographies. Three different forms of the Brundisium diagram have been identified, all of which attempt to show the relationship between the port, the island that protects it from the elements, the sea, and Italy itself.[36] One manuscript, written in Milan in 1452, contains a full text of the *Bellum civile*; illustrated with twelve diagrams, it exemplifies the visual culture that surrounded the poem in the later Middle Ages. The principal scribe, responsible for the text of the poem, supplied the Brundisium diagram in book two, and a relatively sim-

30. *Commenta Bernensia*, ed. Usener, 85–86; *Adnotationes*, 75; *Supplementum Adnotationum* 1: 147; Arnulf of Orléans, *Glosule*, ed. Marti, 145–46.

31. Vatican City, Biblioteca Apostolica Vaticana, MS Vat. Lat 3284, fol. 20r: "dicitur corfu in uulgari et est in mari yonio"; *Commenta Bernensia*, ed. Usener, 86: "Phaeacum ciuitas"; one commentator identified it as Corsica: Endt, "Kommentar zu Lucan," 127.

32. *Adnotationes*, 75.

33. *Supplementum Adnotationum* 1: 148.

34. *Adnotationes*, 74.

35. Cf. Sallust, *Historiarum reliquiae*, 4 fr. 23: "omnis Italia coacta in angustias finditur in duo promunturia."

36. Gautier Dalché, "Les diagrammes topographiques."

ple *mappa mundi* in book nine.[37] The former is a large coloured illustration in the left margin at 2.610–27: Italia is marked, flanked by the "Mare adriaticum" (Adriatic Sea) and the "mare tureneum" (Tyrrhenian Sea), with the "alpes" at its northern-most extent (Figure 6). Two further toponyms, added in another hand, also respond to the text: "corcira" and "illiris" – reversed from their correct positions. Brundisium diagrams usually appear alongside the passage they gloss, although they could on occasion migrate to other parts of the manuscript, even at times leaving the *Bellum civile* altogether.[38] Explanatory, they also have the effect of marking out the passage, drawing attention to its *topographia*, and performing for Lucan's medieval readers the exit from Italy into the waters of the Aegean that Pompey, and the poem itself, were about to take.

Massilia

In the third book of the *Bellum civile*, following Pompey's escape from Italy, Caesar returns to Rome and forces entry to the treasury, while armies from throughout the world flock to assist his rival. Then, leaving Rome, Caesar crosses the Alps, retracing the Rubicon-crossing steps he took in book one, and hurries to do battle in Spain. En route, he passes through Gaul and encounters an obstacle at Massilia, in the form of the city's Greek settlers.

> Ille, ubi deseruit trepidantis moenia Romae,
> agmine nubiferam rapto supereuolat Alpem,
> cumque alii famae populi terrore pauerent,
> Phocais in dubiis ausa est seruare iuuentus
> non Graia leuitate fidem signataque iura
> et causas, non fata, sequi. (*BC* 3.298–303)

> He left the walls of trembling Rome and, taking a column of troops, hastened over the cloud-bearing Alps. When other peoples shuddered with terror at the news, Phocaean warriors dared – not with Greek fickleness – to preserve faith and observe sealed treaties in dangerous times: they dared to follow principles, not fortune.

The Greek (here "Phocaean") settlers refuse to yield to Caesar. This digressive encounter has an analogue in Caesar's own account of the Civil War, and is his-

---

37. London, British Library, MS Additional 11992, fols. 24v and 125r, respectively.
38. Gautier Dalché, "Les diagrammes topographiques," 298–99, 306.

torically accurate, insofar as in 49 BC Caesar did capture Massilia, a city that had been founded by Greek settlers c. 600 BC, and that had remained culturally Greek.[39] But the Massilian episode raises two questions: why are the Greeks in Gaul, and why should Caesar wish to delay his passage by besieging them? In Lucan's account, some answers emerge in a speech delivered by the Massilian men to Caesar:

> Non pondera rerum
> nec momenta sumus: numquam felicibus armis
> usa manus, patriae primis a sedibus exul,
> et post translatas exustae Phocidos arces
> moenibus exiguis alieno in litore tuti,
> inlustrat quos sola fides. (BC 3.337–42)

We are neither of weight nor consequence, never successful in battle, exiled from the first seats of our fatherland, and, after the burned-out citadels of Phocis were translated, we were kept safe by trifling walls on an alien shore. Faith alone distinguishes us.

The Greeks, although translated by war, remain Greek (*Grai, Graia iuventus*), exiles who will not return. Yet in their new city, Massilia, they do not behave like Greeks: "non Graia levitate," they are not fickle, they prefer to proclaim the virtues of faith, law, and principle than to follow fate, events.[40] They inform Caesar that they are prepared to die for freedom (*pro libertate*), as their countrymen, besieged by Carthaginians, once did in the Spanish town of Saguntum (*BC* 3.349–55). Their entreaties are, all the same, vain. Caesar only delays long enough to begin the destruction of Massilia, a siege which will end in a sea battle of outrageous violence, in which the bodies of the dead fill the waves and impede the warring ships; a crust of blood forms over the water. All the same, the dislocations contained in the presence of Greeks in Gaul acting as non-

---

39. *Commentarii*, 1.34–36, 2.6–22. On the origins of Greek Massilia see the lucid overview of Henri Tréziny, "Marseille, une ville ionienne dans l'Occident grec," in *Les territoires de Marseille antique*, ed. Sophie Bouffier and Dominique Garcia (Arles, 2014), 9–18.

40. Compare the contradictory views of the Massilians, and Greeks abroad generally, presented in Livy, *Ab urbe condita libri xxxi–xl* 37.54.21–22, ed. John Briscoe, 2 vols (Stuttgart, 1991), 2: 498: "nec terra mutata mutauit genus aut mores"; and 38.17.12, 2: 537: "Massilia, inter Gallos sita, traxit aliquantum ab accolis animorum." For commentary see Arnaldo Momigliano, *Alien Wisdom: The Limits of Hellenization* (Cambridge, 1975), 50–73, esp. 56, and for the argument that Massilia offers an analogue to Rome see Robert J. Rowland, "The Significance of Massilia in Lucan," *Hermes* 97 (1969): 204–8.

Greeks, allies of Rome now opposing civil war and Caesar, seem to echo the poem's folding of spaces and times. And there is a further complication, noted in at least one commentary: Lucan conflates Phocis, the country in central Greece, with Phocaea, the city in Asia Minor besieged by a Persian army in 540 BC, whose citizens colonized the coasts of Gaul and Spain.[41]

For the commentators there were yet more layers to unravel. It was evident that Phocis was meant to signify a Greek city, and that the "translated citadels" (*translatas arces*) referred to the rebuilding of the city in Massilia by the Greek nomads (*profugi*). The city was the sign of a Greek diaspora, one found not only in Gaul and Spain, but also, as the commentators noted, in Italy.[42] But why had they fled? Several glosses identified their persecutor as the Persian king Cyrus, or his general, Harpagus.[43] One commentary expanded, drawing on the story of the city's foundation contained in Isidore's *Etymologiae*: after Cyrus occupied the Greek cities on the coastline, "the Greeks vowed to flee as far as possible from the Persian empire, to a place where nobody had heard their name. Carried to the furthest shores of Gaul in their boats, defending themselves in armed combat against Gallic ferocity, they built Massilia and named it after their leader."[44] Massilia in this account emerges as a curious site: western Europe's coastline is where the uprooted, the *profugi*, escape their past in spite of hostile natives, only to be destroyed by a Caesarean digression. But for several medieval commentators there were still further resonances. Massilia, after all, was part of their world. "Our city Massilia," one wrote.[45] As Arnulf put it, the Greeks, searching for a land ignorant of their own city, found it "in the direction of St Giles," and built Massilia there.[46] For a medieval audience Massilia carried a trace of Greek-Persian warfare, and conjoined Greece, Rome, and Gaul; but as well as the perverse object of Caesar's ire, it was also part of a landscape now marked by saints.

41. *Commenta Bernensia*, ed. Usener, 109: "'Focidos' autem male posuit. debuit enim 'Foceae' dicere. in quibus subinde peccat. quo apparet eum differentiam ignorasse. est autem Focis regio in qua Delficum est oraculum."

42. *Adnotationes*, 103.

43. *Commenta Bernensia*, ed. Usener, 108; cf. Herodotus, *Histories* 1.163–67, where Phocaea is besieged by Cyrus's general Harpagus, leading to a mass exodus of its inhabitants.

44. *Supplementum Adnotationum* 1: 185: "iuraverunt ut profugerent quam longissime ab imperio Persarum, ubi ne nomen quidem eorum audirent. Atque ita in ultimos Galliae sinus navibus provecti, armisque se adversus Gallicam feritatem tuentes, Massiliam condiderunt et ex nomine ducis nuncupaverunt." Cf. Isidore, *Etymologiae*, 15.1.63. Arnulf of Orléans makes it clear that the requirement to find a land ignorant of their city was part of a pact with Cyrus: Arnulf of Orléans, *Glosule*, ed. Marti, 181.

45. *Supplementum Adnotationum* 1: 182: "MASSILIAM nostram urbem."

46. Arnulf of Orléans, *Glosule*, ed. Marti, 181: "uersus Sanctum Egidium," apparently a reference to the town of Saint-Gilles, to the west of Marseille.

Massilia is the sequel to Brundisium, both in the poem and in the commentaries that surrounded it. Again Caesar surveys a city from outside and attempts to defy nature: he constructs a trench (*fossa*) to cut off water and pastures, while a rampart (*agger*) is fashioned to join his raised vantage point (*tumulus*) to the citadel itself. In the process a sacred grove is desecrated (*BC* 3.375–460). Earth is excavated, the landscape stripped of its features and heaped into a mass. The visual glosses on Massilia preserved in the ninth-century *Commenta Bernensia* respond faithfully to Lucan's narrative of Caesar's assault. One drawing, labelled "Caesar surrounded Massilia just as this picture shows," depicts the "tumulus" from which Caesar views the city, with the ditch (*fossa*) running beneath. A second image, "... Caesar erected towers against Massilia," represents the "twin towers" erected on shaky foundations by the besiegers (Figure 7).[47] The trench (*Fossa*) and the towers (*Turres*) become visual adjuncts to the walled city, simultaneously undermining and overlooking it. All to no avail: like Brundisium, Massilia survives the elaborate constructions of Caesar. Unlike Brundisium, however, it suffers defeat at sea. Its inhabitants no longer flee; their nomadic role is now taken on by Pompey, the escaper who will also meet his end *in alieno litore*.

Rome in Thessaly

The flight of Pompey through Asia Minor and finally into Egypt allowed Lucan to represent a succession of dislocations. Unlike the sieges of Brundisium, Massilia, and Ilerda, these dislocations revolve less around Caesar's distortion of the environment than on the superimposition of the city of Rome itself on foreign spaces, through the displacement either of its political institutions or of its inhabitants. In the fifth book of the *Bellum civile*, the exiled Roman Senate meets in Epirus, on the basis that its power endures even on foreign soil (*BC* 5.17–34: "non unquam perdidit ordo / mutato sua iura solo"). In the following two books Lucan stages the implosion of Roman *imperium* in the climactic encounter between Caesar and Pompey. He first provides a detailed description of Pharsalus, the site of their battle in Thessaly. This location, immanent since its mention in the poem's opening line, is imbued by Lucan with deep mythological and magical significance as well as heavy symbolism. His description begins by establishing the position of five mountains that surround Pharsalus in relation both to the movements of the sun, and to the classical system of winds.

47. Bern, Burgerbibliothek, Cod. 370, fols. 46v ("ita Caesar cinxit massiliam sicut haec pictura testatur"), 48r ("intius picturae similitudinis caesar contra massiliam turres erexit").

Thessaliam, qua parte diem brumalibus horis
attollit Titan, rupes Ossaea coercet;
cum per summa poli Phoebum trahit altior aestas,
Pelion opponit radiis nascentibus umbras;
at medios ignes[48] caeli rapidique Leonis
solstitiale caput nemorosus summouet Othrys;
excipit aduersos zephyros et iapyga Pindus
et maturato praecidit uespere lucem
nec metuens imi borean habitator Olympi
lucentem totis ignorat noctibus Arcton. (BC 6.333–42)

The cliff Ossa encloses Thessaly, in the area [i.e. the south-east] where Titan raises the day in winter hours; when greater heat drags Phoebus through the heights of the sky, Pelion [north-east] opposes its shadows to the emerging rays; but woody Othrys [south] drives off the southern heat of heaven and the midsummer head of fierce Leo; Pindus [west] receives the adverse west wind and the Iapyx [the north-west wind], and cuts off the light by bringing evening to maturity, while the dweller at the foot of Olympus [north], not fearing the north wind, is ignorant of the Great Bear, shining all night.

It was Hercules, Lucan continues, who severed Ossa from Mount Olympus, causing an avalanche and the emergence of Pharsalus from water. Again the poet interweaves a caustic aside – "better to have remained beneath the waves" (*melius mansura sub undis*) (BC 6.349) – reviving the hypothetical erased geography of book four, in which the Civil War battlefields remain or return to primal swamps. Critics have noted Lucan's own manipulation of geographic order in this passage: two of the five mountains (Ossa and Pelion) are incorrectly located; the valley is deliberately styled as devoid of sunlight, in a submerged primeval state that requires sundering violence to create a habitable landscape.[49]

Some medieval readers, such as the humanist chancellor of Florence Coluccio Salutati, sought allegorical readings of this landscape. Ossa represented the human body, Olympus the flames of passion, Othrys human intellect, Pelion the rational soul, and Pindus the multitude of vices. Thessaly itself – Coluccio suggested – was human life, and in separating Ossa from Olympus, body from passions, Hercules had purged it of the oppression of vices.[50] Such high-powered

48. Badalì prints "ignis," but "ignes" has manuscript support.
49. Masters, *Poetry and Civil War*, 151–78 argues persuasively for Lucan's creative, at times deliberately erroneous, use of geography.
50. *De laboribus Herculis* 3.38.6–8, ed. B.L. Ullman (Zürich, 1951), 379–80.

interpretations of the poem depended on a substructure of literalist exposition, in which visual and verbal gloss might align. Many manuscripts of the *Bellum civile* use schematic images to represent Lucan's description of the Thessalian mountains. In general, like the verbal glosses at this point in the poem, such images seek to bring order to the understanding of the passage by showing the mountains (Pelion, Othrys, Pindus, Olympus, and Ossa) in relation to the cardinal points and to each other, as well as features such as "the ditch of Hercules" (*fossa Herculis*) in Mount Olympus. Maps of this sort sometimes reveal the kind of wrestle readers got into with Lucan's work, and perhaps with classical literature more generally. A scrappy diagram from a thirteenth-century manuscript, probably of Italian provenance, which contains extensive fifteenth-century glossing, illustrates this point (Figure 8).[51] Drawn in one of two distinct hands that gloss the page, this sketch of Thessaly is superbly marginal – it literally intersects with the text, and with lines of commentary that gloss the text. There is a significant mistake (east and west are reversed). But the visual gloss works towards an understanding of the passage: Ossa and Pelion are in the east, Olympus in the north, Pindus in the west (or as the diagram has it, "Pindus Yapiga," mountain and north-west wind conjoined), and Othrys in the south. The page is meant to be rotated ("Otthris" is upside-down), the reading of the poem halted. Yet the diagram ultimately complements the poem from which it has sprung. It strips Lucan's elaborate ornamentation down to an underlying scheme so that the literal meaning of the passage may be understood, and its rhetorical effects – significantly marked by the word "topographia" – properly appreciated. The map grafted onto the poem is an essential aid in its comprehension, a manifestation of the process of reading classical verse, and an embodiment of the complex interrelations between commentary and text.

Among the acts of reading demanded by the *Bellum civile* was an appreciation of the role of poetry in defining, and sometimes opposing, nature. The poem soon matches Hercules' landscaping with the description of the nature-bending powers of Thessalian witches. It is an episode that has attracted consistent notoriety amongst Lucan's audiences, intriguing medieval and early modern readers, but eventually disappointing notions of the decorum of classical epic.[52] On the eve of the decisive battle, Pompey's son Sextus seeks counsel from Thessalian

---

51. London, British Library, MS Additional 19891, fol. 50r. Another copy of this diagram appears in Vatican City, Biblioteca Apostolica Vaticana, MS Reg. Lat. 1543, fol. 51v, a late twelfth- or early thirteenth-century school-room manuscript, associated with St Victor in Paris.

52. A rapid overview of reception of the scene appears in Martin Korenjak, *Die Erichthoszene in Lukans Pharsalia* (Frankfurt a.M, 1996), 46–51.

witches: after an account of their supernatural powers (*BC* 6. 413–506), one of their number, Erictho, reanimates a corpse which narrates the varying reactions of Romans in the underworld to the Civil War (*BC* 6. 507–830). In the first of these sections, the reader learns that the witches' magic extends to the ability to alter the climate, to disrupt the interrelationship between the winds and the sea, to stop waterfalls, and to cause rivers to run uphill.

> ... Nilum non extulit aestas,
> Maeander direxit aquas Rhodanumque morantem
> praecipitauit Arar. Summisso uertice montes
> explicuere iugum; nubes suspexit Olympus,
> solibus et nullis Scythicae, cum bruma rigeret,
> dimaduere niues. (*BC* 6.474–79)

> Summer did not see the Nile rise, the Meander straightened its waters and the Arar hurtled into the sluggish Rhone. With stooping peaks mountains levelled their ridges; Olympus looked up and saw clouds, and even as winter grew cold the snows of Scythia melted without the aid of sunlight.

A terrestrial version of the song of Orpheus in hell, the witches' magic allows another world to shimmer into view. The straight Meander, Olympus sitting beneath the clouds, Scythian snows melting and the Nile rising in winter: paradoxically what the magic removes is abnormality, the distinguishing feature. "Hoc contra naturam" noted one commentator: "for the Rhone runs most swiftly, the Arar very slowly; he is saying that the speedy one is sluggish and the lazy one flows rapidly; for in truth the Arar dribbles into the Rhone."[53] The list suggests the acts of categorisation and exception that constitute geographical order, and at the same time the poetic license required to reverse and undo order. "The Meander is the most tortuous river in Asia, about which Ovid [says] 'the Meander plays in curving waves.' So [Lucan] is saying: that spells give the Meander a straight course, which nature denies [it]."[54] As the gloss draws out, the wilful quality of the witches' intervention aligns their craft with poetry: both operate

---

53. *Supplementum Adnotationum* 2: 43: "nam Rhodanus velocissime currit, Arar vero lenissime; dicit ergo velocem morari pigrumque raptim fluere: veraciter enim Arar in Rhodanum cadit."

54. *Supplementum Adnotationum* 2: 43: "Meander fluvius est Asiae flexuosissimus, de quo Ovidius 'curvis ludit Meander in undis.' Dicit ergo: rectum cursum carmina dant, quem natura negat," quoting Isidore, *Etymologiae* 13.21.23, (mis)quoting Ovid's *Metamorphoses* 2.246.

through "carmina," spells/poems/songs that can make and upturn natural order. Geography in the subjunctive mood allows for translations as well as recessions, floods and reversals. That is, land may be moved: cities and peoples transplanted, the order of things not dissolved so much as remixed.

The two most striking examples of transplantation in Lucan's *Bellum civile* see Rome located elsewhere, first in Thessaly and then, following Pompey's death, in Africa. The Thessalian transplantation occurs in the aftermath of the battle of Pharsalus, after a variety of animals feast on the bodies of the dead. Wolves, lions, bears, dogs, cranes, and vultures all take their fill, and the sun, rain, and the passage of time mix what yet remains with Thessalian soils. These bodies are explicitly described as Roman, and Lucan concludes book seven with extended contemplation of the potent notion of mixture. Addressing Thessaly (*Thessalia infelix*), the poet emphasises not only the unfortunate fame that will now attach to the place, but the inextricable connection between the battle and the land:

> Quae seges infecta surget non decolor herba?
> Quo non Romanos uiolabis uomere manes? (*BC* 7. 851–52)

> Is there a crop that will not grow discoloured by the stained turf?
> How will you not profane Roman corpses with the plough?

Still more civil violence, the battle of Philippi in 42 BC, will take place in Thessaly, adding further bones for the ploughman to turn up. At this point, having drawn so vividly the image of soil clogged with Roman remains, irrigated by Roman blood – an image that has its origins in Virgil's *Georgics*[55] – Lucan returns to subjunctive geography to reverse the direction of the passage. Thessaly would be shunned by sailors and ploughmen alike, colonists would settle elsewhere, shepherds and their flocks would be absent, the grass would grow uncut "from our bones" (*de nostris ossibus*):

> ac, uelut inpatiens hominum uel solis iniqui
> limite uel glacie, nuda atque ignota iaceres, [*Aen* 5.871]
> si non prima nefas belli, sed sola tulisses. (*BC* 7. 866–68)

---

55. *Georgics* 1.493–97; discussion in Casali, "*Bellum civile* as an Anti-*Aeneid*," 99–101; Erica Bexley, "Lucan's Catalogues and the Landscape of War," in *Geography, Topography, Landscape: Configurations of Space in Greek and Roman Epic*, ed. Marios Skempis and Ioannis Ziogas (Berlin, 2014), 373–403, at 397–403.

and like land inhospitable to humanity, at the limit of extreme heat or cold, you would "lie naked and unknown," if you were the only war crime, not just the first.

The other scenes of civil war had "made pure" the Thessalian battle fields, Lucan concludes with bitter irony. The geography of dislocation at work in the *Bellum civile* sees Roman bodies fertilizing another soil; that soil is then imagined as a desolate place at the ends of the earth, devoid of humanity, before ultimately being reintegrated into a spatial order determined by human conflict, conjoined with the other sites of violence in a roll-call of battle fields, a geography of military infamy.

Rome in Africa

Rome in Africa, like Rome in Thessaly, is the obverse of a triumphalist narrative. After Pompey's assassination in Egypt, the ninth book of the *Bellum civile* tracks the suffering of the remnants of his army, led into the African desert by the statesman and steadfast opponent of Caesar, Marcus Porcius Cato. In an extended sequence the men march around the Syrtes, endure miseries of heat, wind, and thirst, encounter the oracle of Jupiter Ammon (which Cato pointedly refuses to consult), brave a seemingly endless catalogue of snakes, and experience several varieties of remarkable death before reaching civilization in the form of the city of Leptis. A communal lament sums up their woes towards the end of the ordeal, beginning with a simple yet devastating theme: "bring back Thessaly!" (*reddite Thessaliam*) (*BC* 9.849). Pharsalus would have been better: death in battle preferable to death by snake-bite (even the adders appear to be on Caesar's side); death by the extreme heat of the torrid zone preferable to their present hardships in the land of serpents. Two aspects of Lucan's Africa serve to illustrate the demands the *Bellum civile* made on its readers, and in turn the expectations, frustrations, and innovations his audience brought to the poem: an extended passage on a topographical feature, the Syrtes; and a description of the geographical site of Africa itself.

1. Syrtes
Searching for the kingdoms of the African monarch Juba, an old if untrustworthy ally of Pompey, Cato and his men encounter the Syrtes. These gulfs, extending along the North African coastline from Cyrenaica to Tunisia, were a standard trope of classical and medieval geographical description, which habitually dis-

tinguished a Greater and a Lesser Syrtis.[56] In the hands of poets like Lucan they offered much more than a treacherous landing point. There were, Lucan suggested, two possible explanations for their nature:

> Syrtes uel, primam mundo natura figuram
> cum daret, in dubio pelagi terraeque reliquit
> (nam neque subsedit penitus, quo stagna profundi
> acciperet, nec se defendit ab aequore tellus,
> ambigua sed lege loci iacet inuia sedes:
> aequora fracta uadis abruptaque terra profundo
> et post multa sonant proiecti litora fluctus:
> sic male deseruit nullosque exegit in usus
> hanc partem natura sui); uel plenior alto
> olim Syrtis erat pelago penitusque natabat,
> sed rapidus Titan ponto sua lumina pascens
> aequora subduxit zonae uicina perustae
> et nunc pontus adhuc Phoebo siccante repugnat;
> mox, ubi damnosum radios admouerit aeuum,
> tellus Syrtis erit: nam iam breuis unda superne
> innatat et late periturum deficit aequor. (*BC* 9.303–18)

Either: when nature gave the world its first shape it left the Syrtes in doubt between sea or land (for neither did they completely sink, so that they might accept the waters of the ocean deep, nor did the land repel the sea. Instead by the ambiguous law of the place they lie, an impassable site: sea broken up by shallows, and land sundered by the sea, where the tides resound, thrust forward across many shores: thus nature cruelly forsook this part of itself and cast it out as useless). Or: once, the Syrtis was more full with the high sea and completely covered by water, but burning Titan, nourishing its light with the sea, turned the water near to the torrid zone into a beach; up until now the sea holds back drying Phoebus; soon though, where time the destroyer brings the sun's rays of light, Syrtis will be land: even now a shallow wave floats along the surface, and the doomed sea withdraws everywhere.

The first explanation of the Syrtes sees the region in terms of a primal ambiguity, a fundamental lack of distinction: "there sea is mixed with land, and the place is

---

56. For example, Sallust, *Bellum Iugurthinum*, 78.2–3; Pliny, *Naturalis historia*, 5.26–41; Pomponius Mela, *De chorographia*, 1.35; Strabo, *Geography*, 17.3.20.

both and neither at once," as Arnulf of Orléans put it.[57] The second explanation gives a history to their position between land and sea. On this account, the Syrtes do not so much represent an original chaos, in which the boundaries between elements were indistinct, as constant interaction between earth and water, heat and moisture.[58] Here the active agent is the sun, which first burns up water in equatorial regions (known as the *zona torrida*, or *perusta* – literally, the burned-up zone), and now threatens to do the same to the Syrtes, which once constituted part of the sea; in this instance, it is water rather than land that recedes.

This topographical uncertainty is the starting point for Lucan's styling of Africa as an anti-Rome, in a comparison by no means one-sided. Lucan emphasises Africa's poverty, another ambiguous attribute, it turns out, since it aligns the Africans with Stoic hostility towards luxury, while reducing them to non-productive indigence. It is the Romans who have brought vice. The poet singles out one people for particular attention. The Nasamones are a tough, uncultivated race, literally and figuratively "nudus," "whom barbarous Syrtis nourishes with the world's losses" (quem mundi barbara damnis / Syrtis alit: *BC* 9.440–41). They survive on the nautical perils caused by the Syrtes, so that, Lucan drolly observes, "by means of shipwrecks the Nasamones have commerce with the entire world" (cum toto commercia mundo / naufragiis Nasamones habent: *BC* 9.443–44). The Syrtes start to function as an ironic Pharsalus, drawing the world by accident rather than design, but with the same result: wreckage. Amid the wreckage, Cato and his men take on this not land/not sea in the hope that "bold manhood" (*audax virtus*) may conquer Nature. At first a strong south wind assists by blowing them away from the Syrtes, but the current takes them back, and they find themselves first caught between waves and soil, and then stuck fast yet not ashore, before the survivors of the ordeal reach lake Triton (*BC* 9.348–58).

It was clear to medieval readers that Lucan had deliberately inserted different explanations of the Syrtes, without resolving the matter.[59] He also, as at least one commentary tradition pointed out, had Virgil in mind.[60] At the threshold to the underworld Aeneas had prayed to Phoebus to spare the Trojans. Phoebus has guided Aeneas to "great lands and so many seas," to far flung north African peoples, and to "fields stretched out before the Syrtes" (praetentaque Syrtibus arva: *Aen* 6.60): "now, at last, we take the shores of fleeing Italy" (iam tandem Italiae fugientis prendimus oras: *Aen* 6.61). In one sense this is a narrative of tri-

57. Arnulf of Orléans, *Glosule*, ed. Marti, 446: "est ibi cum terra mare mixtum et est utrumque sed neutrum."

58. Arnulf of Orléans, *Glosule*, ed. Marti, 446.

59. *Supplementum Adnotatianum*, 3: 82: "varias opiniones profert de Syrtibus." Arnulf of Orléans, *Glosule*, ed. Marti, 446.

60. *Commenta Bernensia*, ed. Usener, 298.

umph, of the goal reached at the end of a succession of ordeals. In another, it is a terrified plea that the Trojans may escape their trajectory of misfortune: "let Trojan luck follow us only this far" (hac Troiana tenus fuerit fortuna secuta: *Aen* 6.62). Within it the Syrtes form a counterpoint to the shores of Italy. The primal, shifting sands of the Syrtes become part of the African landscape encountered, and finally rejected, by Aeneas. In the *Bellum civile*, Lucan once again stages an inversion of Virgilian geography, taking his exiles from Rome directly into, rather than around, the Syrtes. This unravelling of *fortuna* was evident to a medieval readership. In his commentary on the *Aeneid*, Servius had explained Virgil's reference to "fields stretched out before the Syrtes" by citing Lucan's description of the Syrtes in book nine: "for seas and lands are uncertain in that place: for which reason Lucan says 'sea broken up by shallows, and land broken up by the sea.'"[61] In the circular way in which commentary sometimes operates, the *Commenta Bernensia* in turn recycled Servius' comment by citing Virgil to explain Lucan's line: "for seas and lands there are uncertain. Thus Virgil, 'fields stretched out before the Syrtes.'"[62] The comparison is revealing. Even as Aeneas and his men skirt the Syrtes and attain Italy, so Cato and his crew approach, enter, and founder upon them, their own fortune to be driven to the ends of the earth.

In medieval literary culture the Syrtes became a metaphor familiar enough to be deployed in a variety of contexts. They were used for changes of fortune (adversity following hard on the heels of prosperity),[63] or religious error and intellectual confusion: the world may seem a placid sea, warned Eriugena, but without divine *clementia* it was "dangerous due to the stretches of the Syrtes (that is, the currents of unknown doctrine)."[64] The Syrtes were frequently linked with Scylla and Charybdis to form a trio of nautical perils.[65] In Walter of Châtillon's twelfth-century epic, the *Alexandreis*, Alexander the Great's entry into Africa occasions deliberate echoes of the *Bellum civile*. Alexander and his men, on a detour from their conquest of Asia, get more than they bargain for when they go searching in

61. Servius, *Commentarii*, 2: 15 (at *Aen* 6.60): "incerta enim sunt illic maria et terrae: unde ait Lucanus aequora fracta vadis abruptaque terra profundo."

62. *Commenta Bernensia*, ed. Usener, 298: "incerta enim illic sunt maria et terrae. ut Virgilius 'praetentaque Syrtibus arua.'"

63. See Stephanus de Borbone, *Tractatus de diversis materiis predicabilibus* 1.9, 2 vols, ed. Jacques Berlioz and Jean-Luc Eichenlaub (Turnhout, 2002), 1: 349; Coluccio, *De laboribus Herculis* 3.33.12–13, ed. Ullman, 359.

64. *Iohannis Scotti seu Eriugenae Periphyseon* 4.744A, ed. Édouard A. Jeauneau (Turnhout, 2000), 5: "tractibus syrtium (hoc est incognitae doctrinae ductibus) periculosus."

65. Isidore treats the Syrtes immediately after Scylla and Charybdis in a section on tides and gulfs: *Etymologiae*, 13.18.4–6. See Walter Map, "De ruina Romae," in *The Latin Poems Commonly Attributed to Walter Mapes*, ed. Thomas Wright (London, 1841), 217–22, at ll. 19–30, 73.

the desert for the oracle of Jupiter. They encounter dry storms, as Walter transplants the imagery of Scylla and Charybdis across the Mediterranean:

> procellas
> Hic Syrtes habuere suas. hic altera sicco
> Scilla mari latrat, hic puluerulenta Caribdis.
> Puluereos uomit ille globos, iacet ille sepultus
> In sabulo.[66]

Here the Syrtes have their well-known storms, here a second Scylla barks on a dry sea, here a dust-covered Charybdis. One soldier vomited particles of dust, another lay buried in the sand.

Walter's Africa is Lucan's Africa: a land of heat and dust, of infertility and death, but also a land with a moral function in relation to Europe. In the hands of Lucan and his successors Africa was not simply anti-Europe, but a *ne plus ultra* of empire and commerce, ambition beached. The Syrtes were its treacherous point of entry: an admixture of elements that held fast and forbad further passage.

2. *Partes*

Africa's position in the *Bellum civile*, at once opposed and inextricably linked to Europe, is well captured in the description Lucan gives of it in book nine. Africa is the third part of the world (*Tertia pars rerum Libye*), the poet announces, following the standard division between the three *partes* of Asia, Europa, and Libya/Africa. But then he goes on: "if you go by winds and sky it will be a part of Europe" (si uentos caelumque sequaris, / pars erit Europae).

> ... Nec enim plus litora Nili
> quam Scythicus Tanais primis a Gadibus absunt,
> unde Europa fugit Libyen et litora flexu
> Oceano fecere locum. Sed maior in unam
> orbis abit Asiam: nam, cum communiter istae
> effundant zephyrum, boreae latus illa sinistrum
> contingens dextrumque noti discedit in ortus
> eurum sola tenens. (*BC* 9.413–20)

66. Walter of Châtillon, *Alexandreis* 3.378–82, ed. Marvin L. Colker (Padua, 1978), 82.

For the shores of the Nile are not further than Scythian Tanais is from Gades in the far west, whence Europe flees Africa and shores made room for the Ocean's influx. But a greater part of the world consists in Asia alone: for, when Europe and Africa pour forth the west wind (Zephyrus), Asia extending to the left of the north wind (Boreas) and to the right of the south wind (Notus), departs to the east holding the east wind (Eurus) in its sole possession.

On one hand Lucan elides the division between Europe and Africa here. There are symmetries between the two *partes*: their rivers, Africa's Nile and Europe's Tanais (the Don) are equidistant from the far west (the Gades, i.e. the entrance to the Mediterranean), and they share a wind. These factors argue for their union, in which, for reasons unexplained, Europe takes priority. On the other hand, the description draws attention to the interposition of Ocean to form the Mediterranean, and the "flight" of Europe from Africa. It reasserts the separation of the two *partes* even as it makes the case (*enim ... nam*) for their contiguity. Two aspects of this brief, and perhaps conflicted, allusion to geography are nevertheless consistent with the rest of the *Bellum civile*. First, Europe and European history is overshadowed by Asia, which in size matches or even exceeds Europe and Africa combined, and which has one wind all to itself and a part share of the north and south winds. Second, Lucan insists on passage away from Rome. In contrast to Virgil's decisive move towards Latium and Rome, Lucan articulates a world image as the action of his poem moves into ever more extreme spaces – the Syrtes, the equatorial torrid zone, and even, in a few delirious moments, the antipodes.[67]

Like other passages in the *Bellum civile*, Lucan's description of Africa in book nine generated visual as well as verbal glosses. Commentators grappled with the poet's apparent ambivalence about the number of parts of the world. As the *Commenta Bernensia* pointed out, Lucan seemed to echo a statement made in Varro's *De lingua Latina*, in which the world was divided in two between Asia and Europe.[68] But the commentary also pointed out that there was authority for dividing the world into three or even – following Timosthenes of Rhodes –

67. References to the antipodes occur at *BC* 8.159–64 (a possible place of refuge for Pompey); 9.876–78 (Cato and his men so deep in Africa that Rome may be literally underfoot: "sub pedibus"); and 10.36–45 (Alexander's ambition to conquer the other side of the world is remembered). See Hiatt, *Terra Incognita*, 28–29, for discussion.

68. Varro, *De lingua latina* 5.31–32, ed. G. Goetz and F. Schoell (Leipzig, 1910), 11. Lucan would also have had Sallust, *Bellum Iugurthinum*, 17.3 in mind: "In diuisione orbis terrae plerique in parte tertia Africam posuere, pauci tantummodo Asiam et Europam esse, sed Africam in Europa."

four parts.[69] In explaining 9.415 – "Europa fugit Libyen" – Arnulf of Orléans argued that Lucan was referring here to the Mediterranean's division of the two land masses, but this left the problem of why Europe should "flee" Libya, and not vice-versa. Lucan's "fugit" disrupts the geometric precision of the tripartite division of the world, and also surely alludes to the rape of Europa. According to Arnulf, though, Lucan said that Europe fled Libya rather than Libya fled Europe "because of the worth (*dignitas*) of Europe, since more worthy flees the less worthy."[70] By supplementing the trope of flight with the concept of *dignitas*, Arnulf arguably added a moral, but also diachronic, resonance to the poet's enigmatic comment. Two lines earlier he used the same word to explain Lucan's suggestion that Africa could be considered part of Europe: "he said Libya could be part of Europe on account of the *dignitas* of Rome, which is in Europe."[71] Rome here may be understood as both the seat of empire, and seat of the papacy, sign of Europe's greater worthiness in both Christian and pre-Christian eras.

In medieval copies of the *Bellum civile* the words "Tertia pars rerum Libye" (Africa is the third part of the world) routinely prompted a world map. Such maps usually identify the tripartite division of the world, along with cardinal points and, following the cues in the passage itself, the winds. Only occasionally did manuscripts contain a more elaborate map, with extensive nomenclature; these images usually appear at the front or back of the codex. In this position they take on a rather different function to that of a straightforward gloss. They invoke, of course, a more detailed geography, one that could be aligned with Lucan's concept of the Civil War as, at once, a Roman and a world conflict. But the alignment was never complete: the more detailed *mappae mundi* in Lucan manuscripts do not act as an index of the poem. Some of their toponyms derive from other sources, such as Sallust's account of north Africa in the *Bellum*

---

69. *Commenta Bernensia*, ed. Usener, 301: "quidam diuiserunt orbem in duas partes, ut Varro, id est Asiam et Europam, quidam in tris Asiam Europam et Africam, ut Alexander [Cornelius Alexander Milesius], quidam in quatuor adiecta Aegypto, ut Timosthenes." Timosthenes's description of the world survives only in fragments, one of which is the remark contained in the *Commenta Bernensia*; his division seems to have been into Asia, Egypt, Libya, and Europe: Emil August Wagner, *Die Erdbeschreibung des Timosthenes von Rhodus* (Leipzig, 1888). The question of division between the *partes* became relatively commonplace in medieval descriptions of the known world. Key discussions can be found in Augustine, *De civitate dei*, 16.17; Orosius, *Historiae*, 1.2.1; Isidore, *Etymologiae*, 14.2.1–3.

70. Arnulf of Orléans, *Glosule*, ed. Marti, 454: "potius dicit fugere Libiam cum etiam Libia fugiat eam pro dignitate Europe, que dignior fugit indigniorem."

71. Arnulf of Orléans, *Glosule*, ed. Marti, 453: "Sed quare dixit Libiam potius esse partem Europe quam Europam Libie, sic soluitur: pro dignitate Rome que est in Europa."

Iugurthinum, and they lack many of the places mentioned by Lucan. Other meanings and interpretations accreted to these images and thereby, subtly, to the poem itself. A world map that appears at the end of one thirteenth-century manuscript of the *Bellum civile* is accompanied by a text that explains the division of the earth in decidedly non-Lucanian terms as the result of the generative activities of the three sons of Noah (Figure 9).[72] On this map, as on all other maps that illustrate the *Bellum civile*, Ilerda and Massilia find no place in Europe. The river Danube and the (medieval) region of Hungary do appear, however, along with explicitly Christian locations such as the earthly paradise. Other regions and cities, such as India, Judaea, Jerusalem, and Rome itself bridge Christian and antique cultures. This and other maps of its kind do not seek a purity of historical geography in the manner of a later, humanist-inflected cartography. Consistent with the verbal glosses of classical texts, they render antiquity comprehensible, but the way to do so was not wholly to sunder it from medieval contexts. Lucan's words, Lucan's winds, Lucan's world remain discernable on the *mappae mundi* in manuscripts of the *Bellum civile*. Yet such maps are critical reformulations of that antique knowledge: distillations, summations, and re-presentations for a later audience that peered, scratched, glossed, allegorized furiously, struggled to comprehend, and in so doing preserved an image of classical geography.

Epilogue: Lucan's *Tristia*

Ovid's journey into exile received at least one detailed cartographic representation during the course of the Middle Ages. A manuscript compiled in the mid-fifteenth century in Norfolk, England, contains a fairly precise attempt to depict the account of the poet's voyage to the Black Sea contained in *Tristia* 1.10 (Figure 10).[73] This map extends from the Adriatic to the "island" of Pontus and the city of Miletus. It contains no obvious reference to Ovid, yet the image makes little sense unless it is read alongside the narrative in the *Tristia*, at which point its function as a visualisation of the itinerary becomes clear. The place names recorded follow *Tristia* 1.10 closely. From Corinth, through Samos, the Helle-

---

72. Copenhagen, Kongelige Bibliotek, Gl. Kgl. S. 2020, fol. 102r; the manuscript's origin is uncertain, but may be German.

73. Dublin, Trinity College Dublin, MS 632, fols. 108v–109r. For extended discussion see Alfred Hiatt, "A Map of Ovid's *Tristia* I.10 in Dublin, Trinity College MS 632," *Journal of the Warburg and Courtauld Institutes* 75 (2012): 31–51.

spont, and Sestos and Abydos, and on to Mesambre and "Bachis," the map faithfully traces the itinerary outlined by Ovid.[74] Finally at the top left of the image appears the site of Ovid's exile, "Pontus insula": the "island" of the Black Sea, or the Black Sea as island. This map emerges from a literary work, yet in its manuscript – which may ultimately derive from the Benedictine monastery of St Albans in Hertfordshire, an institution with a rich historiographical and cartographic legacy – it appears amid a miscellany of information about classical texts, divorced from its crucial context, and with no explanation of what it is. The orthography of several place names testifies to the vagaries of manuscript transmission, and in at least one case a place has moved because of mistakes in copying. According to Ovid, Tempyra is on the coast opposite to "Thracian Samos" (the island of Samothrace, but easily understood as the city of Samos). On the map Samos and Tempyra appear alongside each other, almost certainly because the mapmaker's manuscript read "ab hac *terra* ... est Tempyra" (along from this land, i.e. Thracian Samos, is Tempyra), rather than the original's "ab hac *contra* ... est Tempyra." However, such minor dislocations pale into insignificance by comparison with the dramatic, non-naturalistic step taken by the compiler of this image. For to the map of Ovid's *Tristia* are conjoined three subsidiary images: a map of Sicily, similar in type to the depictions of the island that appear in medieval *mappae mundi*, and two diagrams derived from Lucan's *Bellum civile*, one showing the port of Brundisium and the other the relationship of the Apennines, Sicily, and Italy.

By adding diagrams that glossed the *Bellum civile* to the map of Ovid's exile, the compiler wove together at least two texts and several strands of association. These images do in some sense figure the totality of Ovid's journey from Italy to the Black Sea. On the other hand, the addition of material derived from the *Bellum civile* inevitably adduces non-Ovidian contexts, such as the remarks on the

---

74. The full sequence, with reference to the *Tristia* 1.10, is: Corinth (1.10.9), a "Portus," presumably "portus, Imbria terra, tuos" to which the poet heads (1.10.18); the "Cirincia litora" (Zerynthia litora, 1.10.19); Samos (1.10.20, for Samothrace); "Tentirra" (Tempyra, 1.10.21); the Hellespont (1.10.24); Dardania (1.10.25); "Lapsas" (Lampsacus, 1.10.26); Sestos and Abydos (1.10.28); "Cyzicyn" (for Cyzicos, 1.10.29) opposite Constantinopolis (for Byzantium, 1.10.30). "Cymochi" or "Cyniochi" is apparently a corruption of Ovid's "Thyniacos sinus" of 1.10.35; it is followed by Cyane (Ovid's Cyaneae of 1.10.34), an "urbs Archelas" (derived from 1.10.35–36: "per Apollinis urbem / alta [acta/arta] sub Anchiali moenia"), Mesambre ("Mesembriacos ... arces": 1.10.37), "Obesus" (for Odesos, 1.10.37), "Bachis" (the "arces ... Bacche" of 1.10.37–38), and the "populi alcaciones" ("quos Alcathoi memorant e moenibus ortos / sedibus his profugos constituisse Larem": 1.10.39–40).

extent of the Apennines made by Lucan and a host of classical authorities. The island of Sicily, a key site within the *Aeneid*, perhaps abounds more in Virgilian than Ovidian resonance. Might we even read this image in reverse, from the absent Troy in the vicinity of Dardania to Sicily, and see something of the wanderings of Aeneas and his followers in the third book of the *Aeneid*? Certainly the conjunction of Lucanian matter opens the image up, renders it no longer unilinear – if, in the wake of Ovid's pluralistic reference, it ever was. The image splices together spatial fragments, and duplications and incongruities ensue: the Adriatic appears twice, as does Sicily, once off the coast of Brundisium, and again at the junction of the Adriatic and the Aegean, in both instances out of place.

The map of *Tristia* 1.10 appears at the end of an appendix to a commentary on Ovid's *Metamorphoses* by the chronicler and monk of St Albans, Thomas Walsingham (d. c. 1422). To supplement his commentary on the *Metamorphoses*, Walsingham produced a guide to classical mythology, including genealogies of the descent of the gods, lists of major poets and their works, and notes on topics such as the muses and the Minotaur, as well as classical geography. These topics are illustrated with eight diagrams, ranging from images of the underworld, the Minotaur's labyrinth, and the mountains Parnassus and Cithaeron, to the classical system of winds, planetary circles, and the five terrestrial zones.[75] Two of the diagrams show Thessaly and its five principal mountains, the image that originally illustrated Lucan's *Bellum civile* 6.333–59. The emphasis of Walsingham's appendix is on instruction, and while it may not have been a classroom compilation, it clearly does have a function as a reference tool, drawing on existing images which derive from centuries of glossing ancient texts. The map of Ovid's exile, conceivably Walsingham's own construction, but more likely a later addition to his text,[76] was originally a visual gloss designed to furnish a quite literal interpretation of a passage dense in topographic reference. It takes on a new position in a compilation on myth, at least semi-independent of its origins in the poetry of Ovid and Lucan. But what image is this? A map of the ancient world? A map of a single passage of a poem? A map of a spatial order, once vital, now defunct – or

75. Trinity College Dublin MS 632, fols. 90v–108r. The manuscript is described in M.L. Colker, *Trinity College Library Dublin: Descriptive Catalogue of the Mediaeval and Renaissance Latin Manuscripts*, 2 vols (Aldershot, 1991), 2: 1093–1108.

76. Walsingham's supplement to his commentary on Ovid, the *Archana Deorum*, survives in three medieval manuscripts: Oxford, St John's College, MS 124 (early to mid fifteenth century); London, British Library, MS Lansdowne 728 (second half of the fifteenth century), and Trinity College Dublin MS 632; of these, only the Dublin manuscript has a map, placed at the end of the compilation. For an edition of the *Archana Deorum* see *De Archana Deorum*, ed. Robert A. van Kluyve (Durham, 1968).

of an order once vital, and still fundamental and fascinating for an audience fifteen centuries after the poem's initial publication? The image was all of these things, surely, otherwise it would not have been drawn. The old order had changed, but it had not vanished. The task for the many medieval readers and commentators on ancient texts was to understand that order in relation to their own mutated, mutating geographies.

Dialogue in Hell between Two Readers I

> Ramon Fernandez, tell me, if you know,
> Why, when the singing ended and we turned
> Toward the town, tell why the glassy lights,
> The lights in the fishing boats at anchor there,
> As the night descended, tilting in the air,
> Mastered the night and portioned out the sea,
> Fixing emblazoned zones and fiery poles,
> Arranging, deepening, enchanting night.
>
> Oh! Blessed rage for order, pale Ramon,
> The maker's rage to order words of the sea,
> Words of the fragrant portals, dimly-starred,
> And of ourselves and of our origins,
> In ghostlier demarcations, keener sounds.
>
>   Wallace Stevens, "The Idea of Order at Key West."

WS: Reading that last chapter certainly brought book nine of Lucan's *Civil War* to mind – its monumental length seems to mimic the wanderings of Cato and his men in the desert; the reader doesn't know if it will ever end ...

RF: And yet when the chapter does end, it's as inconclusive as the *Bellum civile*'s book ten, which most people think is unfinished on account of Lucan's untimely death.

WS: I wonder whether some thinking about the nature of order is missing from this discussion.

RF: What do you mean?

WS: We can understand order as monolithic, and we can with an ironic lens see the attempt to impose order as the precondition of a pluralistic disorder. Two names for the same place, two places with the same name, border lines that invite dissolution and contradiction, sea becoming land and vice versa. Identification, categorisation endlessly undone. Yet perhaps that is to misunderstand order. What if it is the other way around, and the precondition of order is multiplicity? The point was neatly made some time ago in an essay by Ernst Cassirer: "The concept of order, in contrast to the unity and rigidity of the concept of being, is from the beginning distinguished by the moment of differentiation and inner multiplicity. ... the manifold is the life-element for order; it is only through this that order can exist and develop."[1] We are now suspicious of order and naturally keen to celebrate disruption; but Cassirer's suggestion that order can support, codify, and even engender pluralism, rather than repress it, might be remembered.

RF: Yet the urge to unstitch order is as ancient as the rage to create it. Remember in Ovid's *Metamorphoses* how in book one the divine maker orders protean Chaos, dividing the elements, shaping the land, arranging the winds, and instituting five terrestrial zones – two snowy, one burning, and two temperate ones for habitation. First Jupiter floods the earth in order to punish humanity. Then, in the next book, Phaeton persuades his father, the sun, to let him drive his chariot. The son loses control of the sun, failing to take the "middle way": the accustomed path is not taken, ice melts, rivers boil, seas shrivel, the earth is scorched, and a return to Chaos is prevented only by Phaeton's plummet to his death. The representation of order immediately invites its transgression – and its restoration comes at a terrible cost. If we turn to non-literary attempts to represent geographical order, like Pliny's or Strabo's or even Ptolemy's, we find that what they describe is incomplete, anachronistic, inconsistent. Geographical order is also retrospective. It tries to account for a state of spatial being which at its cosmic level is open to debate (how many zones are there: five or six? where do they begin?) and which at a terrestrial level is always in flux.

WS: Isn't there a danger here of overemphasising instability, flux, and so forth? Yes, Ptolemy observed the inaccuracy of his predecessors and the necessity of relying on reports, but he also fixed locations according to mathematical princi-

1. Ernst Cassirer, "Mythic, Aesthetic, and Theoretical Space," trans. Donald Phillip Verene and Lerke Holzwarth Foster, *Man and World* 2 (1969): 3–17, at 8, originally published as "Mythischer, ästhetischer und theoretischer Raum," *Zeitschrift für Ästhetik und allgemeine Kunstwissenschaft* 25 (1931): 21–36.

ples. Those co-ordinates survived, they were used through the Middle Ages, by Arabo-Islamic authors as well as Christian ones, and they came to enjoy immense prestige in European geographical thought of the fifteenth and sixteenth centuries.

RF: True, but Ptolemy was never the only game in town. Even when he was "rediscovered" in fifteenth-century Europe thanks to the translation of the *Geography* into Latin, he was read according to existing humanist concerns and not initially celebrated as a mathematical geographer. Before long the translation of Strabo into Latin offered another, and to a certain degree competing, way of understanding and describing space. So maybe what we need is an open, contingent understanding of "order." One that sees spatial order as imperfect and in need of constant renewal, but also recursive: looking back, trying to recover past ways of organising space.

WS: And why not extend the same level of flexibility to chaos, allowing the possibility that disorder may also have constructive moments, may be born out of construction?

RF: Returning to historical contexts, I'm left wondering how meaningful are the distinctions (to some extent observed in this book) between classical, medieval, and humanist spatial orders.

WS: It is fashionable to question such boundaries, but surely you would admit that the differences brought by Christian thought, and by the effort of preserving pre-Christian orders within Christian thought, are real? Similarly, the fault line between humanism and scholastic thought may be staged, but it is impossible to deny – there are new ideological factors in play which lead to the separation of ancient from modern, to the anatomization of the antique.

RF: So then we need to see such distinctions as at once constructed, real, and permeable. And to admit that these temporal distinctions are also spatial ones. The Roman Empire is a space; as is Christendom; as is the humanist "republic of letters," for all its attempts to evade political, sectarian, and geographical borders.

CHAPTER FIVE

Mutatio

Few historical maps have surpassed the *Romani Imperii Imago* of Abraham Ortelius as a statement of political and intellectual authority. First published in 1571, and from 1579 onwards incorporated into Ortelius's great atlas, the *Theatrum Orbis Terrarum*, this was the first map to show the Roman Empire in detail, with modern place names excised (Figure 11). Fundamentally humanist in its sensibility, Ortelius's *Romani Imperii Imago* articulates at once the profound differences between the Roman world and his own, and the translation of political power and spatial dominion from antiquity to modernity. At the top of the map, two medallions contain the heads of Roma and Romulus, accompanied by inscriptions which extol the city's eternal fame, and its destiny to rule over foreign lands.[1] In the frame's lower register a prominent cartouche contains a "brief account of the origin, growth, and height of the Roman Empire" in which the rule of the city extends first "no further than to Portus and Ostia within a radius of 18 miles," then, under the consuls, to all Italy, until it finally swells to the point that its "borders were the ocean in the west, in the north the Rhine and the Danube, in the east the Tigris, and in the south the Atlas mountain range. All of which is shown on this map."[2] At the bottom right of the image a genealogical tree displays the seven kings of Rome from Romulus to Tarquinius Superbus, a line of descent that also marks the rise of the city's political power, topped by the she-wolf suckling her cubs. The assertion of Rome's pre-eminence is unqualified. The reader is invited to understand the history of Rome's political transition from monarchy to repub-

---

1. The inscriptions – "Roma tuum nomen terris fatale regendis" (Rome, your name [is] destined to hold power over lands), and "Romulo urbis aeternae conditori" (to Romulus, founder of the eternal city) – derive from the first-century BC poet Albius Tibullus: *Albii Tibulli aliorumque Carmina* 2.5.57, ed. Georg Luck (Stuttgart, 1988), 61. References to the text of Ortelius's "Romani Imperii Imago" are to the map printed in the *Parergon* contained within the *Theatrum Orbis Terrarum* (Antwerp, 1579).

2. "Originis, Incrementi, et Culminis Imperii Romani, breuis enumeratio": "Primo sub Regibus septem Romulo, Seruio, etc. per annos ducentos et tres supra quadraginta, non amplius quam usque Portum, atque Hostiam, intra decimum octauum miliarium Romanum processit Imperium ... Cuius limites fuere ad Occidentem Oceanus, a Septentrione Rhenus et Danubius, ab Oriente Tigris, a Meridie Atlas mons. quae omnia in hac tabula ... ponuntur."

lic to empire as a narrative of expansion, and to follow that history on the map, moving through Italy, then western Europe, across to north Africa, and finally into the Black Sea and Asia Minor. On later versions of the image, Ortelius buttressed the empire's legitimacy still further by inserting just to the right of the title a sentence from Vitruvius's *De architectura*: "The divine mind established a city of the Roman people in an excellent and temperate region, so that it might take the world into its possession."[3] This sentence encapsulates a species of geographic determinism elaborated in book six of *De architectura*. Using the simile of a stringed instrument (the sambuca, a kind of harp), Vitruvius claimed that Rome was perfectly positioned between northern strength and southern intelligence, or – following his analogy – between the long and the short strings of the sambuca.[4]

Ortelius's *Romani Imperii Imago* is an image of culmination, height, and plenitude, but also one of incompletion. There are lacunae in the genealogy, empty circles that denote missing ancestors and that mark the gaps in the historian's knowledge. Nor is the geographical content of the map without complexity. The image shows the empire at an imagined moment of maximum spatial extent, from Britain to Asia, and as a consequence it leaves the regions beyond the empire – Germania, Sarmatia, the lands of barbarian tribes such as the Getae – devoid of detail. As he must have known, no map of the kind Ortelius produced had ever existed during the Roman Empire. Consciously anachronistic, the *Romani Imperii Imago* nevertheless tries to remove or downplay anachronism, posing as a synchronic map of the empire at a single, never defined, time.

Beyond anachronism, the complications of the *Romani Imperii Imago* encompass a swirl of sixteenth-century ideology and historical debate. The map of the Roman Empire appeared in 1579 as one of just three cartographic images contained in Ortelius's *Parergon,* the appendix to the modern maps in the *Theatrum Orbis Terrarum* (the other two showed the travels of St Paul, and Greece).[5] In the title page to the *Parergon*, Ortelius explained that he had constructed its maps for the benefit of students of ancient history, both profane and sacred.

3. "Diuina mens ciuitatem populi Romani egregia temperataque regione collocauit, uti Orbis terrarum imperio potiretur." Cf. Vitruvius, *De architectura (De l'Architecture)* 6.1.11, ed. Louis Callebat (Paris, 2004), 11: "... uti orbis terrarum imperii potiretur." The Vitruvius quotation was added in 1592: see Marcel van den Broecke, *Ortelius Atlas Maps: An Illustrated Guide*, 2nd ed. (Houten, 2011), 573–75.

4. On Vitruvius and Roman identity see Andrew Wallace-Hadrill, *Rome's Cultural Revolution* (Cambridge, 2008), 144–210.

5. See George Tolias, "Glose, contemplation, et méditation: Histoire éditoriale et fonctions du *Parergon* d'Abraham Ortelius (1579–1624)," in *Les méditations cosmographiques à la Renaissance*, ed. Frank Lestringant (Paris, 2009), 157–86. The *Parergon* swelled dramatically in the succeeding decades, to the extent that by the time of Ortelius's death in 1598 it consisted of thirty maps and two views.

Although he had initially excluded these maps – "for they seemed to have nothing to do with our purpose in this *Theatrum*, in which I intended to show only the site of contemporary places" – the pleas of friends persuaded him to print them "at the foot of this our work, as a Parergon."[6] Ortelius's own description of these maps gives them an ambiguous status: at the end of the work, grafted on, they are also foundational. In showing the world as it was, not as it is, the maps of the *Parergon* enacted the Ortelian motto of "geography the eye of history" and, in the enlarged form of later editions, they constituted, as one recent commentator has aptly put it, no less than "a cartographic and literary archaeology of the western world, an atlas of the Republic of Letters."[7]

The *Romani Imperii Imago* evidently represents one thematic strand of the *Parergon*, that of secular history. Several maps that appeared in subsequent editions developed this strand. By 1595, for instance, in addition to the three introduced in 1579, the *Parergon* boasted maps of Celtic Europe and the British Isles in antiquity, along with (in order) ancient Spain, Gaul, the Netherlands, Germania, Pannonia and Illyria, Italy, Etruria, Latium, Magna Graecia (that is, the southern part of Italy), Sicily, Thrace, Dacia and Moesia, the Black Sea, islands of the Aegean Sea, the campaign(s) of Alexander the Great, Palestine, Judaea and Israel, Ancient Egypt, Africa, the travels of St Paul, Abraham, and Aeneas, along with the *loci amoeni* of Tempe (in Thessaly) and Daphne (near Antioch). In the course of his commentaries on these maps (which appeared on the verso of the double pages on which they were printed in the *Parergon*), Ortelius made clear their significance for the understanding of history. In particular, Ortelius used his commentary on the historical maps to air a theory, buttressed by the pseudo-etymologies of the Dutch physician and lexicographer Joannes Goropius Becanus, that the first inhabitants of Europe were the Celts, and that they were the ancestors of the Germanic peoples. Goropius had maintained that Dutch – not Hebrew, as was more commonly thought – was the language spoken in paradise, and that the ancestors of the modern Dutch, the Cimmerians, were unique among humanity in not having participated in the Tower of Babel.[8] In the maps of Celtic Europe and Germania in the *Parergon*, and in his commentaries thereon, Ortelius propagated a version of this theory, whereby continuities of Celtic (and Cimmerian) culture lingered in the present day, in "common and familiar" words

---

6. *Theatrum* (1579), sig. 91: "nihil enim ad nostrum in hoc Theatro, quo tantum hodiernum regionum situm exhibere proposueram, institutum facere videbantur ... eas in huius nostri operis calcem, tamquam parergon, reieci."

7. Tolias, "Glose, contemplation," 168.

8. Joannes Goropius Becanus, *Origines Antwerpianae, sive Cimmeriorum Becceselana novem libros complexa* (Antwerp, 1569), e.g. 533–41; see John Considine, *Dictionaries in Early Modern Europe: Lexicography and the Making of Heritage* (Cambridge, 2008), 141–45.

such as "Kelt" (printed in Gothic lettering in contrast to the Latin typeface used throughout the rest of the *Theatrum*):

> I think that this Celtic region and its peoples, called Celts by the most ancient Greek writers, is hidden to nobody who studies ancient history. The name Kelt persisted among them, and even now they [i.e. Germans] call each other by this term in common speech.[9]

As this quotation suggests, Ortelius sought to conjoin the linguistic "evidence" of Goropius with classical Greek and Latin sources. The latter could not be bypassed, since they remained the only substantial ancient authority for European history and topography. But they could be reinterpreted in light of the traces of antiquity still discernable in contemporary linguistic forms. This revisionism extended to the very name "Europe." The word "Europa," Ortelius proposed – quoting Goropius – was not derived from the name of the daughter of Agenor seized by Jupiter. It was in fact a Greek version of the original Celtic word, whose first two letters had been reversed in the process of recording speech in writing:

> Our ancestors did not say "europ" but "uerop," by which term they denoted an outstanding multitude of people: this is because "uer," a monosyllable lengthened by a dipthong, means "great," "superior," and that which in whatsoever thing is most outstanding. Some wrote this "ur," without a dipthong, but with a long vowel. So "europ" derived from "uerop" (as Tereus from Terues), and became "Europa."[10]

9. From the revised text accompanying the "Germaniae veteris typus" in the 1595 edition of the *Theatrum*: "Celticam hanc regionem, et Celtos siue Celtas eius populos, a vetustissimis scriptoribus Graecis in primis, vocatos, neminem priscae historiae studiosum latere puto. vnde perdurat apud hos Kelt vocabulum, quo se mutuo in familiari colloquio etiamnum appellitant." A similar point was made in the commentary on "Europa Celtica": "Sin vero, Germanos ipsos audiat, qui hactenus Kelt in familari colloquio sese mutuo nominant." On the texts on the verso of Ortelius's maps see Marcel van den Broecke, "The Significance of Language: The Texts on the Verso of the Maps in Abraham Ortelius, *Theatrum Orbis Terrarum*," *Imago Mundi* 60 (2008): 202–10. Goropius proposed a different etymology for "Celt," identifying it as meaning "money," from the German *Gelt*: Joannes Goropius Becanus, *Opera Ioan. Goropii Becani, hactenus in lucem non edita, nempe: Hermathena, Hieroglyphica, Vertumnus, Gallica, Francica, Hispanica* (Antwerp, 1580), "Gallica," 45–46.

10. The commentary appears on the verso of the double-page map of "Europa Celtica," which was added to 1595 edition of the *Parergon*: "Uerop itaque non Europ, nostri dixerunt, quo excellentem hominum multitudinem denotabant: eo quod Uer monosyllabum per Dipthongon elatum, magnum, excellens, et id quod in quaque re praestantissimum est, sig-

Yet at the same time as he advanced Goropius's radical origin myth, Ortelius also reiterated the more standard theory of *translatio imperii*, one in which the Roman Empire had been translated first to Byzantium (the Greeks), and then to the Franks – or, as Ortelius regarded them, Germans – in the form of Charlemagne. The Holy Roman Empire had thereafter remained in the possession of the Germans, down to the recent emperors Charles V and Philip II. In a brief text that introduced the *Romani Imperii Imago*, Ortelius quoted the fourth-century historian Ammianus Marcellinus's personification of the Roman people from infancy to old age, in which passage into adulthood was marked by the crossing of the Alps, full manhood by the conquest of the world, and senior years by increased tranquillity.[11] Ortelius then added the thought that the Roman *imperium* was part of a sequence of empires, running from the Assyrians, Persians, and Macedonians, and being taken up after the Romans by the Ottomans, Persians, Tartars, and the Empire of Prester John. His map, Ortelius concluded, showed that the rule established by the emperor Charles V (and now maintained by his successor, Philip II) was greater, in terms of geographical extent, than all of them.[12] The purpose of the *Romani Imperii Imago*, then, was to provide a spatial and historical context for the emergent European political power displayed in the *Theatrum*'s maps of the Americas and the east Indies. The blank spaces beyond the extent of the Roman Empire on Ortelius's map corresponded to the blank spaces on the maps of sixteenth-century empires, engaged as they were in the exploration and charting of the New World.

As epitomized by Ortelius's *Romani Imperii Imago*, historical geography was clearly far from straightforward. Any apparent neutrality of view was negated by the uncertainty of the historical record, by the controversial and often tendentious narratives that underlay the map, and by its function as both a reconstruction of the past and commentary on the present. These complexities make it hard to support a triumphalist narrative of Renaissance positivism, in which humanists such as Ortelius swept aside "medieval" error and instilled order and indeed mathematical precision in the presentation of history.[13] Undoubtedly remarkable, innovative and pivotal, Ortelius's map nevertheless responded to pressing problems in the representation of spatial history. Those problems were not new:

nificet: quod alii Ur, citra diphthongon, vocali tamen longa, scribunt. Ex Uerop ergo Europ factum; vt ex Terues Tereus, Europam produxit." Cf. *Origines Antwerpianae*, 1045. Ortelius then cited Goropius's alternative interpretation of "Europa" as "great (*ur*) hope (*hop*) of marriage (*E*)" see *Opera ... non edita*: "Hermathena," 11; "Francica," 105–7.

11. Ammianus Marcellinus, *Res gestae*, 1: 14.6.3–4.

12. *Theatrum* (1579), sig. 92.

13. On the sixteenth-century "mathematization of the world," see David Wootton, *The Invention of Science: A New History of the Scientific Revolution* (London, 2015), 163–210.

they can be found in the work of many earlier authors, humanist and non-humanist alike, who struggled to define the relationship of their own culture to that of the classical texts, images, and other artefacts that they inherited, copied, and adapted. In the following pages I will argue that two intertwined concepts, evident on the *Romani Imperii Imago*, characterise the responses of medieval and early modern geographical thought to the problems of dislocation wrought by historical change. *Translatio* – the translation, or transferral, of political and cultural identity from place to place—promised a profound level of identity between present and past. *Mutatio* – the propensity of human and natural geography to change over the course of time – raised the possibility of the distortion and, at worst, the irrecoverable loss of past forms. These concepts, which articulated but did not equate precisely with the notions of continuity and change, operated across a range of texts from the early Middle Ages onwards. Their significance for spatial representation requires, first, a study of the presence of *mutatio* within standard medieval formulations of the theory of *translatio imperii*, and subsequently, examination of humanist formulations of the translation and mutation of places, peoples, and ideas.

Empires Present and Absent

There is nothing directly comparable to Ortelius's *Parergon* in the Middle Ages. Does this fact indicate a different perception of history on the part of medieval scholars – or worse still, a failure of historical sensitivity? Or were there ways in which medieval historians did attempt to chart the passage from antiquity to modernity? The evidence of medieval geographical writing suggests that, throughout the Middle Ages, the representation of space demanded an investigation of ancient history and literature. By the same token, the study of the past prompted reflection on spatial history, including detailed comparison between different historical periods.[14] Medieval geographical texts also reveal something of the complexity of the concept of *translatio*. The linear model of political and spatial translation from era to era was undoubtedly important to the conceptualisation of history and geography in the Middle Ages. But it was continually dislocated by elements antithetical to the construction of ordered genealogies of

---

14. Fundamental discussions of this topic can be found in Marica Milanesi, "Per una storia della geografia storica," in *I Leponti tra mito e realtà*, ed. Raffaele C. De Marinis and Simonetta Biaggio Simona, 2 vols (Locarno, 2000), 2: 371–83; Patrick Gautier Dalché, "De Pétrarque à Raimondo Marliano: Aux origines de la géographie historique," *Archives d'histoire doctrinale et littéraire du Moyen Âge* 79 (2012): 161–91.

power and cultural descent. Assertions of the movement of peoples and identities across space and time raised questions about the nature of change, about the possibility of disappearance, loss, and corruption, alongside preservation. These assertions, and these questions, engaged both humanistic and non-humanist scholarship up to the time of Ortelius.

The medieval theory of the translation of political power from east to west was grounded in the biblical authority of the book of Daniel. The hinge was the Babylonian king Nebuchadnezzar's dream of a statue with a gold head, breast and arms of silver, stomach and thighs of bronze, iron legs, and feet of iron mixed with clay. Daniel's interpretation of Nebuchadnezzar's dream connected the statue with a succession of kingdoms, each inferior to the last, an echo of the terms in which he praises the Lord after the revelation of the mystery: "he changes [mutat] times and ages; he translates [transfert] and establishes kingdoms."[15] The text of Daniel itself does not articulate this succession in explicitly geographical terms, but exegesis on the book of Daniel connected Nebuchadnezzar's dream with the notion of a historical progression from the Babylonians (gold) to the Medes and Persians (silver), Alexander the Great and the Macedonians (bronze), and the Romans (iron at first, then mixed with clay as the empire descended into civil war and alliances with barbarian races). The conclusion of this progression was to be the eternal rule of Christ at the end of time.[16] While the expression "transferre regnum/imperium" continued to have local meanings, such as the transfer of power within a state, in the works of medieval historians it acquired the sense of profound geopolitical shifts from one world empire to the next.[17] Paulus Orosius's early fifth-century *Historiae adversus paganos* gave this wider political significance a firm footing for subsequent centuries. Orosius identified four major kingdoms at the four cardinal points of the world: Babylon in the East, Carthage in the South, the Macedonian realm of Alexander in the North, and Rome in the West.[18] Other authors preferred to

---

15. Daniel 2:21–22: "Et ipse mutat tempora et aetates; transfert regna, atque constituit."

16. Jerome, *Opera Exegetica: Commentariorum in Danielem Libri III* 1.2.31–35, ed. F. Glorie (Turnhout, 1964), 793–95.

17. Werner Goez, *Translatio Imperii: Ein Beitrag zur Geschichte des Geschichtsdenkens und der politischen Theorien im Mittelalter und in der frühen Neuzeit* (Tübingen, 1958), 30–31. More recent discussion of *translatio imperii* can be found in Cary J. Nederman, "Translatio Imperii: Medieval and Modern," in *Lineages of European Political Thought: Explorations along the Medieval/Modern Divide from John of Salisbury to Hegel* (Washington, DC, 2009), 177–89; Enrico Fenzi, "Translatio studii e translatio imperii: Appunti per un percorso," *Interfaces* 1 (2015): 170–208. For early humanist reception of the concept see Alexander Lee, *Humanism and Empire: The Imperial Ideal in Fourteenth-Century Italy* (Oxford, 2018).

18. Paulus Orosius, *Historiarum adversum paganos libri vii* 2.1–2, ed. C. Zangemeister (Vienna, 1882), 81–85.

divide history between six or even seven kingdoms: the Assyrians, Medes, Persians, Greeks (sometimes sub-divided into Spartans and Athenians), Egyptians, and Romans.[19] Such schemes had an obvious logic for those, like Jerome and Orosius, who were writing while the Roman Empire still maintained a tenuous existence. To make the concept of *translatio imperii* fit events following the collapse of the western empire in the fifth century, however, it was necessary to maintain that the Roman Empire had not ended, merely undergone a series of internal upheavals. By the twelfth century the chronicler Otto of Freising looked back on the fate of the empire with some sorrow, but he nevertheless perceived a continuity of political power:

> the Empire of the Romans, which is compared with iron in Daniel, has as a result of so many changes, especially in our own time, turned from the finest realm into almost the final one, so that as the poet says it scarcely "stands, the shadow of a great name." Transferred from the city of Rome to the [Byzantine] Greeks, from the Greeks to the Franks, from the Franks to the Lombards, from the Lombards back to the German Franks, not only did it grow old with the passage of time, but by its very mobility it acquired manifold filth and various defects, like a pebble tossed here and there in rushing waters.[20]

Battered, worn, antique, and at the end of the line, for Otto empire nevertheless endured in a coherent form. Significantly, Otto turned to the concept of *mutatio* to explain the internal shifts of empire, from Rome to Constantinople in the fourth century, and then in 800 to the Franks under Charlemagne. These shifts, he suggested, were analogous to the *mutationes* undergone by the first, Babylonian, empire when it passed to the Medes and the Persians.[21] In this way the notion of mutation (unregulated change) was subordinated to the broader scheme of *translatio*, in which political power was understood explicitly in terms of space as well as time.

---

19. Goez, *Translatio Imperii*, 36.

20. Otto of Freising, *Chronica sive Historia de duabus civitatibus* 1.prol., ed. A. Hofmeister (Hanover, 1912), 7: "regnum Romanorum, quod in Daniele ... ferro comparatur, ex tot alternationibus, maxime diebus nostris, ex nobilissimo factum est pene novissimum, ut iuxta poetam vix 'magni stet nominis umbra.' Ab Urbe quippe ad Grecos, a Grecis ad Francos, a Francis ad Lonbardos, a Lonbardis rursum ad Teutonicos Francos derivatum non solum antiquitate senuit, sed etiam ipsa mobilitate sui veluti levis glarea hac illacque aquis circumiecta sordes multiplices ac defectus varios contraxit." The references are to Daniel 2:40, and to Lucan, *Bellum civile* 1.135.

21. Otto of Freising, *Historia de duabus civitatibus* 6.22, ed. Hofmeister, 285.

To what extent did the scheme of *translatio imperii* inform the representation of geographical space in the Middle Ages? It has been argued that the translation of empires from east to west, Babylon to Rome, became a key structuring element of medieval world maps.[22] Particular significance has been given in this regard to the work of the twelfth-century theologian Hugh of St Victor. In *De archa Noe*, Hugh notably described the progression of political power after the Biblical flood, from the Assyrians, Chaldaeans, and Medes to the Greeks and finally to the Romans, conceived both chronologically and spatially: "in a straight line from east to west."[23] Might a medieval reader or expositor of a map interpret it "genealogically," starting in the far east and moving west along a vertical axis, identifying features of the map according to the progression of the four world empires and the six ages of man, from Adam to Christ?[24] The eye might follow a line from the earthly paradise, to Noah's Ark, Babel tower, and Chaldaea, then to the barns of Joseph in Egypt, the Twelve Tribes, and Jerusalem, before reaching Rome.

Such an interpretation cannot be excluded from the multiple possibilities open to medieval readers, but equally it should not be privileged too highly. In his own *Descriptio mappe mundi*, which is believed to be a verbal record of a now lost graphic *mappa mundi*,[25] Hugh himself gave no indication that the map should be read in terms of the translation of empires. Instead, in the *Descriptio* he moved from Asia, to Africa and finally to Europe, using the categories of islands, rivers, mountains, provinces and cities, seas, monsters, and peoples.[26] It is true that features such as the earthly paradise, Noah's ark, Babel/Babylon, Jerusalem, and Rome appear on most if not all *mappae mundi*, and are often given particular prominence. Yet some aspects that one would expect to see emphasised if *translatio imperii* were a crucial structuring element of *mappae mundi* are actually rather muted. Troy, for example, so central to many formulations of *translatio*

22. Alessandro Scafi, "Defining *mappaemundi*," in *The Hereford World Map: Medieval World Maps and Their Context*, ed. P.D.A. Harvey (London, 2006), 345–55; and Alessandro Scafi, *Mapping Paradise: A History of Heaven on Earth* (London, 2006), esp. 126–28: "[t]he fundamental east-west progression underlying the *mappae mundi*." Cf. Evelyn Edson, *Mapping Time and Space: How Medieval Mapmakers Viewed Their World* (London, 1997), 98–102.

23. *De archa Noe*, ed. P. Sicard (Turnhout, 2001), 4.9 (678A): "ab oriente in occidentem recta linea decurrente."

24. Scafi, "Defining *mappaemundi*," 347–49.

25. Patrick Gautier Dalché, *La "Descriptio Mappe Mundi" de Hugues de Saint-Victor* (Paris, 1988); but see too the comments of Margriet Hoogvliet, *Pictura et Scriptura: Textes, images et herméneutique des Mappae Mundi (XIIIe–XVIe siècles)* (Turnhout, 2007), 151.

26. *Descriptio Mappe Mundi*, ed. Gautier Dalché, 133–60; cf. Stephen McKenzie, "The Westward Progression of History on Medieval *mappaemundi*," in *The Hereford World Map*, 335–44, esp. 340.

imperii, is often given a rather minor role, as on the Hereford map where the laconic inscription "civitas bellicosa" accompanies the image of a citadel.[27] More importantly, toponyms, natural features, and mirabilia keep distracting any attempts at a straightforward east-west reading. One historian has persuasively argued that "icons of memory," rather than narrative, structure representation on medieval maps.[28] That is, a medieval reader of a *mappa mundi* was less likely to follow a continuous and connected story than to see images and brief texts that invoked and located known historical persons and events. Perhaps the best example of this point is the presence of Alexander the Great on *mappae mundi*. Maps such as Hereford and the Ebstorf *mappa mundi* contain many references to Alexander throughout Asia and in Africa. It would be possible, perhaps, to see all these references as representing the bronze age of the *translatio imperii*. But medieval readers possessed other ways of understanding the Alexander material on maps: most obviously, those traces of his exploits marked the furthest extent of imperial power and knowledge in Asia and Africa, as well as the dangers of imperial overreach, in the spirit of Lucan's criticism of Alexander's "insane" lust for power.[29] Despite the efforts of some scholars to unearth a fundamental principle behind these maps, they remain resolutely eclectic, responding to multiple sources and suiting not one but several agenda.

Mutatio before Humanism

A reading of medieval geographical thought as a simple articluation of *translatio* is also problematic because it ignores the concept of *mutatio*. The consciousness of the change of topographies over time, and especially of places and place names, inevitably complicated narratives of translation. In late antiquity the term *mutatio* referred to a post at which horses might be changed. It is with this signification that it appears frequently on the Peutinger Tables, as it does also in other records of Roman geography, such as the fourth-century *Itinerarium Burdigalense*.[30] But the term also expressed long-standing awareness of more profound

27. *The Hereford Map*, ed. Scott D. Westrem (Turnhout, 2001), 153.

28. Hoogvliet, *Pictura et Scriptura*, 156–59.

29. *Bellum Civile* 10.41–45. On Alexander on medieval *mappae mundi* see Patrick Gautier Dalché, "Quatre notes sur Alexandre et la cartographie médiévale," in *Les voyages d'Alexandre au paradis: Orient et Occident, regards croisés*, ed. Catherine Gaullier-Bougassas and Margaret Bridges (Turnhout, 2013), 213–38; Hoogvliet, *Pictura et Scriptura*, 220–28, 262–64.

30. Annalina and Mario Levi, *Itineraria Picta: Contributo allo studio della Tabula Peutingeriana* (Rome, 1967), 109–11; *Itineraria Romana*, vol. 1: *Itineraria Antonini Augusti et Burdigalense*, ed. Otto Cuntz (1929; repr. Stuttgart, 1990).

kinds of change. Classical authors such as the elder Pliny noted various changes in nomenclature over time, due largely to the movement of peoples (*mutatio incolarum*), but also the result of changes in the administrative division of space (*mutato provinciarum modo*), or the alteration of natural features, such as rivers changing shape, or shifts in the relative positions of seas and lands.[31] In his commentaries on Virgil, Servius was obliged to note changes in toponymy. The opening lines of the *Aeneid* declared the subject of the poem to be "he who, exiled by destiny, first from the shores of Troy came to Italy and the Lavinian coast (*Lavinia litora*)."[32] What and where were those "Lavinia litora"? The reference was to a city, Servius explained, but one that had had three names: first "Lavinum," from Lavinus, brother of Latinus; then "Laurentum," from the laurel found by Latinus; and then "Lavinium" from Lavinia, the wife of Aeneas. The line in Virgil should be "Lavina litora" not "Lavinia," added Servius, because the place was only called Lavinium after Aeneas's arrival.[33] Knowledge of *mutatio* was essential to an informed reading of Virgil's epic, both as a means of establishing the correct state of the text, and as a way of comprehending its dense topographical allusion.

Biblical exegesis equally demanded observation of the change of place names. Eusebius of Caesarea's *Onomasticon*, as transmitted in Jerome's *Liber locorum*, not only identified sites mentioned in the Bible, but also provided the modern toponym if it had changed. "Ailath," mentioned in Genesis, located at the far end of Palestine near the Red Sea, "now in fact is called Aila" (*nunc uero appellatur Aila*); Amman is now Filadelfia, a noble city of Arabia; Fylistiim is now called Ascalon.[34] Here too the role of the commentator was to disambiguate places with the same name. Eusebius observed that one of the sons of Abraham had named the city of "Madiam" (or Madian), that it was located in the desert to the east of the Red Sea, and that another city is homonymous with it – "next to [the river] Arnon and Areopolis, whose ruins are now all that remain."[35] This consciousness of spatial change, and of the possibility for ambiguity within spatial reference, infused standard sources of medieval geography, which identified a number of different causes of *mutatio*.

---

31. See, respectively, Pliny, *Naturalis historia*, 3.71 (population), 3.16 (government).

32. *Aen* 1.1–3, ed. Mynors, 103: "Troiae qui primus ab oris / Italiam fato profugus Lauiniaque uenit / litora"; or, in some manuscripts, "Lauinaque uenit / litora."

33. Servius, *Commentarii*, 1: 8–9 (at *Aen* 1.2). Livy, *Ab urbe condita libri I–V* 1.1.11, ed. R.M. Ogilvie (Oxford, 1974), 5: "Oppidum condunt; Aeneas ab nomine uxoris Lauinium appellat." G. Karl Galinsky, *Aeneas, Sicily and Rome* (Princeton, 1969), 141–90; Lavinium is the modern day Pratica di Mare.

34. Eusebius, *Werke*, vol. 3.1: *Das Onomastikon der biblischen Ortsnamen*, ed. Erich Klostermann (Leipzig, 1904), 7, 25, 167.

35. *Onomastikon*, ed. Klostermann, 125 (in Jerome's translation): "sed et alia ciuitas est homonumos eius iuxta Arnonem et Areopolim, cuius nunc ruinae tantummodo demonstrantur."

In his *Etymologiae*, Isidore of Seville makes several references to changes of place name, or to the simultaneous existence of more than one toponym for the same location. The principal cause of these changes is political fortune, as cities take the name of a conqueror. Samaria, the region of Palestine, accepts its name from a certain town called Samaria, formerly a royal city in Israel, which is now called Sebastia from the name of Augustus.[36] Egypt, which used to be called Aeria, takes its name from Aegyptus the brother of Danaus who ruled there.[37] Sichem, a city of Samaria, which is called Sichima in Latin and Greek, was built by Emor, who named it after his son Sichem. It is now a city of the Samaritans, called Neapolis.[38] An implicit reflection on fortune undoubtedly accompanies such a history of naming. In these examples, the name of the place becomes an extension of royal identity, but that expression of identity is subject to the same processes of mutation as any other place name. Popular, or at least local, naming practices could at times overturn the "correct," imperial name for a place: Isidore reports that his own Hispalis (Seville) was named Julia Romula by its founder, Julius Caesar, but nicknamed "his palis" ("on these stakes") because of its location on stakes in a deep marsh.[39]

The movement of peoples was another reason commonly given for *mutationes locorum*. The introduction to the anonymous eighth-century Ravenna cosmography refers to the *mutatio gentium* caused by conquest, migration, or the barbarous custom of changing the names of homelands, cities, and rivers.[40] The work's twelfth-century follower, Guido da Pisa, similarly identified "invasion or migration in the barbarian manner" as a cause of changes in place names.[41] But change could also be attributed to a mixture of political intervention and linguistic corruption. Guido noted that, following its refoundation by the emperor Trajan, the city Thirrenium had become Traiana "by the shortening of one syllable, and multiplication of another"; subsequently, the syllable "ia" had been jettisoned, leaving the contemporary name of the city as "Tranas."[42]

As this example suggests, medieval commentators on place names were able to give detailed accounts of processes of change. The formulation "olim ... nunc"

36. *Etymologiae* 14.4.22.
37. *Etymologiae* 14.3.27.
38. *Etymologiae* 15.1.21.
39. *Etymologiae* 15.1.71.
40. "Ravennatis Anonymi Cosmographia," 1.1, 1.13, 5.32, in *Itineraria Romana*, vol 2: *Ravennatis anonymi cosmographia et Guidonis geographica*, ed. Joseph Schnetz (1940; repr. Stuttgart, 1990), 2, 12, 109; cf. 5.1, ed. Schnetz, 85.
41. "Guidonis Geographica," in *Itineraria Romana* 2: 119: "incursione vel transmutatione more barbarico aliter numcupentur."
42. *Itineraria Romana* 2: 118: "de Tirheno per tractionem unius et multiplicationem alterius syllabe Traiana est vocata. nunc quoque abiecta ia syllaba Tranas vocatur, ut descriptores philosophi suis in scriptis asserunt." The modern city is Trani. For a brief discussion of this passage, see Guido da Pisa, *Liber Guidonis compositus de variis historiis*, ed. Michele Campopiano (Florence, 2008), lxxiii.

(once ... now) consequently became relatively common in geographical and historical discourse,[43] to the extent that it could not be ignored by proponents of the *translatio imperii*. Otto of Freising wrote to prove "the mutability of (human) affairs," and the inevitable falls of kingdoms and empires, in contradistinction to the immutability of the heavenly kingdom.[44] The final section on Europe in Hugh of St Victor's *Descriptio mappe mundi* shows particular concern for spatial change across time, outlining the regions covered by the term "Gallia Cisalpina" according to ancient historians (*ueteres historiographi*), the ancient leader Brennius's incursion into Italy, and the process of *mutatio* in Gaul.[45] *Translatio imperii* may then in certain guises appear as a manifestation of the principle of *mutatio*, and at its most emblematic level the trope of fortune's wheel, as places move from cities to ruins, and occasionally back again. And yet, when unshackled from the heavily schematic notion of *translatio imperii* – movement from east to west, across space and time to the "end of history" and Apocalypse – the concept of *mutatio* offered the possibility of more unexpected, haphazard, and potentially irrecoverable changes.

Some of the unpredictability of spatial change as conceived in the Middle Ages can be seen in a passage from Gervase of Tilbury's encyclopedia-chronicle, the *Otia imperialia*, compiled for the emperor Otto IV in the early thirteenth century. Towards the end of the second book of the *Otia*, Gervase gives a detailed description of the Holy Land, followed by a list of provinces in the three parts of the world. The chronicler notes that this list, which derives from a certain "Roman register" (probably a version of the mid-fifth-century list of provinces compiled by Polemius Silvius)[46] differs from a list of provinces he had given earlier in book two (2.2–12), which he derived from Orosius, other historians, and the *Provinciale Romanum*, a compilation of ecclesiastical geography produced for the purposes of papal administration. While the previous list included more recent names, this second list is organised "according to the offices of governor or proconsul, prefect or moderator, as they were distinguished in ancient times in the

---

43. A point emphasised by Gautier Dalché, "De Pétrarque à Raimondo Marliano."

44. See as indicative statements *Historia de duabus civitatibus* 5.prol., ed. Hofmeister, 227, "dum mundum, quem pro mutatione sui contempnendum predixerunt"; "nos, qui ad ostendendas mutationes rerum res gestas scribimus" (5.36, ed. Hofmeister, 261); "Sic et regnorum mutationes et ad ultimum inminutiones quis fructus sequatur, Deo ... relinquamus" (7.prol., ed. Hofmeister, 308).

45. *Descriptio mappe mundi* 24–25, ed. Gautier Dalché, 156–58; the description of Gaul draws on Hugh of Fleury, *Historia ecclesiastica*, ed. G. Waitz (Hanover, 1851), 349–64, at 356–57.

46. *Geographi Latini minores*, ed. Riese; *Notitia dignitatum*, ed. Otto Seeck (Berlin, 1876), 254–60.

Roman empire."[47] Having alerted his readers to the differences between the two lists, explicitly conceived as the difference between "antiquitas" and "nouitas,"[48] Gervase warns them not to be confused by any discrepancies they might find:

> Nor should the reader ascribe to ignorance or mendacity the fact that the names we give are sometimes different from those known in our time, since at times we have paid homage to the past, while at other times we have had to fall in with spoken usage. For instance, Babylon was once called Abathanis; Hierapolis is also called Aleppo; Edessa, Rages of the Medes ... So too among the Greeks names have changed: Byzantium, for instance, is now Constantinople; among the Latins, Trinovantum has become London, Agrippina Colonia is called Cologne, Arelas Constantina is called Arles, and the town of the Sadi is now Sées ... Pavia in Italy used to be called Ticinum; Gap in Provence was once called Argentina. In Syria, Bergeberin is an alternative name for Beer-sheba; Jericunthus for Jericho; Diocaesarea for Tiberias ... .[49]

This lengthy and rather disordered list shows no systematic attempt to correlate ancient with modern, but it is nonetheless an impressive demonstration of a historian's awareness of the existence of multiple toponymic forms. Some of these differences represent not so much the change of place name, as the emergence of an alternative form. Some, such as Byzantium-Constantinople, or Agrippina-Cologne, would surely have been familiar to Gervase's readership; others, such as the contemporary Syrian and near eastern nomenclature, perhaps less so. The list of *mutationes* precedes the final chapter of book two of the *Otia*, on the origin of provinces and cities, the descendants of Noah, and the six ages. So the notion of mutation, according to which changes in the names of places reflect

47. Gervase of Tilbury, *Otia Imperialia: Recreation for an Emperor* 2.25, ed and trans. S.E. Banks and J.W. Binns (Oxford, 2002), 524–26: "secundum antiquitus distincta officia presidatuum uel proconsulatuum, prefecturarum et moderationum Romani imperii, ordinauimus ... "

48. *Otia Imperialia* 2.25, ed. and trans. Banks and Binns, 526: "hic antiquitati seruientes, illic nouitati locum dantes."

49. *Otia Imperialia* 2.25, ed. and trans. Banks and Binns, 526–29: "Nec ascribat lector ignorancie uel mendacio quod interdum nomina secus quam hoc tempore se habeant scribimus, cum nunc antiquitati seruierimus, nunc consuetudini loquentium satisfacere nos oportuerit. Ecce enim Babilonia Abathanis olim dicebatur; Ieropolis Halap dicitur, Edissa Rages Medorum ... Sic et apud Grecos nomina mutata sunt, ut Bisantium Constantinopolis; apud Latinos Trinouantum Londonie, Agrippina Colonia, Arelas Constantina, Sadorum nunc Sagium; ... In Italia, Papia Ticinum uocabatur; in Prouincia, Vapincum olim Argentina. In Siria Bergeberim, hoc est Bersabee; Iericunctus, Iereb; Tiberiadis, Dyocesarea ... ."

historical as well as linguistic change, appears adjacent to the ordered narration of human history from Adam to the present day. Unlike *translatio*, which it complements here, the logic of *mutatio* is not necessarily genealogical, since change may be the result of warfare, colonisation, or simply linguistic corruption. The alterations listed by Gervase do indicate continuity across historical change, since places remain in their original location while their names change. But the process is not that of descent. *Mutatio*, whether occasioned by political turbulence, or the steady wearing away of a name over time, lurked as *translatio*'s unstable shadow.

Mapping *mutatio*

Medieval maps, especially those whose size permitted discursive commentary, record *mutationes*, albeit only very selectively. At times a mapmaker noted a change of name of particular historical significance. The inscription "Britannia now called Anglia" (*Britannia nunc dicta Anglia*) on Matthew Paris's second map of Britain, for example, refers to the legend of the foundation of human habitation and kingship on the island by the Trojan exile Brutus.[50] In other cases, mapmakers wanted to acknowledge the multiplicity of names a single place could generate. The thirteenth-century Vercelli *mappa mundi* explained at some length the different names for the region of Thessaly: "this region is called Thessaly from King Thessalus, and Haemonia from Mt. Haemus and Pharsalia from King Pharsalus and Caonia from Caon son of Priam, brother of Helenus, and Molossia from Molossus son of Pyrrhus, and Achaia from King Achaeus."[51] While this inscription is rather unusual within the corpus of medieval maps, it indicates well the array of nomenclature inherited by medieval authors from their sources.

This struggle to assimilate diverse information, and at the same time to account for places and peoples unknown to the classical world within the frame

50. London, British Library, MS Royal 14 C.VII, fol. 5v, a quotation of Henry of Huntingdon's *Historia Anglorum* 1.2, itself echoing Bede's *Ecclesiastical History* 1.1. In all its formulations the map of Britain was intended by Matthew to be read in part for its historical content. Alternative names for the different parts of the island are noted, as are defunct Roman structures such as Hadrian's wall and the Antonine wall: respectively, "murus diuidens anglos et pictos olim" (wall once dividing Angles and Picts), and "murus diuidens scotos et pictos olim" (wall once dividing Scots and Picts): London, British Library, MS Cotton Claudius D.VI, fol. 12v.

51. *Il mappamondo di Vercelli*, section E.IX: "haec regio dicitur tessalia a tessalo rege et hemonia ab hemo monte et pharsalia a pharsalo rege et caonia a caone filio pr[i]ami, frate heleni et Molosia a molose filio pirri et achaia ab acheo rege." The basic elements here are present in Isidore, *Etymologiae*, 14.4.9, 12, 14, with the exception of H(a)emonia and Pharsalia.

of the world image, is best evidenced by the Ebstorf *mappa mundi* (c. 1300). The changes of the names of places and peoples, and the co-existence of different names for the same place, emerge as a consistent interest of the maker(s) of this map, particularly in its depiction of Europe. In part this interest reflects the map's use of source material. The name Europe itself is explained in an inscription in the far north which repeats the account in Isidore's *Etymologiae* of Jupiter's rape of Europa, and reiterates the point that the name Libya (both the name of the grandfather of Europa and the name used to designate Africa) is therefore older than Europa.[52] Similarly, the map follows another of its major sources, Honorius Augustodunensis's *Imago Mundi*, in the Holy Land. There the inscription "Pentapolis is the region in which Sodom and Gomorrha once were. In it are (now) Saracens who are also known as Agareni, and the Nabatei" appears next to a representation of the five cities of Pentapolis destroyed by celestial fire, and repeats Honorius nearly exactly.[53]

In northern and eastern Europe, however, it is possible to read the Ebstorf map as a conscious meditation on the *mutationes* undergone by portions of the Roman Empire (Figure 12). Several Roman provinces or cities are identified, with alternative or earlier names: Lucdunensis Gallia "which was once called Gallia Togata" (*que olim Togata*); Gallia Narbonensis "which was once called Gallia Bracata" (*Narbonensis Gallia que olim Bracata*); and "Agripina which is now the city of Cologne" (*Ag[ripina que nunc] Colonia c.*).[54] The transition from Roman to barbarian rule is most evident in a legend that identifies the ancient province of Pannonia with contemporary Hungary (*Pannonia inferior que nunc Ungaria*), and in a series of inscriptions that identify barbarian peoples along the

52. Hartmut Kugler, *Die Ebstorfer Weltkarte* (Berlin, 2007), 1: 100 (no. 36.3); Isidore, *Etymologiae*, 14.4.1.

53. Kugler, *Ebstorfer Weltkarte*, 1: 94 (no. 33.11): "Pentapolis est regio, in qua fuit olim Sodoma et Gomorra. In ea sunt Saraceni qui et Agareni et Nabatei." Honorius, *Imago Mundi* 1.16, ed. Valierie I.J. Flint, *Archives d'histoire doctrinale et littéraire du Moyen Age* 49 (1982): 7–153, at 57: "In hac est et Pentapolis regio, a .v. civitatibus dicta, in qua olim fuit Sodoma et Gomorra ... In hac quoque Sarraceni a Sarra dicti, qui et Agareni a Agar ... in hac et Nabathei a Nabaioth filio Ismahel dicti"; cf. Gervase of Tilbury, *Otia imperialia* 2.4, ed. Banks and Binns, 204.

54. Kugler, *Ebstorfer Weltkarte*, 1: 132 (no. 52.26); 1: 144 (no. 58.32); 1: 130 (no. 51.13). Medieval authors typically followed classical precursors in dividing Roman Gaul into three provinces – Gallia Narbonensis (sometimes Aquitania), Gallia Lugdunensis, and Gallia Belgica – though the application of the nicknames "togata," "comata," and "bracata" was not consistent. See Pliny, *Naturalis historia* 3.107; Orosius, *Historiarum ... libri vii* 1.2.63–68, ed. Zangemeister, 25–26; Honorius, *Imago mundi* 1.27; Hugh of St Victor, *Descriptio mappe mundi* 25.677, ed. Gautier Dalché, 157; Gervase of Tilbury, *Otia imperialia* 2.10, ed. Banks and Binns, 286.

course of the Danube, from Thrace to the border between Hungary and Bohemia. The words "here are barbarian peoples" (*hic sunt barbarorum gentes*) introduce the series, on the side of the Danube opposite to the legend on the origins of Europa.[55] The naming of these barbarians starts immediately beneath the Isidorean etymology for Europe, with the statement: "Alans, Scythians and Dacians, Anoxobii, Troglodytes, and Sarmatians meet here between the Ocean and the Danube. There are also Quadi and Getae, who were called Callipodi in antiquity."[56] As the reader follows the course of the Danube from north and east to the south and west, further *gentes* are encountered:

> 14 tribes of barbarous Slavs (*Barbarorum gentes XIIII Slavorum*);
> Land of the Bulgars (*Terra Bulgarorum*);
> Region of Raetia and Pannonia of strong men. The Norican territory sparse and less fertile, and adjoined to Raetia which rejoices in its soil, and here there are Huns who are also called Merari (*Retia regio et Pannonia fortium virorum. Noricus ager parcus et minus fertilis, et solo leta coniungitur Retia, et hic sunt Huni qui et Merari[s] vocati*);
> Here was once the land of the Huns (*hic olim terra Hunorum fuit*).
> Here there are Amantini (*Hic sunt Amantini*).[57]

Through these inscriptions the map aligns the old structure of the Roman provinces with the appearance of barbarian peoples, many of which can be claimed as the ancestors of the present-day inhabitants of the region. In its shorthand way, the map invites the reader to understand a process of change, to grasp the context of the historically momentous mutation of Roman power and the articulation of barbarian ethnic identity.

The map also represents invasions and *mutationes* of a more recent vintage. On Ebstorf explicit mention of the movement of people occurs not in relation to an east-west progression, but with regard to the Norman invasions. An inscription, scuffed and nearly illegible, can be discerned on the far north-west corner of the map:

55. Kugler, *Ebstorfer Weltkarte*, 1: 102 (no. 37.2).

56. Kugler, *Ebstorfer Weltkarte*, 1: 100 (no. 36.7): "Alani, Schite et Daci, Anoxobii, Trogodite, Sarmathe hic conveniunt inter occeanum et Danubium. Sunt et Quadi et Gete et qui antiquitus dicuntur Callipodi." The inscription derives in part from Pliny, *Naturalis historia*, 4.80–81; see Kugler's commentary for analogues. The reference to the Callipodi is more puzzling: cf. Pomponius Mela, *De chorographia* 2.1.7, where the Callippidae are a Scythian people, and Jordanes, *Getica* 32, 46, where Callipida (or Callipoda) is a Greek city in Scythia.

57. Respectively, 1: 102 (nos. 37.8; 37.24; 37.27; 37.29; 37.44). These inscriptions appear to derive from Isidore, *Etymologiae* 14.4.5, 14.4.6, and 14.4.16, but with "hic sunt Huni qui et Meraris vocati" seemingly added. The Amantini are menioned in Pliny, *Naturalis historia* 3.148.

Certain Sweones ... are said to be of the Sueui living around these mountains, from which they are now called Alemanni; those who departed from
these mountains for inner Sweonia [Sweden], are called Normans. From
these Normans who live beyond Dania [Denmark], came those Normans
who inhabit France, and from these a third group of Normans was recently
received by Apulia. About the Suevi who live here, Lucan says: "The Elbe
pours forth blond Suevi from the furthest north."[58]

This inscription operates through a sort of envelope pattern, beginning with
the name of one classical people (Sweones), connecting them with another
classical tribe (the Suevi), then updating the name (Alemanni), and introduc-
ing a non-classical people – the Normans – before returning to the appearance
of the Suevi in Lucan. It is in fact (as usual) a rather complex conflation of
sources: the first part seems to be a paraphrase of a description of Sueonia in
Adam of Bremen's eleventh-century history of the bishops of the church of
Hamburg-Bremen;[59] the second sentence, on the Normans, derives from a
scholion to Adam's work.[60] The citation of Lucan was made by Adam too, but
he seems to have taken it not directly from the Roman author but from Isidore's
Etymologiae, which states that "the Suevi were part of the German peoples,
dwelling in the far north. About which Lucan said: '[The Elbe and Rhine] pour
forth blond Suevi from the furthest north.'"[61] Obviously the quotation on a
fourteenth-century map of an eleventh-century source (itself quoting a sev-

---

58. Kugler, *Ebstorfer Weltkarte*, 1: 114 (no. 43.8) (slightly modified): "Sueones
quedam ... dt [dicuntur?] esse Sweuorum circa hec montana habitantium, a quibus illi
nunc Alamanni dicuntur; qui ab istis montanis ad Sweoniam interiorem secesserunt,
Northmanni dicuntur. Ab illis Northmannis, qui trans Daniam habitant, venerunt isti
Northmanni, qui Franciam incolunt, et ab his nuper Apulia suscepit tertios Normannos.
De Suevis qui hic habitant, dicit Lucanus: 'Fundat ab extremo flavos aquilone Suevos
Albis.'" This inscription is evidently badly damaged; the transcription follows Kugler, and
owes much to the reconstruction of Konrad Miller, based on the textual evidence of the
source material.

59. Adam of Bremen, *Gesta Hammaburgensis Ecclesiae Pontificum* 4.21, ed. Bernhard
Schmeidler, 3rd ed. (Hannover, 1917), 250–51: "De Sueonia vero non tacent antiqui auctores Solinus et Orosius, qui dicunt, plurimam partem Germaniae Suevos tenere, necnon
montana eius usque ad Ripheos montes extendi. Ibi est etiam Albis fluvius, de quo Lucanus
meminisse videtur."

60. Scholion 143 on Adam, *Gesta* 4.30, ed. Schmeidler, 263: "Ab illis Nordmannis, qui
trans Daniam habitant, venerunt isti Nordmanni, qui Franciam incolunt, et ab his nuper Apulia suscepit tertios Nordmannos."

61. *Etymologiae* 9.2.98: "Sueui pars Germanorum fuerunt in fine septemtrionis de quibus
Lucanus: 'Fundit ab extremo flauos aquilone Sueuos.'" The citation of Lucan is from *Bellum
civile* 2.51–52.

enth-century source, in turn quoting a first-century source) raises questions about the currency of adverbs such as "now" (*nunc*) and "recently" (*nuper*). But the inscription illustrates abundantly the complex *mutationes* within histories of peoples and places. What begins as a record of the origins of the Alemanni – and both Isidore and Adam make clear the spatial and ethnic significance of the Suevi and their mountain, which constituted the eastern boundary of Germania – is taken over by the story of the Normans, diverting the inscription spatially from the far north-west (where it appears on the map) into France and Apulia. The Normans themselves splinter into three. Such a rapid distillation of ethnography and geography cannot be aptly described by the term "translation," with its connotations of order and agency; we have here something disordered, interlocked, incomplete, defiant of coherent narration. We have *mutatio*.

Humanist *mutatio*

Abraham Ortelius's depiction of the Roman Empire shared much with medieval treatments of spatial change. Like his predecessors, Ortelius sought to identify differences – sometimes minor, sometimes profound – between antiquity and modernity, between "olim" and "nunc." Such differences, which could be discerned through a careful examination of source material, informed the understanding of the contemporary world image and that of past eras, with the result that the two could be compared. But Ortelius's antiquarian mapping was not the product of standard medieval modes of spatial representation. Instead it was a descendant and exemplum of humanist attitudes towards the spaces of antiquity. In its careful detachment of ancient from modern *imago*, in its philological underpinning, in its curatorial presentation of the past, this map of the Roman Empire was the culmination of the sensibilities and practices first developed over two centuries previously by Francis Petrarch and Giovanni Boccaccio, and taken up by their fifteenth-century followers, such as Biondo Flavio and Aeneas Silvius Piccolomini. These humanists were not the first to conceive of *mutatio*, but they did develop distinctive ways of articulating the problem it posed to spatial representation. Such articulations can only simplistically be equated with the birth of modernity, not only because to do so ignores their medieval precursors, but because it elides the particular, and sometimes peculiar, properties of humanist inquiry.

The classic display of erudition in the face of *mutatio* resides in a letter of the chancellor of Florence and second-generation humanist, Coluccio

Salutati.[62] Written in 1403, Coluccio's letter ostensibly responds to the request of his addressee, Domenico d'Arezzo, to identify the name by which Città di Castello in Umbria was known in antiquity. After scouring ancient authorities – Ptolemy, Pomponius Mela, Pliny, Solinus – to no avail, Coluccio turned to the *Dialogues* of Pope Gregory the Great (590–604). There he found a reference to the ancient name of the city, but the two manuscripts of the work in his possession gave two different versions: Trifertina and Tiberrina. Subsequent examination of a further eighteen manuscripts of the *Dialogues* revealed no less than thirteen forms of the name. It all goes to show the instability of writing, Coluccio observed: "this one writes Trifertine, another says Tifertine; this one Tiferne, that one Tiberine, another wants Tuburtine, and yet another Tibertine; another, which I think absurd, has Terbentine, just as others have Tudertine."[63] Humanist endeavour did not give up so easily, however. Re-examination of Pliny, Pomponius Mela, and Ptolemy, along with Guido da Pisa's *Cosmographia*, and, crucially, first-hand observation of an ancient inscription in the city, led Coluccio to conclude that the ancient form of the name was properly "Tifernum." The heroic labour involved in such a task reveals the importance that Coluccio and others attached to establishing spatial correspondences between antiquity and modernity. In the face of the vagaries of multiple sources, careless scribes, and semi-legible manuscripts, the task of erudition was not simply to identify the mutation (what was the place called in antiquity?) but to identify precisely the antique form – to the extent of determining whether its second letter should be "i" or "y." The goal was also to enhance both an understanding of contemporary space in relation to antiquity, and appreciation of the ancient source itself through identification of its modern referent, *mutatis mutandis*. Yet even if a level of precision could be achieved, troubling questions remained. Was there, in fact, a sin-

---

62. See particularly Nathalie Bouloux, *Culture et savoirs géographiques en Italie au XIVe siècle* (Turnhout, 2002), 289–91; the letter is discussed briefly in Berthold L. Ullman, *The Humanism of Coluccio Salutati* (Padua, 1963), 102–3; Ronald G. Witt, *Hercules at the Crossroads: The Life, Works, and Thought of Coluccio Salutati* (Durham, NC, 1983), 235–36 and 421–22; and Elisabetta Guerrieri, "Spunti filologici dall'*Epistolario* di Salutati," in *Coluccio Salutati e l'invenzione dell'umanesimo*, ed. Concetta Bianca (Rome, 2010), 231–81, at 256–59. I have not been able to consult Pierluigi Licciardello, "Un dibattito tra umanisti sull'origine di Città di Castello," *Pagine Altotiberine* 33 (2007): 157–82.

63. Coluccio Salutati, *Epistolario*, ed. Francesco Novati (Rome, 1896), 3: 622–28, at 625: "hic Trifertine scribit, Tifertine dicit alius; ille Tiferne, hic Tiberine; Tuburtine vult alius, vult et alius Tibertine et alius; quod ridiculum arbitror; Terbentine, sicut alii Tudertine." The passage of the *Dialogi* (3.35) concerns the bishop Floridus: see *Gregorii Magni Dialogi Libri IV*, ed. Umberto Moricca (Rome, 1924), 214, which notes manuscript variants and argues for yet another version, "Ferentinae."

gle, immutable ancient form? How could one presume to identify the earliest name a place had held? Was *mutatio*, in other words, an inherent property of place? As Coluccio noted:

> If that city had some other name than the one it now has, who can discover or retrieve why or when the name it once had was changed? What if there is no memory at all of this change, no witness which can with certainty determine by which name the place was formerly known?[64]

The search for correspondences between ancient and contemporary names threw into relief the fundamental uncertainties of historical research: the problem of sources, the evanescent nature of the past. But if consideration of the quest for the original "unchanged" name raised the possibility that the quest might be futile, it nevertheless remained crucial for humanist discourse to define cultural identity in terms of a dialogue between antiquity and modernity.

The dialogic articulation of cultural identity was characteristic of Petrarch, who signed his letters to classical authors using ancient geographical nomenclature. Rather than from France or Italy, he writes to Cicero from "the left bank of the Rhone in Transalpine Gaul," and to Seneca from "the right bank of the Po in Cisalpine Gaul." To Varro he sends a missive from "Rome, world's capital, which was your fatherland, and has become mine"; to Livy from "that part of Italy and in that city in which you were born and in which you are buried, in the vestibule of Justina the virgin and before the very stone of your tomb."[65] As such an act – writing under the sign of the place in its ancient guise – implies, classical spatial formulations offered a platform from which to address antiquity, shared ground between humanist subject and ancient author, with the contemporary readership relied on to supply the modern form.

Petrarch's sense of the presence of ancient space within his own lived environment runs through his writings, evident not only in his many letters but also in texts such as *De gestis Cesaris* (On the deeds of Julius Caesar). There he acknowledges the difficulties posed by changes of names (*nominum mutatio*) but

---

64. Coluccio Salutati, *Epistolario*, ed. Novati, 3: 623: "si nomen unquam habuit illa civitas aliud quam nunc habet, quis invenire vel referre poterit cur vel quando fuerit nomen, quod prius habuerit, immutatum? quod si mutationis huius nulla prorsus est memoria, nullus testis, quis potest certa ratione diffinire quonam nomine prius vocaretur?"

65. Respectively, *Le Familiari*, ed. Rossi, 4: 231 (*Fam* 24.4) ("ad sinistram Rodani ripam Transalpine Gallie"); 4: 237 (*Fam* 24.5) ("in Gallia Cisalpina ad dexteram Padi ripam"); 4: 240 (*Fam* 24.6) ("in capite orbis Roma, que tua fuit et mea patria facta est"); 4: 245 (*Fam* 24.8) ("in ea parte Italie et in ea urbe in qua natus et sepultus es, in vestibulo Iustine virginis et ante ipsum sepulcri tui lapidem").

proceeds to align the regions of Roman Gaul, such as Gallia cisalpina and transalpina, with those of his own day, including Flanders and Brabant, and the cities of Strasbourg, Basel and Constance, so that the reader may grasp the extent of the ancient polity.[66] Where did this humanist concern with *mutatio* leave its sibling, *translatio*? Petrarch's invective against a detractor of Italy ("Contra eum qui maledixit Italie") shows how *mutatio* could be intertwined with *translatio*, and at the same time negate it. The invective is a response to a letter written by the Parisian theologian Jean de Hesdin in late 1369, itself a response to Petrarch's campaign to return the papacy to Rome from its "exile" in Avignon. Seeking to deflect Petrarch's disparagement of France in favour of Italy, Jean had adduced a long list of Italian cities, including Milan, Venice, Pisa, and Turin, that had been founded by foreigners (*alienigene*), several of them Gauls: "why therefore does this man boast so much about their cities, which those foreigners found either non-existant or deserted, due to the wretched state of the Italian people?"[67]

Petrarch's reply did not deny Jean's evidence, but instead amplified and reversed his combatant's premise. First Petrarch pointed out the extensive record of Italians founding cities beyond Italy. Troy itself was founded by a Tuscan; Julius Caesar had founded Paris; Augustus peopled the Rhine valley with colonists. But it is the integral nature of the land, rather than the mutability of peoples, that Petrarch uses to clinch his case:

Such a change (*mutatio*) of settlement changes the people who migrate, rather than the country to which they migrate. Hence, the Gauls migrating to Asia Minor became Asians; and the Italians migrating to Phrygia became Phrygians, but reverted to Italians when they returned to Italy after the fall of Troy. Thus, our own Italians who moved to Gaul or Germany (*in Galliam aut Germaniam translati*) have imbibed the nature of those regions and their barbaric customs. But the inhabitants of Milan, whose city was founded by the Gauls and who were themselves formerly Gauls, are now the gentlest people on earth, and retain no trace of their ancient past. So much does the power of the heavens dominate and influence human minds.[68]

66. Francis Petrarch, *De gestis Cesaris*, ed. Giuliana Crevatin (Pisa, 2003), 10–16.

67. Jean de Hesdin, *Contra Franciscum Petrarcham Epistola*, in Francis Petrarch, *Invectives*, trans. Rebecca Lenoir (Grenoble, 2003), 505–27, at 520: "Cur igitur iste tantum de suis civitatibus gloriatur, quas isti alienigenae, Italicae gentis miseria, aut nullas aut desertas invenerunt?" On Jean de Hesdin, the essential starting point remains Beryl Smalley, "Jean de Hesdin O. Hosp. S. Ioh.," *Recherches de Théologie ancienne et médiévale* 28 (1961): 283–330.

68. Francis Petrarch, *Contra eum qui maledixit Italie* 289–91, ed. Monica Berté (Florence, 2005), 100: "Verum hec sedium mutatio non patriam ad quam pergitur sed pergentes immutat. Itaque et Galli in Asiam Asiatici et Itali in Frigiam profecti Friges et, post

The idea, even ideal, of *translatio* is that essence is carried across, and that while it changes as a result of translation, it retains identity with its former state. Instead, Petrarch dissolves identities in the crucible of fatherland. This is evidently a neat ploy which enables him at once to acknowledge the considerable history of foreign presence and influence in Italy and to assert that Italy remains unchanged in spite of change, that it betrays "no trace" of the foreign or barbarian. Celestial force overwhelms human agency. Such a denial of translation – translation as assimilation – reaffirms the integrity of national boundaries, but at the expense of empire, since its logical extension is the dissolution of Roman/Italian essences beyond Italy.

In less polemical contexts the problems of comprehension posed by ancient sources, and the difficulty of reconciling their evidence with modern geography, led humanists to develop concrete projects involving the simultaneous explication of modern and ancient space. Boccaccio's *De montibus, silvis, fontibus, lacubus, fluminibus, stagnis seu paludibus et de diversis nominibus maris* (On mountains, woods, springs, lakes, rivers, swamps or marshes and different names of the sea) arose out of the fear of misunderstanding the names of natural formations, and the corresponding confusion to the "historical sense" (*sensus hystorialis*) of taking the name of a mountain for a river, a marsh for a mountain, or woods in place of a city or province.[69] Even erudite readers, Boccaccio observed, very often thought a mountain or river of the west was located in the east. *De montibus* is designed to prevent such errors through a series of distinctions, intended not only to establish the proper relationship between names and places, but also to clarify the meaning of topographical terminology – what, for example, is the difference between a *flumen*, a *fluvius*, a *rivus*, and a *torrens*? – a task made more difficult by the propensity of ancient authors themselves to blur the terms. A series of mini geographies emerges, ordered alphabetically, and derived primarily from

---

Troie excidium in Italiam reversi, Itali iterum facti sunt. Sic nostri in Galliam aut Germaniam translati naturam illarum partium imbiberunt moresque barbaricos. Et Mediolanenses, a Gallis conditi atque olim Galli, nunc mitissimi hominum, nullum servant vestigium vetustatis. Ita vis celestis humana vincit ac moderatur ingenia." Trans. from Francis Petrarch, *Invectives*, trans. David Marsh (Cambridge, MA, 2003), 461–63. The influence of Livy, *Ab urbe condita* 38.17.9–10, ed. Ogilvie, 2: 536–37, where the consul Cn. Manlius Vulso uses the trope of degeneration to describe transplanted peoples, plants, and animals, in order to encourage soldiers not to fear the Gauls who have occupied parts of Asia, seems probable: "non tantum semina ad seruandam indolem ualent quantum terrae proprietas caelique sub quo aluntur mutat."

69. Giovanni Boccaccio, *De montibus, silvis, fontibus, lacubus, fluminibus, stagnis seu paludibus et de diversis nominibus maris*, 1.2, ed. Manlio Pastore Stocchi, in *Tutte le opere di Giovanni Boccaccio*, ed. Vittore Branca (Milan, 1998), 8: 1827: "montis nomen pro flumine, dum paludis pro monte, seu silve civitatis vel provincie loco sumitur."

Pliny and Pomponius Mela, though with other classical and some contemporary sources used from time to time. These descriptions of topography included records of alternative names, as well as places lost or ruined.

Boccaccio's approach to geography had some profoundly dislocative effects. A perceptive recent study has pointed out that the alphabetical listing of the mountains, rivers, places, and other topographical features of the world required a "deconstruction" of the world image. If the traditional organisation of geography had been by part or region – and so by contiguity of space – the alphabet organised by contiguity of letter.[70] The toponym was now findable, if you knew what name to look for, but the written word no longer functioned as an analogue to the graphic map. An extract from Boccaccio's *De montibus* illustrates important aspects of this new way of itemizing geography, and certain problems inherent in alphabetical order:

> Mount Ippius according to some is in Bithinia and beneath it was the city of Picopolis; others say it is near Ylion and that in front of it the Greeks lay hidden in ambushes, and from this they proceed to the conclusion that its name derives from horse, which is "ippos" in Greek. Certainly Bithinia borders upon the country around Troy, and this mountain perhaps falls between the regions.
> Mount Ipsizorus is in Macedonia.
> Mount Iraurancos, from which the Danube is said to arise, is in Germany.
> Irmine is a promontory of Achaia.
> Mount Irpinus is in the territory of the Sabines, in which the best horses are produced.[71]

Topography undergoes fragmentation in this list: regions such as Bithinia, Macedonia, Germania, and Achaia no longer serve as the structuring principle of spatial representation, but as referents subordinate to the practice of alphabetization. Naturally, that practice put pressure on orthography. Here the interventions of humanist philology were crucial. Boccaccio followed Petrarch in listing the classical rather than modern form of places – with good reason, since a major function of lists such as the ones compiled for *De montibus* was to elucidate readings of clas-

70. Bouloux, *Culture et savoirs géographiques*, 217–35.

71. *De montibus* 1.289–93, ed. Pastore Stocchi, 1853: "Ippius mons secundum quosdam in Bithinia est et sub eo Picopolis fuit civitas, alii illum dicunt Ylioni propinquum et post eum insidiis latuisse Grecos, et hinc sumptum quod ex equo, qui 'ippos' grece dicitur, prodierint. Sane Bithinia Troadi contermina est, et is forte mons medius inter eas; Ipsizorus mons est Macedonie; Iraurancos mons est Germanie ex quo dicunt Danubium nasci; Irmine promontorium est Achaie; Irpinus mons est Sabinorum in quo optimi nascuntur equi."

sical literature and history. To utilise ancient forms of place names meant interrogating the difference between conflicting sources. Yet it also ran the risk of misreading: Mount "Iraurancos" seems to derive from Solinus's description of the "Hister sent forth from the mountain which overlooks the *Rauraci* of Gaul" (*Hister ... effusus monte qui Rauracos Galliae aspectat*), where the Rauraci are a people, not a mountain.[72] The pressure to taxonomise might, then, have the consequence of creating false knowledge: of adding and then itemising new mistakes.[73] If, within humanist geography, the place name became the focus, one might even say the stage, for at times dazzling philological display, it was also witness to a level of tension about the loss and mutation of place – and paradoxically about the invention of place – that bland declarations of findability conceal.

At the conclusion of *De montibus*, Boccaccio confronted head-on the problem of reconciling ancient with modern geography by imagining objections to his attempt to establish the correct form of classical toponyms. "But maybe someone will say: 'if ... today nearly all names of places have changed and nothing antique remains, why do you not use today's names, where you have the opportunity?' ... another will say, 'you could place both new and old alongside each other.'"[74] In response, Boccaccio noted that a complete record of ancient place names did not exist, although a few were preserved and others could be discerned through conjecture; with regard to the first question, the object of the work was to promote the understanding of ancient books, not to alter them by emending every toponym.[75]

72. *De montibus*, ed. Pastore Stocchi, 2052 n366. Pastore Stocchi notes that the source of the misunderstanding could also be Pliny, *Naturalis historia* 4.79. Julius Solinus, *Collectanea rerum memorabilium* 13.1, ed Th. Mommsen (Berlin, 1895), 90; my italics.

73. See Giulia Perucchi, "Boccaccio lettore del Plinio petrarchesco," *Italia medioevale e umanistica* 54 (2013): 153–211, who details many "voces nullius" in *De montibus* and shows that these non-existent or distorted place-names frequently derived from the copy of Pliny's *Naturalis historia* annotated by Petrarch (now Paris, Bibliothèque nationale de France, MS lat. 6802).

74. *De montibus* 7.123; 125, ed. Pastore Stocchi, 2027–28: "Sed erit forte qui dicat: si adeo rudes tibi erant animo, cum hodie fere locorum nomina permutata sint omnia nec aliquid constet antiquum, cur usus non es, ubi opportunitas exegisset, nominibus hodiernis? ... Poteras, dicet alter, et nova et vetera posuisse." For analysis of the epilogue to *De montibus* see Carla Maria Monti, "La *Genealogia* e il *De montibus*: Due parti di un unico progetto," *Studi sul Boccaccio* 44 (2016): 327–66, esp. 352–54, and for contrast with Petrarch's approach to geographic *mutatio* see Vincenzo Fera, "Storia e filologia tra Petrarca e Boccaccio," in *Petrarca, l'umanesimo e la civiltà europea*, 2 vols, ed. Donatella Coppini and Michele Feo (Florence, 2012), 1: 369–89.

75. *De montibus* 7.123–24, ed. Pastore Stocchi, 2027–28: "Non enim est qui hanc doctrinam tradiderit aut memoriale reliquerit, nisi pauca sint, esto per coniecturas aliqua plura deprehendi possint ... In reliquis potius divinasse necesse erat quam alicuius posse imitari vestigium, quod quidem ego non didici. Et si novissem, libri veterum qui talibus utuntur vocabulis, ad quorum intelligentiam opusculum hoc elaboratum est, omnes erant etiam immutandi, qui labor erat indeficiens, nec est meum, nec etiam honeste alterius esse potest."

To the second, Boccaccio points out that the incomplete state of his knowledge makes it impossible to carry out such an approach with consistent accuracy, and that the need to reconcile ancient toponym with modern space should act as a stimulus to other students.[76] These questions and the responses to them suggest that Boccaccio operated with full awareness, and even under the pressure, of modern or "new" place names. Contemporary space remained a constant presence and point of comparison in the attempt to retrieve the ancient toponym.

In the fifteenth century, no text better expressed the humanist need to distinguish past spatial forms, and to read them alongside and against modern spaces, than Biondo Flavio's *Italia Illustrata*. Biondo, a papal secretary with access to the major Italian courts and a member of an extensive network of humanist intellectuals, began the work in 1447 in response to a request from Alfonso of Aragon, king of Naples, for a "catalogue of the illustrious men of Italy." The catalogue rapidly developed into something more adventurous: a survey of Italy at once historical and, in its essence, topographical.[77] Biondo's approach was simultaneously national and regional. Although he treated Italy from Liguria to Calabria as a coherent unity, he divided his treatise by region. Fundamental to *Italia illustrata* is the comparison between antiquity and modernity, *olim* and *nunc*. As did Petrarch and Boccaccio, Biondo too had recourse to a fairly consistent repertoire of classical sources for identifications of places, contextualisations, and colour: Livy, Pliny, Virgil, and Servius (who is often criticised), above all, but by the mid-fifteenth century also the geographies of Ptolemy and Strabo.[78] The relationship between ancient text and contemporary land cut both ways. Reading the textual source helped to read the land, to learn its history, to make out past – and sometimes lost – forms. But implicitly too the relationship could be reversed: land read in order to understand and explicate a text's knotty surface. That said,

76. *De montibus* 7.125, ed. Pastore Stocchi, 2028: "Iam ultro confessus sum me omnia non novisse, que etiam si novissem satius forte fuerat scripsisse ut factum est, ut aliqualis labor studentium relinqueretur ingeniis, ad hoc ut, dum talia perquirendo fatigabuntur, et memoriam firment et illud ad maiora subliment, et magis delectentur invento."

77. See Pontari's introduction to Biondo Flavio, *Italia illustrata*, ed. Paolo Pontari (Rome, 2011–), 1: 34–88. The work seems to have been completed by 1453, but Biondo revised it after the death of Pope Nicolas V in 1455 and compiled "additions and corrections" in 1462.

78. On Biondo's use of medieval sources, such as the *Liber pontificalis*, Paul the Deacon's *Historia Langobardum*, and the chronicle of Ademar of Chabannes see Ottavio Clavuot, *Biondos "Italia illustrata" – Summa oder Neuschöpfung?: Über die Arbeitsmethoden eines Humanisten* (Tübingen, 1990), 253–302, and 307–22 for a list of Biondo's cited sources. Also Riccardo Fubini, "La geografia storica dell' 'Italia illustrata' di Biondo Flavio e le tradizioni dell'etnografia," in *Storiografia dell'umanesimo in Italia da Leonardo Bruni ad Annio da Viterbo* (Rome, 2003), 53–76; Gautier Dalché, "De Pétrarque à Raimondo Marliano," 178–84.

as the following extract from the description of Tuscany suggests, *Italia Illustrata* retained its original function as a conspectus of those heirs of Roman power, the contemporary Italian nobility:

> Two miles from Baccano lies Campagnano di Roma, a town belonging to the Orsini. Fifteen miles to the right beyond Sutri is the Lacus Traquiniae, now Lago di Anguillara, named for the town overlooking it. From here derive the family of the counts of Anguillara, an ancient one by the lights of present-day Romans; one of them, the Roman senator Orso, with Pandolfo Savelli, gave Petrarch the crown of laurel.[79]

The connections between antiquity and modernity in this short passage are several. Landscape, genealogy, literary fame, and raw political power intertwine under the sign of a stately spatial progression. The prose flows smoothly from a modern town, Baccano (which, we have previously been told, has an ancient name), to a town possessed by a powerful contemporary family, the Orsini; then to a lake whose ancient and modern names are provided, and then back to another family, whose genealogy establishes yet another connection with antiquity, and who unexpectedly divert the flow of spatial and temporal associations to Biondo's own intellectual forebear: Petrarch, the laureate poet himself.

It would, however, be misleading to present *Italia illustrata* as a series of smooth transitions from antiquity to modernity. For the text is punctuated with frank admissions of ignorance. Relatively frequently Biondo acknowledges the inscrutability of the past: the objects that cannot be explained satisfactorily, the places that, although mentioned in a source, appear to have vanished without trace.[80] In his description of the land between lake Velino and the city of Rieti in Umbria, ancient region of the Sabines, Biondo calls this absence of knowledge a "mutatio incomprehensibilis":

---

79. Biondo Flavio, *Italy Illuminated* 1.62, ed. and trans. Jeffrey A. White, 2 vols (Cambridge, MA, 2005–16), 1: 114–15: "Bachanis secundo miliario adiacet Campagnanum, Ursinorum oppidum. Supra Sutrium ad dexteram quinto decimo miliario est lacus Tarquiniae, nunc Anguillariae, ab oppido quod illi imminet dictus: ex quo familia fluxit (ut in Romanis nostrae aetatis vetusta) comitum Anguillariae appellata, e quibus Ursus, cum Pandulpho Sabello urbis senator, Franciscum Petrarcham laurea insignivit." The reference to Pandolfo Savelli appeared in the earliest redaction of Biondo's description of Tuscany but was omitted in later versions.

80. See for example 1.5–9, 2.18–20, 23, 56; 4.71, and Pontari's discussion: *Italia illustrata*, ed. Pontari, 1: 81–85.

There are however a very great number of mountains and fields about which the inhabitants do not know enough, and in which there were many ancient places whose names do not correspond to present-day places, either because they ceased to exist, or because they have undergone an inexplicable mutation into other names (*incomprehensibilis mutatio in aliis*).[81]

Some places change their names so wildly as to become unrecognisable. Biondo's ambition, expressed cogently in the preface to his work, was to give life to the names deleted from memory, and through that to illumine (*illustrare*) the obscure within Italian history. But he went on to admit that all he could hope to achieve was to rescue a few planks from a very great shipwreck: the vessel of antiquity could never be recovered in its entirety.[82] The brief admission of loss in Umbria underscores that sense of incompletion, the impossibility of total recovery, the darkness brought by the passage of time. The legibility of space had its limits.

Biondo's influence can be seen in a range of later fifteenth- and sixteenth-century works that began to develop something approaching a historical geography. In 1458, shortly before he was elected pope, Aeneas Silvius Piccolomini composed a history of Europe which was deeply informed by his knowledge of classical geography, and by his attempts to reconcile the testimony of classical authors such as Pliny, Ptolemy, Pomponius Mela, and Strabo with the political and topographical reality of his own era. Piccolomini, who knew Biondo and his work well, repeated the standard lament about *mutatio*. Not only did classical authorities actively contradict each other's descriptions of provinces, the boundaries of provinces had changed countless times since antiquity, "for the province that was once extensive is now either extinct or very modest, while that which never or scarcely existed then we now see large and flourishing: the ancients did not know Lombardy and Romagna; our times are completely igno-

---

81. *Italy Illuminated* 3.19, ed. White, 1: 228–30 (my translation): "Maximus autem is est montium et camporum globus, quem nec incolae satis norunt, et in quo multa fuerunt prisci vocabuli loca quae praesentibus conferri nequeunt, tum quia interierunt quaedam, tum quia incomprehensibilis mutatio in aliis est facta."

82. *Italy Illuminated* pref.3–4, ed. White, 1: 4. On the possibility that Biondo had in mind an actual attempt to recover a Roman ship from the lago di Nemi see Paolo Pontari, "Alberti e Biondo: Archeologia a Nemi," in *Alberti e la cultura del quattrocento*, ed. Roberto Cardini and Mariangela Regoliosi, 2 vols (Florence, 2007), 1: 495–539. As Fubini has observed, Biondo's preface was modelled on Pliny's letter to Titus at start of the *Naturalis historia*: "La geografia storica," 58.

rant of Insubria, Emilia and Flaminia."[83] However, scholars such as Biondo and Piccolomini were increasingly able to date their sources, and thereby account for the differences they found within them. In his description of Asia, for example, Piccolomini noted that discord between the ancients on matters of geography was due not only to the changing names of mountains, rivers and peoples, but because the authorities belonged to different eras: Strabo was writing under Tiberius Caesar, while Ptolemy described the world at the time of Antoninus Pius.[84] That increased level of precision is reflected in what may be the earliest example of historical geography – if understood in the strict sense of a "past geography concretely reconstructed to facilitate the reading of a particular text"[85] – a lexicon of Gallic and German place names from Caesar's *Commentarii de bello Gallico* (Commentaries on the Gallic Wars), complete with identification of the modern names, locations and inhabitants of each place. This lexicon was compiled around 1470 by Raimondo Marliano, an Italian associate of Cardinal Francesco Tedeschini Piccolomini (the future Pope Pius III and nephew of Aeneas Silvius). In a letter presenting the work, Francesco Piccolomini notes that it arose from discussions with Marliano prompted by his own disquiet at the "changed names" (*mutata nomina*) of places in Caesar's *Commentarii*. Marliano's work aimed to interpret correctly both the ancient place names used by Caesar and the corresponding modern toponyms. It was, Piccolomini made clear, a work in progress: the Cardinal used his knowledge of classical sources to identify several errors in Marliano's list of Italian names. But the outlines of a critical method for the excavation of classical geography and the simultaneous articulation of contemporary space had begun to emerge,[86] and would be consolidated further in works such as Ermolao Barbaro's detailed interrogation of the texts of Pliny and Pomponius Mela.[87]

---

83. Aeneas Silvius Piccolomini, *De Europa* 17, ed. Adrianvs van Heck (Vatican City, 2001), 58: "nam que prouincia latissima quondam fuit, etate nostra aut extincta est aut permodica; contra uero que nulla uel minima extitit, nunc latissimam florentissimamque uidemus. Longobardiam ac Romandiolam non cognouere maiores; nostra tempora Insubriam, Emiliam ac Flaminiam prorsus ignorant." On Biondo's influence on Piccolomini see *Italia illustrata*, ed. Pontara, 1: 208–10.

84. Aeneas Silvius Piccolomini, *Asiae descriptio/Descripción de Asia* 18.8, ed. and trans. Domingo F. Sanz (Madrid, 2010), 144.

85. Gautier Dalché, "De Pétrarque à Raimondo Marliano," 188: "une géographie du passé reconstruite contrètement pour faciliter la lecture d'un texte précis."

86. Gautier Dalché, "De Pétrarque à Raimondo Marliano," 184–88.

87. Ermolao Barbaro, *Castigationes Plinianae et in Pomponiam Melam*, ed. Giovanni Pozzi, 3 vols (Padua, 1973–79).

By the early sixteenth century the emergence of the concept of a "new world" confirmed the tendency to lift classical forms from the detritus of succeeding centuries. The landmark edition of Ptolemy's *Geographia* printed in Strasbourg in 1513 contained two sets of maps, compiled by the German cartographer Martin Waldseemüller in collaboration with the brilliant young poet Matthias Ringmann. The first showed the ancient world, as known to Ptolemy, along with an accompanying text of the *Geographia* which featured corrections to Jacopo Angeli's early fifteenth-century Latin translation based on Ringmann's inspection of Greek manuscripts.[88] The second set of maps showed the modern world, including the new discoveries in the west. *Olim* and *nunc* had come into sharper focus, and could be viewed separately, each in its own representational frame. The process was not simply one of clarification: new sources had been assimilated, and old ones re-examined, with the result that a picture of antiquity could be formed. The path to Ortelius was clear.

How much of a breach with the Middle Ages was the humanist mapping of the ancient world? The consciousness of difference between present and past was nothing new; nor was the attempt to identify change. It may be better to think instead of an intensification of energy, combined with the articulation of a dialogic position and the consequent separation of periods across a temporal divide. The past was addressed from the present; the humanist subject turned to face his ancient forebear – who could speak back with increasing levels of detail, as hitherto unknown or unnoticed sources came into circulation, and as they were examined in an increasingly systematic manner. Yet the concept of *mutatio* had not changed, nor the awareness of its problems. And, as Ortelius was to show, *mutatio* remained entwined with *translatio*, complementing and at times undermining it.

Mutatio incomprehensibilis

The correspondence of Abraham Ortelius reveals the vitality of antiquarian interest in the past in the second half of the sixteenth century. The range is very wide: correspondents comment, as might be expected, on maps, coins, and inscriptions, but also on fossils, plants, and insects, as well as herring and salmon. The geographical interests include Asia and the New World, but the focus of the letters falls on antique geography. Ortelius's *Synonomia*, a catalogue of all place names listed by classical authors, with their modern render-

---

88. Claudius Ptolemy, *Geographiae opus novissima traductione e Grecorum archetypis castigatissime pressum* (Strasbourg, 1513).

ing,[89] and his "historical" maps – the Roman Empire, the *peregrinatio* of Aeneas, Alexander's campaign, the map of the Holy Land – were received with excitement equal to, and perhaps greater than, that generated by his modern maps. Big questions, potentially disturbing and divisive in their implications, lurked around many of the topics raised in the correspondence. These extended beyond concerns about the mutation from ancient to modern names, to more profound questions about original inhabitation, pre- and post-flood – about the history of all creation, not just human. Ortelius and his correspondents discussed these matters against the backdrop, actually at times more a foreground, of extreme civil disturbance and conflict. The two cannot be unconnected. The letters were a means of disseminating news and effecting commercial transactions, even as they preserved intellectual communication across lines of religious and political conflict.

As several of the letters received by Ortelius attest, his maps of antiquity pleased but at times also displeased men of learning. These letters reveal the precise, sometimes parochial, ways in which Ortelius's readers viewed the relationship between the space of classical antiquity and that of their own era. Nicolas Clément de Trèles ("Mosellanus") wrote to Ortelius in 1583 to note that "The interpreters of Caesar's *Commentarii* wrongly call Nancium [Nancy], which is a town of Lorraine, 'Nasium.' The latter lies twelve miles from Nancy, and was built up into a very large town not far from the Meuse river in the province of Bar-le-Duc. Today it is a village, commonly known as 'Nas' [Naix-aux-Forges]. A stone excavated in that place confirms my opinion ... This excerpt comes to you from my notes on Austrasian Kings and Dukes whose inscriptions I transcribed."[90] Some ten years later Manuel

---

89. Initially printed as an appendix to the *Theatrum*, the *Synonymia* was published separately in 1578, then reworked and augmented as the *Thesaurus Geographicus* of 1587; a second edition of the *Thesaurus* appeared in 1596, and Ortelius was still working on it at his death two years later. See Peter H. Meurer, "Synonymia-Thesaurus-Nomenclator: Ortelius' Dictionaries of Ancient Geographical Names," in *Abraham Ortelius and the First Atlas: Essays Commemmorating the Quadricentennial of His Death, 1598–1998*, ed. Marcel van den Broecke et al. (Houten, 1998), 331–46.

90. *Abrahami Ortelii et virorum eruditorum ad eundem et ad Jacobum Colium Ortelianum epistulae*, ed. J.H. Hessels (Cambridge, 1887), 1: 289–91 (Paris, 1 April 1583): "Nancium Lothoringiae oppidum ... male Caesarianorum Commentariorum interpretes dicunt Nasium, a Nancio 12 milliaribus dissitum, quod ex ruderibus urbem amplissimam non procul a Mosa fluvio in Barroducana provincia fuisse colligitur. hodie pagus est, vulgo Nas. eo loci effossus lapis meam sententiam firmat. ...Ex meis adnotationibus in Austrasios Reges et Duces quos epigrammatibus descripsi, excerpta tibi sunt haec." Clément was secretary to the duke of Anjou; his work *Austrasiae reges et duces epigrammatis* appeared in 1591. On the state of Ortelius's correspondence see Joost Depuydt, "New Letters for a Biography of Abraham Ortelius," *Imago Mundi* 68 (2016): 67–78, and for an outline of Ortelius's antiquarian network see Tine Luk Meganck, *Erudite Eyes: Friendship, Art and Erudition in the Network of Abraham Ortelius (1527–1598)* (Leiden, 2017), 1–35.

Barbosa wrote to Ortelius from Oporto, criticising the Portuguese parts of the map of ancient Spain. Not only was the river Cadova depicted on the wrong side of Braga, Ortelius had omitted the towns of "Cinania" ("which today we call Sitania") and "Manliana" ("today Monte Mor o Novo"), both recorded by ancient authorities.[91] The political and intellectual importance of reading maps is perhaps most strikingly distilled in Claes Govaertszoon's sharp criticism of Ortelius for not printing the descriptions that appear on the back of the maps in the *Theatrum* in Dutch, despite the fact that they had appeared in Spanish. Given the state of the Dutch-Spanish conflict in the 1590s these words carry the assertion of national feeling: "Yet I should like to have the ancient and modern names of the countries, cities, mountains, seas, and rivers, either in Dutch or Latin, that they may be bound in my second volume, as otherwise we Dutch do not understand the maps."[92] It was important for a national group, defined by language and shared political interest, to be able to read its geographical space in its antique and modern forms. Ortelius's maps constructed a dialogue, so also a clear distinction, between modernity and antiquity, at a time when the records of antiquity – its texts, but also its physical and linguistic remains – were being eagerly mined for information, to suit more than one agenda.

Compared with the long medieval tradition of reading classical texts and attempting to understand and reconstruct classical spaces, what was different in the sixteenth century was not the capacity or desire to identify change, nor the interest in reading maps to understand ancient history and literature. Geography, under other names, had been the "eye of history" for some time. Undoubtedly, however, the pursuit of ancient sources – now much more readily available – had become more thorough, while print encouraged texts such as the *Parergon* to mushroom from slender appendices into substantial volumes. Perhaps most crucially, the development of the atlas in the course of the sixteenth century saw the separation between antiquity and modernity, the provision of special sections dedicated to maps of the ancient world, rather than the inclusion of multiple temporalities within single maps – a process neatly represented at the south entrance to the Galleria delle Carte Geografiche in the Vatican, constructed in 1578–81, where maps of "Italia Antiqua" and "Italia Nova" face one another.

91. *Epistulae*, ed. Hessels, 1: 568–69 (Oporto, 26 September 1593). Ortelius responded swiftly to this criticism by inserting Cinniana on the Alestes river.

92. *Epistulae*, ed. Hessels, 1: 571–72 (Middelburg, 31 January 1594)(trans. Hessels): "Nochtans soude ick wel de Oude ende Nieuwe Namen vande Landen, Steden, Bergen, Zeen, ende Riuieren, begeren te hebben: Het zy dan in Duytsche off Latinsche sprake: om in myn voorseide tweede volumen gebonden te mogen werden, want anders en verstaen wy Duytschen dickwils de Caerten niet."

Nevertheless, Ortelius's maps present something more complex than modern set against ancient. Many of his statements suggest that Ortelius did not perceive such a great breach with antiquity. After all, deep antiquity was still audible in the everyday speech of Germans, and as the *Romani Imperii Imago* suggested, the land too could be read as an ancient text. That ancient, indigenous connection to Europe seems to speak less of translation than of the stubborn perseverence of peoples and languages, of the continuities embedded in place and speech. At the same time, there was space on Ortelius's maps for discontinuities, for the unrecovered and perhaps irrecoverable. On many of the maps in the *Parergon*, Ortelius provided a list – sometimes a very long list – of the places and peoples, mountains and rivers, that he could not locate on the map. "Places of unknown position" in Ancient Spain, towns in Ancient Gaul that "Caesar describes but does not name," "peoples of unknown position" in Cisalpine Gaul: from Pannonia to Egypt, the majority of antiquarian maps in the *Parergon* record some kind of inaccessible information.[93] On later editions of the *Theatrum* a line was struck through one or two of the hitherto unknown places, to indicate that its location on the map had been found, often thanks to the information of one of Ortelius's correspondents.[94] This admission of incompletion and call for assistance, this expression of Biondo's *mutatio incomprehensibilis*, was the product of the thorough search of ancient records characteristic of humanist investigations of spatial history. Amid the grand projects of translation, with their promise of renewals and relocations, awakenings and linear destiny, dwelled *mutatio*. Mutation, that is, not only of the kind recorded in the familiar "olim ... nunc" formulation, but also mutation in the form of disappearance, of peoples and places now no longer locatable, those who could be neither included nor excluded. This *mutatio* led nowhere but to an appendix of lost knowledge: a home for the untranslated, the ghost-list of history.

93. Examples: on the "Hispaniae Veteris Descriptio": "Hispaniae loca aliquot incognitae positionis"; on the map of "Gallia vetus": "opida Venetorum, que Caesar describit at non nominat"; on the "Pannoniae et Illyrici veteris tabula": "Loca incertae positionis"; on the "Siciliae Veteris Typus": "Veteris Siciliae loca, incertae aut prorsus incognitae positionis"; on the map of "Aegypti reliqua" (i.e. southern Egypt to Ethiopia): "incertae positionis loca"; and on "Africa propria": "Loca incognitae positionis ex varijs antiquae notae auctoribus."

94. For example, in the 1595 edition, Cinniana appears with strikethrough in the list of places of unknown position, and freshly inserted in the "Hispaniae Veteris Descriptio": van den Broecke, *Ortelius Atlas Maps* 588; London, British Library, Maps C.2.d.5.

CHAPTER SIX

Migration, Nation

The representation of peoples was always part of the representation of
geographical space. Names of ethnic groups helped to define space, and could
function in ways identical to toponyms. However, they brought with them the
inherent problem of the representation of movement. In part this was a textual
problem. The static page is not well equipped to show motion across space without recourse to lines, arrows, and similar devices. But it was also a conceptual
problem: since migration is a passage between and through locations, it naturally puts pressure on a unified understanding of location. Where were the
migrants? In their original site, their destination, or eternally en route? The movement of individuals and entire peoples found narrative expression across a range
of medieval genres, from simple itineraries to travel and pilgrimage accounts, to
reworkings of classical epic. Medieval geographical thought thereby memorialised acts of migration without ever establishing the category of the migrant.
Certain groups (the Israelites, the Trojans) were inherently associated with a
historic exodus; others (the Scythians) possessed wandering as a characteristic,
"semper vagantes." Individuals – the evangelist, the saint, the ancestor, the exile,
the pilgrim – could also signify multiple locations.

In concert with purely verbal descriptions, mapmakers responded to the
problem of capturing movement in a variety of ways. Most obviously the itinerary map, known to classical as well as medieval Europe, noted the length of journey between places in terms of both space and time.[1] Yet other adaptations were
possible. In the corpus of *mappae mundi* in manuscripts of Beatus of Liébana's
eighth-century commentary on the *Apocalypse*, three maps use disembodied
heads to mark the regions to which the twelve apostles were assigned, thereby
representing the movement, and martyrdom, of the evangelists throughout the
known world.[2] Elsewhere lines, broken and unbroken, or simply an arrangement

---

1. The Peutinger Tables (see Chapter 2) and Matthew Paris's mid-thirteenth-century
itinerary from St Albans to the Holy Land (Chapter 7) are the obvious examples.

2. The three maps are El Burgo de Osma, Archivo de la Catedral, Codex 1, fols. 34v–35r
(1086); Milan, Biblioteca Ambrosiana, MS F.150 sup., fols. 71v–72r (c. 1200), and the frag-

of toponyms in linear fashion, could serve to show passage. The representation of migration – a *migratio, peregrinatio, transitus,* or simply an *iter* – naturally did not end with the Middle Ages. The desire to document peregrination seems if anything to have intensified in the sixteenth century, above all within the emerging genre of historical geography.

In the following pages two "migrations" serve to illustrate the complexities of the interaction of narratives of movement with spatial representation. These cases indicate the way in which historical figures could be characterised by associations with multiple places in medieval texts across a range of genres. The Bible and the many commentaries upon it encouraged contemplation of the passage of the Israelites from exile to the "promised land"; hagiography presented saints linked both to their place of origin and to their place of martyrdom. In both cases the strands of narrative and interpretation are plural, because the Middle Ages inherited different stories of the same journey, and consequently different understandings of the spatial and temporal dislocations in question. Standing as a counterpoint to these two narratives is the question of nation. If *natio* was an ethnic rather than a spatial concept in the early Middle Ages – an idea that moved with people, rather than inhering to land – the question arises when, if at all, nation began to be conceived in spatial terms in the following centuries; when, in other words, did nations cease to migrate?

THE PASSAGE OF THE ISRAELITES

The first *mansio* is Ramesse, a city at the ends of Egypt. There Israel assembled and entered the desert ... Ramesse means rousing (*commotio*) or thunder (*tonitruum*).

Second *mansio* is Sochot. There they first cooked unleavened bread and fixed their tents. Sochot means tabernacles or tents.

Third *mansio* is Ethan in the wilderness. There God first appeared to the chosen people in a column of fire by night ... Ethan is translated as fortitude or perfection.

---

ment from Lorvão: Lisbon, Arquivo Nacional da Torre do Tombo, MS CXIII/247, fol. 34 bis v (1189). Other maps in the corpus identify the regions to which the apostles were assigned, in fulfilment of the purpose of the map as conceived by Beatus, but the heads themselves may be a later addition: John Williams, "Isidore, Orosius and the Beatus Map," *Imago Mundi* 49 (1997): 7–32, at 23–24; Sandra Sáenz-López Pérez, *The Beatus Maps: The Revelation of the World in the Middle Ages*, trans. Peter Krakenberger and Gerry Coldham (Burgos, 2014), 181–96.

Fourth *mansio* is Fyahirot. It is opposite Belfeson. Fiahirot means noble mouth, Belfeson the lord of the north.

Fifth *mansio* Mara, the third day after the crossing of the Red Sea. Mara means bitterness.

Sixth *mansio* Helym. There they found twelve springs and seventy palms. Helym is translated as strong rams.

Seventh *mansio* the return to the Red Sea, running up against one of its gulfs.

Eighth *mansio* in the wilderness of Syn, which extends to Mount Sinai. Syn means thorn bush or hatred.

Ninth *mansio* Depheca, which means beating.

Tenth *mansio* Alys, which means yeast. In that wilderness Israel murmured against hunger, accepting quail in the evening and manna the morning after.

Eleventh *mansio* Raphydim, which means desolation of the strong or abatement of manna. When the people thirsted here, a spring emerged from the rock Horeb. There Joshua defeated Amalech, and Gethro came to Moses. There certain people, murmuring against the Lord when Moses was absent, made a bull-calf from gold, adoring it.

Twelfth *mansio* Sinai in the wilderness. Sinai means thorn bush. In this *mansio* Moses ascended to the lord on Mount Sinai. And there the lord descended to him, giving him the law written with his own hand on stone tables cut from the same mountain. ...

Thirteenth *mansio* in the caves of desire. ...

Fourteenth *mansio* was Aseroth, in which Aaron the high priest coming upon the place of disfavour, with his sister Maria decried his brother Moses, because he had taken a foreign wife. On that account Aseroth means offence (*offensio*).

Fifteenth *mansio* Rethma. It means noise or juniper. ...

Sixteenth *mansio* Ramoth. It means division of the pomegranate (*mali punici divisio*).

Seventeenth *mansio* Lebna. It means on the side.

Eighteenth *mansio* Rethsa. It translates as bridles (*frenos*).

Nineteenth *mansio* Celatha. It means church.

Twentieth *mansio* Mount Sepher. It means beauty; that is, Christ.

Twenty-first *mansio* Arada. It means miracle.

Twenty-second *mansio* Maceloth. It means in a company (*in coetu*); that is, in church.

Twenty-third *mansio* Caath. It means fear.

Twenty-fourth *mansio* Thare. It means in malice or in pasture.

Twenty-fifth *mansio* Metheha. It translates as sweetness.

Twenty-sixth *mansio* Asmona. It means haste.

Twenty-seventh *mansio* Aseroth. It means chains or discipline (*vincula sive disciplina*).

Twenty-eighth *mansio* Baneiachain. It translates as children of need or of shrill voice.

Twenty-ninth *mansio* Mount Gadgad. It means messenger. Or arming. Or circumcision.

Thirtieth *mansio* Gabathad. It means goodness; that is, Christ.

Thirty-first *mansio* Ebrona. It means passage; that is, world.

Thirty-second *mansio* Asyongaber. It translates as tree of man.

Thirty-third *mansio* the desert of Sin. That is, Cades. That is, Cades Barne. Sin means holy by antiphrasis, like grove (*lucus*) because it scarcely grows light (*minime luceat*). It was there that Maria the sister of Moses and Aaron died, and was buried. There Moses offended God on account of the waters of contradiction. Which is why he was not allowed to cross the Jordan. ...

Thirty-fourth *mansio* Mount Or at the ends of Edom. ...

Thirty-fifth *mansio* Selmona.

Thirty-sixth *mansio* Finon. These two *mansiones* cannot be found in the historical record. Here when Aaron died Israel murmured against the Lord and against Moses, disdaining manna.

Thirty-seventh *mansio* Oboth. It translates as magi or sorcerers.

Thirty-eighth *mansio* Hebar in the ends of Moab. It means heaps of stones for crossings.

Thirty-ninth *mansio* Dibungat. There Israel fought against Sehon king of the Amorrhites and against Og king of Basan. Sehon means temptation of the eyes. Og means conclusion, Basan confusion.

Fortieth *mansio* from Dibungat into Helmon deblataym. It translates as despising of figs or of dishonours. There, very near Jericho, is Thafon, where Moses wrote Deuteronomy. And there is Cademoth the place from which Moses sent legates to Sehon king of the Amorrhites.

Forty-first *mansio* Mount Abarym, opposite the face of Nabo. Mount Abarim means crossing. There Moses died and deserved to be buried by the Lord. But his tomb has never been found. ...

Forty-second *mansio* Moab in the fields above the Jordan near Jericho. ...

Rorgo Fretellus, Descriptio de locis sanctis[3]

---

3. *Rorgo Fretellus de Nazareth et sa description de la terre sainte: Histoire et édition du texte*, ed. P.C. Boeren (Amsterdam, 1980), 12–16.

Told one way, the exodus of the Israelites is the founding narrative of Judaism and Christianity. Enshrined primarily in the biblical books of Exodus and Numbers, it is a story of persecution and divine intervention, of miraculous escapes and sudden punishments, of deserts, seas, and mountains, of rebellion and the realisation of promise. It is simultaneously the narrative of Moses, his people, and their intimate relationship with a God who commands, strikes down, gives law, and finally delivers them to land. Told another way, however, it is a list of numbers and places, and as the third-century Christian exegete Origen freely admitted, numbers and place names were not easy to read. "Take someone who, when the Evangelists or Paul or the psalms are read, happily receives them, freely embraces them, and rejoices as one gathering remedies for his infirmity. If the book of Numbers is read ... this same man will identify nothing of use there, no remedy for his infirmity or salvation of the soul, and he will continually refuse and spit out such heavy and burdensome food ... ."[4]

But what if the story of exodus were read spiritually? Might that heavy food be made somewhat more palatable if the *mansiones* of the Israelites became the staging posts on the story of the soul's journey to God, if the exit from Egypt became the departure from the life of the unbeliever to recognition of divine law, or the soul's flight from the human body? In Origen's allegory, the soul's journey began with "commotio" (rousing, or agitation) in Ramesse, and moved step by step towards the river of God, "so that we might stand next to the flow of wisdom and be fortified by the waves of divine knowledge," with Jesus Christ as our guide.[5] The soul's steps involved purification and labour, vision, temptation, and contemplation, the extinction of desire and the acquisition of law in the desert. This journey was now unequivocally, even aggressively, Christian, its Judaic foundation assimilated: Methca, the twenty-fifth station, meant "new death," so it meant to die and be buried with Christ in order that we might live with him; the forty-two mansiones corresponded to the forty-two generations from Abraham to the birth of Jesus.[6]

---

4. *Homilia in Numeros* 27.1, in *Origenes Werke*, ed. W.A. Baehrens (Leipzig, 1921), 7: 256: "Sed et alius, cum leguntur evangelia vel Apostolus aut psalmi, laetus suscipit, libenter amplectitur et velut remedia quaedam infirmitatis suae inde colligens gaudet. Huic si legatur Numerorum liber et ista maxime loca, quae nunc habemus in manibus, nihil haec ad utilitatem, nihil ad infirmitatis suae remedium aut animae salutem prodesse iudicabit, sed continuo refutabit et respuet tamquam graves et onerosos cibos ... ."

5. *Homilia in Numeros* 27.12, ed. Baehrens, 279: "ad flumen Dei, ut proximi efficiamur fluentis sapientiae et rigemur undis scientiae divinae."

6. *Homilia in Numeros* 27.12, ed. Baehrens, 275 (Methca); 27.3, ed. Baehrens, 259–60 (generations of Christ).

At the heart of that assimilation was the translation of Hebrew names into Greek, and from Greek – thanks to Origen's translator, Rufinus – into Latin. Each toponym had a meaning; that meaning was either itself allegorical, or could be understood allegorically. The interplay of at least three languages allowed commentators critical scope. Eusebius of Caesarea's *Onomasticon*, translated by Jerome from Greek into Latin, contained the literal meanings of place names (where these were known), their geographical locations, and discussion of their significance in biblical history. In his commentary on the journey of the Israelites contained in the *Epistola ad Fabiolam*, Jerome repeated Origen's interpretations of some place names, but also frequently disagreed with them, adducing further possible meanings thanks to his facility with Hebrew. Ramesse did not signify "commotio," but rather "tonitruum gaudii" (thunder-clap of joy); for Jerome, Methca meant "sweetness," the sweet fruit of labour.[7] The orthography of some of the toponyms in circulation had, Jerome observed, been corrupted, leading to mis-interpretations: it was remarkable that erudite men without Hebrew presented fictive explanations of places, as for example when they read Raphaca for Dephca (as Origen had done), and concluded that it meant "curatio" (oversight).[8] Jerome also noted that at least two of the *mansiones* (the thirty-fifth and thirty-sixth) had no historical attestation that he could find.[9] Naturally these disagreements led to differences, sometimes significant, in the understanding of exodus on both the literal and spiritual planes. Whereas Origen thought Moseroth, the twenty-seventh mansio, meant "excludens" (excluding malign thoughts), Jerome translated its meaning as "vincula" or "disciplina." There were two kinds of chain, he explained: the chains that tie an enemy, and the chains of Christ which are voluntary and turn into an embrace (*amplexus*).[10]

After Jerome, both the literal understanding of the biblical text and its allegorical significations were firmly established in medieval Christian thinking about the exodus.[11] The commentaries of Origen and Jerome found their way into the *Glossa ordinaria*, from its compilation in the twelfth century the standard

7. Jerome, "Ad Fabiolam de mansionibus filiorum Israhel per heremum," Epistula 78, in *Sancti Eusebii Hieronymi Epistulae*, ed. I. Hilberg (Vienna, 1996), 49–87, at 53, 71 (78.3; 78.27).

8. "Ad Fabiolam," 78.11, ed. Hilberg, 60.

9. "Ad Fabiolam," 78.37 ed. Hilberg, 78: "in ordine historiae non inueniuntur."

10. "Ad Fabiolam," 78.29, ed. Hilberg, 72; Origen, *Homilia in Numeros* 27.12, ed. Baehrens, 276. Cf. Jerome, *Liber interpretationis Hebraicorum nominum*, ed. P. de Lagarde (Turnhout, 1959), 82: "Maseroth exclusiones uel uincula aut successiones siue disciplinae, quod in nostris codicibus Mazuroth legitur."

11. Substantial treatments, dependent on the exegesis of Origen or Jerome, included pseudo-Ambrose, *De xlii mansionibus filiorum Israel*, Patrologia Latina (PL) 17: 9–40, Isidore of Seville, *Quaestiones in Vetus Testamentum*, PL 83: 207–444, Bede's letter to Acca *De*

medieval commentary on the Bible. The reader was urged to perform his or her own flight from Egypt, understood as a flight from the power of demons, and to follow Moses, "that is, the law of God."[12] The desert and the Red Sea signified the world through which the believer had to pass. The law on first receipt was bitter (*amarus/Mara*) but through the wood of life (*per lignum vitae*) and with spiritual understanding it became sweet, allowing the people to move from the Old Testament to the New, and to the twelve apostolic fonts and the seventy palm trees of the sixth *mansio*. Such a reading enshrined a clear demarcation between Jewish and Christian cultures: the Jews were still at Mara (bitter waters), for God had not yet shown them the wood (i.e. cross), "because unless they shall believe, they will not understand."[13] Moses himself saw the promised land but did not enter because, as the law, he prefigured the advent of Christ and the doctrine of the gospels, yet led no-one to perfection.[14] In the twelfth century, Hugh of St Victor similarly understood the forty-two *mansiones* as the passage of God's people into the Church, figured as the mystic ark of Noah, from "the Egypt of natural law through the desert of written law ... to the promised land of grace."[15] Yet at the level of individual toponyms, the differences within patristic exegesis and the sheer number of subsequent commentators ensured a plurality of interpretations. The same author could associate the Red Sea with the blood of Christ, and consequently baptism, while finding that designating the Jordan as baptism usefully marked the distinction between Moses (Judaism) and Joshua (Christianity).[16] The manifold interpretations of the names of the *mansiones* would fill a heavy book, Peter Damian noted wearily in a letter of 1069; sometimes, he sug-

---

mansionibus filiorum Israel (Epistula 14), PL 94: 699–702, and Rabanus Maurus, *Enarrationes in librum Numerorum*, PL 108: 808–27.

12. PL 113: 224 (Exodus 14:2): "si Moysen, id est legem Dei, sequeris, Aegyptus te insectatur." The source is Origen's fifth homily on Exodus: *Werke*, 6: 188.

13. PL 113: 234 (Exodus 15:27), from Origen's seventh homily on Exodus: *Werke*, 6: 208: "quia nisi crediderint, non intelligent." The quotation is a version of Isaiah 7:9: "Si non credideritis, non permanebitis."

14. PL 113: 504 (Deuteronomy 34:1): "quia lex adventum Christi et doctrinam Evangelii verbis et figuris presignavit, sed neminem ad perfectum duxit."

15. *Libellus de formatione arche* 9–10, ed. P. Sicard (Turnhout, 2001), 155–56: "populus Dei spiritaliter ab Egypto naturalis legis per desertum scripte legis tendit ad terram promissionis gratie."

16. The association of the Red Sea with baptism derived from Paul, 1 Cor 10:2: "et omnes in Moyse baptizati sunt in nube et in mari"; in his sermons Caesarius of Arles confirmed this interpretation, while explaining that the Sea was "red with the blood of Christ" (*Christi sanguine rubicundum*): *Caesarii Arelatensis Opera*, vol. 1: *Sermones*, ed. G. Morin, 2nd ed. (Turnhout, 1953), 397 (sermo 97) and 478–79 (sermo 115) for the Jordan as baptism; see also Isidore of Seville, *Quaestiones in Vetus Testamentum*, PL 83: 341.

gested, it was better to avoid their interior recesses (*archana cubicula*), and present the names simply, like an exterior wall.[17]

However compelling the allegorical interpretation of the exodus of the Israelites, direct contact with Egypt and Palestine continued to inform the literal understanding of scripture. Pilgrimage to the Holy Land had already begun over a century before Jerome translated and commented upon the Bible.[18] It continued during the Middle Ages in spite of – at times, assisted by – the shifting political configuration of the region. Under the banner of the Crusades, for a time Christians gained possession of large swathes of their "terra sancta," including Jerusalem. The first crusade (1096–1101) saw the capture of Jerusalem in 1099, leading some – such as the archdeacon of Antioch, Rorgo Fretellus – to hail its participants as a "second Israel" expelling the Philistines and the Canaanites. Writing at the height of the Latin Kingdom, and from within its ecclesiastical administration, in 1137 or 1138 Fretellus dedicated a description of holy places to a visiting Bohemian pilgrim, the bishop of Olomouc, Jindřich Zdík.[19] In this version of his *Descriptio*, Fretellus gave a list of the forty-two *mansiones* of the Israelites principally derived from Isidore of Seville's *Quaestiones in Vetus Testamentum*, a work itself heavily dependent on Jerome's *Epistola ad Fabiolam*.[20] Fretellus cut down on the allegorical exegesis of his sources, and framed the work within the crusader context: the prologue hails the crusaders as "new Machabees" (*novi Machabei*); the final chapters celebrate the "second Israel's" capture of

17. *Die Briefe des Petrus Damiani*, ed. Kurt Reindel, 4 vols (Munich: Monumenta Germaniae Historica, 1983–93), 4: 115 (no. 160): "non ut earum scrutemur archana cubicula, sed ut in earum nominibus tanquam exteriora parietum simpliciter ostendamus."

18. See E.D. Hunt, *Holy Land Pilgrimage in the Later Roman Empire AD 312–460* (Oxford, 1982), 2–5.

19. *Rorgo Fretellus de Nazareth*, viii–xvii.

20. A different version of Fretellus's text, dedicated to a lord "R" (identified by Hiestand as Rodrigo Gonzalez of Toledo), omits the *mansiones*: see Rudolf Hiestand, "Un centre intellectuel en Syrie du Nord? Notes sur la personnalité d'Aimery d'Antioche, Albert de Tarse et Rorgo Fretellus," *Le Moyen Âge* 100 (1994): 7–36, at 19–36. The complexities of the manuscript tradition of Fretellus are great, as the work was widely copied and incorporated by other authors, such as John of Würzburg, into their own works: see *Rorgo Fretellus de Nazareth*, 2–5, 48–52, 80–83; *Peregrinationes tres: Saewulf, John of Würzburg, Theodericus*, ed. R.B.C. Huygens (Turnhout, 1994), 18–21. The *mansiones* in Fretellus appear in substantially similar form in an anonymous contemporaneous text *De situ urbis Ierusalem*: this work, once attributed to Fretellus, is printed in *Itinera Hierosolymitana Crucesignatorum (saec. XII-XIII)*, ed. Sabino de Sandoli, 4 vols (Jerusalem, 1980), 2: 74–117, at 84–90. On Isidore's use of Jerome, see D.J. Uitvlugt, "The Sources of Isidore's Commentaries on the Pentateuch," *Revue Bénédictine* 112 (2002): 72–100.

Jerusalem under Godfrey of Bouillon.[21] The space of the Holy Land is read at once literally, allegorically, and historically: "regard holy Jerusalem," Fretellus urges, "and contemplate Syon itself, which allegorically figures for us the celestial paradise, and in which now some of the more courageous of Israel, new Machabees that is, watch over the couch of Solomon himself, subduing the Edomite and Amalek."[22] Such success proved to be relatively short-lived. Muslim forces led by Saladin reclaimed the holy city in 1187, and just over a century later the Christians lost their last stronghold in the region with the fall of Acre. Yet military defeats impeded Christian pilgrimage only for a short time: fourteenth-century pilgrims were still able to gain access to Egypt and the Holy Land, where they sometimes found functioning Christian churches and monasteries.

When pilgrims came they remembered the biblical text; at times they read and recited parts of it.[23] They may have recalled passages of exegesis; their own passage was in any case itself an act of exegesis, as were the written and oral accounts they gave of it. Many headed straight for Jerusalem, but many also retraced the footsteps of the sons of Israel, finding signs of exodus still visible. For this was a place of ruins recent and ancient, of imprints. In a twelfth-century reworking of Bede's *De locis sanctis*, Peter the Deacon commented that the wheel marks of Pharaoh's chariots would last forever: they progressed right up to the Red Sea, at which point they disappeared.[24] The 1335 pilgrimage narrative of

21. *Rorgo Fretellus de Nazareth*, 6, 38, 43–44. The celebration of Godfrey was omitted from the later versions of the *Descriptio*. On the relatively widespread representation of the crusaders as "new Machabees" see René Richtscheid, "Die Kreuzfahrer als *novi Machabei*: Zur Verwendungsweise der Makkabäermetaphorik in chronikalischen Quellen der Rhein- und Maaslande zur Zeit der Kreuzzüge," in Campana pulsante convocati: *Festschrift anläßlich der Emeritierung von Prof. Dr. Alfred Haverkamp*, ed. Frank G. Hirschmann and Gerd Mentgen (Trier, 2005), 473–86.

22. *Rorgo Fretellus de Nazareth*, 6: "considera sanctam Iherusalem, contemplare et ipsam Syon, que celestem paradysum allegorice nobis figurat et in qua modo fortiores ex Israel, novi Machabei scilicet, veri Salomonis lectulum excubant, expugnantes inde Ydumeum et Amalech." The "lectulus Salomonis" refers to Song of Songs 3:7 ("En lectulum Salomonis sexaginta fortes ambiunt / Ex fortissimis Israel"). The Edomites and Amalekites were among the traditional enemies of Israel: Deuteronomy 25:17–19; 1 Machabaeorum 5.

23. *Itinerarium Egeriae* 10.7, ed. Aet. Franceschini and R. Weber, in *Itineraria et alia geographica*, 2 vols (Turnhout, 1965), 1: 28–90, at 51. See E.D. Hunt, "The Itinerary of Egeria: Reliving the Bible in Fourth-Century Palestine," in *The Holy Land, Holy Lands, and Christian History*, ed. R.N. Swanson (Woodbridge, 2000), 34–54.

24. Peter the Deacon, *Liber de locis sanctis*, ed. R. Weber, in *Itineraria et alia geographica*, 1: 93–103, at 100–101: "Vestigia autem currus Pharaonis in mediis arenis parent usque in sempiternum." Exodus 14:6–28 for the "currus Pharaonis"; Orosius reported that the tracks of chariots could still be seen on the shore and even in the depths, as far as could be seen; God restored them whenever they were disturbed: Paulus Orosius, *Historiarum adversum paganos libri vii* 1.10.17, ed. C. Zangemeister (Vienna, 1882), 58.

the Augustinian monk Jacopo da Verona records bones in great quantity in seaside caves where Pharaoh and his people were submerged; there too was the place where Moses's sister Maria sang "Cantemus Domino gloriose" (Exodus 15:1–21).[25] On Mount Sinai, Moses had pressed himself against a rock in fear of the Lord: his form was still visible, and pilgrims were allowed to insert themselves into it.[26] The water that Moses struck from the rock Horeb to quell the murmuring of the Israelites still flowed – and pilgrims drank it.[27] You found not the burning bush but the place where it once was and, by the thirteenth century, when the German pilgrim Thietmar described it, a splendid simulacrum in gold, the original having been long since dismembered and spread throughout Christendom. On either side of the bush were two images of Moses himself, one taking his shoes off, the other barefoot.[28] Traces abounded, but they were not always uplifting: you might equally pass through once populous cities now shrunk and squalid, a shadow of their former selves. The pilgrim Egeria, who followed the path of the Israelites in the early 380s, found nothing but ruins at Ramesse, apart from two large statues, said to be of Moses and Aaron.[29] For Burchard of Mount Sion, like Thietmar a thirteenth-century German in the Holy Land, once glorious Jericho now had scarcely eight houses, the traces of the city were paltry, and all the monuments of holy places in it had been totally destroyed.[30]

Distractions of various kinds were at hand for those following the footsteps of the Israelites. The place by the Red Sea where pilgrims saw the wheels of Pharaoh's chariot was by late antiquity an entrepôt called Clesma where you could watch ships sail to and from India and, one sixth-century witness averred, munch on green nuts which were said to come from the earthly paradise; almost a millennium later Petrarch warned the pious against the diverting aromas of eastern merchandise there.[31] Symon Semeonis, an Irishman of the fourteenth

25. *Liber peregrinationis*, ed. Ugo Monneret de Villard (Rome, 1950), 78.

26. *Mag[istri] Thietmari Peregrinatio*, ed. J.C.M. Laurent (Hamburg, 1857), 47 (ch. 23); Jacopo da Verona, *Liber peregrinationis*, ed. Monneret de Villard, 76: "de illo lapide ego recepi cum magno labore."

27. Jacopo da Verona, *Liber peregrinationis*, ed. Monneret de Villard, 72.

28. *Thietmari Peregrinatio*, ed. Laurent, 42 (ch. 18).

29. *Itinerarium Egeriae* 8.2, ed. Franceschini and Weber, 48.

30. Burchard of Mount Sion, *Descriptio Terrae Sanctae*, in *Peregrinatores Medii Aevi Quattuor*, ed. J.C.M. Laurent (Leipzig, 1864), 58.

31. On Clesma/Clysma (modern Suez): *Itinerarium Egeriae* 6.4, ed. Franceschini and Weber, 46; *Itinerarium Antonini Placentini* 41, ed. P. Geyer, in *Itineraria et alia geographica*, 1: 127–74, at 151 for ships and nuts; Peter the Deacon, *Liber de locis sanctis*, ed. Weber, 100–101; Francis Petrarch, *Itinerarium ad sepulcrum Domini nostri Ihesu Christi*, ed. Francesco Lo Monaco (Bergamo, 1990), 80 for smells, albeit without explicit mention of Clesma. Jacopo da Verona mentions pepper, ginger, cinnamon, and "other precious spices" on Red Sea ships:

century, made reference to the sixty-year wandering of the sons of Israel as he set off from Cairo to Jerusalem. But in the desert Symon recorded peoples and hardships unmentioned in Exodus or Numbers: a Sultan and his retinue returning from a hunting expedition, Muslims on pilgrimage to Mecca, dung and sand for pillows at night, and the disconcerting insistence of Saracens and other infidel on answering calls of nature in the manner of women, "such that I scarcely dared to make urine standing in their presence."[32] Those of a classicist bent might find themselves speculating about the location of the tomb of Alexander the Great as well as the body of Catherine of Alexandria, meditating on the source of the Nile as well as the *fons et origo* of their own religion. That at least is what Petrarch did in his *Itinerarium ad sepulcrum Domini nostri* (Journey to the tomb of our Lord), where the flight of the Israelites from the savage rage of Pharaoh into the desert is conjoined with that of Marcus Cato from Caesar "through Libyan Syrtes and the sandy dwellings of snakes."[33] In Petrarch's hands what begins as a tour of the Holy Land derails into Lucan-inspired meditations on fortune. Gazing on the Nile's delta brings to mind Pompey's death there, and the equally bloody fate of the civil war's "victor," Caesar, in Rome: "the world was thus divided between son and father-in-law, so that the Nile washes one cadaver, and the Tiber the other. What fidelity of fortune; what end of human affairs."[34]

The processes of ruination kept returning. From the thirteenth century, after the fall of Jerusalem, pilgrims observed the remains of former Crusader cities and strongholds, as well as more ancient sites. Burchard of Mount Sion surveyed a landscape littered with the fragments of Christian fortifications, or citadels now in Saracen hands, churches converted to mosques. Sebaste no longer possessed a single house, but two churches constructed in honour of John the Baptist still stood there, one inhabited by Greek monks, the other a former cathedral given over to the rites of the Saracens, who – Burchard noted – venerated John.[35] In 1335 Jacopo da

---

Liber peregrinationis, ed. Monneret de Villard, 77. On the historicity of the early reports see Philip Mayerson, "Egeria and Peter the Deacon on the Site of Clysma (Suez)," *Journal of the American Research Center in Egypt* 33 (1996): 61–64.

32. *Itinerarium Symonis Semeonis ab Hybernia ad Terram Sanctam* 81, 85, ed. Mario Esposito (Dublin, 1960), 102: "vix urinam stando in eorum presentia, necessitante me natura, facere audebam, quoniam ipsi sicuti et Saraceni, nunquam nisi ad modum mulierum urinant." (This passage is judiciously omitted from Esposito's English translation).

33. Petrarch, *Itinerarium*, ed. Lo Monaco, 78: "per syrtes Libycas et arenosa loca serpentium," with reference to Lucan's *Bellum civile* 9.

34. Petrarch, *Itinerarium*, Lo Monaco, 84: "sic cum genero partitus orbem, ut illum Nilus, Tibris hunc abluat. O fortune fides, o rerum finis humanarum." Cf. *Bellum civile* 8.851–72.

35. *Descriptio Terrae Sanctae*, ed. Laurent, 52–53.

Verona grieved to find "una execrabilis mosceta Saracenorum" atop Mount Sinai, near to the place where Moses received the law from God – at least, he reflected, it was a small mosque.[36] The multiple times of this Holy Land were addressed, at least by some pilgrims, with notable precision. They readily distinguished between pre-Christian, Judaic, early Christian, Crusader, and Saracen eras. They observed rubble, saw the dirt covering some of the oldest Christian sites, kissed relics, came face to face with saints. Which time were they inhabiting? Unequivocally their own, because it encompassed those preserved relics and vestiges of old times, guarded them to be encountered, witnessed. What was this place? Never, you sense, wholly their own, even when they held it. Unlike Moses, they could do more than view it from afar. They could explore, describe, fight for, cultivate, and occupy the Holy Land. But it was already occupied: not just by the "Saracens," by Jews, by Christians of other denominations, but by the history of their own faith – by God, by saints, by the land itself, brimming with resonances derived from its part in the story of Christianity. The Red Sea; Mount Sion; Ramesse; Soccoth; Jericho: say a name, write a name, and you invoked narratives of profundity. It was a crowded landscape, even if much of the crowd had died long ago.

From the early Middle Ages world maps represented the passage of the Israelites out of Egypt to the promised land. It is not impossible that the inscriptions "Desertum ubi quadraginta annis errauerunt filij israelis ducente Moyse" (desert where the sons of Israel, led by Moses, wandered for forty years) and "Hic legem acceperunt in monte syna" (here on Mount Sinai they received the law) on the Peutinger Tables date from the fourth century, when, it is usually supposed, the map was compiled.[37] If, as has been asserted, the Christian content on the Tables was a later addition, then the reference to the Israelites dates from any time up to around 1200, when the existing copy of the map was made.[38] But the passage of the sons of Israel – "transitus filiorum Israel" – appears on maps in one form or another already by the eighth century,[39] and some version of the exodus continued to be shown right up to the sixteenth century, when it became an important topos within historical geography.[40]

36. Jacopo da Verona, *Liber peregrinationis*, ed. Monneret de Villard, 76.

37. Konrad Miller, *Itineraria Romana: Römische Reisewege an der Hand der Tabula Peutingeriana* (Stuttgart, 1916), 850, 882.

38. See Chapter 2.

39. The world map in Vatican City, Biblioteca Apostolica Vaticana, MS Vat. lat. 6018, fols. 63v–64r, datable to between 762 and 777, has a gap in the Red Sea, which Edson rightly identifies as the *transitus*: Evelyn Edson, *Mapping Time and Space: How Medieval Mapmakers Viewed Their World* (London, 1997), 64.

40. Walter S. Melion, "*Ad ductum itineris et dispositionem mansionum ostendendam*: Meditation, Vocation, and Sacred History in Abraham Oretlius's *Parergon*," *Journal of the Walters Art Gallery* 57 (1999): 49–72. On sacred geography in the sixteenth and seventeenth centuries see Zur Shalev, *Sacred Words and Worlds: Geography, Religion, and Scholarship, 1550-1700* (Leiden, 2012).

Figure 1 Opicinus de Canistris, Map of Europe and Africa anthropomorphized, superimposed. Vatican City, Biblioteca Apostolica Vaticana, MS Vaticanus latinus 6435, fol. 77r. © Biblioteca Apostolica Vaticana; reproduced by permission.

Figure 2 Veronica Lulu, Bessie Doonday, Anna Johns, Wendy Wise, Shirley Brown, Chamia Samuels, Lyn Manson, Daisy Kungah and Kim Mahood, "Paruku" (2007). © Veronica Lulu/Copyright Agency. Licensed by DACS 2019. Photograph: Jason McCarthy, National Museum of Australia.

Figure 3 Cristoforo Buondelmonti, Map of Gallipoli, including Troy and the vestiges of Xerxes' bridge in the foreground, close to a "Turris turchorum fortissima" (very strong Turkish tower), from a manuscript of the *Liber insularum* made in Ghent, in 1482–85. London, British Library, MS Arundel 93, fol. 153r. © The British Library Board.

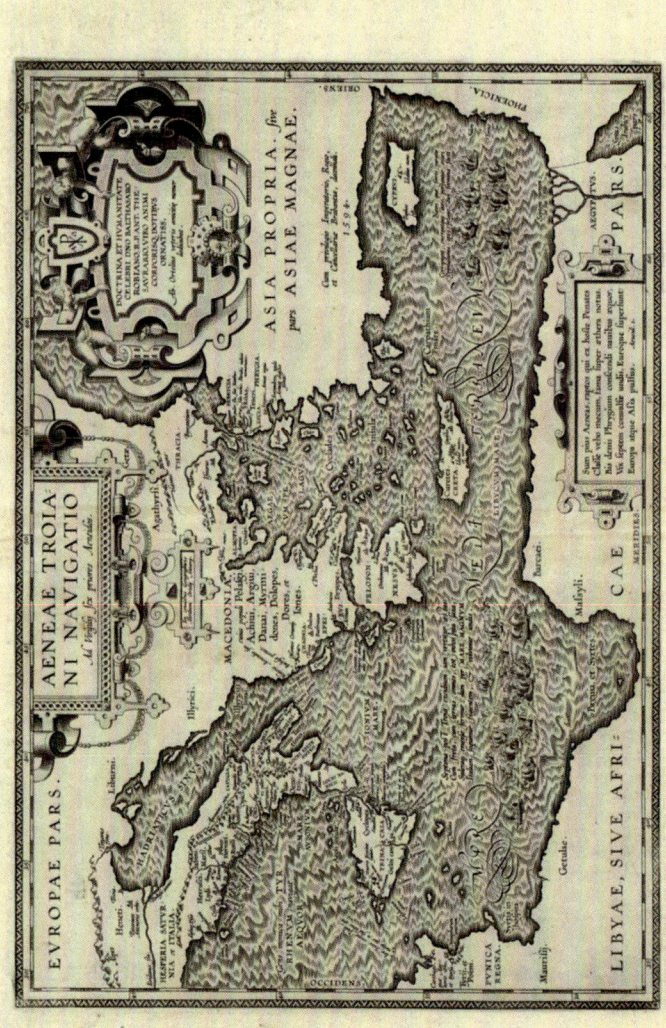

Figure 4 Abraham Ortelius, "Aeneae Troiani Navigatio (Ad Virgilii sex priores Aeneidos)," in *Theatrum Orbis Terrarum* (Antwerp, 1595). London, British Library, Maps C.2.d.5. © The British Library Board.

Figure 5 The Ebstorf *mappa mundi*, detail. East at top. The Black Sea, including "Pontus regio ... in quo Ovidius et Clemens exilio relegantur," beneath Noah's ark. For source, see Figure 34.

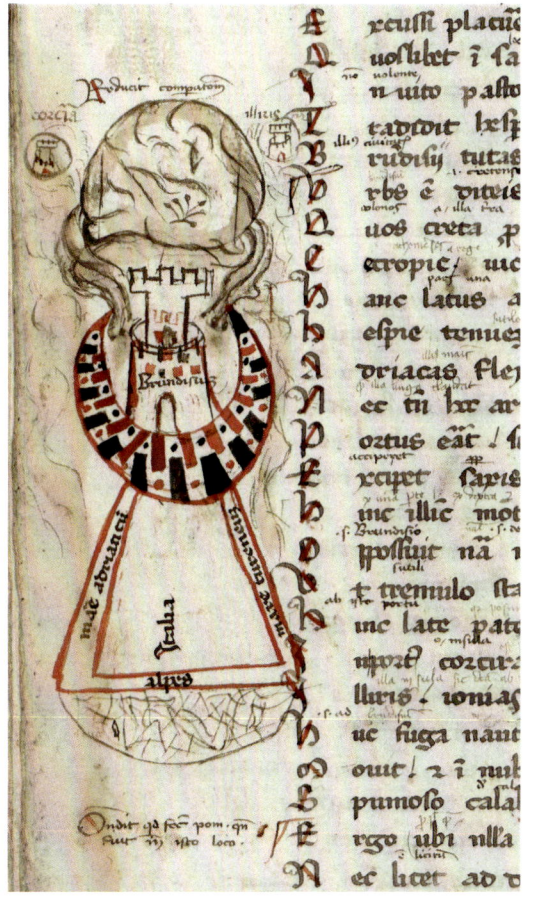

Figure 6 Map of Brundisium, in a manuscript of Lucan, *Bellum civile*, copied in 1452. Oriented to the south-east. London, British Library, MS Additional 11992, fol. 24v. © The British Library Board.

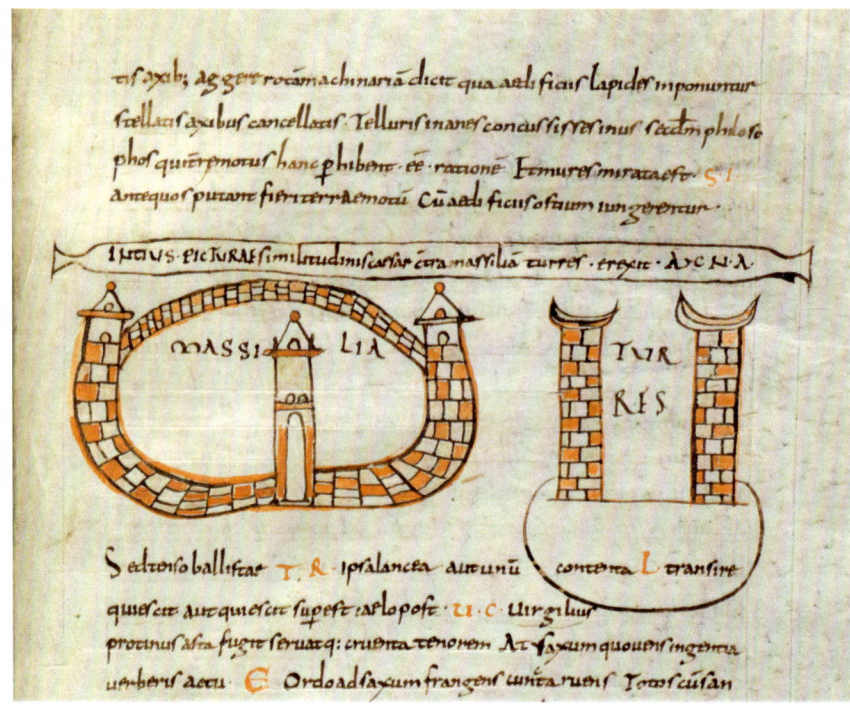

Figure 7 *Commenta Bernensia*, Massilia with Caesar's towers. Bern, Burgerbibliothek Cod. 370 (s. ix), fol. 48r. © Burgerbibliothek Bern. Photograph: Codices Electronici AG.

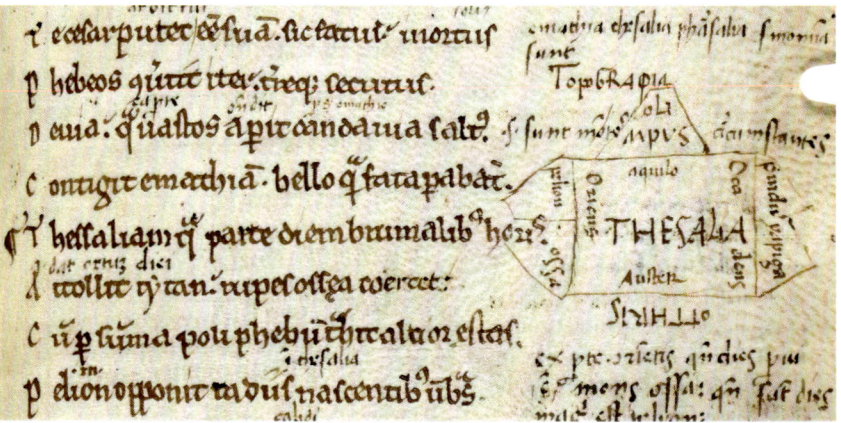

Figure 8 Thessalia, in a thirteenth-century manuscript of Lucan's *Bellum civile*. London, British Library, MS Additional 19891, fol. 50r. © The British Library Board.

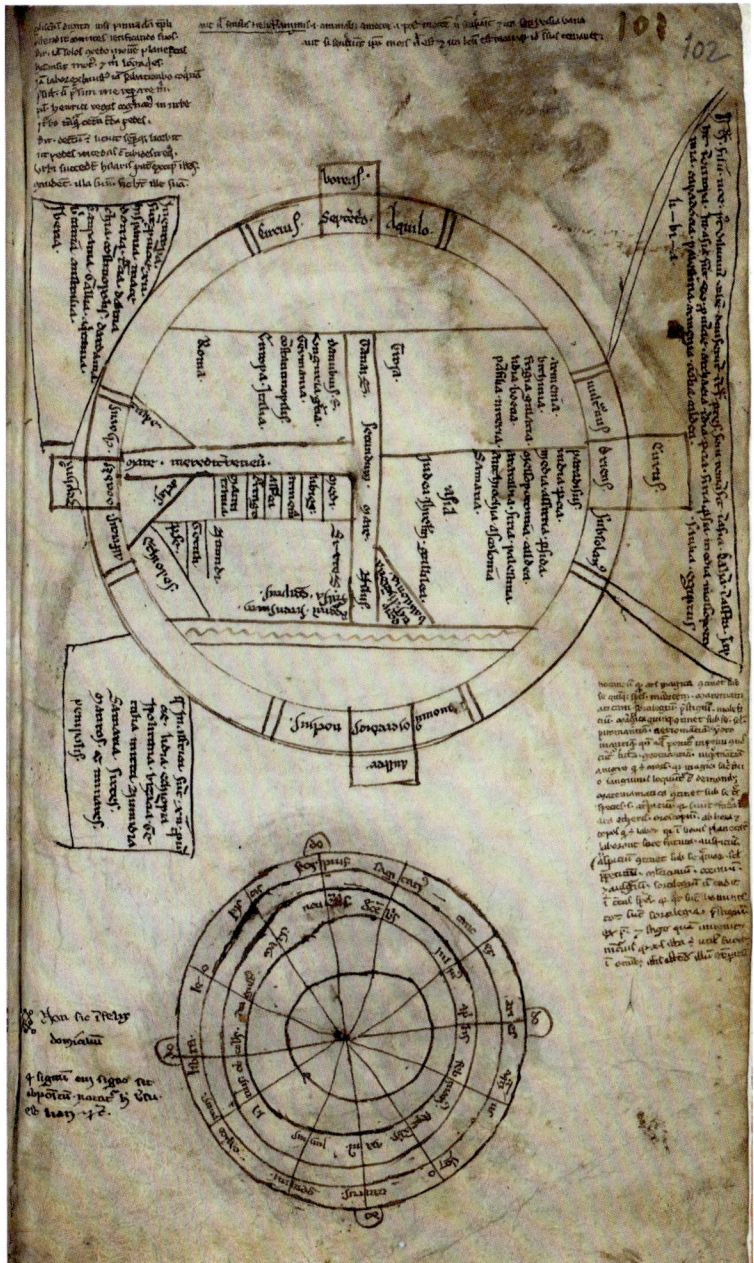

Figure 9 World map at the conclusion of a thirteenth-century copy of Lucan's *Bellum civile*. North is at the top, although the map is probably meant to be read with an east orientation. Three text boxes outside the map describe the division of the known world (Asia, Europe, and Africa) between the three sons of Noah. Copenhagen, Kongelige Bibliotek, Gl. Kgl. S. 2020, fol. 102r.

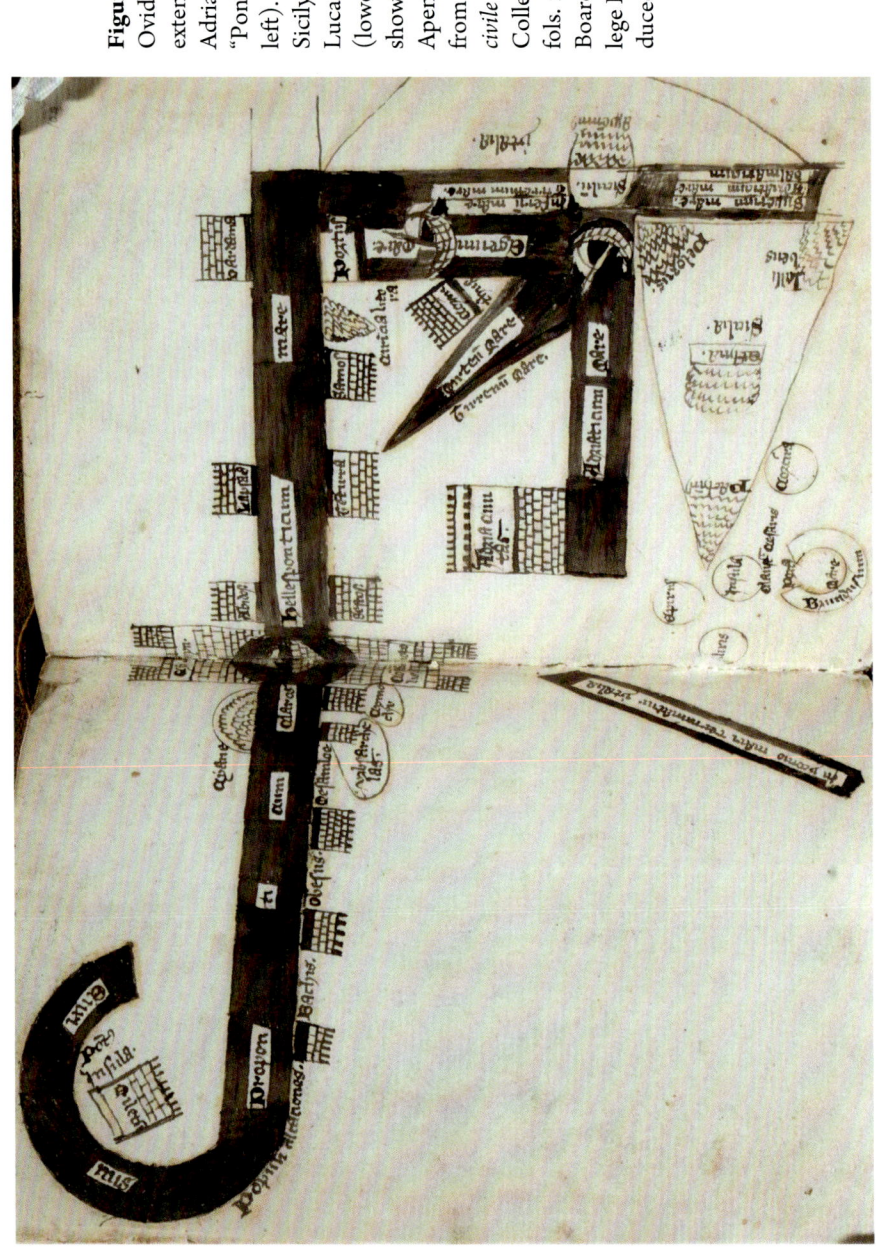

Figure 10 Map of Ovid's *Tristia* 1.10, extending from the Adriatic (lower right) to "Pontus insula" (upper left). Triangular map of Sicily and diagram of Lucan's Brundisium (lower right); diagram showing Sicily, the Apennines, and Italy, from Lucan's *Bellum civile* (far right). Trinity College Dublin MS 632, fols. 108v–109r. © The Board of Trinity College Dublin; reproduced by permission.

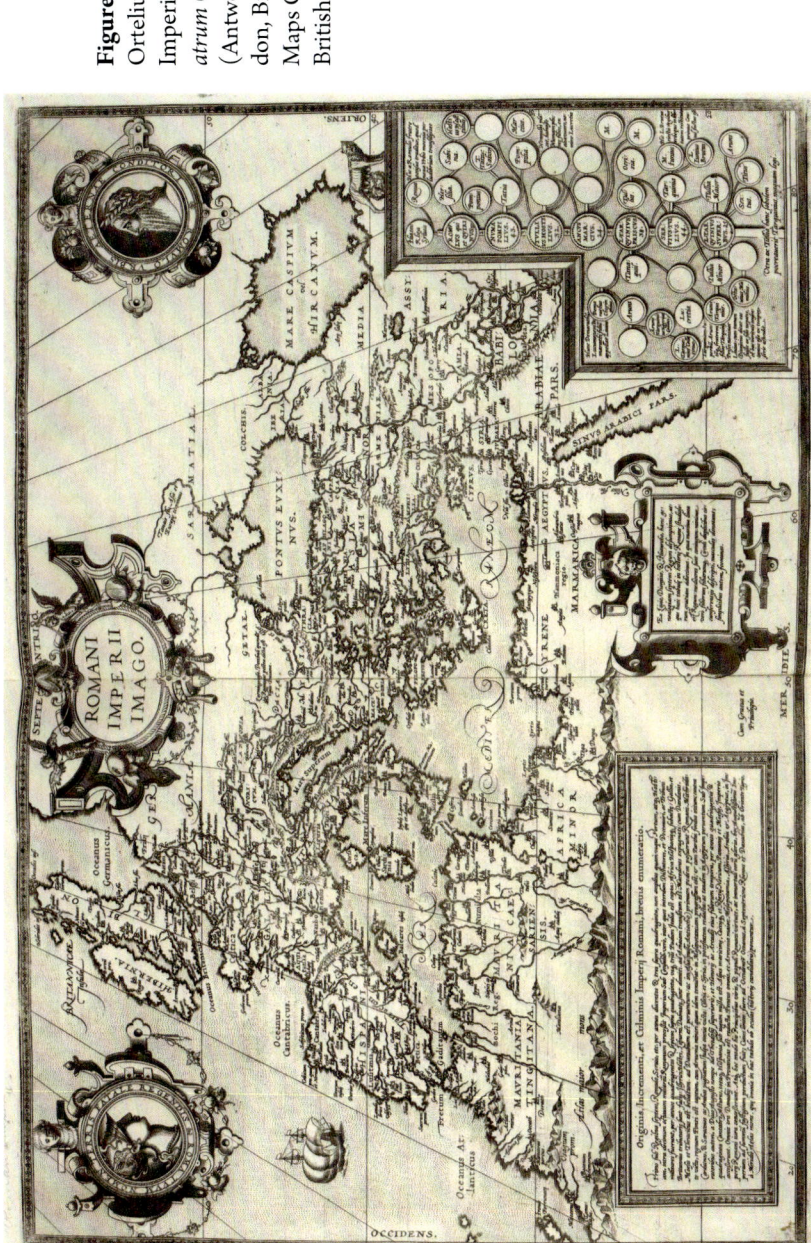

Figure 11 Abraham Ortelius, "Romani Imperii Imago," in *Theatrum Orbis Terrarum* (Antwerp, 1579). London, British Library, Maps C.2.c.12. © The British Library Board.

Figure 12 The Ebstorf *mappa mundi*, detail. East at top. Northern Europe, from Thrace to (Ge)rmania and Scandinavia, with the Danube prominent. For source, see Figure 34.

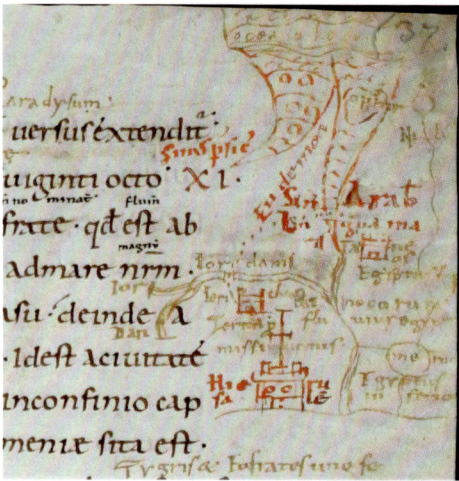

Figure 13 Map of Palestine, Egypt, and the Red Sea added as a gloss to a ninth-century manuscript of Orosius' *Historiae*. A dotted line represents the passage of the Israelites from Egypt across the Red Sea and the Jordan, to Jericho and the "Terra promissionis." St Gall, Stiftsbibliothek St Gallen, MS 621, p. 37. © Stiftsbibliothek St Gallen; reproduced by permission.

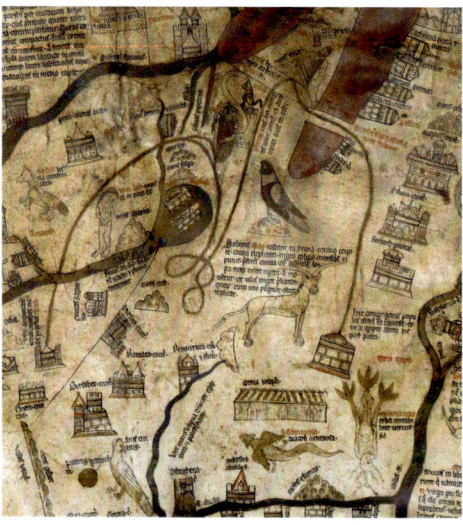

Figure 14 Hereford *mappa mundi*, detail. East at top. The passage of the Israelites across the Red Sea, from Ramesse to Jericho. © Hereford Cathedral.

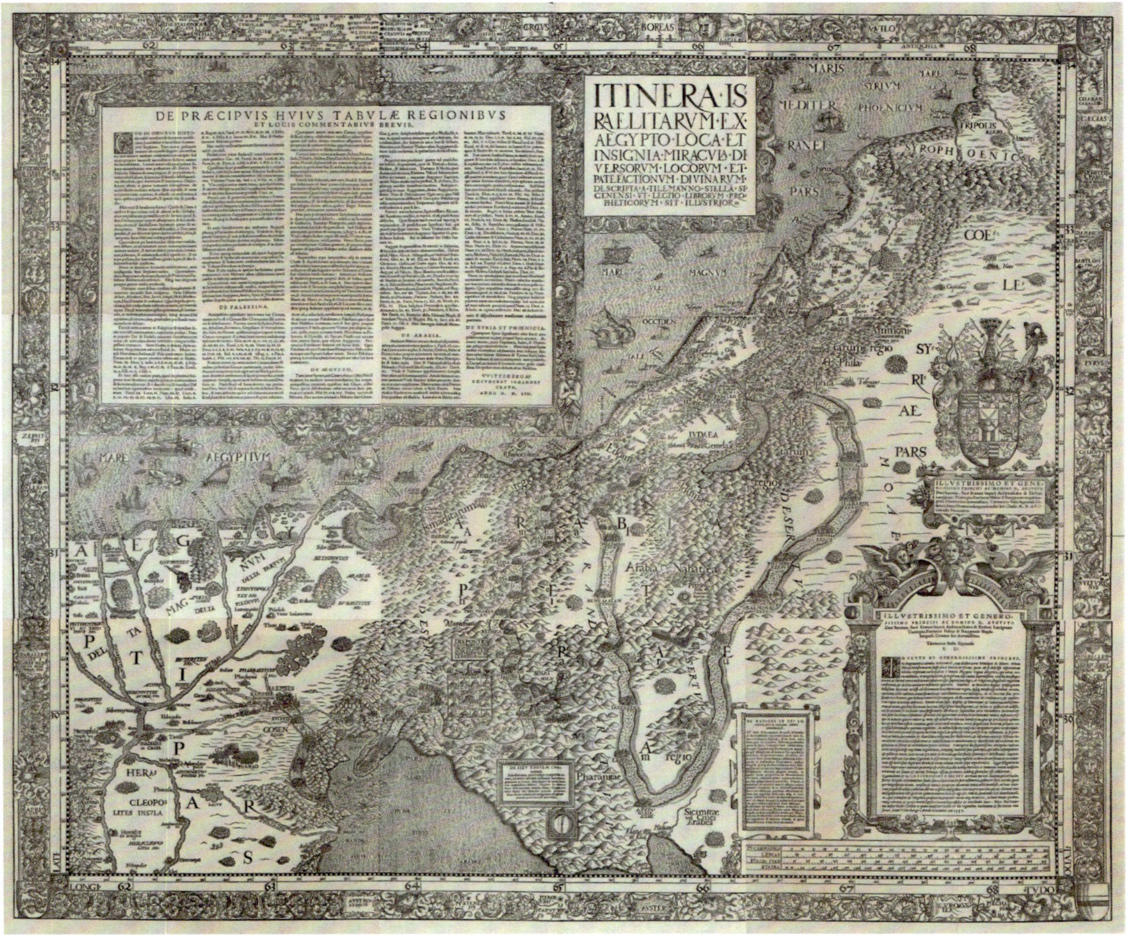

Figure 15 Tilemann Stella, "Itinera Israelitarum ex Aegypto loca et insignia miracula" (1557). The passage of the Israelites from Raemses to the Jordan, with stations numbered. Universitätsbibliothek Basel, Kartenslg AA 104.

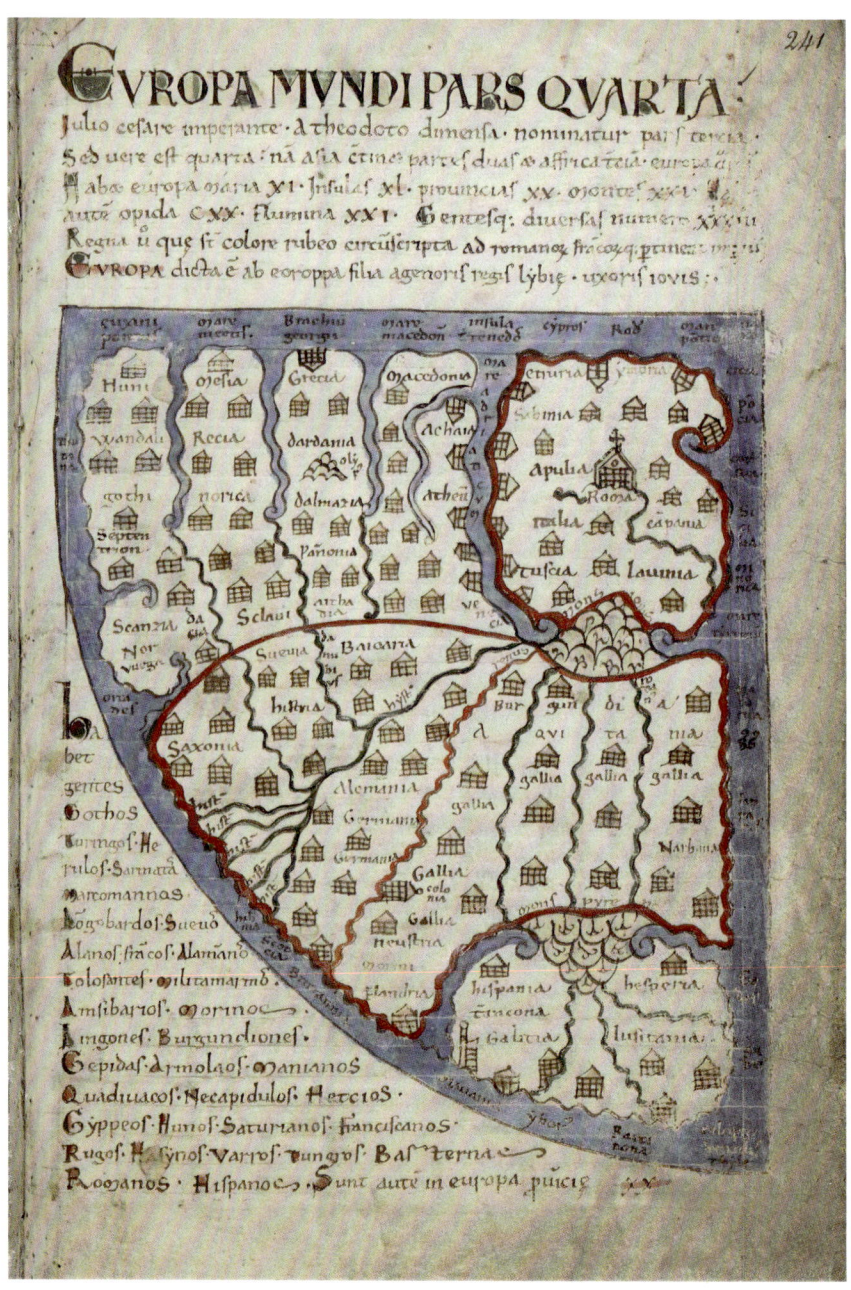

Figure 16 Lambert of St-Omer, "Europa mundi pars quarta," from the autograph manuscript of the *Liber Floridus*. Ghent, University Library, MS 92, fol. 241r. © Universiteitsbibliotheek Gent; reproduced by permission.

Figure 17 Map of the river Maas/Meuse (1357). South at top. The map traces the passage of the Maas/Meuse from Liège (Leodium) to Dordrecht (Dordracum), with particular attention given to the division of the river into the Old and the New Maas/Meuse. Among the towns on the "Antiqua Mosa" is Gertruidenberg (Mons Sancte Gertrudis). The map marks a division between Flanders (Flandria) and Zeeland (Zeelandia) in the west, and between Brabant (Brabantia) and Holland (Hollandia) in the east. Archives de l'Université de Paris Registre 2, vol. 2, fol. 35v. Photograph: Bibliothèque de la Sorbonne.

Figure 18 Matthias Grünewald, "Begegnung von Erasmus und Mauritius" (1521/22). Alte Pinakothek, Munich. © bpk | Bayerische Staatsgemäldesammlungen; reproduced by permission.

Figure 19 El Greco, "Martyrdom of St Maurice and the Theban Legion" (1580–82). El Escorial. © Patrimonio Nacional.

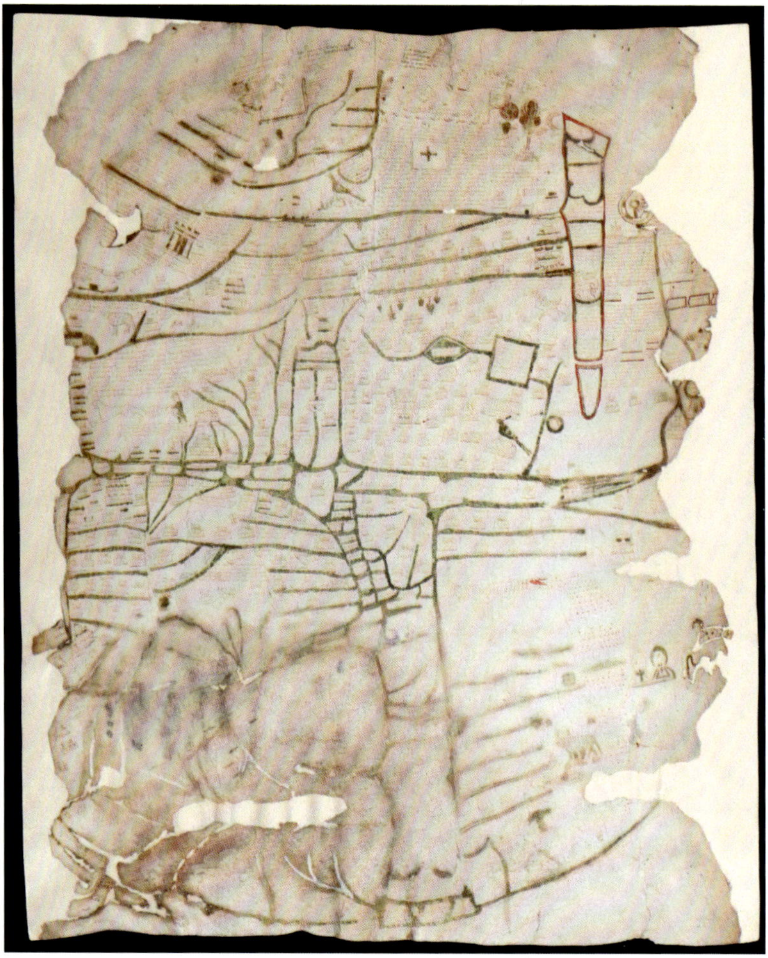

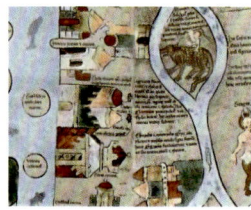

Figure 20 Vercelli *mappa mundi*. East at the top. The inscription describing Thebes is located in the top right of the map, next to the Red Sea. Vercelli, Archivio Capitolare. © Fondazione Museo del Tesoro del Duomo e Archivio Capitolare, Vercelli; reproduced by permission.

Figure 21 The Ebstorf *mappa mundi*, detail. East at top. The inscription describing Thebes (with "Mauritius" rubricated) is located to the left of the Nile. For source, see Figure 34.

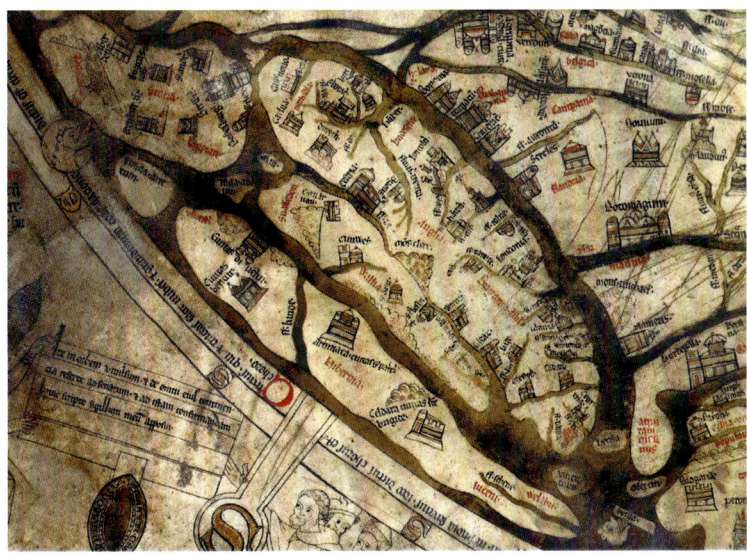

Figure 22 Hereford *mappa mundi*, detail. East at top. The British Isles. © Hereford Cathedral.

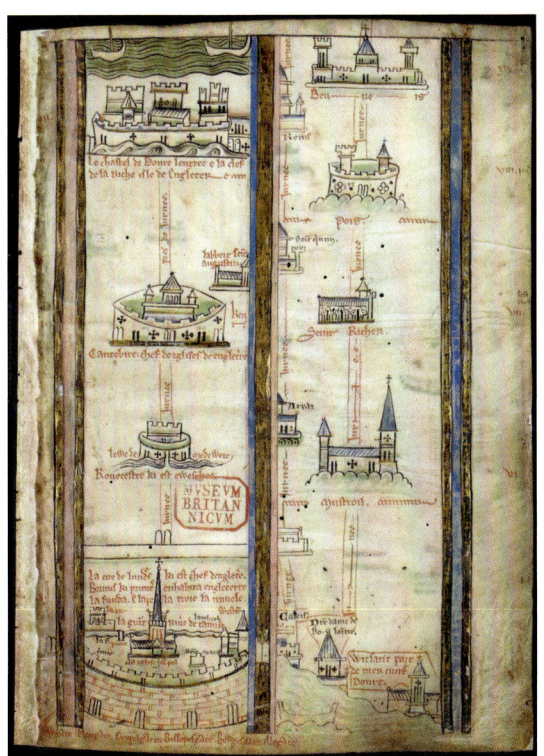

Figure 23 Matthew Paris, Itinerary map showing the route from London (bottom left) to Beauvais (top right), through Rochester, Canterbury, Dover, Wissant, Boulogne, Montreuil, Saint-Riquier, and Póix, with an alternative route from Calais to Reims. London, British Library, Royal 14 C.VII, 2r. © The British Library Board.

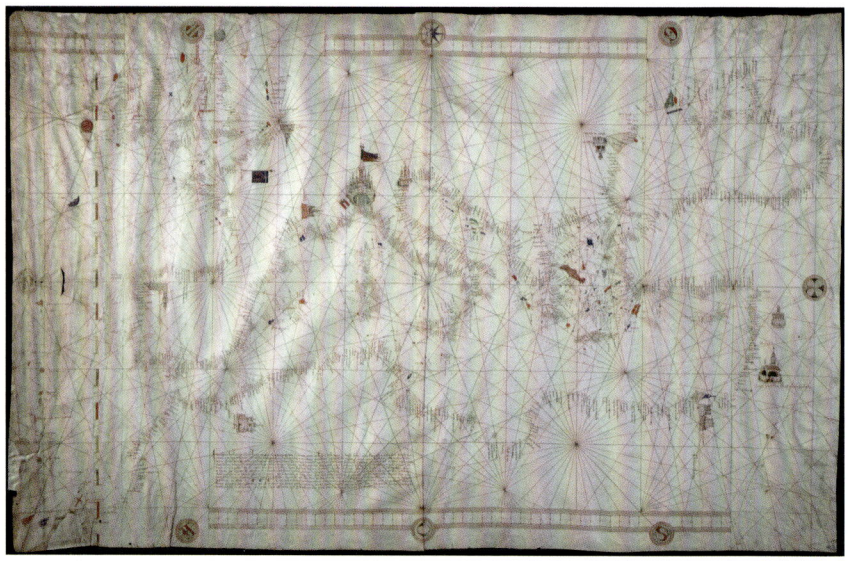

Figure 24 Francesco Beccari, Sea Chart (1403). North at top. The map shows the Mediterranean Sea, the Aegean and Black Seas (right) and the Atlantic coastline (left), with the British Isles at the top left of the image. © Beinecke Rare Book and Manuscript Library, Yale University; reproduced by permission.

Figure 25 World map in Ptolemy, *Geographia* (Ulm, 1482). London, British Library, Maps C.1.d.2. © The British Library Board.

Figure 26 Fra Mauro, *Mappa mundi*. South at the top. © Venice, Biblioteca Nazionale Marciana; reproduced by permission.

Figure 27 Humfrey Lhuyd, "Cambriae Typus Auctore Humfredo Lhuydo Denbigiense Cambrobritanno," in Abraham Ortelius, *Theatrum Orbis Terrarum* (Antwerp, 1573). London, British Library, Maps C.2.c.8. © The British Library Board.

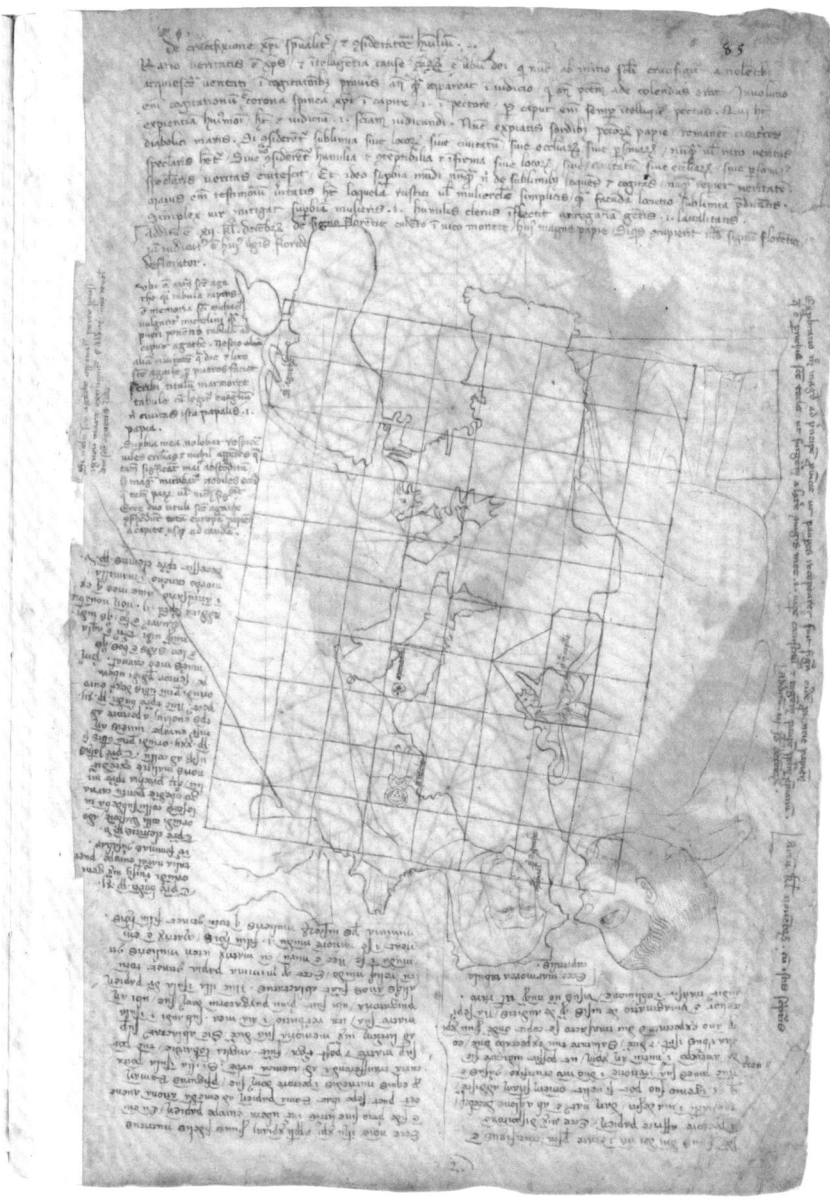

Figure 28 Opicinus de Canistris, Pavia on Europe and Africa. East at the top. A grid plan of the city of Pavia is superimposed on an anthropomorphized map of Europe and Africa. Santa Tecla, represented by a haloed figure, aligns with Avignon, while Santa Maria Capella aligns with North Africa, and appears next to a serpent representing usury. Vatican City, Biblioteca Apostolica Vaticana, MS Vaticanus latinus 6435, fol. 85r. © Biblioteca Apostolica Vaticana; reproduced by permission.

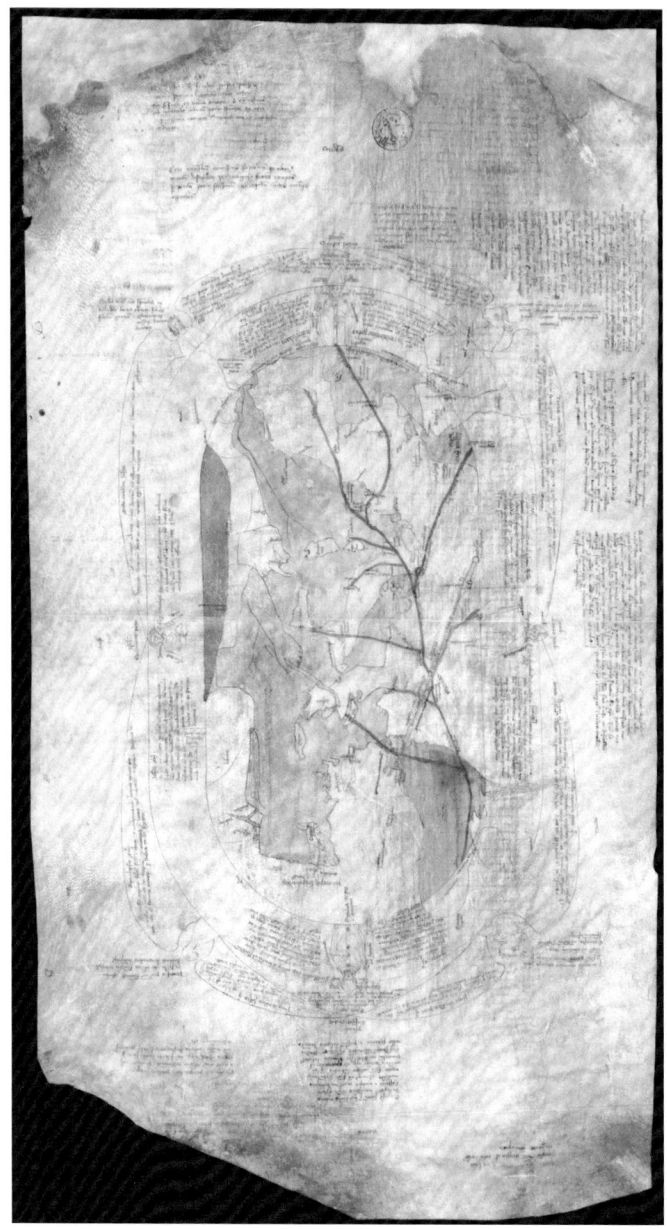

Figure 29 Opicinus de Canistris, Northern Italy on Europe and Africa. West at the top. Opicinus here superimposes a detailed regional map of northern Italy, from Lombardy and the Veneto to Liguria, with an emphasis on its rivers, particularly the Po, onto a map of Europe and Africa. Vatican City, Biblioteca Apostolica Vaticana, MS Palatinus latinus 1993, fol. 4v. © Biblioteca Apostolica Vaticana; reproduced by permission.

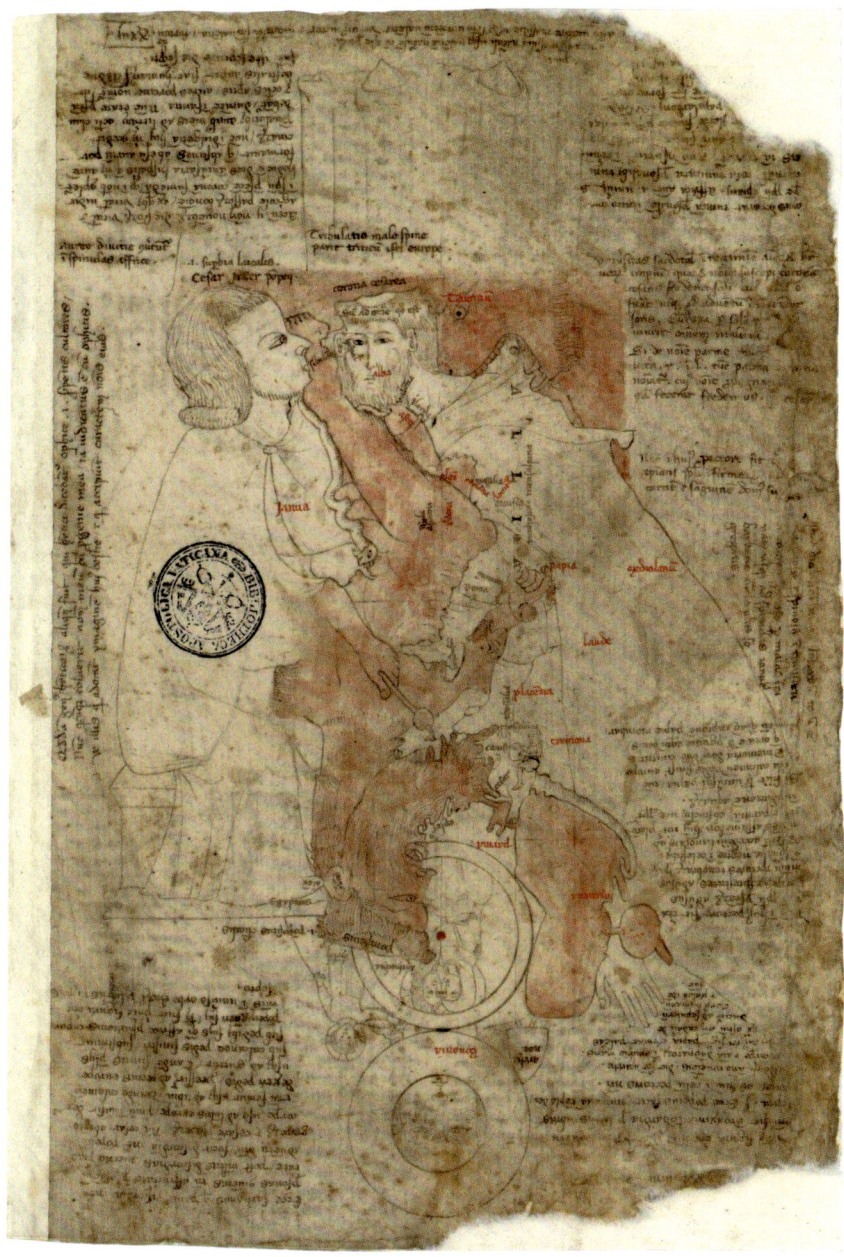

Figure 30 Opicinus de Canistris, Europe and Africa with sites from Lucan, *Bellum civile*. West at the top. Caesar as Africa, the priestly community as Europe, and Pompey as sea monster. Vatican City, Biblioteca Apostolica Vaticana, MS Vaticanus latinus 6435, fol. 87v. © Biblioteca Apostolica Vaticana; reproduced by permission.

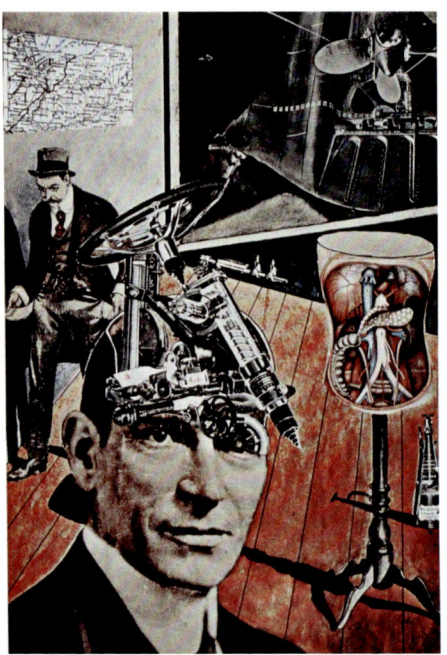

Figure 31 Raoul Hausmann, "Tatlin at Home" (1920). Moderna Museet, Stockholm.

Figure 32 Opicinus de Canistris, Europe and Africa, mirrored, with Northern Italy superimposed. "Occidens mortis" at top of image, with Europe as Apostolic Church and Africa as Judaic Synagogue; "oriens uite" at base, with Europe as universal Christianity and Africa as Judas. Vatican City, Biblioteca Apostolica Vaticana, MS Vaticanus latinus 6435, fol. 76v. © Biblioteca Apostolica Vaticana; reproduced by permission.

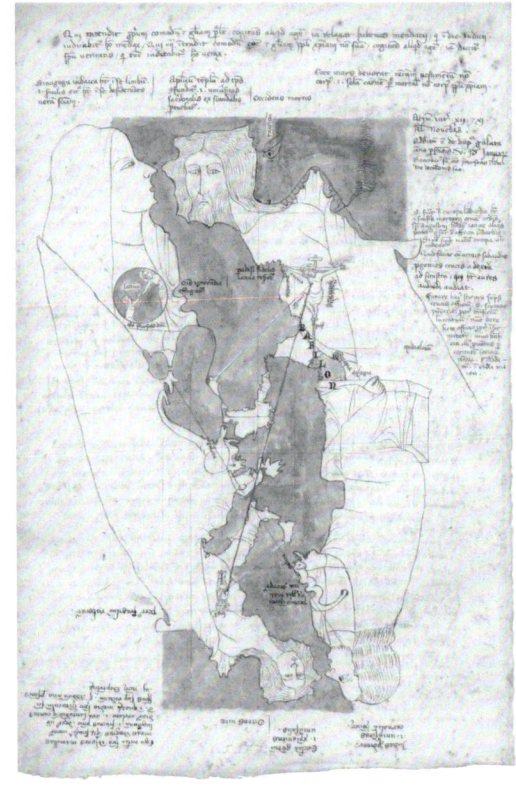

Figure 33 Gulammohammed Sheikh, Mappamundi Suite 1 ("Dwarka," 2003). The Ebstorf *mappa mundi* revitalised with images (clockwise, from top left) of Majnun and the old lady; the poet Kabir; a Pahari dancer; and Mary Magdalene. Digital collage, gouache on inkjet. Photograph courtesy of the artist.

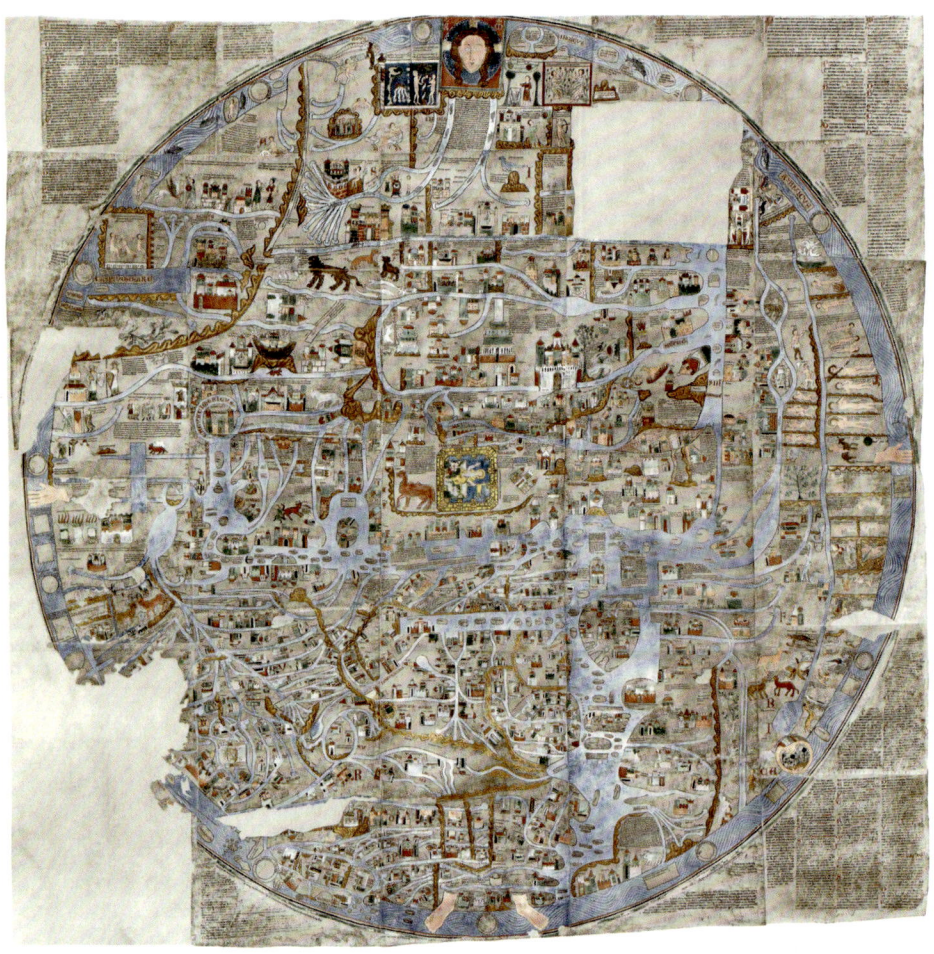

Figure 34 The Ebstorf *mappa mundi*. East at the top. Digital reconstruction by Hartmut Kugler, as published in *Die Ebstorfer Weltkarte*, ed. Hartmut Kugler, 2 vols. (Berlin, 2007).

Figure 35 Gulammohammed Sheikh, Mappamundi Suite 10 ("Magdalene and Majnun II," 2004). Digital collage, gouache on inkjet. Photograph courtesy of the artist.

Figure 36 Majnun and the old lady appear before Layla's tent, from a sixteenth-century copy of Nizami's *Khamsa*. London, British Library, MS Or. 2265, fol. 157v. © The British Library Board.

Figure 37 Gulammohammed Sheikh, Mappamundi Suite 2 ("Looking for Layla," 2003). The Ebstorf *mappa mundi* with Majnun and old woman; Kabir; Mary Magdalene; Pahari dancer. Majnun and the old woman appear throughout. Digital collage, gouache on inkjet. Photograph courtesy of the artist.

Figure 38 Giotto, "Noli me tangere." Chapel of the Magdalene, Assisi. © Photographic Archives of the Sacred Convent of the Basilica of St. Francis in Assisi, Italy.

Figure 39 Giotto, St Francis preaching to the birds. Upper Basilica, Assisi. © Photographic Archives of the Sacred Convent of the Basilica of St. Francis in Assisi, Italy

Figure 40 Gulammohammed Sheikh, Mappamundi Suite 3 ("Marichika," 2003). The Ebstorf *mappa mundi* with Majnun and old woman; Kabir; Mary Magdalene; Pahari dancer. St Francis preaching to birds, and Rama with bow chasing Marica appear throughout. Digital collage, gouache on inkjet. Photograph courtesy of the artist.

Figure 41 Sassetta, St Francis preaching before the Sultan (1437–44). © London, National Gallery; reproduced by permission.

Figure 42 Pandit Seu, Dancing Villagers, c. 1730. The Pahari dancer in Gulammohammed Sheikh's Mappamundi Suite appears in the top left. Los Angeles County Museum of Art (www.lacma.org).

The mapmakers used visual as well as verbal means to show motion. At its most basic, the crossing of the Red Sea could be indicated, mutely, by leaving a gap in the sea's red paint or outline.[41] In some cases a more elaborate line originated in Egypt, crossed the Red Sea, and stopped in the vicinity of the river Jordan. This line is present on a remarkably detailed marginal gloss in a manuscript of Orosius's *Historiae* in the monastery of St Gall (Figure 13). The gloss, an eleventh-century addition to the manuscript made by the monk Ekkehart, is likely to derive from a *mappa mundi* known to have been in the monastery library in the ninth century: it shows a small map of Palestine, Egypt, and the Persian Gulf, and literally tracks exodus from Taneos (Tanis) in Egypt, across the Red Sea and the Jordan, to Jericho in the "terra promissionis."[42] That dotted line is an ancestor of the elaborate passage of the Israelites traced on the Hereford *mappa mundi* (Figure 14). There the itinerary begins in Ramesse – "Hic congregatus populus israel in ramesse exiit de egipto altera die post pasca" – moves east past Soccoth, Etham, and "Phiaroth" to the Red Sea – "Transitus filiorum israel per mare rubrum" – heads sharply west, turns a figure eight and another loop above Mount Oreb, skirts Mount Seir and Mount Fasga, and passes Lot's wife as pillar of salt, before crossing the Jordan and terminating in Jericho.[43]

41. In addition to BAV, MS Vat. lat. 6018, fol. 63v: BL, MS Cotton Tiberius B.V (I), fol. 56v (eleventh century); Munich, Bayerische Staatsbibliothek, Clm 10058, fol. 154v (twelfth century); Cambridge, Corpus Christi College, MS 66, p. 2 (the Sawley Map, late twelfth century); the Vercelli *mappa mundi* (thirteenth century); the Psalter map (London, British Library, MS Additional 28681; thirteenth century); the *transitus* continued to be marked on the *mappae mundi* that accompanied Ranulf Higden's *Polychronicon* in the fourteenth and fifteenth centuries: see for example the Ramsey Abbey *Polychronicon* (London, British Library, MS Royal 14.C.IX, fols. 1v–2r; 2v; fourteenth century); the Evesham *mappa mundi* (London, College of Arms, MS Muniments 18/19; c. 1390); the *Polychronicon* of the Hospital of St Thomas of Acre in Cheapside (London, British Library, MS Royal 14.C.XII, fol. 9v; 1377–1400). This mode of indicating passage is found on several of the more elaborate sea charts of the fourteenth century, which incorporated features of *mappae mundi*, such as Angelino Dulceti's 1339 chart (Paris, Bibliothèque nationale de France, Département des Cartes et Plans, Rés. Ge. B 696) and the Catalan Atlas. Fifteenth-century examples of the *transitus* on charts show an increasingly vestigial line: e.g. Mecia de Viladestes's chart of 1413 (Paris, Bibliothèque nationale de France, Département des Cartes et Plans, Rés. Ge. AA 566), Gabriel de Vallseca's chart of 1449 (Florence, Archivio di Stato, CN 22), and Pere Rossell's chart of 1464 (Nuremburg, Germanisches Nationalmuseum MS La. 4017).

42. Stiftsbibliothek St Gallen, MS 621, p. 37. Heidi Eisenhut, *Die Glossen Ekkeharts IV von St. Gallen im Codex Sangallensis 621* (St Gallen, 2009), 350–53; on the glosses see too Natalia Lozovsky, "Roman Geography and Ethnography in the Carolingian Empire," *Speculum* 81 (2006): 325–64, at 340–46.

43. *The Hereford Map*, ed. Scott Westrem (Turnhout: Brepols, 2001), 117–29, 165, 171 (respectively nos. 287, 286, 285, 279, 278, 399, 259, 260, 254, 381): "Usque ad civitatem Ierico ducebat Moyses populum Israel."

The line seems to have made explicit something that on other maps may have been evident to many medieval observers. Several maps show the basic reference points from which a reader could reconstruct the itinerary of the Israelites: Ramesse the starting point; one or two other *mansiones* prior to the Red Sea, such as Soccoth; then after the transit, Mount Sinai, the Jordan, and Jericho.[44] The persistence of this trace, from some of the earliest known examples of medieval world maps to the latest, suggests its importance as a structuring element. It reveals something of the role of maps in performing a literal exegesis of the biblical text, a function advocated by Cassiodorus as early as the sixth century, still being affirmed by learned commentators at the start of the fourteenth century, and equally strongly endorsed in the sixteenth.[45] Here the passage, here the transit, here Moses received the laws, here the promised land. Such exegesis dwelt alongside other places and other genres: the Hereford map's line steers a course past the two-horned "eale" (when it fights with one horn, it uses the other for defence), drops down past a phoenix (symbol of Christ) and a representation of

44. Within the Beatus *mappa mundi* tradition only the elaborate eleventh-century St Sever *mappa mundi* contains reference to the passage of the Israelites ("Ramesse"; "Transitus filiorum Israel"; "Desertum ubi filii Israel XL annis erraverunt"; "Mons sinai ubi filii Israel legem acceperunt"): Konrad Miller, *Mappae mundi: Die ältesten Weltkarten*, vol. 1: *Die Weltkarte des Beatus* (Stuttgart, 1895), 52–53, 57. The Tournai Palestine map (London, British Library, MS Additional 10049, fol. 64v; twelfth-century, though likely to derive from a much earlier map) has "Ramesse," "Sochoth," and "Phiairoth" prior to the Red Sea, and "desertum cades" thereafter; Hugh of St Victor's description of a *mappa mundi* included the "transitus filiorum Israel per mare Rubrum" near to Thebes; he also lists Ramesses, Socoth, Airoth (Aseroth?), and Delsephon (Belfeson?): *Descriptio Mappe Mundi*, 148. The Ebstorf *mappa mundi* (famously missing part of its depiction of the Red Sea following an illicit nineteenth-century excision) marks "Transitus filiorum Israel" (27/16) alongside "Mons Synai" (27/14), with a break in the colouring of the "Sinus Arabicus" (Arabian Gulf) to indicate the passage. Also by Mount Sinai is a short run of stations and events: "Desertum sur vel Saba," "Marath" (i.e. Mara), "helym" (Elim), "Desertum sin," "Manna hic pluit Dominus" (here the Lord rained manna), "Raphidin," "Cadesbarne" (26/22–27; 30), and eleswhere the stations "Ramasses" (34/11), "Ethant" (27/15), and Jericho (33/20): Hartmut Kugler, *Die Ebstorfer Weltkarte*, (Berlin, 2007), 1: 82–83; 2: 151.

45. Cassiodorus, *Institutiones* 1.25, ed. R.A.B. Mynors (Oxford, 1937), 66; for the fourteenth century see Paolino Veneto's statement at the beginning of the "Tocius orbis divisio" (Paris, Bibliothèque nationale de France, MS lat. 4939, fol. 9r): "Sine autem mundi descripcione ea, que dicuntur de filiis et filiis filiorum Noe ... tam in divinis quam humanis scripturis, dificile est posse ad plenum intelligere vel ymagynari" (without a [pictorial and verbal] description of the world those things that are said about the sons, and the sons of the sons, of Noah ... both in scripture and in profane writings are difficult to understand or visualise completely); for the sixteenth, to cite one example among many, Tilemann Stella's 1557 map of Exodus was expressly produced "vt lectio librorum propheticorum sit illustrior" (so that the reading of the prophetical books might be made clearer).

"Jews" (*Iudei*) worshipping an idol marked "Mahun," rounds Sodom and Gomorrah, and the generic "Saracen city" (*civitas Saraceni*). It starts near an image of a mandrake, passes the "Marsok, transfigured beast" (*bestia transmutata*), and ends in the vicinity of the "Avis cirenus," perhaps the "cinnamolgus," a bird who builds his nests from cinnamon.[46] It is, in essence, a late antique landscape through which Moses and his followers wander, fused from the intersection of biblical and natural history. At the same time, in this line that curved, looped, and finally came to rest, a different kind of story could be read, a metaphysical tale of ascent and purgation: the story of the allegorists. These two readings were not incompatible.

Some *mappae mundi* had, again from an early stage, shown the division of the Holy Land between the tribes of Israel,[47] and from the twelfth century plans showing the Israelites in their desert encampments became a reasonably frequent visual aid to Christian exegesis. Derived from the maps of the Jewish scholar Rashi (Rabbi Shlomo Itzhaki), images of the division of Canaan as set out in Ezekiel 48 and in Numbers 34:2–12, as well as Joshua 13–19, appeared in such texts as Richard of St Victor's biblical commentaries and the widely disseminated *Postillae* of Nicholas of Lyra.[48] The delineation of the territories of the tribes continued to be an important feature of the maps of Palestine produced in the later Middle Ages, as illustrations of pilgrimage narratives or crusading manuals, such as Marino Sanudo's *Liber secretorum fidelium crucis super Terrae Sanctae*.[49] Yet there appears to have been no tradition of representing the exodus in compara-

46. *The Hereford Map*, ed. Westrem, 115–123, 169–173 (respectively nos. 272, 271, 270, 262–63, 397; 426, 249, 405). For a reading of the exodus passage on the Hereford map in the context of contemporary anti-semitism see Debra Higgs Strickland, "Edward I, Exodus, and England on the Hereford World Map," *Speculum* 93 (2018): 420–69.

47. The Cotton world map (BL, MS Cotton Tiberius B.V (I), fol. 56v) incorporates a map of the tribal divisions in the book of Joshua, drawn to illustrate an eighth-century Irish biblical commentary. For the source see Thomas O'Loughlin, "Map and Text: A Mid Ninth-Century Map for the Book of Joshua," *Imago Mundi* 57 (2005): 7–22.

48. Benjamin Z. Kedar, "Rashi's Map of the Land of Canaan, ca. 1100, and its Cartographic Background," in *Cartography in Antiquity and the Middle Ages: Fresh Perspectives, New Methods*, ed. Richard J.A. Talbert and Richard W. Unger (Leiden, 2008), 155–68; Catherine Delano-Smith, "The Exegetical Jerusalem: Maps and Plans for Ezekiel Chapters 40–48," and Hanna Vorholt, "Studying with Maps: Jerusalem and the Holy Land in Two Thirteenth-Century Manuscripts," both in *Imagining Jerusalem in the Medieval West*, ed. Lucy Donkin and Hanna Vorholt (Oxford, 2012), 41–75; 163–99.

49. See Patrick Gautier Dalché, "Cartes, réflexion stratégique et projets de croisade à la fin du XIIIe et au début du XIVe siècle: Une initiative franciscaine?," *Francia* 37 (2010): 77–95. For overview and analysis see P.D.A. Harvey, *Medieval Maps of the Holy Land* (London, 2012); Emmanuelle Vagnon, *Cartographie et Représentations de l'Orient méditerranéen en Occident (du milieu du XIIIe à la fin du XVe siècle)* (Turnhout, 2013).

ble detail. The forty-two *mansiones* were listed within the three arches of an architectural image in Peter of Poitiers's twelfth-century *Compendium historiae in genealogia Christi*, but only a handful of them ever found their way onto a map or illustrative diagram.[50] That changed in the sixteenth century. Then the most notable cartographer of exodus, albeit one among many, was Tilemann Stella, whose "Itinera Israelitarum ex Aegypto loca et insignia miracula" (Passages, places, and renowned miracles of the Israelites out of Egypt) of 1557 was the second map in an intended series of five. Stella's exodus map locates and numbers all forty-two *mansiones*, one after another (Figure 15). No eales are to be seen as the passage of the Israelites winds south from Raemses (*mansiones* 1–4), crosses the Red Sea, follows mountain ranges almost to the Mediterranean (5–26), then loops south again (27–32) and moves steadily through the desert (33–41) until it reaches the Jordan.[51] Now swiftly disseminated and more readily reproduced through the medium of print, maps were fitted to the service of exegetical tendencies Catholic and Protestant alike: Stella was a pupil of Philipp Melanchthon in Luther's Wittenburg in the 1540s, yet his map of the Holy Land was congenial to the generally ecumenical outlook of Ortelius, who published it in the 1570 *Theatrum*.[52]

However much its pleasingly precise account of the progression of Moses and his people across a hostile terrain may seem to signal a new departure in maps of the Holy Land, this particular image is a refinement of a medieval tradition rather than a decisive break from it. The snaking path of the Israelites is in fact no less fanciful on Stella's map than it is on the Hereford *mappa mundi*. The

50. Andrea Worm, "'Ista est Jerusalem': Intertextuality and Visual Exegesis in Peter of Poitiers' *Compendium historiae in genealogia Christi* and Werner Rolevinck's *Fasciculus temporum*," in *Imagining Jerusalem in the Medieval West*, 123–61, esp. 142–46.

51. Basel, Universitäts Bibiliothek, Kartenslg AA 104. The Basel copy of Stella's map, on nine sheets, is apparently the only surviving example of the 1557 printing. A 1559 engraving of the map made by Bernard Van der Putte is also extant (Paris, Bibliothèque nationale de France, Département des Cartes et Plans, Rés. ge. AA 1412). Stella's map derives from the work of the peripatetic scholar Jacob Ziegler, whose maps of the Holy Land were also adapted in Wolfgang Wissenburg's *Descriptio Palestinae nova* (Strasbourg, 1538): see Peter H. Meurer, "Cartography in the German Lands, 1450-1650," in *The History of Cartography*, vol. 3: *Cartography in the European Renaissance*, 2 vols, ed. David Woodward (Chicago, 2007), 2: 1172–1245, at 1218–20. On Stella see Robert W. Karrow, *Mapmakers of the Sixteenth Century and Their Maps: Bio-Bibliographies of the Cartographers of Abraham Ortelius, 1570* (Chicago, 1993), 500–509.

52. "Palestinae sive totius terrae promissionis nova descriptio auctore Tilemanno Stella Sigenens." The map subsequently appeared in Ortelius's *Parergon* of 1595 and subsequent editions: Marcel van der Broecke, *Ortelius Atlas Maps: An Illustrated Guide*, 2nd ed. (Houten, 2011), 508–14 (nos. 170–72).

passage across the Red Sea is identical to the standard *transitus* of the *mappae mundi*, and even if it does not seem ever to have been inscribed on medieval maps, the numbered list of *mansiones* was a familiar element of Christian exegesis. The tomb simply marked "Maria" at the thirty-third *mansio* (*Zin vel Cades Desertum*) on Stella's map may have been innovative in visual terms; but it would have come as no surprise to a medieval audience well versed in verbal articulations of the *mansiones*, such as those of Origen, Jerome, and later adaptors, who would have instantly recognised it as the resting place of the sister of Moses and Aaron. Delicate classicising touches similarly establish a balance between continuity and departure. On the Egyptian coast a tomb of Pompey (*Sepulchrum pompeii*) appears alongside "Casius mons" – where, according to Lucan, the boy king Ptolemy ordered the Roman's death[53] – and not far from a "small city of Hercules" (*Herculis ciuitas parua*). Just as Petrarch's itinerary had strayed from the Holy Land into the classical history of the region, so the reader of Stella's map might reflect that Lucan's charismatic fugitive from Caesar had met his end not far from the twenty-second station of the sons of Israel. But both elements – the *mansiones* and the *sepulchrum Pompeii* – were part of geographical space in the Middle Ages, and the intellectual barriers between them were permeable.

From very early in the history of the religion, most Christians had lived in exile from their Holy Land. One part of that exile, that dislocation, was no doubt painful. Although the sacred sites could be imagined, described, visited, and experienced in the form of relics, they were not immediately present, and they could not be inhabited. But the capacity to be detached from sacred ground yet remain bound to it ensured the very success of the faith. This paradox of Christianity – a religion marked by a very clear notion of sacred space, and by a plethora of places of meaning, but at the same time one independent of direct, personal experience of that space – had allowed it to spread. As it did so, those places did not lessen in significance: instead, their names became familiar, they were reproduced, translocated, and in some cases venerated, because in them the faith resided. So the story of exodus, of the passage to that promised land, acted as a kind of prelude and mirror to the views of those Christians who looked towards the Holy Land from a distance, contemplating its significance and their own relationship towards it, variously troubled and ecstatic, curious and pious, pragmatic and idealistic. The migrant's map that emerged from that ambivalent gaze shows a land plotted, allegorized, topologised, relentlessly eschatologized: a land promised, never liberated, and ultimately never liberating.

---

53. *Bellum civile* 8.470.

NATIONS

In April 2011 I had the pleasure of attending a two-day conference, held at the Austrian Historical Institute in Rome, on the subject of *translatio imperii et studii*. The setting turned out to be as delightful as it was appropriate: the Istituto boasts a sumptuous garden, so enchanting that one barely notices the vast and disfiguring staircase built to furnish Mussolini with a suitably ostentatious route of entry from the Viale delle Belle Arti below. Since the conference schedule allowed generous amounts of time for discussion between participants, with equally generous provision of *espressi* and (in the evening) glasses of sparkling wine, and since the weather was superb – sunny and warm, but not too hot – a mood of relaxed informality soon developed, of the kind highly conducive to intellectual exchange. On the final afternoon of the conference, around 3 pm, I came upon one of the other speakers seated on a shady bench. After checking that his eyes were open, I asked if he would mind answering a question that his paper that morning had raised in my mind. In the following pages I set down the discussion that followed, as clearly as I can recall it.

— The question I wanted to ask as a result of your talk is this: Is the nation a spatial concept in the Middle Ages? If not, what is it, and what relationship does nation have to modes of spatial organisation and division?

B, a grizzled intellectual historian of mature years, stirred and looked at me with barely disguised hostility.

— A rather earnest question for a warm afternoon, he muttered.

An awkward pause followed, during which I contemplated apologising and retreating. But as I was about to do so B, sensing my discomfort, made a conciliatory gesture and began to speak:

— Let me answer obliquely, at first. (You are welcome to sit next to me, by the way). I saw recently an exhibition by the artist Simon Patterson ... "Under Cartel,"[54] as it is called, uses photographs of equestrian monuments to pose a question about the relationship between history and nation. The equestrian monument has its roots in Roman imperial display and propaganda; in more recent experience, however, it is the product of national history – or more precisely, of

---

54. Haunch of Venison Gallery, London, July 13–August 31, 2012.

the need to memorialise national history in the form of the figure of a horse and its rider. The subjects of the statues chosen by Patterson for his exhibition are kings, emperors, presidents, military heroes from classical antiquity (Caligula, Marcus Aurelius) through the Middle Ages (Charlemagne, El Cid, Étienne Marcel, Joan of Arc, Genghis Khan), and up to the nineteenth century (Napoleon, the duke of Wellington, Vittorio Emanuele, and General Georgios Karaiskakis). The genre extends also to anonymity: the "unknown horseman with club" statue of Wiesbaden, and the Royal Scots Greys Monument of Edinburgh. The question is whether these manifestations of national and military history are (now) interchangeable. Using the terminology of international protocols for the transfer of prisoners or hostages, Patterson posits a series of exchanges, some obviously ironically appropriate (the duke of Wellington for Napoleon), some gesturing toward a kind of symmetry of power (Caligula for Genghis Khan), some whimsical (Friedrich III von Preußen for General Karaiskakis), one based on the proliferation of a single identity (George Washington at Valley Forge + George Washington, Union Square, for George Washington, Place d'Iéna, Paris). In the gallery, flashing neon arrows indicate each suggested exchange. Then there is a third element. Beneath each "exchange" Patterson proposes one and sometimes two reserve equestrian monuments, "potential replacements" if one of the statues were to be unavailable for transfer. So if either Jeanne d'Arc of the Place des Pyramides, Paris, or the statue of the Cid in Burgos were to be indisposed, Count Ramon Berenguer III "the Great" from the Gothic Quarter of Barcelona could be used instead. If Charlemagne outside Notre-Dame de Paris could not be exchanged with Marcus Aurelius of the Piazza del Campidoglio, Rome, then Frederick the Great of Sanssouci, Postdam, would fill in. One might ponder the alignments implicit in such configurations. Charlemagne—Marcus Aurelius—Frederick the Great; France—Rome—Prussia. Jeanne d'Arc—El Cid—Ramon Berenguer; France—Castile—Catalonia. But the flashing arrows ask not to be pressed too hard. The point and the question is about the loss of meaning, about the curious invisibility of many if not all of these statues, about the antiquated status of the genre. Would anyone notice? The answer is clearly yes and no, because not all the statues are of equal significance: some of the proposed transfers would be polemical, others of little or no moment. The more profound question concerns the way in which such monuments define and give identity to place. At the time of their creation they must have seemed emphatic signifiers of identity. But the international nature of the genre leads to banality, and from there to an ephemeral hollowness, until finally these horses and their riders are ready to be picked off by a playful cosmopolitanism: to be displaced, rotated, unmoored. The visual language of nationalism and militarism has changed (not vanished), and Patterson reminds us that such change leaves debris, detritus, vestiges.

B paused, and I found myself unable to think of anything to say. Luckily, he resumed:

— But let's think about the Middle Ages, since that is what you asked about. I don't suppose you recall Isidore of Seville's definition of "natio," do you?

As it happened I had just finished a translation of book nine of the *Etymologiae*, so yes – in fact I did recall it. B smiled and I wondered whether he somehow knew of my translation, as yet unpublished. Reddening, I began haltingly, but gradually spoke with more confidence ...

— In book nine Isidore outlines the concepts of *gens* (which you could translate variously as people, tribe, nation, race) and *natio*. He says that a *gens* is a multitude descended from a single origin. But he adds that a *gens* forms a particular grouping which is distinct from another *natio*, as in "the people of Greece," "of Asia." Then he moves on to etymologies: "gentilitas" comes from *gens*; a *gens* is also so called on account of the generations of families, that is from "giving birth" (*gignendo*), just as *natio* comes from "being born" (*nascendo*).

In the next section Isidore invokes the story of the division of the earth between the three sons of Noah. Fifteen of the *gentes* among whom the earth was divided descend from Japhet, thirty-one from Cham, twenty-seven from Sem; the same number of tongues were dispersed through the earth, and as they increased they filled provinces and islands. A bit later he explicitly says that *nationes* which are defined by their own blood relationships (*cognationibus*) are called *gentes*.[55]

— What do you notice about these statements?

Again I hesitated. Frowning, I replied ...

---

55. Isidore of Seville, *Etymologiae/Étymologies* 9.2.1–2, ed. and trans. Marc Reydellet (Paris, 1984), 41–43: "Gens est multitudo ab uno principio orta, siue ab alia natione secundum propriam collectionem distincta, ut Greciae, Asiae. Hinc et gentilitas dicitur. Gens autem appellata propter generationes familiarum, id est a gignendo, sicut natio a nascendo. Gentes autem a quibus diuisa est terra quindecim sunt de Iafeth, triginta et una de Cham, uiginti et septem de Sem, quae fiunt septuaginta tres, uel potius, ut ratio declarat, septuaginta duae, totidemque linguae, quae per terras esse coeperunt quaeque crescendo prouincias et insulas inpleuerunt"; 9.4.4, ed. Reydellet, 157: "Genus aut a gignendo et progenerando dictum aut a definitione certorum prognatorum, ut nationes quae propriis cognationibus terminatae gentes appellantur."

— Well, one might say that the concept of nation is a shadow of *gens*. It runs alongside, but is also secondary. Isidore is primarily thinking about peoples, and it's hard to discern much if any difference between his use of *gens* and *natio*; the two are basically synonyms. "Nation" is probably an acceptable translation of *gens*, as well as *natio*, but that's where the problems start. What do we understand by nation? What did Isidore understand by *gens* and *natio*? (And let's not forget that he himself was obviously working with terminology inherited from the Bible, Augustine, Orosius, and a host of other authorities, Christian and non-Christian).

Isidore certainly does think of peoples in spatial terms: "people of Greece," "people of Asia," and so on. But the spatial boundaries he suggests remain very vague. Language and genealogy are much stronger as defining agents – following Augustine, after the flood the number of *gentes* was equal to the number of languages on earth; peoples are an extension of family.[56] Since the generations of peoples with their many languages have filled terrestrial space, islands and provinces derive their identity from the populations and tongues within them, not the other way around. The borders are not geographic but ethnographic: nations are defined ("terminatae" is the word used – limited, marked off) by blood, by birth, but not by space.

— Alright then, said B. Let's accept, for a moment, that you are right, and that in late antiquity nation is primarily an ethnographic concept, one that moves with people. So then, the question we might ask is: when does nation begin to be expressed in spatial terms – when do nations develop borders, spatial rather than (or as well as) genetic limits?

— Exactly, I said. That was the question I started with.

— Actually, said B, it is a far more precise and useful formulation of your initial sally.

Trying to hide my irritation at his haughty manner, I smiled wanly. B continued, now staring fixedly ahead and warming to his theme.

— What does recent debate among classicists about the construction of the Roman Empire as a geographical entity have to tell us? They are now saying – and the argument seems to me persuasive – that the spatial ends of the empire should

56. Augustine of Hippo, *De civitate dei* 16.6, ed. B. Dombart and A. Kalb, Corpus Christianorum Series Latina 47–48 (Turnhout, 1955), 2: 507.

be understood in terms of frontiers rather than borders. Frontiers were not political barriers but social, cultural, and moral definitions of community and alterity, the very opposite of the fixed frontiers of ethnicity and territoriality created by the rise of the nation-state.[57] The Romans certainly marked boundaries (using stones, cadasters, and monuments of various kinds), but these shifted back and forth over the course of the empire. More important was the space of the frontier – a zone, not a line – which expressed Roman identity and power ...

— Think of the Peutinger Tables, I exclaimed.

— I do. Particularly when I am writing articles about them. But I would be interested to know what you make of them in the context of frontiers, he remarked placidly, yet with an unmistakeable hint of menace.

— I know much less than you do, of course, I stammered. But I mentioned them because the Tables show an image of the late Roman world. An image, dating perhaps from the third or fourth century AD, that extends from southern Britain to India, stretched out across almost seven metres of parchment. As I recall, there are three basic planes that structure the map. The central one runs through Gaul, Italy, then Macedonia, Asia Minor, Mesopotamia, and finally India. To the south there is a strip that extends along North Africa, Egypt, Palestine, then desert, Babylon and Taprobana. To the north the strip runs from Britain through Germania, Pannonia, the Adriatic, the Black Sea, and Scythia. Of course these strips are interconnected in various ways, and the most striking feature of the map at first glance is the network of routes marked on it, with distances from place to place consistently indicated. There are provinces and peoples on the map. Yet evidently it is not quite the administrative map that once existed, or at least that has been imagined by scholars keen to reconstruct "the Roman map of the world." Instead the dominant mode is that of the itinerary. We have routes, rivers, mountain ranges, deserts, marshes, *fines* – ends, limits, but very vaguely defined ones, without the precision of a line. Surely in the end it is the continuity of space, of the empire, that emerges from this map ... the borders are primarily natural and the purpose of the map is to articulate the routes across them.

B inclined his head to one side.

---

57. C.R. Whittaker, *Rome and its Frontiers: The Dynamics of Empire* (London, 2004); Mark W. Graham, *News and Frontier Consciousness in the Late Roman Empire* (Ann Arbor, 2006).

— Be careful, he warned, of that glib assumption that the only borders in the ancient and early medieval world were natural ones. We can appreciate the falsity of such a view by returning to Isidore. For it is in Isidore that we see the profound imprint left by Roman spatial organisation on medieval intellectual life. There is a striking passage in book fourteen of the *Etymologiae*, which seemed so telling to me that I committed it to memory some years ago during a particularly tedious summer holiday in Dorset. Isidore is talking about provinces, and he says that "a *patria* is so called because it is common to all who are born in it." *Terra* is one of the four elements, but its plural form – *terrae* – signifies a particular part of the world: like Africa, or Italy. Then he adds the term *loca* – a synonym of *terrae* – meaning something like areas or expanses. The point is that these expanses, these *spatia*, contain provinces, in the same way that the body contains limbs, or a house contains rooms. You have an area – he gives the example of Asia – and within that area there are provinces (like, Phrygia), then within the provinces there are regions, a *regio* or *conventus*, and finally you get to cities.[58] Much of what he says derives from Servius's commentary on the *Aeneid*, but the point is that Isidore stitches together various statements by Servius and one or two other authors to construct a hierarchy of spatial division, which he connects explicitly with Roman provincial organisation. The *provincia* is a direct political intervention in spatial order, used by a central power to demarcate and ultimately control territory. But what happens to that evocative notion of the *patria*, the native land "common to all born in it"? It's quickly left behind, if not erased, by the distinctions between *locus, provincia, regio,* and *civitas*. Evidently Roman provincial organisation offered a means of mapping a large area, not necessarily in the sense of producing a pictorial map, but in the sense of sub-division, the construction of interlocking categories. And those categories were not defined by the *natio* or the *patria*: in fact, they were probably deliberately designed to submerge or contain such dangerous concepts.

— What about borders?

— To some extent these can be found in the *Etymologiae*. Often they are indeed natural. The description of Gaul, for example, notes that it is protected by the Alps to the east, enclosed by Ocean to the west, and delimited by the Pyrenees to the south and the Rhine to the north.[59] But take Phrygia. It is bordered by the Hellespont to the west, it's true, but to the north, south, and east its borders are

58. *Etymologiae XIV: De Terra* 14.5.19–22, ed. and trans. Olga Spevak (Paris, 2011), 97–99.

59. *Etymologiae* 14.4.25, ed. Spevak, 69–77.

formed by neighbouring regions: Galatia, Lycaonia, and Lydia.[60] It's all about the establishment of contiguities. To a certain extent these borders are administrative, repeating Roman provincial organisation, but by Isidore's time the context and the function have changed. Post-empire, this set of relations remains the most comprehensive taxonomy of space. But I'd argue that it exists as a legacy of the power under whose auspices it was constructed – the footprint or memory of empire.

— Hmm. So, it's fair to say that over the course of the Middle Ages no method of spatial delineation emerged to replace in a comprehensive way the Roman model?

— Agreed. What happened was more interesting: various polities – the Carolingian Empire and the Holy Roman Empire, other powerful kingdoms, and the papacy – constituted territorial entities. That is, they came to administer and define their own spaces. However, except for the papacy the administrative structures of these polities either did not last or were spatially limited. The papacy adopted the provincial structure of the Roman Empire, revised and expanded it; then later religious orders, such as the friars, followed suit. This allowed for a fluidity of representation: maps continued to show long defunct Roman provinces, because following Orosian precepts they attempted to reveal history as well as space on the map, but also because information about spatial configurations was only relatively slowly disseminated, and not in an orderly fashion. In other words, in the absence of systematic mapping of, for example, North Africa, the Arabian peninsula, Asia, and actually parts of Europe too, the Roman model remained useful.

A voice suddenly came from directly behind us.

— Useful, yes, but you are talking only about administrative and perhaps antiquarian geographies.

B and I both started and turned abruptly. Behind us was C, a distinguished looking woman of uncertain age and indeed nationality.

— May I join you? I have only heard the last few minutes of your very stimulating conversation, the topic of which is of considerable interest to me.

Without waiting for a response, she perched on what I had previously taken for a garden ornament, but which on closer inspection revealed itself to be a low stool.

60. *Etymologiae* 14.3.41, ed. Spevak, 45; cf. Pliny, *Naturalis historia* 5.145; Solinus, *Collectanea rerum memorabilium* 40.9, ed. Theodor Mommsen (Berlin: 1895), 167–68.

— You imply that I neglect other kinds of geographies? B offered, somewhat icily.

— But of course. What, for example, of the genre of the *laus patriae*? Don't you have there native lands described in explicitly spatial terms? You will no doubt be familiar with the early twelfth-century "laus Flandrie" of Petrus Pictor, edited by Van Aker in the *Corpus Christianorum* series.

— No doubt, said B drily.

— Then you will recall that the poem is a forty-four-line paean to Flanders, clearly conceived as a political entity, and compared to several other places and realms.

— Naturally, B smiled thinly. But for the sake of our young friend here, perhaps you will be so good as to enumerate those comparisons.

— You have not read the poem? C turned to me with surprise.

— I have ... heard of it, I muttered, reddening once more.

— No matter. I will summarise for you. "Flandria, super omnes terra beata" (land blessed above all others), is described initially as "Gallorum decus et robur generale / Et timor Anglorum" (glory and strongest part of the Gauls and terror of the English). The English have cause to fear it, as we learn that Flanders seeks (or perhaps just rivals) the imperial sceptre. And it has been making useful marriage alliances with the Holy Roman Empire, with the French, with the Danes, with Apulia, with the duke of Antioch, and even with the English themselves. It has a treaty with the Burgundians, and helped to repel the Parthians (Turks, in one manuscript) from Jerusalem. Indeed Flanders, a land that is potent under its Count Robert, is the standard-bearer for the Crusades. For reasons that are unclear, the poet has suffered some form of exile, and he tells us that he longs to return to his native land. The final four lines see him address Flanders as, in order, "terra piorum," "terra bonorum," "terra proborum," and finally "terra meorum" (land of the devout, of the good, of the upright, land of my people).[61]

— The word *natio* is not used?

---

61. *Petri Pictoris Carmina*, ed. L. Van Acker (Turnhout, 1972), xxv–xli, 57–58.

— No – and the reference to Flanders as "decus Gallorum" suggests that ethnically it is conceived as Gallic, but politically poised between European powers. (For Pirenne, you know, Flanders was the model of a single society formed of two distinct populations, one *de race romane* and the other *de race teutonique*).[62]

— Flanders is then perhaps a region, but not a nation?

— In the poem it is described repeatedly as a *terra*. Politically at this time (around 1110) it is a county, and there are several references to the counts of Flanders. Emotionally, it is the poet's *patria*, his homeland. Technically, as you imply, it does not qualify as a nation, because the terminology that would allow us to identify it as such is not there. But then perhaps our terminology needs to be rethought.

B had closed his eyes, and appeared to be about to commence his postponed mid-afternoon nap. All of a sudden, though without opening his eyes, he spoke:

— A reader of this poem who knew nothing of Flanders would, after perusing it, be none the wiser about a single aspect of Flemish topography. It is, in fact, a zero in terms of spatial representation, and therefore irrelevant to our discussion of nation.

There was a short pause. I cast a quick glance at C, but observed only a slight tightening of her jaw.

— And yet, she said calmly, the poetry of Petrus Pictor is intimately connected with a work that, in terms of spatial representation, is very much more than zero. I refer to the *Liber Floridus* of Lambert of St Omer.

At this I started.

— The autograph manuscript of the *Liber Floridus*, she continued, contains no less than eight poems attributed to Petrus, who was a native of St Omer, albeit apparently an exiled one. It is true that "De laude Flandrie" is absent. Nevertheless, the maps of Lambert give us a remarkably clear idea of how Flanders might

---

62. Henri Pirenne, *Histoire de Belgique*, 5th ed, 4 vols (Brussels, 1948–52), 1: 72; for recent thoughts, see Élodie Lecuppre-Desjardin, *Le Royaume inachevé des ducs de Bourgogne (XIVe–XVe siècles)* (Paris, 2016), 313–44.

have been conceived spatially in relation to the rest of Europe. But perhaps – turning to me – you recall them better than I do.

— Not at all, I said hastily – though it is true that I find the *Liber Floridus* particularly fascinating.

— Of course, muttered B. It's full of pictures and the Latin isn't too taxing ...

— In any case, resumed C, we know – do we not – that this remarkable encyclopedia was compiled by Lambert, a secular canon of the Church of Our Lady, by 1121. It gathers together various kinds of information available within the evidently learned community of St Omer at the time. Natural history, genealogy, political history (the deeds of the counts of Flanders and the Crusades were of particular interest to Lambert), cosmology, time-reckoning, and eschatology: all find their place within the pages of this book – which is, as B remarks, prolifically illustrated. There are several maps in the *Liber Floridus*, but one in particular is relevant to our discussion.

— The map of Europe? I murmured.

— Exactly. It is remarkable firstly because maps of single continents, or *partes mundi*, as they were called in the Middle Ages, are almost unknown at this time. More striking is the presentation of Europe, in the form – I have recently been persuaded of this – of a hand held upwards and facing the viewer (Figure 16). This is more likely to be a mnemonic device, I think, than the right hand of God in benediction, as some have speculated.[63] On the "thumb," if one may call it that, is Italy, with Rome central, prominent, and marked by a church. The fingers show stretches of land from Macedonia to Venice (index finger); Grecia through Pannonia to Archadia (middle finger); Mesia to the Sclavi (ring finger); the little finger shows northern peoples – the Huns (*Huni*), Vandals (*Wandali*), and Goths (*Gothi*) – and ends in Scandinavia with Scanzia, Denmark and Norway. The palm of the hand is structured by three rivers and a mountain range: the Danube, Rhine, Rhone, and the Pyrenees. Within it Germania and Gallia are given particular prominence, but so too are regions: Saxonia, Sueuia, Histria, and Baioaria (Bavaria) on one side of the Danube; and, to the west of the Rhine, Bur-

---

63. Hartmut Kugler, "Europa pars quarta: Der Teil und das Ganze im 'Liber floridus,'" in *Europa im Weltbild des Mittelalters: Kartographische Konzepte*, ed. Ingrid Baumgärtner and Hartmut Kugler (Berlin, 2008), 45–61, at 55–59.

gundia, Aquitania, Neustria, and, yes, Flandria. At the foot of the hand sits Spain and Lusitania.

Now, the text around this map is extremely interesting. It begins by stating that Europe is a fourth part of the world, because Asia accounts for half, and Africa the remaining quarter. It lists the number of seas, islands, provinces, mountains, towns, rivers, and the peoples (thirty-three, apparently) within Europe. Nothing too exciting about this – it's an adaptation of a cosmography which claimed to derive from a survey of the known world commissioned by Julius Caesar.[64] The next bit is unusual, though: Lambert tells us that he has marked in red the kingdoms (*regna*) which pertain to the Roman and Frankish Empires. Italy is indeed bordered in red, and on the other side of the Alps a red line extends from the Mediterranean coast of Gaul, along the Atlantic coast of Europe as far as Saxony, before curving through central Europe until it returns to the Alps. The Rhine too is marked in red. I think the point here is that one may see on the map the boundaries of the Carolingian Empire overlaid on the foot – or hand – print of the ancient Roman Empire.

— So the lines in red mark the Frankish Empire of the ninth century?

— Yes, more or less, and the image was probably meant to be consulted alongside a genealogy and history of the Frankish kings compiled by Lambert – a text that includes discussion of the division of the Frankish Empire between the successors of Charlemagne. Now, some have seen the map as fitting into Lambert's ideas about the coming of Antichrist (because according to one apocalyptic text the division of all the kingdoms formerly ruled by the Roman Empire from their erstwhile mistress was a pre-requisite for the end-times).[65] Others think the image is meant to assert papal authority (Rome's new power) over Europe's secular rulers.[66] All I would say is that the map is clearly conceived as emanating from the Roman Empire; this is acknowledged in the surrounding text, which refers to the measurement of the world "Julio cesare imperante." So it is very far from a map of Europe in Lambert's own time. But neither is it a "map of the

64. "Cosmographia olim Aethici dicta," in *Geographi Latini minores*, ed. Alexander Riese (Heilbronn, 1878; repr. Hildesheim, 1964), 71–103.

65. Albert Derolez, *The Autograph Manuscript of the Liber Floridus: A Key to the Encyclopedia of Lambert of Saint-Omer* (Turnhout, 1998), 151–52.

66. Claudius Sieber-Lehman, "Regna colore rubeo circumscripta," in *Grenzen und Raumvorstellungen*, ed. Guy P. Marchal (Zürich, 1996), 79–91, at 84–85; Patrick Gautier Dalché, "Représentations géographiques de l'Europe – septentrionale, centrale et orientale – au Moyen Âge," in *Europa im Weltbild des Mittelalters*, 63–79, at 70.

Roman Empire" or even a "map of Europe in the age of Charlemagne." It is instead a composite of all three.

— And Flanders?

— A region within Gallia, nestling against the sea. There are of course *gentes* – peoples – on the map, and all around it: the list of those thirty-three European peoples (which since it is derived from late antique sources does not include the Flemish!) appears beneath the map.

— I feel sure that C will soon reveal the point of this lengthy description, sighed B.

It was C's turn to smile wanly.

— My impression was that you and A here were talking about borders, boundaries, and frontiers. You were proposing the absence of nations in the precise modern sense – that is, as spatial entities with clearly defined and agreed borders, not to mention some form of unifying government and a notion of citizenship. Instead you thought the early medieval idea of nation could only be understood as a synonym, or near synonym, for people. Lambert's map of Europe largely supports your hypothesis. When Lambert thinks about spatial division and representation he thinks of peoples, of natural features, and he thinks of provinces, kingdoms, and empires. But this map does also show the capacity – his capacity – to draw borders: often natural ones, but on occasion – as with the line that runs from Saxony to the Adriatic, excluding Scandinavia, the Slavs, and Venice, while including Saxony, Suevia, and Bavaria – the red line is man-made.

And antiquity and modernity are not divorced: the Huns and the Vandals find themselves alongside the Goths, in among some Roman provinces. The map shows "Lauinia" in Italy (a reference to the town supposedly founded by Aeneas in honour of his wife), but also "Venecia," a foundation that post-dates the Empire. Hesperia, the antique name for Spain, sits across the Pyrenees from Neustria (Normandy). I think from the content and tone of the *Liber Floridus* it is obvious that Lambert himself and presumably his fellow canons would have looked at the inscription "Flandria" and been conscious of the position of their *patria* (dare we say their nation?) within European space and history.

— All well and good, said B. We are speculating, but what you conjecture is not implausible. Though I would caution against eliding *patria* and *natio* as freely as you seem to want to do.[67] However, I wish to ask A – who has some pretensions to being a historian of cartography (again: pictures, easy Latin) – whether he is aware of a single instance of a national map in anything approaching the modern sense from the entire span of the European Middle Ages?

— If by "national map" you mean a map whose primary function is to display the extent of a nation-state, with little or nothing beyond its borders, then the answer is that only very late in the Middle Ages do we have maps that could be said to resemble a modern map of, let's say, France, or Italy, or ... the Republic of Botswana.

— Or even – B interjected – maps that show the defined borders of several nations, rather than the kind of mix of peoples and provinces that we have heard about on Lambert's map of Europe.

— There are certainly some candidates, though, as I say, from later in the Middle Ages. The Franciscan Paolino Veneto produced at least two maps of Italy in the first quarter of the fourteenth century, which show the whole peninsula.[68] These are remarkable but not isolated examples, and maps like them may have inspired the "situs Italiae," a map of Italy whose place names reveal its origins in the humanist geography of the fourteenth and fifteenth centuries. By the end of the fifteenth century maps of the peninsula were pretty commonplace, at least in elite circles: according to an inventory of his Florence palazzo taken in 1492, Lorenzo dei Medici had two maps of Italy along with four *mappae mundi*, two of the Holy Land, and several other cartographic items.[69] Beyond Italy, the story seems roughly similar. There is, from about the middle of the fifteenth century, an image explicitly described by its maker (or at least its copyist) as a figure that

67. Thomas Eichenberger, *Patria: Studien zur Bedeutung des Wortes im Mittelalter (6.-12. Jahrhundert)* (Sigmaringen, 1991); Pierre Monnet, "La *patria* médiévale vue d'Allemagne, entre construction impériale et identités régionales," *Le Moyen Âge* 107 (2001): 71–99.

68. Bernard Degenhart and Annegrit Schmidt, *Marino Sanudo und Paolino Veneto: Zwei Literaten des 14. Jahrhunderts in ihrer Wirkung auf Buchillustrierung und Kartographie in Venedig, Avignon und Neapel* (Tübingen, 1973), 83–87; Nathalie Bouloux, *Culture et savoirs géographiques en Italie au XIVe siècle* (Turnhout, 2002), 101–6.

69. For the "situs Italiae" see Marica Milanesi, "Antico e moderno nella cartografia umanistica: Le grandi carte d'Italia nel Quattrocento," *Geographia antiqua* 16–17 (2007–8): 153–76; on Lorenzo dei Medici and others see Nathalie Bouloux, "La géographie à la cour (Italie, XVe siècle)," and Marica Milanesi, "Cartografia per un principe senza corte: Venezia nel quattrocento," *Micrologus* 16 (2008): 171–88; 189–216, respectively.

"contains all the realm of France."[70] A map of Flanders from 1452 represents the region from the perspective of an Italian merchant, with an emphasis on rivers, canals, and cities.[71] In Germany too the fifteenth century sees the production of a map, often attributed to the learned Cardinal Nicholas of Cusa, which shows Germania. Admittedly this last is far more a representation of a region – and a very broad swathe of Europe at that, from Norway in the north to the Adriatic in the south, and the Low Countries in the west to the Black Sea in the east – but it is generated by the desire to show an idea that is at least at some level national, or proto-national: the idea of Germany. This map owes an obvious conceptual debt to Ptolemy's *Geographia*, which as you know was only widely disseminated within learned circles in Europe after it was translated into Latin in the first decade of the fifteenth century.[72] The *Geographia*'s regional maps could be combined with its world image to form a sort of atlas: it ultimately provided a frame to which national – as well as regional – maps could be appended. During the sixteenth century, editions of the *Geographia* arguably started to look like a bit like collections of national maps – albeit produced for the cosmopolitan audience of the republic of letters.

— And Matthew Paris's thirteenth-century maps of Britain, now so widely reproduced as to have become banalities. Are they "national maps"? asked B in a tired voice.

— Like the later "Gough" map of Britain, strictly speaking no, since in charting Scotland, the Orkneys, and Ireland, as well as England and Wales, they show more than one kingdom. But I think what we are concluding here is that nation and region may not always be easy concepts to extract from one another at this point. Sometimes mapmakers clearly had the idea of showing a particular realm, a *regnum*. At others they seem to have been more interested in showing Britannia, Italia, or magna Germania – something that was by no means a single polit-

---

70. Camille Serchuk, "*Ceste figure contient tout le royaulme de France*: Cartography and National Identity in France at the End of the Hundred Years War," *Journal of Medieval History* 33 (2007): 320–38; Nathalie Bouloux, "From Gaul to the Kingdom of France: Representations of French Space in the Geographical Texts of the Middle Ages (Twelfth–Fifteenth Centuries)," in *Space in the Medieval West: Places, Territories, and Imagined Geographies*, ed. Meredith Cohen and Fanny Madeline (Farnham, 2014), 197–217.

71. Bruges, Openbare Bibliotheek, MS 685, fols. 211v–212r.

72. Meurer, "Cartography in the German Lands," 1183–88; cf. Gautier Dalché, *La Géographie de Ptolémée en Occident (IVe–XVIe siècle)* (Turnhout, 2009), 211.

ical entity – indeed in the case of Italy and Germany, something that would have to wait until the nineteenth century to attain the dubious privilege of nationhood. Britannia is interesting in this regard, in that it is an island, hence a spatial entity with very clearly defined natural borders. As an island, it perhaps lends itself to a map. Yet it is an island notably subdivided into separate kingdoms, counties or provinces, principalities. The border between England and Scotland was more or less continuously in dispute, and like that between England and Wales best thought of in terms of marches, frontier zones rather than lines. While the territorial ambition of the kings of England at times encompassed the entire island, and beyond to Ireland and the continent, those ambitions remained unfulfilled. Around the middle of the fifteenth century John Hardyng, a chronicler and energetic forger of documents, made a map of Scotland to facilitate an English invasion. In his chronicles and forgeries Hardyng worked hard to assert the English claim to overlordship of Scotland, and indeed the entire island: in mapping Scotland he saw himself delineating a realm that was by rights part of England.[73] But his plans came to nothing. In fact it is striking how rarely medieval islands – Crete, Sicily, Sardinia, Majorca, for instance, with Ireland and Iceland complicated counter-examples – are the site of unitary political or proto-national identities. Perhaps the problem was that they were too easily invaded, whether by military forces or by merchants, too easily annexed to larger polities and spheres of influence.

In almost all these cases of regional mapping what is shown has very strong historical content. The mapmaker does not wish to show "the nation as it is now." Instead, he wants to show something in its historical dimension: something that might be termed a nation, but more accurately perhaps a *situs*, a *provincia*, or even just a *locus*. A viewer might look at one of these images and understand the history of the area – its relationship to the Roman Empire, for example; who founded it; where it gets its name from – as well as its present site and the topographical features (rivers, mountains, seas, islands, lakes and so forth) that have defined, and continue to define, its form. To that degree, there seems to be a continuity with the cartographic practice of a Lambert of St Omer in the twelfth century. Perhaps most striking of all is the lack of evidence of official governmental sponsorship of anything like national mapping until the fifteenth century. The Gough map may – possibly – be an exception to that rule, and we know that King Robert of Naples possessed a "pictura Italiae," probably a copy of Paolino

73. Alfred Hiatt, "Beyond a Border: The Maps of Scotland in John Hardyng's *Chronicle*," in *The Lancastrian Court: Proceedings of the 2001 Harlaxton Symposium*, ed. Jenny Stratford (Donington, 2003), 78–94.

Veneto's map of Italy.[74] But even in the fifteenth century what rulers seem to have wanted was maps of disputed territory, like the map of Burgundy commissioned by Philip the Good in 1444 to settle a disagreement with the king of France, or the maps of Pomerania occasioned by the conflict between the Teutonic Knights and the king of Poland, or the map of the border between the lands of the marquis of Mantua and the duke of Ferrara jointly commissioned by these magnates in 1473.[75] These examples (and there are several others) show the dramatic rise in administrative and juridical mapping in the fifteenth century, and the level of interest in regional mapmaking expressed by powerful patrons – but I think it's safe to say that energetic sponsorship of cartography along national lines really only seems to have begun in any kind of systematic way in the sixteenth century.

B looked pleased with my answer. Yet C appeared troubled.

— I seem to recall, she said, once seeing a reproduction of a fourteenth-century map of the border between Picardy and the Netherlands. Do you know this image?

I thought for a moment.

— Perhaps, yes. Do you mean the rather sketchy map that was produced to settle a legal dispute about a student at the University of Paris sometime in the 1350s?

— 1357, growled B.

---

74. Biondo Flavio, *Italy Illuminated* 6.68 and 6.77, ed. and trans. Jeffrey A. White, 2: 342 and 2: 354.

75. F. de Dainville, "Cartes et contestations au XVe siècle," *Imago Mundi* 24 (1970): 99–121; P.D.A. Harvey, "Local and Regional Cartography in Medieval Europe," in *The History of Cartography*, vol. 1: *Cartography in Prehistoric, Ancient, and Medieval Europe and the Mediterranean*, ed. J.B. Harley and David Woodward (Chicago, 1987), 464–501; *Luca Fancelli, architetto: Epistolario gonzaghesco*, ed. Corinna Vasić Vatovec (Florence, 1979), 381–88; Patrick Gautier Dalché, "Limite, frontière et organisation de l'espace dans la géographie et la cartographie de la fin du Moyen Âge," in *Grenzen und Raumvorstellungen*, ed. Marchal, 93–122; Léonard Dauphant, *Le royaume des quatre rivières: L'espace politique français (1380–1515)* (Seyssel, 2012), 117–28, 143–50, 175–90, 387–91.

— The map essentially shows the river Maas or Meuse, with certain points along either side of it (Figure 17). Flanders is marked. (Odd, the way we keep coming back to Flanders.) As you know, students in medieval universities had to belong to a "nation," but the term was used rather differently to the way we apply it today. The "nation" in the context of the medieval university did operate spatially – that is, where you came from determined which nation you belonged to. But at the same time it was used rather generically. So for example by the mid-thirteenth century at the University of Paris there were four "nations": the French, the Norman, the Picard, and the English.[76] All students had to belong to a nation, with the result that many students from diverse regions and hence diverse ethnicities were for administrative purposes classed within a particular nation. The "English" nation at the university of Paris included students who came from what is now part of the Netherlands, and who had presumably never been to England in their lives. This particular student came from Geertruidenberg, a town just south of the river Meuse, so the question was whether he should be part of the Picard nation, or "English." The point of the map – which was drawn by one of the "English" masters (one Willelmus de Spyny, himself described as "Scotus") – may have been to elucidate the evidence of a witness. This witness was a student from the region in question, who asserted that customarily men from south as well as north of the Meuse had joined the English nation. He gave a rather detailed account of the course of the river, including its division at a certain point into the "old" and "new" Meuse, and he identified several of the towns on its course. This is what the map shows, as well as what appear to be borderlines between Flanders and Zeeland, and Brabant and Holland. No other maps of precisely this kind survive, and it does not seem to have acted as evidence in itself. Ironically perhaps, the commissioners who heard the case ruled in favour of the Picards that the river actually should function as the border between the nations: that is, with some exceptions, students from south of the Meuse were Picard; those to its north, English.[77] The river, they claimed, also marked a linguistic division, between Germanic and Romance: or as they said, it was where the "lingua theotonica" met the "lingua gallica." All the same, the map is very interesting. It's not a national map, but ...

76. Pearl Kibre, *The Nations in the Mediaeval Universities* (Cambridge, 1948); Nathalie Gorochov, "Genèse et organisation des nations universitaires en Europe aux XIIe et XIIIe siècles," in *Nation et nations au Moyen Âge* (Paris, 2014), 273–86.

77. Bibliothèque de la Sorbonne, Archives de l'Université de Paris Registre 2, vol. 2, fol. 35v; Gray C. Boyce, "The Controversy over the Boundary between the English and Picard Nations (1356–58)," in *Études d'histoire dédiées a la mémoire de Henri Pirenne* (Brussels, 1937), 55–66.

— But this other concept of nation is one we should consider, is it not? suggested C.

B began to speak quickly and confidently.

— Naturally. There is a fascinating malleability of the term *natio* in the last centuries of what we call the Middle Ages. Just think of the Council of Constance.

He looked at us meaningfully. There was a pause before he continued.

— I see from the blank expression on your faces – or rather the transparent attempt to feign familiarity – that you require a bald summary of this pivotal event. So. The purpose of the Council (1414–18) is usually held to have been three-fold. First, to resolve the papal schism, which had been initiated in 1378 when two popes were elected, and exacerbated in 1409 by the election of a third claimant at the Council of Pisa. Second, the extirpation of heresy. And third, the reform of the Church in its head and members. (The Council succeeded in the first and, given its condemnation of John Wyclif and execution of Jan Hus and Jerome of Prague, second of these objectives; the third was postponed – fatally, it turned out – until the next century). The key point is that, in a practice that had begun in the thirteenth century, the Council was constituted by nations. These were similar in some ways to the "nations" that made up medieval universities. There were initially four principal nations at the Council: Italian; German; French; English; then five when the Spanish joined the Council after "their" pope was deposed. Each nation voted as a unit, but comprised representatives of smaller kingdoms, regions, and ethnic groupings who met to discuss each issue (and who often bitterly resented each other). Thus the German nation at the Council included the Holy Roman Empire, Hungary, Dalmatia, Croatia, Denmark, Norway, Sweden, Bohemia, and Poland; the "Gallic nation" included Burgundians, as well as Provence, the duchy of Savoy, Dauphine, and Lorraine.[78]

---

78. On nations at Constance: Louise R. Loomis, "Nationality at the Council of Constance: An Anglo-French Dispute," *American Historical Review* 44 (1939): 508–27; Hans-Joachim Schmidt, *Kirche, Staat, Nation: Raumgliederung der Kirche im mittelalterlichen Europa* (Weimar, 1999), esp. 476–84; Robert N. Swanson, "*Gens secundum cognationem et collectionem ab alia distincta?* Thomas Polton, Two Englands, and the Challenge of Medieval Nationhood," in *Das Konstanzer Konzil als europäisches Ereignis: Begegnungen, Medien und Rituale,* ed. Gabriela Signori and Birgit Studt (Ostfildern, 2014), 57–87; David Wallace, "Constance," in *Europe: A Literary History, 1348–1418,* ed. David Wallace, 2 vols (Oxford, 2016), 2: 655–82.

— And the English?

— Exactly. As ever, the English were the troublemakers of Europe. At the Council, the question of the coherence and the extent of the English nation was raised in dramatic fashion. Specifically, in 1416–17 the right of the English nation to equal status with the Gallic, German, Italian, and Spanish nations was strongly attacked by the French delegation, led by the Cardinal and *homme de lettres*, Pierre d'Ailly.[79] The motivations for the attack were without doubt political, to do with the tactical alliance formed between the Germans and English, and supported by the Holy Roman emperor elect, Sigismund. But they need not detain us: the point is that the idea of the *natio* came under pressure. The contention of the French was that the "natio Anglicana," though indeed a nation (*natio particularis*), was simply too small and too homogenous to deserve equality with the other four principal European nations (*nationes principales*). Hence, the French provocatively suggested, it should be incorporated within the German nation.

— That would have gone down well, C remarked.

— The response of the English was certainly indignant. It was probably written by Thomas Polton, one of the four official notaries of the Council; in any case, it stressed the geographical size of Britain, its many provinces and dioceses, its ecclesiastical significance, based on the antiquity of Christianity there, and the multiplicity of its languages – five (English, Welsh, Irish, Gascon, and Cornish), unlike the single language of the Gallic nation. "Beside duchies, lands, islands, and lordships, in great number," the reply ran, "there are eight kingdoms [that comprise the English nation], namely England, Scotland, and Wales – which three make up greater Britain – then the Kingdom of the Isle of Man, and in Ireland, next to England, four great and noble kingdoms," referring to Connaught, Galway, Munster, and Meath.[80]

    As this exchange shows, at the Council of Constance it was important for English delegates to assert the significance and harmony of what they termed in their reply to the French the "English or British nation" (*natio anglicana sive Britannica*): a regional grouping inclusive of Scotland, Wales, and Ireland. I find it

79. *Magnum Œcumenicum Constantiense Concilium de universali Ecclesiae reformatione, unione, et fide*, ed. Hermann von der Hardt, 7 vols (Frankfurt, 1696–1742), 5: 57–75.

80. *Magnum Œcumenicum Constantiense Concilium*, 5: 86: "praeter Ducatus, terras, ac insulas, et dominia in numero copioso, sunt regna 8, videlicet Anglia, Scotia, Wallia, quae tria majorem integrant Britanniam, regnum etiam de mari et in Hibernia, juxta Angliam, quatuor regna magna et notabilia ... ." For the suggested emendation of "mari" to "Man" see Loomis, "Nationality," 524 n52.

rather interesting that their claims to be a principal nation required them to elide the concepts of England and Britain, but at the same time to retain a sense of the particularity of the English nation. Well, *plus ça change ...*

In any case, the defining feature of the late medieval nation – at least, the *natio principalis* – would seem to have been its capacity to contain multitudes. Clearly we are dealing with a relatively fluid concept, and one that continued to be defined by ethnography, language, and administrative subdivision (how many dioceses, how many kingdoms). Spatial definitions hovered at the fringes of this debate. The English reply concluded by proposing a counter to the French method of determining the status of a nation, one based on the cardinal points: north (England, Wales, Scotland, Ireland, Denmark, Sweden, Norway); east (Germany, Hungary, Bohemia, Poland), south (Italy and those on Cyprus and Crete obedient to the pope), and west (France and Spain).[81] Naturally no-one took this suggestion seriously, but it served to show the way maps could be re-drawn.[82]

So – B said, turning towards me – let me finally make an answer to your, or I should say, our question. In the nineteenth century the nation could be described as a "spiritual principle";[83] a century later it had become an "imagined community";[84] debates continue as to the nature and origins of nations and national consciousness.[85] But my view is that nation is entirely different in the Middle Ages. That it does not exist as a clearly defined spatial concept until after the end of the fifteenth century – and even then, that it develops slowly and unpredictably. That we needlessly impose our own notions on an earlier era when we start trying to uncover nations and nationalism in the Middle Ages. I fully grant that things begin to look somewhat different in the fifteenth and even four-teenth century; but what is stirring then will only begin to be realised much later. I am thinking of what may be termed "humanist nationalism," such as we see in Biondo's *Italia illustrata*, or in Conrad Celtis's famous address to Germans.[86]

81. *Magnum Œcumenicum Constantiense Concilium*, 5: 94–96.

82. *Magnum Œcumenicum Constantiense Concilium*, 5: 91–92.

83. Ernest Renan, *Qu'est-ce qu'une nation?* (Paris, 1882), 25.

84. Benedict Anderson, *Imagined Communities: Reflections on the Origin and Spread of Nationalism*, 2nd ed. (London, 1991).

85. The tip of an iceberg: Patrick J. Geary, *The Myth of Nations: The Medieval Origins of Europe* (Princeton, 2002); *Regna and Gentes: The Relationship between Late Antique and Early Medieval Peoples and Kingdoms in the Transformation of the Roman World*, ed. Hans-Werner Goetz, Jörg Jarnut, and Walter Pohl (Leiden, 2003); Anthony D. Smith, *The Antiquity of Nations* (Cambridge, 2004); Caspar Hirschi, *The Origins of Nationalism: An Alternative History from Ancient Rome to Early Modern Germany* (Cambridge, 2012).

86. Conrad Celtis, *Oratio in gymnasio in Ingelstadio publice recitata*, ed. Johannes Rupprich (Leipzig, 1932).

A concept of nation is present for these men, but one that does not accord with contemporary political boundaries and that insistently refers to and takes its inspiration from the past – from the *Italia* at the time of the Roman Empire, or the *Germania* of Tacitus. The great age of nationalism is the nineteenth century, and we would do well to see the Middle Ages as something else: an age in which realms, provinces, regions, areas, cities, towns, and islands all co-existed and competed as ways of defining space, and in which the spaces of the past inevitably informed, and structured, any attempt to define the spaces of the present. Only by discarding the unhelpful concept of nation can we fully appreciate the rich variety – the unpredictability, the error-strewn instability – of medieval spatial conceptions.

As B was talking I noticed that the shade in which we had begun our conversation had vanished, and my head (protected only by vestiges of hair) was in danger of scorching in the still potent late afternoon sun. I suggested we might move inside, if my companions could bear to leave the warmth. They readily agreed, and we retreated to the cool and dark wood-panelled library where the papers had been delivered. There, once our eyes had adjusted to the light, we found to our relief a table laid out with cups, saucers, and small biscuits along with a freshly brewed jug of coffee. I thought for a moment that our discussion had come to a natural end, and was about to ask my colleagues if they knew the name of the restaurant in Trastevere where we were to dine that night, when C put down her espresso and started talking rapidly.

— I spent a few years in Thailand you know, she began. ... Around the time I was there a book by a bright young historian came to my attention. It is entitled *Siam Mapped*, by Thongchai Winichakul, and it has achieved a certain kind of reflected glory: it turns out that Thongchai's study of the role of cartography in the formation of Thai nationhood provided an important prompt to Benedict Anderson's thinking on maps. Anderson had said nothing much about maps in the first edition of his famous book on nations; in the second edition, however, he acknowledged the importance of the map (as well as the census and the museum) in the imagination and definition of a nation. Thongchai developed this idea further with specific reference to Thailand.[87] He noted the fusion in the late nineteenth century of two hitherto distinct concepts, under the pressure of British and French imperialisms, as well as the Thai monarchy's own desire to exert and extend control. *Prathet* (traditionally "a piece of the earth's surface without any

87. Thongchai Winichakul, *Siam Mapped: A History of the Geo-Body of a Nation* (Honolulu, 1994).

specific qualification of size, population, or power") came to mean "nation, country"; and it was fused with *chat* (literally and traditionally "birth, commonality by birth") to form the word *chatprathet* or *prathetchat*, meaning nation, country.[88] Is this analogous to the more gradual shift in European usage of *natio* from "people" to "nation"? For Thongchai the formation of Thai nationhood was coterminus with the definition of the national "geo-body," a body represented and constructed by the map. He identified firm links between mapping and military conquest, but more profoundly, the role of the map in the twentieth century in the construction of Thai national identity: the map is the image of the nation, signifies it, but also constitutes its body, above all defining its limits. Not only do these observations resonate strikingly with Isidore's comparison of an expanse of land to the human body, they seem to me to raise some questions. If an intimate connection between nation and map is not present in the Middle Ages, what political or ethnographic function do medieval maps have? Is nationalist mapping of the post-medieval period in fact about claiming the map, shaping the universalising discourse of cartography, a discourse that has always aimed at the description of the entire world? And do medieval mapping practices suggest possibilities for the construction of maps in the twenty-first century – for the dissolution and reformation of geo-bodies, for maps without nations, without borders, but *with* history? Or, perhaps more modestly, for a plurality of modes of spatial representation: maps on which more than one definition of the nation may be read. In the case of disputed territories, for example, might we allow, even encourage, maps to show more than one border?

And, she smiled, as for our discussion. Rather than discarding nation as a concept, on the grounds that it is useless for understanding medieval spatial representation, we should turn the tables. Let us use the multiple senses of *natio* in the Middle Ages to interrogate and loosen our own already precarious sense of what nation might be. To do this will not commit to anachronistic folly; it will instead create a true connection between the distant past and the present, with the hope that the study of the past may reinvigorate not only our understanding of the present, but also the practices that inform our daily lives.

B opened his mouth to reply, but at that moment a bell began ringing loudly and continuously. Time had flown, and the champagne hour was upon us. We moved outside again, where the first bottle of *Sekt* was in the process of being uncorked.

88. *Siam Mapped*, 49–50, 134–35.

ST MAURICE: THEBES ON THE RHONE

On July 13, 2004, the *Neue Zürcher Zeitung* reported that the head of the Coptic Church, Pope Shenouda III, had visited the Swiss town of St Maurice.[89] The visit was not casual. Shenouda wished to honour the town's eponymous saint, along with a group of martyrs he believed to be not only his countrymen, but the ancestors of Christian worship in Egypt.[90] The story that informed his visit is roughly as follows.

In the second-last decade of the third century AD, a man from the ancient Egyptian city of Thebes, serving in the Roman army, was assigned to military service in western Europe. The soldier, Mauritius, formed part of a legion of Thebans, all of whom were Christian. Once in Europe, the Roman emperor Maximian required the Theban legion either (the sources vary) to pursue rebellious Gauls or to persecute Christians. The emperor insisted that the men sacrifice to Roman deities; when they refused, he ordered that they be decimated; when they persisted in their faith, he ordered a second decimation, and finally the destruction of the entire legion. The site of the massacre was called Agaunus, in an Alpine valley near to the source of the Rhone river. It was difficult of access, but a *locus amoenus* all the same.

In this place, according to the *vitae*, the bodies of the Thebans stayed for around a century. Then Theodore, bishop of nearby Octodurum (Martigny), discovered the remains of some of the martyrs, including Maurice, and built a basilica in their honour by a cliff near the river. Soon afterwards, in 397, the relics of St Maurice were solemnly translated to Tours, where St Martin, the bishop, incorporated them into the cathedral. A monastery, about which records are sketchy, was operating on or near the site of the massacre during the fifth century. By 515, it had been refounded by Sigismund, soon to become the king of Burgundy,[91] setting in train the eventual transformation of Agaunus (sometimes Acaunus) into the modern town of St Maurice.

In the 440s Eucherius, the bishop of Lyon, recorded the story of Mauritius in the form of a moving *passio*, a work that exerted enormous influence in prop-

89. "Koptischer Patriarch zu Besuch in der Schweiz," *Neue Zürcher Zeitung*, 13 July 2004, p. 13.

90. For a summary of the early history of the Copts see Alastair Hamilton, *The Copts and the West, 1439–1822* (Oxford, 2006), 9–22.

91. Sigismund's foundation, along with the ceaseless liturgy established at the monastery, was commemorated by Avitus of Vienne's *Homilia 25: Opera*, ed. R. Peiper (Berlin, 1883), 145–46; see too the *Vita abbatum agaunensium*, ed. Bruno Krusch, in *Passiones vitaeque sanctorum aevi Merovingici* (Hannover, 1920), 331–32; Sigismund became king in 516.

agating the legend, thanks in part to its eventual insertion into the official liturgy for the feast of the deposition of the martyrs. Eucherius began by noting the relative importance of Agaunus: "if a particular place or town is held to be famous on account of a single martyrdom ... how much reverence should be devoted to that holy place Agaunus, in which so many thousands of martyrs are reputed to have been slaughtered for Christ?"[92] Emphasising the vicious character of Maximian, Eucherius assured his readers of the piety of the Thebans, men who knew how to render unto God those things that were of God, and Caesar's to Caesar: faithful to the Empire, but more faithful still in their devotion to Christ.[93] The show-stopping centrepiece of the *Passio Acaunensium martyrum* is the Thebans' proud plea to the emperor, shaped by the rules of classical rhetoric: "We are your soldiers, Emperor, but we freely confess ourselves the servants of God. To you we owe military service; to him, our innocence. From you we took a stipend; from him, the origin of life."[94] Maximian's response to such eloquent obduracy was to order its annihilation, with the result that, as Eucherius put it, the Theban Legion joined the legions of angels in heaven.[95]

The source of this narrative has been a matter of some puzzlement to scholars interested in the tradition. Although there is tentative evidence for the presence of a Theban legion within the Roman army during this period,[96] few outside the Catholic and Coptic churches are able to maintain faith in the historicity of the massacre. An arresting theory, first advanced in the middle of the nineteenth

92. *Passio Acaunensium martyrum* 1, ed. Bruno Krusch, in *Passiones vitaeque sanctorum aevi Merovingici et antiquiorum aliquot* (Hannover, 1896), 32–41, at 33: "si pro martyribus singulis loca singula, quae eos possident, vel singulae urbes insignes habentur ... quanta excolendus est reverentia sacer ille Acaunensium locus, in quo tot pro Christo martyrum milia ferro caesa referuntur?"

93. *Passio Acaunensium martyrum* 3, ed. Krusch, 33–34; Matthew 22:21; Mark 12:17; Luke 20:25.

94. *Passio Acaunensium martyrum* 9, ed. Krusch, 36: "Milites sumus, imperator, tui, sed tamen servi, quod libere confitemur, Dei. Tibi militiam debemus, illi innocentiam; a te stipendium laboris accepimus, ab illo vitae exordium sumpsimus." See Jean-Louis Feiertag, "Les sources littéraires du plaidoyer des Thébains adressé à l'Empereur dans la *Passio Acaunensium Martyrum* (chap. 9) attribuée à Eucher de Lyon (BHL 5737–5739)," in *Mauritius und die Thebäische Legion/Saint Maurice et la légion Thébaine*, ed. Otto Wermelinger et al. (Fribourg, 2005), 255–64 on this passage's sources and influences.

95. *Passio Acaunensium martyrum* 11, ed. Krusch, 37.

96. The early fifth-century *Notitia dignitatum* lists a legion of "Thebaei" in Italy: for the argument that this is the legion in Eucherius's *passio* see David Woods, "The Origin of the Legend of Maurice and the Theban Legion," *Journal of Ecclesiastical History* 45 (1994): 385–95.

century,[97] and taken up again in the twentieth,[98] saw the origins of the story in a kind of transference by homonym. The narrative of Maurice of Agaunus was, so the theory went, in fact that of his fellow saint and namesake, Maurice of Apamea, and confusion between the two – or more likely deliberate recycling, with Theodore of Martigny the prime suspect – led to the relocation of the Theban legion from Greece to its more remarkable resting place in the Alps. Ingenious and satisfying though such a scenario is, more recent research has championed the "piste ambrosienne." On this view, the invention of the legend and its relics bear all the hallmarks of Ambrose, the bishop of Milan (374–397), a vigorous promoter of the cults of various saints. The name Maurice was not the product of confusion or transposition, but a deliberate choice made for its association with the adjective "maurus" (Moor), and hence with Africa, Egypt, and Thebes.[99]

The precise number of Thebans martyred at the foot of the Alps was a matter of some concern for later hagiographers, who held different views on the size of a Roman legion: 6,666 had a pleasingly auspicious significance for some commentators, while others favoured slightly more modest estimates (Eucherius thought 6,600).[100] That Maurice was the leader of the Thebans there was no doubt. The names of others, some of whom had managed to flee to nearby regions, were also known. Eucherius noted the presence alongside Maurice of a certain Candidus, "senator militum" (apparently a cavalry officer), and one Exsuperius, the "campidoctor" (drill-master).[101] There were Ursus and Victor, who, having survived the massacre, were martyred in Solodurum (Solothurn), a *castrum* on the Aare river not far from the Rhine.[102] There was Innocent, whose body – according to an early interpolation to the legend left by Eucherius – the Rhone revealed in the early fifth century, so that he could be reunited with the

97. Friedrich Wilhelm Rettberg, *Kirchengeschichte Deutschlands* (Göttingen, 1846), 1: 100–101.

98. Denis van Berchem, *Le Martyre de la Légion Thébaine: Essai sur la formation d'une légende* (Basel, 1956), 42–44.

99. Jean-Michel Carrié, "Des Thébains en Occident? Histoire militaire et hagiographie," in *Mauritius und die Thebäische Legion*, 9–35, at 24–25.

100. *Passio Acaunensium martyrum* 3, ed. Krusch, 33; Eric Chevalley, "La Passion anonyme de Saint Maurice d'Agaune: Édition critique," *Vallesia* 45 (1990): 37–120, at 96 (6666 in some manuscripts of this text).

101. *Passio Acaunensium martyrum* 8, ed. Krusch, 35.

102. Victor and Ursus were noted by Eucherius, *Passio Acaunensium martyrum* 14, ed. Krusch, 38, though this may be a later interpolation: see Hans Reinhard Seeliger, "Die Ausbreitung der Thebäer-Verehrung nördlich und südlich der Alpen," in *Mauritius und die Thebäische Legion*, 211–25, at 214. Eucherius records another Victor, a veteran who comes upon perpetrators of the massacre dividing the spoils and is murdered after declaring himself a Christian: *Passio Acaunensium martyrum* 12, ed. Krusch, 37–38.

other holy martyrs in the basilica of St Maurice.[103] There were Theban women too. Verena left Thebes in pursuit of the Legion, learned in Milan of the murder of the soldiers, searched for their graves, lived for a time as a hermit, and ended up performing holy works in Zurzach on the Rhine.[104] Regula, along with her brother Felix, was martyred in Zürich. The cult, in other words, spread beyond its immediate origins, first within Burgundian Gaul along the Rhone to Vienne and Lyon, and west to Auxerre and Tours; then into the southernmost German lands, including the monastery of St Gall, whose founder brought relics of Maurice with him when he established his hermitage in 612. (The "St Galler Klosterplan," a famous diagram of an ideal monastery designed for the abbot of St Gall in the early ninth century, includes an altar dedicated to St Maurice).[105] By the middle of the sixth century the legend had established firm roots in upper Italy (especially Piedmont), marked by the connection of the Turin martyrs Adventius, Octavius, and Solutor with the Thebans; in later times the royal house of Savoy became an energetic promoter of the cult.[106] Gradually too the Thebans drifted in the opposite direction, deeper within the German-speaking lands, up the Rhine to Cologne (where Gereon was martyred with 318 companions) and Bonn (where Cassius and Florentius suffered similar fates), and north-east to the Elbe, where Magdeburg became a centre of devotion to the martyrs.[107] As part of this process of diffusion, local cults appear to have been assimilated, earlier saints "Thebanised" – as in Cologne, where Gereon only appears to have become Theban in the mid-ninth century, or in the Stiftskirche St Viktor in Xanten am Niederrhein, where some fourth-century martyrs were identified with the Thebans by the time of the late tenth-century "Passio sanctorum Gereonis, Victoris, Cassii et Florentii Thebaeorum martyrum," but possibly not long before.[108]

More, and stranger, transformations were on the way. At some point in the later Middle Ages (certainly by the twelfth century) the belief arose that Maurice and the other Thebans had been black. It is as a moor, with black face and red lips, that the saint was depicted on the facade of Magdeburg cathedral around 1250.[109]

103. *Passio Acaunensium martyrum* 19, ed. Krusch, 40–41.

104. Adolf Reinle, *Die heilege Verena von Zurzach: Legende, Kult, Denkmäler* (Basel, 1948).

105. Seeliger, "Ausbreitung," 213–16.

106. Seeliger, "Ausbreitung," 217–20.

107. Seeliger, "Ausbreitung," 221–25.

108. Carola Jäggi, "Die Verehrung der Thebäerheiligen in Spätantike und Frühmittelalter: Was sagen die archäologischen Quellen?," in *Mauritius und die Thebäische Legion*, 173–91.

109. See Jean-Jacques Aubert, "L'insignificance de la négritude: Maurice le Maure," in *Mauritius und die Thebäische Legion*, 57–66, at 58–59.

The inference was both geographical and etymological, with its clearest statement in Isidore's *Etymologiae*, in which, commenting on varieties of horses, Isidore noted that the Greek word for black was "mauros."[110] The iconographic tradition of the black Maurice spread gradually within central Europe and Scandinavia. It reached Bohemia and Austria in the mid-fourteenth century under the influence of the emperor Charles IV, a keen promoter of the cult, and thereafter found its way to the Baltic. There the black Maurice was adopted as an emblem both by the bloodthirsty Teutonic Order and by a group of merchants in Talinn and Riga, the self-styled "blackheads."[111] In southern and western Europe, Maurice remained white, and a rather different etymology for the saint's name was given in the influential collection of lives compiled in the thirteenth century by Jacobus de Voragine: "Mauritius is so called from 'sea/bitter' (*a mari*) and 'cis,' which means discharging or hard, and 'us' which is interpreted as a counsellor or one who hurries."[112] For Jacobus, the Isidorean etymology (*mauros niger est*: "the *mauros* is black") required an allegorical interpretation: "black in contempt for his own person."[113]

Firmly implanted within Catholic consciousness, Maurice was an intriguing, provocative presence there. Certainly a strong element of his success was the appeal at an elite level, to rulers, or at least to those hoping to flatter them. Appropriated early on by the Burgundians, then by the Merovingians,[114] and Carolingians,[115] for the Ottonians Maurice was "tocius regni summus patronus," and the saint's sword and especially his lance were adopted as imperial sym-

---

110. *Etymologiae* 12.1.55, ed. Lindsay: "Mauron niger est; nigrum enim Graeci μαυρον vocant" ([the horse called] Mauros is black; for the Greeks call black "mauros").

111. Gude Suckale-Redlefsen, *Mauritius: Der heilige Mohr/ The Black Saint Maurice* (Houston, 1987), 69.

112. Jacobus de Voragine, *Legenda aurea*, ed. Giovanni Paolo Maggioni, 2 vols (Florence, 1998), 2: 965: "Mauritius dicitur a mari et cis, quod dicitur uomens uel durus, et us, quod interpretatur consiliator uel festinans." Jacobus explains that Maurice was bitter because of his experience of hardship and distance from his homeland, "discharging" in the sense of shedding superfluous things, "hard" in the suffering of torture, a "counsellor" in his encouragement of fellow soldiers, and "hurrying" through the zeal and increase of good works.

113. *Legenda aurea*, 2: 965: "niger per sui despectionem."

114. For Agaunus as a "model of episcopal and royal synergy" for Burgundian and Merovingian rulers see Barbara H. Rosenwein, "One Site, Many Meanings: Saint-Maurice d'Agaune as a Place of Power in the Early Middle Ages," in *Topographies of Power in the Early Middle Ages*, ed. Mayke de Jong and Frans Theuws (Leiden, 2001): 271–90, at 284.

115. Charlemagne allegedly carried Maurice's banner into battle in Spain: William of Malmesbury, *Gesta Regum Anglorum* 2.135.5, ed. and trans. R.A.B. Mynors, R.M. Thomson, and M. Winterbottom (Oxford, 1998), 1: 218.

bols.[116] In the early thirteenth century Gervase of Tilbury cited the legend of the Thebans in support of the validity of secular imperial power, with Pope Innocent III's excommunication of the Holy Roman emperor Otto IV in 1210 particularly in mind: "Take heed, therefore, Your Holiness, when you command me not to obey my earthly ruler. I gladly render obedience to you, as the guardian of my soul, in what belongs to God; but I shall also obey my earthly ruler in what touches the lawful exercise of his authority."[117] By the end of the fifteenth century Maurice could boast patronage of the Order of the Golden Fleece (for the Burgundians), and the short-lived Order of the Crescent (for the Angevins), as well as the Royal House of Savoy. But the attraction was surely bitter-sweet. Maurice and his men are "noble in virtue and vigorous in battle, but more noble in faith";[118] a warrior saint, yes, but also the first saint of civil disobedience, of passive resistance to imperial command. "See – we bear arms and yet we do not resist, because we choose to die rather than to kill, and to die innocent rather than to live guilty."[119] Very occasionally, artists depicted Maximian himself crushed beneath Maurice's feet.[120]

Two representations of Maurice, from either end of the sixteenth century, early- and post-Reformation, capture something of the saint's ambiguous relationship to royal, imperial, and ecclesiastical power. For the foundation of a new church in the central German town of Halle, Matthias Grünewald painted a startling "Begegnung von Erasmus und Mauritius" (Meeting of Erasmus and Mauritius) (1521/22) (Figure 18). The image is imbued with contemporary reference. Maurice the Moor wears the splendid coronation armour of the Holy Roman emperor Charles V, crowned with a diadem, one gloved hand on sword. He addresses the appraising third-century Bishop-Saint Erasmus, a portrait of

116. See Laura Hibbard Loomis, "The Holy Relics of Charlemagne and King Athelstan: The Lances of Longinus and St Mauricius," *Speculum* 25 (1950): 437–56 on Maurice's lance and standard.

117. *Otia imperialia* 3.35, ed. and trans. S.E. Banks and J.W. Binns (Oxford, 2002), 632–33: "Attende igitur, sanctissime papa, qui mandas ne principi pareant. Pareo libens in hiis que Dei sunt tibi ut anime custodi; parebo et principi in hiis que ius tangunt imperii." (Translation from Banks and Binns).

118. *Passio Acaunensium martyrum* 3, ed. Krusch, 33: "viri in rebus bellicis strenui et virtute nobiles, sed nobiliores fide."

119. *Passio Acaunensium martyrum* 9, ed. Krusch, 37: "Tenemus, ecce! arma et non resistimus, quia mori quam occidere satis malumus, et innocentes interire, quam noxii vivere praeoptamus." Seeliger, "Ausbreitung," 223 points out Maurice's appeal as a missionary saint, due to Eucherius's account of the legion's conversion of a non-Christian *faber*.

120. Notably the statue of Maurice in the choir of Magdeburg Cathedral from c. 1220, and the statue (possibly influenced by the Magdeburg example) by Konrad von Einbeck (1411) in Halle's Moritzkirche: see Suckale-Redlefsen, *Mauritius*, 43, 73.

Albrecht von Brandenburg, contemporary pluralist bishop and founder of the new church.[121] Black and white, secular and ecclesiast, saint and saint stand apparently in dialogue. But there is something less than amicable about Erasmus's rigid posture, crozier held with a grip of iron, in response to Maurice's fluid, importunate demeanour.

Towards the end of the century, from 1580–82, El Greco worked on a monumental altarpiece of the Theban martyrdom for Philip II of Spain. Destined for the Escorial, the image shows Maurice in conversation with his fellow Theban soldiers, including Exsuperius (with banner) and Candidus (with back turned) on a rocky outcrop (Figure 19). Light falls from heaven on their upturned palms, as the slaughter commences beneath them. It has been conjectured that El Greco painted the features of Maurice to resemble those of Philip, and modelled some of the other Thebans (such as the pair of soldiers in modern dress, gazing at the viewer) on contemporary noblemen.[122] If so, the gesture failed to please the monarch, who ordered a replacement altarpiece almost immediately. Nevertheless Maurice and the Thebans remained figures of contemporary relevance, now emblems of the Counter-Reformation and imperial defence of the faith against heresy. The rocks and crags of the painting's landscape, according to one modern commentator, "evoke the *cigarrales* on the outskirts of Toledo more than the mountains of Helvetia."[123]

"Streams of holy blood flow"

Curiously enough, the vast spread of the Theban legend never vitiated the central aspect of its power: the spatial dislocation inherent in the physical presence – and destruction – of north Africans in Europe. It is surely significant that the Thebans encounter their grisly fate at the source of a river, in a part of Europe at once pivotal and obscure, rocky and pleasant, mountainous and fluid. In a story of the transmission of Christianity from its roots in the east to what was to become its base in the west, the narrative finds its point of gravity in the

---

121. Alte Pinakothek, Munich; for discussion see Suckale-Redlefsen, *Mauritius*, 94–99; Ludwig Grote, *Die Erasmus-Mauritius-Tafel* (Stuttgart, 1957).

122. Opinions differ on this point: see Margit Kern, "A Question of Conscience: El Greco's *Martyrdom of St. Maurice and the Theban Legion*," in *El Greco: The First Twenty Years in Spain*, ed. Nicos Hadjinicolaou (Rethymno, 2005), 95–122; José Álvarez Lopera, *El Greco: Estudio y Catálogo*, vol. 2.1 (Madrid, 2007), 141–47.

123. José Álvarez Lopera, "Martyrdom of St Maurice and the Theban Legion," in *El Greco: Identity and Transformation: Crete, Italy, Spain*, ed. José Álvarez Lopera (Milan, 1999), 380–82, at 381; Álvarez Lopera, *El Greco*, 143.

conjunction of the Alps and the Rhone, at the meeting point of Rome, Gaul and Germany.

Agaunus, Eucherius noted, lies almost sixty miles from the city of Geneva, and fourteen miles from the head of Lac Léman, into which the Rhone flows. The town is located in a valley, between Alpine peaks, where the river allows the traveller only a narrow, rocky path.[124] A similar point is made in an anonymous *passio* of the Legion, composed no later than the mid-eighth century, and probably earlier: "in this place the course of the river Rhone is compressed by great cliffs, such that, without the possibility of passage, necessity teaches the route of the journey to be by makeshift bridges."[125] Two vital elements inform this topography. The overhanging, compressing nature of the rocks, protecting and confining the place of the martyrdom, is a feature of both the earliest *passiones*: "beneath overhanging rocks, a small place indeed, but delightful."[126] A number of allegorical meanings may be inferred, most obviously the rocky, troublesome path of true faith. Eucherius's other known works, including *De contemptu mundi* and *De laude eremi*, support an interpretation of the landscape as a manifestation of a neo-Stoic aesthetic in the service of a monastic ideal, in which the *locus amoenus* is cut off from the world, reminiscent of the desert monasticism associated explicitly with Egypt.[127]

Even more striking, though, is the role of the river. Undoubtedly the Rhone is a crucial part of the story, one that works to irrigate the inherent harshness of Alpine monasticism. Emphasised by Eucherius, the image of the river flowing with blood[128] was quickly taken up by poets. Venantius Fortunatus, perhaps writing in 589 to celebrate the translation of relics of the Theban saints at the time of the dedication of the restored cathedral of St Martin at Tours, revelled in the aquatic nature of the carnage:

124. *Passio Acaunensium martyrum* 5, ed. Krusch, 34; the formulaic aspects of this description are documented by Beat Näf, "Eucherius von Lyon, Theodor von Octodurus und ihre Legionäre: Zu den historischen Bedingungen einer hagiographischen Geschichtsdeutung," in *Mauritius und die Thebäische Legion*, 95–118, at 101–2.

125. "La Passion anonyme," ed. Chevalley, 98: "Quo in loco ita vastis rupibus Rhodani fluminis cursus artatur ut commeandi facultate subtracta constratis pontibus viam fieri itineris necessitas imperaret"; for the dating of this text see Chevalley, "La Passion anonyme," 45–92.

126. "La Passion anonyme," ed. Chevalley, 98: "imminentibus saxis parvus quidem [locus] sed amoenus."

127. See Näf, "Eucherius von Lyon," 101–2; Michaela Zelzer, "Zur Überlieferung und Rezeption der Passio Acaunensium Martyrum," in *Mauritius und die Thebäische Legion*, 325–30, at 329–30.

128. *Passio Acaunensium martyrum* 11, ed. Krusch, 37: "fluxerunt pretiosi sanguinis rivi."

Hortantes se clade sua sic ire sub astra
alter in alterius caede natauit heros.
Adiuuit rapidas Rhodani fons sanguinis undas
tinxit et alpinas ira cruenta niues.[129]

Urging themselves to rise up to the stars from their slaughter, one hero swims
in another's gore. The fountain of blood swells the rapid waves of the Rhone
[or: the source of the Rhone swells the rapid waves of blood], and bloody ire
dyes the alpine snows.

The nature of the source is ambiguous. The "fons" may refer either to the bodies of the martyrs (fons sanguinis), or to the river (Rhodani fons). If, as seems likely,
the ambiguity is deliberate, Venantius wanted to present blood and Rhone as
interchangeable – and intermingled – elements, so that the river is now of blood,
and at the same time the holy blood of the martyrs becomes the river. The poem's
opening, according to which "faith pierces hearts, overturning cold, kindling fiery
battles among the icy cliffs,"[130] finds an echo in the subsequent contrast of gore
with snow, adding the visual impact of colour to the clash of heat with cold. The
specificity of place (the Alps, the Rhone) forms the basis for the remainder of
the poem, in which, while slipping in a reference to their relics left on earth,
Venantius envisages the ascent of the legion to the light of heaven and their presence at the Last Judgement.[131]

In the ninth century, Walahfrid Strabo took the bloody river further, letting
it flow all the way to the Mediterranean in claiming the legend for Gaul, and in
many ways making explicit the trope of Venantius. "Felix Gallia," begins Walahfrid, consciously echoing the fourth-century poet Prudentius, whose "Felix Tarraco" (Happy Tarraco) is one of fourteen hymns composed to honour Spanish
and Roman martyrs.[132] Walahfrid (c. 809–49), abbot of Reichenau, and tutor to

129. "De sanctis agaunensibus," in Poèmes, 3 vols, ed. Marc Reydellet (Paris, 1994–
2004), 1: 70–71, ll. 11–14, and pp. 190–91 on the possible connection with the relics at Tours.
Gregory of Tours claimed to have personally rediscovered the martyrs' relics in the basilica
of St Martin: Gregorii Episcopi Turonensis Libri Historiarum X 10.31.18, ed. Bruno Krusch and
Wilhelm Levison (Hannover: Hahn, 1951), 534–35.
130. "De sanctis agaunensibus," ll. 3–4, ed. Reydellet, 70: "frigore depulso, succendens
corda peregit / rupibus in gelidis feruida bella fides."
131. "De sanctis agaunensibus," ll. 19–28, ed. Reydellet, 71.
132. "Ymnus de agaunensibus martyribus," in Poetae Latini Aevi Carolini, ed. E. Dümmler, 4 vols. (Berlin, 1881–1923), 2: 367–69; "Hymnus in honorem beatissimorum martyrum
Fructuosi episcopi Augurii et Eulogii," in Aurelii Prudentii Clementis Carmina, ed. M. P. Cunningham (Turnhout, 1966), 314–20. On the geographical thought of Walahfrid see Patrick
Gautier Dalché, "Représentations géographiques savantes, constructions et pratiques de

Charles, son of Louis the Pious, proceeds to enact a series of spatial manoeuvres designed to position the Carolingian Empire as the pious heir to Rome, at the centre of the Christian faith. Gaul's happiness, he asserts, lies in its status as Rome's "sister and consort," but it is superior to the imperial capital, for it has been "anointed by the gore of martyrs."[133] Here the Rhone emerges as a crucial symbol for the simultaneous transmission and protection of the faith. Walahfrid observes the Thebans' transmission of the faith from east to west: "they reveal to western fields the faith that they imbibed in eastern lands."[134] Then, in a clear echo of Eucherius's *Passio*, Walahfrid sees the river as actually consecrated by Theban blood:

> Caeduntur gladiis, replentur ipsae
> valles corporibus, fluuntque rivi
> sacri sanguinis, ipse per cruorem
> sanctorum Rhodanus sacratus exit.
>
> Hinc iam nobilior, suoque maior
> excursu, mare cum decore magnum
> maiori petit, omne Galliarum
> regnum de nece martyrum coronans.[135]

They are felled by swords, the valleys are filled with bodies, and streams of holy blood flow; the Rhone departs, itself sanctified by the blood of saints. From here now it is larger and more noble in its current when it seeks the great sea with greater grace, crowning the entire realm of the Gauls with the slaughter of martyrs.

Bodies dissolve in water, the river and by extension realm receive and transmit the faith: the blood finally performs the function of coronation, as regal and religious imagery fuse. Place remains important: Walahfrid sketches the Rhone's journey from Alps to Mediterranean, and immediately returns to Agaunus, "felix Agaunus," once obscure, now renowned.[136] A later hagiographic tradition will insist that quan-

---

l'espace," in *L'espace géographique au Moyen Âge*, 77–103, at 79–84; Lozovsky, "Roman Geography," 345–46.

133. "Ymnus de agaunensibus martyribus," ll. 4, 6, ed. Dümmler, 367: "Romanae soror urbis atque consors"; "illita martyrum cruore."

134. "Ymnus de agaunensibus martyribus," ll. 23–24, ed. Dümmler, 367: "quam terris Orientis imbiberunt, / castris occiduis fidem recludunt."

135. "Ymnus de agaunensibus martyribus," ll. 73–80, ed. Dümmler, 368.

136. "Ymnus de agaunensibus martyribus," ll. 85–88, ed. Reydellet, 368.

tities of the martyrs' blood remained in the soil at Agaunus, so much that when, some decades after the massacre, St Martin of Tours struck the ground, a stream of St Maurice's blood emerged.[137] But the point of the poems was to extend the reach of the martyrs' blood, from its Alpine shedding through Gaul, and along the course of the Rhone to southern Europe, without ever forgetting its eastern origins.

Thus established, the conjunction of mountains and river remained fundamental to later literary representations, although not without further twists. In Walter of Châtillon's twelfth-century epic, the *Alexandreis*, the legend of Maurice and the Theban legion acquired a strange, disorienting function. As the poem stands in most manuscripts, Walter mentions the event in two separate books, as a point of contrast to eastern geography. In book two, in order to survey terrain near the town of Issus, Alexander's rival Darius climbs a mound frequented by nymphs and satyrs. There a fountain enriches the valley beneath:

> Qualiter Alpinis spumoso uertice saxis
> Descendit Rodanus, ubi Maximianus eoos
> Extinxit cuneos cum sanguinis unda meatum
> Fluminis adiuuit fusa legione Thebea
> Permixtusque cruor erupit in ethera spreto
> Aggere terrarum totumque rigauit Agaunum.[138]

just as the Rhone descends from Alpine rocks with frothing eddy, where Maximian destroyed the eastern troops, when a wave of blood flowing from the Theban legion furthered the river's flow, and the churned bloodstream burst forth into the air from the scorned bank, irrigating all Agaunus.

In book five, Alexander pursues Darius like a star, or rather:

> Quantus ab Alpinis spumoso uertice saxis
> Erumpit Rodanus, ubi Maximianus eoos
> Extinxit cuneos cum sanguinis unda meatum
> Fluminis adiuuit fusa legione Thebea
> Permixtusque cruor erupit in ardua spreto
> Aggere terrarum totumque rigauit Agaunum.[139]

---

137. The legend may be no earlier than the twelfth century: Sharon Farmer, *Communities of Saint Martin: Legend and Ritual in Medieval Tours* (Ithaca, 1991), 232–35.

138. Walter of Châtillon, *Alexandreis* 2.318a–f, ed. Marvin L. Colker (Padua, 1978), 51–52.

139. *Alexandreis* 5.313–18, ed. Colker, 134.

as much as the Rhone bursts forth from Alpine rocks with frothing eddy, where Maximian destroyed the eastern troops, when a wave of blood flowing from the Theban legion furthered the river's flow, and the churned bloodstream burst forth on high from the scorned bank, irrigating all Agaunus.

In both passages Walter borrows the verb "adiuuit" (furthered, helped) from Venantius; he shares with the earlier poets the notion of the waves flowing with blood, mixture to the point of dissolution.[140] He adds a sense of the scene's combination of natural and human violence: the eruption of the Rhone, frothing, mirrors Maximian's "extinction" of the troops, while blood cascades beyond the river's bounds, drenching Agaunus in its entirety. The possibility for ironic reversal surely appealed to Walter. It cannot be just chance or convenience that causes him to specify that the troops were "eastern," or to align in a mere six lines the Alps, the Rhone, Agaunus, and Thebes. The incursion into Asia of Alexander's troops, explicitly characterised in the poem as representatives of Europe and the west, receives a momentary and startling counterpoint in the story of the massacre of Egyptian soldiers at the foot of the Alps. The near identical nature of the two passages suggests either an early scribal interpolation or error, or that Walter meant to cancel one set of lines but failed to do so.[141] Nevertheless, in the text as it was copied the two positions of the analogy are intriguing. In book two a relatively straightforward application sees the eastern fountain compared to the western river. In book five, however, Alexander himself is figured as the Rhone erupting from the Alpine rocks, but presumably also, as the excursus continues, as the bloodied Rhone, flooding Darius/Agaunus. In the flamboyant hands of Walter, then, the legend of Maurice, itself a narrative of spatial dislocation, was subject to further dislocations: it became a means of disrupting the spatial logic of the story of Alexander, a way of inviting the reader to see contiguous narratives of violence, east in west and west in east.

---

140. "De sanctis agaunensibus," ll. 13–14, ed. Reydellet, 71: "Adiuuit rapidas Rhodani fons sanguinis undas / tinxit et alpinas ira cruenta niues."

141. Colker appears to regard the passage in book two as an interpolation on manuscript evidence: *Alexandreis*, ed. Colker, 51; Heinrich Christensen on stylistic grounds suggests that the passage originally appeared in book two and was interpolated into book five: *Das Alexanderlied Walters von Châtillon* (Halle, 1905), 77–78 n2. Pritchard views the repetition as authorial: *The Alexandreis*, trans. R. Telfryn Pritchard (Toronto, 1986), 30 n77. The absence of the book five version of the passage from an early commentary on the poem (as contained in Zürich, Zentralbibliothek, MS Rh.98) and some manuscripts (e.g. Berlin, Staatsbibliothek Preussischer Kulturbesitz, MS Hamilton 20) would support Christensen's case.

Men, Places, Names, Peoples

In remembering St Maurice, medieval maps attempted to hold his multiple spatial reference points. Two surviving world maps, and one smaller map of Palestine and environs, refer to Maurice, enough to affirm that a tradition of recording the saint within the world image existed on at least one strand of *mappae mundi*. All three maps mention Maurice as part of a description of Thebes in Egypt. In its most succinct form, an inscription simply cites Thebes as the origin of the saint: "hence from Thebes the legion of Maurice" (*Thebe hinc Mauricii legio*).[142] But the more expansive inscriptions on these maps link Egypt with Burgundy, and implicitly the Nile with the Rhone. The inscriptions in Egypt that describe Thebes on the thirteenth-century Vercelli map and the Ebstorf map (c. 1300) are similar (Figures 20 and 21); both derive principally from Honorius Augustodunensis's *Imago Mundi*.

> *Vercelli*: hi proveniti a thebe, unde a thebe civitate cognominatur; cadmus, agenoris filius eam et constituit querens sororem suam *a Ioue raptam* et thebas secundum illam quam in boetia construxit nominavit et regio ab illa civitate nominem accepit ... hac fuit princeps beatus mauritius qui passus est *sub* maximiano imperatore apud agaunum ab ista dicuntur thebani. ab illa quae est in boethia dicuntur thebani.[143]

> The inhabitants came from Thebes, for which reason [the city] is named after the [original] city of Thebes. Cadmus, son of Agenor, built the city seeking his sister, who had been abducted by Jupiter, and he named it Thebes after the Thebes which he had constructed in Boeotia; the region took its name from that city ... In this city the blessed Maurice was a centu-

142. BL, MS Additional 10049, fol. 64v. Formerly known as the "Jerome" map of Palestine, this map and its companion map of Asia in the same manuscript have no direct connection with Jerome; they were added at the end of a copy of his "Liber de locis" in the twelfth century at the abbey of St Martin in Tournai: see Harvey, *Medieval Maps of the Holy Land*, 40–59. On the basis of the Mauritius inscription, Patrick Gautier Dalché has posited that the Tournai maps ultimately derive from a *mappa mundi* created by Eucherius of Lyon; one link in the chain is a verbal description of a map, which includes the incription "Thebas, de qua ciuitate erat legio sancti Mauricii, ubi est et desertum Thebaidos, in quo erat sedes anachoritarum. Est et in hac Egypto Phyairoth iuxta quam est transitus filiorum Israel per mare Rubrum": "Eucher de Lyon, Iona, Bobbio: Le destin d'une *mappamundi* de l'antiquité tardive," *Viator* 41 (2010): 1–22. Though attractive, the argument is necessarily speculative.

143. *Il mappamondo di Vercelli (1191–1218?)*, ed. Carlo F. Capello (Turin, 1976), section K: XVI. Italics indicate letters supplied.

rion, who was martyred by Emperor Maximian at Agaunus. The inhabitants are called Thebans after that city; they are called Thebans from the city which is in Boeotia.

Ebstorf: Thebe civitas, quam Cathmus, Agenoris filius, in Egyptum veniens edificavit et Thebas secundum illam quam in Boemia construxerat nominavit, regioque nomen ab illa mutuavit id est Thebaida. In hac Mauritius principabatur et ab hac Thebei dicuntur. Hic Arabes etiam et commercia undique subeunt.[144]

The city of Thebes, which Cadmus, son of Agenor, built when he came into Egypt. He named it Thebes after the city which he had constructed in Bohemia, and the region took its name from the city, i.e. Thebaida. In this [city] Mauritius served as a centurion and from it Thebans derive their name. Here too Arabs come, along with merchandise from everywhere.

Details blur. Isidore of Seville had stated in his *Etymologiae* that when Jupiter abducted Europa, her brother Cadmus had searched in vain for her. Fearing the anger of their father, he chose the path of exile, followed the footsteps of a cow, and where it came to rest founded a city which he named Thebes, in a region which he called Boeotia after the name for a cow (*bos*).[145] Isidore clearly distinguished the Egyptian and the Boeotian Thebes, "although they were built by the same person," and remarked that Arabs "from everywhere" conducted business in the Egyptian city.[146] Honorius followed Isidore in identifying Cadmus as the founder of both Thebes, but added the reference to Maurice and the Thebans (implicitly of the Legion): "in this city Maurice served as a centurion and from this city the Thebans derive their name."[147] The inscription on the Vercelli map blends Honorius with Isidore, implying that Cadmus's search for his sister took him to Egypt rather than Asia Minor, and it expands Honorius's terse reference to Maurice by adding the place of his martyrdom. On the Ebstorf map too there is a further Maurician trace. Perched by the source of the Rhone, a building is

144. Kugler, *Ebstorfer Weltkarte*, 1: 82 (20.19).

145. *Etymologiae* 14.4.11, ed. Spevak, 61–63.

146. *Etymologiae* 15.1.35, ed. Lindsay, 153: "Thebae autem et Boeotiae sunt et Aegyptiae, uno tamen auctore conditae." Isidore's remark about Arabs derives from Solinus, *Collectanea* 32.40, ed. Mommsen, 146–47: "ad quos commercia Arabes Indique subvehunt." "Undique" (from everywhere) is a common manuscript variant for "Indique" (and Indians).

147. *Imago mundi* 1.17, ed. Flint, 57: "in hac Mauricius principabatur, et ab hac Thebei dicuntur."

labelled "Monasterium sancti Mauritii."[148] The presence of the monastery at Agaunus/St Maurice on the map is unusual, and can be explained by the special significance that Maurice held, as patron saint of the north-German nunnery for which the map was produced.[149] The Ebstorf map complements the origins of the saint in Egypt – where his name appears to have been rubricated – with the presence in Europe of the monastery that marks the site of his martyrdom.

On Ebstorf, however, disambiguation of the two Thebes ended in further ambiguity: according to its inscription, Bohemia, not Boeotia, was the site of Cadmus's original city.[150] Even if Bohemia is present only due to the wild-card of scribal error, the multiplication of spatial reference is typical of Thebes. Were there, after all, just two cities of that name? Commentators on Walter of Châtillon's *Alexandreis* were not sure. In manuscripts of the poem from the thirteenth century onwards, one frequently-repeated gloss attempted to explicate Walter's reference to the Theban martyrs in books two and five of his poem:

> There are two Thebes. One Egyptian and the other Greek. From the Thebes of Egypt came a certain legion of soldiers led by Mauritius with his companions.[151]

Clear enough, except that another version of this gloss added a third Thebes:

> Note that there are three Thebes, one in Greece whose inhabitants are Thebans, another in Egypt whose inhabitants are Thesbites, another in the east whose inhabitants are Thebei, from which Blessed Mauricius came. Whence the verse "India bears Thebei, Greece Thebani, Egypt a Thesbidus: men, places, names, peoples."[152]

It is not uncommon to find glosses in the same manuscript of the *Alexandreis* asserting the different number of Thebes within the space of a few

148. Kugler, *Ebstorfer Weltkarte*, 1: 134 (53.7).

149. Kugler, *Ebstorfer Weltkarte*, 2: 295; Jürgen Wilke, *Die Ebstorfer Weltkarte*, 2 vols (Bielefeld, 2001), 1: 185–86.

150. Kugler, *Ebstorfer Weltkarte*, 2: 125 for commentary.

151. Wolfenbüttel, Herzog August Bibliothek, MS 38.2 Aug. 4°, fol. 20v: "due sunt thebe. vna egiptiaca et alia greca. de thebis egypti uenit quidam legio militum cui prefuit beatus mauricius cum sociis suis."

152. Novara, Archivio Capitolare, MS 44 (cxxxii), fol. 70v: "Nota quod tres sunt Thebe, una in Grecia a qua dicuntur Thebani, alia in Egipto a qua dicuntur Thesbita, alia in oriente a qua dicuntur Thebei. quo fuit beatus Mauricius. Vnde uersus India Thebeos, Thebanos Grecia nutrit Thesbidus Egiptus: homines, loca, nomina, gentes."

pages.[153] So what? Simply that the mutant tradition of the third Thebes – the far eastern, Indian, one – pushed Maurice even further away from Europe, made him more precisely an inversion of Alexander. And simply that Thebes, restless city, kept multiplying, precisely because encyclopedists, mapmakers, and commentators tried to pin it and its simulacra down. And if, on these inscriptions, Cadmus understandably figures as the founder, and the point of connection with classical myth, it is Maurice who emerges as the city's second famous son, the Christian emblem and supplement. He is a strange offshoot of the story of Thebes, transferring and displacing the city's fortune to the foot of the Alps, where it will be commemorated, institutionalised, and read within a history of late imperial violence and Christian suffering: a cornerstone of shifting identities, dynastic, national, and ecclesiastical. Until, centuries later, another Egyptian – mindful of his religion's troubled present and its rich, turbulent past – came to revisit the relics and attained a few column inches in the *Neue Zürcher Zeitung*.

153. E.g. Paris, Bibliothèque nationale de France, MS lat. 8116, fols. 19v, 57r; Novara, Archivio Capitolare 44, fols. 24r, 70v; Wolfenbüttel, HAB, MS 38.2 Aug. 4°, fols. 20v, 60r.

CHAPTER SEVEN

Maps and Vulgar Tongues

In Buenos Aires, while losing his sight, Jorge Luis Borges began to learn Old English. Many years later, he recalled the intoxicating effect of his first encounter with the language. He and a group of students decide to study a literature and language they do not know. On their first meeting, the group experience "what always happens when one studies a language," the force of new words, each one of which "stood out as though it had been carved."[1] But for Borges, and for his students too, there is something poignant about the nature of Old English.

> Finding ourselves with the Romans in a text of the North, we were moved. You must remember we knew nothing of the language; each word was a kind of talisman we unearthed. We found two words. And with those two words we became almost drunk. [...] I thought: "I am returning to the language my ancestors spoke fifty generations ago; I am returning to that language; I am reclaiming it. It is not the first time I speak it; when I had other names this was the language I spoke." Those two words were the name of London, "*Lundenburh*," and the name of Rome, which moved us even more, thinking of the light that had fallen on those northern islands, "*Romeburh*." I think we left crying, "Lundenburh, Romeburh ... " in the streets.
> So I began my study of Anglo-Saxon, which blindness brought me.[2]

1. Borges, "La ceguera," in *Siete noches* (México, 1980), 143–60, at 150: "Cada una de las palabras resalta como si estuviera grabada ..."; translated by Eliot Weinberger, in Borges, *The Total Library: Non-Fiction 1922–1986* (London, 2000) 473–83, at 477.
2. "La ceguera," 150–51: "Encontrarnos con los romanos en un texto del Norte, nos conmovió. Recuerden ustedes que no sabíamos nada del idioma, que lo leíamos con lupa, que cada palabra era una suerte de talismán que recobrábamos. Encontramos dos palabras. Con esas dos palabras estuvimos casi ebrios [...] Yo pensaba: 'estoy volviendo al idioma que hablaban mis mayores hace cincuenta generaciones; estoy volviendo a ese idioma, estoy recuperándolo. No es la primera vez que lo uso; cuando yo tenía otros nombres, yo hablé este idioma.' Esas dos palabras fueron el nombre de Londres; *Lundenburh*, Londresburgo, y el nombre de Roma, que nos emocionó más aún, por pensar en la luz de Roma que había caído sobre esas islas boreales perdidas, la *Romeburh*, la *Romaburgo*. Creo que salimos a la calle gritando *Lundenburh, Romeburh* ... Así empezó el estudio del anglosajón, al que me llevó la ceguera." "Blindness," trans. Weinberger, 478.

The anecdote comes in the middle of a lecture entitled "Blindness" (*La ceguera*), and seems to offer a form of consolation. Borges is at pains to dispel any inclination to perceive his blindness as calamitous or even unfortunate. It is to be appreciated as irony, since his sight began to deteriorate at the time of his appointment as Director of the National Library in Buenos Aires: the "magnifica ironia" of God gives him books and night, "libros y la noche," at the same time. Learning Old English introduces the power of sound, and its revelation of a lost heritage, as vision founders. "I thought: I have lost the visible world but now I am going to recuperate another, the world of my distant ancestors ... ."[3]

At a fundamental level the anecdote depends on the nature of place names. The toponym contains histories, preserves idiom, invokes memories and mythologies. The talismanic words inebriate Borges and his students because of their foreign nature but – for him, at least – the conviction of the deep familiarity of the language is equally dizzying. Given such freight, can place names be translated? Yes and no, Borges seems to suggest. The names of places move between languages, acquire and lose suffixes, become portals that move their speakers. Yet their strangeness, their distillation of history and preservation of light, also depends on a resistance to translation. "Romeburh" is a translation of "Roma," but also no translation.

As "Blindness" implies, the story of medieval spatial representation is one of the meeting of languages, of the adaptation of place names – of their preservation, and disappearance. The two preceding chapters have considered the concepts of *translatio* and *mutatio* – translation as preservation, translation as change, and change as anti-translation – as well as narratives of human movement, identity and borders. This chapter argues that language is a vital element in the question of spatial dislocation. In Christian Europe during the Middle Ages, Latin – the language of religious, political, and cultural authority – occupied a hegemonic position with regard to vernacular tongues. However, the study of spatial representation shows a long history of interaction between Latin and vernacular forms. Predictably enough, place names move from vernacular languages into Latin, and from Latin into the vernacular. Yet movement occurs not just between Latin and the vernacular but also from one vernacular language to another, to the point that it is sometimes difficult to tell to which language a toponym belongs.

The following pages treat the long history of interaction between Latin and vernacular spatial representation up to 1600, starting with one of the most precocious early translations of Latin geography, before considering medieval maps as an index of the role of language in describing space. Different genres of map use languages differently, but there are no absolutes. On *mappae mundi* Latin is

---

3. "La ceguera," 150: "Pensé: he perdido el mundo visible pero ahora voy a recuperar otro, el mundo de mis lejanos mayores"; "Blindness," trans. Weinberger, 477.

the dominant language, but the use of vernacular toponyms is far from infrequent; on sea charts, vernacular languages dominate, but Latin is still present. The question of the status and hierarchy of languages ultimately leads back to the humanist representation of space. The final part of this chapter argues that spatial representation played a telling role in humanist debates about the status of Latin in regard to "vulgar tonuges." Yet even here, despite repeated assertions of the superiority of the classical language, the attempt to rescue a history of space could lead to the excavation of vernacular languages as the equal, at times the antecedent, of Latin. The languages of place names reveal differences – different histories, different claims to land – but also interaction, literal or figural translation, misunderstanding, corruption. Dislocation occurs at the level of language; maybe it starts there.

" ... and the name of Rome, which moved us even more"

In the second decade of the fifth century Paulus Orosius began his histories "against the pagans" with a detailed description of the known world.[4] The purpose of the history was to detail the disasters that were endemic to the Roman Empire, with the specific intention of debunking the notion that Christianity had fatally weakened Rome's power. The geography Orosius provided was therefore essentially a Roman one, extending across a swathe of the known world from the columns of Hercules in the west to India, and from Scythia in the north to Ethiopia, but with significant gaps the further one progressed away from the Mediterranean basin. Orosius wrote in Latin, the language of empire, but also the language of the works of the Christian intellectuals Augustine and Jerome, to whom he had gravitated in North Africa and the Holy Land.

A little under five centuries later, Orosius's history was rendered into English. The *Old English Orosius* seems to have been connected with a programme, initiated by King Alfred in the late ninth century, of the revitalisation of learning by means of vernacular translations.[5] The other translations associated with this programme, such as the Old English versions of Boethius's *De consolatione philosophiae*, Gregory the Great's *Cura pastoralis*, and Augustine of Hippo's *Soliloquia*, range from relative fidelity to the original text to

---

4. See the discussion of Orosius in Chapter 2.

5. David Pratt, *The Political Thought of King Alfred the Great* (Cambridge, 2007), 115–29; Susan Irvine, "English Literature in the Ninth Century," in *The Cambridge History of Early Medieval English Literature*, ed. Clare A. Lees (Cambridge, 2013), 209–31.

free adaptation and at times alteration; the *Old English Orosius* falls somewhere between these poles. This mixture of fidelity and innovation is nowhere
more evident than in its translation of the geographical description at the
opening of the *Historiae*. The translator followed Orosius's division of the
world into three *partes*, then his account of Asia from India to the Near East.
When it comes to the description of Europe the geography initially adopts
the Orosian manner of defining places by reference to the points of the com-
pass – "be westan," "be eastan," "suð þanon," "be norþan him," "be suþaneas-
tan" (to the west; to the east; south of there; to its north; to the south-east) –
a process that results in a web of interconnected localities. Many place names
remain entirely or essentially unchanged. Europa is Europe, Asia is Asia, Africa
is Affrica; Parthia is Parthia, Mesopotamia is Mesopotamia; the "Rubrum
Mare" is translated literally as "se Reada Sæ." Yet many names are transformed, with the result that Rome's world begins to acquire an unmistakably
Saxon inflection. The Mediterranean – Orosius's "Mare Nostrum" or "Mare
Magnum" – becomes the "Wendelsæ," while "Oceanus," the body of water
which surrounds all three *partes*, is in Old English the "garsæcg" which lies
outside "all the circle of this earth."[6] Germania is still Germania, but whereas
Orosius mentioned that the region possessed fifty-four peoples and moved
on without offering further detail, the Old English text records a wealth of
ethnonyms: "Eastfrancan" (the East Franks), "þa Ealdseaxan" (the Old Sax-
ons, who stayed on the Continent rather than migrating to Britain),
"Maroaras" (Moravians), "Bægware" (Bavarians), "Bæme" (Bohemians),
"Þyringas" (Thuringians), "Frisan" (Frisians), "Dene" (Danes), "Sweon"
(Swedes), "Burgendan" (the inhabitants of the island of Bornholm), and the
"Cwenas," after whom the northern branch of ocean above *Germania* is des-
ignated "Cwensæ."[7] These names appear as part of a coherent verbal map of
Germania and its environs. The mode of description remains broadly consis-
tent with that of Orosius: the Old English text uses nine peoples as pivots,

6. *The Old English Orosius* 1.1, ed. Janet Bately (London, 1980), 8: "ealne þisne ymbh-
wyrft þises middangeardes ... swa swa Oceanus utan ymbligeþ, þone [mon] garsæcg hateð."
The Wendelsæ in the *Old English Orosius* incorporates seas connected to the Mediterranean:
the Adriatic, Tyrrhenian, and Black Seas. The term appears also in Old High German ("wen-
til-séo"). The etymology of "garsæcg" is uncertain: see *The Dictionary of Old English: A to H*,
ed. Angus Cameron et al. (Toronto, 2016), s.v. "gār-secg": http://www.doe.utoronto.ca
[accessed 4/6/2019].

7. *Old English Orosius* 1.1, ed. Bately, 12; Orosius depicts the "Saxones" at 7.25.3 and
7.32.10 in an unflattering light, but does not mention them in book one. On the "Cwenas" see
Bately's comments (*Old English Orosius*, 166), and Irmeli Valtonen, *The North in the* Old English Orosius: *A Geographical Narrative in Context* (Helsinki, 2008), 386–402.

identifying the regions around them by reference to cardinal points.[8] The description begins with the East Franks, moves north to the Old Saxons, then south-east to the Moravians, further east and north-east as far as the Sarmatians and the "land of women" (possibly the Amazons),[9] then north-west to Scandinavia. As well as peoples, the description makes use of natural features such as the Alps, the rivers Danube, Rhine and Elbe, and the North Sea (the text's "Ostsæ") to provide a schematic yet comprehensive account. Roughly contemporary Latin texts indicate that the energetic verbal mapping of the *Old English Orosius*'s account of Germania and environs was not unprecedented. Comparable descriptions include the sketch of the Baltic and outline of the *regnum Francorum* before and after Charlemagne contained in Einhard's biography of the emperor, and the list of fifty-seven peoples unknown to classical ethnography compiled in the anonymous ninth-century *Descriptio civitatum ad septentrionalem plagam Danubii* (Description of cities to the north of the Danube).[10] Yet there is no obvious source for the *Old English Orosius*'s description – certainly there is nothing similar in Old English, nor any other European vernacular language prior to the twelfth century. Nor does any graphic map of Germania survive with this level of detail, from this period.

This striking intervention in the geography of Orosius sits alongside another in the Old English text: the unexpected insertion of the descriptions of Scandinavian lands by two otherwise unknown men, Ohthere and Wulfstan. The insertion comes at the mention of "Northmenn" (Norwegians), when the *Old English Orosius* suddenly announces that "Ohthere told his lord, King Alfred, that he dwelt northernmost of all the Northmen."[11] An account of Ohthere's travels in

8. Noted by Bately, *Old English Orosius*, lxviii–lxix; E.D. Laborde, "King Alfred's System of Geographical Description in his Version of Orosius," *The Geographical Journal* 62 (1923): 133–39 (the attribution of the *Old English Orosius* to Alfred himself is no longer accepted); Valtonen, *North in the* Old English Orosius, 320–22. The peoples are the East Franks, Old Saxons, Moravians, then (with a reduced level of detail) the Dalemintzi, South Danes, North Danes, Osti, Burgendan, and Swedes.

9. See Bately's comments on the uncertainty of this term: *Old English Orosius*, 173–74. Godden translates the Old English "mægða lond" as "the Magyars": *The Old English History of the World: An Anglo-Saxon Rewriting of Orosius*, ed. and trans. Malcolm R. Godden (Cambridge, MA, 2016), 35, but this meaning is otherwise unattested for "mægd" (normally "maiden," "woman," or, with long vowel, "tribe," "people").

10. Einhard, *Vita Karoli Magni* 12, 15, ed. G.H. Pertz, rev. G. Waitz, 6th ed (Hanover, 1911), 15, 17–18; *Descriptio civitatum ad septentrionalem plagam Danubii*, ed. Bohuslav Horák and Dušan Trávníček, *Rozpravy Československé Akademie Věd* 66 (1956): 1–73.

11. *Old English Orosius* 1.1, ed. Bately, 13: "Ohthere sæde his hlaforde, Ælfrede cyninge, þæt he ealra Norðmonna norþmest bude." On the probability that the reports of Ohthere and Wulfstan were inserted very early in the history of the text's transmission see Janet Bately, "The Orosius," in *A Companion to Alfred the Great*, ed. Nicole Guenther Discenza and Paul E. Szarmach (Leiden, 2015), 313–43.

the far north of Europe follows, complemented by a sequel from Wulfstan, again begun without fanfare (*Wulfstan sæde* ...), in which details of the Baltic emerge. Both narratives introduce places and peoples which had not been recorded by Orosius, nor by any other classical or late antique Latin authority. Ohthere navigates a sometimes precarious path among the northmen, the Beormas and the Finnas, prolific whalers and hunters of reindeer, who appear to speak the same language.[12] Wulfstan travels from Hedeby past the Vistula to the land of the "Este," where the richest men drink mare's milk and where, prior to cremation, a horse race determines the distribution of a dead man's property.[13] This supplement ends as abruptly as it begins: following Wulfstan's testimony, the text resumes its Orosius-directed description of Europe south of the Danube, the "land of the Greeks" (*Creca land*), and western Europe from Italy, through Gallia and Hispania, as far as Britain.[14] Here too the Old English paraphrases, truncates, and omits some aspects of Orosius's text, such as the description of the province of Gallia Lugdunensis, while adding new peoples such as the Basques (*Wascan*) and the Burgundians (*Burgende*), and glossing Ireland as "Igbernia, þæt we Scotland hatað" (Hibernia, which we call Scotland).[15]

The exercise of rendering Orosian geography into English seems, then, to have inspired two kinds of supplement: the verbal map of the region, and the first-person narratives of Ohthere and Wulfstan. The first adopts the mode of the Latin source text but turns it towards ethnic geography; the second opens further possibilities for spatial and ethnographic representation by means of the eye-witness report, and crucially adduces the presence of King Alfred. Is it the use of the vernacular that allows such licence? Perhaps. A very similar kind of expansion could certainly be imagined in Latin. One only needs to think of Solinus's transformation of Pliny's *Naturalis historia* to realise that translation into the vernacular is not a precondition for serious adaptation. Nevertheless, the aesthetic and intellectual effects of the *Old English Orosius*'s geography are palpably different to the original. The translator has taken Orosius's anonymous "fifty-four peoples" and left Germania defined by the spatial interrelations of nearly thirty peoples, expressed in the idiom of a Germanic language with its love of the impersonal (*þe mon hætt*: which one calls), its industrious prepositions (*be, binnan, geond, oþ þa, be westan him*: by, within, through(out), as far as, to its west), and its distinctive ethnonyms. The care and creativity evident in this expansion

12. *Old English Orosius* 1.1, ed. Bately, 14–16. Valtonen, *North in the* Old English Orosius, 373–83.

13. *Old English Orosius*, 1.1, ed. Bately, 17. Valtonen, *North in the* Old English Orosius, 402–47.

14. *Old English Orosius*, 1.1, ed. Bately, 18–19.

15. *Old English Orosius*, 1.1, ed. Bately, 19; on "Scotland" for Ireland see Bately's comments: *Old English Orosius*, 194.

of Orosius's description does not seem to equate to domestication, nor necessarily to a deep interest in an imagined Germanic homeland, nor yet the desire to express symbolic political control over the region by textual means.[16] Instead it might attest something different: the connections between Anglo-Saxon literary, political, and ecclesiastical culture with the places described; the appropriation of Frankish models for representing and updating classical space; and the extension of that updated map of Germania farther into the lands to the north, incorporating lucrative possibilities for trade and commerce. Far from nostalgic (the old homeland) or narrowly political (realms for Alfred to influence), the vernacular geography of the *Old English Orosius* revises and retells European space in terms of its peoples, placing and naming them, describing their customs and their economies. Neither predictable nor programmatic, the translation of the *Old English Orosius* includes elements that are not translations at all, voices piping up and falling silent, and a fundamental commitment to accretion in which classical nomenclature is preserved alongside new places and peoples. These complex literary and linguistic transactions do not so much witness light falling from Rome on lost northern parts, as the reciprocal sheen of a section of the world in part unknown to Latin geography, and in part in need of updating. Such an image would hardly have moved Borges and his students to cry aloud in the street, but he at least might have appreciated its ambition, its mysteries and inevitable errors.

The *Old English Orosius* is a precocious example of the translation and embellishment of Latin world geography into a vernacular language. As it suggests, interaction between languages was far from a case of unidirectional transference from Latin to vernacular. Many "Latin" toponyms are, after all, simply latinizations of vernacular place names.[17] This was particularly true in the Germanic languages: Frankenfurt (Old High German *Franchonô furt*) becomes Francofurtum, Hammaburg becomes Hamburgum or Ham(m)aburgensis, Hereford (Old English *here* [army] + ford) becomes Herefordia or Her(e)fordensis, Norwich (Old English *Northwic* ["north town"]) becomes Norwicum or Norwicensis. Yet at times it was unnecessary or impractical to latinize the vernacular. In

---

16. See, for example, Daniel Anlezark, "The Anglo-Saxon World View," in *The Cambridge Companion to Old English Literature*, ed. Malcolm Godden and Michael Lapidge, 2nd ed. (Cambridge, 2013), 66–81, at 71–72; Fabienne L. Michelet, *Creation, Migration, and Conquest: Imaginary Geography and Sense of Space in Old English Literature* (Oxford, 2006), 132–39.

17. "Reverse" word borrowings from vernacular languages to Latin typically occur in relation to local or regional features, including terrain: Michael Herren, "Latin and the Vernacular Languages," in *Medieval Latin: An Introduction and Bibliographical Guide*, ed. F.A.C. Mantello and A.G. Rigg (Washington, DC, 1996), 122–29, at 127.

book three of his influential early twelfth-century *Imago Mundi*, Honorius Augustodunensis recorded the construction of "Babinberc" (Bamberg) by Henry, duke of Bavaria.[18] Since Honorius is known to have spent a significant portion of his life in Regensburg, the appearance of a German toponym within his Latin text is hardly surprising. Manuscript variants (Babinburc, Babenberch, Babinberch)[19] indicate the relative ease with which scribes could distort place names, but they also raise the possibility that scribes were less respectful of the orthography of toponyms than that of other vocabulary, more willing to insert the forms with which they were familiar.[20] It is evident, at any rate, that elements of vulgar speech were already embedded in "Latin" geographical descriptions. As with the reverse example – the vulgarisation of Latin names – as a loan word, the proper noun acquires the capacity to be aligned grammatically within a language, to be made a consistent and assimilable member, rather than an intrusion.[21]

By the twelfth century, as their literatures developed, Romance languages also began to co-opt and adapt Latin spatial representation. French descriptions of a world map appear in texts such as the *Roman de Thèbes* (c. 1150), where a "mappamonde" is depicted on the tent of King Adrastus. The *Roman de Troie* (c. 1165) of Benoît de Sainte-Maure provides an account of the origin of the Amazons which leads on to a sketch of the geography of the east, and in the *Roman d'Alexandre* (1185) the world map this time appears on Alexander's tent.[22] The toponyms on display in these brief excurses are usually only lightly vernacularised, as in the following description of thirteen provinces of Asia from the *Roman de Troie*:

> En cest Oriëntal partie, –
> De ço ne redotons nos mie, –
> A treize provinces contees:
> Oëz come els sont devisees.

18. *Imago Mundi* 3.38, ed. Valerie I.J. Flint, *Archives d'histoire doctrinale et littéraire du Moyen Âge* 49 (1982): 7–153, at 150.

19. *Imago Mundi*, ed. Flint, 150 n106.

20. Roger Wright, *A Sociophilological Study of Late Latin* (Turnhout, 2002), 314–15.

21. See Richard Ingham, "Mixing Languages on the Manor," *Medium Ævum* 78 (2009): 80–97, esp. 86.

22. *Le Roman de Thèbes*, ed. Guy Raynaud de Lage, 2 vols (Paris, 1966–67), 1: 132–34 (ll. 4217–68); *The Medieval French Roman d'Alexandre*, vol. 1: *Text of the Arsenal and Venice Versions*, ed. Edward C. Armstrong and Milan S. La Du (Princeton, 1937), 161–63 (ll. 3441–83); *The Medieval French Roman d'Alexandre*, vol. 3: *Version of Alexandre de Paris*, ed. Edward C. Armstrong and Alfred Foulet (Princeton, 1949), 203–4 (ll. 2020–70). See Margriet Hoogvliet, *Pictura et Scriptura: Textes, images et herméneutique des Mappae Mundi (XIIIe–XVIe siècles)* (Turnhout, 2007), 90–91.

Perse, Inde, Isaure e Azonis;
La quinte *Sine*, ço m'est vis;
La siste a non *Apamena,*
L'autre *Mesopotamia;*
Phenice, Assire, Commacine;
L'onzime apelent *Palestine;*
Sire, la plus chaude, l'ardant,
E *Mede*, que mout par est grant.[23]

In this eastern part, about which doubt us not one bit, thirteen provinces are numbered: see how they are arranged. Perse, Inde, Isaure and Azonis; the fifth is Sine, I believe; the sixth is called Apamena, the others Mesopotamia, Phenice, Assire, Commacine; the eleventh is called Palestine; Sire, the hottest, the burning, and Mede, which is very large.

The Latin source for Benoît was the *Cosmographia* of pseudo-Aethicus, an early medieval text which claimed to represent a survey of the world commissioned by Julius Caesar, and which presented convenient lists of seas, islands, mountains, rivers, provinces, towns, and peoples. The list of Asian provinces in the *Cosmographia* is little different to that in the *Roman de Troie*, except that the three Syrian provinces of the Latin text have been turned into six in the vernacular version: Persis, India, Isauria, Adonis, Syria Appamea, Mesopotamia, Phenice, Syria Palestina, Commagene (Commacene is a manuscript variant), Media Syria.[24]

This incorporation of learned geography into vernacular literary texts slightly predates the emergence of encyclopedic works in Romance tongues in the thirteenth century. At that time, varieties of the French language in particular began to be used in a more consistent way as a vehicle of learned expression, and geographic description was not an insignificant part of this vernacular learning. Gossouin de Metz's *Image du monde* (mid-thirteenth century) and Brunetto Latini's *Livres dou tresor* (c. 1266) provide only the best-known examples of vernacular texts which are, in whole or part, "books of nature."[25] This emergence of extended

23. Benoît de Sainte-Maure, *Le Roman de Troie*, ed. Léopold Constans, 6 vols (Paris, 1904–12), 4: 10–11 (ll. 23283–94); my emphasis. "Sine" is rendered "syre" or "sire" in some manuscripts, which may be the better reading.

24. *Cosmographia of pseudo-Aethicus*, in *Geographi Latini minores*, ed. Alexander Riese (Heilbronn, 1878; repr. Hildesheim, 1964), 71–103, at 78.

25. Hoogvliet, *Pictura et Scriptura*, 91–95, 99–100; Leena Löfstedt, "Observations sur la toponymie dans la traduction en ancien français du Decretum Gratiani," in *Latin et langues romanes*, ed. Sándor Kiss et al. (Tübingen, 2005), 547–60; Michel Salvat, "Le ciel des vulgarisateurs: Note sur les traductions du *De proprietatibus rerum*," in *Observer, lire, écrire le ciel au Moyen Age*, ed. Bernard Ribémont (Paris, 1991), 301–13.

scholarly writing in the vernacular was consolidated in the following century in works such as Nicolas Oresme's *Livre du ciel et du monde*, the *Book of Sir John Mandeville*, and the Castilian *Libro del conosçimiento*, all translations or compilations with significant geographic or cosmographic content.

Maps and Vulgar Tongues

Spatial description permitted a permeable Latinity, in which vernacular writing appeared alongside Latin, not in a spirit of competition, but as a coherent and complementary mode of expression. Maps, in this regard, reflect the wider textual culture of which they formed part. World maps written primarily in Latin often contain at least some vernacular place names, particularly in regions of local significance to the audience. The Cotton world map, which was produced in England in the first half of the eleventh century, provides the earliest example of the use of vernacular toponyms on a *mappa mundi*. The overwhelming majority of toponyms and ethnonyms on the Cotton map are in Latin, but there are five names in Old English. Most identify places and peoples in the general vicinity of England: "Suðbryttas" (Bretons, literally "South British") across the Channel; "Sleswic" further north and east; "Island" (presumably Iceland) and two peoples, the "Neronorroen" (Norwegians) and the "Scridefinnas," in the Scandinavian area.[26] The presentation of the north-west part of the world is linguistically mixed: standard Latin place names such as "Britannia," "Hibernia," "Lundona," and "Wintonia" (Winchester) appear alongside the vernacular. These vernacular names suggest that the map's maker and intended audience were English, or English-speaking, and they articulate a regional knowledge more current than that contained in Latin sources, most notably Orosius, that inform other parts of the map.[27]

The two outstanding examples of monumental *mappae mundi* – the Hereford map, and the Ebstorf *mappa mundi*, both now dated to c. 1300 – show a significant presence of vernacular place names corresponding to the regions in which they were produced. Of the 1091 inscriptions on the Hereford map, eighty-

26. For a transcription of the map's inscriptions see P. McGurk, "The Mappa Mundi," in *An Eleventh-Century Anglo-Saxon Illustrated Miscellany (British Library Cotton Tiberius B.V. Part I)*, ed. P. McGurk, D. N. Dumville, M. R. Godden, A. Knock (Copenhagen, 1983), 79–86.

27. For Icelandic examples of mixed Latin and vernacular toponymy see Rudolf Simek, *Altnordische Kosmographie: Studien und Quellen zu Weltbild und Weltbeschreibung in Norwegen und Island vom 12. bis zum 14. Jahrhundert* (Berlin, 1990); Dale Kedwards, "Cartography and Culture in Medieval Iceland" (PhD diss., University of York, 2014).

one toponyms appear on the part of the map that represents the British Isles (Figure 22). Roughly half of these are in English. English names include cities and towns (*edenburgh, Snotingham, oxenford, hereford, baþe* [Bath]), rivers (*vse, auen, de* [Dee], *Medey* [Medway]), and one mountain (*mons cleoe*). Latin is preferred for the names of nations (*Anglia, Scocia, Wallia*), counties (*Norhumbria, Wircestria, Cornubia*), and usually for cities with particular ecclesiastical significance (*Sanctus andreas* [St Andrews], *Eboracia* [York], *duremia* [Durham], *Lincolnia, canturia* [Canterbury], *Ahrmaca civitas Sancti Patricii* [Armagh, city of St Patrick]).[28] But vernacular place names are not restricted to Britain: an unusually high number are found in central Europe, including "Straburh," "Salzeburgh," and "Magaddesburg" (Magdeburg).[29] The Ebstorf map reveals a similar linguistic picture: there are at least forty-four vernacular place names, concentrated in the north German region where the map was produced. Ebstorf itself appears as "Ebbekesstorp," and German names extend into parts of modern Russia (*Kiwen*), Italy (*Fauenz* for Faenza), Holland (*hec regio vocatur Hollant*), and Britain (*Euerwic* for York).[30] The use of Latin and vernacular languages on these sections of the Hereford and Ebstorf maps is neither hierarchical, nor rigorously categorized. The maps were predominantly written in Latin, but the vernacular identifies certain places and natural features, particularly those within the areas familiar to the makers and audience of these maps.

Mixture is similarly the rule on regional maps, where mapmakers often preferred vernacular languages for place names, if not inscriptions. Matthew Paris, the chronicler and monk of St Albans, is perhaps the outstanding thirteenth-century example of a regional mapmaker. His maps of Britain, Palestine, and his itinerary from St Albans to the Holy Land, amply demonstrate the use of the three great languages of later medieval England: Latin, French, and English. The place names on Matthew's maps of Britain are predominantly in English, but – as in a number of other examples of regional maps – Latin is used for longer inscriptions and geographical features. These maps accordingly show mixture even at a minute level, with constructions such as "castrum dinkeual" (Dunkeld) or "Oske

28. *The Hereford Map*, ed. Scott D. Westrem (Turnhout, 2001), 297–325 (nos. 756–837).

29. *The Hereford Map*, ed. Westrem, 223 (no. 543), 229 (no. 559), 245 (no. 603). The *Expositio Mappe Mundi*, a twelfth-century Latin description of a *mappa mundi* which was clearly related to the Hereford map, similarly contains a number of German toponyms ("Straisburch," "Salzeburch," "Magarburch"), some of which are not found on the Hereford map ("Slessic"): see Gautier Dalché's edition of the *Expositio: Du Yorkshire à l'Inde: Une 'géographie' urbaine et maritime de la fin du XIIe siècle (Roger de Howden?)* (Geneva, 2005), 162–63.

30. Hartmut Kugler, *Die Ebstorfer Weltkarte* (Berlin, 2007), respectively 1: 128, 102, 120, 140, 142 (nos. 50.12, 37.25, 46.15, 56.3, 57.3).

fluuius" (river Usk), in which a Latin noun (for castle, river, mountain, island) accompanies a vernacular place name.[31] Matthew's itinerary maps, by contrast, show the emergence of the vernacular as a language of topographic description. On these maps, which plot a journey from St Albans to southern Italy, and from there to the Holy Land, French is the dominant language in England and Italy as well as in France (*Lundres, Rouecestre, Cantebire chef de iglises de engleterre, la pou* [Po], *la terre de poille* [Puglia]), with Latin used sparingly in connection with ecclesiastical establishments or topographical features (*Puteres abbacia; Russelun monticulus*) (Figure 23).[32] It is only within the walls of Jerusalem that inscriptions appear solely in Latin – "Templum Domini"; "Templum Salomonis"; "Civitas Jerusalem", "civitas omnium civitatum dignissima" – while Matthew uses French immediately outside the city's walls, suggesting the ultimate assertion of a hierarchy between the two languages, the holy city protecting the language of the liturgy and the Bible within its walls.[33] In all, the large quantity of French on the itinerary and map of Palestine suggests that the itinerary was designed for readers from a French-speaking aristocratic milieu with connections to the monastery, and with an interest in pilgrimage and crusade.[34]

Like regional maps, local maps resist simple conclusions, and do not conform to straightforward chronologies. While there are occasional examples of local maps written in the vernacular, the high proportion produced for legal and administrative purposes seems to have encouraged a preference for vernacular place names, with Latin retained for longer inscriptions and paratext.[35] In general,

31. Matthew's map of Britain survives, in whole or part, in four manuscripts: BL, MS Cotton Claudius D.VI, fol. 12v ("castrum dinkeual"; "oske fluuius"); Cambridge, Corpus Christi College, MS 16, fol. iv verso ("castrum dinkeual"; "Oske fluuius"); London, British Library, MS Cotton Julius D. VII, fols. 50v–51r, 52v–53r (originally a single sheet, then folded in four to form part of a codex) ("Castrum Dinkeual"); BL, MS Royal 14 C.VII, fol. 5v contains neither toponym.

32. Examples taken from BL, MS Royal 14 C.VII, fols. 2r–4r; Cambridge, Corpus Christi College, MS 26, fols. i recto–iii recto.

33. BL, MS Royal C.VII, fol. 5r; P.D.A. Harvey notes the higher proportion of Latin in this version of the map: *Medieval Maps of the Holy Land* (London, 2012), 90.

34. See Salvatore Sansone, *Tra cartografia politica e immaginario figurativo: Matthew Paris e l'Iter de Londinio in Terram Sanctam* (Rome, 2009), 131–39.

35. The map of the region of Aardenburg in Zeeland from 1307 is written entirely in Flemish. For local maps generally see Paul Fermon, "Cartes et plans à grande échelle," in *La Terre: Connaissance, représentations, mesure au Moyen Âge*, ed. Patrick Gautier Dalché (Turnhout, 2013), 581–624, and 600–602 for the Aardenburg map; *Local Maps and Plans from Medieval England*, ed. R.A. Skelton and P.D.A. Harvey (Oxford, 1986). For commentary on the language of local maps and other genres see P.D.A. Harvey, "Cartography and its Written Sources," in *Medieval Latin*, 388–94.

local and regional maps show a higher proportion of vernacular place names than can be found on world maps, but in many examples Latin remains the "matrix" language, used for discursive elements, and for generic topographical and architectural features.[36] The intermixture of tongues found in medieval spatial representation can only partially be described as "translation." More often the model is one of the co-habitation, combination and mutual influence of languages and registers, in which the informal vocabulary of inhabitants and travellers was accommodated to the formal description codified in maps, written itineraries, and other texts. The results at the level of the individual toponym were unpredictable. While certain place names seem to have invited translation, others remained essentially unchanged as they moved between languages, thereby becoming the particular property of no single tongue. And there is a third category: the place name that originates in no single language, but that is the product of an interstitial space between languages. Some striking exampes of this phenomenon of the place name without a language emerge in the most obviously vernacular genre of medieval maps, the sea chart.

Vulgar to Vulgar: The Sea Chart Tradition

The later Middle Ages saw the emergence of a genre of maps, the sea chart, in which – in a reversal of the pattern of *mappae mundi* – the predominant languages were vernacular ones. This position of relative independence from Latin seems to have been the result of the origins and purpose of these maps. Sea charts have no known classical antecedents. While there is good evidence that charts existed by the early 1200s,[37] the earliest surviving example of a sea chart, the *Carte Pisane*, can only tentatively be dated to the second half of the thir-

---

36. On the "Gough" map of Britain, recently redated to c. 1390–1410 (though copied from a model dating to the 1290s and with an additional "layer" in south-east England apparently added in the second half of the fifteenth century), the overwhelming majority of toponyms is in English, but Latin is used for longer inscriptions and for generic terms such as "Earldom," "bridge," "castle," "mountain," "forest," "water," "ford," "river," and region ("plaga") throughout the map: for transcription see Edward J.S. Parsons, *The Map of Great Britain circa A.D. 1360 Known as the Gough Map* (Oxford, 1958), 21–37; for redating and caveats concerning Parsons's transcription, see Catherine Delano-Smith et al., "New Light on the Medieval Gough Map of Britain," *Imago Mundi* 69 (2017): 1–36.

37. Patrick Gautier Dalché, *Carte marine et portulan au XIIe siècle: Le* Liber de existencia riveriarum et forma maris nostri Mediterranei *(Pise, circa 1200)* (Rome, 1995).

teenth century.[38] The fourteenth century and particularly the fifteenth century provide a much richer store of these maps: from before 1500 there are around 180 datable sea charts and atlases, over half of which can be assigned to named chart-makers.[39] Key characteristics of sea charts are production on vellum sheets, which could be bound together to form an atlas; an emphasis on coastal outlines, with rel-atively few inland toponyms; a network of sixteen or thirty-two winds represented by the presence of "rhumb lines," designed to assist the plotting of a ship's course; and the presence of a scale bar. The standard format of the earliest sea charts com-prises the entire Mediterranean basin and the Black Sea coasts, and includes parts of North Africa and Asia Minor. Some, though not all, sea charts show the Atlantic, and in certain instances extend as far as Scandinavia and the North Sea.

The nexus between merchants and mariners has long been identified as fun-damental to the sea chart tradition.[40] The corpus of surviving sea charts consists primarily of maps constructed by people working with vernacular languages, sometimes with fairly low levels of competence in Latin. But just as it would be wrong to see *mappae mundi* as entirely Latinate, so it would be wrong to regard sea charts as entirely vernacular. Records of the use and production of sea charts indicate strongly that the makers and audience for these texts included priests, monks, and university scholars – men, in other words, with an often sophisti-cated knowledge of Latin.[41] The one known chart of the Genoese priest Gio-vanni da Carignano (active 1306–30) used Latin as its default language, and included legends such as "Hic fuerunt amazones, femine bellatrices" (here were Amazons, female warriors), derived from the *mappa mundi* tradition.[42] Carig-

38. The dating of the *Carte Pisane* (Paris, Bibliothèque nationale de France, Départe-ment des Cartes et Plans, Rés. ge. B 1118) is contested, as is its priority among surviving sea charts, but a late thirteenth-century date remains most plausible: see Tony Campbell, "A Detailed Reassessment of the Carte Pisane: A Late and Inferior Copy, or the Lone Survivor from the Portolan Charts' Formative Period?": http://www.maphistory.info/CartePisane-TEXT.html.[accessed 4/6/2019].

39. Tony Campbell, "Portolan Charts from the Late Thirteenth Century to 1500," in *The History of Cartography*, 1: 370–463, at 373, 432, 449–56; compare the lists of known charts, atlases, and chart makers in Ramon J. Pujades i Bataller, *Les Cartes portolanes: La representació medieval d'una mar solcada/Portolan Charts: The Medieval Representation of a Ploughed Sea* (Barcelona, 2007), 63–65, 68–70, 236–40.

40. Piero Falchetta, *Marinai, mercanti, cartografi, pittori: Ricerche sulla cartografia nautica a Venezia (sec. XIV–XV)* (Venice, 1995).

41. For English evidence see Alfred Hiatt, "'From Hulle to Cartage': Maps and the Sea," in *The Sea and Englishness in the Middle Ages: Maritime Narratives, Identity and Culture*, ed. Sebastian Sobecki (Cambridge, 2011), 133–57.

42. The map was destroyed in World War II; it is reproduced in Youssouf Kamal, *Mon-umenta Cartographica Africae et Aegypti*, 5 vols (Leiden, 1926–53), vol. 4.1, fols. 1137v–1138r, and Pujades, *Portolan Charts*, 328–29, with discussion on 517.

nano's chart is unusual, but beyond the vernacular coastal toponymy that distinguishes sea charts, it is not hard to find the presence of Latin inscriptions. Latin is often used for the designation of regions, kingdoms, and some geographical features in the interior, as well as more detailed inscriptions, particularly on expensive charts. In addition, sea charts frequently carry a signature, recording the name of the mapmaker and the date and place of production. These signatures are typically in Latin, if sometimes of a quality that reveals strong vernacularising elements, as in the Venetian brothers Francesco and Domenico Pizzigano's use of "compoxuid" for "composuit" and "Venexia" for "Venetia" in their signature on a 1367 chart: "MCCC.L.X.VII. Hoc opus compoxuid franciscus ex pizigano veneciarum cum doming. pizigano. In Venexia meffecit die XII decembris" (1367. Francesco Pizzigano of the Venetians prepared this work with Domenico Pizzigano. Made in Venice on the 12th day of December).[43]

Closer examination of the place names on sea charts shows, furthermore, that it is unhelpful to oppose Latin to vernacular in any rigid way, because the vernacular is itself a fluid and multifarious category. These maps come from a period before the codification and nationalisation of vernacular languages. The production of sea charts took place overwhelmingly in the mercantile ports of Genoa, Venice, and Palma de Majorca, and as a result the languages that, broadly speaking, dominate the toponomy of sea charts are the Ligurian and Venetian vernaculars, as well as Catalan. The earliest surviving portolano – that is, a written, non-cartographic, compilation of coastal place names – for the Mediterranean region, *Lo compasso da navigare*, uses a form of Italian close to the Tuscan vernacular.[44] However, the evidence of surviving charts reveals the persistent combination of different languages. The *Carte Pisane*, probably roughly contemporaneous with *Lo compasso*, has been described as "a linguistic mixture" dominated by Italian dialects, but marked by the influence of non-Italian vernaculars, such as Catalan.[45] Venetian chartmakers from Pietro Vesconte onwards produced maps which generally contained a high level of specifically Venetian forms, but their vernacular cannot be described as solely or purely Venetian, since the maps contain Genoese, Catalan, and Latin elements. The Majorcan chartmakers of the fourteenth century were clearly working with

43. Pujades, *Portolan Charts*, 250 for reproduction of the signatures of the Pizzigano brothers' 1367 chart, Francesco's 1373 chart, and other signatures; 494 for comment.

44. Simonetta Conti, "Portolano e carta nautica: Confronto toponomastico," *Imago et mensura mundi: Atti del IX congresso internazionale di storia della cartografia*, ed. Carla Clivio Marzoli, 2 vols (Rome, 1985), 1: 55–60, at 58. The *portolani* were predominantly written in vernacular languages, although there are examples of the genre in Latin: see the texts assembled in Konrad Kretschmer, *Die italienischen Portolane des Mittelalters: Ein Beitrag zur Geschichte der Kartographie und Nautik* (Berlin, 1909), 235–552.

45. Pujades, *Portolan Charts*, 489; Conti, "Portolano e carta nautica," 59.

Italian models, and they appear to have taken different approaches to the Italianate elements that they inherited. While the late fourteenth-century Jewish master chart-maker Abraham Cresques tended to leave Italianate forms unchanged,[46] other Majorcan cartographers, such as Pere Rossell, adapted and translated more freely. Yet the movement was not simply from the Italian languages into Catalan. In the fifteenth century there is evidence of transmission in the opposite direction. Maps that were predominantly written in Italian vernaculars – such as the 1403 chart of the Genoese Francesco Beccari (Figure 24) – started to include Catalan names such as Puig de Santa Maria (*lo puyg*) and Benidorm (*bendormi*),[47] and in the course of the fifteenth century Catalan forms such as "londres," "bruges," "cologna," "portegal," "florentza," "napols," and "palerm" became increasingly widely used on maps produced outside of Majorca.[48]

Some sense of this linguistically fluid picture can be derived from a comparison of individual place names across the corpus of surviving charts. One particular category of place name is that of the "hagiotoponym," that is, a place named after a saint. Because a single saint frequently had multiple places named after him or her, such names can uncover different regionally- and linguistically-inflected approaches to place names taken by mapmakers. A comparison of Sveti Juraj in the Northern Adriatic with Sant Jordi d'Alfama in Catalonia (both versions of St George) reveals, broadly speaking, four versions of the same toponym.[49] The first category is Latin – "sanctus georgius" – which appears on an anonymous Genoese map from the first quarter of the fourteenth century (Florence, Biblioteca Riccardiana, MS 3827).[50] There are three vernacular versions. The Venetian form "san zorzo/ç[i]orç[i]o" is evident from the second half of the fourteenth century in the maps of the Pizzigano brothers, and thereafter throughout the fifteenth century, with the exception of the atelier of Grazioso Benincasa, which consistently marks both places "san giorgio" (possibly a reflection of Benincasa's origins in a noble Ancona family).[51] The Catalan "san[t]

46. Vicenç M. Rosselló i Verger, "Els italianismes de les cartes portolanes mallorquines," in *Estudis de llengua i literatura en honor de Joan Veny*, ed. Josep Massot i Muntaner, 2 vols (Barcelona, 1997), 1: 39–62, at 46–48.

47. Pujades, *Portolan Charts*, 388–93, 495. A similar picture emerges from the analysis of wind names on sea charts: Philipp Billion, *Graphische Zeichen auf mittelalterlichen Portolankarten: Ursprünge, Produktion und Rezeption bis 1440* (Marburg, 2011), 48–57.

48. Rosselló i Verger, "Els italianismes de les cartes portolanes mallorquines," 49.

49. The following analysis is based on the useful table provided by Pujades, *Portolan Charts*, 350–97.

50. Pujades, *Portolan Charts*, 350–51, 386–77. The Riccardiana map uses "sancti georgi" for the Adriatic place and "sanctus georgius" for the Catalan.

51. Pujades, *Portolan Charts*, 351–57; 393.

jordi" is first used for the Catalonian town by the Majorcan mapmaker Guillem Soler in his charts from the second half of the fourteenth century, although he retained the Venetian-influenced "san zorzo" for the Adriatic place.[52] During the fifteenth century, Majorcan chartmakers seem to use the Catalan form outside of the region of Catalonia more often than their fourteenth-century predecessors: Gabriel de Vallseca and, in some of his maps, Pere Rossell, designate the Adriatic place "san[t] jordi."[53] Overall, the shifting nature of these toponyms attests, firstly, to a move away from the use of Latin in the early fourteenth-century examples to more unambiguously vernacular forms by the fifteenth century. At the same time, the evidence of these place names indicates the extent to which mapmakers copied the designs and toponyms of earlier models. Since models were transmitted across spatial borders – from the north Italian port cities to Palma de Majorca, and back – they also crossed linguistic borders.

Sea charts witness the passage of place names not just between Romance languages, but also from Germanic languages, from tongues such as English with a mixture of Germanic and Romance components, and from non Indo-European languages such as Arabic into Italianate or Catalan vernaculars.[54] The place names along the coastlines of England and Scotland, for example, were subject to often unpredictable transformations. In general, they underwent a process of Italianisation. Thus the town of Hull (or as it sometimes appears in Middle English, "Hulle") on the north-east coast of England is consistently rendered "u/vllo" on fourteenth- and fifteenth-century sea charts, through the loss of the initial "h" and the addition of a final vowel. The south-coast ports of Plymouth, Falmouth, and Portsmouth become, respectively, "priamua" or "premua," "fala/emua," and "portamua."[55] More complex is the transformation of the town on the south-eastern coast of England called Winchelsea, a name derived from the Anglo-Saxon *winceles* + *eg* ("island of the river bend"). Starting with Pietro Vesconte's chart of 1313, this place appears variously on sea charts of the fourteenth and fifteenth centuries as Ginsellexe, Guinsalexea, G(u)insalexio, Gixalixeo, and

52. Pujades, *Portolan Charts*, 394, 374–75.

53. Pujades, *Portolan Charts*, 376–77, though neither is completely consistent. See too Rosselló i Verger, "Els italianismes de les cartes portolanes mallorquines," 49.

54. Cairo appears on sea charts as "Car," "Cayre," "Chaire," but also "Al caira," "Al cayra": Billion, *Graphische Zeichen*, 286.

55. For example, Florence, Biblioteca Riccardiana, MS 3827 (Genovese, first quarter of the fourteenth century); Florence, Prince Filippo Corsini (A. Dulceti, 1330); London, British Library, MS Additional 18665, fols. 1v–2r (Venetian, second quarter of the fifteenth century); London, British Library, MS Additional 18454, fols. 2v–3r (Grazioso Benincasa, 1463). These forms appear consistently on Italian *portolani*: see Kretschmer, *Die italienischen Portolane*, 565–66.

Vizalixeo.[56] These forms seem to represent assimilation to Venetian dialect. From the four-syllable Middle English form "Winchelese(e)" the initial "w" is transcribed by a "g" or "gu"; the palatal "ch" becomes a sibilant "s"; the "e" of the second syllable mutates to an "a," the final "s" is represented by a "x," with the addition of a final "o" or "a." Such forms suggest a process of initial transcription of an oral source (a Venetian mariner?), followed by copying from one written exemplar to the next.

Transcriptions of this kind could, however, lead to confusions of meaning. Two place names that appear regularly on the coasts of England on medieval sea charts are "sancta polla" and "san duci" (in the Majorcan ateliers "s. dux").[57] These are the towns of "Poole" and "Sandwich," which have been sanctified, in one case because of apparent confusion of "Poole" with "Paulo" or "Paula," and in the other because an initial transliteration as "sanuis" mutated, through the re-insertion of "d," into fifteenth-century forms such as "san duihi/o" (Beccari), and slightly later to "san dux/duci/tuci."[58] Such errors indicate that the transmission of place names between languages might have rendered maps quite baffling to certain audiences, which would not have recognised the curious new forms that their own local geography had taken. Yet it is likely that, however far removed from their original vernacular forms, places such as "Guinsalexio" and "san dux" would have been understood and recognised within the mercantile centres of Europe that made and used sea charts. Such toponyms became established features of a cartographic repertoire, in some cases entering the *mappa mundi* tradition.[59] The lively linguistic mix at work within medieval sea charts finally reveals something different, per-

56. "Ginsalexeo": Pietro Vesconte, 1313 (Paris, Bibliothèque nationale de France, Département des Cartes et Plans, Rés. ge. DD 687); "Ginsellexe": Pietro Vesconte, chart of 1318 (Venice, Museo Correr, port. 28); "Guinsalexea": Angelino Dulceti, 1339 (BnF, Rés.Ge. B 696); "Gixalexio": Francesco Cesanis, 1421 (Venice, Museo Correr, port. 13); "Ginsalesio": Pere Rossell, mid fifteenth century, copy of 1489 (London, British Library, MS Egerton 73); "Vizalixeo": Anonymous Venetian, second quarter of the fifteenth century (BL, MS Additional 18665).

57. P. Vesconte, chart of 1318 (Venice, Museo Correr, port. 28): "sancta pola," "san uis"; G. Soler, chart of 1385 (Florence, Archivo di Stato, CN3): "sancta polla," "sanuis"; Anonymous Majorcan, last quarter of the fourteenth century (Florence, Biblioteca nazionale centrale, port. 22): "Sancto polla," "Sanuix"; F. Beccari, chart of 1403 (New Haven, Beinecke Rare Book and Manuscript Library, Art Store 1980.158): "Santa polla," "San duihi"; B. Beccari, chart of 1435 (Parma, Biblioteca Palatina, II.21.1613): "santa polla," "S. duiho"; G. de Vallseca, chart of 1439 (Barcelona, Museo Marítimo, Inv. 3236): "S. poli," "S. dux"; G. Beninincasa, 1463 (BL, MS Additional 18454, fols. 2v–3r): "sancta polla"; "Sanduci."

58. Noted by Rosselló i Verger, "Els italianismes de les cartes portolanes mallorquines," 48.

59. Fra Mauro has "Falamua" and "P[or]temua" on the south coast of Britain, as well as "Antona" (for Southampton): *Fra Mauro's World Map*, ed. and trans. Piero Falchetta (Turnhout, 2006), 581 (nos. 2214–16); the Catalan Atlas (1375), and the Catalan world map in the Biblioteca Estense similarly use a coastal toponomy derived from sea charts.

haps even contradictory, to translation: the emergence of names, such as Guin-salaxeo or san dux, that do not properly belong to any language.[60] In the act of describing space, these words became caught between languages – caught but nevertheless comprehensible to medieval audiences.

Humanism and Vulgar Tongues: Dante to Ortelius

Around 1305 the man who would become known as the father of Italian litera-ture wrote a strange apology for the use of the vernacular as a vehicle for elo-quence. The strangeness of Dante Alighieri's De vulgari eloquentia resides not only, not even principally, in the fact that he chose to write his defence of il vol-gare in Latin. It lies rather in the deep ambivalence, even hostility, expressed by Dante for his subject. Far from defending or elevating vernacular languages, Dante in fact ridicules them, exalting instead a constructed, "noble" vernacular worthy of literary composition. It is only by reference to the standard of Latin, rather than in their own right and on their own terms, that vernacular languages can be validated. The implications of De vulgari eloquentia for the usage of the vernacular in maps and geographical texts may seem obscure and indirect. How-ever, if the text is read as a form of spatial description two points become evi-dent. First, a language cannot be understood without reference to its habitat, its borders: the places where it is or was spoken. Second, the names of places con-sequently can become highly charged signs of linguistic status. Dante's unfin-ished treatise can be considered the first in a series of works that gave serious consideration to the history of languages, including the history of place names. Here too, what initially appears to be humanist reassertion of the superiority of Latin in the face of insurgent vernacular usage turns out on closer inspection to be a more complicated process of accommodation.

Dante begins De vulgari eloquentia by defining "common speech" (vulgaris locutio) as that which infants acquire by imitating their nurse, rather than through study. He immediately distinguishes this language of childhood from another, secondary, speech: "that which the Romans called gramatica," a language that must be studied, and which few have the time and the dedication to master.[61] It

60. On the "untranslatable" see Simon Gaunt, Marco Polo's Le Devisement du Monde: Narrative Voice, Language and Diversity (Cambridge, 2013), 102–11.

61. Dante Alighieri, De vulgari eloquentia 1.1.3, ed. Pier Vincenzo Mengaldo (Padua, 1968), 3: "alia locutio secundaria nobis, quam Romani gramaticam vocaverunt." On the com-plex question of Dante's shifting use of "locutio" see the helpful discussion in Stefano Gensini, "Attraverso il De vulgari eloquentia. A proposito di due edizioni recenti," Studi Danteschi 77 (2012): 277–91, at 281–84.

is common speech, Dante contends, that is the more noble. It was common, not grammatical, speech that was used in Eden; it is common speech that extends through the world, albeit in a post-Babel state of division. Against the artificial form of Latin, the quality of common speech is "natural."[62] In book one of *De vulgari eloquentia* Dante attempts to account for the division of the primal human idiom – which he alleged to be Hebrew – into so many forms. He presents a justly famous threefold regional division of the languages of Europe: the language of those who respond in the affirmative with *iò*, which extends from the mouth of the Danube to England, and is subdivided among Slavs, Hungarians, Teutons, Saxons, English, and other nations; another language from the border of Hungary through eastern Europe and beyond, into Asia; the third, the language of *oc, oïl, sì*, that of the Hispanics, French, and Italians.[63] As Dante freely acknowledges, this last language has numerous subdivisions. After all, languages differ within the same region, even within the same city: not only do the Milanese speak differently to the Veronesi, and the Romans to the Florentines, but in Bologna the people of "Borgo di San Felice" even have a different speech to those of "Strada Maggiore."[64]

In order better to characterise these differences within the language of *sì*, Dante sketches out a verbal map of Italy, one which strikingly invokes the description of Italy in book two of Lucan's *Bellum civile*:

We say firstly that Latium is divided in two parts, right and left. If someone asks what the dividing line is, we quickly respond that it is the ridge of the Apennines which distils water to the shores on either side through long channels – just as water-pipes drain a roof into different gutters on this side and that – as Lucan describes in book two: the right side has the Tyrrhenian Sea as its trough, while the left side falls into the Adriatic. The regions of the right

62. *De vulgari eloquentia* 1.1.4, ed. Mengaldo, 4. Compare Dante, *Convivio* 1.5, ed. Franca Brambilla Ageno, 2 vols (Florence, 1995), 2: 20–23, where Latin is unchanging, sovereign, beautiful, the language of art; the vernacular mutable, servile, the language of use. On Dante's use of Babel see Arno Borst, *Der Turmbau von Babel: Geschichte der Meinungen über Ursprung und Vielfalt der Sprachen und Völker*, 4 vols (Stuttgart, 1957–63), 2.2: 869–75; Irène Rosier-Catach (with Ruedi Imbach), "La Tour de Babel dans la philosophie du langage de Dante," in *Zwischen Babel und Pfingsten: Sprachdifferenzen und Gesprächsverständigung in der Vormoderne (8.–16. Jahrhundert)*, ed. Peter von Moos (Zürich, 2008), 183–204.

63. *De vulgari eloquentia* 1.8.3–6, ed. Mengaldo, 12–13.

64. *De vulgari eloquentia* 1.9.2–5, ed. Mengaldo, 14–15. Strada Maggiore was located within the second circle of Bologna's city walls; Borgo San Felice was enclosed within the third circle; the latter probably represented a form of the vernacular "più periferica e popolare": *De vulgari eloquentia*, ed. and trans. Mirko Tavoni, in Dante Alighieri, *Opere*, gen. ed. Marco Santagata (Milan, 2011), 1: 1220n.

are Apulia, but not all of it; Rome; the Duchy of Spoleto; Tuscany; and the march of Genoa [Liguria]. The regions of the left are part of Apulia; the march of Ancona; Romandiola [Romagna]; Lombardy; the march of Treviso with the Venetians.[65]

Dante adopts Lucan's view of Italy from the north, with the Apennines dividing "right" (west coast) from "left" (east coast), Tyrrhenian from Adriatic seas. In Lucan the view from the north coincides with the passage of Caesar from Gaul to Brundisium in pursuit of Pompey. But where Lucan's description is primarily a catalogue of rivers, hyperbolic and panegyric, designed to set in stark relief the violent desires of Caesar (*in arma furens*),[66] in *De vulgari eloquentia* Dante substitutes a brief account of the regions of Italy, followed by characterisation of their various forms of speech. Languages, in the manner of waters, come to define the territory. What emerges in Dante is a kind of linguistic civil war, an epic struggle not between Caesar and Pompey, but between the low, the diluted, the indigent, weak, and coarse on the one hand, and the courtly and refined on the other. The Sicilian and Apulian vernaculars are crude and barbaric, and eloquent and high-minded speakers prefer not to use them.[67] In Tuscany just a few know the highest form of the vernacular (*excellentia vulgaris*), the Genoese overuse the letter z, in Romagna the vernacular is soft – that is, feminine.[68] By contrast, the language of Brescia, Verona, Vicenza, and Padua is "hairy" (*yrsutum et yspidum*), the speech of people who say "nof" for nove and "vif" for vivo.[69] The Venetians, with one exception (the poet Aldebrandino dei Mezzabati di Padova), have failed to

65. *De vulgari eloquentia* 1.10.4–5, ed. Mengaldo, 17: "Dicimus ergo primo Latium bipartitum esse in dextrum et sinistrum. Si quis autem querat de linea dividente, breviter respondemus esse iugum Apenini quod, ceu fistule culmen hinc inde ad diversa stillicidia grunda[n]t, aquas ad alterna hinc inde litora per ymbricia longa distillat, ut Lucanus in secundo describit: dextrum quoque latus Tyrenum mare grundatorium habet, levum vero in Adriaticum cadit. Et dextri regiones sunt Apulia, sed non tota, Roma, Ducatus, Tuscia et Ianuensis Marchia; sinistri autem pars Apulie, Marchia Anconitana, Romandiola, Lombardia, Marchia Trivisiana cum Venetiis." Mengaldo and other editors print "grundat," but "grundant" is found in two of the three earliest manuscripts and, with comma placed before "aquas," makes better sense of "fistule" (by some editors unsatisfactorily emended to "fictile"): cf. *De vulgari eloquentia*, ed. Aristide Marigo, 3rd ed (Florence, 1957), 80–82, esp. n27. Tavoni translates "fistule culmen" as "il colmo della vena acquifera" (i.e. the top of the water-bearing lode), with long supporting note, but does not consider "grunda[n]t": *De vulgari eloquentia*, 1: 1243–45n.

66. *Bellum civile* 2.396–429.

67. *De vulgari eloquentia* 1.12, ed. Mengaldo, 20–22.

68. *De vulgari eloquentia* 1.13–14, ed. Mengaldo, 22–23.

69. *De vulgari eloquentia* 1.14.4–5, ed. Mengaldo, 23–24.

"turn away from the mother tongue towards the courtly vernacular."[70] And while the Bolognese have the most beautiful speech, one enriched by the co-mixture of other vernaculars, including that of Lombard invaders, their gutteral sounds (adopted from Ferrara and Modena) prevent the possibility of a truly refined vernacular.[71] Trent, Turin, and Alessandria, meanwhile, are too close to the frontiers of Italy to have a pure speech and consequently their vernaculars are not really Italian.[72] At the end of this rapid linguistic and geographical tour, the idealised vernacular described by Dante emerges as a powerful, yet absent, symbol for political unity. It is the imagined language of an imagined court, a language of government, justice, and charity, and one that also supports poetic composition (*poeta esserere*). It is a language alienated from the mother tongue, or the vernacular of fathers, even from one's own (*a proprio*) speech and thought: a language around which the "herd of municipal vernaculars" would turn.[73] Speech, power, and poetry are thereby brought together in *De vulgari eloquentia*, and it is Lucan's description of Italy prior to the rupture of Caesar that helps Dante to define spatially an area that he will then anatomize linguistically. Somehow the verbal map performs the trick of holding the diversity of lands, peoples, and tongues within a conceptual unity.

Many of the arguments over the status of the vernacular that peppered European intellectual life in the fourteenth and fifteenth centuries seem caught within the scope of Dantean ambivalence.[74] *De vulgari eloquentia* was barely known in the years after Dante's death, but all the same it articulated two paths that numerous authors faced: that of the acceptance and use of the vernacular as a viable means of literary and scientific expression, and that of insistence on its cultural and practical inferiority to Latin. It is not hard to find examples of those taking the second path, although these cases are often more complex than they appear at first glance. In 1313 the Dominican Pere Marsili broke off from his translation of a chronicle of the deeds of Jaime I of Aragon from Catalan into Latin (*Chronica illustrissimi regis Aragonum domini Iacobi*) to explain to his readers why he had

70. *De vulgari eloquentia*, 1.14.6–7, ed. Mengaldo, 24: "divertere a materno et ad curiale vulgare intendere."

71. *De vulgari eloquentia*, 1.15.2–4, ed. Mengaldo, 24–25: "ad vulgare aulicum."

72. *De vulgari eloquentia*, 1.15.7, ed. Mengaldo, 26: "propter aliorum commixtionem esse vere latium negaremus."

73. *De vulgari eloquentia* 1.18.1, ed. Mengaldo, 29: "sic et universus municipalium grex vulgarium vertitur et revertitur ... ."

74. The obvious contrast is with Dante's own defense of the use of the vernacular in the *Convivio* 1.5–13, written shortly before *De vulgari eloquentia*. On the contradictions of *De vulgari eloquentia* see Albert Russell Ascoli, "'Neminem ante nos': Historicity and Authority in the *De vulgari eloquentia*," *Annali d'Italianistica* 8 (1990): 186–231.

retained vernacular terms for winds instead of using Latin ones. His audience, he feared, would find "ridiculous" his use of a "vernacular and base vocabulary" (*uulgari et rudi uocabulo*). However, he explained, he had been compelled to employ the vernacular terminology so that the majority of his readers could understand him: "for few would have comprehended me" if he had used the Latin names for winds, such as "Africus" and "Vulturnus."[75] In other words, Pere Marsili had, apparently reluctantly, bowed to common usage rather than insisting on linguistic consistency in his work. At the same time the fact that he felt the need to issue an apology of this kind indicates the lower status of the vernacular in the eyes of at least some authors and readers, as well as the increasing difficulty involved in avoiding it, even in a Latin text.

On the other hand, a slew of translations into several European languages in the fourteenth century emphasised the validity of the vernacular, typically citing the practical utility of translation (particularly into prose), its cultural pedigree (the translation of the Bible into Greek and Latin being the most obvious point of reference), and its compatibility with religious orthodoxy.[76] The more considered exponents of translation from Latin to vernacular languages were certainly conscious of the particular difficulties posed by place names. John Trevisa's introductory "Epistle" to his English translation of Ranulf Higden's Latin *Polychronicon* acknowledged changes to the original, such as altering the grammar of certain passages, or adding occasional words of explanation. Trevisa insisted, though, that:

> somme wordes and names – of cuntreys, of londes, of citees, of watris, of ryvers, of mounteyns and hilles, of persons and of places – mot be ysett and stonde for hemself in her owne kynde [nature] (as *Asia, Europa, Affrica*, and

75. Patrick Gautier Dalché, "Pere Marsili, une carte majorquine (1313) et l"ardua controversia' des vents," *Itineraria* 5 (2006): 153–70, at 168: "nominibus uentorum uulgaribus usus sum, ne pluribus legentibus uentos et nomina occultarem. Pauci enim me intellexissent, si dixissem 'affricum impediuisse regem recedentem de Salodio, qui uulturno in recta linea opponitur ... '."

76. See *The Idea of the Vernacular: An Anthology of Middle English Literary Theory, 1280–1520*, ed. Jocelyn Wogan-Browne et al. (University Park, 1999). On the complex nature of the rise of vernaculars in Europe see, *inter alia*, Serge Lusignan, *Parler vulgairement: Les intellectuals et la langue française aux XIIIe et XIVe siècles* (Paris, 1986); *La résistable ascension des vulgaires: Contacts entre latin et langues vulgaires au bas Moyen Âge*, ed. Benoit Grevin, *Mélanges de l'École française de Rome, Moyen Âge* 117.2 (2005): 447–718; *Tous vos gens à Latin: Le latin, langue savante, langue mondaine (XIVe–XVIIe siècles)*, ed. Emmanuel Bury (Geneva, 2005); Anne Grondeux, "La notion de langue maternelle et son apparition au Moyen Âge," in *Zwischen Babel und Pfingsten*, 339–56; Ardis Butterfield, *The Familiar Enemy: Chaucer, Language and Nation in the Hundred Years War* (Oxford, 2009).

Siria; Mount Athlas, Syna and *Oreb; Marach, Jordan,* and *Arnon; Beethlem, Nazareth, Jerusalem,* and *Damascus; Hanibal, Risyn, Assuerus* and *Cirus* and many siche wordes and names).[77]

Trevisa has, all the same, translated several of the toponyms he lists, which does not necessarily contradict his point that they "stand for themselves in their own nature." Here again the principle of vernacularising place names for a local audience seems to pertain. In his translation it is particularly in Britain and northern Europe that Trevisa substitutes vernacular toponyms for Higden's Latin originals, or inserts a gloss to update: "in Gaius Iulius Cesar his tyme Gallia, þat is Fraunce, was i-made soget" (in Gaius Julius Caesar's time Gallia, that is France, was made subject).[78]

This trend towards increased use of the vernacular, even to the point of the replacement of Latin as the standard language of maps and other forms of spatial representation, met resistance on a number of fronts. Earlier Latin texts were frequently copied without significant vernacularisation of place names, while at the beginning of the fifteenth century the resources of Latin toponymy were considerably enriched. The *Geographia* of Ptolemy, as translated by the Florentine Jacopo Angeli in the first decade of the fifteenth century, helped to disseminate and consolidate an ancient nomenclature, particularly for regions beyond Europe.[79] As the text and maps of the *Geographia* became well known through much of Europe in the second half of the fifteenth century, so did its place names – originally Greek, now Latin. Some of these were of course already standard Latin place names, such as Hispania, Gallia, Germania, Pannonia, and many more. But other names, not necessarily totally new, but formulated in distinctive ways, derived unmistakably from the *Geographia* and became commonplace (Figure 25): "India intra Gangem fluvium," and its sibling "India extra Gangem fluvium" (India within/beyond the Ganges river); "Scithia extra imaum montem" (Scythia beyond the Imaus mountains); "Aurea chersonesus" (Golden Peninsula); "Serica regio"; "Sina"; "Ethiopia sub egipto" (Ethiopia beneath Egypt), "Ethiopia interior." These toponyms could be found in texts and on maps explicitly imitative of Ptolemy, but they also circulated more freely, becoming part of a shared geographic language. This image of the world and its nomenclature was so ingrained within learned circles by the early sixteenth century that

77. "Epistle to Thomas, Lord Berkeley," ed. Stephen Shepherd, in *The Idea of the Vernacular,* 134–35, at 135.

78. Ranulph Higden, *Polychronicon,* ed. Churchill Babington, 9 vols. (London, 1865–86), 1: 287; cf. Higden's Latin, 286: "Tandem Gallia, sub Julio Caesare subacta ... ."

79. See Patrick Gautier Dalché, *La géographie de Ptolémée en Occident (IVe–XVIe siècle)* (Turnhout, 2009).

when, in the course of a translation of Columbus's letter from Jamaica, the Venetian Alessandro Zorzi sketched a map of the world to represent details of the explorer's fourth voyage, he used Ptolemaic toponyms for the old world (*Aethiopia, India interior Gangem, India Extra Gangem Fluvium, Sinarum situs, Aurea chersonesus*) and vernacular (predominantly Italian) to represent the discoveries in the new world.[80]

The authority attributed to Ptolemy as a "cosmographus," an ancient *auctor*, meant that his work acquired a definitive cast. Yet the response to such authority was far from slavish, and in some cases it was not even deferential. The fifteenth-century reception of Ptolemy's *Geographia* entailed critical confrontation with other sources, ancient and modern. In some cases that process resulted in a mixture of Latin and vernacular toponymy,[81] but it also carried the possibility of outright rejection of Ptolemaic names. The most eloquent opponent of the necessity of following Ptolemy's representation of the world and its nomenclaure was the Camaldolese mapmaker Fra Mauro. A characteristically proud affirmation, located off the Atlantic coast of France on Fra Mauro's world map (Figure 26), articulates succinctly his reasons for not using Latin place names:

In questa opera per necessità ho convenuto usar nomi moderni e vulgari perché al vero se io havesse fato altramente pochi me haveria inteso salvo che qualche literato, avegna che ancora lor non possa acordar hi autori cum quel che hora se pratica.

In this work I decided to use modern, vernacular names out of necessity because truly if I had done otherwise few would have understood me, except certain lettered men, and even they cannot reconcile the [Latin] authorities with what now is practised.[82]

The declaration that Latin could reach only a few was a standard trope of the defence of the vernacular. Yet it is significant that Fra Mauro expressed his rejection of Ptolemy's toponomy by uniting the modern with the vulgar and opposing these concepts implicitly to the antique (Latin) place names of "autori." Fra

80. Florence, Biblioteca nazionale centrale, Banco Rari 234, fol. 60v. It has been suggested that Zorzi copied a map of Bartolomeo Columbus: on Zorzi's compilation see Luciano Formisano, "La compilazione di viaggi di Alessandro Zorzi: Firenze, Biblioteca Nazionale Centrale, B.R. 233-236," in *Vespucci, Firenze e le Americhe*, ed. Giuliano Pinto et al. (Florence, 2014), 441–56.

81. See Gautier Dalché, *La géographie de Ptolémée en Occident*, esp. 189–214.

82. *Fra Mauro's World Map*, ed. and trans. Piero Falchetta (Turnhout, 2006), 577 (no. 2202) [translation modified].

Mauro rejected a learned and perhaps specifically humanistic standard which would, for example, attempt to eliminate corruptions of antique place names. In favouring instead the modern and vulgar, Fra Mauro acknowledged fully the problems posed to a mapmaker by linguistic diversity, without attempting to resolve them. In an inscription regarding the Baltic Sea, he draws attention to his choice between competing place names:

> Questo colfo, el qual Tolomeo non mete, ha piusor nomi, e si dito lubech, prusico, sarmatico, germanico, e perché questo ultimo nome è più chiaro, però ho notado colfo germanico.

> This gulf, which is not found in Ptolemy, has several names, being called Lübeck, Prussian, Sarmatian, German, and because this last name is the most famous I have recorded it as the German Gulf.[83]

In this instance the mapmaker firstly notes the absence of Ptolemaic authority, then lists four possible alternatives. He chooses the name that is the best known (*più chiaro*), and hence the best point of reference for his non-scholarly, vernacular readers. As the map of Fra Mauro indicates, by the mid-fifteenth century, in cartographically active parts of Europe, vernacular mapping was taking precedence over Latin. The outreach to a wider audience, the influence of vernacular sources, the resistance to classicizing models, made the choice of vulgar tongues preferable. In the case of Fra Mauro, it is clear that it was not simply the availability of vernacular sea charts that encouraged the Camaldolese to use Venetian throughout his map, but his membership of an order that in the middle of the fifteenth century was busily translating into the vernacular key works of religious life, including the Bible, the Golden Legend, and a *laudario*.[84] The tangible presence of a vernacular cartographic and intellectual culture in Venice at the middle of the fifteenth century, coupled with the diffusion of Venetian throughout the courtly and mercantile centres of Europe and beyond, made Fra Mauro's choice of language not simply explicable, but obvious.[85]

Again, however, it would be dangerous to assert too rigid a division between vernacular and humanist Latin geography. In fact, the relationship between Latin and vulgar place names within humanist culture was itself complex and not always

83. *Fra Mauro's World Map*, ed. Falchetta, 707 (no. 2862) [transcription and translation modified].

84. Angelo Cattaneo, *Fra Mauro's Mappa Mundi and Fifteenth-Century Venice* (Turnhout, 2011), 228–34.

85. Cattaneo, *Fra Mauro's Mappa Mundi*, 232–34. See too Marica Milanesi, "Cartografia per un principe senza corte," *Micrologus* 16 (2008): 189–216, at 209–16.

oppositional. In the first place, the humanists inherited a learned tradition of rendering geographical description in vernacular verse, the outstanding early example of which is Gossouin's *L'image du monde*. Tuscan examples of this tradition include the fourteenth-century *Dittamondo* of Fazio degli Uberti (where Solinus acts as a guide), *La sfera* of Goro Dati, and in the late fifteenth century Francesco Berlinghieri's learned adaptation of the *Geographia* "in lingua florentina." Berlinghieri's "Le sette giornate della geographia" (1478–82), in which Ptolemy now performs the role of guide, features the regular modernisation of Ptolemaic place names.[86] Humanists increasingly used modern, vernacular names to gloss toponyms in classical Latin texts,[87] while surviving examples of humanist-inflected maps of Italy show both Latin and modern vernacular Italian place names, even if Latin remains the language of learned discourse surrounding and informing these maps.[88]

Secondly, the aim of humanists such as Giovanni Boccaccio and Biondo Flavio was not to dismiss or suppress vernacular place names, but to interrogate both modern and classical geography so as to bring the two into alignment. The work of Biondo can be understood in the context of the fierce fifteenth-century debate about the nature of the relationship between Latin and vulgar tongues. This debate, seen most clearly and polemically in the exchanges between Biondo and Leonardo Bruni, raised difficult questions about languages, their co-existence, interactions, and divisions. Had Latin, once, been a vernacular? If not, what language had ancient Romans commonly spoken? Were the ancient authors who wrote in Latin using their mother tongue, or a language of erudition? One thing that most participants agreed on was that the barbarian invasions that eventually terminated the Roman Empire had inevitably affected both Latin and vernacular tongues.[89]

86. Francesco Berlinghieri, *Geographia* (Florence, 1482), e.g. "per lo strecto galipolitano / quale hellesponto antichamente appello" [1.13]; "Sobto a Leuci & questi porre e bene / Longoni & hoggi Langre oue si face / Andomatunno che Borgogna tiene" [2. "Gallia Belgica"]; "Da germinando fu decta Germania / o da similituone fraterna / quale ha co galli: hoggi e decta alamania" [2. "Germania Magna"]; "Molossa decta inprima hoggi Albania" [3.23].

87. A good example is provided by the fifteenth-century glosses on Lucan's *Bellum civile* in BAV, MS Vat. lat. 3284.

88. Marica Milanesi, "Antico e moderno nella cartografia umanistica: Le grandi carte d'Italia nel Quattrocento," *Geographia antiqua* 16–17 (2007–8): 153–76, at 161–63.

89. Leonardo Bruni Aretino to Biondo (7 May 1435), in *Lettres familières*, ed. and trans. Laurence Bernard-Pradelle, 2 vols (Montpellier, 2014), 2: 148–62 (Ep. 6.15); Blondus Flavius, *De verbis Romanae locutionis*, ed. Fulvio Delle Donne (Rome, 2008); Leon Battista Alberti, *I libri della famiglia*, in *Opere Volgari*, vol. 1, ed. Cecil Grayson (Bari, 1960), 153–56 (Proemio del Libro Terzo). These and other key texts are gathered in Mirko Tavoni, *Latino, Gram-*

The debate over the history of Latin and its relationship to the Italian vernaculars demanded reflection not only on changes over time, but also on Latin's geographical extent. In the prologues to his *Elegantiae Linguae Latinae*, the brilliant, sharp-tongued Roman Lorenzo Valla told a story of the rise and spread of Latin through the world. Latin had marched with the Roman Empire, and it had flourished as a – perhaps *the* – great imperial glory. In the reach and unity of their language, Valla thought, the Romans had surpassed the Greeks, whose tongue was divided into different dialects. A good in itself, comparable to grain, oil, and wine, the Latin language acted as a foil to violence and military conquest, promoting friendship and peace to soften the wars and blood.[90] It was not undone by contact with the native languages of conquered peoples, but neither did it eliminate their use. Latin conferred splendour on these languages, as a gem set in a gold ring is turned into an ornament.[91] However, the irruption of the Gauls, and worse still the Goths, had inflicted on Latin the same sorry fate the barbarian invaders had wrought on Rome. Burdened, corrupted, occupied – it was up to Valla, a self-styled second Camillus, to liberate the city and its tongue once more.[92] So the *Elegantiae* sought to identify the correct usage of Latin, based on classical models, and thereby reclaim a lost standard.

A less heroic – but more subtle – account of Latin emerged towards the end of the fifteenth century in the writing of another Roman, the grammarian Paolo Pompilio. Pompilio devoted a chapter of his short tract "De accentibus" to the many differences of pronunciation across Latin-speaking Europe. The French,

---

matica, Volgare: Storia di una questione umanistica (Padua, 1984); see also Riccardo Fubini, "La coscienza del latino negli umanisti," and "Postcriptum," in *Umanesimo e secolarizzazione da Petrarca a Valla* (Rome, 1990), 1–53; Angelo Mazzocco, *Linguistic Theories in Dante and the Humanists: Studies of Language and Intellectual History in Late Medieval and Early Renaissance Italy* (Leiden, 1993); Giuseppe Patota, "Latino e volgare, latino nel volgare," in *Il Latino nell'età dell'umanesimo*, ed. Giorgio Bernardi Perini (Florence, 2004), 109–66. On Biondo's attitude to language and the *Italia illustrata* see Paolo Pontari, "'Nedum mille qui effluxerunt annorum gesta sciamus': L'Italia di Biondo e l'"invenzione' del Medioevo," in *A New Sense of the Past: The Scholarship of Biondo Flavio (1392–1463)*, ed. Angelo Mazzocco and Marc Laureys (Leuven, 2016), 151–75.

90. Lorenzo Valla, *De linguae latinae elegantia*, ed. and trans. Santiago López Moreda, 2 vols (Cáceres, 1999), 1: 56–64; the deficiencies of this edition are noted by Clementina Marsico, *Per l'edizione delle Eleganti di Lorenzo Valla: Studio sul V Libro* (Florence, 2013), 34–38.

91. *De linguae latinae elegantia*, ed. López Moreda, 58.

92. *De linguae latinae elegantia*, ed. López Moreda, 60–64, esp. 62: "Camillus nobis, Camillus imitandus est, qui signa, ut inquit Vergilius, in patriam referat, eamque restituat." Livy styled Marcus Furius Camillus the "second founder" of Rome for his actions following the city's sack by Gauls in 390 BC (*Ab urbe condita*, 5.49); in book six of the *Aeneid*, Virgil has Aeneas see Camillus in the underworld "signa referens" (*Aen* 6.825), bearing the standards back to Rome.

observed Pompilio, "ioticize," mixing "i" with "u," pronouncing "Lucanus" as "Lucanius," while the Genoese "zeticize," so that "Juno" becomes "Zuno" and "gens," "zens." Spain abounds in vices ("forsam" for "forsan," "atus" for "aptus," "esto" for "sto" and "isse" for "ipse"), the Germans turn "d" into "t" ("Teus" not "Deus" and "tominus" for "dominus"), and the British mix up the sounds of "e" and "i," so "fecit" sounds like "ficet" and "pisces" like "pescis."[93] The contagion had even spread from the provinces to Rome itself, Pompilio sighed, leading to "betacisms" such as "binea" for "vinea," as well as missing consonants: "Coscius pro Conscius et mannare, cantanno, amanni pro mandare, cantando, amandi."[94] In his notebooks Pompilio explained these varieties as the product of history. Latin had once been a common tongue: "latinum sermonem olim promiscuum fuisse."[95] The proof was its presence throughout Europe, and in parts of Asia and Africa too. The language was spoken in Scandinavia, across the Danube, in Judaea, on the shores of the Caspian: "I believe because of the colonies founded there by the Romans, or rather because of the journeyings of the Latin language, which, it is reckoned, rhetoricians at some point even transmitted as far as Thule."[96] An informant had given Pompilio an account of the Latin spoken in north Africa, revealing in the process striking similarities with the Latin of Sardinia.[97] Geography, from this perspective, acted as the enemy of purity, but also as a strange preserver of old connections otherwise obscured by political change. In such a view, modern and ancient place names were less opposed concepts than different points within a ruptured continuum.

Debates about the relationship between Latin and vulgar tongues naturally took on different inflections across the Alps. For German humanists, the situation was strangely inverted. The humanist project at the end of the fifteenth and early sixteenth centuries, as advanced by the "archhumanist" Conrad Celtis and his followers, required the establishment of the boundaries of ancient Germa-

---

93. "De accentibus" was printed as part of Pompilio's *Syllabae* (Rome, 1488), dedicated to Cesare Borgia. The chapter "De Iotacismo et Labdacismo et Zetacismo aliisque uitiis pronuntiandi apud multas nationes" appears on fols. 50r–51r (the work is unpaginated). For discussion see Carlo Dionisotti, *Gli umanisti e il volgare fra Quattro e Cinquecento* (Florence, 1968; repr. Milan, 2003), 31–33.

94. "De accentibus," fol. 50r–v.

95. Paulus Pompilius, "Latinum sermonem olim promiscuum fuisse," ed. Tavoni, in *Latino, Grammatica, Volgare*, 301.

96. Pompilius, "De antiquitate linguae latinae," ed. Tavoni, in *Latino, Grammatica, Volgare*, 297–300, at 299: "credo propter colonias eo a Romanis deductas, ac potius propter linguae latinae peregrinationes, quae vel in Thilen usque rethoras suos existimata est quandoque transmisisse."

97. Pompilius, "Latinum sermonem olim promiscuum fuisse," 301.

nia.[98] The key sources of the antique toponomy of Germany were texts of the Roman Empire, written either in Latin or Greek: Caesar's *Civil Wars*, Tacitus's *Germania*, Pomponius Mela's *De chorographia*, Pliny's *Naturalis historia* and the geographies of Ptolemy and Strabo, both now accessible in Latin translation. The Italians could either conceive of Latin in a familial relation with the Italian vernaculars, in which the corruption of Latin by barbarian invasions had resulted in contemporary vernaculars, or in an adversarial relation, in which the vulgar tongues of modern Italy had descended from a vernacular that existed in ancient Rome alongside Latin. But few filiations could be found between Latin and German, let alone Greek and German. The alien nature of Latin seemed to some humanists to pose dangers to a correct understanding of Germania's spatial history. The Alsatian Jakob Wimpfeling feared that modern Germans could misunderstand or garble Latin toponomy: they might hear the monastery of St John and St Nicholas *in undis* (between the waters) as *zu den Hunden* (to the dogs), "finis terrae" (land's end) as "finstern sternen" (dark stars), and "alta ripa" ("high shore") as Altrip, a city on the west bank of the Rhine.[99] Nor was classical Latin easy to align with contemporary German place names. Who, observed the cartographer Martin Waldseemüller, "with his finger will point out on the River Rhine the cities of Ganodurum, Augusta Raurica, Elcebus and Borbetomagus recorded by Ptolemy?"[100] Conversely, educated readers might stumble over the harsh sounds of German names rendered into Latin. In his *Brevis Germanie Descriptio* of 1512, the Nuremberg schoolmaster and future opponent of Luther, Johannes Cochlaeus, apologised to his readers for the obstacles to Latin eloquence posed by the necessary use of a large number of German toponyms and ethnonyms; to soften the discordant notes he adjusted toponyms by adding or

98. Gernot Michael Müller, *Die "Germania generalis" des Conrad Celtis: Studien mit Edition, Übersetzung und Kommentar* (Tübingen, 2001), 359–86. On the relationship between German and Latin in the fourteenth and fifteenth centuries see Klaus Wriedt, "Latein und Deutsch in den Hansestädten vom 13. bis zum 16. Jahrhundert," and Ulrich Andermann, "Albert Krantz (1448–1517): Bemerkungen zum Verhältnis von lateinischer und volkssprachlicher Gelehrsamkeit am Beispiel eines norddeutschen Humanisten," in *Latein und Nationalsprachen in der Renaissance*, ed Bodo Guthmüller (Wiesbaden, 1998), respectively 287–313, 315–43.

99. Jakob Wimpfeling, *Germania*, in Emil von Borries, *Wimpfeling und Murner im Kampf um die ältere Geschichte des Elsasses: Ein Beitrag zur Charakteristik des deutschen Frühhumanismus* (Heidelberg, 1926), 124.

100. See Waldseemüller's address "Ad Lectorem" at the beginning of the section "In Claudii Ptolemei Supplementum": Claudius Ptolemy, *Geographiae opus novissima traductione e Grecorum archetypis castigatissime pressum* (Strasbourg, 1513): "Quis enim iuxta Rhenum Flauium [sic], Canodurum, Augustam rauricum, Elcebum et Berthomagum urbes a Ptolemaeo commemoratas digito monstrabit."

altering letters, and in rare cases entirely translated them.[101] "Amberga" and "Bamberga" stood for "Amberg" and "Bamberg," "Landa" for "Landau," while in the second category Königsberg became "Mons Regius," and Saarbrücken "Sarapontum."[102] The old dilemma remained: the new names were in the vernacular and hard to express pleasingly in Latin; the ancient names were obsolete, and intelligible only to a few, but for the sake of understanding history they could not be jettisoned.[103] Or could they? Cochlaeus approvingly drew his readers' attention to Erhard Etzlaub's 1501 map of *Germania*, marked with German, not Latin names, "in which it is possible to see the distances between cities and the courses of rivers depicted even more accurately than in the maps of Ptolemy."[104] The path to a fully vernacular "modern" geography – held separate from the ancient record of space preserved in Ptolemy and other authors – was evident. Such a modern geography could represent national boundaries in a linguistic rather than a political sense – the *lingua*, and therefore the *gens*. For vulgar tongues, as Dante had grasped, could mark borders, or as one early fifteenth-century German chronicler put it with striking clarity: "the ancients used to divide provinces according to frontiers and the [natural] boundaries provided by rivers, mountains, woods and seas, but moderns commonly determine such borders using differences of speech."[105] So it was that language had come to play a crucial role in the definition of space.

The cartography that emerged in the works of Waldseemüller and others in humanist Europe by the beginning of the sixteenth century was, then, one in which Latin, far from being discarded, retained its cultural and political capital as the language of ancient record. Still the default language of international scholarship, it remained the necessary means to recuperate the space of antiquity. Nevertheless, in the fields of maritime, and local and regional cartography, "vulgar tongues" had long since established themselves as legitimate languages of modern maps, not only in combination with Latin, but wholly independent of it. By the time of Ortelius, the divisions between Latin and vernacular geography had consolidated to the point that his *Theatrum* had to be printed in multiple lan-

101. Johannes Cochlaeus, *Brevis Germanie Descriptio* (1512), ed. and trans. Karl Langosch (Darmstadt, 1960), 162.

102. *Brevis Germanie Descriptio*, ed. Langosch, respectively 102, 144, 108, 132, 160.

103. *Brevis Germanie Descriptio*, ed. Langosch, 66, 162.

104. *Brevis Germanie Descriptio*, ed. Langosch, 90: "in qua cernere licet urbium distantias fluviorumque cursus exactius certe quam vel in Ptolomei tabulis."

105. *Cosmidromius Gobelini Person*, ed. Max Jansen (Münster, 1900), 3: "antiqui considerabant divisiones provinciarum secundum limites et terminos fluminum, moncium et silvarum ac marium, sed vulgares moderni attendunt tales distinctiones secundum differencias idiomatum."

guages to serve an expanded, linguistically diverse market. But the separation, and interplay, of languages could occur also at the very level of the map itself. The most spectacular example of the careful, yet politically and historically charged, recuperation of classical Latin alongside vernacular toponymy is Humfrey Lhuyd's map of Wales, which Ortelius published in the *Theatrum* of 1573 (Figure 27).[106] For Lhuyd, a learned antiquary and parliamentarian who served in the household of the Earl of Arundel, place names revealed occluded histories. They showed the former extent across Britain of the "Cambri" – Lhuyd's ancestors, for whom he rejected the English term "Welsh" – and their priority to both Romans and Saxons. The British, he explained to Ortelius in a letter about the Isle of Anglesey ("De Mona Insula"), had possessed the entire island before the arrival of the Angles. Pushed to the furthest parts of the island (*in angustias terrarum*), they kept their language – *lingua Britannica* – alive, and in so doing they preserved the ancient names of regions, cities, rivers, islands, and peoples.[107] In a description of Britain sent to Ortelius along with his maps, Lhuyd finds the old British tongue infiltrating Latin, since the Romans frequently derived their place names from the native inhabitants. Such infiltration was not, he thought, restricted to Wales. Dover comes from the British word for water, "dwr"; all Latin placenames in Britain beginning or ending in "lan" or "lam" must be a corruption of the old British "phan," meaning river.[108]

The map printed by Ortelius presents Latin, Welsh, and English in parallel. Lhuyd carefully identifies the languages with different letters: L for Latin, B for Welsh/British, A for English. Several places and regions are represented by all three languages, often illustrating the derivation of Latin toponomy from Welsh, with English the interloper: Cambria (L), Cambry (B), Wales (A); Venedotia (L), Gwynedhia (B), Northwales (A); Mona insula (L), Mon (B), Anglesey (A). In his introduction to the map, Ortelius followed Lhuyd (by time of publication recently deceased) in drawing attention to the antiquity of the Welsh language, and to its survival in the speech and writing of the populace, as well as in a recently printed vernacular Bible and Book of Common Prayer.[109] Part of the carefully structured appeal of the map for the erudite sixteenth century reader, then, was

106. "Cambriae Typus Auctore Humfredo Lhuydo Denbigiense Cambrobritanno," *Theatrum Orbis Terrarum* (Antwerp, 1573).

107. "De Mona Insula," in Abraham Ortelius, *Theatrum Orbis Terrarum* (Antwerp, 1570), sig. aii verso: "ut Regiones, Civitates, Fluvii, Insulae et Populi, apud nostrates nomina obtinent antiqua."

108. *Commentarioli Britannicae Descriptionis Fragmentum* (Cologne, 1572), fols. 12r, 19r: "... facile crediderim loca quae a Latinis in lan, vel lam desinunt vel incipiunt, olim a phanis Britannice dicta fuisse."

109. "Cambria siue Wallia," *Theatrum Orbis Terrarum* (Antwerp, 1573), fol. 9r.

its mix of languages, and thereby its articulation of history. Latin is the language of presentation, of discursus, of historical commentary. The vernaculars play against it and against each other – English the language of the invader, the coloniser, the realm; Welsh the language of the early inhabitants, colonised, preserved. All three tongues are contemporary, all three representative of historical processes, held in a kind of creative tension, the vernacular as important in the sixteenth century as it had been in the ninth. No mere counterpart of Latin, it could be asserted as a precursor and at times even the origin of the language of the Romans: "each name a kind of talisman unearthed."

Dialogue in Hell between Two Readers II

WS: Has this author become too fond of the ellipsis?

RF: Yes, but perhaps some sense can be made. Looking back over the *disiecta membra* of the past three chapters, the common ground appears to be *mutatio*. Or in other words the fact that the ancient spatial order was never jettisoned. It was preserved, explicated, added to, but it continued to form the basis of geographical thinking into the fifteenth century and beyond. *Mutatio* is the textual problem that arises from trying to reconcile the space of the past with the space of the present.

WS: And the "medieval" response, if one can call it that, is to mix these two spaces, while being conscious of the differences between them. While the humanist response is to separate the two, attempting to clarify and purify the ancient order, thereby creating a more homogenous space for modernity?

RF: Obviously it wasn't always so neat, and it wasn't the case that the chronologically mixed non-humanist mode of accommodating *mutatio* vanished as soon as Petrarch began holding forth. On the contrary, it took at least a century and a half for humanist practices – the *tabula antiqua* sitting opposite the *tabula moderna* – to become the norm, helped by the discoveries in the New World for which no classical nomenclature existed.

WS: I can see that the vernacular is part of the story of *mutatio*, because while the ancient language with its toponyms and its way of describing space is preserved, vernacular languages emerge and gain credibility of their own as agents of spatial representation, sometimes in competition with, sometimes as a complement to, Latin. What has mutated is, at a fundamental level, language, and hence space, since it is primarily through language that space is represented. But as for the Israelites, St Maurice, nation – how do you make sense of those scattered limbs?

RF: There is an obvious connection between Exodus and the topic of nation. The Israelites are in biblical terms the original nation, and a significant part of their identity derives from the narrative of exile, flight, and journey to the promised land. (It could be argued that this picks up the thread of Aeneas and the Trojans from Chapter 3). Medieval nations are peoples not places, but increasingly peoples that require some form of spatial definition, a "where" that informs who they are – and who they were. Saints too give meaning to space, in ways that – like a river – can cut across regional or proto-national boundaries, or that can be co-opted to serve dynastic, imperial, and ultimately nationalist narratives.

WS: Hence St Maurice, the Thebans, and the Rhone. But I wonder whether it is possible to take this analysis a bit further. There is an Ortelius map that the author hasn't considered in any depth: the travels of St Paul. This map, which also appeared in the *Parergon*, and which was a bit of a favourite among sixteenth-century historical cartographers, is in its way as much a fiction as the "Image of the Roman Empire." It shows the places to which Paul travelled, based on the narrative contained in the Acts of the Apostles. However contrived, might it tell us something about the new space that Christianity constructs? Paul's world is, in one sense, the old Roman world, with its great cities (Tarsus, Antioch, Ephesus, Corinth, Thessalonica, Caesarea, Jerusalem, and Rome itself) and provinces (Cilicia, Lycaonia, Pamphylia, Syria, Macedonia, Judaea), but he transforms it into the space of the nascent church. He, the believer, the convert, the founder – Jew, Christian, Roman – is the mobile centre of a network of places, preaching, fleeing, cajoling, and correcting them into some form of unity. The final books of the New Testament seem to obey a spatio-temporal sequence. The time of expansion (Acts, especially if we include apocrypha), with the embrace of the extent of the known world; the time of foundation and consolidation (Epistles), in which the regional identity of the church is established; the time of temporal and spatial dissolution (Apocalypse). Spatial definition is crucial for Christianity but so is mobility, its peripatetic urge never contained within the realm of believers, its republic of letter writers and readers.

Among the most prodigious of those writers and readers was Jerome. Thinking about these questions, what sense can we make of Eusebius's *Onomasticon*, and Jerome's translation of it, the *Liber de locis*? These works can be read in terms of dislocation, of the movement from a secular spatial order to a Christian one, a movement that necessarily takes place across languages, and that hence invites error, correction, and error-within-correction. But they could also be read in terms of location, in which the co-ordinates by which places are given identity are historical and linguistic rather than mathematical. Just as Ptolemy's co-ordinates enable his readers, to a greater or lesser degree, to construct maps, so Eusebius and Jerome give textual coherence to a space, organise it alphabetically, and enable it to be reproduced, albeit not necessarily in map form. So the emphasis on dislocation should not distract attention from the conscious – and effective – ordering of space.

RF: Granted, but all orderings invite correction and supplementation. One example is the remarkable pair of maps found at the conclusion of a manuscript, made in Tournai in the twelfth century, right after the text of Jerome's *Liber de locis*. The first is a map of Asia and the eastern Mediterranean; on its verso is a map of Palestine, which in fact extends as far as Egypt and India, and which includes a reference to St Maurice.[1] For some time wrongly attributed to Jerome himself, these images are almost certainly copies of maps produced in late antiquity. Their purpose is not exactly, or not primarily, illustrative. They do not always correspond in particular detail to Jerome's texts, and one could only incompletely and with difficulty refer to the maps while consulting the *Liber de locis*. Rather the logic is that of compilation and juxtaposition: a visual representation of Asia and the Holy Land alongside a verbal ordering of the places of scripture. Whether as map or list, the Roman world is foundational only to the extent that it is remade.

WS: So again we return to an idea of order that must be flexible enough to encompass the representation of non-Christian history as the condition of possibility for Christianity. Not only that. This ordering of the world – the descriptions of Orosius, Isidore, and the copying and adaptation of Pliny and Solinus, to name only the most obvious – had to allow for, or be made to allow for, the secular impulses which established new polities, those *gentes* becoming gradually but not necessarily nations. It had to absorb and adapt to the mutation of the world image caused by new languages, to allow passage between vulgar and not so vulgar tongues. You can choose to see this world order swelling and bursting, to be replaced by the mathematical map of modernity; or you might instead perceive the replacement of one order with its roots in antiquity by another (Ptolemaic) order of similar vintage. Either way, beyond a certain point medieval world images come to signify a discarded order.

RF: Yet discards not only survive, they sometimes enjoy a curious vitality. In certain hands they can even acquire a numinous force.

---

1. BL, MS Additional 10049, fols. 64r, 64v.

CHAPTER EIGHT

Opicinus Dada

In 1334 a papal scribe in the city of Avignon suffered a severe mental and physical breakdown. The man was nearly 40. He had been born in the north Italian town of Lomello, near Pavia, where in the 1320s he became a parish priest. In 1328 he left Pavia, apparently forced into exile by persistent warfare between partisans of the pope and supporters of the Holy Roman emperor. In Avignon, seat of the papacy since 1309, he found favour and employment, assisted by his authorship of a tract advocating the pre-eminence of papal rule over the temporal power of the emperor. But in 1334 something dramatic happened to the scribe: he believed himself to be near death, he lost his memory, and he endured visionary dreams and a series of "temptations."

The next year "the heavens opened" for Opicinus de Canistris. God permitted him to understand "misteria."[1] The nature of these mysteries was profound: they concerned the relationship between time and space, flesh and the soul, between the Church and the world, Christ and Christians, sin, salvation, and divine judgement. More unusually, his "conversion" allowed Opicinus to "discern images of Africa, Europe and the sea."[2] Illness affected his ability to write, but he found that he could draw. For the next three years he filled "almost innumerable leaves of parchment – both big ones of larger format and small pieces of lesser dimension – with different kinds of images and circles about the world and other figures of mystery."[3] In 1337 Opicinus composed a kind of treatise, designed in part to accompany and to explain his remarkable and persistent visions. He continued to annotate this treatise throughout 1338, and as late as

---

1. Muriel Laharie, ed. and trans., *Le journal singulier d'Opicinus de Canistris (1337–vers 1341): Vaticanus latinus 6435*, 2 vols (Vatican City, 2008), 2: 896 (fol. 85v).

2. *Vaticanus latinus 6435*, ed. Laharie, 2: 780 (fol. 75v): "Dominus aperire mihi dignatus est intellectum preuia ratione paulatim ad discernendas ymagines Affrice, Europe et maris."

3. *Vaticanus latinus 6435*, ed. Laharie, 2: 522 (fol. 53r): "Per hos tres annos continuos multa et quasi innumerabilia folia cartarum – tam magna maioris forme quam parua minoris peciole – diuersis et uariis modis ymaginum et rotarum super descriptione orbis terrarum et aliarum figurarum misterii in tanta uarietate experientie cuiuscumque ... ."

1341, after which, apart from two leaves (the latest from 1350), he seems to have ceased work on these unclassifiable texts.

Opicinus's account of his illness and its aftermath can be found in two manuscripts and one fragment, all of which came to light in the twentieth century.[4] These manuscripts, which are written in his own hand, preserve a series of images, accompanied by Opicinus's extensive commentary. The recurring image was at base a sea chart, which depicted the coastlines of Europe, North Africa, and Asia Minor with some precision.[5] In the hands of Opicinus, however, this was no ordinary map. Europe and Africa took on human form, along with an assortment of companions. The Mediterranean could become a bearded man, associated with the devil, with the Adriatic as his right arm; in the Atlantic, the leonine head of the *Tarasconus*, a mythical beast of the Rhone defeated by St Martha, might appear gnawing on Europe's shoulders. Gender could be switched. In one manuscript (Palatinus latinus 1993) anthropomorphized Europe is consistently male and Africa female. In the other (Vaticanus latinus 6435) no fixed pattern emerges: the two appear as male or female depending on the requirements of allegory. The geo-body of Europe was most evolved in Opicinus's thought: Spain the head, Gaul the chest, Lombardy the stomach "as far as the loins," Italy the right leg, the Balkans the left, Venice the testicles or vulva. Sometimes naked, sometimes clothed, Europe and Africa were depicted in states of social and occasionally sexual intimacy, and in a variety of relations to their monstrous intermediaries.

4. The two manuscripts are Vatican City, Biblioteca Apostolica Vaticana, MSS Palatinus latinus 1993 and Vaticanus latinus 6435. For the former see Richard Salomon, *Opicinus de Canistris: Weltbild und Bekenntnisse eines avignonesischen Klerikers des 14. Jahrhunderts*, 2 vols (London, 1936). Vaticanus latinus 6435 has been transcribed and translated by Laharie, *Le journal singulier d'Opicinus de Canistris*. The fragment is Vatican City, Biblioteca Apostolica Vaticana, MS Barberinianum lat. 2999: for reproduction, transcription, and commentary see Michele Feo, "La 'peciola' ritrovata (*fragmentum Barberinianum Lat.* 2999)," in *Omaggio ad Augusto Campana*, ed. Cino Pedrelli (Cesena, 2003), 222–348.

5. The chart used by Opicinus has not been conclusively identified and it may not be possible to do so. One of his comments (Vaticanus latinus MS 6435, fol. 59r) indicates that at Avignon he had access to both Genovese and Majorcan *mappae maris*, and the appearance of parts of Scandinavia on some of his images suggests that he used more than one model; the charts of Pietro Vesconte and Angelino Dulceti have been advanced as possible candidates. Still less can be said about the models for Opicinus's regional map of Lombardy and his city plan of Pavia, both of which he may have brought with him to Avignon. See Roberto Almagià, *Monumenta Cartographica Vaticana*, 4 vols (Vatican City, 1944–55), 1: 97–98.

With Europe and Africa his key terms, Opicinus developed an array of original allegories.[6] Some of these figurations follow the pattern of Europe as virtue and Africa as sin, but others are more complex, and several escape any easy assignation of meaning. The two *partes* appear, variously, as Adam (Europe) and Eve (Africa), faith and infidelity, Christianity and Babylon, the universal church and Judas, the priestly community and lay pride, Boethius and the muse of poetry.[7] As these identities suggest, Opicinus used Europe and Africa to dramatize different facets of Christian institutional and spiritual life. They appear as the sacramental and material church, "caritas dei in universo" and "caritas universalis in deum," the spiritual and servile church, as St Thomas and Martha, apostolic church and synagogue, prostration of the lord's temple and Opicinus himself.[8] The writing that surrounds, glosses, and informs Opicinus's images articulates these and many other significations. But the radicalism of Opicinus did not stop at allegory. A significant proportion of the images contain a further twist: onto the map of the world, Opicinus superimposed another image, sometimes a regional map of Lombardy, sometimes a map of the city of Pavia, very occasionally a map of the Holy Land. In certain instances Opicinus even superimposed one or more copies of the entire map on itself. Naturally, the intermingling of these distinct spatial orders – civic, regional, and ecumenical – allied to a specular logic expressed in the repeated mirroring of images, could not but reveal certain mystical alignments. For Opicinus "every locality assumes doubleness of position and meaning,"[9] and sometimes more than doubleness. That capacity to superimpose spaces of different magnitudes and to view them through each other gave rise to a contingent geography in which the human body is the mediating term. The conjunctions that arise are playful, potentially shocking, but also redolent with meaning: "if the vulva of Ocean [Gibraltar] was in the minor world [i.e. if the world map were superimposed on the map of Lombardy]," Opicinus observed, "it is Cuneo in Piedmont, and England is Biella del Canavese. If the vulva of Ocean was in Pavia it is the Pertusi gate, and England is the Marenca gate, or thereabouts."[10]

6. On Opicinus's use of allegory and allegoresis see Karl Whittington, *Body-Worlds: Opicinus de Canistris and the Medieval Cartographic Imagination* (Toronto, 2014), 61–101; Jörg-Geerd Arentzen, *Imago Mundi Cartographica: Studien zur Bildlichkeit mittelalterlicher Welt- und Ökumenekarten unter besonderer Berücksichtigung des Zusammenwirkens von Text und Bild* (Munich, 1984), 310–18.

7. Respectively, Palatinus latinus MS 1993, fol. 2r; Vaticanus latinus MS 6435, fols. 73v, 74v, 76v, 87v, 71v.

8. Respectively, Vaticanus latinus MS 6435, fols. 54r, 61v, 69v, 71r, 76v, 79v.

9. Pierluigi Tozzi, *La città e il mondo in Opicino de Canistris (1296–1350 ca.)* (Varzi, 1996), 74.

10. *Vaticanus latinus 6435*, ed. Laharie, 2: 826 (fol. 79v): "Si uulua occeani fuerit in minori mundo, est cunium Pedemontium et Anglia est bugella Canapitii. Si uulva occeani fuerit in Papia, est porta Pertusi, et Anglia est porta Marenca uel circa." Tozzi, *La città e il mondo*, 74, 80.

Such conjunctions and superimpositions were not restricted to the generation of meaning at local or regional level. On several occasions Opicinus's images make use of zonal maps, showing the world from pole to pole. Two zones in particular captured his interest: the temperate zone of the northern hemisphere (containing the known world of Europe, Africa, and Asia), and the central, torrid zone, which he associated with inextinguishable hellfire.[11] One image shows Opicinus himself lying on the length of this central zone, apparently figuring his damnation "had the Lord not struck me" (*Nisi me Dominus percussisset*). From his belly, which is at the same time the centre of the torrid zone, runs a line labelled "Pugio Phinees," a reference to the dagger used by the zealous Phinees to transfix two fornicating Israelites during the flight from Egypt, thereby appeasing God's wrath.[12] The meaning of the image seems to be that God's striking of the sinning body of Opicinus replicates the blow of Phinees and portends both personal and a more universal salvation. Here and elsewhere the movement from world to region to city to body allows for multiple alignments, whose meaning was never purely spatial. Topography, ultimate sign of the world and of sin, was at the core of Opicinus's visions, but it was not the sole purpose or destination. "Hoc dico non locis sed moribus," he was fond of saying: I speak not about the places themselves but about their moral significance. Knowledge of the world without knowledge of its mystical meaning was vain, empty.[13]

There is no record of any medieval reception of Opicinus's visions, except his own note that at the surprise visit of a "simple priest from Lombardy" he was forced to cover one of his maps quickly, lest the sight of a naked female belly shock his guest.[14] A note from the late sixteenth century concerning one of the manuscripts reveals incomprehension of the meaning of its contents though, perhaps, appreciation of their mystical nature.[15] It was only from the first half of the twentieth century that the manuscripts received scholarly attention, first as an example of the *Weltbild* of a remarkable individual, though one ultimately a prod-

11. Palatinus latinus MS 1993, fols. 9r; 9v; 13r; 17r; Salomon, *Opicinus*, 196; Victoria Morse, "A Complex Terrain: Church, Society, and the Individual in the Works of Opicino de Canistris (1296–ca. 1354)" (PhD diss., University of California, Berkeley, 1996), 237–54.

12. Numbers 25:7–8, where it is specified that the two are transfixed "in locis genitalibus." The image appears on the fragment Barberinianum lat. MS 2999, fol. 108r; Feo, "La 'peciola' ritrovata," 272–73, 319–21.

13. E.g. Vaticanus latinus MS 6435, fols. 2v, 3r, 5r, 7v, 30v, 32v, 38r, 43v, etc.

14. *Vaticanus latinus 6435*, ed. Laharie, 2: 912 (fol. 87r): "Hora qua hoc agebatur, necesse habui operire quodam folio papiri uentrem mulieris propter superuentionem Lombardi presbiteri simplicis, ne scandalizaretur ob hoc."

15. Archivio Segr. Vaticano, Indice 146, fol. 52r: "Liber plenus variis figuris, quae vix intelligi possunt, pertinent vero ad civitatem Papiensem et ad alias partes ecclesiae cum multis misteriis"; citation from Almagià, *Monumenta Cartographica Vaticana*, 1: 96.

uct of his time;[16] then as evidence of a psychotic and probably schizoid personality.[17] Over the last two decades the view of Opicinus as psychotic – while still attracting advocates – has been opposed by attempts to locate him within the traditions of medieval piety. Such readings draw attention variously to his particular urban experience, his powerful sense of self-recrimination, his vision of the universal Church,[18] and the daring, experimental qualities of his artistry.[19] Most recently, a subtle analysis has understood Opicinus as a symptom at once of the political, religious, and cultural upheaval of north Italy in the early fourteenth century, and of the tensions resident in the institutionalisation of Christian belief and practice.[20] The following pages draw on several of these studies, but they do not seek to explain Opicinus, or to reach firm conclusions about his work. They certainly make no attempt to diagnose him. They try instead to follow the movement between different spaces generated by his supple superimpositions, and to understand the nature of the geographic "vision" that emerged from such manipulation of spatial order. They also seek to hold his surprising oeuvre in apposition to the emergence of a radical artistic movement of the twentieth century and, at the same time, to the superimpositions of space in the

16. Salomon, *Opicinus*. The discovery of Vaticanus latinus MS 6435, and the work of Ernst Kris, led Salomon significantly to revise his view of Opicinus, now emphasising his "psychical crisis" and the "monotonous variation of themes" across the two manuscripts: "A Newly Discovered Manuscript of Opicinus de Canistris," *Journal of the Warburg and Courtauld Institutes* 16 (1953): 45–59; "Aftermath to Opicinus de Canistris," *Journal of the Warburg and Courtauld Institutes* 25 (1962): 137–46.

17. Ernst Kris, "A Psychotic Artist of the Middle Ages," in *Psychoanalytic Explorations in Art* (London, 1953), 118–27; Guy Roux and Muriel Laharie, *Art et folie au Moyen Âge: Aventures et énigmes d'Opicinus de Canistris (1296–vers 1351)* (Paris, 1997). Laharie and Roux's conviction that Opicinus suffered from a psychotic condition ("paraphrenia"), marked by "the prevalence of the imagination" and megalomania, is restated in the introduction to Laharie's edition of Vaticanus latinus MS 6435; it heavily influences her translation at a number of points.

18. Morse, "A Complex Terrain"; Victoria Morse, "Seeing and Believing: The Problem of Idolatry in the Thought of Opicino de Canistris," in *Orthodoxie, christianisme, histoire*, ed. Susanna Elm, Éric Rebillard, and Antonella Romano (Rome, 2000), 163–76; Catherine Harding, "Opening to God: The Cosmographical Diagrams of Opicinus de Canistris," *Zeitschrift für Kunstgeschichte* 61 (1998): 18–39; Tozzi, *La città e il mondo*; Feo, "La 'peciola' ritrovata"; Michele Feo, "Il nome di Opizzino," in *Margarita amicorum: Studi di cultura europea per Agostino Sottili*, ed. Fabio Forner et al., 2 vols (Milan, 2005), 1: 255–79.

19. Whittington, *Body-Worlds*; Karl Whittington, "Experimenting with Opicinus de Canistris (1296–ca.1354)," *Gesta* 51 (2012): 147–73; Karl Whittington, "Queer," *Studies in Iconography* 33 (2012): 157–68.

20. Sylvain Piron, *Dialectique du monstre: Enquête sur Opicino de Canistris* (Brussels, 2015).

thought of his most famous contemporary, Francis Petrarch. Again, the objective is not to use Petrarch and twentieth-century art to understand Opicinus, but to use all three better to understand the representation of spatial dislocation.

Non locis sed moribus

What is the effect of superimposition in the oeuvre of Opicinus? What did he see in the alignment of city, region, and world? In three of Opicinus's images, which appear on successive pages in Vaticanus latinus MS 6435, a plan of Pavia, divided into 80 squares, overlies his base map, with its anthropomorphized Europe and Africa.[21] The conflated presence of city and world allows Opicinus to distinguish between the parts of Pavia that fall within Europe and Africa as "European Pavia" and "African Pavia," and to locate his own experience therein. Across the three images the correspondences shift, but the overriding theme is of Pavia's corruption through its adherence to the Empire rather than the papacy, as well as its abandonment to the "sign of the florin." From the second decade of the fourteenth century, the city had come increasingly under the control of the Milanese Visconti family and their pro-imperial ("Ghibelline") allies. Pavia received the troops of the emperor-elect Louis of Bavaria in 1327; in that year the city was placed under papal interdict, having suffered the same fate ten years previously.[22] Against this frequently-invoked backdrop of capitulation to outside forces, certain key reference points emerge on Opicinus's maps to construct a narrative of personal, if not urban, redemption. Santa Tecla, the parish of the Canister family in the western part of the old city of Pavia,[23] appears in the first image (fol. 84r) on the left shoulder of Europe, in danger of being devoured by the monster of the Atlantic; in the next (fol. 84v), marked by the designs of a basket, Santa Tecla aligns with Pavia on the map of Europe and figures "the broken basket for collecting the dung of the sea."[24] On the third in the series Santa Tecla now aligns with Avignon between the breasts of Europe (the "parrochia" of Pavia meeting the "province/Provence of the Pope"); the parish is surmounted by a haloed figure which represents the servant faithful to the name of Jesus Christ and the

21. Vaticanus latinus MS 6435, fols. 84r, 84v, 85r.

22. Piron, *Dialectique du monstre*, 60–61; John Law, "The Italian North," in *The New Cambridge Medieval History*, vol. 6: *c. 1300–1415*, ed. Michael Jones (Cambridge, 2000), 442–68, at 449.

23. Morse, "A Complex Terrain," 56.

24. *Vaticanus latinus 6435*, ed. Laharie, 2: 886 (fol. 84v): "de canistro rupto ad colligenda stercora maris."

Christian people (Figure 28).[25] Similarly Santa Maria Capella, where Opicinus served as a parish priest before his exile from Pavia, appears in all three images. It dominates "African" (southern) Pavia, nearly aligning with Hippo (and hence the memory of St Augustine), but is disfigured by a serpent representing the crooked path of usury.[26] On the final map, Santa Maria Capella contains the figure of Christ on the cross, though the serpent of usury still runs through the parish. Like the serpent, the quarter of Pavia called "Moneta" (the Mint) figures the city's spiritual and carnal depravity. On the first map this district aligns with Pavia itself ("behold the Pavian whore has in its belly a quarter called Moneta"), while on the third the sign of the florin marks Moneta in order to represent Florence, "the one who deflowers this flowering virgin."[27] The first image, Opicinus explains, represents Pavia not as a carnal whore, but as a spiritual adulterer, copulating with a foreign seducer (the emperor), like a parish that hears a preacher from outside rather than its own *rector*.[28] The second shows the Pavia which is governed by progeny of the meat-market, called "Becarie" in the vernacular – entirely carnal, it has no part of the universal Church.[29] The third, an image structured by the alignment of the crucified Christ and the loyal Christian servant, the parishes of Santa Maria Capella and Santa Tecla, and the two breasts of St Agatha, reveals that little Pavia contains the whole world in itself, as the womb of a woman contains an entire child.[30]

Among the many remarkable inscriptions that surround and inform these maps, one stands out for its alignment of the life of Opicinus, the office of the papacy and the popes themselves, the human body, and the spaces of the city and the world. In a text added on November 4, 1337, "on the birthday of my grandmother who died from a cancerous illness in her breast in the time of Pope Clement V," Opicinus chronicles his life in terms of the popes who have reigned since his youth, and their birthplaces.[31] When Benedict XI (1303–4), born in

25. *Vaticanus latinus 6435*, ed. Laharie, 2: 890 (fol. 85r).

26. *Vaticanus latinus 6435*, ed. Laharie, 2: 876 (fol. 84r): "Hec uia a manu Cartaginis deorsum exercet usurariam prauitatem"; elsewhere in the manuscript the figure represents the "worm of conscience": 2: 610–11 (fol. 61r): "uermis conscientie qui a pectore Affrice carnalibus pascebatur occulte."

27. *Vaticanus latinus 6435*, ed. Laharie, 2: 874 (fol. 84r): "Ecce meretrix Papiensis habet in uentre uicum qui dicitur Moneta"; 2: 890 (fol. 85r): "illud signum Florentie, iam iudicatus est huius uirginis floride deflorator."

28. *Vaticanus latinus 6435*, ed. Laharie, 2: 876 (fol. 84r).

29. *Vaticanus latinus 6435*, ed. Laharie, 2: 886 (fol. 84v). The Beccaria family dominated Pavian political life for much of the first half of the fourteenth century. Aligned with the Visconti and the emperor, they provided an obvious target for Opicinus's condemnation.

30. *Vaticanus latinus 6435*, ed. Laharie, 2: 892 (fol. 85r).

31. *Vaticanus latinus 6435*, ed. Laharie, 2: 892 (fol. 85r): "in anniuersario aue mee que ex morbo cancerino in mamilla decessit tempore Clementis pape V."

Treviso "next to the genitals of Europe" (i.e. Venice), was pope, Opicinus was a boy, who lived among women. In the time of Clement V (1305–14), born in the "Gascon neck," he was nearing maturity (*adolescens*) and submitted his own neck to the yoke of his parents. When John XXII (1316–34), born in the left breast of Europe (Cahors), became pope, Opicinus was a young man who flew from one breast to the other, a reference to his emigration from Pavia to Avignon. Now, in the time of Benedict XII (1334–42), who hails from the right breast of Europe (Saverdun, near Toulouse), Opicinus is a *senior* who has lost the breasts of his carnal mother.[32]

The correspondences established by Opicinus are at times witty, at times portentous, and at others opaque. He was a relentless punner, alert to word play not only in Latin but also in the various local dialects with which he was familiar. On one map the toponym "Medie Barbe" identifies the *cittadino* of the Mezzabarba in Pavia, and is located halfway along the beard of the diabolic sea-man;[33] the reference to baskets around Santa Tecla is a play on the Canister family name (*canistrum*, basket).[34] Etymologies served to confirm his somatic reading of space: Genoa (*Ianua*/gates), Francia (*frank*/free), Pavia (*Papa*/pope – that is, the "true" Pavia, a daughter of the pope, rather than his adversary, the Pavia of Opicinus's day),[35] Lombardy (*lumbi*/loins), and Tunisia (*Tunicium*/tunic) were all toponyms that could be invested with particular meaning.

But if we are encouraged to read the city as world, on top of world, are we also invited to do the reverse: to read Europe and Africa as urban space, set within the frame of Pavia? Some of Opicinus's comments suggest that Pavian space already carries with it habitual or customary traces of other places. "I remember," he notes alongside one map, "that when I was growing I was at the Thessalonica of Pavia and in my artlessness I composed vernacular poems about the works of Antichrist."[36] Opicinus has indeed marked "Thessalonica" in red, in its correct

---

32. *Vaticanus latinus 6435*, ed. Laharie, 2: 892 (fol. 85r).

33. *Vaticanus latinus 6435*, ed. Laharie, 2: 886 (fol. 84v); Tozzi, *La città e il mondo*, 80.

34. Morse, "A Complex Terrain," 47, 56–57. Piron suggests that the Canister family emblem might have been a coiled viper, in the form of a basket: *Dialectique du monstre*, 55; also Feo, "La 'peciola' ritrovata," 330.

35. Salomon, *Opicinus*, 230; see too the etymologies Opicinus gave for Pavia (*Papia*) in his description of the city, published as *Anonymi ticinensis liber de laudibus civitatis ticinensis*, ed. R. Maiocchi and F. Quintavalle, Rerum Italicarum Scriptores 11.1 (Città di Castello, 1903), 50–51. On etymologies in Opicinus generally see Piron, *Dialectique du monstre*, 131–32.

36. *Vaticanus latinus 6435*, ed. Laharie, 2: 878 (fol. 84r): "Recolo me adolescentem commorantem Thessalonice Papiensi ex simplicitate mea fecisse rithimos uulgares de operibus Antichristi."

place on the map of Europe, but it seems likely that this toponym also describes an area well known to Pavesi in the central-eastern corner of the city, and also called by the name of "Thessalonica."[37] The layers multiply, invert: Thessalonica is within the city, a part of local knowledge, but also without, in its formal geographical position. Opicinus's vision of Pavia-in-the-world invokes his memories of the city, but he represents it as a sign of human corruption, rather than affection or even *campanilismo*: it has been taken over by imperial, anti-papal forces, and as a result now falls outside the universal church. Moving rapidly from urban to world space, Opicinus asserts that the cardinal virtues associated with the city walls (and marked, accordingly, on his maps) now lie beyond the Lombard region: "behold the virtue of Temperance in the torrid zone at the back of Africa; Fortitude in Egyptian Alexandria; Justice in Paris, France; and Prudence in the island of Ponza facing Rome."[38] This is ostensibly a comment on the depravity of the city, but the logic of the image argues for an understanding of Pavia as equivalent to the sinning world. Opicinus himself is the exemplum of this simultaneity of space: an exile, writing from outside the city walls, his past ("my parish") and his name (canister, the basket) are figured within. The dynamism of the image of Pavia-as-world/world-as-Pavia lies in the constant movement and interaction between the two concepts.

In Opicinus's superimposition of regional, rather than urban, space on the world it is the river system of Lombardy that provides structure, instead of the city grid. The relationship between the two spaces is subtly different. In the absence of the grid, which had the effect of clearly demarcating the space of the intramural city, the regional and world schemes of spatial description interpenetrate each other much more profoundly: the rivers disfigure the world map, threatening to be read within its scheme, and unexpected juxtapositions abound (Figure 29).[39] In these images Venice typically appears twice: once in the world space, once in the map of Lombardy. World Venice coincides with regional Pavia, confirming their shared identity as the "vulva Europae." On the most detailed of Opicinus's regional/world superimpositions, the Tyrrhenian Sea irrigates the Maghreb.[40] In the area of the Holy Land, Antioch and Jerusalem are located in the vicinity of Lombardy.[41] This is clearly no accident. Maps and certain inscriptions in Palat-

---

37. Tozzi, *La città e il mondo*, 81.

38. *Vaticanus latinus 6435*, ed. Laharie, 2: 886 (fol. 84v): "Ecce uirtus Temperantie in torrida plaga a tergo Affrice, Fortitudo in Alexandria Egypti, Iustitia in Parisius Francie et Prudentia in insula Poncia ante Romam."

39. The superimposition of regional and world spaces occurs in both of Opicinus's manuscripts: Palatinus latinus MS 1993, fols. 2r, 4v, 8v, 10v, 18r; Vaticanus latinus MS 6435, fols. 71r, 76v, 87v.

40. Palatinus latinus MS 1993, fol. 4v.

41. E.g. Vaticanus latinus MS 6435, fol. 87v; Palatinus latinus MS 1993, fol. 4v.

inus latinus MS 1993 make clear Opicinus's equation of northern Italy with Judaea, with the imputation that if Lombardy has corrupted the entire world, then redemption of this region and the world is possible.[42] Following a logic that delights in spiritual, moral, and topographic congruence, the rivers Ticino and Po are equated with the sources of the Jordan river, and the Agogna – a stream that runs between the rivers, and on which is situated Opicinus's birth place, Lomello – is the "agonia" of birth, whose product (a blind lion-cub, which will transform into a man) will turn the "wandering whore" into a chaste woman.[43] So even as Lombardy is superimposed on the entire Mediterranean basin, the area surrounding the Holy Land is superimposed on Lombardy.[44] Nevertheless, Opicinus's goal was surely not the confusion of two spaces, but the exposition of their immanent correspondences. Here, as in his representations of Pavia-on-world, the use of different coloured inks for the toponyms (typically red for one set of toponyms and brown for another) reveals Opicinus's desire at once to distinguish and to overlay two spatial entities.

Perhaps Opicinus's greatest challenge to conventional geographical readings, however, was to superimpose the three *partes mundi* on each other. In these images Opicinus took his standard map of Europe, Africa, and Asia Minor and overlaid a copy of the same map, reversed, so that each of the three *partes* appears twice, intersecting with the reverse image in curious ways. The techniques of doubling and reversing seem to celebrate rather than undermine the logic of continental division. The idea of the discrete *pars mundi* is not disputed, nor its integrity – but it is given another way of meaning. Again, the correspondences revealed by the map carry significances at once etymological, political, and eschatological. On one folio of the Vaticanus manuscript (fol. 77r) there are two depictions of Europe and Africa (Figure 1). One, coloured red, represents the couple as an allegory of the "damnation of the seducer and the seduced" (*dampnatio seductricis et seducte*); the other shows Europe as the "church free of the seducer" (*ecclesia libera a seductore*) next to the seducer, in the form of a bearded monk. The dialectic that underlies the page is the contrast between old and new man, the seducing flesh and the unseduced spirit. A note records the dislocated geography of the superimposed maps: the island of Cyprus appears next to France,

42. Palatinus latinus MS 1993, fols. 2r, 4v, 8v, 18r; Salomon, *Opicinus*, 63–65; see Piron, *Dialectique du monstre*, 132–34.

43. Palatinus latinus MS 1993, fol. 2r; Salomon, *Opicinus*, 159: "Habens itaque agoniam parturientis intra ventrem pregnantem intra Ior Padi et Dan Ticini." The connection is actualised on the map on fol. 4v: "fluvius Padus in Ior"; "fluvius Ticinus in Dan". The blind lion-cub is elsewhere explained as the heathen world that will attain illumination through baptism: Salomon, *Opicinus*, 193.

44. Cf. Vaticanus latinus MS 6435, fol. 54r.

Rhodes in the Rhone, Crete in the belly of Pavia according to the Cretan prophet,[45] Achaia next to Rome, Sicily near Hungary, the remaining two islands of the papal patrimony (Sardinia and Corsica) not far from the "fork" of Corinth ... both Britains possess the Holy Land, because they abound in ecclesiastical incomes more than others.[46] In visual articulation of Opicinus's theorising about the roles of north Italian cities, Pavia is represented as the female womb (*matrix feminea*), and Milan the virile rod in the stomach of the woman. Venice, meanwhile, is associated with the testicles and the vulva at one and the same time. The "revolutio" (revolution) of the body of Europe reveals the "illusions of the loins, that is of the Lombards, who were converted into the seed of the infidel pomegranate/of Granada, disfiguring the jaw": disloyal to the pope, infidel Lombardy finds itself in Spain, aligned with Muslim Granada.[47] Just as male and female can be superimposed, so can the *partes mundi*. The world can be doubled, quadrupled, north placed over south and south over north. It can be reduced to the size of a city, or a region, and the city or region expanded to fill the world. Place, in the thought of Opicinus, is never singular.

Given this multiplicity of spatial meaning in his visions, it is perhaps not surprising that, of all classical authors, Opicinus turned to Lucan. On what is now the final page in Vaticanus latinus 6435, Christian and pre-Christian history align in a way unprecedented in Opicinus's previous schema, for the image is, in part, a map of the *Bellum civile* (Figure 30). No other classical work of literature makes such a contribution to an image in one of Opicinus's manuscripts.[48] In the map, Caesar appears as Africa, representing lay arrogance and whispering into the ear of a Europe tonsured, but labelled "corona caesarea" (imperial crown): this, it seems, is the "universitas sacerdotalis" (priestly community), a figure elsewhere

45. Opicinus presumably refers here to Paul's letter to Titus 1:12, which contains the famous words of a prophet that Cretans are "always liars, evil beasts, lazy bellies (*ventri pigri*)." The prophet's remark is previously given by Opicinus (on Vaticanus latinus 6435, fol. 79v), following remarks about Crete, Venice, and St Mark's testicles: see Feo, "Il nome di Opizzino," 276–77.

46. *Vaticanus latinus 6435*, ed. Laharie, 2: 794 (fol. 77r).

47. *Vaticanus latinus 6435*, ed. Laharie, 2: 808 (fol. 78r): "Ecce quod reuolutio corporis Europe patitur in dextra maxilla illusiones lumborum, id est Lombardorum qui conuersi sunt in semen infidelis granate deturpantis maxillam." See Whittington, *Body-Worlds*, 157–67 for discussion of this page. The remark about the "seed/semen of the infidel" appears to explain the appearance of an enormous ejaculating phallus off the coast of Spain in certain images in the Vaticanus manuscript (fols. 53v, 68v, 69v, 84r, 84v, 87v).

48. Papal Avignon appears to have been relatively well endowed with copies of Lucan: see Birger Munk Olsen, "L'étude des classiques à Avignon au XIVe siècle," in *Avignon and Naples: Italy in France-France in Italy in the Fourteenth Century*, ed. Marianne Pade et al. (Rome, 1997), 13–25.

aligned with Opicinus himself,[49] and one which has the true authority (*imperium*) over souls. Pompey is the sea monster of the Mediterranean, and a punning figuration of "clerical pomp" (*Pompeius id est pompositas clericalis*).[50] Satan, states one of the notes surrounding the image, places discord between persons once close to each other. So he did with Caesar and Pompey. Once Caesar had obtained the body of Europe "as far as its loins" (i.e. Gaul), he "invaded the right leg down to the tibia" (i.e. Italy to the Tiber), and then to the "right heel" (Brundisium) before returning to Europe's chest and throat (the campaigns in Gaul and Spain). When the battles beneath the left heel (Pharsalia) were over, he covered Pompey's head beneath Europe's feet in Pharaonic Africa (Egypt).[51] The narrative of the Civil War informs the geo-body of Europe, and it is clear that the narrative Opicinus has in mind is Lucan's. The toponyms in brown correspond in significant part to those places particularly emphasised in the *Bellum civile*: Ariminum, Brundisium, Massilia, Ilerda, and of course Thessalia. To these Opicinus has added places of Christian importance that do not appear in Lucan's poem: Antioch, Ephesus, and Jerusalem, as well as Noah's ark.

There is some irony in the fact that Opicinus created, perhaps for the first time, something no surviving manuscript of Lucan's *Bellum civile* has yet been found to possess: a map showing key sites of the Civil War. This map, in no way intended as an aid for reading Lucan, is instead directed towards allegorical ends. We are invited to read Europe as priesthood in its pure form, beset by the vices of arrogance and material display from both the lay (Caesar-Africa) and clerical (head of Pompey-sea monster) worlds. Onto these significations Opicinus imposes the now familiar regional map of Lombardy, the second "image of struggle," we are told, and one related to the imminent second coming of Christ. Opicinus conceives the struggle between the emperor and pope in apocalyptic, specifically Pauline, terms as a battle "in this breast" (Lombardy) in which the

49. *Vaticanus latinus 6435*, ed. Laharie, 1: 308 (fol. 32r).

50. Piron argues for the development of Opicinus's thought, in line with the policies of Benedict XII, against clerical wealth and ambition: *Dialectique du monstre*, 110–18. There is a faint echo here of Opicinus's pro-papal tract, where "Roman freedom" – that is, of the Roman church – is held to derive from the apostles, and not from the pomp of secular princes (*ex gentilium principum pompa*): *De preeminentia spiritualis imperii*, ed. Richard Scholtz, in "Unbekannte politische Streitschriften aus der Zeit Ludwigs des Bayern (1327–1354)," *Bibliothek des Kgl. Preussischen Historischen Instituts in Rom* 9 and 10 (1911–14): 1: 37–43; 2: 89–104, at 95.

51. *Vaticanus latinus 6435*, ed. Laharie, 2: 916 (fol. 87v): "Nam Cesar, obtento corpore usque ad lumbos Europe, primum inuasit dextrum femur usque ad tibiam; deinde calcaneum dextri pedis processit [et] ad pectus Europe usque ad guttur. Tandem finitis preliis sub calcaneo pedis sinistri, substrauit sub pedibus suis (quasi Affrice pharaonis) caput Pompeii generi sui."

"people of the perfecti" (*populus perfectorum*) contend "against principalities and powers (*aduersus principes et potestates*), against the rulers of the darkness of the world, against spiritual wickedness in celestial matters."[52] History, then, is not forgotten or absent from the images of Opicinus. Instead it serves to inform his understanding of present and future time. Lucanic geography, marked by invasion, violence, and death, is read at once quasi-typologically as the map of the "first struggle," prefiguring the second (and last) of the end of time, here conceived in terms of regional space. But these ancient and contemporary geographies are not held at arm's length. They are conjoined above all by the figure of Caesar – both Julius Caesar and subsequent Holy Roman emperors, such as Frederick II, who adopted his title – and they are meant to be appreciated for their continuities across Christian and pre-Christian eras. One comment moves from recalling the role of Ilerda in support of Pompey to imagining an alliance between St Victor of Marseille and St Vincent of Valencia in which – puns in full flow – winner (*victor*) and winning (*vincentius*) might be one with valour (*valentia*).[53] Around the idea of "dissension" or "conflict" (*certamen*), the image pivots to act as a meditation on secular and ecclesiastical power: on the struggle for control of bodies and places, on subjection to power, and on power's ultimate dissolution.

Opicinus Dada

Opicinus worked with charts, although he was not a cartographer. But it should not be thought that he was uninterested in the map as a map, as a visual representation of the earth. On the contrary, it was precisely the capacity of the map to represent the world, the region, and the city in graphic form that excited his attention. He saw that, as an image, the map could be made flexible: because it described the world, it could become a tool of revelation, a "testimonium." The two manuscripts compiled by Opicinus are not depictions of visions in the manner of a Hildegard of Bingen or a Joachim of Fiore.[54] Although they contain many allegorical elements, they are not precisely allegories, nor *cartes moralisées*.[55] Like

52. *Vaticanus latinus 6435*, ed. Laharie, 2: 920 (fol. 87v). *Ad Ephesios* 6:12.

53. *Vaticanus latinus 6435*, ed. Laharie, 2: 920 (fol. 87v): "Ilerde fauore Pompeii uulga- [...] papelardoni. Sed Sanctus Vin[...] habet forte [...] unita cum Massilia naturali usque Valentiam naturalem cum Aste partiali [...] a Sancto Victore Massilie usque Sanctum Vincentium Valentie, ut unus Victor et Vincentius cum sancta ualentia (id est fortitudine)."

54. Hildegard of Bingen, *Scivias*, ed. A. Führkötter and A. Carlevaris, 2 vols (Turnhout, 1978); Marjorie Reeves and Beatrice Hirsh-Reich, *The Figurae of Joachim of Fiore* (Oxford, 1972).

55. Salomon, *Opicinus*, 78.

other Italian autograph manuscripts of the thirteenth and fourteenth centuries, they are modelled on the documentary register.[56] As *testimonia*, they bear witness to the world, to the church, to secular power, and to Opicinus himself.[57] The superimposition of map and human body made the map figural, pregnant with allegory, but its shape remained. The body was fitted to the map and not vice-versa. And the superimposition of map on map opened up yet further possibilities for Opicinus: it allowed him to display the congruence of apparently distinct places, to defy scale even while respecting it, to show the workings of sacred time within the secular, the carnal.

Dislocation asks us to see two places in the same place at the same time. The spatial logic of the city or the region coincides with the spatial logic and expression of the world. But it also invites the dissolution of those logics. It offers the doubled, tripled, even quadrupled map as a single statement, rather than two or more statements to be disentangled and read separately. Reading through spatial order makes the signifying potential of the superimposed map all the greater. Places which "are" distant now lie alongside one another. A parish church in a northern European town appears to the south of Carthage. Jerusalem is located in the British Isles. These dislocations were not irrational but the manipulation – even the conclusion – of rational knowledge. For it was rational knowledge of the material world, the description of the nature of things as expressed in the sea chart, that inspired and enabled Opicinus to document immaterial relations. The depiction of the real, the literal, formed the basis for the revelation of its mystical significance. Revelation was performed thanks to a whole series of literary dislocations – metaphor, allegory, typology – but also, Opicinus seems to insist, as the result of his own experience of illness, collapse and mystical "opening," crucially linked to his *spatial* experience as a Pavese in Avignon, a Lombard in Provence. Because for the migrant and the exile, above all, experience can encompass more than one place at one time.

In the twentieth century a fugitive and traumatised "anti-art" also crafted a language based on the principles of superimposition and dislocation. The collage or montage was one of the principal resources of Dadaism, then Surrealism and, in the Soviet Union, Constructivism. More than a technique, collage came to identify some of the central impulses of the movements that emerged in Europe and America during and immediately after the First World War. The very terms used to describe the practices express something of their nature and motivations. In both collage, from the French "colle" (glue), and montage (from the

56. Morse, "A Complex Terrain," 159–60; see further Piron, *Dialectique du monstre*, 79–89.

57. *Vaticanus latinus 6435*, ed. Laharie, 2: 872 (fol. 83v): "De testimoniis personalibus et localibus"; Salomon, *Opicinus*, esp. 169–72, 183–87, 190–200, 242–44, 252–54, 261–72.

French for "mounting," "putting up"; German "montieren"), the emphasis was on the assemblage of diverse, previously constructed, objects by a "monteur," a fitter or mechanic, rather than an artist. Collage and montage denied single-point perspective – fundamental to the self-conception of Western art since the sixteenth century – and they disrupted the notion of visual unity. Collage had already emerged as an important element in pre-war Cubist and Futurist painting, and forms of montage, including photomontage, undoubtedly pre-dated the Dadaists. But the direct and indirect experience of war seems to have made all the more urgent a form of expression based on the compilation of pre-existing fragments. Among the Berlin Dadaists such as Raoul Hausmann and John Heartfield, montage had a consciously political function, one explicitly connected to the use of photographic elements. George Grosz, looking back to the origin of photomontage in 1916, affirmed its utilization of the detritus of popular culture and its context in war-time repression of freedom of speech: "On a piece of cardboard we pasted a mishmash of advertisements for hernia belts, student song-books and dog food, labels from schnaps- and wine-bottles, and photographs from picture papers, cut up at will in such a way as to say, in pictures, what would have been banned by the censors if we had said it in words."[58] Certainly in its Soviet incarnation montage became, briefly, synonymous with post-revolutionary (anti-) art: painting was farewelled, and in film as well as plastic art, emphasis fell on the construction rather than the creation of picture. Yet the left had no monopoly on montage. Its two great popular manifestations were in propaganda and advertising, both of which were equally open to manipulation by conservative or reactionary forces: as the 1920s and 30s were to show, collage could serve Fascists as well as Communists. The meaning and purpose of collage or montage cannot, then, be understood in terms of fixed political positions. Instead, two concerns – both formal and social – may be said to be at the base of collage/montage: the commitment to transformation of vision;[59] and the question of realism.

It was realism and the response to the real, according to Louis Aragon, that defined collage. Aragon made a crucial distinction between Cubist collage, which he saw as realistic, and the collage of Max Ernst, to which he assigned the status of poetry.[60] Surrealism was, as a consequence, not a denial of the real, but a heightened representation of it.[61] The language of vision and representation cer-

58. Hans Richter, *Dada: Art and Anti-Art*, trans. David Britt (London, 1965), 117; Richter does not give a reference for this quotation.

59. Dawn Ades, *Photomontage*, 2nd ed. (London, 1986), 17.

60. "Max Ernst, peintre des illusions" [1923], in Louis Aragon, *Les Collages* (Paris, 1965), 27–33.

61. Ades, *Photomontage*, 135–36.

tainly recurs frequently in the rhetoric of the practitioners of collage. What emerges from the multiple accounts of the genesis of photomontage, for example, is the expression of an intense desire to attain reality, to see the new age properly. For László Moholy-Nagy photography offered a "new vision." The camera, in achieving the representational goal of post-medieval Western art, had brought it to an end, and opened the way to more direct, emotive – and indeed, Moholy-Nagy thought, more medieval – modes of perception.[62] Ernst described his discovery of collage in terms of transcendence, but again with an emphasis on heightened vision. In 1919 he had come across an illustrated catalogue, where "I found brought together elements of figuration so remote that the sheer absurdity of that collection provoked a sudden intensification of the visionary faculties in me and brought forth an illusive succession of contradictory images, double, triple and multiple images, piling up on each other with the persistence and rapidity which are peculiar to love memories and visions of half-sleep."[63] The catalyst of the First World War seems to have led the *collageur* or *monteur* to feel dissatisfaction at traditional modes of representation not because they were realistic, but precisely because they were not realistic enough. In denying the multiplicity of perspective, in denying the principles of mass-reproduction that defined the machine age, in denying the fractured and compiled nature of reality as found in the illustrated magazine, the newspaper, the picture postcard, in denying, also, violence and disjunction, in denying the very disunity of reality, conventional representational art – landscape painting, portraiture, Expressionism – was itself anti-real and the work of the *monteur* was to see, show, and respond to a new reality. That reality was defined by mechanism, by motion – Moholy-Nagy described "a new *kinetic* concept of spatial articulation, vision in motion"[64] – as well as by "sheer absurdity." And it may be that this central position of the real in the Dadaist and Surrealist engagement with and against art helps to explain the lingering presence in their work of maps and map fragments.

Hausmann's "Tatlin at Home" (1920) shows Dadaist montage at its most provocative (Figure 31). In the forefront is the machine. The eponymous Tatlin, creator of the famous *Monument to the Third International*, has a steering wheel and motor engine superimposed on his upper head, implying its existence in the interior of his skull. A propeller at the top left of the image seems to be set in con-

---

62. László Moholy-Nagy, "A New Instrument of Vision" (1932), in *Moholy-Nagy*, ed. Richard Kostelanetz (New York, 1970), 50–54 (originally published in *Telehor* [Brno, 1936], trans. F.D. Klingender and P. Morton Shand).

63. Max Ernst, *Beyond Painting* (New York, 1948), 14.

64. "In Defense of 'Abstract' Art," *Journal of Aesthetics and Art Criticism* 4 (1945); reprinted in *Moholy-Nagy*, 44–46, at 46. (Emphasis in original.)

trast with the anatomised torso beneath. Hausmann's Tatlin was proclaimed as icon of the new "machine art," a man "who only had machines in his head."[65] Yet at least two non-machine elements in the image complicate this interpretation. Behind Tatlin a man turns out his pockets, perhaps as a commentary on post-war poverty. Above him appears a wall map of Pomerania (now north-east Germany and Poland), extending from Berlin at its south-west corner to Rügen on the Baltic Sea coast, and east to the Brahe (Brda) river. The railway line from Berlin to the town of Kolberg (Kołobrzeg) on the north coast is heavily marked, perhaps to indicate an itinerary. This map is, of course, just one – and perhaps the least noticeable – element of the montage. Its function is in part self-referential: "Tatlin at Home" was first exhibited in Berlin at the International Dada Fair in 1920. More particularly, Hausmann claimed that he and Hannah Höch invented photomontage while on holiday on the Baltic coast in 1917 or 1918 (in Gribow according to Höch, or Heidebrink according to Hausmann).[66] The two observed how the face of their landlord had been pasted onto a lithograph of a young grenadier in a patriotic scene featuring Kaiser Wilhelm II; this kitsch populist act apparently inspired their more radical image. But if the map gestures to the alleged origin of photomontage, it also possesses other resonances. It is certainly suggestive of militarism. Elsewhere at the 1920 International Dada Fair, Hausmann's "dada siegt!" contained at the top of its assemblage the word "DADA" superimposed on a map of the northern hemisphere, jokingly (and perhaps bitterly) mimicking the language of war. In "Tatlin at home" the map also carries echoes of tourism, of holidays as well as fraught borders and territorial disputes. It seems at the same time reminiscent of the pedagogical function of the classroom map: its torn right corner suggests its frayed, used, state, aligning it with the penniless Bürger beneath. Part of the world of machine-man and machine-art, itself standardised and mechanised, the map of Pomerania is also a throwback to a previous age. It is not, itself, a machine, and its lines and toponyms seem to provide a dim reminder of elements otherwise absent from the image: land and sea.

What relation, if any, does the collage of the early twentieth century have with the texts of Opicinus de Canistris? It is not my intention to assert identity between Opicinus's work and that of a *monteur*, nor to argue that montage helps us to understand the purpose and meanings of the images he produced. To make this comparison is itself a superimposition that runs the risk of superficiality – laying the modern on the medieval in the hope that something will align. Yet the

65. Ades, *Photomontage*, 28. The image's central photograph is not actually of Vladimir Tatlin, but of a man who "automatically" reminded Hausmann of Tatlin.

66. Ades, *Photomontage*, 19–20; Richter, *Dada*, 117.

comparison of modern with medieval was not foreign to the Dadaists themselves, and they made the point that, in turning their backs on what had led to their own time, they were turning towards something earlier – towards the "primitive" or the medieval – as well as towards the future. As a consequence it is possible to see affinity between Opicinus and Dada, and through affinity to understand the function of spatial dislocation, whether in the fourteenth or twentieth century.[67] Two areas of convergence and sympathy stand out: the use of repeated images to create meaning across a body of work, and the complex engagement with the real.

Opicinus operated with the concept of the series. Given the nature of the manuscripts that he left, it seems clear that if he intended his images to be read at all, he intended them to be read as contiguous rather than isolated documents. The permutations of Europe and Africa through his visual imagination demanded expression through repetition and variation. In the twentieth century it was precisely the reproducibility of the photograph that made it seem attractive to those seeking a "new structure of vision." The series, Moholy-Nagy thought, is no longer a "picture," so the canons of pictorial aesthetics did not apply to it: "the separate picture loses its identity as such and becomes a detail of assembly, an essential structural element of the whole which is the thing itself."[68] The map in Opicinus's work must be reproduced, copied again and again, with its essential elements left intact. It is not a photograph. But nor does it function any more as "a map of the Mediterranean basin." Surrounded by glosses, by calendars, transfigured by the superimposition of human bodies, by allusions to past, contemporary and future events, the map is surely for Opicinus "a detail of assembly." Montage may have seemed to many viewers to confuse, to cover, to paste over, but the *monteurs* spoke not of obfuscation but of vision, even revelation – sometimes documentary in nature, sometimes quasi-mystical, such as Ernst's "love memories and visions of half-sleep." In part this revelation involved an assault on the viewer's sensibilities and expectations. In the Russian avant-garde, for example, El Lissitzky sought to challenge and even defeat the viewer's perception of correct orientation, in order to compel "a continuous beholding process through which orientation would be perpetually renegotiated from multiple sides of the same work."[69] Opicinus's flamboyant mirrorings and reversals similarly demand multiple orientations. His images must be turned, rotated, viewed from

---

67. The discussion of Opicinus's work in relation to *art brut* goes back to Kris, "A Psychotic Artist." For consideration of Opicinus with regard to Antonin Artaud, see Piron, *Dialectique du monstre*, 121, 168.

68. "A New Instrument of Vision," 54.

69. Jeffrey Weiss, "Dis-Orientation: Rothko's Inverted Canvases," in *Seeing Rothko*, ed. Glenn Phillips and Thomas Crow (Los Angeles, 2005), 135–57, at 144–45.

different angles. East remains perhaps the privileged direction for him, but no way is up. Transformation – seeing differently – was as central to the meaning of collage and photomontage as revelation was for Opicinus.

It is the engagement with the real that does most to connect the work of Opicinus to the dislocations of twentieth-century anti-art. He used the map repeatedly precisely because it represented cities, regions, seas: the world. That reality needed to be seen, he thought, in eschatological terms, as part of a divine ordering of space and time; it needed to be witnessed. And as part of this process the familiar had to be made unfamiliar: city aligned with region, with world; world aligned with region, city. It was *dépaysement* – disorientation, but in more banal settings a change of scene or scenery, often with positive connotations – that André Breton, Aragon and others identified as central to surrealism, and in particular "the reconciliation of the real and the marvellous or miraculous." In an essay from 1930 Aragon expanded on Breton's remark (in the introduction to Ernst's *La femme 100 têtes*) that "La surréalité sera d'ailleurs fonction de notre volonté de dépaysement complet de tout" (surreality will be moreover a function of our will to total disorientation/displacement):

> The dead displaced (*dépaysés*) from the grave, giants displaced by their height, sylphs by lightness, roses by the season. The miracle is an unexpected disorder, a surprising lack of proportion. And it is in this respect that it is the negation of the real, and that the reconciliation of the real and the marvellous (*la conciliation du réel et du merveilleux*) becomes accepted as miracle. The new relation thus established is surrealism, defined one thousand times, and always definable in different ways, this real line that connects all the potential images (*les images virtuelles*) that surround us.[70]

The project of revelation, of conversion, in Opicinus can also be described, suggestively if not precisely, by these words. The witness of "mysterii" and their connection with the real, the all-encompassing nature of revelation, the unexpected and thrilling aspects of disorientation, all describe Opicinus as well as Sur – or super – realism.

---

70. "La peinture au défi" (1930), reprinted in Aragon, *Les Collages*, 35–72, at 41: "Les morts dépaysés du tombeau, les géants dépaysés par la taille, les sylphes par la légèreté, les roses par la saison. Le miracle est un désordre inattendu, une disproportion surprenante. Et c'est à cet égard qu'il est la négation du réel, et qu'il devient une fois accepté miracle, la conciliation du réel et du merveilleux. Le nouveau rapport ainsi établi est la surréalité, mille fois définie, et toujours différemment définissable, cette ligne réelle qui relie toutes les images virtuelles qui nous entourent." André Breton, "Avis au lecteur" [1929], in Max Ernst, *La femme 100 têtes* (Paris, 1956) [unpaginated].

Antagonisms, re- and disorientations, superimpositions, surprise, spectacle, revelation. If these traits speak of an affinity between Opicinus and the *collageur* and *monteur* of the twentieth century, should we, however, deny any spiritual sympathy between the self-absorbed Dadaist and the equally self-absorbed Avignonese scribe? Certainly the evangelical fervour of Opicinus seems far from the iconoclastic posture of Dadaism and its relations and descendents. But the relation between Dada and religion is complex,[71] and the writings of Aragon, of Moholy-Nagy, of Hausmann all reveal sympathy for the era before the Renaissance. Aragon identified a "period of stability" dating from the invention of oil painting in fourteenth-century Flanders by Jean de Bruges, which permitted the introduction of perspective and "fixed the limits of debate up to our own day." Troubled by Impressionism in the nineteenth century, it was only in the twentieth that art had undergone "dramatic revision."[72] Moholy-Nagy thought that pre-Renaissance painting, unburdened by the need to illustrate reality, "expressed moods, devotion, wonder, and ecstasy with the sensuous and emotional power of colour."[73] This emphasis on feeling, on sense, emerges strongly in Hausmann's affirmation of the Middle Ages:

I am not aware of an opposition between a Gothic cathedral and the metro, apart from their different directions: one being above the surface, the other below; but what does that matter? In the Gothic cathedrals there were often many people; just as in the metro. Thinking of the leaf of a lime tree, it matters little whether one identifies the leaf's veins with the system of pipes of the Gothic cathedrals, or of the metro – the Gothic cathedrals were constructions of spiritual channeling, just like the metro which channels us from experience to experience; the system of veins of the lime tree leaf perhaps also serves its spiritual consciousness.[74]

71. While adopting a posture of irreverence, Dadaists such as Ernst and Kurt Schwitters frequently reprised religious themes and contexts in their work. Schwitters's "Merzbau," based on the idea of a cathedral and comprising reliquaries and other facets of Catholic worship, is an obvious example: see Alexander Nagel, *Medieval Modern: Art out of Time* (London, 2012), 263–74.

72. Aragon, *Les Collages*, 11–13.

73. "In Defense of 'Abstract' Art," 45

74. Raoul Hausmann, *Courrier Dada* [1958], rev ed. Marc Dachy (Paris, 1992), 130: "je n'ai pas connaissance d'un contraste entre une cathédrale gothique et le métro, à part une opposition de leurs directions: l'une étant au-dessus de la surface, l'autre au-dessous de la surface; mais qu'est-ce que cela signifie? Dans les cathédrales gothiques il y avait souvent beaucoup de gens; de même que dans le métro. Pensons à la feuille de tilleul, il importe peu que l'on identifie les canaux de la feuille avec le système de tuyaux des cathédrales gothiques ou du métro – les cathédrales gothiques étaient des constructions de canalisation spirituelle, tout comme le métro qui nous conduit d'expérience en expérience, et le système des canaux de la feuille de tilleul sert peut-être aussi à sa conscience spirituelle."

Medieval architecture is enlisted here in Hausmann's opposition to Expressionism, but it also serves as a means of articulating modernity as a channelling of experience, drawing together the natural and the man-made, the spiritual and the material, above and underground, in ways thoroughly congenial to an Opicinian aesthetic. The perception of shared functions in apparently disparate forms seems to characterise both the art of Opicinus and that of Dada: a rejection of traditional modes of categorisation as inadequate and even blind. Was there any serious basis to the anti-traditionalists' embrace of the medieval? Did Aragon, Breton, Hausmann, or Moholy-Nagy know much more than they had learned at school or seen in the streets and museum galleries of Europe? Quite possibly not: their view is superficial, unresearched. But what matters more than what they knew is their instinctive perception of affinity, their sense that an era of representation had come to an end, and that, standing at the beginning of something new, they could locate a portion of their own spirit in the pre-history of representation, in art before art:

> And as we do not want to be Expressionists, but people who still live in the Middle Ages, people who, in the metro, in the face of the invariability of life, feel a cold shiver of profound respect run the length of their backs, we should still think that there is more than a possibility of comparison between our era, the Middle Ages, and the green leaf in the shape of a heart.[75]

If Avignon Were Babylon

Opicinus de Canistris and Francis Petrarch seem, at first glance, to have shared little. One was an obscure scribe, the other – laureate poet – an author of pan-European fame. One was an ardent supporter of the papal cause, the other a scathing critic of the papacy who urged the Holy Roman emperor to conquer Italy. One saw Avignon as a site of spiritual renewal, the other as a cesspit of depravity. One was forgotten until a twentieth-century rediscovery, the other accorded a more or less continuous place of centrality within the history of letters. Rather than mutual antagonism, so great are the differences between the terms of Opicinus's and Petrarch's thought and work that it is easier to conceive

---

75. Hausmann, *Courrier Dada*, 131: "Et comme nous ne voulons pas être des expressionistes, mais des gens qui vivent encore au Moyen Âge, des gens qui dans le métro sentent devant l'invariabilité de la vie leur couler le long du dos un frisson froid de profond respect, il nous faut encore penser qu'il y a plus d'une possibilité de comparaison entre notre époque, le Moyen Âge et la feuille verte en forme de cœur."

of their relation as one of mutual incomprehension. But for a few years they shared a city.

From April 1329 to 1337, and again from 1351–52, both lived in Avignon; then, some years after Opicinus's death, Petrarch spent time in Pavia, staying in the city from time to time between 1363 and 1369, and even describing it in a letter to Boccaccio that curiously echoes the lengthier account of Pavia given by Opicinus over thirty years previously.[76] No evidence has been found to show conclusively that the two ever met, or were even aware of each other's work. All the same, they had mutual acquaintances, even mutual friends. And one does not have to look too hard through the voluminous writings of Petrarch to discern *dépaysement*. Petrarch's spatial formulations should not be equated with the cartographic transformations of Opicinus, and it would be hazardous to assert influence in either direction. Instead, a comparison between the superimpositions of Opicinus and Petrarch reveals alignment, contradiction – and occasionally intersection of thought.

The most famous of Petrarch's superimpositions is so notorious that it often escapes examination. His description of the tenure of the papacy in Avignon as its "Babylonian captivity" continues to have currency today. But the complexity of this conjunction is not immediately apparent. The rationale for Petrarch's condemnation of Avignon as the "new Babylon" was given limpid form in one of his letters to the Florentine Francesco Nelli, written in 1352, and later preserved in the collection known as "Liber sine nomine" (Book without a name), a volume that contains Petrarch's most forceful critiques of papal corruption in Avignon. The letter to Nelli begins with a reference to Psalm 136 ("Super flumina Babylonis"), establishing a sermon-like theme of exile, but also of geographic division. Petrarch knows that Nelli will be puzzled: there are only two Babylons – the Assyrian city where Semiramis flourished, and the Egyptian Babylon founded by Cambyses and still in existence.[77] Is Petrarch referring to Rome, styled by some authors – including those as authoritative as Augustine[78] – as another Babylon? Certainly not. It is the western Babylon, lying on the Rhone as the others lie on

76. *Lettres de la Vieillesse*, ed. Nota, 5.1 (2: 115–25); Angelo Cerri, "Francesco Petrarca a Pavia," in *Storia di Pavia*, vol. 3.1: *Dal libero comune alla fine del principato indipendente 1024–1535* (Milan, 1992), 451–95; for other brief comparisons between Opicinus and Petrarch see Piron, *Dialectique du monstre*, 14, 87; Feo, "La 'peciola' ritrovata," 309–10.

77. *Liber sine nomine* 10, edited in Paul Piur, *Petrarcas "Buch ohne Namen" und die päpstliche Kurie: Ein Beitrag zur Geistesgeschichte der Frührenaissance* (Halle, 1925), 197–201, at 197.

78. Augustine, *De civitate dei* 18.2, ed. B. Dombart and A. Kalb (Turnhout, 1955), 594 ("Babylonia, quasi prima Roma"); 18.22, ed. Dombart and Kalb, 612 ("ciuitas Roma uelut altera Babylon et uelut prioris filia Babylonis").

the Euphrates or the Nile, a true "city of confusion" (Gen 11:9), that he has in mind. Here another Nimrod (the pope) rules the land and builds towers to reach heavens (the papal palace); here can be found a new Semiramis and a second Cambyses; here too there is a labyrinth to add to those reported by Pliny in Egypt, Crete, Lemnos, and Clusium in Italy – one worse than all of them.[79] But the only thread out of this Avignonese labyrinth is gold – the gold for which Christ is sold.[80]

The Avignonese Babylon of the letter to Nelli appears also in a letter of the same year, written to another Florentine, Lapo da Castiglionchio. Here again Babylon is located in the west, by the "wild Rhone, like the boiling Cocytus or Tartarean Acheron, where the meagre heritage of fishermen once ruled, [now] to a remarkable degree forgetful of its origin."[81] The apostles provide a damning contrast with their successors, who are weighed down with gold and purple. Instead of overturned boats, luxurious palaces are constructed; feasts consumed in place of the sparse haul from fishing nets on the Sea of Galilee. Once established, Avignon as Babylon can function as a shorthand for ecclesiastical vice, but also for Petrarch's own position of exclusion from the Holy Land: "I an angry exile from Jerusalem, between and above the rivers of Babylon, have written these things to you in great haste."[82] The complexities of Avignon-Babylon lie in its layering of multiple spatial identities, as well as its conflation of historical period. Petrarch carefully separates two historical Babylons, one of which still exists, bridging antiquity and modernity, and imagines Avignon as simultaneously Assyrian and Egyptian. The two ancient Babylons seem also to figure separate textual traditions: one Biblical, the other the pagan literature of classical antiquity. Petrarch's explicit reference to Augustine's description of Rome as a second Babylon enriches and complicates his act of dislocation. Augustine is at once a model for the articulation of criticism through deployment of geographical analogy, and an authority to be rerouted. Petrarch cannot allow that Rome resembles Babylon except in its former imperial status (and even in this Rome was different: it ruled the world, not just the east). At some level, however, Petrarch's anal-

---

79. *Liber sine nomine* 10, ed. Piur, 198–200. As Piur (199n) observes, the reference to "uesanior Cambisses" evokes Lucan's comparison of Alexander the Great to "insane Cambyses" (Vaesanus ... Cambyses): *Bellum civile* 10.279–80. Pliny, *Naturalis historia* 36.13 for the labyrinths.

80. *Liber sine nomine* 10, ed. Piur, 200–201.

81. *Liber sine nomine* 5, ed. Piur, 185: "ferox Rodanus estuanti Cocyto uel Tartareo simillimus Acheronti, ubi piscatorum inops quondam regnat hereditas, mirum in modum oblita principii."

82. *Liber sine nomine* 9, ed. Piur, 196: "Hec tibi raptim Hierosolymitanus exul inter et super flumina Babilonis indignans scripsi."

ogy turns back on himself. Avignon stands for his own spiritual and political alienation: it is, after all, from where he writes. Revealingly, his letter to Lapo da Castiglionchio begins with a different dislocation. Petrarch notes that he has experienced two versions of Mt Parnassus: "one is in Italy, the other in Gaul ... I was
happier on the Italian Parnassus ... Now the Gallic world has me and the western
Babylon."[83] The mountain moves with the man, it seems, but the conceit speaks
clearly of a vagrant, exilic identity perpetually looking from the outside in, and
perpetually correlating the space of antiquity with that of modernity.

That position of exilic vagrancy appears to have been for Petrarch emblematic of literary transmission. In 1360, now returned to Italy, he wrote a letter to
Homer. This missive, part of a series sent to the authors of classical antiquity,
muses on literary fortune and influence, particularly Homer's influence on Virgil, and the tenuous knowledge of Greek literature that can currently be found in
the Latin west. Yet all is not lost: though few read Greek, Homer's works are even
now being translated into Latin in Florence by a "mutual friend," Leonzio Pilato.
Petrarch imagines Homer's distress and tries to console his fellow poet: "You
weep, when you may just as well laugh, because a mutual friend, whom you regard
as a Thessalian and I consider a Byzantine, has forced you to wander as a foreigner, or if you prefer, to live as an exile within the flourishing walls of my
patria."[84] As Ovid and the *Tristia*, the author becomes the work, and textual transmission a process of relocation through time and space. But notable too is
Petrarch's insistence on precision of spatial reference, on the record of mutation.
Homer's Thessalian is now Petrarch's "Byzantine," or perhaps more accurately
"native of Constantinople." The different perspectives of the same region amount
to another act of superimposition in which ancient and contemporary toponym
are held together, an articulation of the posture of address to antiquity figured by
Petrarch in this letter written to a shade from "the upper world, between the very
famous rivers Po, Ticino, Adda and others, from which middle position some
derive the name Milan (*Mediolanum*)."[85]

83. *Liber sine nomine* 5, ed. Piur, 184–85: "alter in Italia est, alter in Galliis ... In Ausonio
Helicone felicior fui ... Nunc me Gallicus orbis habet et occidentalis Babilon."

84. *Le Familiari* 24.12.30, ed. Vittori Rossi, 4 vols. (Florence, 1933–42), 4: 253–63, at
260–61: "fles unde ridere par fuerat –, quod comunis amicus, quem tu thesalum facis ego
bizantinum rebar, te intra florentes patrie mee muros peregrinari, sive ita mavis, exulare
coegerit." On the complex question of Leonzio's origins see Antonio Rollo, *Leonzio lettore
dell'Ecuba nella Firenze di Boccaccio*, vol. 2 of *Petrarca e il mondo greco*, ed. Michele Feo et al.
Quaderni Petrarcheschi 12–13 (2002–3), 7–21, and 8 n6 for the argument that "bizantinus"
should be understood as "constantinopolitanus."

85. *Le Familiari* 24.12.43, ed. Rossi, 4: 263: "Apud superos, medio amnium clarissimo-
rum Padi Ticini Ardue aliorumque, unde quidam Mediolanum dici volunt ... ."

Petrarch at no stage in his long career took a map of Europe and North Africa, copied it, reversed it, and superimposed a map of Lombardy on it. Nor did he represent Africa and Europe as male and female, draw the head of a monster in the Atlantic tearing off Europe's clothing, depict a sea monster ejaculating off the coast of Spain, add an image of Christ on the cross, and surround the whole with mystical allegorisations. So far as we know, he perceived neither Pavia nor Venice as the vulva of Europe. Geography could not, for him, serve as an intimation of material and spiritual history. But it could be manipulated to rhetorical and autobiographical effect. Like Petrarch, Opicinus thought about the relationship between Avignon and Babylon. What he saw, however, was not identity. One of the more striking maps from the Vaticanus manuscript expresses a very different relationship (Figure 32).[86] The mirroring of *partes* on this image means that Europe and Africa interchange positions, and genders. At one end of the image, "west, of death," a male Europe represents the Apostolic church next to Africa as the "Judaic synagogue"; at the other end of the image, "east, of life," a female Europe is universal Christianity, while Africa is "the traitor Judas, that is the community of carnal men."[87] Superimposed on the mirrored maps of Europe and Africa is a map of northern Italy, with toponyms written in red. Pavia is figured as a vulva, Genoa (Ianua) located in the breast of Africa. The crucified Christ appears simultaneously in Asia, in the vicinity of Babylon, but also (viewing the image in the other direction) with his head next to Avignon (Avinio) and the base of the cross in Lombardy. The toponym at the right of his waist is "Lomellum" (Lomello), birthplace of Opicinus. From Christ's side wound a line of blood extends diagonally across the image to the figure of a child with a halo, located in the equivalent part of the mirrored map, and marked "Papia." A nearby inscription written in the voice of Ecclesia records the presence of two "inner breasts," representing the fruit of penitence and charity, and a "little dwelling of the Holy Spirit on the Rhone."[88] Instead of a betrayal of apostolic Christianity, then, Opicinus found himself to be living in its innermost bosom. In his vision it is Lombardy, and in particular Pavia, held by empire, that corresponds to Babylon.

Exiles in Avignon, looking towards Italy, contemplating the sweep of Christian history, repeatedly documenting their thoughts, Opicinus and Petrarch saw differently. Both men sought correspondences, analogies, allegories in geography –

86. Vaticanus latinus MS 6435, fol. 76v.

87. *Vaticanus latinus 6435*, ed. Laharie, 2: 792 (fol. 76v): "Iudas proditor, id est uniuersitas carnalium hominum." On Opicinus and Judas, see Feo, "La 'peciola' ritrovata," 324–30.

88. *Vaticanus latinus 6435*, ed. Laharie, 2: 792 (fol. 76v): "habitaculum Sancti Spiritus super Rodanum."

but Petrarch would not distort geographical order by reading cities on regions and on and over maps of the world. By the same token what is missing from Opicinus's superimpositions is a desire to hold classical and modern space apart, so that the two can engage in eloquent dialogue. As I have indicated, classical history is not absent from Opicinus's texts and image, but it is the history of Christianity in the world and its manifestation in the Church, from creation to judgement, that informs the maps of the Vaticanus and Palatinus manuscripts. More obedient, more devout, certainly more respectful of ecclesiastical authority, Opicinus produced *dépaysement* more radical, more unsettling and intense, than those of his sometime fellow denizen of the papal city. The brilliance of his work lies in its observance of spatial orders, even as it repeats, figures, overlays and thereby dislocates order. This geography in which place is repeated and transfigured speaks from the present to what was and will be. It is a geography in which the real must be revealed – in which "a sudden intensification of the visionary faculties" might result in new testaments, new maps.

CHAPTER NINE

Ebstorf in Baroda: The *Mappae Mundi* of Gulammohammed Sheikh

In the first decade of the twenty-first century a number of artists, working on different continents and with different media, began to fashion creative responses to medieval maps. Those responses were, in different ways, playful and for the most part gently provocative, unmooring preconceptions about the fixed nature of geographical space, and the distinction between modern and medieval ways of representing it. Grayson Perry's "Map of Nowhere" (2008) reinvented the Ebstorf *mappa mundi*, recasting the artist as a Christ-like figure presiding over an allegorised topography. Perry's earlier "Balloon" (2004) is a "transcription" of the Hereford *mappa mundi*, in which figures from the London art world populate the medieval image.[1] The Ebstorf map – a monumental *mappa mundi* created around 1300 in north Germany – similarly infused Olivier Ruellet's "Memory/Territory" (2006–7), in which conflated maps of the Paris Metro, the London Underground, and France underpinned the artist's meditations on travel. In New York, Joyce Kozloff's "JEEZ" (2011–12) also responded to the Ebstorf map by adding 125 images of Christ, sourced from various parts of the world, to the map's own depiction of the deity. Kozloff's previous work included seventy-two Knowledge frescos and globes (1998–2000), reinterpretations of maps and globes primarily from the "Age of Discovery," but also from the Middle Ages, including the twelfth-century world map of the Islamic cartographer al-Idrīsī. For all of these artists the presence of subjectivity, history, and memory on medieval maps appears to have had a liberating effect. More than that, medieval maps do not exclude the human body from their frame, and they offer intriguing alignments with the itinerary, one function of which is to record the body's interaction with space. Geographical space – on the medieval map as on the modern artwork – is malleable, at times corporeal. This is not to say that it does not express a reality. It is simply that the realities expressed are those of memory, of argument, of belief, and of imagination, as well as of topography. Crucially, these

1. Jacky Klein, *Grayson Perry* (London, 2009), 222.

realities are expressed *on* the map, thereby connecting (and in the case of the twenty-first-century artwork, reconnecting) the record of geographic reality with the experience and the associations of space.

Arguably the most complex of all recent artistic responses to medieval maps has come from the Gujarati scholar and poet Gulammohammed Sheikh. As with Kozloff, Perry, and Ruellet, the Ebstorf world map has been the catalyst for new work: Sheikh's *Mappamundi Suite*, a series of images composed primarily in 2003–4 but still subject to adaptation and supplementation, comprises multiple reworkings of the medieval map. To construct his contemporary *mappae mundi*, Sheikh scanned a photographic reproduction of the Ebstorf *mappa mundi*, manipulated the digitised map to form a collage with other images, then printed it, adding paint and yet further images to its surface. The basic form of the map remains: its rivers, mountains, and cities are still legible. But its frame and crucial aspects of its content have changed. The original showed Christ's face at the top of the map, his hands at the far north and south of the world image, and his feet at the west; on most versions of Sheikh's *mappa mundi* the saviour has been decapitated, though his limbs linger. Instead of Jesus, four principal figures surround the map (Figure 33). At the top right of the image sits the fifteenth-century poet Kabir; beneath him whirls a dancer from the Pahari region of north India. To the left of the map, two figures represent the theme of thwarted longing: Giotto's *noli me tangere*, his painting of Mary Magdalene with arms outstretched towards Christ after the resurrection, and a Mughal-era image from the popular story of Majnun (the mad) and his beloved Layla, in which Majnun, emaciated and driven insane by love, is led by an old woman to Layla's tent. Within several of the maps two other icons recur: an image from the third Kanda of the *Ramayana*, in which Rama pursues a deer, and a depiction of St Francis preaching to the birds, also attributed to Giotto. Such an ensemble is evidently dislocative, but in what sense and to what effect?

Born in Surendranagar, Gujarat, in 1937, Sheikh studied in the early 1960s at the Royal College of Art, London. Disillusioned by the dominance of minimalism and Pop Art, he developed a profound interest in fourteenth- and fifteenth-century Flemish and Italian painting, and at the same time began to examine with some intensity the rich collection of Indian and Persian miniatures held in London institutions such as the Victoria and Albert Museum.[2] Sheikh was

2. For outline biography see Gayatri Sinha, *The Art of Gulammohammed Sheikh* (New Deli, 2002), as well as the important collection *Contemporary Art in Baroda*, ed. Gulammohammed Sheikh (New Delhi, 1997), the reflections in Laetitia Zecchini, "'More Than One World': An Interview with Gulammohammed Sheikh," *Journal of Postcolonial Writing* 53 (2017): 69–82, and most recently Chaitanya Sambrani, ed., *At Home in the World: The Art and Life of Gulammohammed Sheikh* (New York, 2019).

struck by the formal and thematic similarities between these traditions. His return to India in 1967 to take up a post at the Maharaja Sayajirao University, Baroda, facilitated the development of an artistic style in which Indian and Western pictorial techniques and images freely interact. A frequent theme of his work and thought is the interpenetration of times: "returning to India and visiting my hometown," he has written, "I saw accretions of time past still alive in interaction with elements of change, unharmonized yet vital."[3] Increasingly – against a backdrop of intensifying sectarian violence – Sheikh's mixture of styles has assumed significance as a means of asserting the principle of religious tolerance and opposition to dogmatism. Sheikh's work is characterised by bright colours, by a resistance to single-point perspective, and by the use of visual quotations and "splinters" within each image, never at the expense of legibility and cohesion. In the painting "Ek Achambha Dekha Re Bhai" (2001) "the face of Kabir becomes a proto landscape, in which monks and angels, yogis and bodhisattvas, the prophet and pilgrims traverse in a historical quest,"[4] while in "Numens" (2001) the artist inserts sacred buildings, including the destroyed Babri masjid of Ayodhya, onto a repainting of the "Thebaid" attributed to Gherardo Starnina (c. 1410). Already in 1981 Sheikh had proclaimed (or acclaimed) the continual telescoping and reunion of traditional and modern, private and public, the inside and outside: "as times and cultures converge," he wrote, "the citadels of purism explode."[5]

Map as Crossroads

Perhaps the first point that should be made about Sheikh's *mappa mundi* suite is that its foundation, the Ebstorf map, is itself far from a stable text. Lost, found, copied, destroyed, re-made, its own curious story is embedded in Sheikh's new maps. The *mappa mundi* was constructed around 1300 for the Benedictine nunnery of Ebstorf, situated between the towns of Braunschweig and Lüneburg in Lower Saxony. It consisted of thirty parchment sheets, sewn together. The richly detailed image they presented included around 1330 inscriptions, ranging from single words to lengthy descriptions, accompanying hundreds of pictures.[6] Ele-

3. Gulammohammed Sheikh, "Among Several Cultures and Times," in *Contemporary Indian Tradition: Voices on Culture, Nature, and the Challenge of Change*, ed. Carla M. Borden (Washington, DC, 1989), 107–20, at 115.

4. Sinha, *Art of Gulammohammed Sheikh*, 15.

5. "Among Several Cultures and Times," 107.

6. Wilke estimates "altogether almost 2,345 text and image entries": Jürgen Wilke, *Die Ebstorfer Weltkarte*, 2 vols. (Bielefeld, 2001), 1: 11 (based on M. Warnke, "Die Ebstorfer Weltkarte: Der Computer als Medium für selbstbestimmtes Lernen," *Computer und Unterricht* 5 (1992), 2); some inscriptions have been lost.

ments of its form resemble other medieval *mappae mundi*. The map is centred on Jerusalem, and the three *partes* of Asia, Africa, and Europe are divided by the Mediterranean, the Nile, and a combination of the Don and the Black Sea. It is the product of an intellectual milieu informed by the bestiary, by encyclopedic texts "on the nature of things," by romance literature, saints' lives, and the literature and practice of pilgrimage.[7] Some of these diverse influences crystallise in the map's extensive paratext, the writing that surrounded the world image, and that acted as a form of commentary on it (Figure 34). This commentary begins in the top left corner with a section of text on the name and nature of "celum" (sky, heavens, firmament), and proceeds to the right with a chunk of text on the earthly paradise. On the other side of Christ's head, texts inform the reader about the shape of the earth (*Orbis a rotunditate*), and God's creation of it (*Prima die*), illustrated by a schematic representation of the three *partes*. In the far right corner, a brief statement describes the map itself. According to this account, the term "mappa" equates to "forma" (figure, shape, image), and the origin of the world map lies in a survey of the entire world commissioned by Julius Caesar. The resulting image offers "no small utility" to readers, direction to travellers, and "the love of freely contemplating (*speculatio*) the things along the way."[8] The meaning of this brief and somewhat enigmatic statement can be understood in at least two ways. The most obvious is that it suggests a programme of spiritual reading, in which the "traveller" seeks moral direction and a passage from the earthly to the heavenly. On this understanding the map may tend towards allegory. But an alternative is to read the instruction in less exalted terms, as an invi-

---

7. Useful discussions of the map include Wilke, *Ebstorfer Weltkarte*, vol. 1; Margriet Hoogvliet, *Pictura et Scriptura: Textes, images et herméneutique des Mappae Mundi (XIIIe–XVIe siècles)* (Turnhout, 2007), 45–50, 164–68, 183–96, 221–23; Patrick Gautier Dalché, "À propos de la mappemonde d'Ebstorf," *Médiévales* 55 (2008): 163–70; Marcia Kupfer, "Reflections on the Ebstorf Map: Cartography, Theology and *Dilectio Speculationis*," in *Mapping Medieval Geographies: Cartography and Geographical Thought in the Latin West and Beyond, 300–1600*, ed. Keith D. Lilley (Cambridge, 2013), 100–26.

8. Hartmut Kugler, *Die Ebstorfer Weltkarte*, 2 vols (Berlin, 2007), 1: 21 (7.1): "Mappa dicitur forma. Inde mappa mundi id est forma mundi. Quam Julius Cesar missis legatis per totius orbis amplitudinem primus instituit; regiones, provincias, insulas, civitates, syrtes, paludes, equora, montes, flumina quasi sub unius pagine visione coadunavit; que scilicet non parvam prestat legentibus utilitatem, viantibus directionem rerumque viarum gratissime speculacionis dilectionem." This passage has been much discussed: see for example Uwe Ruberg, "Mappae mundi des Mittelalters im Zusammenwirken von Text und Bild," in *Text und Bild: Aspekte des Zusammenwirkens zweier Künste in Mittelalter und früher Neuzeit*, ed. Christel Meier and Uwe Ruberg (Wiesbaden, 1980), 530–85, at 565–67; Cornelia Herberichs, " ... *quasi sub unius pagine visione coadunavit*: Zur Lesbarkeit der Ebstorfer Weltkarte," in *Text-Bild-Karte: Kartographien der Vormoderne*, ed. Jürg Glauser and Christian Kiening (Freiburg i.Br., 2007), 201–17: 212–14; Kupfer, "Reflections on the Ebstorf Map."

tation to unstructured, even leisured, looking: something close to browsing. The map is useful, practical, but the things along the path of utility provide enjoyment. Does such a reading run the risk of encouraging an anachronistic modern (mis)understanding of the ordered, hierarchical nature of medieval reading practices? Perhaps; but perhaps too we need to hesitate before denying the Middle Ages the textual freedoms we readily ascribe to modernity.

It is precisely the plurality of possible readings that makes even a relatively well documented example of a medieval world map such as the Ebstorf *mappa mundi* so hard to classify. For, despite the best efforts of several twentieth- and twenty-first century scholars and editors, the purpose of the Ebstorf map remains uncertain. It seems likely that it was displayed within the nunnery at Ebstorf, but it is not clear where or how. Was its function pedagogic? Liturgical (since the inscriptions near the hands and feet of Christ contain liturgical quotations)?[9] Did the map act as a gift from or to the duchy of Braunschweig-Lüneburg? Was it an *Andachtsbild* (devotional image) for pilgrims visiting the graves of the ninth-century "Ebstorf martyrs," sites of veneration from the fourteenth century, and perhaps earlier? The martyrs' tombs appear on the map, where, in combination with the image of Christ rising from the sepulchre in Jerusalem, they may constitute a theme of grave veneration.[10] Like several other maps, the Ebstorf *mappa mundi* could be read in order to see the local space where the map was produced and displayed, in relation to the world.[11] The central and northern European area is significantly expanded to include much more information than appears on other contemporary *mappae mundi*. At the same time, the complexity of the map makes insistence on a purely or even primarily localist significance appear excessive. On the Ebstorf map, for example, the twelve winds are represented with some care around the surface of the earth.[12] They are ethnographically significant: each wind circle contains a hexameter, which links it to a particular part of the world, and in some instances to a particular people (the British, Ruthenians, Goths, the Seres, Indi-

---

9. As pointed out by Kugler, *Ebstorfer Weltkarte*, 2: 22.

10. Kugler, *Ebstorfer Weltkarte*, 2: 64–65; Wilke, *Ebstorfer Weltkarte*, 1: 185–91. Other graves/tombs on the map include those of Darius, Philip, Bartholomaus, and St Thomas.

11. See Kugler, *Ebstorfer Weltkarte*, 2: 63–67 for a summary of possibilities. Wilke, *Ebstorfer Weltkarte*, raised serious problems with the once prevalent view that the map was originally produced by the chronicler Gervase of Tilbury in the first half of the thirteenth century, in order to accompany his *Otia imperialia*; for a tenacious, if unconvincing, defence of this thesis see Armin Wolf, "The Ebstorf *Mappamundi* and Gervase of Tilbury: The Controversy Revisited," *Imago Mundi* 64 (2012): 1–27.

12. Kugler, *Ebstorfer Weltkarte*, 2: 29–30.

ans).[13] It seems legitimate to understand these wind inscriptions as representations of the movement of air, to be visualised across the far-from-static surface of the image in its entirety.

The original map can no longer provide answers to questions about its function. It was rediscovered at Ebstorf in 1830, having apparently lain unnoticed among Catholic detritus for the best part of three centuries following the reform of the nunnery during the sixteenth century. It quickly attracted attention on its reappearance, however, to the extent that part of it (the Red Sea area, no doubt attractively coloured) was swiftly removed by "an unknown evil-doer."[14] The map was photographed at the end of the nineteenth century, losing in the process some parts of its fabric, while acquiring creative additions at the hands of its editors, who published two somewhat contradictory images of the artefact.[15] However distorted, these photographic records became crucial when, in the night of October 8–9, 1943, the Ebstorf map was destroyed as a result of an Allied bombing raid on Hanover. The loss of the artefact was keenly felt, not least in the Ebstorf Kloster itself,[16] and four facsimile reproductions of the original, based on late nineteenth-century collotype tables, were produced between 1951 and 1953. These tables, scanned and electronically conjoined, also form the basis for the digital reconstruction of the map published as part of its 2007 edition.[17] The original is lost, but its simulacra abound. For a text that before 1830 was literally unknown this fate seems far from tragic.

Its twenty-first century incarnation at the hands of Gulammohammed Sheikh has multiplied the spectral map even further. The "suite" of fourteen *mappae mundi* created by Sheikh can be roughly divided into two or three basic types.[18] The most frequent version of the *mappa mundi* displays the four icons at

13. Kugler, *Ebstorfer Weltkarte,* 1: 18: Aquilo ("Sese Meotides stringent Aquilone paludes"); Septentrio: Goti ("Quos algore ferit Gotos Septentrio querit"); Vulturnus: Seres ("Gentes tectorum mulces, Vulturne, Serorum"); Subsolanus: Indii ("Explicat Eoos se Subsolanus ad Indos"), etc.

14. Georg Heinrich Wilhelm Blumenbach, "Beschreibung der ältesten bisher bekannten Landkarte aus dem Mittelalter, in Besitze des Klosters Ebstorf," *Vaterländisches Archiv für hannoverisch-braunschweigische Geschichte* (1834): 2–21, at 2: "ein unbekannter Frevler."

15. Ernst Sommerbrodt published photographs of the map in atlas form in 1891; the lithographs of the map as a whole that were published by Konrad Miller in 1896 and again in 1900 differ in several ways from that of Sommerbrodt. Both editors freely invented in some sections: Kugler, *Ebstorfer Weltkarte,* 2: 3–9.

16. Dieter Brosius, "Die Ebstorfer Weltkarte von 1830 bis 1943: Ergänzungen zu ihrer Überlieferungsgeschichte," in *Ein Weltbild vor Columbus,* ed. Hartmut Kugler and Eckhard Michael (Weinheim, 1991), 23–40.

17. See Kugler, *Ebstorfer Weltkarte,* 1: 5–6.

18. See the appendix itemising the *Mappamundi Suite* at the conclusion of this chapter.

the corners: Majnun and the old woman; Kabir; Mary Magdalene; and the Pahari dancer (*Mappamundi Suite* 1–7). These icons threaten to enter into the fabric of the image, and on several of the maps Sheikh has repeatedly inserted one or more image (either Majnun and the old woman, or the images of Rama hunting and St Francis preaching) through the interior. Sheikh's *mappae mundi* contain a number of openings in the fabric of the map which the artist has filled with swatches of colour, or patched with other images. Conversely, Sheikh has filled a number of the lesions of the original, such as the vacant Red Sea area, and the frayed northern European section. The second type of *mappa mundi* in the suite appears as a disc on a bed of clouds with two figures on either side of the map: demons in two instances (*Mappamundi Suite* 9: "Turmoil within"; and 12: "Beyond Borders"), while in two other examples the Magdalene engages in a sort of implied dialogue with Majnun and his captor, the old woman (*Mappamundi Suite* 8 and 10: "Magdalene and Majnun") (Figure 35). The third version of the map has no framing imagery, or inserted icons, but sees much of the content of the original replaced by a collage of images, including in one instance a sixteenth-century European world map (*Mappamundi Suite* 14: "Troubled Terrains"; cf. *Mappamundi Suite* 13: "Whose World"). In a final, and entirely appropriate, irony, in 2003–4 four female weavers in Melbourne, Australia, recreated one of Sheikh's *mappae mundi* as a tapestry, with a form and with dimensions that closely resemble those of the original map.[19]

Evidently a meditation on the Ebstorf map and the representation of the world more generally,[20] the "suite" may appear to be a programmatic proclama-

19. Australian Tapestry Workshop (formerly Victorian Tapestry Workshop), "Mappamundi" (2004). The tapestry, which measures 3.025 x 3.6m, was made for display in the Sidney Myer Asia Centre, University of Melbourne.

20. Other works by Sheikh from this period explicitly refer to mapping and/or the legends imported to the *Mappamundi* Suite: "Vasl: Meeting of Layla and Majnun," 2000 (with Nilima Sheikh); "Looking for Layla/Siege/The Nation and the State," 2000; "Mapping: the Nation and the State," 2001; "Whose World is it Anyway!," 2003; and "Tiranga Bharat I and II," 2003. "Journeys," one of four multiple-panelled *kaavad* (portable "shrines" used by itinerant Rajasthani storytellers), made by Sheikh in 2002–4, includes images from the *Mappamundi* Suite, as does the eight-foot-high shrine entitled "Kaavad: Home" made subsequently. Two further images, exhibited at the Kochi Biennale in 2014–15, supplement the original *Mappamundi* Suite, this time reorienting the central image of the Ebstorf map around the figures of Gandhi and Vasco da Gama. The introduction of these figures (and others, including Jesuit missionaries in Asia) falls outside the scope of the present study. Contextualisation of the *Mappamundi* Suite and its constituent images can be found in Peter Maddock, "The Imagini [*sic*] Mundi of Gulammohammed Sheikh: An Exercise in the Dedifferentiation of the Global and Local Ecumene," *Third Text* 20 (2006): 539–53 (though Maddock's discussion of classical and medieval European maps must be treated with caution); Karin Zitzewitz, "Past

tion of tolerance, of religious and social pluralism, and of the shared traditions that underlie sometimes warring faiths. Yet there is an alternative reading. The *mappa mundi* suite can be seen not simply as the expression of a benign tolerance, but as an image sequence with darkly polemical undercurrents, an explosive attack on religious and aesthetic "citadels of purism" through the convergence of times and peoples.

Map against the World?

Sheikh's *mappa mundi* suite is instantly notable for its combination of images that are genuinely pluralist, a meeting of traditions on and around the world picture. These images are far from uncontroversial. Each of the icons imported onto the Ebstorf map by Sheikh contains a hint, and in some cases much more than a hint, of transgression against religious orthodoxy. No single individual or deity could be granted the centrality that the original map accords to Christ, but Kabir, seated at the top right and apparently casting an amused glance across the earth, is perhaps the suite's presiding spirit.[21] The very person of Kabir, a weaver with a Muslim name whose poems declare his worship of the Hindu deity Ram, embodies religious pluralism. Aspects of his biography remain uncertain. He seems likely to have been born into the Hindu weaver caste, the relatively low status of which may have encouraged significant levels of conversion to Islam in the thirteenth and fourteenth centuries.[22] The oeuvre of Kabir is far from clearly defined, with large amounts of pseudonymous material present in the canon. As a result, generalisation about the nature of his verse requires some caution.[23] There are a num-

Futures of Old Media: Gulammohammed Sheikh's Kaavad: Traveling Shrine: Home," *Borderlines* (*Comparative Studies of South Asia, Africa and the Middle East*) (11 March 2016); and Marcia Kupfer, "Worlds Enmeshed," in *At Home in the World*, ed. Sambrani (New York, 2019), 278–93. My thanks to Marcia Kupfer for sharing her article with me in advance of publication.

21. On the seventeenth-century Mughal miniature used by Sheikh see Prabhakar Machwe, *Kabir* (New Delhi, 1968), 16.

22. Jodh Singh, *Kabir* (Patiala, 1971); Charlotte Vaudeville, *A Weaver Named Kabir: Selected Verses With a Detailed Biographical and Historical Introduction* (New Delhi, 1993), 39–65.

23. The verse has not been subject to critical editing until relatively recently: see Vaudeville, *A Weaver Named Kabir*, 131–47, which significantly revises the position taken in her *Kabir*, vol. 1 (Oxford, 1974); for the argument that "Kabir" should be understood as a community of authors see *Kabir: The Weaver's Songs*, trans. Vinay Dharwadker (London, 2003), 58–72. Recent editions are implicitly or explicitly critical of the influential selection made in *One Hundred Poems of Kabir*, trans. Rabindranath Tagore, with Evelyn Underhill (London, 1915; reprinted 1961).

ber of different Kabirs – variously pithy, ecumenical, anti-Brahmin, respectful of authority, bhakti, Sufi, Yogic – and some of the most frequently cited examples of his verse are likely to be para-Kabirian at best. Nevertheless, it is possible to say that, while profoundly religious, Kabir's poetry is at the same time deeply hostile to religious hierarchy and authority. Brahmins are a particular target, but so too are Islamic conventions that deflect rather than nurture religious feeling.

> If you are a Brahman,
> born from a Brahmani,
> Why didn't you enter this world
> through a different path?
>
> If you are a Turk,
> born from a Turkini,
> Why didn't God Himself
> circumcise you in the womb?
>
> Says Kabir,
> there are no low-born:
> This man alone is vile
> who does not invoke Ram.[24]

The sharp criticism of the formal elements of both faiths created a space for Kabir that could not be assimilated wholly into either Hinduism or Islam. It is not coincidental that some of Kabir's verses are preserved among the corpus of Sikh sacred writing, the *Gurū Granth*. In fact, the influences on Kabir's thought seem to have come from religious movements that crossed sectarian lines. He is frequently associated with bhakti, a particularly vigorous form of devotion centred on suffering, love, and yearning for union with the divine. But Kabir's bhakti is inflected with notions derived from Sufism as well as from Tantric yoga, an offshoot from Buddhism in which the individual seeks a state of bliss or "non-conditionment" associated with the concept of the void, freed from the bonds of the material world.[25] As a figure who in some sense exists on the borders of at least

24. Vaudeville, *A Weaver Named Kabir*, 219. Vaudeville glosses entering the world through a "different path" as entering in some way other than vaginal birth, and explains with regard to the next verse that Kabir was opposed to circumcision.

25. William J. Dwyer, *Bhakti in Kabīr* (Patna, 1981); Pradeep Bandyopadhyay, "The Uses of Kabir: Missionary Writings and Civilisational Difference," in *Images of Kabir*, ed. Monika Horstmann (New Delhi, 2002), 9–31; John Stratton Hawley, *Three Bhakti Voices: Mirabai, Surdas, and Kabir in Their Time and Ours* (Oxford, 2005), 267–332. On the significance of Kabir and bhakti for Sheikh see Zecchini, "'More Than One World'," 80.

three or four established religions, drawing from all of them, criticizing all of them, Kabir provokes.

> Wonderful are the deeds of the All-merciful –
> worthless the Veda and the Koran!
> False is the Koranic Law and the sacred Thread;
> neither Turk nor Hindu ever grasped that mystery.
> The enigma of the Mind, they cannot unravel –
> yet, in their folly, they keep talking of two Religions!
> From a mixture of earth and water
> was this universe born:
> When the Sabda is re-absorbed into the Void,
> what then will "Caste" mean?[26]

Some of these qualities of provocation and renunciation are embodied by three other figures in Sheikh's suite: Majnun, Mary Magdalene, and St Francis. The story of Majnun and Layla exists in many different versions, having been subject to multiple retellings since it first became popular in ninth-century Arabic poetry. Possibly the most influential medieval version of the story was its adaptation in the hands of the Persian author Nizami, who constructed a single narrative poem in 1188, which he included as one of five stories in his *Khamsa*. "Majnun," the mad one, is the name given to Qays, a young man from a good family who as an adolescent falls profoundly in love with Layla, a girl of the same age from a different tribe. Although his love is reciprocated, Qays's excessive behaviour (in particular, the composition of verse extolling Layla and his love for her) alarms Layla's father, and he refuses to allow the pair to marry. Qays's response is to become ever more "Majnun." He leaves society and family, lives alone in a mountainous wasteland, and continues to write poetry. In a climactic scene his father takes him to the kaaba at Mecca and advises him to pray to Muhammad to cast out his infatuation with Layla. Instead Majnun prays for the intensification of his love: "if I am drunk with the wine of love, let me drink even more deeply."[27] On one reading, Majnun transgresses the central tenets of Islamic culture and belief: he deserts his family, disobeys his father, pursues secular love, and associates with animals, including unclean ones such as dogs.[28] Even if Majnun is read as affirm-

26. Vaudeville, *A Weaver Named Kabir*, 154. The sacred thread is the *janeu* or *upavīta*, worn by men belonging to the three higher varnas (i.e. castes or social classes); *Sabda* is word or sound, but also by extension poetic composition.

27. Nizami, *The Story of Layla and Majnun*, trans. R. Gelpke, E. Mattin and G. Hill (Oxford, 1966), 44.

28. Michael W. Dols, *Majnūn: The Madman in Medieval Islamic Society*, ed. Diana E. Immisch (Oxford, 1992), esp. 314–53.

ing, rather than transgressing, Islam – a proposition supported by the story's widespread popularity within Islamic societies – he does so in the role of an outsider figure, the ascetic who endures madness, exile and, in the scene chosen by Sheikh, a form of captivity.[29]

This scene is particularly complex. In the version of Nizami, Majnun comes upon an old woman leading a dervish in chains as a means of begging for money.[30] Majnun replaces the dervish, and permits the woman to lead him around the desert. When the two encounter settlements at oases, Majnun recites his love poems, cries out "Layla," bangs head and body against stones, and dances around "like a drunken madman, while the woman punished him."[31] Inevitably they find themselves outside the tent of Layla herself. Majnun utters a lament – "You have left me to myself, sharing with me nothing but your grief ... I am your prisoner; you be my judge" – tears off his chains, and returns to the mountains, typically frustrating any hopes for the lovers' union.[32] The gesture of replacing the dervish is curiously performative: Majnun appears before Layla in a kind of disguise that is at the same time a true representation of his imprisoned, and impassioned, state. In the sumptuous sixteenth-century depiction of the scene used by Sheikh, the degraded nature of the prisoner/beggar is emphasised by a group of children who chase behind him, throwing stones (Figure 36).[33] And in Sheikh's "suite" this moment of willed humiliation spreads across the surface of the earth: on *Mappamundi Suite 2* ("Looking for Layla") Majnun reappears everywhere from India to Sicily to Scandinavia, reiterating the moment at which, more dervish than the dervish, his identity is simultaneously asserted and dissolved (Figure 37).

The posture of Mary Magdalene, who appears opposite Majnun in mute dialogue on two of the *mappae mundi* in Sheikh's suite, is even more obviously one of unfulfilled yearning. This image, familiar within Western medieval

---

29. Ali Asghar Seyed-Gohrab, *Laylī and Majnūn: Love, Madness and Mystic Longing in Nizāmī's Epic Romance* (Leiden, 2003), esp. 109–40 for questioning of Dols's thesis; see also André Miquel and Percy Kemp, *Majnûn et Laylâ: L'amour fou* (Paris, 1984) on Nizami's "Persianisation" of the legend.

30. In the version of the sixteenth-century Baghdadi poet Fūzūli, an old man leads another man who is pretending to be his prisoner; Majnun reproaches them, arguing that only the mad, not the sane, should be chained, and offering himself as a genuine madman. Fūzūli, *Leylā and Mejnūn*, trans. Sofi Huri (London, 1970), 226–27 (ch. 44).

31. *Layla and Majnun*, trans. Gelpke, 104.

32. *Layla and Majnun*, trans. Gelpke, 104–5.

33. London, British Library, MS Or. 2265, fol. 157v. On iconography in Nizami manuscripts more generally see Adel T. Adamova, "The Hermitage Manuscript of Nizami's *Khamsa* Dated 835/1431," in *Islamic Art* 5 (2001): 53–132.

iconography, is based on an event described only in the gospel of John, in which Mary Magdalene sees Christ after his resurrection, but fails to recognise him. Jesus asks her whom she seeks (*quem quaeris*); she mistakes him for a gardener (*hortulanus*), and asks where he has placed her lord. When he addresses her as "Maria," she responds by calling him "Rabboni" ("which means master"), and he utters the words "Noli me tangere, nondum enim ascendi ad Patrem meum" (do not touch me, for I am not yet risen to my father).[34] The iconography heightens the emotional intensity of the scene by showing the Magdalene kneeling with arms extended, expanding upon the implication carried by the Vulgate's "tangere" that she attempted to touch Christ (the original Greek verb, ἅπτομαι, may simply indicate movement towards him).[35] The particular *noli me tangere* chosen by Sheikh comes from the chapel of the Magdalene in Assisi (Figure 38), where it appears opposite a "Raising of Lazarus," in which the Magdalene weeps before Christ in a similarly kneeling posture, though not with arms outstretched. It shows some significant differences to another *noli me tangere* painted by Giotto, in the Arena Chapel, Padua, where the Magdalene's hair is covered, and where her gesture appears less imploring. The hair is significant: a veritable icon of the saint, it is with her hair that she dries Christ's feet.[36] After the resurrection – according to a tradition originating in the ninth century – she becomes "hairy Mary," an ascetic living naked, whose decency is preserved by locks that flow from head to toe.[37] A reformed sinner (commonly understood to mean a prostitute), a devoted disciple whose physical contact with the deity is both permitted and denied, on the margins and finally outside of society, she has more in common with Majnun than meets the eye, and it is the unexpected congruence of their stories that seems to inform Sheikh's use of their images.

It was her penitence for past sins, and her removal from the world, that made Mary Magdalene particularly venerated within the Franciscan movement, to the

34. John 20:11–18.

35. See the discussion in Reimund Bieringer, "Touching Jesus? The Meaning of mē mou háptou in Its Johannine Context," in *To Touch or Not to Touch? Interdisciplinary Perspectives on the* Noli me tangere, ed. Reimund Bieringer, Karlijn Demasure and Barbara Baert (Leuven, 2013), 61–81.

36. Luke 7:38; John 11:2. On the iconography of Mary Magdalene see, *inter alia*, Eve Borsook, *The Mural Painters of Tuscany: From Cimabue to Andrea del Sarto*, 2nd ed (Oxford, 1980), 14–19; Moshe Barasch, *Giotto and the Language of Gesture* (Cambridge, 1987), 169–82; Barbara Baert, *Noli me tangere: Mary Magdalene: One Person, Many Images* (Leuven, 2006); and Baert, *Interspaces between Word, Gaze and Touch: The Bible and the Visual Medium in the Middle Ages* (Leuven, 2011).

37. Baert, *Interspaces*, 20.

extent that Francis could be perceived as a second Magdalene.[38] The Magdalene chapel at Assisi was commissioned by the town's Franciscan bishop, Teobaldo Pontano, who appears clutching the Magdalene's hand just beneath the *noli me tangere*. The story of Francis's life narrated in the upper church at Assisi includes another image used repeatedly in Sheikh's *mappa mundi* cycle, Francis preaching to the birds (Figures 39 and 40). Like so many aspects of the Franciscan tradition, this famous incident is susceptible to different interpretations. The biography of the saint produced by Bonaventure and given official status in 1266 explains that Francis came upon a gathering of birds near the town of Bevagna. He hastened towards them, and they in turn converged on him. His preaching consisted of an admonition to his "bird brothers" to praise their creator for granting them feathers, wings, and the purity of the air. The birds responded with gestures of rapt attention and only departed once Francis had made the sign of the cross.[39] The story serves to illustrate both Francis's skill in preaching and his embrace of God's creation in its entirety. However, in the acts of St Francis compiled between 1327 and 1337 by the obscure friar Ugolino of Monte Santa Maria and an anonymous assistant[40] – a work that gained widespread influence through its Italian translation as *Fioretti* (little flowers) – the story acquired an explicitly geographical significance. In this version, at the end of the sermon the birds rise into the air with marvellous song, and then, upon the sign of the cross made by Francis, divide into four parts, flying to the east, west, south, and north.[41] The image holds the tensions endemic to Franciscanism from its very inception. A merchant who to the dismay of his wealthy father renounces the pursuit of worldly goods in order to repair the Catholic Church, Francis himself is a figure at once transgressive and orthodox, singular and institutionalised. There are parallels here again with the life of Majnun, another father-rejecter who enjoys a special bond with animals, constantly rescuing them from the snares of hunters, and whose wildness risks making him unrecognisable as a human being. In one account of his life, rebuked for not conforming to an established monastic order, whether Benedictine, Augustinian, or Cistercian, Francis declares that God called him through the path of humility, showed him the path of simplicity, and instructed him to be

38. Katherine Ludwig Jansen, *The Making of the Magdalen: Preaching and Popular Devotion in the Later Middle Ages* (Princeton, 2000), 138.

39. Bonaventura de Balneoregio, *Legenda maior Sancti Francisci* 12.3, in *Fontes Franciscani*, ed. Enrico Menestò and Stefano Brufani (Assisi, 1995), 881–82.

40. For discussion of authorship and date see Enrico Menestò's introduction to the *Actus Beati Francisci et Sociorum Eius*, in *Fontes Franciscani*, ed. Menestò and Brufani, 2075–79.

41. *Actus Beati Francisci et Sociorum Eius* 16.30–33, ed. Menestò and Brufani, 2122; *I Fioretti di San Francesco*, ed. Luigina Morini (Milan, 1979), 109 (ch. 16).

"a new madman (*pazzus*) in the world"; the friars should follow no other way.[42] The scene of Francis preaching to the birds can be read accordingly as a moment of radical disorientation (*majnun, pazzus*), in which discourse with animals reveals the narrowness of preaching's normal focus on humanity alone, in the process demonstrating the saint's preternatural powers.

At the same time, the theme of evangelism connects the preaching to the birds with another image, one well known to Sheikh, who has cited it as a formative influence: Sassetta's painting of St Francis preaching before the Sultan, a panel of the altarpiece made for the church of San Francesco in Borgo San Sepolcro in 1437–44 (Figure 41). This episode too is a defining one for the Franciscans, emblematic of the revival of the apostolic mission to convert the infidel. Here again, where most Latin biographies struggled with the evident failure of the mission to convert anybody or – preferably – to secure Francis's status as a Christian martyr, Ugolino and the *Fioretti* added spice to an otherwise bland narrative. In Bonaventure's account, an unnerved Sultan declines Francis's offer to walk through fire to prove the truth of Christianity.[43] But the alternative version introduces a seductive woman who meets Francis in a hostelry and invites him to perform a most wicked deed with her. "I accept; let's go to bed," he rather surprisingly replies – but it turns out that the bed he has in mind is fiery in a very literal sense. When Francis is neither burned nor even bronzed by an enormous blaze, the amazed temptress converts to Christianity on the spot, eventually followed by the Sultan himself.[44] Sassetta's image in fact largely follows the more sober Latin accounts, but it departs from them in showing Francis actually stepping into the fire before the mostly alarmed Saracen audience—one of whom, young, beardless, bare-headed and probably male, looks at the saint with something approaching attraction.

The aspect of Sassetta's craft that particularly struck Sheikh was the painting's clarity of colour in the absence of cast shadows, encapsulating a moment in Western art before the ideology of linear perspective "overran the intimate realism of this provincial terrain."[45] Sheikh has identified continuities between this

---

42. *Compilatio Assisiensis* ch. 18, in *Fontes Franciscani*, ed. Menestò and Brufani, 1497–98: "Et dixit Dominus michi, quod volebat, quod ego essem unus novellus pazzus in mundo; et noluit nos ducere Deus per aliam viam, quam per istam scientiam."

43. *Legenda maior* 9.8, ed. Menestò and Brufani, 860–61.

44. *Actus Beati Francisci et Sociorum Eius* 27.8–24, ed. Menestò and Brufani 2143–45; *I Fioretti*, ed. Morini, 130–31 (ch. 24): "Io accetto, andiamo a letto."

45. "Among Several Cultures and Times," 111. In fact Sassetta appears to have deployed perspective techniques, albeit not entirely consistently, in the Borgo San Sepolcro altarpiece: see Koichi Toyama, "Light and Shadow in Sassetta: The Stigmatization of Saint Francis and the Sermons of Bernardino da Siena"; and Roberto Bellucci and Cecilia Frosinini, "'Cum suis

stage of European painting and Indian art, continuities he felt especially intensely on his return to India from Europe as a young man: "Somewhere the luminosity of Sassetta's interiors overlapped with the procession of [the Muslim saint] Gebanshah Pir, and moving along the overused streets and repeatedly touched walls brought recollections of the streets of Siena Ambrogio [Lorenzetti] had painted."[46] The *mappa mundi* suite may in the final analysis be an argument about the plasticity of artistic traditions, and about the capacity of visual representation to comment upon and enter into the world. The point too is that faiths have no monopoly on art: that images, like narratives, may move between traditions.

Precisely such fluidity characterises the iconography of Rama, who like Francis appears repeatedly through the *mappa mundi* suite. As narrated in the *Ramayana*, the golden deer he hunts is in fact the demon Marica, who has been sent by the scheming Ravana to tempt Rama away from his wife, Sita. Ultimately slain by Rama, Marica is able to impersonate the hero with his dying breath, calling out to Sita in the voice of her husband and setting off a course of events that leads to her abduction.[47] An epic of extraordinary popularity, endlessly retold throughout Asia,[48] the *Ramayana* was notably translated and sumptuously illustrated at the Mughal court of the emperor Akbar (1556–1605). This crosspollination of a Hindu narrative with Muslim artistic traditions can be seen as a critical act of accommodation, even coalescence between the two faiths. Subsequent depictions of the *Ramayana* – such as the deluxe seventeenth-century manuscript from the Pahari region (in the Punjab hills) which is the source of Sheikh's image of Rama and Marica – translated Mughal style into local idiom.[49] And it may be in this spirit of creative interaction that a Pahari dancer appears on many versions of Sheikh's *mappa mundi*. This image, usually attributed to the Guler artist

---

depitis proportionibus': Perspective and Geometry in Sassetta's Borgo San Sepolcro Altarpiece," in *Sassetta: The Borgo San Sepolcro Altarpiece*, ed. Machtelt Israëls, 2 vols (Leiden, 2009), respectively 1: 305–15; 1: 359–69.

46. "Among Several Cultures and Times," 115–16.

47. *Aranyakāṇḍa*, ed. Robert P. Goldman, trans. Sheldon I. Pollock, vol. 3 of *The Rāmāyaṇa of Vālmīki: An Epic of Ancient India*, 6 vols (Princeton, 1991), 169–90.

48. Paula Richman, ed., *Many Rāmāyaṇas: The Diversity of a Narrative Tradition in South Asia* (Berkeley, 1991); Vidya Dehejia, ed., *The Legend of Rama: Artistic Visions* (Bombay, 1994); Gauri Parimoo Krishnan, ed., *Ramayana in Focus: Visual and Performing Arts of Asia* (Singapore, 2010).

49. Bahu-Shangri Ramayana, Kulu. National Museum, New Delhi. Sheikh has celebrated this image for its dissolution of the boundary between viewer and narrative. Gulammohammed Sheikh, "Visualising the Ramayana: Reading Pictures," in *Indian Painting: Themes, Histories, Interpretations: Essays in Honour of B.N. Goswamy*, ed. Mahesh Sharma and Padma Kaimal (Ahmedabad, 2013), 79–91, at 90: "Entranced by the mirages of Marica materialising and disappearing, the viewer is left sharing the golden space of the pursuer."

Pandit Seu and dated to c. 1730, is thought to represent the influence of Mughal
miniatures on local Pahari artistic tradition (Figure 42).[50] Seven men, apparently
villagers, dance flamboyantly to the music of four musicians. In genre, composition, and in the gestures of the dancers, the image strongly resembles a contemporaneous painting, "Dancing devotees" (or "Dancing Derwishes"), in which a
similar number of men, turbans flying, dance vigorously – perhaps too vigorously, since one has fallen and another is being assisted from the fray. It has been
noted that "Dancing devotees" seems to depict a convergence of faiths: the
"dervishes" appear alongside a yogi and Hindus with caste marks on their fore-
heads.[51] Similarly, Pandit Seu's depiction of the dancing villagers has been associated with Besakhi, a "bacchanalian" farmers' festival unique in that it was celebrated alike by Hindus, Muslims, and Sikhs.[52] Seen in this context, the lone
Pahari dancer represents the ecstatic fusion of religious practice, and the annihilation of sectarian identity. In local devotional practice, the image suggests, the
"citadels of purism" in the form of the tenets of faith determined by elites (castes,
priests, popes and other heads of churches) explode – or rather, they never
existed.

Yet for all their shared, pan-religious resonances, this agglomeration of
images within Sheikh's *mappa mundi* suite leads to something unexpected and
perhaps contradictory: the renunciation of the world. Is renunciation not a characteristic of Majnun, of Francis, of Mary Magdalene, all of whom go naked and
live in solitary exile? Does not Rama, noted for his asceticism, fatally leave his
wife as a result of seeking the golden deer – a separation that in at least one major
version of the *Ramayana* is never completely remedied? This renunciation of the
world is not simply a matter of ascetic denial, however. For the renunciation is not

50. Los Angeles County Museum of Art. Acc. no. M.77.19.24. W.G. Archer, *Indian
Paintings from the Punjab Hills: A Survey and History of Pahari Miniature Painting*, 2 vols (New
Delhi and London, 1973), 1: 148–49 (where the image is not attributed to Pandit Seu); B.N.
Goswamy and Eberhard Fischer, *Pahari Masters: Court Painters of Northern India* (Oxford,
1992), 226 (where it is attributed to Pandit Seu).

51. For comparison of the two images see Archer, *Indian Paintings from the Punjab Hills*,
1: 148; F.S. Aijazuddin, *Pahari Paintings and Sikh Portraits in the Lahore Museum* (Karachi
and London, 1977), 26; Goswamy and Fischer, *Pahari Masters*, 226; Roy C. Craven, Jr, "Manaku: A Guler Painter," and Vishwa Chander Ohri, "Pandit Seu and His Sons Manaku and
Nainsukh," in *Painters of the Pahari Schools*, ed. Vishwa Chander Ohri and Roy C. Craven, Jr
(Mumbai, 1998), respectively 46–67; 149–66; esp. 59, 164–65. Sheikh adapts "Dancing
Dervishes" in one of his *kaavad*, "Musings and Miscellanies," which also includes the same
images of Kabir and Majnun and the old lady quoted in the *Mappamundi Suite*; similarly, the
"shrine" entitled "Ayodhya" is centred around the imagery of Rama's chase of the deer.

52. Archer, *Indian Paintings from the Punjab Hills*, 1: 148, citing the description in
Prakash Tandon's autobiography, *Punjabi Century: 1857–1947* (Berkeley, 1968), 57–58.

so much of worldly objects as of the self. In Kabir's verse the loss of the "I" is a repeated theme.

> Repeating "Thou, Thou," I became Thou,
> In me, no "I" remained:
> Offering myself unto thy Name,
> wherever I look, Thou art![53]

Following bhakti principles, the body tends to be viewed as an obstacle to union with a supreme reality – a forest, according to one Kabirian "padh," in which the grazing deer of lust must be shot by the mind.[54] Yet more than lust alone, it is the dissolution of self, the melting of the hailstone in the pond, that is the precondition of enlightenment:

> It was a good thing, hail fell on the ground,
> for it lost its selfhood:
> Melting, it turned into water
> and rolled down to the pond.[55]

The Pahari dancer's pose of ecstatic celebration surely refers to this moment of dissolution. The devotee (of love, of God) seeks not just to remove him or herself from the world but to lose individual identity, to merge with another. The dervish is overpowered by ecstasy, responds with uncontrolled and unplanned movements, experiences a "passing away from self."[56] Where does this leave the world? Transient, impermanent: a temporary host to tumultuous passions and thwarted desire?

That understanding of the world and the self might have seemed wholly congenial to the makers of the Ebstorf map, who lived one or two generations after Francis and who were immediate contemporaries to the decoration of his church at Assisi. The attraction of an ascetic radicalism that yearned for self-annihilation was not so very far from their own orientations. Such impulses had existed within Christianity since its earliest days. They certainly would have comprehended the technique of quoting images on the surface of the *mappa mundi*, of

---

53. Vaudeville, *A Weaver Named Kabir*, 173.

54. Dwyer, *Bhakti in Kabir*, 151–53.

55. Vaudeville, *A Weaver Named Kabir*, 178–79.

56. Ahmet T. Karamustafa, *God's Unruly Friends: Dervish Groups in the Islamic Later Middle Period 1200–1550* (Salt Lake City, 1994; republished Oxford, 2006), 31.

importing faces, figures, and narratives to the world picture – because that was their technique, too. True, it is as an image rather than as description of the world that the Ebstorf map generates creative responses. It is within the category of art, not science, that it flourishes in the twenty-first century. But it flourishes: other eras and other articulations of faith have been added to the *mappa mundi*'s own self-conscious articulation of its descent from Roman geography, its union of Caesar's survey with Christ's ministry, death and resurrection. Perhaps then it is only in a restricted sense that the *mappa mundi* suite of Gulammohammed Sheikh falls outside the category of science. Ebstorf in Baroda offers a way of knowing the nature of things across borders, times, and faiths: a world new and old, alive with narrative, spinning towards the void.

Appendix: The *Mappamundi Suite* of Gulammohammed Sheikh

Mappamundi Suite 1 ("Dwarka"), 2003: Majnun with old woman; Kabir; Mary Madgdalene; Pahari dancer.

Mappamundi Suite 2 ("Looking for Layla"), 2003: Majnun with old woman; Kabir; Mary Madgdalene; Pahari dancer. Majnun and the old woman appear throughout.

Mappamundi Suite 3 ("Marichika"), 2003: Majnun with old woman; Kabir; Mary Madgdalene; Pahari dancer. St Francis preaching to birds and Rama with bow chasing Marica appear throughout.

Mappamundi Suite 4 ("Marichika II"), 2003: Majnun with old woman; Kabir; Mary Madgdalene; Pahari dancer. Rama and St Francis appear throughout.

Mappamundi Suite 5 ("Lands Divided"), 2003: Majnun with old woman; Kabir; Mary Madgdalene; Pahari dancer. Rama and St Francis appear throughout.

Mappamundi Suite 6 ("Distant Destinations"), 2004: Majnun with old woman; Kabir; Mary Madgdalene; Pahari dancer. Rama and St Francis appear throughout.

Mappamundi Suite 7 ("Distant Destinations II"), 2004: Majnun with old woman; Kabir; Mary Madgdalene; Pahari dancer. Rama and St Francis appear throughout.

Mappamundi Suite 8 ("Magdalene and Majnun"), 2004. The map appears as a disc on a bed of cloud. Mary Magdalene (left centre) and Majnun with old woman (right centre).

Mappamundi Suite 9 ("Turmoil Within"), 2004. Map as a disc on a bed of cloud. Two demonic figures appear to the left and right of the frame.

Mapppamundi Suite 10 ("Magdalene and Majnun II"), 2004. Map as a disc on a bed of cloud. Mary Magdalene (left centre) and Majnun with old woman (right centre). The images of the Magdalene and Majnun and the old woman are replicated at the centre of the map.

Mappamundi Suite 11 ("Fortress"), 2003: World as a circular fortress. Kabir; St Francis.

Mappamundi Suite 12 ("Beyond Borders"), 2003: Rama; St Francis; demons.

Mappamundi Suite 13 ("Whose World"), 2004: The map appears without accompanying icons. Collage of numerous images and "quotations" within.

Mappamundi Suite 14 ("Troubled Terrains"), 2004: Map appears without accompanying icons. Collage of numerous images and "quotations" within.

Six Questions

You might be guilty of writing the same essay about eight times over (sometimes without even changing the names and texts, though at least each chapter has a different title). Despite all that reiteration one feels compelled to ask, once again: what is dislocation? You haven't really explained it. Is it an experience? A phenomenon? A concept? An act? A trope? Well, you are going to say, it is all of those things and more. It is noun, verb, adjective. One can be dislocated, one can dislocate, one can perceive and represent dislocation. But that is far too fuzzy. Ultimately, you never defined your key term. And without definition your analysis was destined to remain sketchy, rootless – dislocated, actually.

The danger in striving for a high level of analytical precision is that you attempt to achieve something that did not – and does not – exist. The texts that represent dislocation did not classify it in strict terms. Of course, we can identify numerous types of dislocation for which there were names: exile, *relegatio, translatio, mutatio* ... but without an overarching signifier. That doesn't mean that dislocation did not exist – quite the opposite – but it should suggest why it becomes very difficult and even self-defeating to designate dislocation a phenomenon but not a trope (for example). Nobody was thinking in those terms, and ultimately I question the imposition of excessive rigour on material – but also experience – that is heterogeneous and ill-defined.

In lieu of a definition, it may be helpful to return to collage, itself a noun-verb capable of multiple applications. I explored what I took to be an ancestor of Dadaist collage in the form of the extraordinary corpus of texts and images compiled by Opicinus de Canistris. But there was another, more obvious and more contemporary relative – the "dreamwork" of Sigmund Freud. Unsurprisingly, perhaps, the late nineteenth- and early twentieth-century construction of the unconscious perceived the importance of the overlapping and blurring of places, and their disambiguation. Freud, prompted by a dream in which he confused Rome with Prague, considered the composite structures (*Mischbildungen*) that make up dreams. In some dreams, he concludes, the process of uniting two objects – places, or more frequently persons – into a composite is a failure: "two representations are superimposed and produce something in the nature of a contest between the two visual images."[1] Freud's section on "absurd" dreams develops further the question of the superimposition of places in dreams. There he recounts a particularly striking dream of his own:

> On account of certain events which had occurred in the city of Rome, it had become necessary to remove the children to safety, and this was done. The scene was then in front of a gateway, double doors in the ancient style (the "Porta Romana" at Siena, as I was aware during the dream itself). I was sitting on the edge of a fountain and was greatly depressed and almost in tears. A female figure – an attendant or nun – brought two boys out and handed them over to their father, who was not myself. The elder of the two was clearly my eldest son; I did not see the other one's face. The woman who brought out the boy asked him to kiss her good-bye. She was noticeable for having a red nose. The boy refused to kiss her, but, holding out his hand in farewell, said "AUF GESERES" to her, and then "AUF UNGESERES" to the two of us (or to one of us). I had a notion that this last phrase denoted a preference.[2]

Freud's interpretation of his dream runs as follows:

> This dream was constructed on a tangle of thoughts provoked by a play which I had seen, called *Das neue Ghetto*. The Jewish problem [*Die Judenfrage*], concern about the future of one's children, to whom one cannot give a country [*Vaterland*] of their own, concern about educating them in such a way that they can move freely across frontiers – all of this was easily recognizable among the relevant dream-thoughts.
>
> *"By the waters of Babylon we sat down and wept."* Siena, like Rome, is famous for its beautiful fountains. If Rome occurred in one of my dreams, it was necessary for me to find a substitute [*irgendeinen Ersatz*] for it from some locality known to me. Near the Porta Romana in Siena we had seen a large and brightly lighted building. We learned that it was the *Manicomio*, the insane asylum. Shortly before I had the dream I had heard that a man of the

---

1. *The Complete Psychological Works of Sigmund Freud*, trans. James Strachey, vols. 4–5: *The Interpretation of Dreams* (London, 1953), 324; *Gesammelte Schriften*, vol. 2: *Die Traumdeutung* (Leipzig, 1925), 324: "die beiden Darstellungen überdecken einander und erzeugen etwas wie einen Wettstreit der visuellen Bilder."
2. *Interpretation of Dreams*, 441–42.

same religious persuasion as myself had been obliged to resign the position which he had painfully achieved in a State asylum.[3]

The richness of this dream, and the fluid nature of dreams in general, leads to a striking set of spatial conjunctions, moving from the local to the biblical and transcontinental. From the primary conjunction of Siena-Rome, in which the "Roman" gate (the gate leading to and from Rome) becomes a metonym for Rome itself, Freud's interpretation draws out implied presences. The most crucial of these is his Jewish identity. This is what allows fountains, and the act of weeping, to conjoin Siena with Babylon, via Psalm 137 (itself mediated here through Swinburne's "Super Flumina Babylonis").[4] Freud's subsequent discussion of the dream identifies "Geseres" as a Hebrew word meaning "doom," or colloquially "wailing," and associates the nonsense word "Ungeseres" with unleavened bread, and the flight of Israelites out of Egypt. The "Judenfrage," to be without a *patria/Vaterland*, while living within them, provokes the desire to be "freizügig" – free of movement, and perhaps in particular free to move beyond the invisible walls of the "new ghetto" dramatized in Theodore Herzl's play of 1897.[5]

Freud goes some way to addressing the odd role of Rome in the dream in an earlier passage, in which he discloses a series of dreams about the city. In the first he sees the Tiber from a railway carriage; in the second he beholds mist-shrouded Rome from a distant hill, a view he relates to the Israelites' sight of the promised land, though subsequent analysis reveals that the city in the dream is in fact Lübeck; in the third, he is inside a mysteriously rural version of the city, whose lilies and streams turn out to derive from his memories of a visit to Ravenna. In the fourth dream, Freud is surprised to find Rome full of German posters; it is, also, Prague, where the status of the German language is a matter of controversy.[6] The dreams signify a longing: at the time of *Die Traumdeutung*'s initial publication in 1899 Freud had never succeeded in visiting Rome, ostensibly for practical health-related reasons, but implicitly because of a phobia induced by its overwhelming mixture of classical and Catholic associations. Some of those associations are evident in the "Geseres/Ungeseres" dream, although they remain underexplored: Freud does not comment on the nun, while the significances of the gate – *porta* – as the link between Siena and Rome, and the fountains – *fontes*

---

3. *Interpretation of Dreams*, 442; *Die Traumdeutung*, 370.

4. Didier Anzieu, *Freud's Self-Analysis*, trans. Peter Graham (London, 1986), 260.

5. Strachey's translation of "daß sie freizügig werden können" as "that they can move freely across frontiers" is problematic; compare *The Interpretation of Dreams*, trans. Joyce Crick (Oxford, 1999), 283: "able to move freely from place to place."

6. *Interpretation of Dreams*, 193–98.

– as symbols of origin as well as passage go unremarked. His interest, instead, is in the "absurd" word "(Un)geseres," and his contemplation of it brings forth a "sudden association," and a further set of spatial dislocations. "Geseres/Unge-seres" turns out to derive from an incident that occurred "during the previous Easter, [when] my Berlin friend [Wilhelm Fliess] and I had been walking through the streets of Breslau, a town in which we were strangers."[7] Breslau/Wrocław, a city with a complex Polish and German heritage (and now Livonian, following the mass movements of peoples during the twentieth century), only serves to intensify the spatial sprawl of the dream's significations. A map of Freud's dream would need to show Rome and Siena, but also Vienna, Berlin, and Breslau, and it should depict the flight of the Israelites too. In short, it would resemble a medieval *mappa mundi*.

Spaces mix freely in the unconscious; the point here is not to identify thereby some kind of truth of human experience, but rather to view Freud's account of his dream and his commentary on it as a paradigm for the intermingling of spatial forms. There is the movement of association brought by a place and its name – Rome-Romana; the logic of contiguity – gate-fountain-asylum; the matrix of identity – Jewish-Israel-ghetto-flight; and then the irruptive passage of nonsense – Breslau (Berlin)-(Vienna)-Siena. And finally the question of language's mediation of space: in this case German, but with Hebrew, Yiddish, Latin, and Italian contributing to the mix. Freud decodes the dream through meditation on the crucial prefix "un"; a prefix that appears to deny identification, to signify a state of non-belonging. Obviously, this dream and its interpretation do not tell us what dislocation "is." But they suggest what it can be, as well as some of its propensities towards the impossible, the erroneous, the layered, and at the same time the real.

This is suggestive (or frustratingly digressive?) but the mention of Swinburne's poem prompts me to comment that you have presented a rather secular Middle Ages. The most obvious medieval locus of dislocation – Jerusalem – barely features.

There are many different versions of the Middle Ages, and I readily agree that someone expecting the Middle Ages of cloisters, cathedrals, and devotional intensity might be taken aback at the relative lack of emphasis on the Holy Land, or on exegesis (despite the discussion of Exodus and the Book of Numbers, not to mention saints' lives, and a wide range of Christian authors). This does not pretend in any way to be a comprehensive discussion of dislocation in medieval geographical thought; it offers one perspective only. However, it is worth empha-

7. *Interpretation of Dreams*, 443–44.

sising that the works of classical authors, and therefore luminous figures such as Aeneas and Alexander, Julius Caesar and Gnaeus Pompey – as well as Moses and St Maurice – were also part of the Middle Ages. If we are going to stop drawing firm lines between periods of history, and look at the entire mix of texts that constitute a given historical moment, then we will also have to stop drawing firm lines between the secular and the sacred too. With regard to Jerusalem, it is important to understand that its centrality was constructed over the course of the Middle Ages, undoubtedly given particular impetus by the success of the First Crusade. The representation of Jerusalem at the centre of *mappae mundi*, never the norm, only occurs with any degree of consistency from the thirteenth century.[8] The importance of spatial representation of the Holy Land is unquestionable; but it must be seen as part of the much broader area of medieval spatial representation, which after all encompassed not only the entire known world, but also the antipodes and the celestial spheres. That said, one way of reading the materials gathered together in this book – the reception of classical geography, the themes of *mutatio* and *translatio*, narratives of migration and "nation," revelatory superimposition and collage – is to see each of them as the product of the single greatest agent of dislocation, one whose intellectual, moral, and physical effects lasted for well over a millennium and ultimately affected all parts of Europe: the Christianisation of the Roman world. Medieval geographical thought, however "secular" it may appear, needs to be understood with that precondition in mind.

To someone who has followed "the spatial turn" over the past three decades or more there seem to be some striking absences from your thinking, not to mention your bibliography. What of Lefebvre's "production of space," of Foucault (there's scarcely a heterotopia in sight here), of de Certeau's spatial practices (and there are many others ...)?[9] You might also say a word or two about philosophically-inflected work

8. Ingrid Baumgärtner, "Die Wahrnehmung Jerusalems auf mittelalterlichen Weltkarten," in *Jerusalem im Hoch- und Spätmittelalter: Konflikte und Konfliktbewältigung-Vorstellungen und Vergegenwärtigungen*, ed. Dieter Bauer et al. (Frankfurt, 2001), 271–334; Marcia Kupfer, "The Jerusalem Effect: Rethinking the Centre in Medieval World Maps," in *Visual Constructs of Jerusalem*, ed. Bianca Kühnel, Galit Noga-Banai, and Hanna Vorholt (Turnhout, 2014), 353–65.

9. Henri Lefebvre, *The Production of Space*, trans. Donald Nicholson-Smith (Oxford, 1991); Michel Foucault, "Questions on Geography," in *Power/Knowledge: Selected Interviews and Other Writings, 1972–77*, ed. Colin Gordon, trans. Colin Gordon et al. (Brighton, 1980), 63–77; Foucault, "Of Other Spaces," trans. Jay Miskowiec, *Diacritics* 16 (1986): 22–27; Michel de Certeau, *The Practice of Everyday Life*, trans. Steven Rendall (Berkeley, 1984). For the use of dislocation within political philosophy see Ernesto Laclau, *New Reflections on The*

specifically on geography and even cartography which you don't so much as acknowledge.

You are right that there is now a large body of work on space, place, and the necessity of adding a spatial dimension to our understanding of history, philosophy, literature, and art. I certainly agree with the commitment of the "spatial turn" i) to challenge the privileged position of time in western thought by breaking down the artificial division between space and time, and ii) to insist on the produced and non-transparent nature of space. However, I have found it difficult to respond to the work done on this topic, despite its apparent relevance to my concerns. In the first place, the treatment of the Middle Ages in this corpus (if one can compress a diverse and far from uniform series of contributions in this way) is problematic. The overwhelming temporal focus of writers on space and spatiality is on modernity. It is the modern, and modernity's discourses of space and place that preoccupy the field. Where medieval practices and representations appear at all, they are almost always treated as the foil to modernity: the thing that modernity replaced. The effect is inevitably simplifying. The Middle Ages is characterised by place not space; by an absence of accuracy; by a lack of interest in reality. Representative examples: "For the real scandal of Galileo's work lay not so much in his discovery, or rediscovery, that the earth revolved around the sun, but in his constitution of an infinite, and infinitely open space. In such a space the place of the Middle Ages turned out to be dissolved";[10] "... the adventurous avenue toward infinite space opened up decisively after the thirteenth century in the West. The closely confining circuit of place-as-perimeter dissolved and the vista of a New World of Space began to captivate the ablest minds of the succeeding period";[11] "the first medieval maps included only the rectilinear marking out of itineraries ... along with the stops one was to make and distances calculated in hours or in days";[12] "Der Grundvorgang der Neuzeit ist die Eroberung der Welt als Bild" (The founding event of the modern age is the conquest of the

---

Revolution of Our Time (London, 1990), esp. 39–73. For a helpful overview of the "spatial turn" within medieval studies, with an emphasis on Anglophone and French scholarship, see Meredith Cohen, Fanny Madeline, and Dominique Iogna-Prat, "Introduction," in *Space in the Medieval West*, ed. Cohen and Madeline, 5–13.

10. Foucault, "Of Other Spaces," 23.

11. Edward S. Casey, *The Fate of Place: A Philosophical History* (Berkeley, 1997), 115. The hyperbolic nature of this statement is unfortunate given the attention Casey devotes to classical and late medieval texts throughout his history. The result is a teleology more complex than that presented by Foucault in "Of Other Spaces," but still reliant on the space-place binarism and the unhelpful notion of the dissolving Middle Ages.

12. De Certeau, "Spatial Stories," in *The Practice of Everyday Life*, 120.

world as picture).[13] It seems to me that these characterisations are not merely unfortunate slips by authors whose interests and expertise lie elsewhere, but a fundamental problem in their theses.[14] To put it simply, if they are wrong about the Middle Ages (where people think about space as well as place, a binarism that is not, in the final analysis, particularly helpful;[15] where there is interest in both accuracy and reality, albeit not necessarily on the terms of the twenty-first century; where the itinerary function of maps was not primary; where a subject might view and even make the world-as-picture), then they are wrong about modernity. Modernity – a force, an idea, a period that these authors often attempt to combat, sometimes enlisting the medieval to do so – is less monolithic, more heterogenous and mixed than the "spatial turn" usually allows; and so was the Middle Ages. Given this problem (in many ways the problem of periodisation, rarely addressed in literature of the "spatial turn"), and the very different nature of the approach I wished to take to classical and medieval material, it seemed necessary *not* to engage with this body of writing, many of whose starting points and historical assumptions I do not share, or which I feel should be opened to question. (*Despite that writing's interests in, for example, exile, dislocation, or super-imposition?* — But these are so frequently claimed as typically or essentially modern experiences; what happens when we allow them a longer history than that?) It was better, in other words, to work from the ground of classical, medieval, and later sources, rather than to respond to a set of arguments at odds with, or even on a different topic entirely to my own findings. I acknowledge that for many readers that failure to engage will represent a regrettable absence.

But as a result of this absence your work seems politically and philosophically rather innocent. Have you not evacuated your study of any serious consideration of the role of power in effecting dislocations, or more bluntly in dislocating people and things? You write about Ovid's exile but you hardly mention the emperor Augustus and the force of imperial will that put him into exile (even though Ovid himself mentions it incessantly in his exile poetry). You playfully invoke the idea of migration, yet you don't address real migrants (medieval or not), just fictional ones. There is a lived experience of dislocation that you entirely ignore. Serious consideration of it would require you to engage with the structures of power that require dislocation. And incidentally,

13. Martin Heidegger, "Die Zeit des Weltbildes," in *Gesamtausgabe*, vol. 5: *Holzwege*, ed. Friedrich-Wilhelm von Herrmann (Frankfurt am Main, 1977), 75–113, at 94; "The Age of the World Picture," in *The Question Concerning Technology and Other Essays*, trans. William Lovitt (New York, 1977), 115–54, at 89.

14. Medievalists of course are not immune from simplification of their own period.

15. See the critique of the space-place binarism in Doreen Massey, *For Space* (London, 2005), esp. 62–71.

such consideration would have informed and enlivened your discussion of literature and intellectual history. In short, one misses an analysis that thinks about epistemic power in relation to geographical literature.

What makes spatial dislocation possible? If it is the existence of disorder within order, or at the conjunction of different orders, where does order come from, and whose is it?

I think that the threads of thought about epistemic power and spatial representation are present in my discussion, albeit not always brought into the light. Drawing some of these threads together, it is possible to provide a very brief historical outline of spatial order in relation to structures of power. As I have indicated, classical order was not complete, nor was it completely imperial; yet it contained immensely rich reserves of information and offered a memorable and workable structure for comprehending and representing geographical space. As a result, that order was reiterated through the Middle Ages after its condition ceased to exist. In the classical and medieval periods there was certainly a pedagogy of spatial order: even if "the geography lesson" as such did not exist, spatial representation was sufficiently embedded in mainstream disciplines and forms of art to ensure the steady perpetuation and innovation of geographical thought in educational settings. We are a long way from the emergence of national geographies, however. There were institutions – royal courts, monasteries, and then fraternal organisations, universities, independent scholars, and finally printers – which were sites for the production of geographical space, but the process was not systematic. Similarly, it is certainly possible to discern historical change in the paradigms for spatial representation, without insisting on rigid or unidirectional models ("progress" from medieval to modern, the triumph of the practical mind over myopic monasticism, etc.). Sea charts, to give one frequently cited example of a "modern" innovation, were produced in workshops for commercial purposes, yet they interacted with existing forms of representation such as the *mappae mundi,* and circulated at the papal curia (where Opicinus took them in original directions). As for humanism, Petrarch, Boccaccio and followers attached themselves to courts yet maintained an identity independent of any single noble patron. The printing press perhaps exacerbated rather than transformed this situation. In the sixteenth century the printer/cosmographer served an international clientele, usually while soliciting the support of powerful noblemen. That stance is the default position of humanism: high-minded, often transgressive, sometimes provocative, but comfortable in the service of power.

As this rapid overview indicates, the alignment between power structures and spatial order was never exact. Those structures undoubtedly did generate order at certain points – an imperial province, an ecclesiastical diocese, a realm or a duchy are all formations of power, often interlinked and often with shared spatial ancestry.[16] Yet spatial representation was rarely directed from above or instrumentalised prior to the sixteenth century, and even then it remained decentred. Undoubtedly space inhabited and informed knowledge structures: Orosius introduces history with the description of the world; Isidore includes geographies in his *Etymologiae*; Bede refers repeatedly to models of ecumenical and global space; the "encyclopedias" of the twelfth and thirteenth centuries have to include places, provinces, and regions, their peoples and properties, among the "nature of things." This makes space both significant and relatively unremarkable: no more and no less than a part of the structure of knowledge. In the final analysis, however, if we are searching for the relationship between epistemic power and spatial dislocations, it might be most productive to examine the mobilisation of history. In other words, the question would then be about space as a historical formation. If we accept the proposition that space and history are not opposed concepts in the Middle Ages – history is expressed in spatial terms, while space is understood as imbued with and inextricable from history – then how does space signify in historical terms? What types of spatial history are narrated? Which aspects of the history of spaces, and the spatial dimension of history, are remembered, and which erased? Any answers to these questions need to take into consideration the history of dislocations presented here: the problem of *mutatio*; resistance to translation; the thrills of superimposition.

What about the role of maps in your discussion? Why do you so often fail to integrate them? Quite frequently you have a separate section in each chapter that deals with them, rather than reading them alongside non-graphic texts. It is as if you want to see them as part of a whole which you label "geographical thought" or "spatial representation," but when it comes down to it you end up saying something to the effect of "oh, and as for the maps ... " What status do they have for you?

They are a genre within spatial representation. First it is important to understand that there is a continuity between written descriptions of the world without any graphic element and maps that contain visual elements as well as words. So we have to allow for a fundamental fluidity between verbal and pictorial description, and that fluidity should dissuade us from decontextualising maps – from seeing

16. For the para-Foucauldian construction "imperial formations," on which I am loosely drawing here, see *Imperial Formations*, ed. Ann Laura Stoler, Carole McGranahan, and Peter C. Perdue (Santa Fe, 2007).

them apart from the many texts and images that surrounded them in medieval manuscripts, as well as the architectural spaces in which they were viewed (cathedrals, chapter houses, refectories, libraries, halls, bedrooms, and so on). At the same time, because I do think that maps can be considered a genre (akin to a literary genre, like epic, which is itself not at all fixed in its boundaries, but which does usefully describe certain shared traits) it has made sense to discuss them together. Their status is not that of an afterthought (rather, they are often at the heart of the analysis), but throughout I have wanted to emphasise the level of textual complexity within medieval – and no doubt early modern – maps. Their relationship to classical and late antique texts is often profound; they can function as a visual gloss, but also as an adaptation or a point of reflection on an authoritative text. At the same time, there are medieval and early modern maps that are independent of prior textual authority, or at least dependent on multiple textual sources. As a result, they can be unstable and interesting texts that have their own way of doing things. This is an aspect of maps that I tried to bring out in my discussion of the language of geographical description, for example.

Perhaps we can end by taking a step or two back. As you are no doubt aware, recent political events have placed the concept of Europe under a certain amount of pressure. Some of the pressure has arisen because of tensions between national and supranational bodies, but at a more fundamental level there are difficult questions of identity: who is and is not a European, where does Europe begin and end, does Europe contain, enable, or oppose, the many identities of its peoples? History is deployed (or forgotten) in various ways in the debates that surround the "question of Europe." Scholarship, meanwhile, has begun to search for new ways of understanding European history in terms of the relationships – whether co-operative, mercantile, or antagonistic – between European peoples and states and the regions that surround or interact with Europe: North Africa, the Near East, the spaces of the Mediterranean and Atlantic, and further afield still.[17] At the same time, the notion of a period called the Middle Ages, is – as you have yourself pointed out in this book – far from stable: when did it end and begin? Given this background it is interesting – but also problematic – that you have chosen to define your work through use of the term "European Middle Ages." Did the "European Middle Ages" ever exist? What meaning does it have now?

The answer to your penultimate question is a simple one: no. This term, and others designed to express roughly the same concept, are and always were labels of convenience. Of course things were much more messy.

17. For an inclusive, multi-centred definition of "Europe" see David Wallace, ed., *Europe: A Literary History, 1348–1418* (Oxford, 2016).

In thinking about the meaning of the "European Middle Ages" we could start with Gulammohammed Sheikh's proposition about the co-existence of times: he observed "accretions of time past still alive in interaction with elements of change, unharmonized yet vital."[18] This was a comment made some time ago, slightly pre-dating Bruno Latour's essay of 1991.[19] Both ask us to accept the non-absolute nature of modernity, or in Latour's terms "non-modernity" or "amodernity." (Neither, it could be added, derive from arcane theorising but from lived and observed experience – in Sheikh's case Gujarat of the 1970s; in Latour's the fall of the Berlin Wall and environmental disaster already looming in 1989). There is a point here that is often overlooked, which is that a rejection of the narrative of the inevitable triumph of modernity at the expense of past cultures also entails a rejection of the notion that "traditional" societies are timeless or outside of history. For this reason I reject the notion that medieval spatial representation was static and unchanging, and at the same time I reject the notion of a revolutionary breach between medieval and (early) modern spatial representation. The "Middle Ages" had to be constructed, and it is significant that its construction was essentially a negative one, designed to set it in opposition to two other constructions – classical antiquity and modernity.[20]

The key question though concerns the adjective. For there are difficulties however you try to describe the "Middle Ages." These are in part difficulties of space and language. There is a need to acknowledge a plurality of Middle Ages: the medieval period of the Latin west co-existed with contemporaries in Byzantium, in the Arab world, in Slavonic lands, to say nothing of farther removed regions. Hence monoliths such as "the Middle Ages" – Le Moyen Âge, Das Mittelalter, Il medioevo – are unsatisfactory. A linguistic and cultural signifier such as *Latin* would seem to exclude vernacular languages, even if monumental examples such as E.R. Curtius's *European Literature and the Latin Middle Ages* in fact dealt at some length with vernacular texts. Use of relative terms such as "Western" requires an understanding of "west" that encompasses parts of the north of Europe in the vicinity of the Arctic Circle, while extending deep into the eastern

18. Gulammohammed Sheikh, "Among Several Cultures and Times," in *Contemporary Indian Tradition: Voices on Culture, Nature, and the Challenge of Change*, ed. Carla M. Borden (Washington, DC, 1989), 107–20, at 115.

19. Bruno Latour, *We Have Never Been Modern*, trans. Catherine Porter (Harlow, 1993).

20. Theodor E. Mommsen, "Petrarch's Conception of The 'Dark Ages'," *Speculum* 17 (1942): 226–42; Eugenio Garin, "Medio Evo e tempi bui: Concetto e polemiche nella storia del pensiero dal XV al XVIII secolo," in *Concetto, storia, miti e immagini del Medio Evo*, ed. Vittore Branca (Florence, 1973), 199–224; Jean-Michel Dufays, "*Medium tempus* et ses équivalents: Aux origines d'une terminologie de l'âge intermédiaire," *Il Pensiero Politico* 21 (1988): 237–49.

Mediterranean, and halting abruptly at Gibraltar.[21] But "European" is no less problematic as a descriptor. For while medieval geographical texts were able to provide perfectly clear descriptions of where Europe began and ended (the Mediterranean; the Tanais river; the Western and Northern Ocean), Europe was never a cultural or even religious unity. In his version of Urban II's sermon at the Council of Clermont in 1095, William of Malmesbury sketched an alarmist picture of the constricted nature of Christianity within Europe. Inhabitants in the glacial northern islands could hardly be counted as Christians; Spain and the Balearics had long ago fallen to Muslim rule; the Turk and Saracen pressed from the east.[22] Even allowing for the propagandist intent of the passage, the volatile nature of Christian Europe, always bemoaning shrinkage, but always intending expansion, is clear. Can one meaningfully speak of "medieval European" history, culture, literature, and art? Absolutely, since it is necessary to describe the shared culture that existed, and that was not limited by the particularities of language, political organisation, or ethnic identity. Yet the conjunction of "European" and "Middle Ages" only finally has validity when understood in terms that are far from absolute. After all, the materials gathered in the preceding pages show the very considerable importance of non-Europe to "European" texts. Palestine, Egypt, North Africa, Asia Minor all played a significant role in spatial representation and the articulation of a "European" spatial identity. To the famous pairings of Rome and Carthage, Babylon and Avignon, Jerusalem and more or less anywhere, we can add Thebes and Ebstorf, "African" Pavia. Because of Ovid, certain educated medieval readers thought about the Black Sea; because of Lucan, they carefully considered the topography of Thessaly and the Syrtes. Europe's intellectual past sprawled beyond its borders, such as they existed. So too did its present and future. In that imaginative sense, then, as well as the physical one, *European* must be considered a very loose adjective, one comprised of many dislocations.

21. R.W. Southern, *Western Society and the Church in the Middle Ages* (Harmonsdworth, 1970); Andreas Fischer and Ian Wood, eds., *Western Perspectives on the Mediterranean: Cultural Transfer in Late Antiquity and the Early Middle Ages, 400–800 AD* (London, 2014).

22. William of Malmesbury, *Gesta Regum Anglorum: The History of the English Kings* 4.347.6–7, ed. and trans. R.A.B. Mynors, R.M. Thomson, and M. Winterbottom, 2 vols. (Oxford, 1998), 1: 600–602.

Bibliography

This bibliography is divided into three sections: manuscripts, primary sources, and secondary works. The primary sources consulted in this volume span a wide range of materials. They include the standard classical and medieval authors and texts, studies containing editions of texts (such as those attributed by Patrick Gautier Dalché to Hugh of St Victor and Roger de Howden), facsimiles of maps, collections of conciliar records, and anthologies, as well as literary and foundational works by twentieth-century writers.

Manuscripts

Barcelona, Museo Marítimo, Inv. 3236
Berlin, Staatsbibliothek
    Preussischer Kulturbesitz, Lat. 2 34-I
    Preussischer Kulturbesitz, MS Hamilton 20
Bern, Burgerbibliothek, Cod. 370
Bruges, Openbare Bibliotheek, MS 685
Cambridge, Corpus Christi College
    MS 16
    MS 26
    MS 66
Copenhagen, Kongelige Bibliotek
    Gl. Kgl. S. 2015 4°
    Gl. Kgl. S. 2020
Dublin, Trinity College Dublin, MS 632
El Burgo de Osma, Archivo de la Catedral, Codex 1
Florence, Archivo di Stato, CN3
Florence, Biblioteca nazionale centrale
    Banco Rari 234
    port. 22
Florence, Biblioteca Riccardiana, MS 3827
Florence, Prince Filippo Corsini Collection, chart of Angelino Dulceti
Freiburg, Universitätsbibliothek, MS 380
Lisbon, Arquivo Nacional da Torre do Tombo, MS CXIII/247

London, British Library
    MS Additional 10049
    MS Additional 11992
    MS Additional 18454
    MS Additional 18665
    MS Additional 19891
    MS Additional 28681
    MS Cotton Claudius D.VI
    MS Cotton Julius D.VII
    MS Cotton Tiberius B.V (1)
    MS Egerton 73
    MS Lansdowne 728
    MS Royal 14 C.VII
    MS Royal 14.C.IX
    MS Royal 14.C.XII
    MS Or. 2265
London, College of Arms, MS Muniments 18/19
Milan, Biblioteca Ambrosiana
    MS F.150 sup.
    MS A 79 inf.
Munich, Bayerische Staatsbibliothek
    Clm 4593
    Clm 10058
New Haven, Beinecke Rare Book and Manuscript Library, Art Store 1980.158
    (Francesco Beccari, chart of 1403)
Novara, Archivio Capitolare, MS 44 (cxxxii)
Nuremburg, Germanisches Nationalmuseum, MS La. 4017
Oxford, St John's College, MS 124
Paris, Bibliothèque de la Sorbonne, Archives de l'Université de Paris, Registre 2, vol. 2
Paris, Bibliothèque nationale de France
    Département des Cartes et Plans, Rés. ge. AA 566
    Département des Cartes et Plans, Rés. ge. DD 687
    Département des Cartes et Plans, Rés. ge. B 696
    Département des Cartes et Plans, Rés. ge. B 1118
    MS esp. 30
    MS lat. 4850
    MS lat. 4939
    MS lat. 6802
    MS lat. 8116
    MS lat. 8255
Parma, Biblioteca Palatina, II.21.1613
St Gall, Stiftsbibliothek St Gallen, MS 621

Vatican City, Biblioteca Apostolica Vaticana
  MS Barberinianum lat. 2999
  MS Palat. lat. 1993
  MS Reg. lat. 1543
  MS Vat. lat. 3225
  MS Vat. lat. 3284
  MS Vat. lat. 6018
  MS Vat. lat. 6435
Venice, Museo Correr
  port. 13
  port. 28
Wolfenbüttel, Herzog August Bibliothek, MS 38.2 Aug. 4°
Zürich, Zentralbibliothek, MS Rh.98

Primary Sources

Accessus ad Auctores. Ed. R.B.C. Huygens. Leiden: Brill, 1970.
Accessus Ovidiani. Ed. Gustavus Przychocki. Kraków: Nakładem Akademii Umiejętności, 1911.
Actus Beati Francisci et Sociorum Eius. In *Fontes Franciscani*, ed. Enrico Menestò and Stefano Brufani. Assisi: Edizioni Porziuncola, 1995.
Adam of Bremen. *Gesta Hammaburgensis Ecclesiae Pontificum*. Ed. Bernhard Schmeidler. Monumenta Germaniae Historica Scriptores Rerum Germanicarum 2. Hannover: Hahn, 1917.
Adnotationes super Lucanum. Ed. Ioannes Endt. Leipzig: Teubner, 1909.
Pseudo-Aethicus. "Cosmographia olim Aethici dicta." In *Geographi Latini minores*, ed. Alexander Riese, 71–103. Heilbronn, 1878; repr. Hildesheim: Georg Olms, 1964.
Alberti, Leon Battista. *I libri della famiglia*. In *Opere Volgari*, ed. Cecil Grayson. Volume 1. Bari: Laterza, 1960.
Almagià, Roberto. *Monumenta Cartographica Vaticana*. 4 vols. Vatican City: Biblioteca Apostolica Vaticana, 1944–55.
Ambrose. *Opera V: Expositio Psalmi CXVIII*. Ed. M. Petschenig. Vienna: Tempsky, 1913.
Pseudo-Ambrose. *De xlii mansionibus filiorum Israel*. In Patrologia Latina 17: 9–40. Paris, 1879.
Ammianus Marcellinus. *Res gestae*. Ed. Wolfgang Seyfarth. 2 vols. Leipzig: Teubner, 1978.
Antoninus Placentinus. *Itinerarium Antonini Placentini*. Ed. P. Geyer. In *Itineraria et alia geographica*, 1: 127–74. Corpus Christianorum Series Latina 175–76. 2 vols. Turnhout, Brepols, 1965.
Araṇyakāṇḍa. Ed. Robert P. Goldman. Trans. Sheldon I. Pollock. Volume 3 of *The Rāmāyaṇa of Vālmīki: An Epic of Ancient India*. 6 vols. Princeton: Princeton University Press, 1991.

Aristotle. *Meteorologica*. Trans. H.D.P. Lee. London: Heinemann, 1952.

Arnulf of Orléans. *Glosule super Lucanum*. Ed. Berthe M. Marti. Rome: American Academy in Rome, 1958.

Arrian. "Periplus of the Pontus-Euxine." In *Il Periplo del Ponto Eusino di Arriano e altri testi sul Mar Nero e il Bosforo: Spazio geografico, mito e dominio ai confini dell'Impero romano*, ed. Stefano Belfiore. Venice: Istituto Veneto di Scienze, Lettere ed Arti, 2009.

Arrigo da Settimello. *Elegia*. Ed. Clara Fossati. Florence: SISMEL-Edizioni del Galluzzo, 2011.

Augustine of Hippo. *De civitate dei*. Ed. B. Dombart and A. Kalb. 2 vols. Corpus Christianorum, Series Latina 47–48. Turnhout: Brepols, 1955.

Avitus of Vienne. *Opera*. Ed. R. Peiper. Monumenta Germaniae Historica Auctorum Antiquissimorum 6. Berlin: Weidmann, 1883.

Baudri de Bourgueil. *Poèmes*. Ed. and trans. Jean-Yves Tilliette. 2 vols. Paris: Les Belles Lettres, 1998–2002.

Becanus, Joannes Goropius. *Opera Ioan. Goropii Becani, hactenus in lucem non edita, nempe: Hermathena, Hieroglyphica, Vertumnus, Gallica, Francica, Hispanica*. Antwerp: Plantin, 1580.

—. *Origines Antwerpianae, sive Cimmeriorum Becceselana novem libros complexa*. Antwerp: Plantin, 1569.

Bede. *Bede's Ecclesiastical History of the English People*. Ed. Bertram Colgrave and R.A.B. Mynors. Oxford: Clarendon Press, 1969.

—. *De mansionibus filiorum Israel*. In Patrologia Latina 94: 699–702. Paris, 1862.

Benoît de Sainte-Maure. *Le Roman de Troie*. Ed. Léopold Constans. 6 vols. Paris: Firmin-Didot, 1904–12.

Berlinghieri, Francesco. *Geographia*. Florence, 1482.

Bernardus Silvestris. *Commentum super sex libros Eneidos Virgilii*. Ed. Julian Ward Jones and Elizabeth Frances Jones. Lincoln and London: University of Nebraska Press, 1977.

Bianchi, Phil, Peter Bridge, Ethel Bianchi, and Angela Teague, eds. *Royal Commission to Inquire into the Treatment of Natives by the Canning Exploration Party 15 January – 5 February 1908*. Carlisle: Hesperian Press, 2010.

Biondo Flavio. *De verbis Romanae locutionis*. Ed. Fulvio Delle Donne. Rome: Istituto storico italiano per il Medio Evo, 2008.

—. *Italia illustrata*. Ed. Paolo Pontari. Rome: Istituto storico italiano per il Medio Evo, 2011– . Ed. and trans. as *Italy Illuminated* by Jeffrey A. White. 2 vols. Cambridge, MA: Harvard University Press, 2005–16.

Boccaccio, Giovanni. *De montibus, silvis, fontibus, lacubus, fluminibus, stagnis seu paludibus et de diversis nominibus maris*. Ed. Manlio Pastore Stocchi. In *Tutte le opere di Giovanni Boccaccio*. Volume 8. Milan: Mondadori, 1998.

—. *Esposizioni sopra la Comedia di Dante*. Ed. Giorgio Padoan. Milan: Mondadori, 1965.

Bonaventura de Balneoregio. *Legenda maior Sancti Francisci*. In *Fontes Franciscani*, ed. Enrico Menestò and Stefano Brufani. Assisi: Edizioni Porziuncola, 1995.

Borges, Jorge Luis. "La ceguera." In *Siete noches,* 143–60. México: Fondo de Cultura Económica, 1980.

—. *El libro de arena.* Buenos Aires: Emecé, 1975. Trans. as *The Book of Sand* in *The Book of Sand and Shakespeare's Memory* by Andrew Hurley. London: Penguin, 2001.

—. *The Total Library: Non-Fiction 1922–1986.* Trans. Eliot Weinberger. London: Penguin, 2000.

Buondelmonti, Cristoforo. *Liber insularum archipelagi.* Ed. Gabr. Rud. Ludovicus de Sinner. Leipzig: Reimer, 1824. Ed. and trans. as *Liber insularum archipelagi: Transkription des Exemplars Universitäts und Landesbibliothek Düsseldorf Ms. G13* by Karl Bayer. Wiesbaden: Reichert, 2007.

Burchard of Mount Sion. *Descriptio Terrae Sanctae.* In *Peregrinatores Medii Aevi Quattuor,* ed. J.C.M. Laurent. Leipzig: Hinrichs, 1864.

Caesarius of Arles. *Opera.* Vol. 1: *Sermones.* Ed. G. Morin. 2nd ed. Corpus Christianorum, Series Latina 103. Turnhout: Brepols, 1953.

Cassiodorus. *Institutiones.* Ed. R.A.B. Mynors. Oxford: Clarendon Press, 1937.

Celtis, Conrad. *Oratio in gymnasio in Ingelstadio publice recitata.* Ed. Johannes Rupprich. Leipzig: Teubner, 1932.

Cicero. *De oratore.* Ed. K. Kumaniecki. Leipzig: Teubner, 1969.

—. *De re publica.* Ed. J.G.F. Powell. Oxford: Clarendon Press, 2006.

Cleomedes. *Caelestia.* Ed. Robert Todd. Leipzig: Teubner, 1990.

Cochlaeus, Johannes. *Brevis Germanie Descriptio (1512).* Ed. and trans. Karl Langosch. Darmstadt: Wissenschaftliche Buchgesellschaft, 1960.

Commenta Bernensia M. Annaei Lucani. Ed. Hermann Usener. Leipzig: Teubner, 1869. Repr. Hildesheim: Olms, 1967.

Compilatio Assisiensis. In *Fontes Franciscani,* ed. Enrico Menestò and Stefano Brufani. Assisi: Edizioni Porziuncola, 1995.

Corippus. *In laudem Iustini/Éloge de l'empéreur Justin II.* Ed. and trans. Serge Antès. Paris: Les Belles Lettres, 1981.

—. *Iohannidos, seu, De bellis Libycis libri VIII.* Ed. J. Diggle and F.R.D. Goodyear. Cambridge: Cambridge University Press, 1970.

Cosmidromius Gobelini Person. Ed. Max Jansen. Münster: Aschendorffschen Buchhandlung, 1900.

Dante Alighieri. *La Commedia secondo l'antica vulgata.* Ed. Giorgio Petrocchi. 4 vols. Milan: Mondadori, 1966–67.

—. *The Divine Comedy,* vol. 1: *Inferno.* Trans. Charles S. Singleton. Princeton: Princeton University Press, 1970.

—. *Convivio.* Ed. Franca Brambilla Ageno. 2 vols. Florence: Casa Editrice Le Lettere, 1995.

—. *De vulgari eloquentia.* Ed. Aristide Marigo. 3rd ed. Florence: Le Monnier, 1957.

—. *De vulgari eloquentia.* Ed. Pier Vincenzo Mengaldo. Padua: Antenore, 1968.

—. *De vulgari eloquentia.* Ed. and trans. Mirko Tavoni. In *Opere,* ed. Marco Santagata. Milan: Mondadori, 2011.

—. *Monarchia.* Ed. Pier Giorgio Ricci. Milan: Mondadori, 1965.

Descriptio civitatum ad septentrionalem plagam Danubii. Ed. Bohuslav Horák and Dušan Trávníček. *Rozpravy Československé Akademie Věd* 66 (1956): 1–73.

Dicuil. *Liber de mensura orbis terrae.* Ed. J.J. Tierney. Dublin: Dublin Institute for Advanced Studies, 1967.

Dionysius of Byzantium. "Navigation on the Bosforus." In *Il* Periplo del Ponto Eusino *di Arriano e altri testi sul Mar Nero e il Bosforo: Spazio geografico, mito e dominio ai confini dell'Impero romano*, ed. Stefano Belfiore. Venice: Istituto Veneto di Scienze, Lettere ed Arti, 2009.

Dracontius. *Oeuvres.* Ed. and trans. Claude Moussy and Colette Camus. Vols 1 and 2. Paris: Les Belles Lettres, 1985–88.

Die Ebstorfer Weltkarte. Ed. Hartmut Kugler. 2 vols. Berlin: Akademie Verlag, 2007.

Egeria. *Itinerarium Egeriae.* Ed. Aet. Franceschini and R. Weber. In *Itineraria et alia geographica*, 1: 28–90. Corpus Christianorum, Series Latina 175–76. 2 vols. Turnhout, Brepols, 1965.

Einhard. *Vita Karoli Magni.* Ed. G.H. Pertz. Rev. G. Waitz. 6th ed. Monumenta Germaniae Historica Scriptores Rerum Germanicarum 25. Hannover: Hahn, 1911.

Eratosthenes. *Eratosthenes' Geography.* Trans. Duane W. Roller. Princeton: Princeton University Press, 2010.

Eriugena. *Periphyseon. Liber quartus.* Ed. Edouard A. Jeauneau. Corpus Christianorum, Continuatio Mediaevalis 164. Turnhout: Brepols, 2000.

Ermolao Barbaro. *Castigationes Plinianae et in Pomponiam Melam.* Ed. Giovanni Pozzi. 3 vols. Padua: Antenore, 1973–79.

Eusebius. *Werke*, 3.1: *Das Onomastikon der biblischen Ortsnamen.* Ed. Erich Klostermann. Leipzig: Hinrichs'sche Buchhandlung, 1904.

Expositio totius mundi et gentium. Ed. Jean Rougé. Paris: Cerf, 1966.

Filelfo, Francesco. *De exilio / On Exile.* Ed. Jeroen de Keyser. Trans. W. Scott Blanchard. Cambridge: Harvard University Press, 2013.

I Fioretti di San Francesco. Ed. Luigina Morini. Milan: Rizzoli Editore, 1979.

Fra Mauro's World Map. Ed. and trans. Piero Falchetta. Turnhout: Brepols, 2006.

Freud, Sigmund. *The Complete Psychological Works of Sigmund Freud.* Trans. James Strachey. Vols. 4–5: *The Interpretation of Dreams.* London: Hogarth Press, 1953.

—. *Gesammelte Schriften.* Vol. 2: *Die Traumdeutung.* Leipzig: Internationaler Psychoanalytischer Verlag, 1925.

—. *The Interpretation of Dreams.* Trans. Joyce Crick. Oxford: Oxford University Press, 1999.

Fulcher of Chartres. *Historia Hierosolymitana (1095–1127).* Ed. Heinrich Hagenmeyer. Heidelberg: Winter, 1913.

Fulgentius. "Expositio Virgilianae continentiae secundum philosophos moralis." In *Opera*, ed. Rudolf Helm. Leipzig: Teubner, 1898.

Fūzūlī. *Leylā and Mejnūn.* Trans. Sofi Huri. London: Allen and Unwin, 1970.

Gautier Dalché, Patrick. *La 'Descriptio Mappe Mundi' de Hugues de Saint-Victor.* Paris: Études Augustiniennes, 1988.

—. *Du Yorkshire à l'Inde: Une 'géographie' urbaine et maritime de la fin du XIIe siècle (Roger de Howden?)*. Geneva: Droz, 2005.

Géographes grecs, vol. 1. Ed. and trans. Dider Marcotte. Paris: Les Belles Lettres, 2000.

Geographi Latini minores. Ed. Alexander Riese. Heilbronn, 1878; repr. Hildesheim: Olms, 1964.

Gervase of Tilbury. *Otia imperialia: Recreation for an Emperor*. Ed. and trans. S.E. Banks and J.W. Binns. Oxford: Clarendon Press, 2002.

Glossa ordinaria. In Patrologia Latina 113. Paris, 1879.

Gower, John. *Vox clamantis*. In *The Complete Works of John Gower*, ed. G.C. Macaulay. Vol. 4: *The Latin Works*, 3–314. Oxford: Clarendon Press, 1902.

Gregory of Tours. *Libri Historiarum X*. Ed. Bruno Krusch and Wilhelm Levison. Monumenta Germaniae Historica Scriptores rerum Merovingicarum 1.1. Hannover: Hahn, 1951.

Gregory the Great. *Dialogi Libri IV*. Ed. Umberto Moricca. Rome: Istituto Storico Italiano, 1924.

Guido da Pisa. *Expositiones et Glose super Comediam Dantis*. Ed. Vincenzo Cioffari. Albany: SUNY Press, 1974.

—. *Liber Guidonis compositus de variis historiis*. Ed. Michele Campopiano. Florence: SISMEL-Edizioni del Galluzzo, 2008.

Hausmann, Raoul. *Courrier Dada* [1958]. Rev ed. Marc Dachy. Paris: Allia, 1992.

Hegesippus. *Historiae Libri V*. Ed. V. Ussani. 2 vols. Vienna: Hölder-Pichler-Tempsky, 1932–60.

Henry of Huntingdon. *Historia Anglorum: The History of the English People*. Ed. and trans. Diana Greenway. Oxford: Clarendon Press, 1996.

Heraclitus. *Heraclitus: The Cosmic Fragments*. Ed. G.S. Kirk. Cambridge: Cambridge University Press, 1962.

The Hereford Map. Ed. Scott D. Westrem. Turnhout: Brepols, 2001.

Herodotus. *Historiae*. Ed. N.G. Wilson. 2 vols. Oxford: Clarendon Press, 2015.

Higden, Ranulf. *Polychronicon*. Ed. Churchill Babington. 9 vols. London: Longman, 1865–86.

Hildegard of Bingen. *Scivias*. Ed. A. Führkötter and A. Carlevaris. 2 vols. Turnhout: Brepols, 1978.

Honorius Augustodunensis. *Imago mundi*. Ed. Valerie I.J. Flint. *Archives d'histoire doctrinale et littéraire du Moyen Âge* 49 (1982): 7–153.

Horace. *Opera*. Ed. D.R. Shackleton Bailey. Stuttgart: Teubner, 1985.

Hugh of Fleury. *Historia ecclesiastica*. Ed. G. Waitz, Monumenta Germaniae Historica Scriptores 9, 349–64. Hanover: Hahn, 1851.

Hugh of St Victor. *De archa Noe; Libellus de formatione arche*. Ed. P. Sicard. Corpus Christianorum, Continuatio Mediaevalis 176. Turnhout: Brepols, 2001.

—. *Didascalicon de studio legendi: A Critical Text*. Ed. Charles Henry Buttimer. Washington, DC: Catholic University Press, 1939.

—. *See also under* Gautier Dalché, Patrick *above*

Isidore of Seville. *Etymologiarum sive originum libri xx.* Ed. W.M. Lindsay. 2 vols. Oxford: Clarendon Press, 1911.

—. *Etymologiae IX: Les langues et les groupes sociaux.* Ed. and trans. Marc Reydellet. Paris: Les Belles Lettres, 1984.

—. *Etymologiae XIV: De Terra.* Ed. and trans. Olga Spevak. Paris: Les Belles Lettres, 2011.

—. *Quaestiones in Vetus Testamentum.* In Patrologia Latina 83: 207–444. Paris, 1862.

Itinera Hierosolymitana Crucesignatorum (saec. XII–XIII). Ed. Sabino de Sandoli. 4 vols. Jerusalem: Franciscan Printing Press, 1978–84.

Itineraria Romana. Vol. 1. Ed. Otto Cuntz. 1929; repr. Stuttgart: Teubner, 1990.

Itineraria Romana. Vol. 2. Ed. Joseph Schnetz. 1940; repr. Stuttgart: Teubner, 1990.

Jacobus de Voragine. *Legenda aurea.* Ed. Giovanni Paolo Maggioni. 2 vols. Florence: SISMEL-Edizioni del Galluzzo, 1998.

Jacopo da Verona. *Liber peregrinationis.* Ed. Ugo Monneret de Villard. Rome: Libreria dello Stato, 1950.

Jean de Hesdin. *Contra Franciscum Petrarcham Epistola.* In Francis Petrarch, *Invectives,* trans. Rebecca Lenoir, 505–27. Grenoble: Millon, 2003.

Jerome. *Adversus Iovinanum.* In Patrologia Latina 23: 211–338. Paris, 1883.

—. *Commentariorum in Danielem Libri III.* In *Opera,* vol. 1.5, ed. F. Glorie. Corpus Christianorum, Series Latina 75A. Turnhout: Brepols, 1964.

—. *Epistulae.* Ed. I. Hilberg. 3 vols. Vienna: Österreichischen Akademie der Wissenschaften, 1996.

—. *Liber interpretationis Hebraicorum nominum.* In *Opera,* vol. 1.1, ed. P. de Lagarde. Corpus Christianorum, Series Latina 72. Turnhout: Brepols, 1959.

John of Salisbury. *Policraticus.* Ed. Clement Webb. 2 vols. Oxford: Clarendon Press, 1909.

Jordanes. *De origine actibusque Getarum.* Ed. Francesco Giunta and Antonino Grillone. Rome: Istituto storico per il Medio Evo, 1991.

Julius Caesar. *Commentarii.* Ed. Alfred Klotz. 2 vols. Leipzig: Teubner, 1952–57.

Kabir. *Kabīr.* Ed. and trans. Charlotte Vaudeville. Vol. 1. Oxford: Clarendon Press, 1974.

—. *Kabir: The Weaver's Songs.* Trans. Vinay Dharwadker. London: Penguin, 2003.

—. *One Hundred Poems of Kabir.* Trans. Rabindranath Tagore, with Evelyn Underhill. London: Macmillan, 1915.

—. *A Weaver Named Kabir: Selected Verses With a Detailed Biographical and Historical Introduction.* Ed. and trans. Charlotte Vaudeville. New Delhi: Oxford University Press, 1993.

Kamal, Youssouf. *Monumenta Cartographica Africae et Aegypti.* 5 vols. Leiden, 1926–53.

Landino, Cristoforo. *Comento sopra la Comedia.* Ed. Paolo Procaccioli. 4 vols. Rome: Salerno Editrice, 2001.

—. *Disputationes Camaldulenses.* Ed. Peter Lohe. Florence: Sansoni, 1980.

Leonardo Bruni Aretino. *Lettres familières.* Ed. and trans. Laurence Bernard-Pradelle, 2 vols. Montpellier: Presses Universitaires de la Méditerranée, 2014.

Lhuyd, Humfrey. *Commentarioli Britannicae Descriptionis Fragmentum.* Cologne, 1572.

—. "De Mona Insula." In Abraham Ortelius, *Theatrum Orbis Terrarum.* Antwerp, 1570.

Livy. *Ab urbe condita libri I–V*. Ed. R.M. Ogilvie. Oxford: Clarendon Press, 1974.

—. *Ab urbe condita libri XXXI–XL*. Ed. John Briscoe. 2 vols. Stuttgart: Teubner, 1991.

Lucan. *Bellum Civile*. In *Lucani Opera*, ed. Renato Badalì. Rome: Istituto Poligrafico e Zecca dello Stato, 1992.

—. *De Bello Ciuili Book I*. Ed. Paul Roche. Oxford: Oxford University Press, 2009.

—. *Bellum civile (Pharsalia) Libro IV*. Ed. Paolo Esposito. Naples: Loffredo, 2009.

Macrobius. *Commentarii in Somnium Scipionis,* 2 vols. Ed. and trans. M. Armisen-Marchetti. Paris: Les Belles Lettres, 2001–3.

—. *Saturnalia*. Ed. and trans. Robert A. Kaster. 3 vols. Cambridge: Harvard University Press, 2011.

Il mappamondo medioevale di Vercelli (1191–1218?). Ed. Carlo F. Capello. Turin: Fanton, 1976.

Martianus Capella. *De nuptiis Philologiae et Mercurii*. Ed. James Willis. Leipzig: Teubner, 1983.

"Martyrium S. Clementis." In Patrologia Graeca 2: 617–32. Paris, 1891.

The Medieval French Roman d'Alexandre, vol. 1: *Text of the Arsenal and Venice Versions*. Ed. Edward C. Armstrong and Milan S. La Du. Princeton: Princeton University Press, 1937.

The Medieval French Roman d'Alexandre, vol. 3: *Version of Alexandre de Paris*. Ed. Edward C. Armstrong and Alfred Foulet. Princeton: Princeton University Press, 1949.

Moholy-Nagy, László. "In Defense of 'Abstract' Art" [1945]. In *Moholy-Nagy*, ed. Richard Kostelanetz, 44–46. New York: Praeger, 1970.

—. "A New Instrument of Vision" [1932]. In *Moholy-Nagy*, ed. Richard Kostelanetz, trans. F.D. Klingender and P. Morton Shand, 50–54. New York: Praeger, 1970.

Neue Zürcher Zeitung. "Koptischer Patriarch zu Besuch in der Schweiz." 13 July, 2004.

Nizami. *The Story of Layla and Majnun*. Trans. R. Gelpke, E. Mattin, and G. Hill. Oxford: Bruno Cassirer, 1966.

Notitia dignitatum. Ed. Otto Seeck. Berlin: Weidmann, 1876.

The Old English History of the World: An Anglo-Saxon Rewriting of Orosius. Ed. and trans. Malcolm R. Godden. Cambridge: Harvard University Press, 2016.

The Old English Orosius. Ed. Janet Bately. Early English Text Society, supplementary series 6. London: Oxford University Press, 1980.

Opicinus de Canistris. *De preeminentia spiritualis imperii*. Ed. Richard Scholtz. In "Unbekannte politische Streitschriften aus der Zeit Ludwigs des Bayern (1327–1354)." Bibliothek des Kgl. Preussischen Historischen Instituts in Rom 9 and 10 (1911–14): 1: 37–43; 2: 89–104.

—. *Le journal singulier d'Opicinus de Canistris (1337–vers 1341): Vaticanus latinus 6435*. Ed. and trans. Muriel Laharie. 2 vols. Vatican City: Biblioteca Apostolica Vaticana, 2008.

—. *Liber de laudibus civitatis ticinensis*. Ed. R. Maiocchi and F. Quintavalle. Rerum Italicarum Scriptores 11.1. Città di Castello: Lapi, 1903.

Origen. *Werke*. Vols 6–7: *Homilien zum Hexateuch*. Ed. W.A. Baehrens. Leipzig: Hinrichs'sche Buchhandlung, 1920–21.

Orosius, Paulus. *Historiarum adversum paganos libri vii.* Ed. C. Zangemeister. Vienna: C. Geroldi filium, 1882. Ed. and trans. as *Histoires (contre les païens)* by Marie-Pierre Arnaud-Lindet. 3 vols. Paris: Les Belles Lettres, 1990–91.

Ortelius, Abraham. *Abrahami Ortelii et virorum eruditorum ad eundem et ad Jacobum Colium Ortelianum epistulae.* Ed. J.H. Hessels. Cambridge: Cambridge University Press, 1887.

—. *Theatrum Orbis Terrarum.* Antwerp, 1570; 1573; 1579; 1595; 1601.

Otto of Freising. *Chronica sive Historia de duabus civitatibus.* Ed. A. Hofmeister. Monumenta Germaniae Historica Scriptores rerum Germanicarum 45. Hanover: Hahn, 1912.

Ovid. *Ex Ponto libri qvattvor.* Ed. J.A. Richmond. Leipzig: Teubner, 1990.

—. *Heroides.* Ed. G.P. Goold. Trans. Grant Showerman. 2nd ed. Cambridge: Harvard University Press, 1977.

—. *Metamorphoses.* Ed. R.J. Tarrant. Oxford: Clarendon Press, 2004.

—. *Tristia.* Ed. John Barrie Hall. Stuttgart and Leipzig: Teubner, 1995. Ed. and trans. Georg Luck. 2 vols. Heidelberg: Carl Winter Universitätsverlag, 1967.

Pseudo-Ovid. *De vetula: Untersuchungen und Text.* Ed. Paul Klopsch. Leiden: Brill, 1967.

Passio Acaunensium martyrum. Ed. Bruno Krusch. In *Passiones vitaeque sanctorum aevi Merovingici et antiquiorum aliquot,* 32–41. Monumenta Germaniae Historica Scriptorum rerum Merovingicarum 3. Hannover: Hahn, 1896.

The Periplus Maris Erythraei. Trans. Lionel Casson. Princeton: Princeton University Press, 1989.

Peter Damian. *Die Briefe des Petrus Damiani.* Ed. Kurt Reindel. Monumenta Germaniae Historica, Die Briefe der deutschen Kaiserzeit 4. 4 vols. Munich: Monumenta Germaniae Historica, 1983–93.

Peter the Deacon. *Liber de locis sanctis.* Ed. R. Weber. In *Itineraria et alia geographica,* 1: 93–103. Corpus Christianorum, Series Latina 175–76. 2 vols. Turnhout: Brepols, 1965.

Petrarch, Francis. *Contra eum qui maledixit Italie.* Ed. Monica Berté. Florence: Casa Editrice Le Lettere, 2005.

—. *De gestis Cesaris.* Ed. Giuliana Crevatin. Pisa: Scuola Normale Superiore, 2003.

—. *Le Familiari.* Ed. Vittorio Rossi. 4 vols. Florence: Sansoni, 1933–42.

—. *Invectives.* Ed. and trans. David Marsh. Cambridge, MA: Harvard University Press, 2003.

—. *Itinerarium ad sepulcrum Domini nostri Ihesu Christi.* Ed. Francesco Lo Monaco. Bergamo: Lurbina, 1990.

—. *Lettere disperse.* Ed. Alessandro Pancheri. Parma: Fondazione Pietro Bembo/Ugo Guanda, 1994.

—. *Liber sine nomine.* In *Petrarcas 'Buch ohne Namen' und die päpstliche Kurie: Ein Beitrag zur Geistesgeschichte der Frührenaissance,* ed. Paul Piur. Halle: Niemeyer, 1925.

—. *Rerum Senilium Epistolae: Lettres de la Vieillesse.* Ed. Elvira Nota. Trans. Frédérique Castelli, François Fabre, Antoine de Rosny, and Laure Schebat. 5 vols. Paris: Les Belles Lettres, 2002–13.

Petrus Pictor. *Carmina.* Ed. L. Van Acker. Corpus Christianorum, Continuatio Mediaevalis 25. Turnhout: Brepols, 1972.

Piccolomini, Aeneas Silvius. *Asiae descriptio/Descripción de Asia*. Ed. and trans. Domingo F. Sanz. Madrid: Consejo Superior de Investigaciones Científicas, 2010.

—. *De Europa*. Ed. Adrianvs van Heck. Vatican City: Biblioteca Apostolica Vaticana, 2001.

Pietro Alighieri. *Il 'Commentarium' di Pietro Alighieri*. Ed. Roberto della Vedova and Maria Teresa Silvotti. Florence: Olschki, 1978.

Plato. *Phaedo*. Ed. C.J. Rowe. Cambridge: Cambridge University Press, 1993.

—. *The Republic*. Ed. James Adam. 2nd ed. Cambridge: Cambridge University Press, 1963.

—. *Timaeus, Critias, Cleitophon, Menexenus, Epistles*. Trans. R.G. Bury. Cambridge: Harvard University Press, 1929.

Pliny the Elder. *Naturalis Historiae Libri XXXVII*. Ed. C. Mayhoff. 6 vols. Leipzig: Teubner, 1892–1909.

—. *Histoire naturelle*. Vol. 6.4: *L'Asie africaine sauf l'Égypte, les dimensions et les climats du monde habité*. Ed. and trans. Jehan Desanges. Paris: Les Belles Lettres, 2008.

Plutarch. *De placitis philosophorum*. In *Œuvres morales*, vol. 12.2: *Opinions des philosophes*. Ed. and trans. Guy Lachenaud. Paris: Les Belles Lettres, 1993.

Poetae Latini Aevi Carolini. Ed. E. Dümmler, 4 vols. Monumenta Germaniae Historica Poetae Latini medii aevi 1–4. Berlin: Weidmann, 1881–1923.

Pompilius, Paulus. *Syllabae*. Rome, 1488.

Pomponius Mela. *De chorographia libri tres*. Ed. Piergiorgio Parroni. Rome: Edizioni di storia e letteratura, 1984.

Priscian. *La Périégèse de Priscien*. Ed. Paul van de Woestijne. Bruges: De Tempel, 1953.

Prudentius. *Carmina*. Ed. M.P. Cunningham. Corpus Christianorum, Series Latina 126. Turnhout: Brepols, 1966.

Ptolemy, Claudius. *Geographiae opus novissima traductione e Grecorum archetypis castigatissime pressum*. Strasbourg, 1513.

—. *Handbuch der Geographie*. Ed. and trans. Alfred Stückelberger, Florian Mittenhuber, and Gerd Graßhoff. 3 vols. Basel: Schwabe Verlag, 2006–9.

Quintilian. *Institutionis oratoriae libri duodecim*. Ed. M. Winterbottom. 2 vols. Oxford: Clarendon Press, 1970.

Rabanus Maurus. *Enarrationes in librum Numerorum*. In Patrologia Latina 108: 808–27. Paris, 1864.

Roger de Howden: *see under* Gautier Dalché, Patrick *above*

Le Roman de Thèbes. Ed. Guy Raynaud de Lage. 2 vols. Paris: Champion, 1966–67.

Rorgo Fretellus. *Rorgo Fretellus de Nazareth et sa description de la terre sainte: Histoire et édition du texte*. Ed. P.C. Boeren. Amsterdam: North Holland Publishing Company, 1980.

Sallust. *Historiarum reliquiae*. Ed. B. Maurenbrecher. Leipzig: Teubner, 1891–93.

—. *Iugurtha*. Ed. L.D. Reynolds. Oxford: Clarendon Press, 1991.

Salutati, Coluccio. *De laboribus Herculis*. Ed. B.L. Ullman. Zürich: Thesauri Mundi, 1951.

—. *Epistolario*. Ed. Francesco Novati. 4 vols. Rome: Istituto Storico Italiano, 1891–1911.

Seneca. *Naturalium quaestionum libros*. Ed. Harry M. Hine. Stuttgart: Teubner, 1996.

Servius. *In Vergilii carmina Commentarii.* Ed. G. Thilo and H. Hagen. 3 vols. Leipzig: Teubner, 1881–87.

Pseudo-Skylax. *Pseudo-Skylax's Periplous: The Circumnavigation of the Inhabited World.* Ed. and trans. Graham Shipley. Exeter: Bristol Phoenix Press, 2011.

Solinus, Julius. *Collectanea rerum memorabilium.* Ed. Theodor Mommsen. 2nd ed. Berlin: Weidmann, 1895.

Statius. *Silvae.* Ed. E. Courtney. Oxford: Clarendon Press, 1990.

Stella, Tilemann. "Itinera Israelitarum ex Aegypto loca et insignia miracula." Basel, Universitätsbibiliothek, Kartenslg AA 104. 1557.

Stephanus de Borbone. *Tractatus de diversis materiis predicabilibus.* Ed. Jacques Berlioz and Jean-Luc Eichenlaub. Corpus Christianorum, Continuatio Mediaevalis 124. Turnhout: Brepols, 2002.

Stevens, Wallace. *The Collected Poems of Wallace Stevens.* New York: Knopf, 1954.

Strabo. *Geography.* Ed. and trans. H.L. Jones. 8 vols. London: Heinemann, 1917–33.

—. *The Geography of Strabo.* Trans. Duane W. Roller. Cambridge: Cambridge University Press, 2014.

Supplementum Adnotationum super Lucanum. Ed. G.A. Cavajoni. 3 vols. Milan: Cisalpino-Goliardica, 1979–84; Amsterdam: Hakkert, 1990.

Symon Semeonis. *Itinerarium Symonis Semeonis ab Hybernia ad Terram Sanctam.* Ed. Mario Esposito. Dublin: Dublin Institute for Advanced Studies, 1960.

Tacitus. *Annales.* Ed. H. Heubner. 2 vols. Stuttgart: Teubner, 1983.

Theodoric. *De locis sanctis.* In *Peregrinationes tres: Saewulf, John of Würzburg, Theodericus,* ed. R.B.C. Huygens. Corpus Christianorum, Continuatio Mediaevalis 139. Turnhout: Brepols, 1994.

Thietmar. *Peregrinatio.* Ed. J.C.M. Laurent. Hamburg: Nolte und Köhler, 1857.

Tibullus, Albius. *Carmina.* Ed. Georg Luck. Stuttgart: Teubner, 1988.

Trevisa, John. "Epistle to Thomas, Lord Berkeley." Ed. Stephen Shepherd. In *The Idea of the Vernacular: An Anthology of Middle English Literary Theory, 1280–1520,* ed. Jocelyn Wogan-Browne, Nicholas Watson, Andrew Taylor, and Ruth Evans, 134–35. University Park: Pennsylvania State University Press, 1999.

Valla, Lorenzo. *De linguae latinae elegantia.* Ed. and trans. Santiago López Moreda. 2 vols. Cáceres: Universidad de Extremadura, 1999.

Van der Putte, Bernard. "Itinera Israelitarum ex Aegypto loca et insignia miracula," after Tilemann Stella. Paris, Bibliothèque nationale de France, Département des Cartes et Plans, Rés. ge. AA 1412. 1559.

Varro. *De lingua latina.* Ed. G. Goetz and F. Schoell. Leipzig: Teubner, 1910.

Venantius Fortunatus. *Poèmes.* Ed. and trans. Marc Reydellet. 3 vols. Paris: Les Belles Lettres, 1994–2004.

Vibius Sequester. *De fluminibus fontibus lacubus.* Ed. R. Gelsomino. Leipzig: Teubner, 1967.

Virgil. *Opera.* Ed. R.A.B. Mynors. Oxford: Clarendon Press, 1969.

Vita abbatum agaunensium. In *Passiones vitaeque sanctorum aevi Merovingici,* ed. Bruno

Krusch. Monumenta Germaniae Historica Scriptorum rerum Merovingicarum 7. Hannover: Hahn, 1920.

Vitruvius. *De architectura (De l'Architecture)*. Book 6. Ed. and trans. Louis Callebat. Paris: Les Belles Lettres, 2004.

von der Hardt, Hermann, ed. *Magnum Œcumenicum Constantiense Concilium de universali Ecclesiae reformatione, unione, et fide.* 7 vols. Frankfurt, 1696–1742.

Walahfrid Strabo. "Ymnus de agaunensibus martyribus." In *Poetae Latini Aevi Carolini*, ed E. Dümmler, 2: 367–69. 4 vols. Berlin: Weidmann, 1884.

Walsingham, Thomas. *De Archana Deorum*. Ed. Robert A. van Kluyve. Durham: Duke University Press, 1968.

Walter Map. *The Latin Poems Commonly Attributed to Walter Mapes*. Ed. Thomas Wright. London: Camden Society, 1841.

Walter of Châtillon. *Alexandreis*. Ed. Marvin L. Colker. Padua: Antenore, 1978. Trans. as *The Alexandreis* by R. Telfryn Pritchard. Toronto: Pontifical Institute of Mediaeval Studies, 1986.

William of Malmesbury. *Gesta Regum Anglorum: The History of the English Kings*. Ed. and trans. R.A.B. Mynors, R.M. Thomson, and M. Winterbottom. 2 vols. Oxford: Clarendon Press, 1998.

Wimpfeling, Jakob. *Germania*. In Emil von Borries, *Wimpfeling und Murner im Kampf um die ältere Geschichte des Elsasses: Ein Beitrag zur Charakteristik des deutschen Frühhumanismus*. Heidelberg: C. Winters Universitätsbuchhandlung, 1926.

Wissenburg, Wolfgang. *Descriptio Palestinae nova*. Strasbourg, 1538.

Wogan-Browne, Jocelyn, Nicholas Watson, Andrew Taylor, and Ruth Evans, eds. *The Idea of the Vernacular: An Anthology of Middle English Literary Theory, 1280–1520*. University Park: Pennsylvania State University Press, 1999.

Secondary Works

Adamova, Adel T. "The Hermitage Manuscript of Nizami's *Khamsa* Dated 835/1431." *Islamic Art* 5 (2001): 53–132.

Ades, Dawn. *Photomontage*. 2nd ed. London: Thames and Hudson, 1986.

Ahl, Frederick. *Lucan: An Introduction*. Ithaca: Cornell University Press, 1976.

Aijazuddin, Fakir Sayed. *Pahari Paintings and Sikh Portraits in the Lahore Museum*. Karachi: Oxford University Press; London: Sotheby, 1977.

Álvarez Lopera, José. *El Greco: Estudio y Catálogo*. Vol. 2.1. Madrid: Fundación Arte Hispánico, 2007.

—. "Martyrdom of St Maurice and the Theban Legion." In *El Greco: Identity and Transformation: Crete, Italy, Spain*, ed. José Álvarez Lopera, 380–82. Milan: Skira, 1999.

Andermann, Ulrich. "Albert Krantz (1448–1517): Bemerkungen zum Verhältnis von lateinischer und volkssprachlicher Gelehrsamkeit am Beispiel eines norddeutschen

Humanisten." In *Latein und Nationalsprachen in der Renaissance*, ed. Bodo Guthmüller, 315–43. Wiesbaden: Harrassowitz, 1998.

Anderson, Benedict. *Imagined Communities: Reflections on the Origin and Spread of Nationalism.* 2nd ed. London: Verso, 1991.

Anlezark, Daniel. "The Anglo-Saxon World View." In *The Cambridge Companion to Old English Literature*, ed. Malcolm Godden and Michael Lapidge, 66–81. 2nd ed. Cambridge: Cambridge University Press, 2013.

Anzieu, Didier. *Freud's Self-Analysis.* Trans. Peter Graham. London: Hogarth Press, 1986.

Apps, Arwen. "Source Citation and Authority in Solinus." In *Solinus: New Studies*, ed. Kai Brodersen, 32–42. Heidelberg: Antike, 2014.

Arad, Pnina. "Is Calvary Worth Restoring? The Way of the Cross in Romans-sur-Isère, France." In *Between Jerusalem and Europe: Essays in Honour of Bianca Kühnel*, ed. Renana Bartal and Hanna Vorholt, 154–72. Leiden: Brill, 2015.

Aragon, Louis. *Les Collages.* Paris: Hermann, 1965.

Archer, William George. *Indian Paintings from the Punjab Hills: A Survey and History of Pahari Miniature Painting.* 2 vols. Delhi: Oxford University Press; London: Sotheby, 1973.

Arentzen, Jörg-Geerd. *Imago Mundi Cartographica: Studien zur Bildlichkeit mittelalterlicher Welt- und Ökumenekarten unter besonderer Berücksichtigung des Zusammenwirkens von Text und Bild.* Munich: Fink, 1984.

Ascoli, Albert Russell. "'Neminem ante nos': Historicity and Authority in the *De vulgari eloquentia.*" *Annali d'Italianistica* 8 (1990): 186–231.

Asso, Paolo, ed. *Brill's Companion to Lucan.* Leiden: Brill, 2011.

Aubert, Jean-Jacques. "L'insignificance de la négritude: Maurice le Maure." In *Mauritius und die Thebäische Legion/Saint Maurice et la légion Thébaine: Actes du colloque international Fribourg, Saint-Maurice, Martigny, 17–20 septembre 2003*, ed. Otto Wermelinger, Philippe Bruggisser, Beat Näf and Jean-Michel Roessli, 57–66. Fribourg: Academic Press Fribourg, 2005.

Aujac, Germaine. *Ératosthène de Cyrène, le pionnier de la géographie: Sa mesure de la circonférence terrestre.* Paris: C.T.H.S., 2001.

Baert, Barbara. *Interspaces between Word, Gaze and Touch: The Bible and the Visual Medium in the Middle Ages.* Leuven: Peeters, 2011.

—. *Noli me tangere: Mary Magdalene: One Person, Many Images.* Leuven: Peeters, 2006.

Baglio, Marco, Antonietta Nebuloni Testa, and Marco Petoletti, eds. *Le Postille del Virgilio Ambrosiano.* 2 vols. Rome: Antenore, 2006.

Bandyopadhyay, Pradeep. "The Uses of Kabir: Missionary Writings and Civilisational Difference." In *Images of Kabir*, ed. Monika Horstmann, 9–31. New Delhi: Manohar Publishers, 2002.

Barasch, Moshe. *Giotto and the Language of Gesture.* Cambridge: Cambridge University Press, 1987.

Baswell, Christopher. *Virgil in Medieval England: Figuring the Aeneid from the Twelfth Century to Chaucer.* Cambridge: Cambridge University Press, 1995.

Bately, Janet. "The Orosius." In *A Companion to Alfred the Great*, ed. Nicole Guenther Discenza and Paul E. Szarmach, 313–43. Leiden: Brill, 2015.

Baumgärtner, Ingrid. "Die Wahrnehmung Jerusalems auf mittelalterlichen Weltkarten." In *Jerusalem im Hoch- und Spätmittelalter: Konflikte und Konfliktbewältigung- Vorstellungen und Vergegenwärtigungen*, ed. Dieter Bauer, Klaus Herbers, and Nikolas Jaspert, 271–334. Frankfurt: Campus Verlag, 2001.

Beagon, Mary. *The Elder Pliny on the Human Animal: Natural History Book 7*. Oxford: Clarendon Press, 2005.

Beaune, Colette. "L'utilisation politique du mythe des origines troyennes en France à la fin du Moyen Âge." In *Lectures médiévales de Virgile*, 331–55. Rome: École française de Rome, 1985.

Bellucci, Roberto and Cecilia Frosinini. "'Cum suis depitis proportionibus': Perspective and Geometry in Sassetta's Borgo San Sepulcro Altarpiece." In *Sassetta: The Borgo San Sepolcro Altarpiece*, ed. Machtelt Israëls, 1: 359–69. 2 vols. Leiden: Primavera Press, 2009.

Bettini, Maurizio. "Ghosts of Exile: Doubles and Nostalgia in Vergil's *parva Troia* (*Aeneid* 3.294ff)." *Classical Antiquity* 16 (1997): 8–33.

Bexley, Erica. "Lucan's Catalogues and the Landscape of War." In *Geography, Topography, Landscape: Configurations of Space in Greek and Roman Epic*, ed. Marios Skempis and Ioannis Ziogas, 373–403. Berlin: de Gruyter, 2014.

Bianchetti, Serena, Michele R. Cataudella, and Hans-Joachim Gehrke, eds. *Brill's Companion to Ancient Geography: The Inhabited World in Greek and Roman Tradition*. Leiden: Brill, 2016.

Bieringer, Reimund. "Touching Jesus? The Meaning of mē mou háptou in Its Johannine Context." In *To Touch or Not to Touch? Interdisciplinary Perspectives on the* Noli me tangere, ed. Reimund Bieringer, Karlijn Demasure, and Barbara Baert, 61–81. Leuven: Peeters, 2013.

Billion, Philipp. *Graphische Zeichen auf mittelalterlichen Portolankarten: Ursprünge, Produktion und Rezeption bis 1440*. Marburg: Tectum, 2011.

Bischoff, Bernhard. "Eine mittelalterliche Ovidlegende." *Historisches Jahrbuch* 71 (1952): 268–73.

Bispham, Edward. "Pliny the Elder's Italy." In *Vita Vigilia Est: Essays in Honour of Barbara Levick*, ed. Edward Bispham and Greg Rowe, 41–67. London: Institute of Classical Studies, 2007.

Blumenbach, Georg Heinrich Wilhelm. "Beschreibung der ältesten bisher bekannten Landkarte aus dem Mittelalter, im Besitze des Klosters Ebstorf." *Vaterländisches Archiv für hannoverisch-braunschweigische Geschichte* (1834): 1–21.

Borsook, Eve. *The Mural Painters of Tuscany: From Cimabue to Andrea del Sarto*. 2nd ed. Oxford: Clarendon Press, 1980.

Borst, Arno. *Der Turmbau von Babel: Geschichte der Meinungen über Ursprung und Vielfalt der Sprachen und Völker*. 4 vols. Stuttgart: Hiersemann, 1957–63.

Bosi, Fausto. "Sulla descrizione dell'area pontica nella Naturalis Historia di Plinio." In

Plinio il vecchio sotto il profilo storico letterario, 231–38. Como: Banca Briantea, 1982.

Bouloux, Nathalie. *Culture et savoirs géographiques en Italie au XIVe siècle*. Turnhout: Brepols, 2002.

—. "From Gaul to the Kingdom of France: Representations of French Space in the Geographical Texts of the Middle Ages (Twelfth-Fifteenth Centuries)." In *Space in the Medieval West: Places, Territories, and Imagined Geographies*, ed. Meredith Cohen and Fanny Madeline, 197–217. Farnham: Ashgate, 2014.

—. "La géographie à la cour (Italie, XVe siècle)." *Micrologus* 16 (2008): 171–88.

Boyce, Gray C. "The Controversy over the Boundary between the English and Picard Nations (1356–58)." In *Études d'histoire dédiées a la mémoire de Henri Pirenne*, 55–66. Brussels: Nouvelle Société d'Éditions, 1937.

Braidotti, Cecilia, ed. *Le vite antiche di M. Anneo Lucano*. Bologna: Pàtron, 1972.

Bresc-Bautier, Geneviève. "Les imitations du S. Sepulcre de Jérusalem (IXe–XVe siècles)." *Revue d'histoire de la spiritualité* 50 (1974): 319–42.

Breton, André. "Avis au lecteur." [1929]. In Max Ernst, *La femme 100 têtes*. Paris: Éditions de l'Œil, 1956.

Brodersen, Kai. "Mapping Pliny's World: The Achievement of Solinus." *Bulletin of the Institute of Classical Studies* 54 (2011): 63–88.

—. "A Revised Handlist of Manuscripts Transmitting Solinus' Work." In *Solinus: New Studies*, ed. Kai Brodersen, 201–8. Heidelberg: Antike, 2014.

Brosius, Dieter. "Die Ebstorfer Weltkarte von 1830 bis 1943: Ergänzungen zu ihrer Überlieferungsgeschichte." in *Ein Weltbild vor Columbus*, ed. Hartmut Kugler and Eckhard Michael, 23–40. Weinheim: VCH, 1991.

Burckhardt, Jacob. *Die Kultur der Renaissance in Italien: Ein Versuch*. Basel: Schweighauser, 1860.

Bury, Emmanuel, ed. *Tous vos gens à Latin: Le latin, langue savante, langue mondaine (XIVe–XVIIe siècles)*. Geneva: Droz, 2005.

Butterfield, Ardis. *The Familiar Enemy: Chaucer, Language and Nation in the Hundred Years War*. Oxford: Oxford University Press, 2009.

Campbell, Tony. "A Detailed Reassessment of the Carte Pisane: A Late and Inferior Copy, or the Lone Survivor from the Portolan Charts' Formative Period?" Updated 4 January 2018. http://www.maphistory.info/CartePisaneTEXT.html.

—. "Portolan Charts from the Late Thirteenth Century to 1500." In *The History of Cartography. Volume 1: Cartography in Prehistoric, Ancient, and Medieval Europe and the Mediterranean*, ed. J.B. Harley and David Woodward, 370–463. Chicago: University of Chicago Press, 1987.

Carey, Sorcha. *Pliny's Catalogue of Culture: Art and Empire in the Natural History*. Oxford: Oxford University Press, 2003.

Carrié, Jean-Michel. "Des Thébains en Occident? Histoire militaire et hagiographie." In *Mauritius und die Thebäische Legion/Saint Maurice et la légion Thébaine: Actes du colloque international Fribourg, Saint-Maurice, Martigny, 17–20 septembre 2003*, ed. Otto Wermelinger, Philippe Bruggisser, Beat Näf and Jean-Michel Roessli, 9–35. Fribourg: Academic Press Fribourg, 2005.

Carty, John. "Drawing a Line in the Sand: The Canning Stock Route and Contemporary Art." In *Yiwarra Kuju: The Canning Stock Route*, 23–31. Canberra: National Museum of Australia Press, 2010.

Casali, Sergio. "The *Bellum Civile* as an Anti-*Aeneid*." In *Brill's Companion to Lucan*, ed. Paolo Asso, 81–109. Leiden: Brill, 2011.

Casey, Edward S. *The Fate of Place: A Philosophical History.* Berkeley: University of California Press, 1997.

Cassell Anthony K. *The* Monarchia *Controversy.* Washington, DC: Catholic University of America Press, 2004.

Cassirer, Ernst. "Mythic, Aesthetic, and Theoretical Space." Trans. Donald Phillip Verene and Lerke Holzwarth Foster. *Man and World* 2 (1969): 3–17. Originally published as "Mythischer, ästhetischer und theoretischer Raum." *Zeitschrift für Ästhetik und allgemeine Kunstwissenschaft* 25 (1931): 21–36.

Catón, José Maria Fernández. *Las Etimologías en la tradición manuscrita medieval.* León: Centro de estudios e investigacion 'San Isidoro', 1966.

Cattaneo, Angelo. *Fra Mauro's Mappa Mundi and Fifteenth-Century Venice.* Turnhout: Brepols, 2011.

Cerri, Angelo. "Francesco Petrarca a Pavia." In *Storia di Pavia.* Vol. 3.1, *Dal libero comune alla fine del principato indipendente 1024–1535*, 451–95. Milan: Banca del Monte di Lombardia, 1992.

Chevalley, Eric. "La Passion anonyme de Saint Maurice d'Agaune: Édition critique." *Vallesia* 45 (1990): 37–120.

Chibnall, Marjorie. "Pliny's *Natural History* and the Middle Ages." In *Empire and Aftermath: Silver Latin II*, ed. Thomas Allen Dorey, 57–78. London: Routledge, 1975.

Christensen, Heinrich. *Das Alexanderlied Walters von Châtillon.* Halle: Verlag der Buchhandlung des Waisenhauses, 1905.

Clavuot, Ottavio. *Biondos 'Italia illustrata' – Summa oder Neuschöpfung?: Über die Arbeitsmethoden eines Humanisten.* Tübingen: Niemeyer, 1990.

Cohen, Meredith, Fanny Madeline, and Dominique Iogna-Prat. Introduction to *Space in the Medieval West: Places, Territories, and Imagined Geographies*, ed. Meredith Cohen and Fanny Madeline, 1–20. Farnham: Ashgate, 2014.

Colker, Marvin L. *Trinity College Library Dublin: Descriptive Catalogue of the Mediaeval and Renaissance Latin Manuscripts.* 2 vols. Aldershot: Scolar Press, 1991.

Comparetti, Domenico. *Virgilio nel medio evo.* Rev. ed. 2 vols. Florence: Seeber, 1896.

Considine, John. *Dictionaries in Early Modern Europe: Lexicography and the Making of Heritage.* Cambridge: Cambridge University Press, 2008.

Conti, Simonetta. "Portolano e carta nautica: Confronto toponomastico." In *Imago et mensura mundi: Atti del IX congresso internazionale di storia della cartografia*, ed. Carla Clivio Marzoli, 1: 55–60. 2 vols. Rome: Istituto della Enciclopedia Italiana, 1985.

Courcelle, Pierre. *Lecteurs païens et lecteurs chrétiens de l'Énéide: I. Les témoignages littéraires.* Paris: Institut de France, 1984.

Cova, Pier Vincenzo, ed. *Il libro terzo dell'Eneide.* 2nd ed. Milan: Vita e Pensiero, 1998.

Craven, Roy C., Jr. "Manaku: A Guler painter." In *Painters of the Pahari Schools*, ed. Vishwa Chander Ohri and Roy C. Craven, Jr, 46–67. Mumbai: Marg, 1998.

Crone, Gerald R. "New Light on the Hereford Map." *Geographical Journal* 131 (1965): 447–62.

Curtius, Ernst Robert. *European Literature and the Latin Middle Ages*. Trans. Willard R. Trask. London: Routledge, 1953.

Dainville, François de. "Cartes et contestations au XVe siècle." *Imago Mundi* 24 (1970): 99–121.

Dauphant, Léonard. *Le royaume des quatre rivières: L'espace politique français (1380–1515)*. Seyssel: Champ Vallon, 2012.

Davenport, Carly. "The Story behind the Canning Stock Route Project." In *Yiwarra Kuju: The Canning Stock Route*, 3–11. Canberra: National Museum of Australia Press, 2010.

de Certeau, Michel. *The Practice of Everyday Life*. Trans. Steven Rendall. Berkeley: University of California Press, 1984.

Degenhart, Bernard, and Annegrit Schmidt. *Marino Sanudo und Paolino Veneto: Zwei Literaten des 14. Jahrhunderts in ihrer Wirkung auf Buchillustrierung und Kartographie in Venedig, Avignon und Neapel*. Tübingen: Ernst Wasmuth, 1973.

Dehejia, Vidya, ed. *The Legend of Rama: Artistic Visions*. Bombay: Marg, 1994.

Delano-Smith, Catherine. "The Exegetical Jerusalem: Maps and Plans for Ezekiel Chapters 40–48." In *Imagining Jerusalem in the Medieval West*, ed. Lucy Donkin and Hanna Vorholt, 41–75. Oxford: The British Academy, 2012.

Delano-Smith, Catherine, Peter Barber, Damien Bove, Christopher Clarkson, P.D.A. Harvey, Nick Millea, Nigel Saul, William Shannon, Christopher Whittick, and James Willoughby. "New Light on the Medieval Gough Map of Britain." *Imago Mundi* 69 (2017): 1–36.

Depuydt, Joost. "New Letters for a Biography of Abraham Ortelius." *Imago Mundi* 68 (2016): 67–78.

Derolez, Albert. *The Autograph Manuscript of the Liber Floridus: A Key to the Encyclopedia of Lambert of Saint-Omer*. Turnhout: Brepols, 1998.

Dewar, Michael. "Laying It on with a Trowel: The Proem to Lucan and Related Texts." *Classical Quarterly* 44 (1994): 199–211.

Dickinson, R.J. "The *Tristia*: Poetry in Exile." In *Ovid*, ed. J.W. Binns, 154–90. London: Routledge and Kegan Paul, 1973.

The Dictionary of Old English: A to H. Ed. Angus Cameron, Ashley Crandell Amos, and Antonette diPaolo Healey. Toronto: Dictionary of Old English Project, 2016. http://www.doe.utoronto.ca.

Diller, Aubrey. *The Textual Tradition of Strabo's Geography*. Amsterdam: Hakkert, 1975.

Dionisotti, Carlo. *Gli umanisti e il volgare fra Quattro e Cinquecento*. Florence: Le Monnier, 1968.

Dols, Michael W. *Majnūn: The Madman in Medieval Islamic Society*. Ed. Diana E. Immisch. Oxford: Clarendon Press, 1992.

Donkin, Lucy. "Earth from Elsewhere: Burial in *terra sancta* beyond the Holy Land." In *Natural Materials of the Holy Land and the Visual Translation of Place 500–1500*, ed. Renana Bartal, Neta Bodner, and Bianca Kühnel, 109–26. London: Routledge, 2017.

Dougherty, Carol. *The Poetics of Colonization: From City to Text in Archaic Greece*. Oxford: Oxford University Press, 1993.

Dueck, Daniela. *Strabo of Amasia: A Greek Man of Letters in Augustan Rome*. London: Routledge, 2000.

Dufays, Jean-Michel. "*Medium tempus* et ses équivalents: Aux origines d'une terminologie de l'âge intermédiaire." *Il Pensiero Politico* 21 (1988): 237–49.

Dwyer, William J. *Bhakti in Kabīr*. Patna: Associated Book Agency, 1981.

Edson, Evelyn. *Mapping Time and Space: How Medieval Mapmakers Viewed Their World*. London: British Library, 1997.

Ehlen, Thomas. "Bilder des Exils–das Exil als Bild: Ästhetik und Bewältigung in lyrischen Texten." In *Exil, Fremdheit und Ausgrenzung in Mittelalter und früher Neuzeit*, ed. Andreas Bihrer, Sven Limbeck, and Paul Gerhard Schmidt, 151–232. Würzburg: Ergon, 2000.

Eichenberger, Thomas. *Patria: Studien zur Bedeutung des Wortes im Mittelalter (6.–12. Jahrhundert)*. Sigmaringen: Thorbecke, 1991.

Eisenhut, Heidi. *Die Glossen Ekkeharts IV von St. Gallen im Codex Sangallensis 621*. St Gallen: Verlag am Klosterhof, 2009.

Endt, Johannes. "Ein Kommentar zu Lucan aus dem Mittelalter." *Wiener Studien* 32 (1910), 123–55 and 272–95.

Ernst, Max. *Beyond Painting*. New York: Wittenborn, Schultz, 1948.

Esposito, Paolo. "Early and Medieval *Scholia* and *Commentaria* on Lucan." In *Brill's Companion to Lucan*, ed. Paolo Asso, 452–63. Leiden: Brill, 2011.

—. "Sulla prima fase della fortuna lucanea." *Giornale italiano di filologia* 66 (2014): 163–81.

—. "Virgilio e Servio nella scoliastica lucanea." In *Gli scolii a Lucano ed altra scoliastica latina*, ed. Paolo Esposito, 25–77. Pisa: Edizioni ETS, 2004.

Falchetta, Piero. *Marinai, mercanti, cartografi, pittori: Ricerche sulla cartografia nautica a Venezia (sec. XIV–XV)*. Venice: Atento Veneto, 1995.

Farmer, Sharon. *Communities of Saint Martin: Legend and Ritual in Medieval Tours*. Ithaca: Cornell University Press, 1991.

Feiertag, Jean-Louis. "Les sources littéraires du plaidoyer des Thébains adressé à l'Empereur dans la *Passio Acaunensium Martyrum* (chap. 9) attribuée à Eucher de Lyon (BHL 5737–5739)." In *Mauritius und die Thebäische Legion/Saint Maurice et la légion Thébaine: Actes du colloque international Fribourg, Saint-Maurice, Martigny, 17–20 septembre 2003*, ed. Otto Wermelinger, Philippe Bruggisser, Beat Näf and Jean-Michel Roessli, 255–64. Fribourg: Academic Press Fribourg, 2005.

Fenzi, Enrico. "Petrarca e l'esilio: Uno stile di vita." In *Écritures de l'exil dans l'Italie médiévale*, ed. Anna Fontes Baratto and Marina Gagliano, 365–402. Paris: Presses Sorbonne Nouvelle, 2013.

—. "*Translatio studii* e *translatio imperii*: Appunti per un percorso." *Interfaces* 1 (2015): 170–208.

Feo, Michele. "Il nome di Opizzino." In *Margarita amicorum: Studi di cultura europea per Agostino Sottili*, ed. Fabio Forner, Carla Maria Monti, and Paul Gerhard Schmidt, 1: 255–79. 2 vols. Milan: Vita e Pensiero, 2005.

—. "La 'peciola' ritrovata (*fragmentum Barberinianum Lat.* 2999)." In *Omaggio ad Augusto Campana*, ed. Cino Pedrelli, 222–348. Cesena: Società di Studi Romagnoli, 2003.

Fera, Vincenzo. "Storia e filologia tra Petrarca e Boccaccio." In *Petrarca, l'umanesimo e la civiltà europea*, ed. Donatella Coppini and Michele Feo, 1: 369–89. 2 vols. Quaderni Petrarcheschi 15–16 (2005–6). Florence: Le Lettere, 2012.

Fermon, Paul. "Cartes et plans à grande échelle." In *La Terre: Connaissance, représentations, mesure au Moyen Âge*, ed. Patrick Gautier Dalché, 581–624. Turnhout: Brepols, 2013.

Filippini, Célia, and Anne-Marie Telesinski. "Métaphores et métamorphoses de l'exil dans le *Canzoniere* de Pétrarque." In *Écritures de l'exil dans l'Italie médiévale*, ed. Anna Fontes Baratto and Marina Gagliano, 141–55. Paris: Presses Sorbonne Nouvelle, 2013.

Fischer, Andreas, and Ian Wood. *Western Perspectives on the Mediterranean: Cultural Transfer in Late Antiquity and the Early Middle Ages, 400–800 AD.* London: Bloomsbury, 2014.

Fischli, Walter. *Studien zum Fortleben der* Pharsalia. Lucerne: Haag, 1945.

Fontaine, Jacques. *Isidore de Seville et la culture classique dans l'Espagne wisigothique.* 3 vols. Paris: Études Augustiniennes, 1959–83.

Formisano, Luciano. "La compilazione di viaggi di Alessandro Zorzi: Firenze, Biblioteca Nazionale Centrale, B.R. 233–236." In *Vespucci, Firenze e le Americhe: Atti del convegno di studi, Firenze, 22–24 novembre 2012*, ed. Giuliano Pinto, Leonardo Rombai, and Claudia Tripodi, 441–56. Florence: Olschki, 2014.

Foucault, Michel. "Of Other Spaces." Trans. Jay Miscowiec. *Diacritics* 16 (1986): 22–27.

—. "Questions on Geography." In *Power/Knowledge: Selected Interviews and Other Writings, 1972–77*, ed. Colin Gordon, trans. Colin Gordon, Leo Marshall, John Mepham, and Kate Soper, 63–77. Brighton: Harvester Press, 1980.

Frings, Irene. "Mantua me genuit – Vergils Grabepigramm auf Stein und Pergament." *Zeitschrift für Papyrologie und Epigraphik* 123 (1998): 89–100.

Fubini, Riccardo. "La geografia storica dell' 'Italia illustrata' di Biondo Flavio e le tradizioni dell'etnografia." In *Storiografia dell'umanesimo in Italia da Leonardo Bruni ad Annio da Viterbo*, 53–76. Rome: Edizioni di storia e letteratura, 2003.

—. *Umanesimo e secolarizzazione da Petrarca a Valla.* Rome: Bulzoni, 1990.

Gaertner, Jan Felix. "The Discourse of Displacement in Greco-Roman Antiquity." In *Writing Exile: The Discourse of Displacement in Greco-Roman Antiquity and Beyond*, ed. Jan Felix Gaertner, 1–20. Leiden: Brill, 2007.

—. "Ovid and the 'Poetics of Exile': How Exilic is Ovid's Exile Poetry?" In *Writing Exile: The Discourse of Displacement in Greco-Roman Antiquity and Beyond*, ed. Jan Felix Gaertner, 155–72. Leiden: Brill, 2007.

Galinsky, G. Karl. *Aeneas, Sicily and Rome*. Princeton: Princeton University Press, 1969.

Gallo, Ernest. *The* Poetria Nova *and Its Sources in Early Rhetorical Doctrine*. The Hague: Mouton, 1971.

Garin, Eugenio. "Medio Evo e tempi bui: Concetto e polemiche nella storia del pensiero dal XV al XVIII secolo." In *Concetto, storia, miti e immagini del Medio Evo*, ed. Vittore Branca, 199–224. Florence: Sansoni, 1973.

Gaunt, Simon. *Marco Polo's Le Devisement du Monde: Narrative Voice, Language and Diversity*. Cambridge: Brewer, 2013.

Gautier Dalché, Patrick. "À propos de la mappemonde d'Ebstorf." *Médiévales* 55 (2008): 163–70.

—. *Carte marine et portulan au XIIe siècle: Le* Liber de existencia riveriarum et forma maris nostri Mediterranei *(Pise, circa 1200)*. Rome: École française de Rome, 1995.

—. "Cartes, réflexion stratégique et projets de croisade à la fin du XIIIe et au début du XIVe siècle: Une initiative franciscaine?" *Francia* 37 (2010): 77–95.

—. "De la glose à la contemplation: Place et fonction de la carte dans les manuscrits du haut Moyen Âge." *Settimane di studio del Centro italiano di studi sull'alto medioevo* 41 (1994): 693–771.

—. "De Pétrarque à Raimondo Marliano: Aux origines de la géographie historique." *Archives d'histoire doctrinale et littéraire du Moyen Âge*, 79 (2012): 161–91.

—. "Les diagrammes topographiques dans les manuscrits des classiques latins (Lucain, Solin, Salluste)." In *La Tradition Vive: Mélanges d'histoire des textes en l'honneur de Louis Holtz*, ed. Pierre Lardet, 291–306. Paris and Turnhout: Brepols, 2003.

—. "L'enseignement de la géographie dans l'antiquité tardive." *Klio* 96 (2014): 144–82.

—. *L'espace géographique au Moyen Âge*. Florence: SISMEL-Edizioni del Galluzzo, 2013.

—. "Eucher de Lyon, Iona, Bobbio: Le destin d'une *mappamundi* de l'antiquité tardive." *Viator* 41 (2010): 1–22.

—. *La Géographie de Ptolémée en Occident (IVe–XVIe siècle)*. Turnhout: Brepols, 2009.

—. "L'héritage antique de la cartographie médiévale: Les problèmes et les acquis." In *Cartography in Antiquity and the Middle Ages: Fresh Perspectives, New Methods*, ed. Richard J.A. Talbert and Richard W. Unger, 29–66. Leiden: Brill, 2008.

—. "Limite, frontière et organisation de l'espace dans la géographie et la cartographie de la fin du Moyen Âge." In *Grenzen und Raumvorstellungen*, ed. Guy P. Marchal, 93–122. Zürich: Chronos, 1996.

—. "Mappemonde, milieu du VIIIe siècle." In *Le Scriptorium d'Albi: Les manuscrits de la Cathédrale Sainte-Cécile (VIIe–XIIe siècle)*, ed. Matthieu Desachy, 24–27. Rodez: Rouergue, 2007.

—. "Pere Marsili, une carte majorquine (1313) et l'"ardua controversia' des vents." *Itineraria* 5 (2006): 153–70.

—. "Quatre notes sur Alexandre et la cartographie médiévale." In *Les voyages d'Alexan-*

dre au paradis: Orient et Occident, regards croisés, ed. Catherine Gaullier-Bougassas and Margaret Bridges, 213–38. Turnhout: Brepols, 2013.

—. "Le renouvellement de la perception et de la représentation de l'espace au XIIe siècle." In *Renovación intelectual del occidente europeo (siglo XII)*, 169–218. Pamplona: Gobierno da Navarra, 1998.

—. "Représentations géographiques de l'Europe – septentrionale, centrale et orientale – au Moyen Âge." In *Europa im Weltbild des Mittelalters: Kartographische Konzepte*, ed. Ingrid Baumgärtner and Hartmut Kugler, 63–79. Berlin: Akademie, 2008.

—. "La trasmissione medievale e rinascimentale della Tabula Peutingeriana." In *Tabula Peutingeriana: Le antiche vie del mondo*, ed. Francesco Prontera, 43–52. Florence: Olsckhi, 2003.

—. See also under Primary Sources

Geary, Patrick J. *The Myth of Nations: The Medieval Origins of Europe*. Princeton: Princeton University Press, 2002.

Gensini, Stefano. "Attraverso il *De vulgari eloquentia*: A proposito di due edizioni recenti." *Studi Danteschi* 77 (2012): 277–91.

Ghisalberti, Fausto. "Mediaeval Biographies of Ovid." *Journal of the Warburg and Courtauld Institutes* 9 (1946): 10–59.

Goetz, Hans-Werner, Jörg Jarnut, and Walter Pohl, eds. *Regna and Gentes: The Relationship between Late Antique and Early Medieval Peoples and Kingdoms in the Transformation of the Roman World*. Leiden: Brill, 2003.

Goez, Werner. *Translatio Imperii: Ein Beitrag zur Geschichte des Geschichtsdenkens und der politischen Theorien im Mittelalter und in der frühen Neuzeit*. Tübingen: Mohr, 1958.

Gormley, Catherine M., Mary A. Rouse, and Richard H. Rouse. "The Medieval Circulation of the *De chorographia* of Pomponius Mela." *Mediaeval Studies* 46 (1984): 266–320.

Gorochov, Nathalie. "Genèse et organisation des nations universitaires en Europe aux XIIe et XIIIe siècles." In *Nation et nations au Moyen Âge*, 273–86. Paris: Publications de la Sorbonne, 2014.

Goswamy, B.N. and Eberhard Fischer. *Pahari Masters: Court Painters of Northern India*. Oxford: Oxford University Press, 1992.

Gotoff, Harold C. *The Transmission of the Text of Lucan in the Ninth Century*. Cambridge, MA: Harvard University Press, 1971.

Graham, Mark W. *News and Frontier Consciousness in the Late Roman Empire*. Ann Arbor: University of Michigan Press, 2006.

Grevin, Benoit, ed. *La résistible ascension des vulgaires: Contacts entre latin et langues vulgaires au bas Moyen Âge. Mélanges de l'École française de Rome, Moyen Âge* 117.2 (2005): 447–718.

Grondeux, Anne. "La notion de langue maternelle et son apparition au Moyen Âge." In *Zwischen Babel und Pfingsten: Sprachdifferenzen und Gesprächsverständigung in der Vormoderne (8.–16. Jahrhundert)*, ed. Peter von Moos, 339–56. Zürich: LIT, 2008.

Grote, Ludwig. *Die Erasmus-Mauritius-Tafel*. Stuttgart: Reclam, 1957.

Guerrieri, Elisabetta. "Spunti filologici dall'*Epistolario* di Salutati." In *Coluccio Salutati e l'invenzione dell'umanesimo,* ed. Concetta Bianca, 231–81. Rome: Edizioni di storia e letteratura, 2010.

Hamilton, Alastair. *The Copts and the West 1439–1822.* Oxford: Oxford University Press, 2006.

Harding, Catherine. "Opening to God: The Cosmographical Diagrams of Opicinus de Canistris." *Zeitschrift für Kunstgeschichte* 61 (1998): 18–39.

Harvey, P.D.A. "Cartography and Its Written Sources." In *Medieval Latin: An Introduction and Bibliographical Guide,* ed. F.A.C. Mantello and A.G. Rigg, 388–94. Washington, DC: Catholic University of America Press, 1996.

—. "Local and Regional Cartography in Medieval Europe." In *The History of Cartography.* Vol. 1: *Cartography in Prehistoric, Ancient, and Medieval Europe and the Mediterranean,* ed. J.B. Harley and David Woodward, 464–501. Chicago: University of Chicago Press, 1987.

—. *Medieval Maps of the Holy Land.* London: British Library, 2012.

Hawley, John Stratton. *Three Bhakti Voices: Mirabai, Surdas, and Kabir in Their Time and Ours.* Oxford: Oxford University Press, 2005.

Heidegger, Martin. "Die Zeit des Weltbildes." In *Gesamtausgabe.* Vol. 5: *Holzwege,* ed. Friedrich-Wilhelm von Herrmann, 75–113. Frankfurt am Main: Vittorio Klostermann, 1977. Trans. as "The Age of the World Picture" by William Lovitt in *The Question Concerning Technology and Other Essays.* New York: Garland, 1977.

Henderson, John. *Fighting for Rome: Poets and Caesars, History and Civil War.* Cambridge: Cambridge University Press, 1998.

Herberichs, Cornelia. "*... quasi sub unius pagine visione coadunavit*: Zur Lesbarkeit der Ebstorfer Weltkarte." In *Text-Bild-Karte: Kartographien der Vormoderne,* ed. Jürg Glauser and Christian Kiening, 201–17. Freiburg i.Br.: Rombach, 2007.

Herren, Michael. "Latin and the Vernacular Languages." In *Medieval Latin: An Introduction and Bibliographical Guide,* ed. F.A.C. Mantello and A.G. Rigg, 122–29. Washington, DC: Catholic University of America Press, 1996.

Hexter, Ralph J. *Ovid and Medieval Schooling: Studies in Medieval School Commentaries on Ovid's* Ars Amatoria, Epistulae ex Ponto, *and* Epistulae Heroidum. Munich: Arbeo-Gesellschaft, 1986.

—. "Ovid and the Medieval Exilic Imaginary." In *Writing Exile: The Discourse of Displacement in Greco-Roman Antiquity and Beyond,* ed. Jan Felix Gaertner, 209–36. Leiden: Brill, 2007.

Hiatt, Alfred. "Beyond a Border: The Maps of Scotland in John Hardyng's *Chronicle.*" In *The Lancastrian Court: Proceedings of the 2001 Harlaxton Symposium,* ed. Jenny Stratford, 78–94. Donington: Shaun Tyas, 2003.

—. "'From Hulle to Cartage': Maps and the Sea." In *The Sea and Englishness in the Middle Ages: Maritime Narratives, Identity and Culture,* ed. Sebastian Sobecki, 133–57. Cambridge: Brewer, 2011.

—. *The Making of Medieval Forgeries: False Documents in Fifteenth-Century England.* London: British Library, 2004.

—. "A Map of Ovid's *Tristia* I.10 in Dublin, Trinity College MS 632." *Journal of the Warburg and Courtauld Institutes* 75 (2012): 31–51.

—. *Terra Incognita: Mapping the Antipodes before 1600*. London: British Library, 2008.

Hiestand, Rudolf. "Un centre intellectuel en Syrie du Nord? Notes sur la personnalité d'Aimery d'Antioche, Albert de Tarse et Rorgo Fretellus." *Le Moyen Âge* 100 (1994): 7–36.

Higgs Strickland, Debra. "Edward I, Exodus, and England on the Hereford World Map." *Speculum* 93 (2018): 420–69.

Hillard, Tom. "Prosopographia Shared by Pliny and Solinus: The Question of Solinus' Source(s)." In *Solinus: New Studies*, ed. Kai Brodersen, 43–74. Heidelberg: Antike, 2014.

Hirschi, Caspar. *The Origins of Nationalism: An Alternative History from Ancient Rome to Early Modern Germany*. Cambridge: Cambridge University Press, 2012.

Homburger, Otto. *Die illustrierten Handschriften der Burgerbibliothek Bern: Die vorkarolingischen und karolingischen Handschriften*. Bern: Burgerbibliothek Bern, 1962.

Hoogvliet, Margriet. *Pictura et Scriptura: Textes, images et herméneutique des Mappae Mundi (XIIIe–XVIe siècles)*. Turnhout: Brepols, 2007.

Horsfall, Nicholas. "Aeneas The Colonist." *Vergilius* 35 (1989): 8–27.

—. *Virgil, Aeneid 3: A Commentary*. Leiden: Brill, 2006.

Hunt, E.D. *Holy Land Pilgrimage in the Later Roman Empire AD 312–460*. Oxford: Clarendon Press, 1982.

—. "The Itinerary of Egeria: Reliving the Bible in Fourth-Century Palestine." In *The Holy Land, Holy Lands, and Christian History*, ed. R.N. Swanson, 34–54. Woodbridge: Boydell Press, 2000.

Ibsen, Henrik. *The Wild Duck*. In *Ibsen*, vol. 6, ed. and trans. James Walter McFarlane. London: Oxford University Press, 1960.

Ingham, Richard. "Mixing Languages on the Manor." *Medium Ævum* 78 (2009): 80–97.

Inglebert, Hervé. "Isidore de Séville en son monde: Lieux, peuples, époques." *Antiquité Tardive* 23 (2015): 109–22.

Irvine, Susan. "English Literature in the Ninth Century." In *The Cambridge History of Early Medieval English Literature*, ed. Clare A. Lees, 209–31. Cambridge: Cambridge University Press, 2013.

Jacob, Christian. *La Description de la terre habitée de Denys d'Alexandrie ou la leçon de géographie*. Paris: Albin Michel, 1990.

Jäggi, Carola. "Die Verehrung der Thebäerheiligen in Spätantike und Frühmittelalter: Was sagen die archäologischen Quellen?" In *Mauritius und die Thebäische Legion/Saint Maurice et la légion Thébaine: Actes du colloque international Fribourg, Saint-Maurice, Martigny, 17–20 septembre 2003*, ed. Otto Wermelinger, Philippe Bruggisser, Beat Näf and Jean-Michel Roessli, 173–91. Fribourg: Academic Press Fribourg, 2005.

Jansen, Katherine Ludwig. *The Making of the Magdalen: Preaching and Popular Devotion in the Later Middle Ages*. Princeton: Princeton University Press, 2000.

Janvier, Yves. *La Géographie d'Orose.* Paris: Les Belles Lettres, 1982.

Kahn, Charles H. *The Art and Thought of Heraclitus: An Edition of the Fragments with Translation and Commentary.* Cambridge: Cambridge University Press, 1979.

Kallendorf, Craig. *In Praise of Aeneas: Virgil and Epideictic Rhetoric in the Early Italian Renaissance.* Hanover, NH: University Press of New England, 1989.

Karamustafa, Ahmet T. *God's Unruly Friends: Dervish Groups in the Islamic Later Middle Period 1200–1550.* Salt Lake City: University of Utah Press, 1994; Oxford: Oneworld Publications, 2006.

Karrow, Robert W. *Mapmakers of the Sixteenth Century and Their Maps: Bio-Bibliographies of the Cartographers of Abraham Ortelius, 1570.* Chicago: Speculum Orbis Press, 1993.

Kaster, Robert A. *Guardians of the Language: The Grammarian and Society in Late Antiquity.* Berkeley: University of California Press, 1988.

Kedar, Benjamin Z. "Rashi's Map of the Land of Canaan, ca. 1100, and Its Cartographic Background." In *Cartography in Antiquity and the Middle Ages: Fresh Perspectives, New Methods,* ed. Richard J.A. Talbert and Richard W. Unger, 155–68. Leiden: Brill, 2008.

Kedwards, Dale. "Cartography and Culture in Medieval Iceland." PhD diss., University of York, 2014.

Keith, Alison. "Ovid in Lucan: The Poetics of Instability." In *Brill's Companion to Lucan,* ed. Paolo Asso, 110–32. Leiden: Brill, 2011.

Kern, Margit. "A Question of Conscience: El Greco's *Martyrdom of St. Maurice* and the *Theban Legion.*" In *El Greco: The First Twenty Years in Spain,* ed. Nicos Hadjinicolaou, 95–122. Rethymno: University of Crete, 2005.

Kibre, Pearl. *The Nations in the Mediaeval Universities.* Cambridge: Medieval Academy of America, 1948.

Klein, Jacky. *Grayson Perry.* London: Thames and Hudson, 2009.

Knauer, Georg. *Die Aeneis und Homer: Studien zur poetischen Technik Vergils mit Listen der Homerzitate in der Aeneis.* Göttingen: Vandenhoeck & Ruprecht, 1964.

Korenjak, Martin. *Die Ericthoszene in Lukans Pharsalia.* Frankfurt a.M.: Lang, 1996.

Krautheimer, Richard. "Introduction to an 'Iconography of Medieval Architecture.'" *Journal of the Warburg and Courtauld Institutes* 5 (1942): 1–33.

Kretschmer, Konrad. *Die italienischen Portolane des Mittelalters: Ein Beitrag zur Geschichte der Kartographie und Nautik.* Berlin: Mittler, 1909.

Kris, Ernst. "A Psychotic Artist of the Middle Ages." In *Psychoanalytic Explorations in Art,* 118–27. London: Allen and Unwin, 1953.

Krishnan, Gauri Parimoo, ed. *Ramayana in Focus: Visual and Performing Arts of Asia.* Singapore: Asian Civilisations Museum, 2010.

Kugler, Hartmut. "Europa pars quarta: Der Teil und das Ganze im 'Liber floridus.'" In *Europa im Weltbild des Mittelalters: Kartographische Konzepte,* ed. Ingrid Baumgärtner and Hartmut Kugler, 45–61. Berlin: Akademie, 2008.

Kühnel, Bianca. "Virtual Pilgrimages to Real Places: The Holy Landscapes." In *Imagining Jerusalem in the Medieval West,* ed. Lucy Donkin and Hanna Vorholt, 243–64. Oxford: Oxford University Press, 2012.

Kühnel, Bianca, Galit Noga-Banai, and Hanna Vorholt, eds. *Visual Constructs of Jerusalem*. Turnhout: Brepols, 2014.

Kupfer, Marcia. "The Jerusalem Effect: Rethinking the Centre in Medieval World Maps." In *Visual Constructs of Jerusalem*, ed. Bianca Kühnel, Galit Noga-Banai, and Hanna Vorholt, 353–65. Turnhout: Brepols, 2014.

—. "Medieval World Maps: Embedded Images, Interpretive Frames." *Word and Image* 10 (1994): 262–88.

—. "Reflections on the Ebstorf Map: Cartography, Theology and *Dilectio Speculationis*." In *Mapping Medieval Geographies: Cartography and Geographical Thought in the Latin West and Beyond, 300–1600*, ed. Keith D. Lilley, 100–126. Cambridge: Cambridge University Press, 2013.

—. "Worlds Enmeshed." In *At Home in the World: The Art and Life of Gulammohammed Sheikh*, ed. Chaitanya Sambrani, 278–93. New York: Columbia University Press, 2019.

Laborde, Edward D. "King Alfred's System of Geographical Description in His Version of Orosius." *The Geographical Journal* 62 (1923): 133–39.

Laclau, Ernesto. *New Reflections on the Revolution of Our Time*. London: Verso, 1990.

La Fontaine, Monique. "Listening to Country: The Inseparable Links between Family and Dreaming on the 'Canning Stock Road.'" In *Yiwarra Kuju: The Canning Stock Route*, 13–21. Canberra: National Museum of Australia Press, 2010.

La Fontaine, Monique, and Elisha Buttler, eds. *Ngurra Kuju Walyja: One Country, One People. The Canning Stock Route Project, 2006–2011*. Perth: FORM, 2011.

Lapidge, Michael. *The Anglo-Saxon Library*. Oxford: Oxford University Press, 2006.

—. "Lucan's Imagery of Cosmic Dissolution." *Hermes* 107 (1979): 344–70.

Lascu, Nicolae. *Ovide: Le poète exilé à Tomi*. Constantza: Musée d'Archéologie de Constantza, 1974.

Latour, Bruno. *We Have Never Been Modern*. Trans. Catherine Porter. Harlow: Longman, 1993.

Law, John. "The Italian North." In *The New Cambridge Medieval History*. Vol. 6: *c. 1300–1415*, ed. Michael Jones, 442–68. Cambridge: Cambridge University Press, 2000.

Lecuppre-Desjardin, Élodie. *Le Royaume inachevé des ducs de Bourgogne (XIVe–XVe siècles)*. Paris: Belin, 2016.

Lee, Alexander. *Humanism and Empire: The Imperial Ideal in Fourteenth-Century Italy*. Oxford: Oxford University Press, 2018.

Lefebvre, Henri. *The Production of Space*. Trans. Donald Nicholson-Smith. Oxford: Blackwell, 1991.

Leigh, Matthew. *Lucan: Spectacle and Engagement*. Oxford: Clarendon Press, 1997.

Le Roy Ladurie, Emmanuel. *Montaillou: Village occitan de 1294 à 1324*. Paris: Gallimard, 1975.

Levi, Annalina and Mario Levi. *Itineraria Picta: Contributo allo studio della Tabula Peutingeriana*. Rome: 'L'Erma' di Bretschneider, 1967.

Lightfoot, J.L. Introduction to Dionysius Periegetes, *Description of the Known World*. Trans. J.L. Lightfoot. Oxford: Oxford University Press, 2014.

Löfstedt, Leena. "Observations sur la toponymie dans la traduction en ancien français du Decretum Gratiani." In *Latin et langues romanes: Études de linguistique offertes à József Herman à l'occasion de son 80ème anniversaire*, ed. Sándor Kiss, Luca Mondin, and Giampaolo Salvi, 547–60. Tübingen: Niemeyer, 2005.

Loomis, Laura Hibbard. "The Holy Relics of Charlemagne and King Athelstan: The Lances of Longinus and St Mauricius." *Speculum* 25 (1950): 437–56.

Loomis, Louise R. "Nationality at the Council of Constance: An Anglo-French Dispute." *American Historical Review* 44 (1939): 508–27.

Loupiac, A. *La poétique des éléments dans* La Pharsale *de Lucain*. Brussels: Latomus, 1998.

Lozovsky, Natalia. *"The Earth Is Our Book": Geographical Knowledge in the Latin West ca. 400–1000*. Ann Arbor: University of Michigan Press, 2000.

——. "Roman Geography and Ethnography in the Carolingian Empire." *Speculum* 81 (2006): 325–64.

Lusignan, Serge. *Parler vulgairement: Les intellectuals et la langue française aux XIIIe et XIVe siècles*. Paris: Vrin, 1986.

Machwe, Prabhakar. *Kabir*. New Delhi: Sahitya Akademi, 1968.

Maddock, Peter. "The Imagini Mundi of Gulammohammed Sheikh: An Exercise in the Dedifferentiation of the Global and Local Ecumene." *Third Text* 20 (2006): 539–53.

Mahé-Simon, Mathilde. "Servius et le nom de l'Italie." In *Servius et sa réception de l'Antiquité à la Renaissance*, ed. Monique Bouquet and Bruno Méniel, 89–100. Rennes: Presses Universitaires de Rennes, 2011.

Maraglino, Vanna, ed. *La Naturalis Historia di Plinio nella tradizione medievale e umanistica*. Bari: Cacucci, 2012.

Marcotte, Didier. "La climatologie d'Ératosthène à Poséidonios: Genèse d'une science humaine." In *Sciences exactes et sciences appliquées à Alexandrie*, ed. Gilbert Argoud and Jean-Yves Guillaumin, 263–77. Saint-Étienne: Publications de l'Université de Saint-Étienne, 1998.

——. "Ptolémée et la constitution d'une cartographie régionale." In *La invención de una geografía de la Península Ibérica*, ed. Gonzalo Cruz Andreotti, Patrick Le Roux, and Pierre Moret, 161–72. Madrid: Centro de Ediciones de la Diputación de Málaga, 2007.

Marshall, P.K. "Servius." In *Texts and Transmission: A Survey of the Latin Classics*, ed. L.D. Reynolds, 385–88. Oxford: Clarendon Press, 1983.

Marsico, Clementina. *Per l'edizione delle Elegantie di Lorenzo Valla: Studio sul V Libro*. Florence: Firenze University Press, 2013.

Massey, Doreen. *For Space*. London: SAGE Publications, 2005.

Masters, Jamie. *Poetry and Civil War in Lucan's Bellum Civile*. Cambridge: Cambridge University Press, 1992.

Mattia, Eleonora. "L'illustrazione delle 'Metamorfosi' di Ovidio nel codice Panciatichi 63 della Biblioteca Nazionale di Firenze." *Rivista di storia della miniatura* 1–2 (1996–97): 45–54.

Mayerson, Philip. "Egeria and Peter the Deacon on the Site of Clysma (Suez)." *Journal of the American Research Center in Egypt* 33 (1996): 61–64.

Mazzocco, Angelo. "Dante, Bruni and the Issue of the Origin of Mantua." *Modern Language Notes* 127 (2012): 257–63.

—. *Linguistic Theories in Dante and the Humanists: Studies of Language and Intellectual History in Late Medieval and Early Renaissance Italy.* Leiden: Brill, 1993.

Mazzotta, Giuseppe. *The Worlds of Petrarch.* Durham: Duke University Press, 1993.

McGurk, Patrick. "The Mappa Mundi." In *An Eleventh-Century Anglo-Saxon Illustrated Miscellany (British Library Cotton Tiberius B.V. Part I),* ed. Patrick McGurk, David N. Dumville, Malcolm R. Godden, and Ann Knock, 79–86. Copenhagen: Rosenkilde and Bagger, 1983.

McKenzie, Stephen. "The Westward Progression of History on Medieval *mappaemundi.*" In *The Hereford World Map: Medieval World Maps and Their Context,* ed. P.D.A. Harvey, 335–44. London: British Library, 2006.

Meganck, Tine Luk. *Erudite Eyes: Friendship, Art and Erudition in the Network of Abraham Ortelius (1527–1598).* Leiden: Brill, 2017.

Melion, Walter S. "*Ad ductum itineris et dispositionem mansionum ostendendam*: Meditation, Vocation, and Sacred History in Abraham Oretlius's *Parergon.*" *Journal of the Walters Art Gallery* 57 (1999): 49–72.

Merrills, A.H. *History and Geography in Late Antiquity.* Cambridge: Cambridge University Press, 2005.

Merrills, Andy. *Roman Geographies of the Nile: From the Late Republic to the Early Empire.* Cambridge: Cambridge University Press, 2017.

Meurer, Peter H. "Cartography in the German Lands, 1450–1650." In *The History of Cartography.* Vol. 3: *Cartography in the European Renaissance,* ed. David Woodward, 1172–1245. 2 vols. Chicago: University of Chicago Press, 2007.

—. "Synonymia-Thesaurus-Nomenclator: Ortelius' Dictionaries of Ancient Geographical Names." In *Abraham Ortelius and the First Atlas: Essays Commemorating the Quadricentennial of His Death, 1598–1998,* ed. Marcel van den Broecke, Peter van der Krogt, and Peter Meurer, 331–46. Houten: HES, 1998.

Michelet, Fabienne L. *Creation, Migration, and Conquest: Imaginary Geography and Sense of Space in Old English Literature.* Oxford: Oxford University Press, 2006.

Milanesi, Marica. "Antico e moderno nella cartografia umanistica: Le grandi carte d'Italia nel Quattrocento." *Geographia antiqua* 16–17 (2007–8): 153–76.

—. "Cartografia per un principe senza corte: Venezia nel quattrocento." *Micrologus* 16 (2008): 189–216.

—. "Per una storia della geografia storica." In *I Leponti tra mito e realtà,* ed. Raffaele C. De Marinis and Simonetta Biaggio Simona, 2: 371–83. 2 vols. Locarno: Dadò, 2000.

Milham, Mary Ella. "Solinus." In *Catalogus translationum et commentariorum: Mediaeval and Renaissance Latin Translations and Commentaries: Annotated Lists and Guides.* Vol. 6. Ed. F. Edward Cranz. Washington, DC: Catholic University of America Press, 1986.

Miller, Konrad. *Itineraria Romana: Römische Reisewege an der Hand der Tabula Peutingeriana.* Stuttgart: Strecker und Schröder, 1916.

—. *Mappae mundi: Die ältesten Weltkarten.* 6 vols. Stuttgart: Jos. Roth'sche Verlagshandlung, 1895–98.

Miquel, André, and Percy Kemp. *Majnûn et Laylâ: L'amour fou.* Paris: Sindbad, 1984.

Momigliano, Arnaldo. *Alien Wisdom: The Limits of Hellenization.* Cambridge: Cambridge University Press, 1975.

Mommsen, Theodor E. "Orosius and Augustine." In *Medieval and Renaissance Studies*, ed. Eugene F. Rice, 325–48. Ithaca: Cornell University Press, 1959.

—. "Petrarch's Conception of The 'Dark Ages.'" *Speculum* 17 (1942): 226–42.

Monnet, Pierre. "La *patria* médiévale vue d'Allemagne, entre construction impériale et identités régionales." *Le Moyen Âge* 107 (2001): 71–99.

Monti, Carla Maria. "La *Genealogia* e il *De montibus*: Due parti di un unico progetto." *Studi sul Boccaccio* 44 (2016): 327–66.

Morris, Colin. "Bringing the Holy Sepulchre to the West: S. Stefano, Bologna, from the Fifth to the Twentieth Century." In *The Church Retrospective*, ed. R.N. Swanson, 31–59. Woodbridge: Boydell Press, 1997.

Morse, Victoria. "A Complex Terrain: Church, Society, and the Individual in the Works of Opicino de Canistris (1296–ca. 1354)." PhD diss., University of California, Berkeley, 1996.

—. "Seeing and Believing: The Problem of Idolatry in the Thought of Opicino de Canistris." In *Orthodoxie, christianisme, histoire*, ed. Susanna Elm, Éric Rebillard, and Antonella Romano, 163–76. Rome: École française de Rome, 2000.

Mortensen, Lars Boje. "The Diffusion of Roman Histories in the Middle Ages: A List of Orosius, Eutropius, Paulus Diaconus, and Landolfus Sagax Manuscripts." *Filologia Mediolatina* 6–7 (1999–2000): 101–200.

Müller, Gernot Michael. *Die 'Germania generalis' des Conrad Celtis: Studien mit Edition, Übersetzung und Kommentar.* Tübingen: Niemeyer, 2001.

Mund-Dopchie, Monique. *Ultima Thulé: Histoire d'un lieu et genèse d'un mythe.* Geneva: Droz, 2009.

Munk Olsen, Birger. *L'étude des auteurs classiques latins aux XIe et XIIe siècles.* 4 vols. Paris: CNRS, 1982–2014.

—. "L'étude des classiques à Avignon au XIVe siècle." In *Avignon and Naples: Italy in France-France in Italy in the Fourteenth Century*, ed. Marianne Pade, Hannemarie Ragn Jensen, and Lene Waage Petersen, 13–25. Rome: 'L'Erma' di Bretschneider, 1997.

—. "Ovide au Moyen Âge (du IXe au XIIe siècle)." In *Le strade del testo*, ed. Guglielmo Cavallo, 67–96. Bari: Adriatica Editrice, 1987.

Murphy, Trevor. *Pliny the Elder's* Natural History: *The Empire in the Encyclopedia.* Oxford: Oxford University Press, 2004.

Myers, Micah Y. "Lucan's Poetic Geographies: Center and Periphery in Civil War Epic." In *Brill's Companion to Lucan*, ed. Paolo Asso, 399–415. Leiden: Brill, 2011.

Naas, Valérie. *Le projet encyclopédique de Pline l'Ancien.* Rome: École française de Rome, 2002.

Näf, Beat. "Eucherius von Lyon, Theodor von Octodurus und ihre Legionäre: Zu den historischen Bedingungen einer hagiographischen Geschichtsdeutung." In *Mauritius und die Thebäische Legion/Saint Maurice et la légion Thébaine: Actes du colloque international Fribourg, Saint-Maurice, Martigny, 17–20 septembre 2003*, ed. Otto Wermelinger, Philippe Bruggisser, Beat Näf and Jean-Michel Roessli, 95–118. Fribourg: Academic Press Fribourg, 2005.

Nagel, Alexander. *Medieval Modern: Art out of Time*. London: Thames and Hudson, 2012.

Narducci, Emanuele. *Lucano: Un'epica contro l'impero*. Rome: Laterza, 2002.

—. *La provvidenza crudele: Lucano e la distruzione dei miti augustei*. Pisa: Giardini, 1979.

National Museum of Australia. *Yiwarra Kuju: The Canning Stock Route*. Canberra: National Museum of Australia Press, 2010.

Nauert, Charles G., Jr. "Caius Plinius Secundus." In *Catalogus Translationum et commentariorum: Mediaeval and Renaissance Latin Translations and Commentaries: Annotated Lists and Guides*, ed. F. Edward Cranz, 4: 297–422. Washington, DC: Catholic University of America Press, 1980.

Nederman, Cary J. *Lineages of European Political Thought: Explorations along the Medieval/Modern Divide from John of Salisbury to Hegel*. Washington, DC: Catholic University of America Press, 2009.

Nicolet, Claude. *Space, Geography, and Politics in the Early Roman Empire*. Ann Arbor: The University of Michigan Press, 1991.

Nicolet, Claude, and Patrick Gautier Dalché. "Les 'Quatre Sages' de Jules César et la 'Mesure du Monde' selon Julius Honorius: Réalité antique et tradition médiévale." *Journal des savants* (1986): 157–218.

Nolhac, Pierre de. *Le Virgile du Vatican et ses peintures*. Paris: Klincksieck, 1897.

Ohri, Vishwa Chander, "Pandit Seu and His Sons Manaku and Nainsukh." In *Painters of the Pahari Schools*, ed. Vishwa Chander Ohri and Roy C. Craven, Jr, 149–66. Mumbai: Marg, 1998.

O'Loughlin, Thomas. "Map and Text: A Mid Ninth-Century Map for the Book of Joshua." *Imago Mundi* 57 (2005): 7–22.

Ousterhout, Robert. "The Church of S. Stefano: A 'Jerusalem' in Bologna." *Gesta* 20 (1981): 311–21.

—. "Flexible Geography and Transportable Topography." In *The Real and Ideal Jerusalem in Jewish, Christian and Islamic Art*, ed. Bianca Kühnel, 393–404. Jerusalem: Hebrew University of Jerusalem, 1998.

Oxford English Dictionary. 3rd ed. Oxford: Oxford University Press, 2000.

Parsons, Edward J.S. *The Map of Great Britain circa A.D. 1360 Known as the Gough Map*. Oxford: Oxford University Press, 1958.

Passalacqua, Marina. *I codici di Prisciano*. Rome: Edizioni di storia e letteratura, 1978.

Patota, Giuseppe. "Latino e volgare, latino nel volgare." In *Il Latino nell'età dell'umanesimo*, ed. Giorgio Bernardi Perini, 109–66. Florence: Olschki, 2004.

Pavlock, Barbara. "Paradox and the Journey in the Dedicatory Preface of Solinus' *Collectanea*." In *Solinus: New Studies*, ed. Kai Brodersen, 24–31. Heidelberg: Antike, 2014.

Perucchi, Giulia. "Boccaccio lettore del Plinio petrarchesco." *Italia medioevale e umanistica* 54 (2013): 153–211.

Philipp, Hans. *Die historisch-geographischen Quellen in den Etymologiae des Isidorus von Sevilla*. 2 vols. Berlin: Weidmann, 1912–13.

Pirenne, Henri. *Histoire de Belgique.* 5th ed. 4 vols. Brussels: Renaissance du livre, 1948–52.

Piron, Sylvain. *Dialectique du monstre: Enquête sur Opicino de Canistris.* Brussels: Zones sensibles, 2015.

Pontari, Paolo. "Alberti e Biondo: Archeologia a Nemi." In *Alberti e la cultura del quattrocento,* ed. Roberto Cardini and Mariangela Regoliosi, 1: 495–539. 2 vols. Florence: Edizioni Polistampa, 2007.

—. "'Nedum mille qui effluxerunt annorum gesta sciamus': L'Italia di Biondo e l'invenzione' del Medioevo." In *A New Sense of the Past: The Scholarship of Biondo Flavio (1392–1463),* ed. Angelo Mazzocco and Marc Laureys, 151–75. Leuven: Leuven University Press, 2016.

Pratt, David. *The Political Thought of King Alfred the Great.* Cambridge: Cambridge University Press, 2007.

Prontera, Francesco. *Geografia e storia nella Grecia antica.* Florence: Olschki, 2011.

Pujades i Bataller, Ramon J. *Les Cartes portolanes: La representació medieval d'una mar solcada/Portolan Charts: The Medieval Representation of a Ploughed Sea.* Barcelona: Institut Cartogràfic de Catalunya, 2007.

Racine, Félix. "Teaching with Solinus: Martianus and Priscian." In *Solinus: New Studies,* ed. Kai Brodersen, 157–70. Heidelberg: Antike, 2014.

Radicke, Jan. *Lucans poetische Technik: Studien zum historischen Epos.* Leiden: Brill, 2004.

Reeve, Michael D. "Agrimensores." In *Texts and Transmission: A Survey of the Latin Classics,* ed. L.D. Reynolds, 1–6. Oxford: Clarendon Press, 1983.

—. "The Editing of Pliny's *Natural History.*" *Revue d'histoire des textes,* n.s. 2 (2007): 107–79.

—. "Notitia dignitatum." In *Texts and Transmission: A Survey of the Latin Classics,* ed. L.D. Reynolds, 253–57. Oxford: Clarendon Press, 1983.

Reeves, Marjorie, and Beatrice Hirsh-Reich. *The* Figurae *of Joachim of Fiore.* Oxford: Clarendon Press, 1972.

Reinle, Adolf. *Die heilege Verena von Zurzach: Legende, Kult, Denkmäler.* Basel: Holbein, 1948.

Renan, Ernest. *Qu'est-ce qu'une nation?* Paris, 1882.

Rettberg, Friedrich Wilhelm. *Kirchengeschichte Deutschlands.* Vol. 1. Göttingen: Vandenhoeck und Ruprecht, 1846.

Reynolds, L.D. "The Elder Pliny." In *Texts and Transmission: A Survey of the Latin Classics,* ed. L.D. Reynolds, 307–16. Oxford: Clarendon Press, 1983.

Reynolds, Susan. "Medieval *origines gentium* and the Community of the Realm." *History* 68 (1983): 375–90.

Richman, Paula, ed. *Many Rāmāyanas: The Diversity of a Narrative Tradition in South Asia.* Berkeley: University of California Press, 1991.

Richmond, John. "Manuscript Traditions and the Transmission of Ovid's Works." In *Brill's Companion to Ovid,* ed. Barbara Weiden Boyd, 443–83. Leiden: Brill, 2002.

Richter, Hans. *Dada: Art and Anti-Art.* Trans. David Britt. London: Thames and Hudson, 1965.

Richtscheid, René. "Die Kreuzfahrer als *novi Machabei*: Zur Verwendungsweise der Makkabäermetaphorik in chronikalischen Quellen der Rhein- und Maaslande zur Zeit der Kreuzzüge." In *Campana pulsante convocati: Festschrift anläßlich der Emeritierung von Prof. Dr. Alfred Haverkamp*, ed. Frank G. Hirschmann and Gerd Mentgen, 473–86. Trier: Kliomedia, 2005.

Roller, Duane W. *Ancient Geography: The Discovery of the World in Classical Greece and Rome*. London: I.B. Tauris, 2015.

Rollo, Antonio. *Leonzio lettore dell'Ecuba nella Firenze di Boccaccio*. Vol. 2 of *Petrarca e il mondo greco*, ed. Michele Feo, Vincenzo Fera, Paola Megna, and Antonio Rollo. *Quaderni Petrarcheschi* 12–13 (2002–3): 7–21.

Roselló i Verger, Vicenç M. "Els italianismes de les cartes portolanes mallorquines." In *Estudis de llengua i literatura en honor de Joan Veny*, ed. Josep Massot i Muntaner, 1: 39–62. 2 vols. Barcelona: Abadia de Montserrat, 1997.

Rosenwein, Barbara H. "One Site, Many Meanings: Saint-Maurice d'Agaune as a Place of Power in the Early Middle Ages." In *Topographies of Power in the Early Middle Ages*, ed. Mayke de Jong and Frans Theuws, 271–90. Leiden: Brill, 2001.

Rosier-Catach, Irène (with Ruedi Imbach). "La Tour de Babel dans la philosophie du langage de Dante." In *Zwischen Babel und Pfingsten: Sprachdifferenzen und Gesprächsverständigung in der Vormoderne (8.–16. Jahrhundert)*, ed. Peter von Moos, 183–204. Zürich: LIT, 2008.

Roux, Guy, and Muriel Laharie. *Art et folie au Moyen Âge: Aventures et énigmes d'Opicinus de Canistris (1296–vers 1351)*. Paris: Léopard d'Or, 1997.

Rowland, Robert J. "The Significance of Massilia in Lucan." *Hermes* 97 (1969): 204–8.

Ruberg, Uwe. "Mappae mundi des Mittelalters im Zusammenwirken von Text und Bild." In *Text und Bild: Aspekte des Zusammenwirkens zweier Künste in Mittelalter und früher Neuzeit*, ed. Christel Meier and Uwe Ruberg, 530–85. Wiesbaden: Reichert, 1980.

Sáenz-López Pérez, Sandra. *The Beatus Maps: The Revelation of the World in the Middle Ages*. Trans. Peter Krakenberger and Gerry Coldham. Burgos: Gil de Siloé, 2014.

Salomon, Richard. "Aftermath to Opicinus de Canistris." *Journal of the Warburg and Courtauld Institutes* 25 (1962): 137–46.

—. "A Newly Discovered Manuscript of Opicinus de Canistris." *Journal of the Warburg and Courtauld Institutes* 16 (1953): 45–59.

—. *Opicinus de Canistris: Weltbild und Bekenntnisse eines avignonesischen Klerikers des 14. Jahrhunderts*. 2 vols. London: Warburg Institute, 1936.

Salvat, Michel. "Le ciel des vulgarisateurs: Note sur les traductions du *De proprietatibus rerum*." In *Observer, lire, écrire le ciel au Moyen Age*, ed. Bernard Ribémont, 301–13. Paris: Klincksieck, 1991.

Sambrani, Chaitanya, ed. *At Home in the World: The Art and Life of Gulammohammed Sheikh*. New York: Columbia University Press, 2019.

Sanford, Eva Matthews. "The Manuscripts of Lucan: *Accessus* and *Marginalia*." *Speculum* 9 (1934): 278–95.

Sansone, Salvatore. *Tra cartografia politica e immaginario figurativo: Matthew Paris e l'Iter de Londinio in Terram Sanctam*. Rome: Istituto storico italiano per il Medio Evo, 2009.

Savage, John J.H. "The Manuscripts of Servius' Commentary on Virgil." *Harvard Studies in Classical Philology* 45 (1934): 157–204.

—. "The Manuscripts of the Commentary of Servius Danielis on Virgil." *Harvard Studies in Classical Philology* 43 (1932): 77–121.

Scafi, Alessandro. "Defining *mappaemundi*." In *The Hereford World Map: Medieval World Maps and Their Context*, ed. P.D.A. Harvey, 345–55. London: British Library, 2006.

—. *Mapping Paradise: A History of Heaven on Earth*. London: British Library, 2006.

Schmidt, Hans-Joachim. *Kirche, Staat, Nation: Raumgliederung der Kirche im mittelalterlichen Europa*. Weimar: Böhlaus, 1999.

Schmidt, Peter Lebrecht. "Solins Polyhistor in Wissenschaftsgeschichte und Geschichte." *Philologus* 139 (1995): 23–35.

Schülper, Sabine. "Ovid aus der Sicht des Balderich von Bourgueil, dargestellt anhand des Briefwechsels Florus-Ovid." *Mittellateinisches Jahrbuch* 14 (1979): 93–117.

Seeliger, Hans Reinhard. "Die Ausbreitung der Thebäer-Verehrung nördlich und südlich der Alpen." In *Mauritius und die Thebäische Legion/Saint Maurice et la légion Thébaine: Actes du colloque international Fribourg, Saint-Maurice, Martigny, 17–20 septembre 2003*, ed. Otto Wermelinger, Philippe Bruggisser, Beat Näf and Jean-Michel Roessli, 211–25. Fribourg: Academic Press Fribourg, 2005.

Serchuk, Camille. "*Ceste figure contient tout le royaulme de France*: Cartography and National Identity in France at the End of the Hundred Years War." *Journal of Medieval History* 33 (2007): 320–38.

Seyed-Gohrab, Ali Asghar. *Laylī and Majnūn: Love, Madness and Mystic Longing in Nizāmī's Epic Romance*. Leiden: Brill, 2003.

Shalev, Zur. *Sacred Words and Worlds: Geography, Religion, and Scholarship, 1550–1700*. Leiden: Brill, 2012.

Sharpe, R., J.P. Carley, R.M. Thomson, and A.G. Watson, eds. *English Benedictine Libraries: The Shorter Catalogues*. London: The British Library, 1996.

Sheikh, Gulammohammed. "Among Several Cultures and Times". In *Contemporary Indian Tradition: Voices on Culture, Nature, and the Challenge of Change*, ed. Carla M. Borden, 107–20. Washington, DC: Smithsonian Institution Press, 1989.

—, ed. *Contemporary Art in Baroda*. New Delhi: Tulika, 1997.

—. "Visualising the Ramayana: Reading Pictures." In *Indian Painting: Themes, Histories, Interpretations: Essays in Honour of B.N. Goswamy*, ed. Mahesh Sharma and Padma Kaimal, 79–91. Ahmedabad: Mapin Publishing, 2013.

Sieber-Lehman, Claudius. "Regna colore rubeo circumscripta." In *Grenzen und Raumvorstellungen*, ed. Guy P. Marchal, 79–91. Zürich: Chronos, 1996.

Simek, Rudolf. *Altnordische Kosmographie: Studien und Quellen zu Weltbild und Weltbeschreibung in Norwegen und Island vom 12. bis zum 14. Jahrhundert*. Berlin: de Gruyter, 1990.

Singh, Jodh. *Kabir*. Patiala: Punjabi University, 1971.

Sinha, Gayatri. *The Art of Gulammohammed Sheikh*. New Deli: Roli Books, 2002.

Skelton, R.A., and P.D.A. Harvey, eds. *Local Maps and Plans from Medieval England*. Oxford: Clarendon Press, 1986.

Smail, Daniel Lord. *Imaginary Cartographies: Possession and Identity in Late Medieval Marseille.* Ithaca: Cornell University Press, 1999.

Smalley, Beryl. "Jean de Hesdin O. Hosp. S. Ioh." *Recherches de Théologie ancienne et médiévale* 28 (1961): 283–330.

Smith, Anthony D. *The Antiquity of Nations.* Cambridge: Polity, 2004.

Southern, R.W. *Western Society and the Church in the Middle Ages.* Harmondsworth: Penguin, 1970.

Spevak, Olga. "Isidore de Séville: Le livre XIV des *Etymologiae* et la tradition étymologique." *Revue des Études Latines* 87 (2009): 231–48.

Stoler, Ann Laura, Carole McGranahan, and Peter C. Perdue, eds. *Imperial Formations.* Santa Fe: School for Advanced Research Press, 2007.

Suckale-Redlefsen, Gude. *Mauritius: Der heilige Mohr/The Black Saint Maurice.* Houston: Menil Foundation, 1987.

Swanson, Robert N. "*Gens secundum cognationem et collectionem ab alia distincta*? Thomas Polton, Two Englands, and the Challenge of Medieval Nationhood." In *Das Konstanzer Konzil als europäisches Ereignis: Begegnungen, Medien und Rituale,* ed. Gabriela Signori and Birgit Studt, 57–87. Ostfildern: Thorbecke, 2014.

Talbert, Richard J.A. *Rome's World: The Peutinger Map Reconsidered.* Cambridge: Cambridge University Press, 2010.

Tandon, Prakash. *Punjabi Century: 1857–1947.* Berkeley: University of California Press, 1968.

Tarrant, R.J. "Lucan." In *Texts and Transmission: A Survey of the Latin Classics,* ed. L.D. Reynolds, 215–18. Oxford: Clarendon Press, 1983.

—. "Ovid." In *Texts and Transmission: A Survey of the Latin Classics,* ed. L.D. Reynolds, 257–84. Oxford: Clarendon Press, 1983.

Tavoni, Mirko. *Latino, Grammatica, Volgare: Storia di una questione umanistica.* Padua: Antenore, 1984.

Tesoriero, Charles, ed. *Lucan.* Oxford: Oxford University Press, 2010.

Tilliette, Jean-Yves. "Savants et poètes du moyen âge face à Ovide: Les débuts de l'*aetas Ovidiana* (v. 1050–v. 1200)." In *Ovidius redivivus: Von Ovid zu Dante,* ed. Michelangelo Picone and Bernhard Zimmermann, 63–104. Stuttgart: Metzler und Poeschel, 1994.

Tinelli, Elisa. "La *Naturalis Historia* di Plinio nel *De natura rerum* di Beda il Venerabile." In *La* Naturalis Historia *di Plinio nella tradizione medievale e umanistica,* ed. Vanna Maraglino, 77–104. Bari: Cacucci, 2012.

Tola, Éléonora. *La métamorphose poétique chez Ovide:* Tristes et Pontiques: Le poème inépuisable. Louvain: Peeters, 2004.

Tolias, George. "Glose, contemplation, et méditation: Histoire éditoriale et fonctions du *Parergon* d'Abraham Ortelius (1579–1624)." In *Les méditations cosmographiques à la Renaissance,* ed. Frank Lestringant, 157–86. Paris: PUPS, 2009.

Toyama, Koichi. "Light and Shadow in Sassetta: The Stigmatization of Saint Francis and the Sermons of Bernardino da Siena." In *Sassetta: The Borgo San Sepolcro Altarpiece,* ed. Machtelt Israëls, 1: 305–15. Leiden: Primavera Press, 2009.

Tozzi, Pierluigi. *La città e il mondo in Opicino de Canistris (1296–1350 ca.)*. Varzi: Edizioni Guardamagna, 1996.

Trapp, J.B. "Ovid's Tomb: The Growth of a Legend from Eusebius to Laurence Sterne, Chateaubriand and George Richmond." *Journal of the Warburg and Courtauld Institutes* 36 (1973): 35–76.

Tréziny, Henri. "Marseille, une ville ionienne dans l'Occident grec." In *Les territoires de Marseille antique*, ed. Sophie Bouffier and Dominique Garcia, 9–18. Arles: Errance, 2014.

Uitvlugt, D.J. "The Sources of Isidore's Commentaries on the Pentateuch." *Revue Bénédictine* 112 (2002): 72–100.

Ullman, Berthold L. *The Humanism of Coluccio Salutati*. Padua: Antenore, 1963.

Vagnon, Emmanuelle. *Cartographie et Représentations de l'Orient méditerranéen en Occident (du milieu du XIIIe à la fin du XVe siècle)*. Turnhout: Brepols, 2013.

Valtonen, Irmeli. *The North in the Old English Orosius: A Geographical Narrative in Context*. Helsinki: Société Néophilologique, 2008.

van Berchem, Denis. *Le Martyre de la Légion Thébaine: Essai sur la formation d'une légende*. Basel: Friedrich Reinhardt, 1956.

van den Broecke, Marcel. *Ortelius Atlas Maps: An Illustrated Guide*. 2nd ed. Houten: HES & de Graaf, 2011.

—. "The Significance of Language: The Texts on the Verso of the Maps in Abraham Ortelius, *Theatrum Orbis Terrarum*." *Imago Mundi* 60 (2008): 202–10.

Van Nuffelen, Peter. *Orosius and the Rhetoric of History*. Oxford: Oxford University Press, 2012.

Vatovec, Corinna Vasić. *Luca Fancelli, architetto: Epistolario gonzaghesco*. Florence: Uniedit, 1979.

Venesky, Laura. "Jerusalem Refracted: Geographies of the True Cross in Late Antiquity." In *Natural Materials of the Holy Land and the Visual Translation of Place 500–1500*, ed. Renana Bartal, Neta Bodner, and Bianca Kühnel, 64–75. London: Routledge, 2017.

Videau-Delibes, Anne. *Les Tristes d'Ovide et l'élégie Romaine: Une poétique de la rupture*. Paris: Klincksieck, 1991.

von Moos, Peter. "Lucain au Moyen Âge." In *Entre histoire et littérature: Communication et culture au Moyen Âge*. Florence: SISMEL-Edizioni del Galluzzo, 2005.

Vorholt, Hanna. "Studying with Maps: Jerusalem and the Holy Land in Two Thirteenth-Century Manuscripts." In *Imagining Jerusalem in the Medieval West*, ed. Lucy Donkin and Hanna Vorholt, 163–99. Oxford: The British Academy, 2012.

Wagner, Emil August. *Die Erdbeschreibung des Timosthenes von Rhodus*. Leipzig: Frankenstein and Wagner, 1888.

Walde, Christine, ed. *Lucans Bellum Civile: Studien zum Spektrum seiner Rezeption von der Antike bis ins 19. Jahrhundert*. Trier: Wissenschaftlicher Verlag, 2009.

Wallace, David. "Constance." In *Europe: A Literary History, 1348–1418*, ed. David Wallace, vol. 2, 655–82. 2 vols. Oxford: Oxford University Press, 2016.

—, ed. *Europe: A Literary History, 1348–1418*. 2 vols. Oxford: Oxford University Press, 2016.

Wallace-Hadrill, Andrew. *Rome's Cultural Revolution*. Cambridge: Cambridge University Press, 2008.

Waswo, Richard. "Our Ancestors, the Trojans: Inventing Cultural Identity in the Middle Ages." *Exemplaria* 7 (1995): 269–90.

Weingarten, Susan. *The Saint's Saints: Hagiography and Geography in Jerome*. Leiden: Brill, 2005.

Weiss, Jeffrey. "Dis-Orientation: Rothko's Inverted Canvases." In *Seeing Rothko*, ed. Glenn Phillips and Thomas Crow, 135–57. Los Angeles: Getty Publications, 2005.

Werner, Shirley. "On the History of the *Commenta Bernensia* and the *Adnotationes super Lucanum*." *Harvard Studies in Classical Philology* 96 (1994): 343–68.

Wetherbee, Winthrop. *Platonism and Poetry in the Twelfth Century: The Literary Influence of the School of Chartres*. Princeton: Princeton University Press, 1972.

Whittaker, C.R. *Rome and Its Frontiers: The Dynamics of Empire*. London: Routledge, 2004.

Whittington, Karl. *Body-Worlds: Opicinus de Canistris and the Medieval Cartographic Imagination*. Toronto: Pontifical Institute of Mediaeval Studies, 2014.

—. "Experimenting with Opicinus de Canistris (1296– ca.1354)." *Gesta* 51 (2012): 147–73.

—. "Queer." *Studies in Iconography* 33 (2012): 157–68.

Wilke, Jürgen. *Die Ebstorfer Weltkarte*. 2 vols. Bielefeld: Verlag für Regionalgeschichte, 2001.

Williams, Gareth D. *Banished Voices: Readings in Ovid's Exile Poetry*. Cambridge: Cambridge University Press, 1994.

—. "Ovid's Exilic Poetry: Worlds Apart." In *Brill's Companion to Ovid*, ed. Barbara Weiden Boyd, 337–81. Leiden: Brill, 2002.

Williams, John. "Isidore, Orosius and the Beatus Map." *Imago Mundi* 49 (1997): 7–32.

Winichakul, Thongchai. *Siam Mapped: A History of the Geo-Body of a Nation*. Honolulu: University of Hawaii Press, 1994.

Witt, Ronald G. *Hercules at the Crossroads: The Life, Works, and Thought of Coluccio Salutati*. Durham, NC: Duke University Press, 1983.

Wogan-Browne, Jocelyn, et al.: *see under* Primary Sources

Wolf, Armin. "The Ebstorf *Mappamundi* and Gervase of Tilbury: The Controversy Revisited." *Imago Mundi* 64 (2012): 1–27.

Wolf, Kordula. *Troja – Metamorphosen eines Mythos: Französische, englische und italienische Überlieferungen des 12. Jahrhunderts im Vergleich*. Berlin: Akademie, 2009.

Woods, David. "The Origin of the Legend of Maurice and the Theban Legion." *Journal of Ecclesiastical History* 45 (1994): 385–95.

Wootton, David. *The Invention of Science: A New History of the Scientific Revolution*. London: Allen Lane, 2015.

Worm, Andrea. "'Ista est Jerusalem': Intertextuality and Visual Exegesis in Peter of Poitiers' *Compendium historiae in genealogia Christi* and Werner Rolevinck's *Fasciculus temporum*." In *Imagining Jerusalem in the Medieval West*, ed. Lucy Donkin and Hanna Vorholt, 123–61. Oxford: The British Academy, 2012.

Wriedt, Klaus. "Latein und Deutsch in den Hansestädten vom 13. bis zum 16. Jahrhundert." In *Latein und Nationalsprachen in der Renaissance*, ed. Bodo Guthmüller, 287–313. Wiesbaden: Harrassowitz, 1998.

Wright, Neil. "'Industriae Testimonium': William of Malmesbury and Latin Poetry Revisited." *Revue Bénédictine* 103 (1993): 482–531.

—. "Twelfth-Century Receptions of a Text: Anglo-Norman Historians and Hegesippus." *Anglo-Norman Studies* 31 (2009): 177–95.

Wright, Roger. *A Sociophilological Study of Late Latin*. Turnhout: Brepols, 2002.

Zecchini, Laetitia. "'More Than One World': An Interview with Gulammohammed Sheikh." *Journal of Postcolonial Writing* 53 (2017): 69–82.

Zelzer, Michaela. "Zur Überlieferung und Rezeption der Passio Acaunensium Martyrum." In *Mauritius und die Thebäische Legion/Saint Maurice et la légion Thébaine: Actes du colloque international Fribourg, Saint-Maurice, Martigny, 17–20 septembre 2003*, ed. Otto Wermelinger, Philippe Bruggisser, Beat Näf and Jean-Michel Roessli, 325–30. Fribourg: Academic Press Fribourg, 2005.

Ziolkowski, Jan, and Michael C.J. Putnam, eds. *The Virgilian Tradition: The First Fifteen Hundred Years*. New Haven: Yale University Press, 2008.

Ziolkowski, Theodore. *Ovid and the Moderns*. Ithaca: Cornell University Press, 2005.

Zitzewitz, Karin. "Past Futures of Old Media: Gulammohammed Sheikh's Kaavad: Traveling Shrine: Home." *Comparative Studies of South Asia, Africa and the Middle East: Borderlines*, 11 March, 2016. https://cssaamejournal.org/borderlines/past-futures-of-old-media/.

Index

References to figures appear in italics, prior to references to page numbers. Works of unknown authorship are indexed by title. The many peoples mentioned in the book can be found grouped under *gentes* (biblical; classical and late antique; and medieval). Readers may also find it convenient to consult other grouped entries, among them animals; empires; languages; manuscripts; maps; mountains; rivers; saints; sea charts; and seas and oceans.